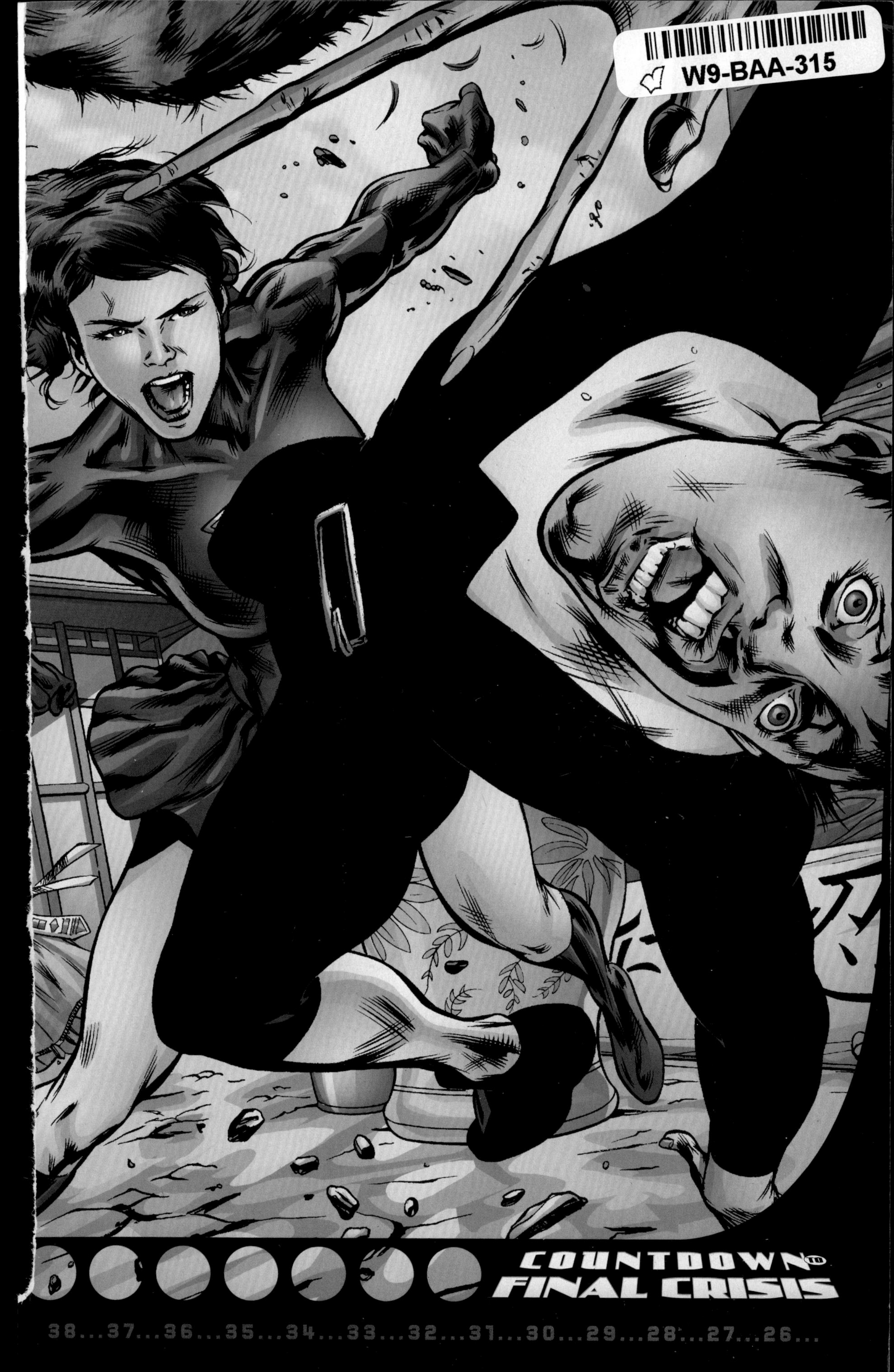
COUNTDOWN TO
FINAL CRISIS
38...37...36...35...34...33...32...31...30...29...28...27...26...

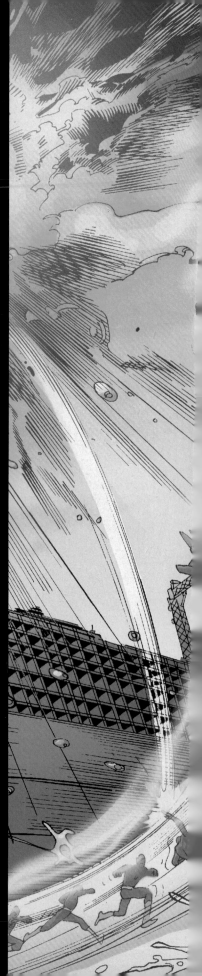

## PAUL DINI With...

Justin Gray &
Jimmy Palmiotti
Adam Beechen
Tony Bedard
Sean McKeever
Writers

Keith Giffen
Story Consultant

Jesus Saiz
David Lopez
Mike Norton
Jim Calafiore
Manuel Garcia
Carlos Magno
Al Barrionuevo
Pencillers

Jimmy Palmiotti
Jon Hillsman II
Rod Ramos
Jack Purcell
Mark McKenna
Jay Leisten
Art Thibert
Inkers

Jared K. Fletcher
Ken Lopez
Travis Lanham
Letterers

Tom Chu
Alex Bleyaert
Pete Pantazis
Hi-Fi
Rod Reis
Colorists

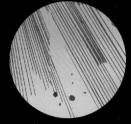

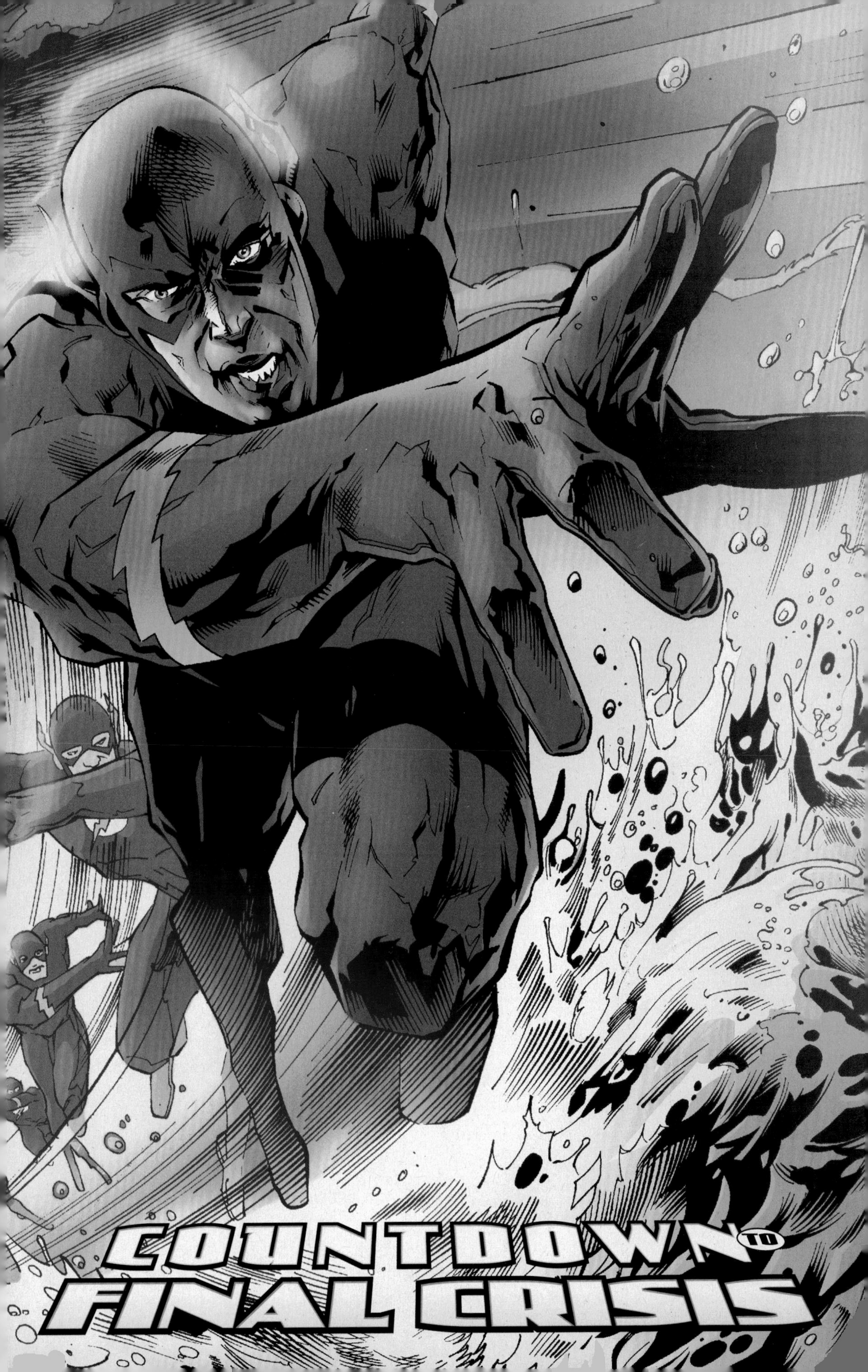
COUNTDOWN TO
FINAL CRISIS

**Dan DiDio** Senior VP-Executive Editor  **Mike Marts  Mike Carlin** Editors-original series  **Jeanine Schaefer** Associate Editor-original series  **Elisabeth Gehrlein** Assistant Editor-original series  **Bob Joy** Editor-collected edition  **Robbin Brosterman** Senior Art Director  **Louis Prandi** Art Director  **Paul Levitz** President & Publisher **Georg Brewer** VP-Design & DC Direct Creative  **Richard Bruning** Senior VP-Creative Director  **Patrick Caldon** Executive VP-Finance & Operations  **Chris Caramalis** VP-Finance  **John Cunningham** VP-Marketing  **Terri Cunningham** VP-Managing Editor  **Alison Gill** VP-Manufacturing  **David Hyde** VP-Publicity  **Hank Kanalz** VP-General Manager, WildStorm  **Jim Lee** Editorial Director-WildStorm  **Paula Lowitt** Senior VP-Business & Legal Affairs  **MaryEllen McLaughlin** VP-Advertising & Custom Publishing  **John Nee** Senior VP-Business Development  **Gregory Noveck** Senior VP-Creative Affairs  **Sue Pohja** VP-Book Trade Sales  **Steve Rotterdam** Senior VP-Sales & Marketing  **Cheryl Rubin** Senior VP-Brand Management  **Jeff Trojan** VP-Business Development  DC Direct,  **Bob Wayne** VP-Sales

Cover art by **Ed Benes** and **Rod Reis**

**COUNTDOWN TO FINAL CRISIS VOLUME 2** Published by DC Comics. Cover, text and compilation Copyright © 2008 DC Comics. All Rights Reserved. Originally published in single magazine form as COUNTDOWN 38-26. Copyright © 2007 DC Comics. All Rights Reserved. All characters, their distinctive likenesses and related elements featured in this publication are trademarks of DC Comics. The stories, characters and incidents featured in this publication are entirely fictional. DC Comics does not read or accept unsolicited submissions of ideas, stories or artwork. DC Comics, 1700 Broadway, New York, NY 10019. A Warner Bros. Entertainment Company. Printed in Canada. First Printing. ISBN:978-1-4012-1824-9.

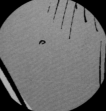

## PREVIOUSLY...

There are 52 dimensions, each with it's own Earth and each with their own guardians of history known as the Monitors. It is their duty to ensure the universes are kept separate and ignorant of each other's existence. If beings should start crossing over it would weaken the Source walls, which would then eventually collapse and cause the universes to merge — causing infinite chaos!

**JIMMY OLSEN** — Superman's Pal began an investigation into the murder of the costumed anti-hero Joker's Daughter. Hitting nothing but dead ends, Olsen's journey took him to Gotham City, where he was attacked by Batman's most vicious foe, Killer Croc. In dire peril, the young reporter was amazed when he saved himself using a super-power he's never possessed before — super stretching ability. He soon began to display other amazing talents such as super speed and becoming a human porcupine. With no idea of the origin or extent of his newfound endowments, Jimmy fashioned a costume and is now ready to begin his crime-fighting career as Mr. Action.

**HOLLY ROBINSON AND HARLEY QUINN —** The former Catwoman, on the run and looking to make a fresh start in Metropolis, sought refuge in a women's shelter run by Themyscira, Wonder Woman's homeland. There she met Harleen Quinzel, better known as the Joker's girlfriend, Harley Quinn, and the two became fast friends. After witnessing a single mother being turned away, Holly demanded to speak to the goddess Athena who explained that the shelter is only meant for special candidates and convinced Holly to take part in a self esteem workshop.

**MARY MARVEL** — Once one of the world's mightiest mortals, Mary Batson came out of a year-long coma and found herself powerless and abandoned by her friends and family. Despondent and searching for her new destiny, Mary went to Gotham City, where she was attacked by thugs and rescued by her former nemesis, Black Adam. Wanting to teach the young girl a lesson in power and corruption, Adam gave Mary all of his mystic abilities. The all-new Mary Marvel began an unusually aggressive war on crime, which caught the attention of some very powerful beings. She met with her brother Billy, who explained that the rules of magic have changed and he now IS the power of Shazam. Realizing that there is no longer a place for her in the Marvel Family, Mary renounced her brother but soon realized she needs a mentor to help her control her more powerful magic abilities. She sought out Zatanna, the Justice League's resident magician, unaware that she is also being watched by the new lord of darkness, Eclipso.

**HARATE HID** — A member of the 31st century Legion of Super-Heroes, Val Armorr remained quarantined in the present due to a virus he is carrying. Knowing a Great Disaster is on the horizon, but not sure of its exact nature, Val and his teammate Una seek out Oracle, rumored to be the 21st century's greatest source of information. After breaking into her headquarters, they learn Oracle is preoccupied with a crisis of her own — someone is trying to steal the secret identities of all of Earth's super-heroes from her database.

**DONNA TROY AND JASON TODD** — Jason Todd, in the guise of the Red Hood, witnessed the murder of Duela Dent — the Joker's Daughter — by one of the Monitors, who then turned his attention to Jason. The executioner stated that both Jason and Duela were displaced refugees in the Multiverse and as such must be purged. However, another Monitor (who would later be nicknamed "Bob") rescued Red Hood. At Duela's gravesite, Jason met Donna Troy, another possible traveler from a different universe. The pair were attacked by Forerunner, the savage new assassin of the Monitors. Bob saved them and the duo joined him on his quest to save the planet from the Great Disaster. Bob believes the only person who can stop the disaster is the missing Atom, Ray Palmer. Palmer has been gone for over a year and was succeeded by Ryan Choi. Now Donna, Jason, Ryan and Bob are scouring the micro worlds-within-worlds, the Nanoverse, trying to find some clue to Ray's whereabouts.

**PIED PIPER AND THE TRICKSTER** — Bart Allen had returned from a secret dimensional adventure four years older and inherited the identity of the Flash. In response, his nemesis Inertia reunited the Rogues, a team of Flash-villains including Heat Wave, Mirror Master, Captain Cold, Abra Kadabra, Weather Wizard and two formerly reformed villains Trickster and Pied Piper, to end the new speedsters career. Bart was killed in the ensuing battle. This put the Rogues on everyone's most-wanted list, including the Teen Titans, Justice League and the Suicide Squad. Most of the villains, are now in custody, but Trickster and Pied Piper (who are shackled together) escaped the confinement of the Squad and are still running for their lives…

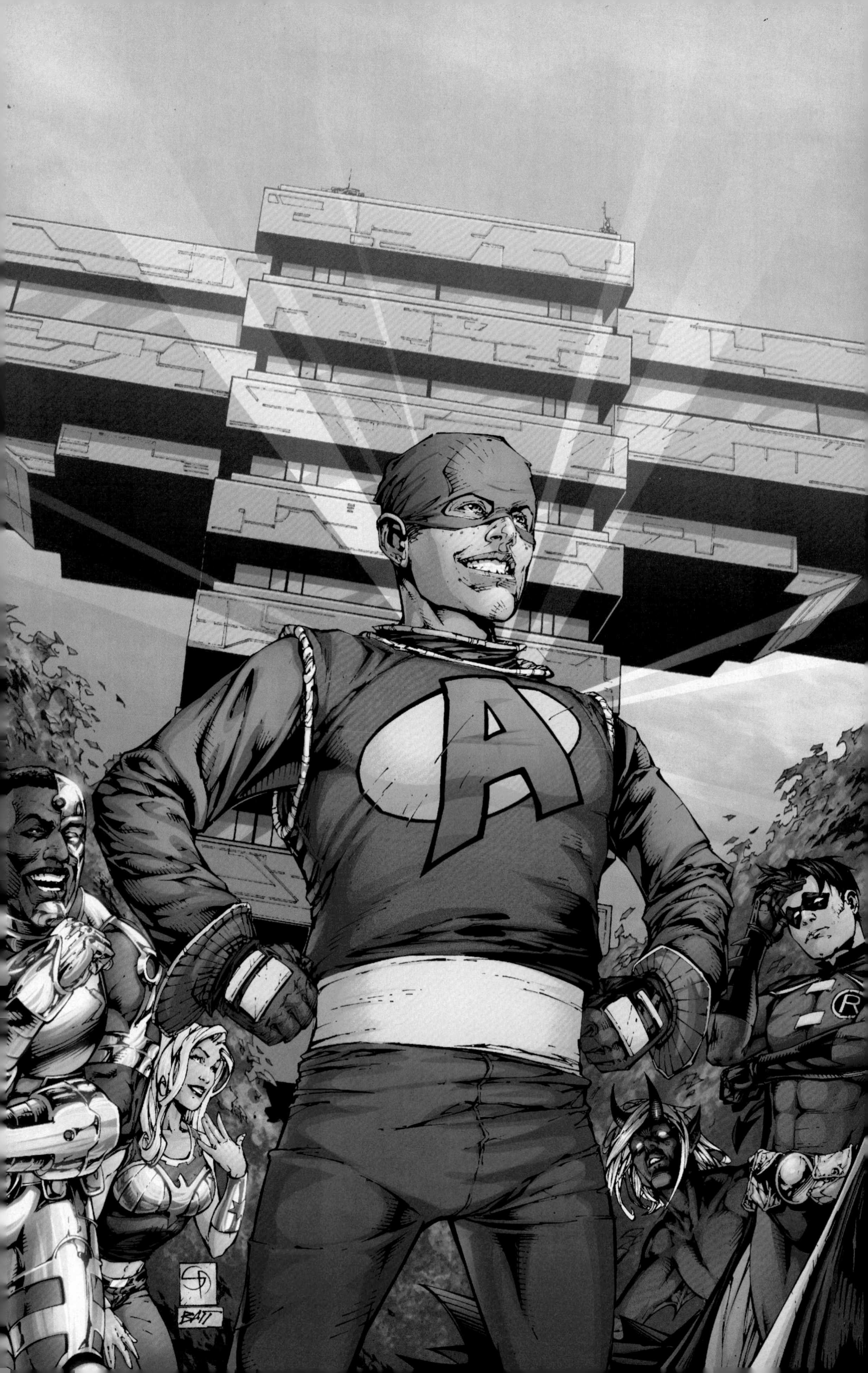

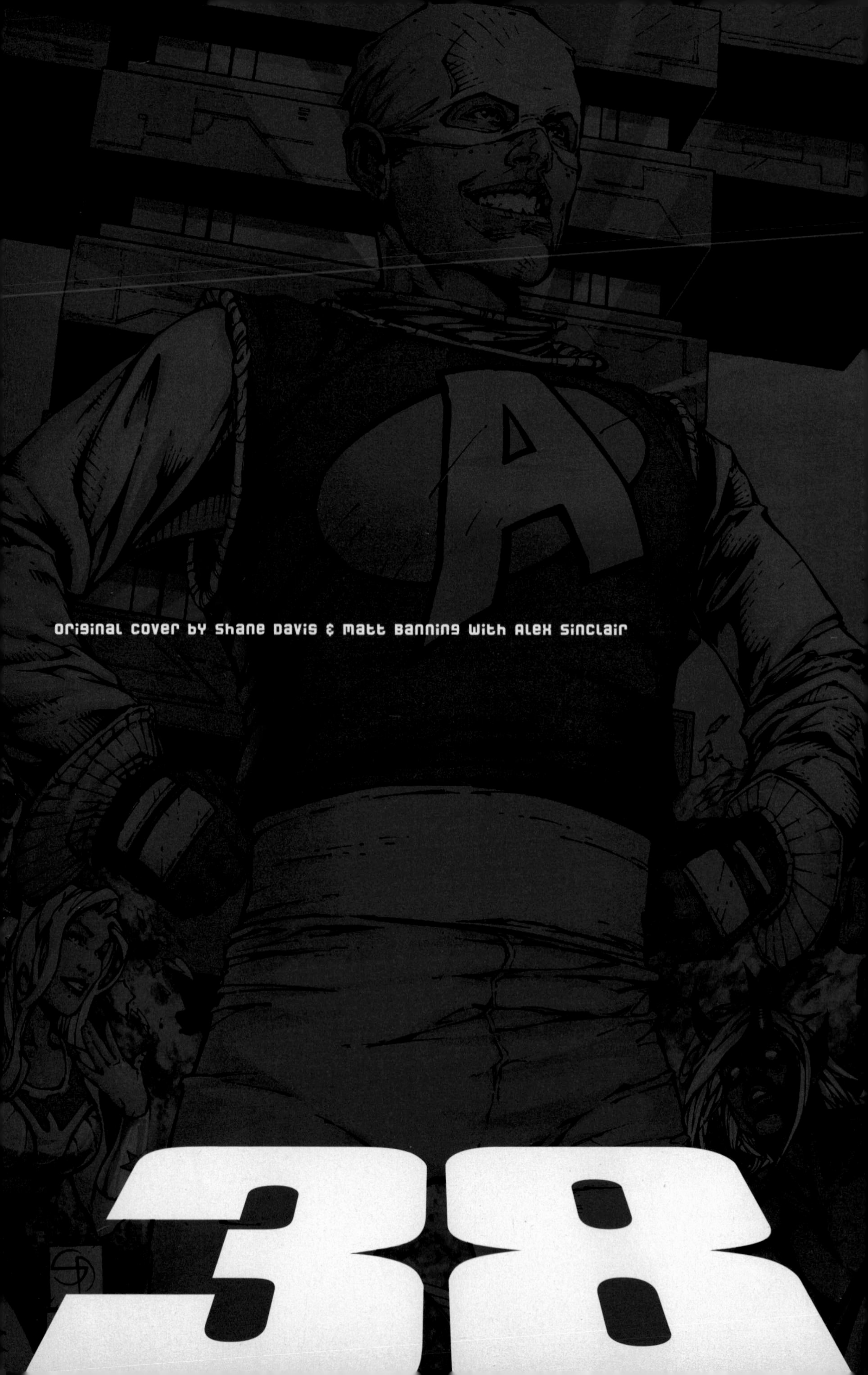
38

original cover by Shane Davis & Matt Banning with Alex Sinclair

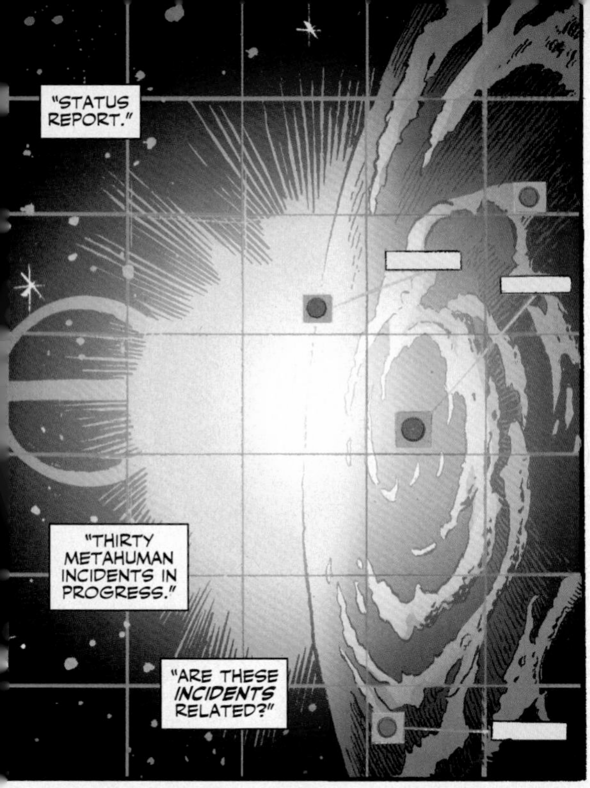
"STATUS REPORT."
"THIRTY METAHUMAN INCIDENTS IN PROGRESS."
"ARE THESE INCIDENTS RELATED?"


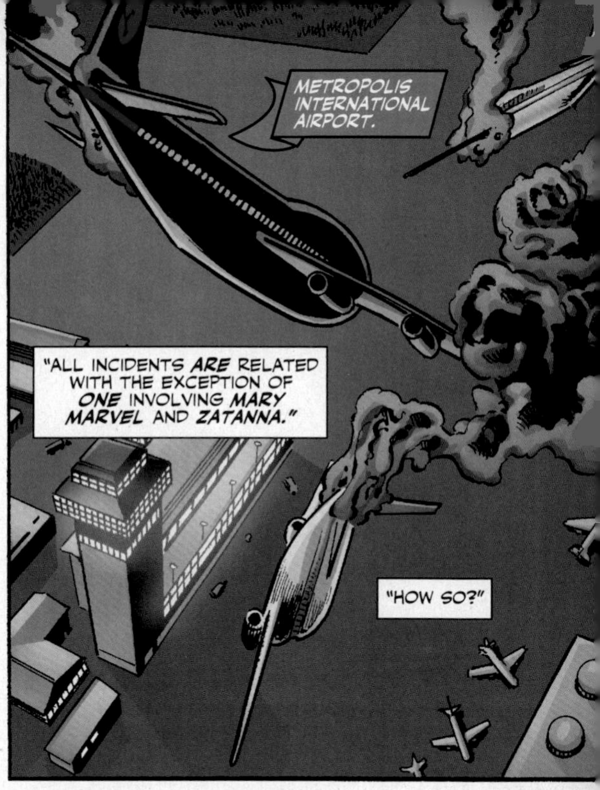
METROPOLIS INTERNATIONAL AIRPORT.
"ALL INCIDENTS ARE RELATED WITH THE EXCEPTION OF ONE INVOLVING MARY MARVEL AND ZATANNA."
"HOW SO?"


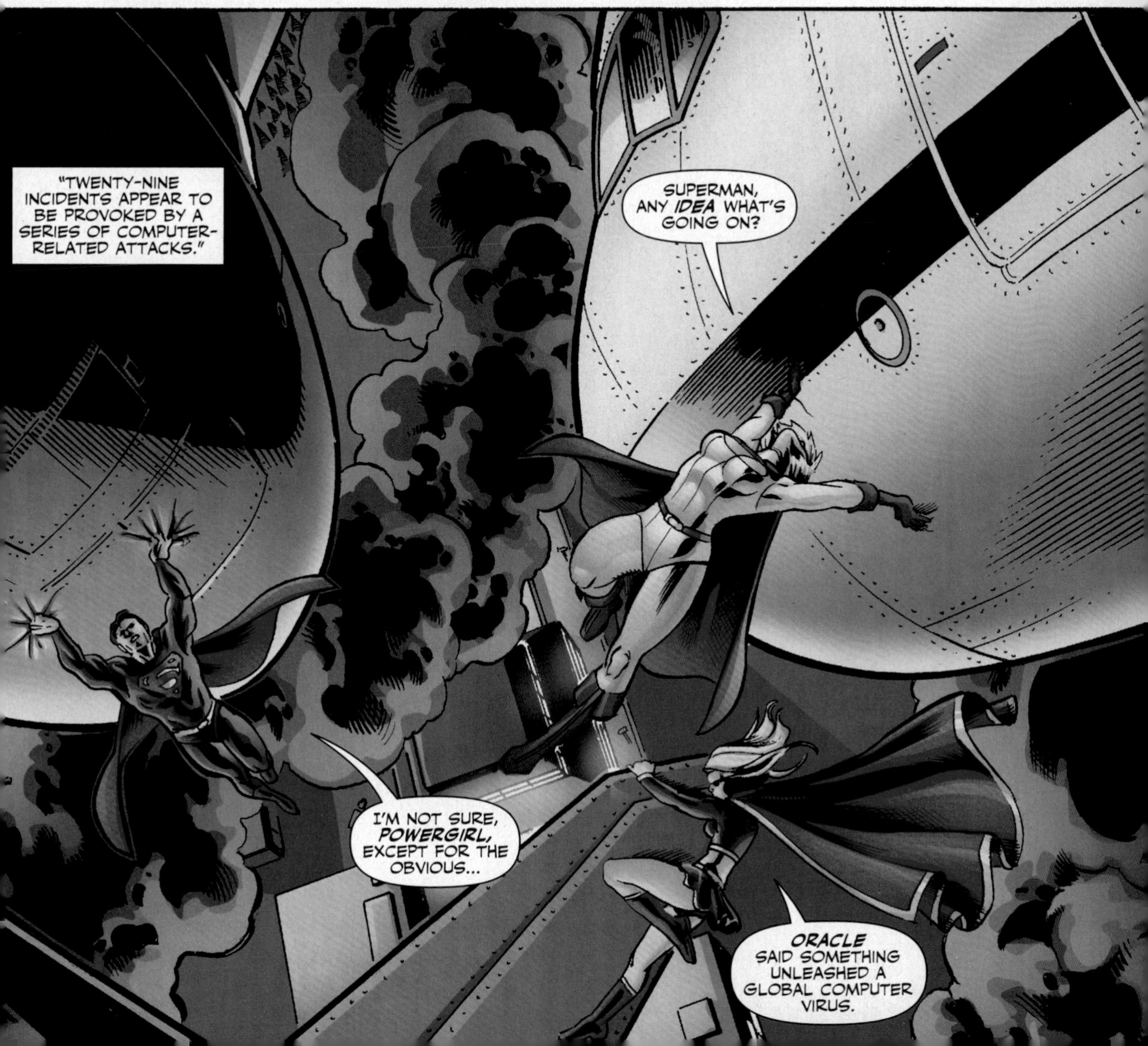
"TWENTY-NINE INCIDENTS APPEAR TO BE PROVOKED BY A SERIES OF COMPUTER-RELATED ATTACKS."
SUPERMAN, ANY IDEA WHAT'S GOING ON?
I'M NOT SURE, POWERGIRL, EXCEPT FOR THE OBVIOUS...
ORACLE SAID SOMETHING UNLEASHED A GLOBAL COMPUTER VIRUS.

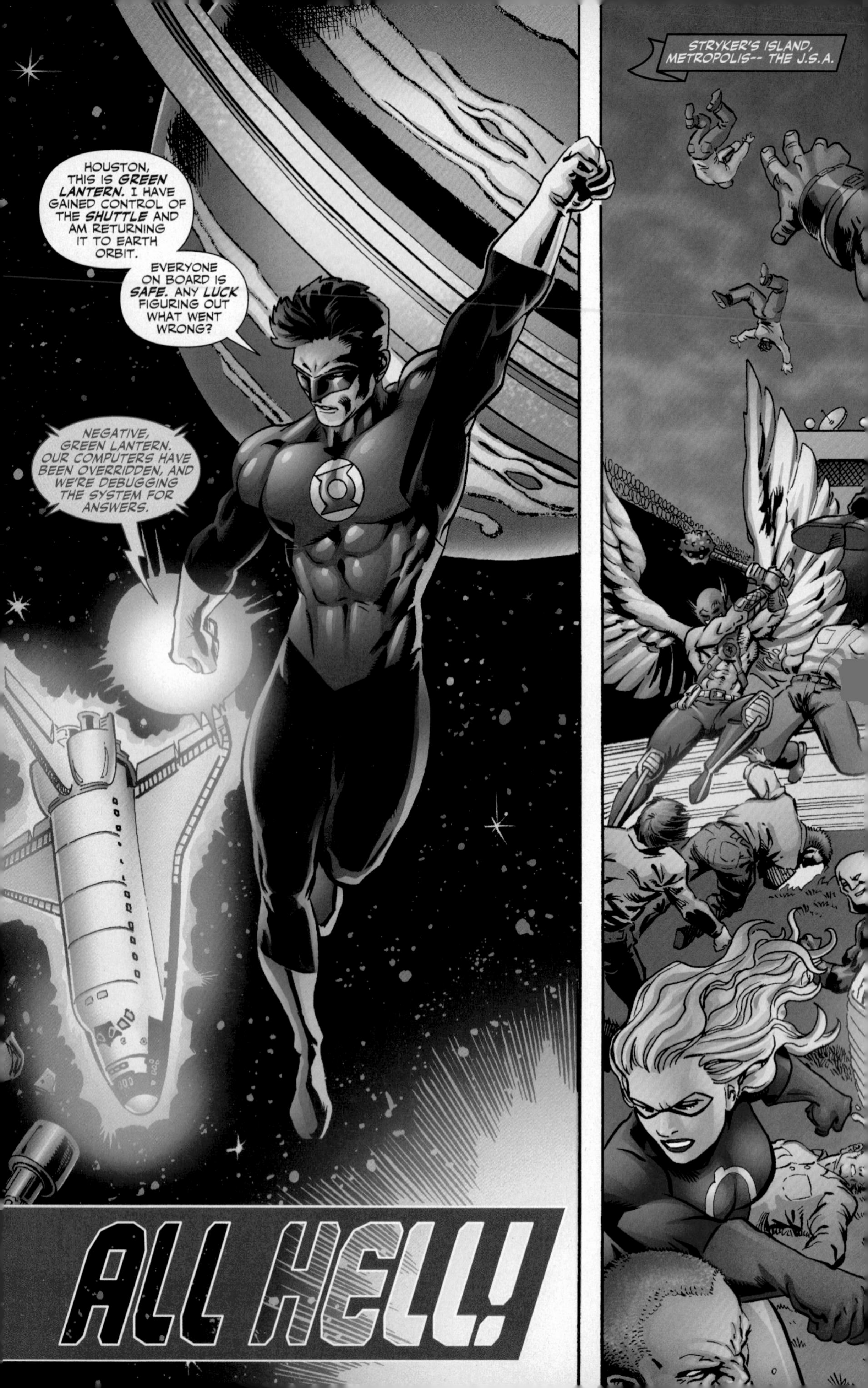

HOUSTON, THIS IS GREEN LANTERN. I HAVE GAINED CONTROL OF THE SHUTTLE AND AM RETURNING IT TO EARTH ORBIT.
EVERYONE ON BOARD IS SAFE. ANY LUCK FIGURING OUT WHAT WENT WRONG?
NEGATIVE, GREEN LANTERN. OUR COMPUTERS HAVE BEEN OVERRIDDEN, AND WE'RE DEBUGGING THE SYSTEM FOR ANSWERS.
ALL HELL!
STRYKER'S ISLAND, METROPOLIS-- THE J.S.A.

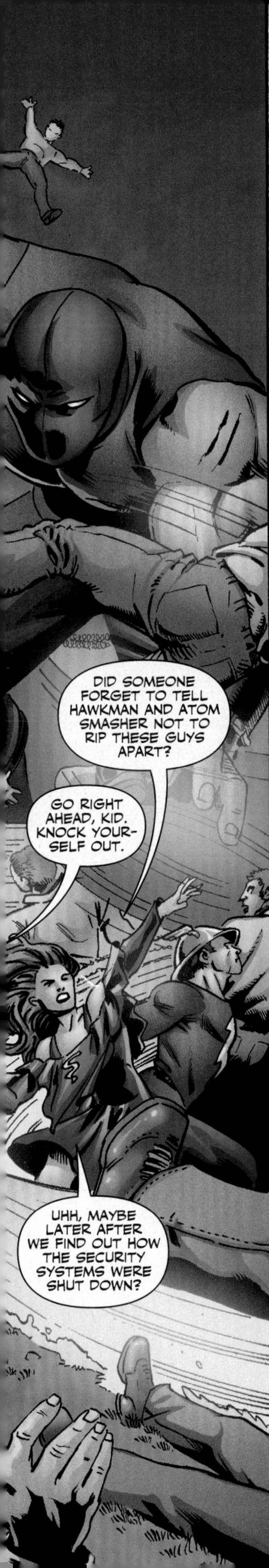
DID SOMEONE FORGET TO TELL HAWKMAN AND ATOM SMASHER NOT TO RIP THESE GUYS APART?
GO RIGHT AHEAD, KID. KNOCK YOURSELF OUT.
UHH, MAYBE LATER AFTER WE FIND OUT HOW THE SECURITY SYSTEMS WERE SHUT DOWN?

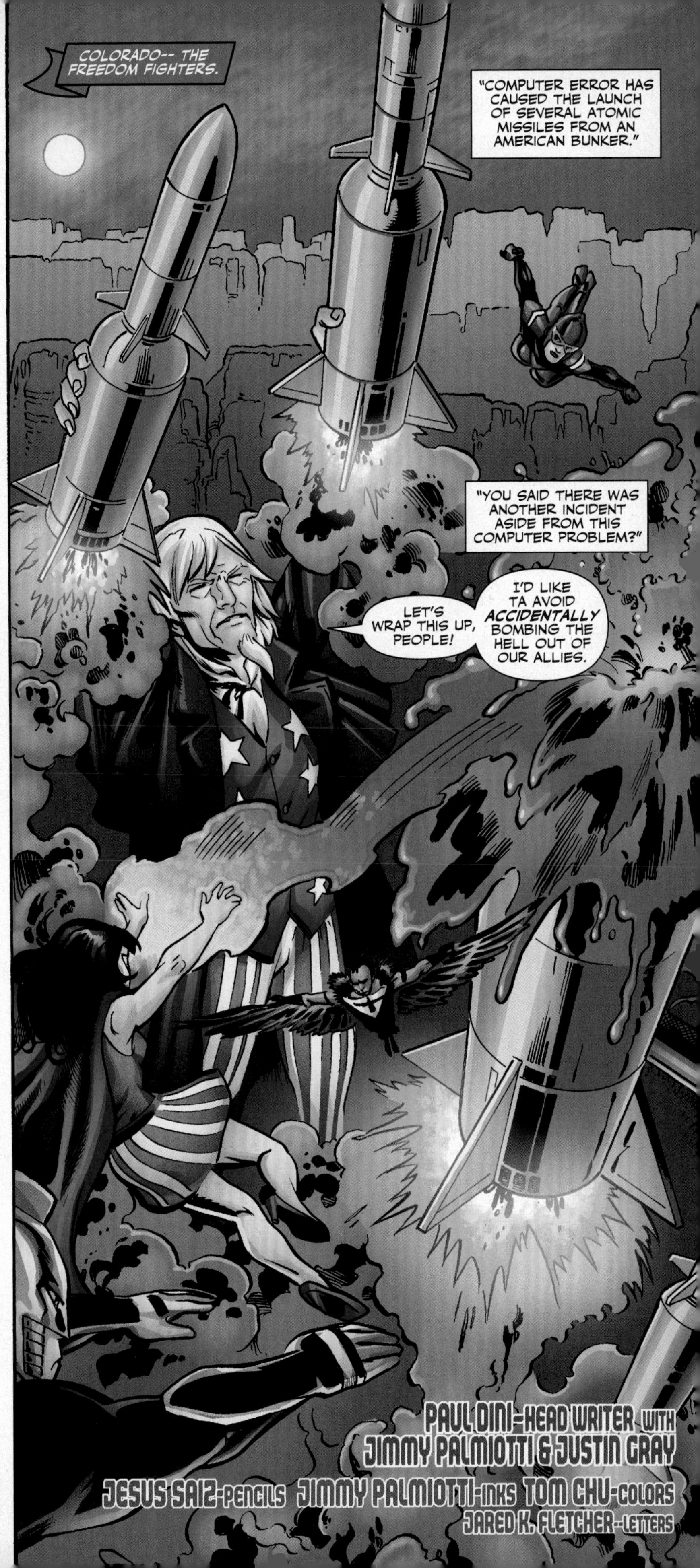
COLORADO-- THE FREEDOM FIGHTERS.
"COMPUTER ERROR HAS CAUSED THE LAUNCH OF SEVERAL ATOMIC MISSILES FROM AN AMERICAN BUNKER."
"YOU SAID THERE WAS ANOTHER INCIDENT ASIDE FROM THIS COMPUTER PROBLEM?"
LET'S WRAP THIS UP, PEOPLE!
I'D LIKE TA AVOID ACCIDENTALLY BOMBING THE HELL OUT OF OUR ALLIES.
PAUL DINI-HEAD WRITER WITH JIMMY PALMIOTTI & JUSTIN GRAY
JESUS SAIZ-PENCILS JIMMY PALMIOTTI-INKS TOM CHU-COLORS
JARED K. FLETCHER--LETTERS

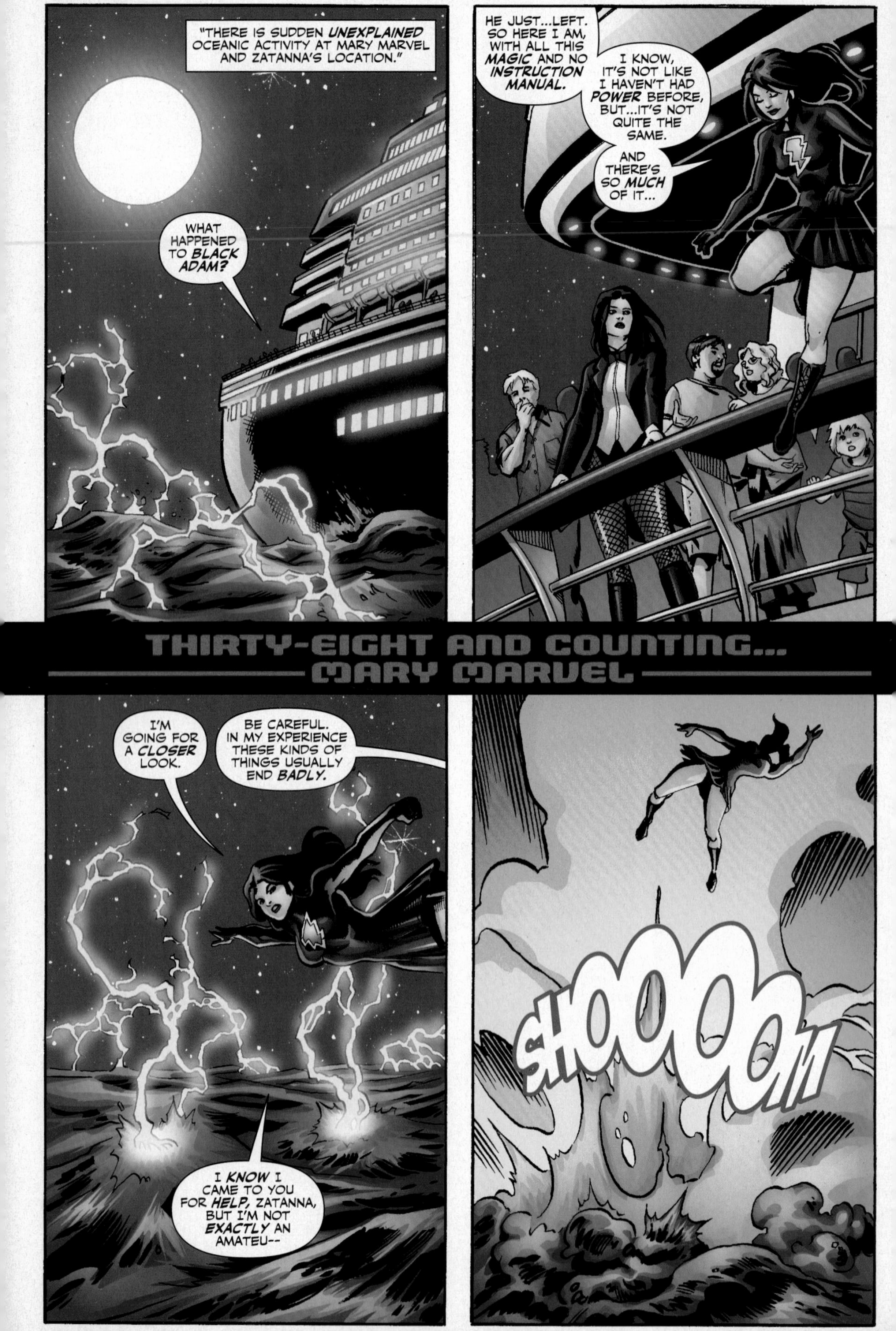
"THERE IS SUDDEN UNEXPLAINED OCEANIC ACTIVITY AT MARY MARVEL AND ZATANNA'S LOCATION."
WHAT HAPPENED TO BLACK ADAM?
HE JUST...LEFT. SO HERE I AM, WITH ALL THIS MAGIC AND NO INSTRUCTION MANUAL.
I KNOW, IT'S NOT LIKE I HAVEN'T HAD POWER BEFORE, BUT...IT'S NOT QUITE THE SAME.
AND THERE'S SO MUCH OF IT...
THIRTY-EIGHT AND COUNTING...
MARY MARVEL
I'M GOING FOR A CLOSER LOOK.
BE CAREFUL. IN MY EXPERIENCE THESE KINDS OF THINGS USUALLY END BADLY.
I KNOW I CAME TO YOU FOR HELP, ZATANNA, BUT I'M NOT EXACTLY AN AMATEU--
SHOOOOM

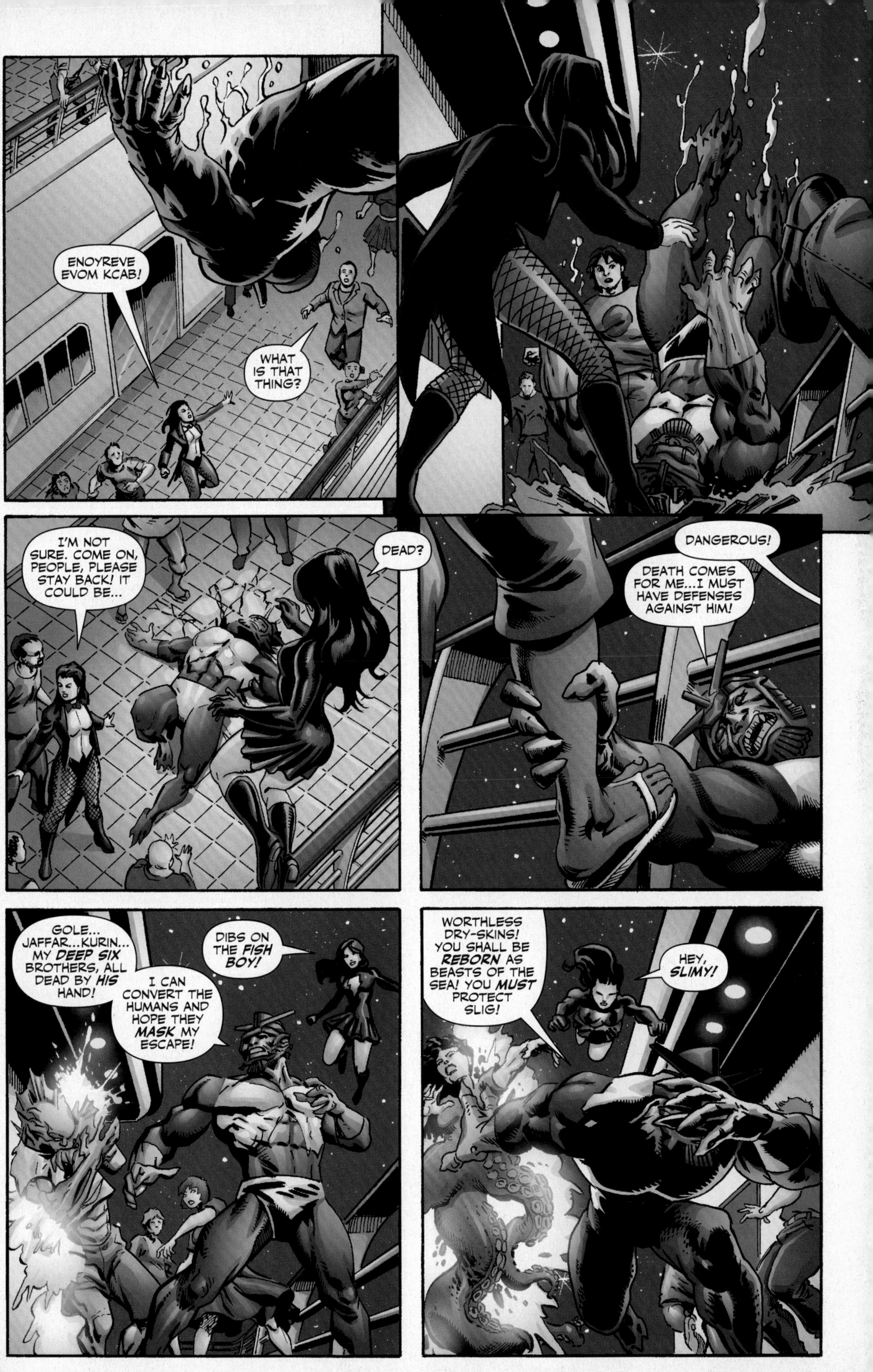
ENOYREVE EVOM KCAB!
WHAT IS THAT THING?
I'M NOT SURE. COME ON, PEOPLE, PLEASE STAY BACK! IT COULD BE...
DEAD?
DANGEROUS!
DEATH COMES FOR ME...I MUST HAVE DEFENSES AGAINST HIM!
GOLE... JAFFAR...KURIN... MY DEEP SIX BROTHERS, ALL DEAD BY HIS HAND!
I CAN CONVERT THE HUMANS AND HOPE THEY MASK MY ESCAPE!
DIBS ON THE FISH BOY!
WORTHLESS DRY-SKINS! YOU SHALL BE REBORN AS BEASTS OF THE SEA! YOU MUST PROTECT SLIG!
HEY, SLIMY!

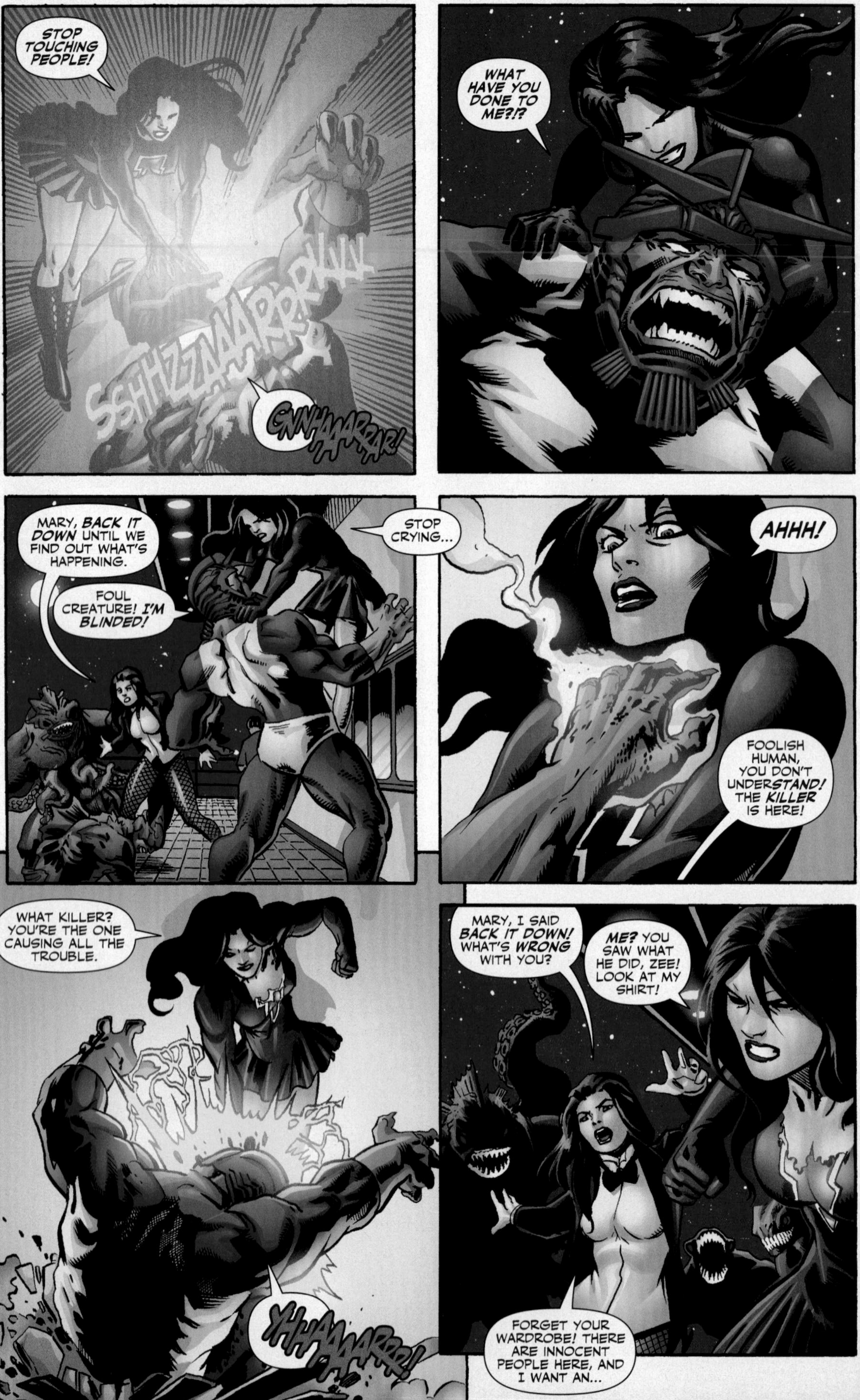
STOP TOUCHING PEOPLE!
SSHHZZZAARRRRAAAA
GNNHAAARRAR!
WHAT HAVE YOU DONE TO ME?!?
MARY, BACK IT DOWN UNTIL WE FIND OUT WHAT'S HAPPENING.
FOUL CREATURE! I'M BLINDED!
STOP CRYING...
AHHH!
FOOLISH HUMAN, YOU DON'T UNDERSTAND! THE KILLER IS HERE!
WHAT KILLER? YOU'RE THE ONE CAUSING ALL THE TROUBLE.
YHHAAARRR!
MARY, I SAID BACK IT DOWN! WHAT'S WRONG WITH YOU?
ME? YOU SAW WHAT HE DID, ZEE! LOOK AT MY SHIRT!
FORGET YOUR WARDROBE! THERE ARE INNOCENT PEOPLE HERE, AND I WANT AN...

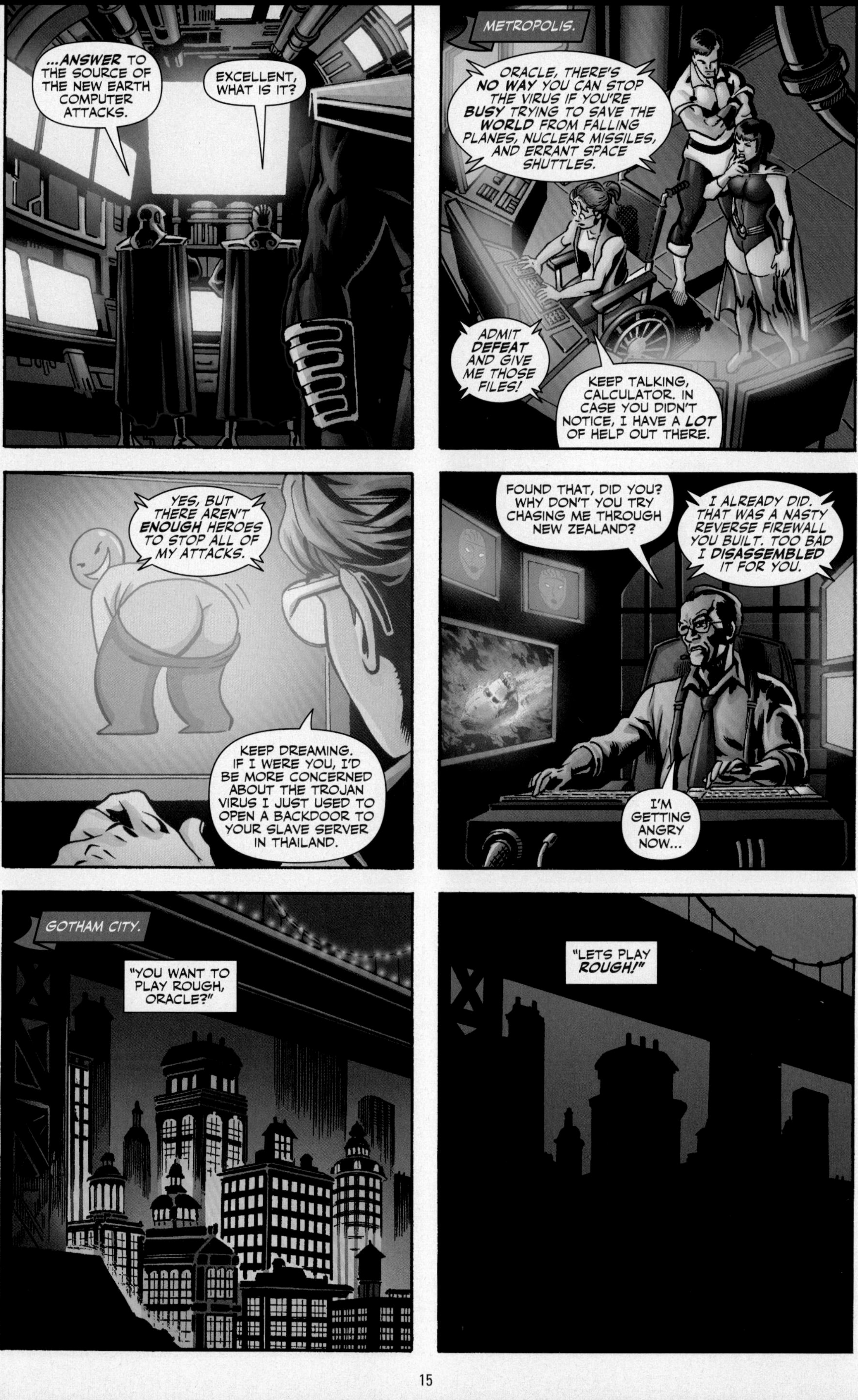
...ANSWER TO THE SOURCE OF THE NEW EARTH COMPUTER ATTACKS.
EXCELLENT, WHAT IS IT?
METROPOLIS.
ORACLE, THERE'S NO WAY YOU CAN STOP THE VIRUS IF YOU'RE BUSY TRYING TO SAVE THE WORLD FROM FALLING PLANES, NUCLEAR MISSILES, AND ERRANT SPACE SHUTTLES.
ADMIT DEFEAT AND GIVE ME THOSE FILES!
KEEP TALKING, CALCULATOR. IN CASE YOU DIDN'T NOTICE, I HAVE A LOT OF HELP OUT THERE.
YES, BUT THERE AREN'T ENOUGH HEROES TO STOP ALL OF MY ATTACKS.
KEEP DREAMING. IF I WERE YOU, I'D BE MORE CONCERNED ABOUT THE TROJAN VIRUS I JUST USED TO OPEN A BACKDOOR TO YOUR SLAVE SERVER IN THAILAND.
FOUND THAT, DID YOU? WHY DON'T YOU TRY CHASING ME THROUGH NEW ZEALAND?
I ALREADY DID. THAT WAS A NASTY REVERSE FIREWALL YOU BUILT. TOO BAD I DISASSEMBLED IT FOR YOU.
I'M GETTING ANGRY NOW...
GOTHAM CITY.
"YOU WANT TO PLAY ROUGH, ORACLE?"
"LETS PLAY ROUGH!"

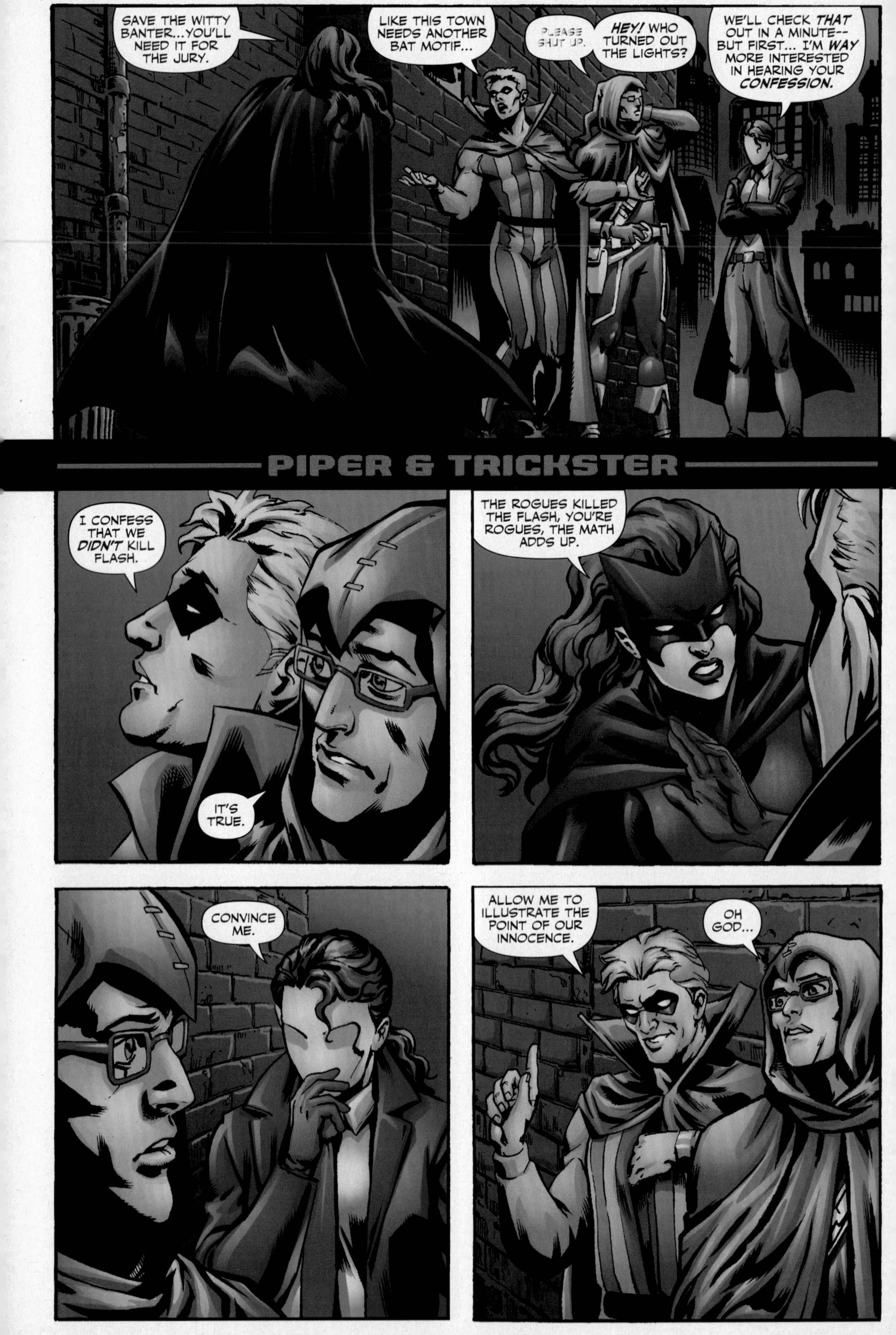
SAVE THE WITTY BANTER...YOU'LL NEED IT FOR THE JURY.
LIKE THIS TOWN NEEDS ANOTHER BAT MOTIF...
PLEASE SHUT UP.
HEY! WHO TURNED OUT THE LIGHTS?
WE'LL CHECK THAT OUT IN A MINUTE-- BUT FIRST... I'M WAY MORE INTERESTED IN HEARING YOUR CONFESSION.
PIPER & TRICKSTER
I CONFESS THAT WE DIDN'T KILL FLASH.
IT'S TRUE.
THE ROGUES KILLED THE FLASH, YOU'RE ROGUES, THE MATH ADDS UP.
CONVINCE ME.
ALLOW ME TO ILLUSTRATE THE POINT OF OUR INNOCENCE.
OH GOD...

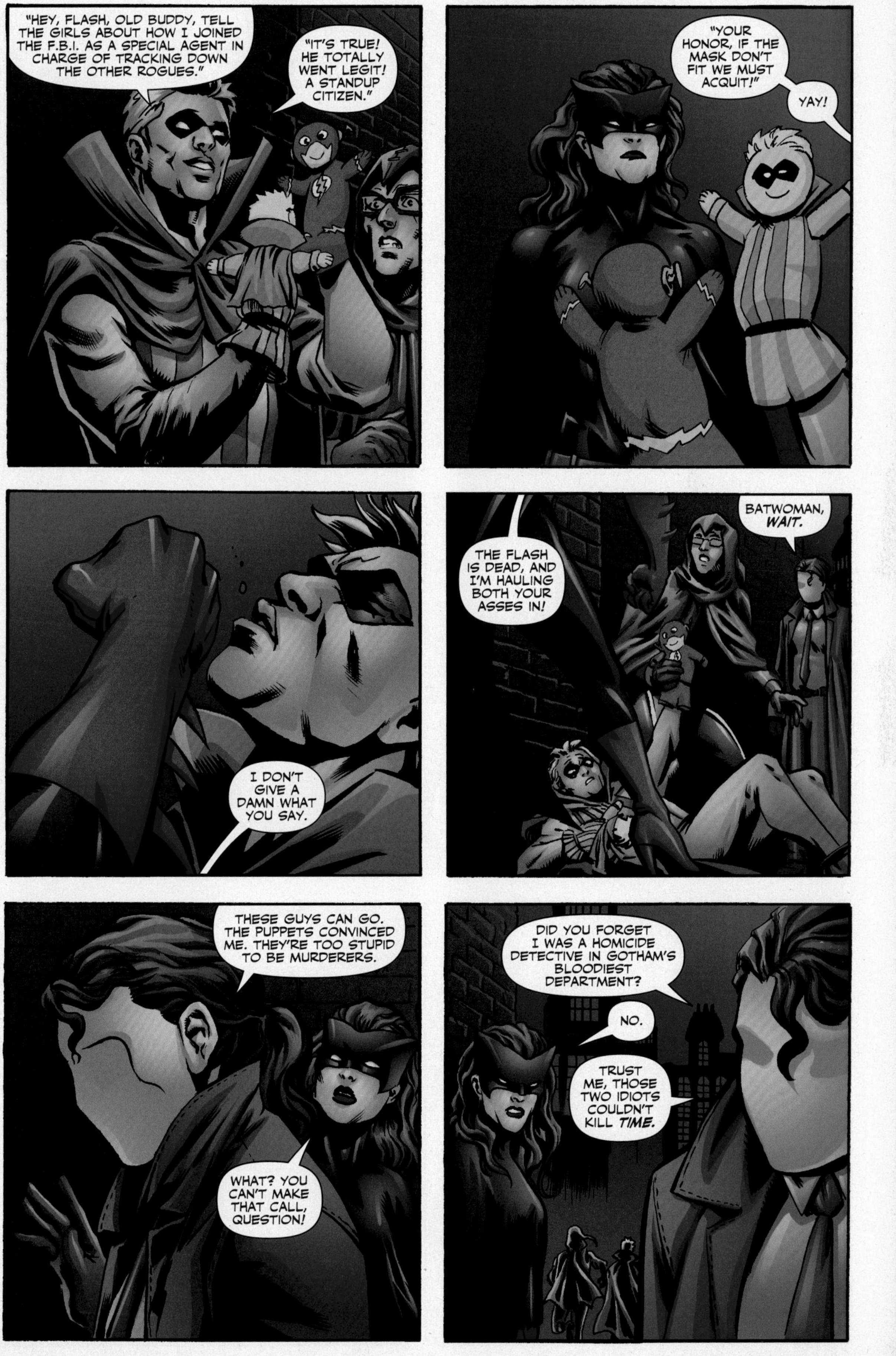
"HEY, FLASH, OLD BUDDY, TELL THE GIRLS ABOUT HOW I JOINED THE F.B.I. AS A SPECIAL AGENT IN CHARGE OF TRACKING DOWN THE OTHER ROGUES."
"IT'S TRUE! HE TOTALLY WENT LEGIT! A STANDUP CITIZEN."
"YOUR HONOR, IF THE MASK DON'T FIT WE MUST ACQUIT!"
YAY!
I DON'T GIVE A DAMN WHAT YOU SAY.
THE FLASH IS DEAD, AND I'M HAULING BOTH YOUR ASSES IN!
BATWOMAN, *WAIT.*
THESE GUYS CAN GO. THE PUPPETS CONVINCED ME. THEY'RE TOO STUPID TO BE MURDERERS.
WHAT? YOU CAN'T MAKE THAT CALL, QUESTION!
DID YOU FORGET I WAS A HOMICIDE DETECTIVE IN GOTHAM'S BLOODIEST DEPARTMENT?
NO.
TRUST ME, THOSE TWO IDIOTS COULDN'T KILL *TIME.*

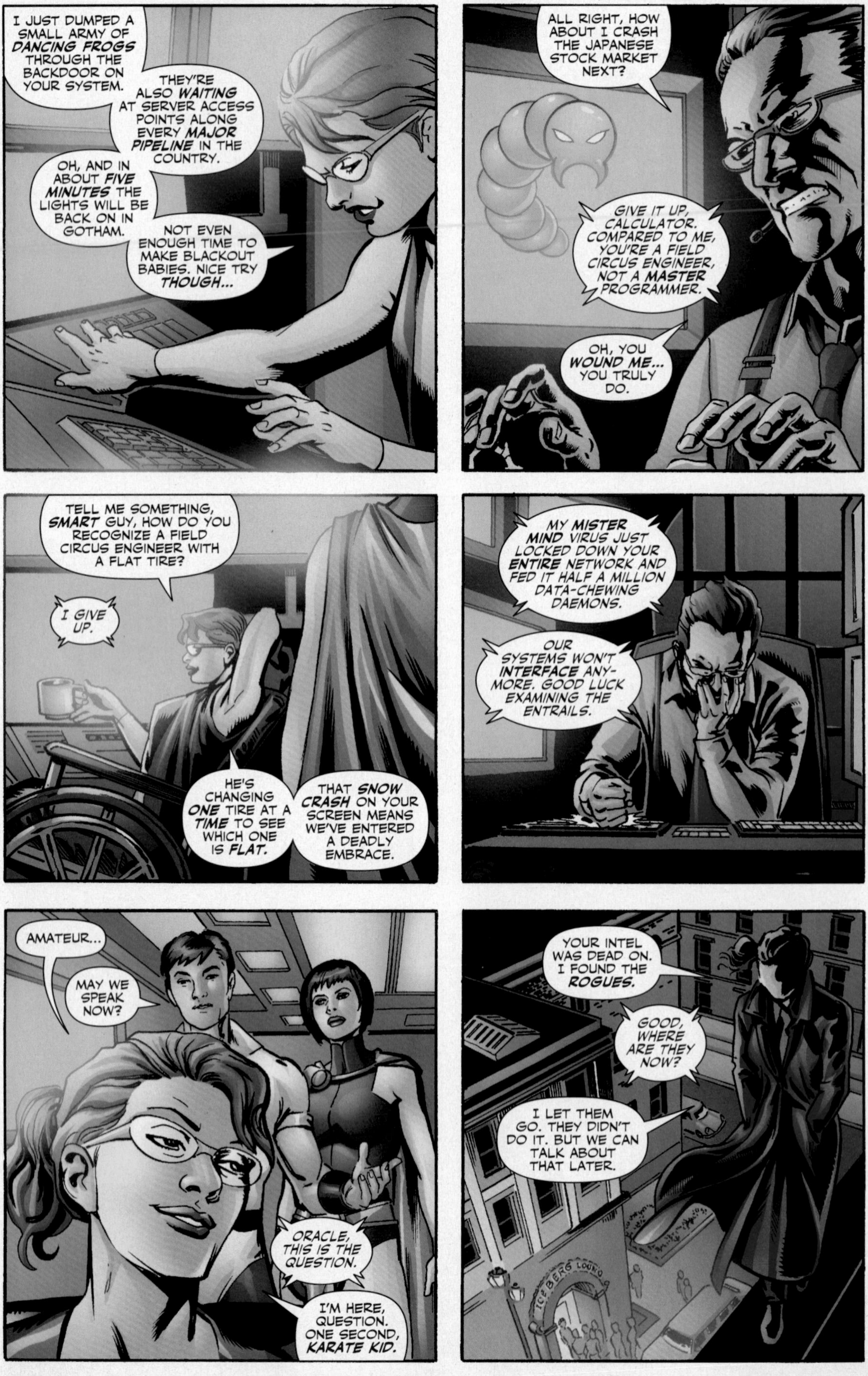
I JUST DUMPED A SMALL ARMY OF DANCING FROGS THROUGH THE BACKDOOR ON YOUR SYSTEM.
THEY'RE ALSO WAITING AT SERVER ACCESS POINTS ALONG EVERY MAJOR PIPELINE IN THE COUNTRY.
OH, AND IN ABOUT FIVE MINUTES THE LIGHTS WILL BE BACK ON IN GOTHAM.
NOT EVEN ENOUGH TIME TO MAKE BLACKOUT BABIES. NICE TRY THOUGH...
ALL RIGHT, HOW ABOUT I CRASH THE JAPANESE STOCK MARKET NEXT?
GIVE IT UP, CALCULATOR. COMPARED TO ME, YOU'RE A FIELD CIRCUS ENGINEER, NOT A MASTER PROGRAMMER.
OH, YOU WOUND ME... YOU TRULY DO.
TELL ME SOMETHING, SMART GUY, HOW DO YOU RECOGNIZE A FIELD CIRCUS ENGINEER WITH A FLAT TIRE?
I GIVE UP.
HE'S CHANGING ONE TIRE AT A TIME TO SEE WHICH ONE IS FLAT.
THAT SNOW CRASH ON YOUR SCREEN MEANS WE'VE ENTERED A DEADLY EMBRACE.
MY MISTER MIND VIRUS JUST LOCKED DOWN YOUR ENTIRE NETWORK AND FED IT HALF A MILLION DATA-CHEWING DAEMONS.
OUR SYSTEMS WON'T INTERFACE ANY-MORE. GOOD LUCK EXAMINING THE ENTRAILS.
AMATEUR...
MAY WE SPEAK NOW?
ORACLE, THIS IS THE QUESTION.
I'M HERE, QUESTION. ONE SECOND, KARATE KID.
YOUR INTEL WAS DEAD ON. I FOUND THE ROGUES.
GOOD, WHERE ARE THEY NOW?
I LET THEM GO. THEY DIDN'T DO IT. BUT WE CAN TALK ABOUT THAT LATER.
ICEBERG LOUNGE

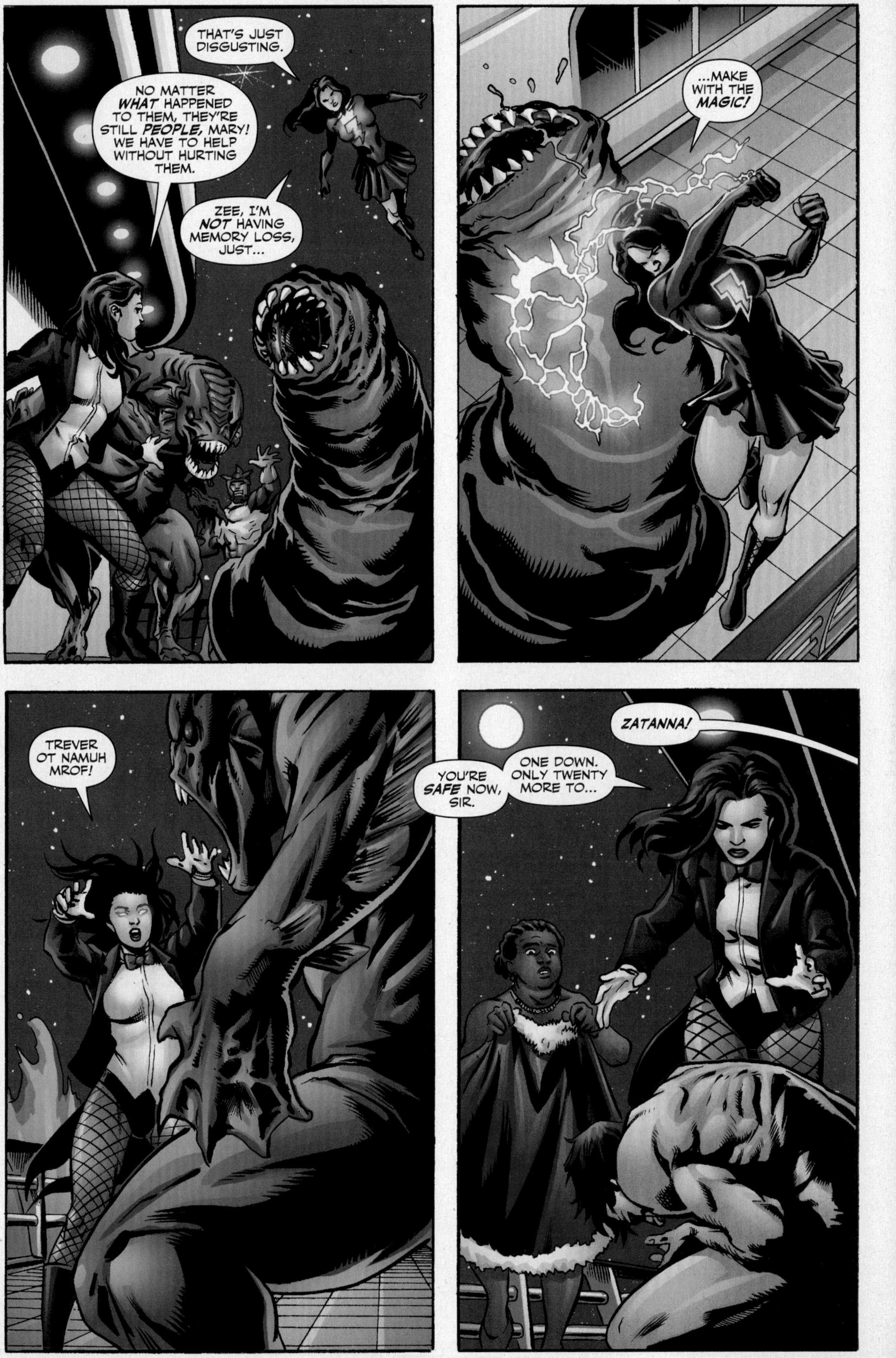
THAT'S JUST DISGUSTING.
NO MATTER *WHAT* HAPPENED TO THEM, THEY'RE STILL *PEOPLE,* MARY! WE HAVE TO HELP WITHOUT HURTING THEM.
ZEE, I'M *NOT* HAVING MEMORY LOSS, JUST...
...MAKE WITH THE *MAGIC!*
TREVER OT NAMUH MROF!
YOU'RE *SAFE* NOW, SIR.
ONE DOWN. ONLY TWENTY MORE TO...
*ZATANNA!*

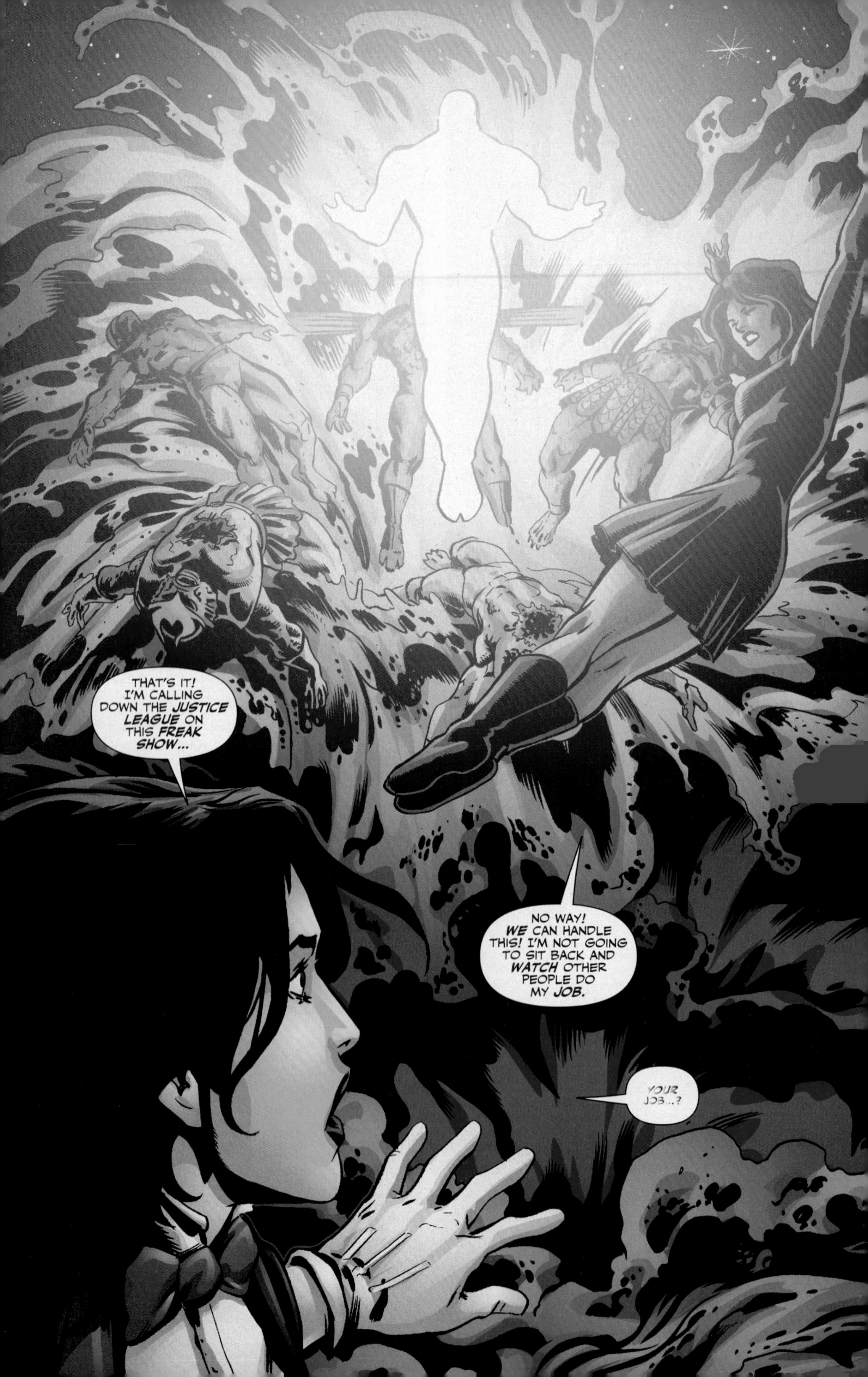
THAT'S IT! I'M CALLING DOWN THE JUSTICE LEAGUE ON THIS FREAK SHOW...
NO WAY! WE CAN HANDLE THIS! I'M NOT GOING TO SIT BACK AND WATCH OTHER PEOPLE DO MY JOB.
YOUR JOB...?

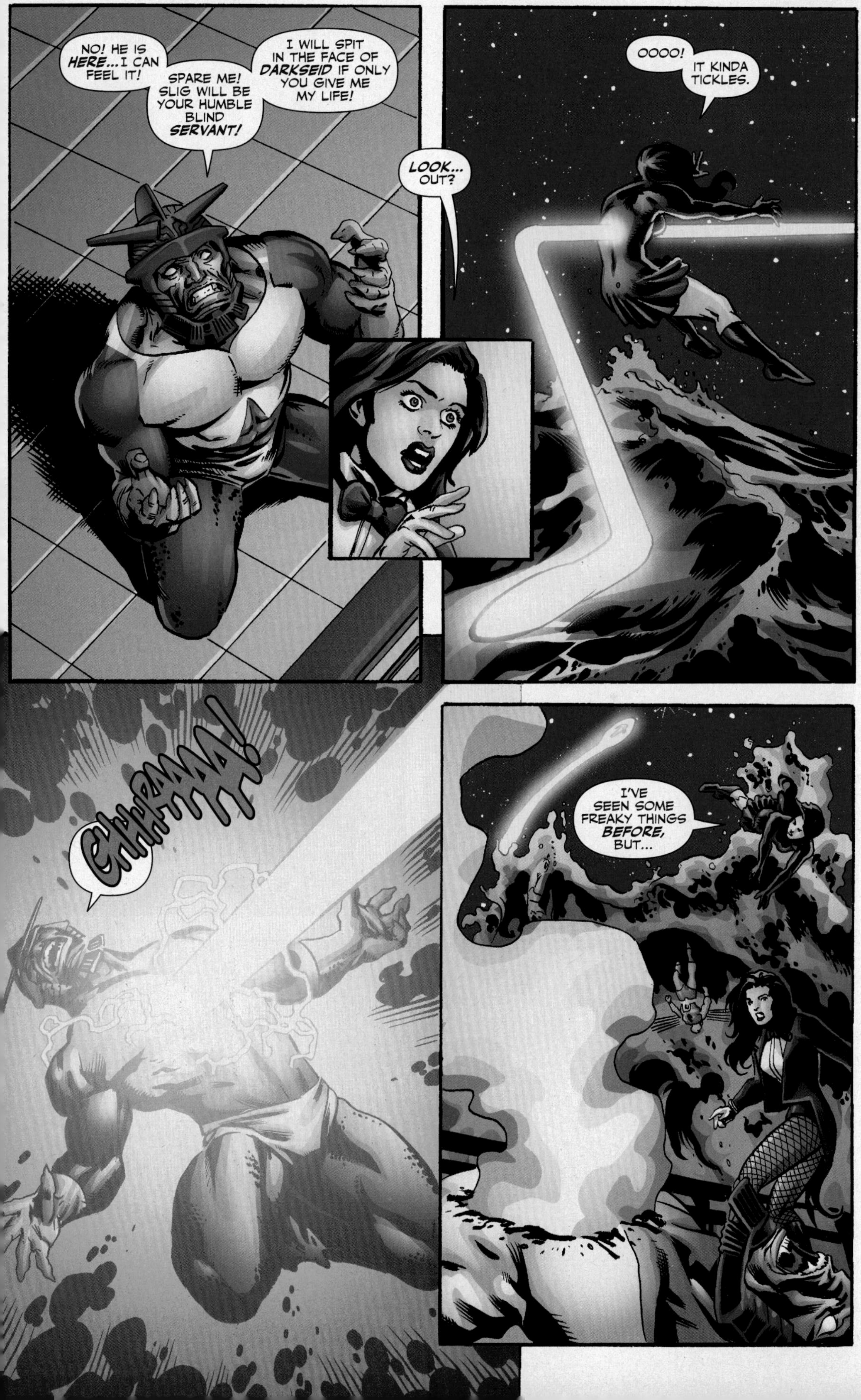
NO! HE IS *HERE*...I CAN FEEL IT!
SPARE ME! SLIG WILL BE YOUR HUMBLE BLIND *SERVANT!*
I WILL SPIT IN THE FACE OF *DARKSEID* IF ONLY YOU GIVE ME MY LIFE!
*LOOK...* OUT?
OOOO! IT KINDA TICKLES.
CHHRAAAA!
I'VE SEEN SOME FREAKY THINGS *BEFORE,* BUT...

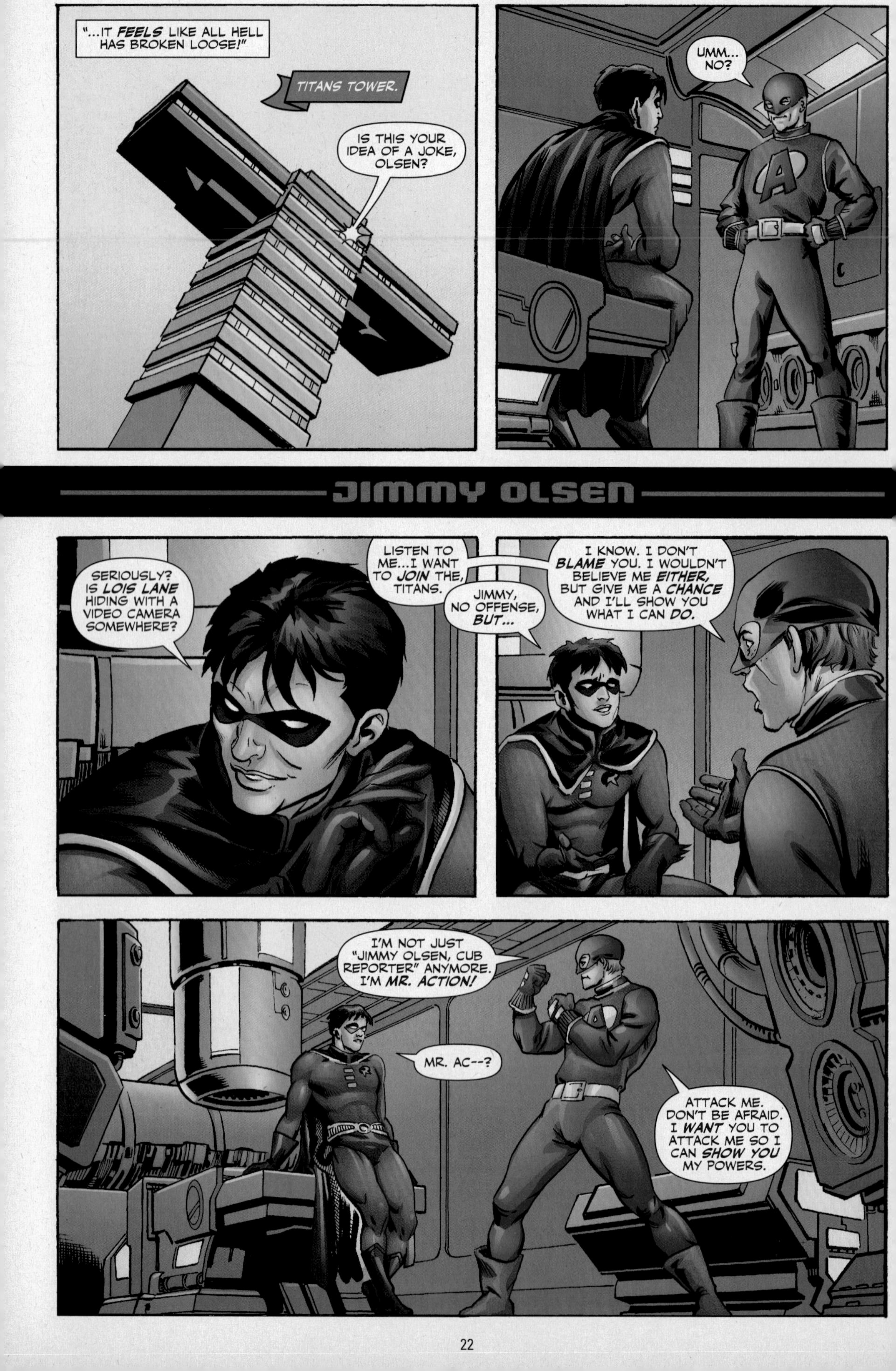
"...IT *FEELS* LIKE ALL HELL HAS BROKEN LOOSE!"
TITANS TOWER.
IS THIS YOUR IDEA OF A JOKE, OLSEN?
UMM... NO?
JIMMY OLSEN
SERIOUSLY? IS *LOIS LANE* HIDING WITH A VIDEO CAMERA SOMEWHERE?
LISTEN TO ME...I WANT TO *JOIN* THE TITANS.
JIMMY, NO OFFENSE, *BUT...*
I KNOW. I DON'T *BLAME* YOU. I WOULDN'T BELIEVE ME *EITHER,* BUT GIVE ME A *CHANCE* AND I'LL SHOW YOU WHAT I CAN *DO.*
I'M NOT JUST "JIMMY OLSEN, CUB REPORTER" ANYMORE. I'M *MR. ACTION!*
MR. AC--?
ATTACK ME. DON'T BE AFRAID. I *WANT* YOU TO ATTACK ME SO I CAN *SHOW YOU* MY POWERS.

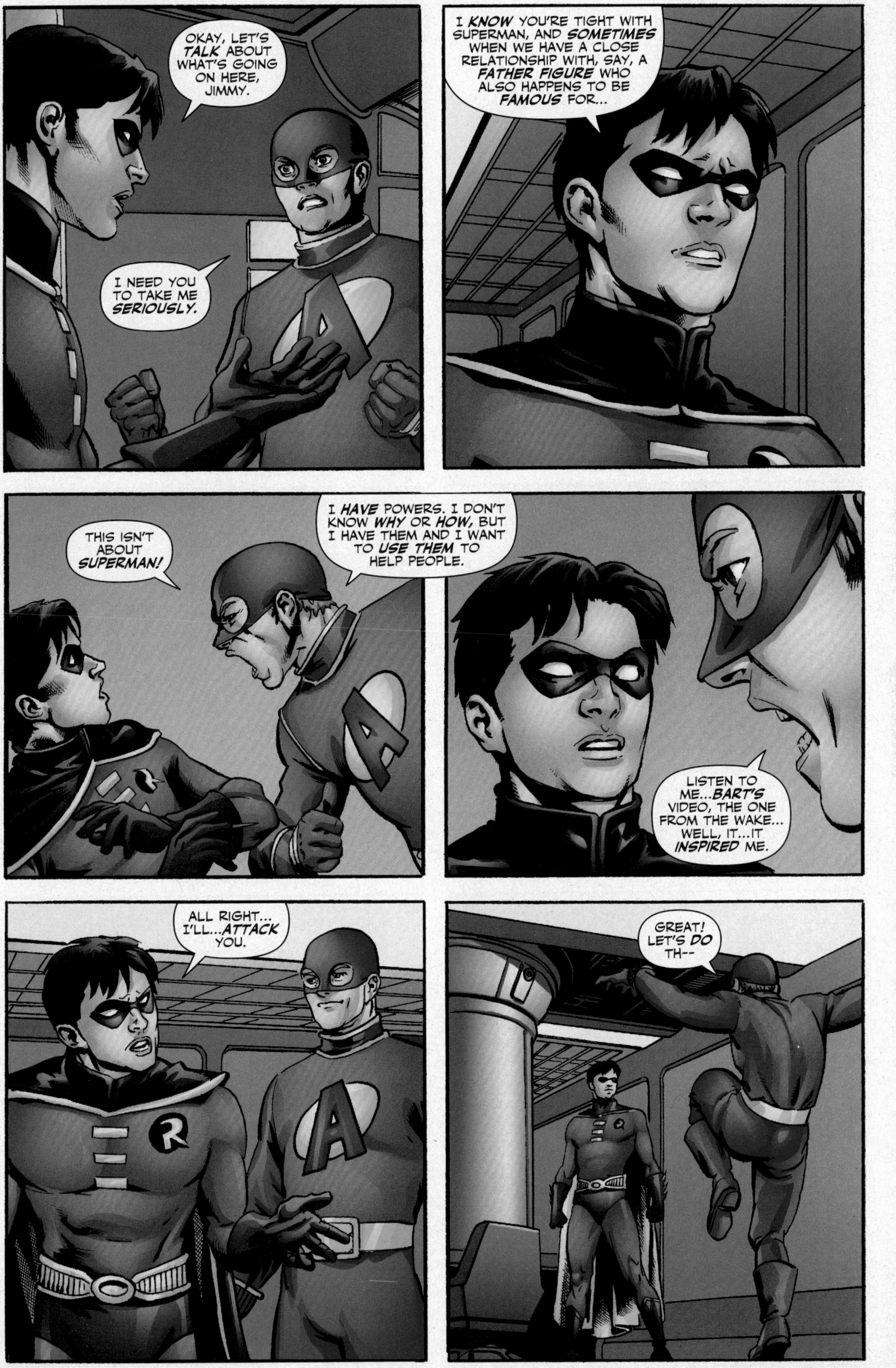
OKAY, LET'S TALK ABOUT WHAT'S GOING ON HERE, JIMMY.
I NEED YOU TO TAKE ME SERIOUSLY.
I KNOW YOU'RE TIGHT WITH SUPERMAN, AND SOMETIMES WHEN WE HAVE A CLOSE RELATIONSHIP WITH, SAY, A FATHER FIGURE WHO ALSO HAPPENS TO BE FAMOUS FOR...
THIS ISN'T ABOUT SUPERMAN!
I HAVE POWERS. I DON'T KNOW WHY OR HOW, BUT I HAVE THEM AND I WANT TO USE THEM TO HELP PEOPLE.
LISTEN TO ME...BART'S VIDEO, THE ONE FROM THE WAKE... WELL, IT...IT INSPIRED ME.
ALL RIGHT... I'LL...ATTACK YOU.
GREAT! LET'S DO TH--

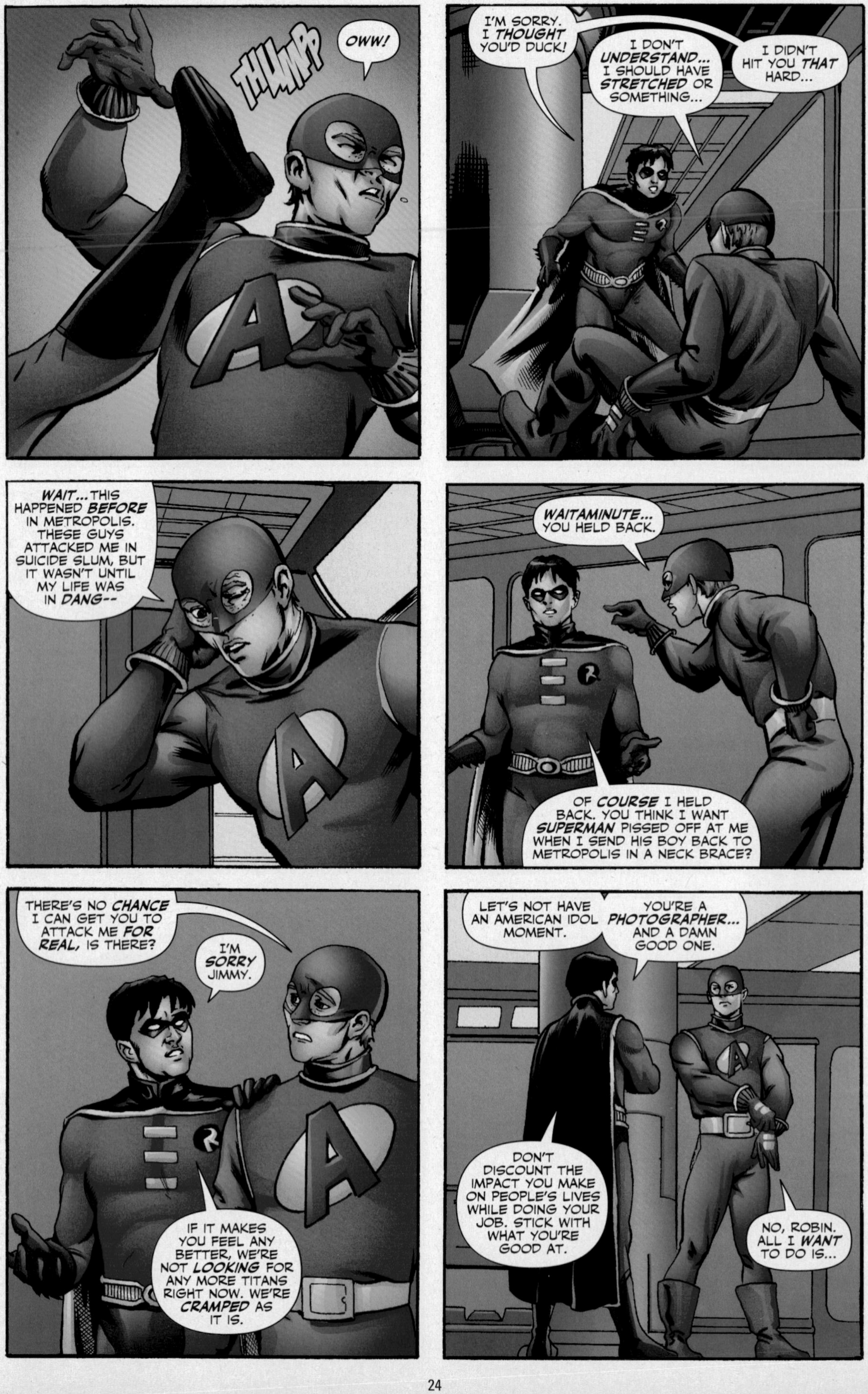
THUMPP
OWW!
I'M SORRY. I THOUGHT YOU'D DUCK!
I DON'T UNDERSTAND... I SHOULD HAVE STRETCHED OR SOMETHING...
I DIDN'T HIT YOU THAT HARD...
WAIT... THIS HAPPENED BEFORE IN METROPOLIS. THESE GUYS ATTACKED ME IN SUICIDE SLUM, BUT IT WASN'T UNTIL MY LIFE WAS IN DANG--
WAITAMINUTE... YOU HELD BACK.
OF COURSE I HELD BACK. YOU THINK I WANT SUPERMAN PISSED OFF AT ME WHEN I SEND HIS BOY BACK TO METROPOLIS IN A NECK BRACE?
THERE'S NO CHANCE I CAN GET YOU TO ATTACK ME FOR REAL, IS THERE?
I'M SORRY JIMMY.
IF IT MAKES YOU FEEL ANY BETTER, WE'RE NOT LOOKING FOR ANY MORE TITANS RIGHT NOW. WE'RE CRAMPED AS IT IS.
LET'S NOT HAVE AN AMERICAN IDOL MOMENT.
YOU'RE A PHOTOGRAPHER... AND A DAMN GOOD ONE.
DON'T DISCOUNT THE IMPACT YOU MAKE ON PEOPLE'S LIVES WHILE DOING YOUR JOB. STICK WITH WHAT YOU'RE GOOD AT.
NO, ROBIN. ALL I WANT TO DO IS...

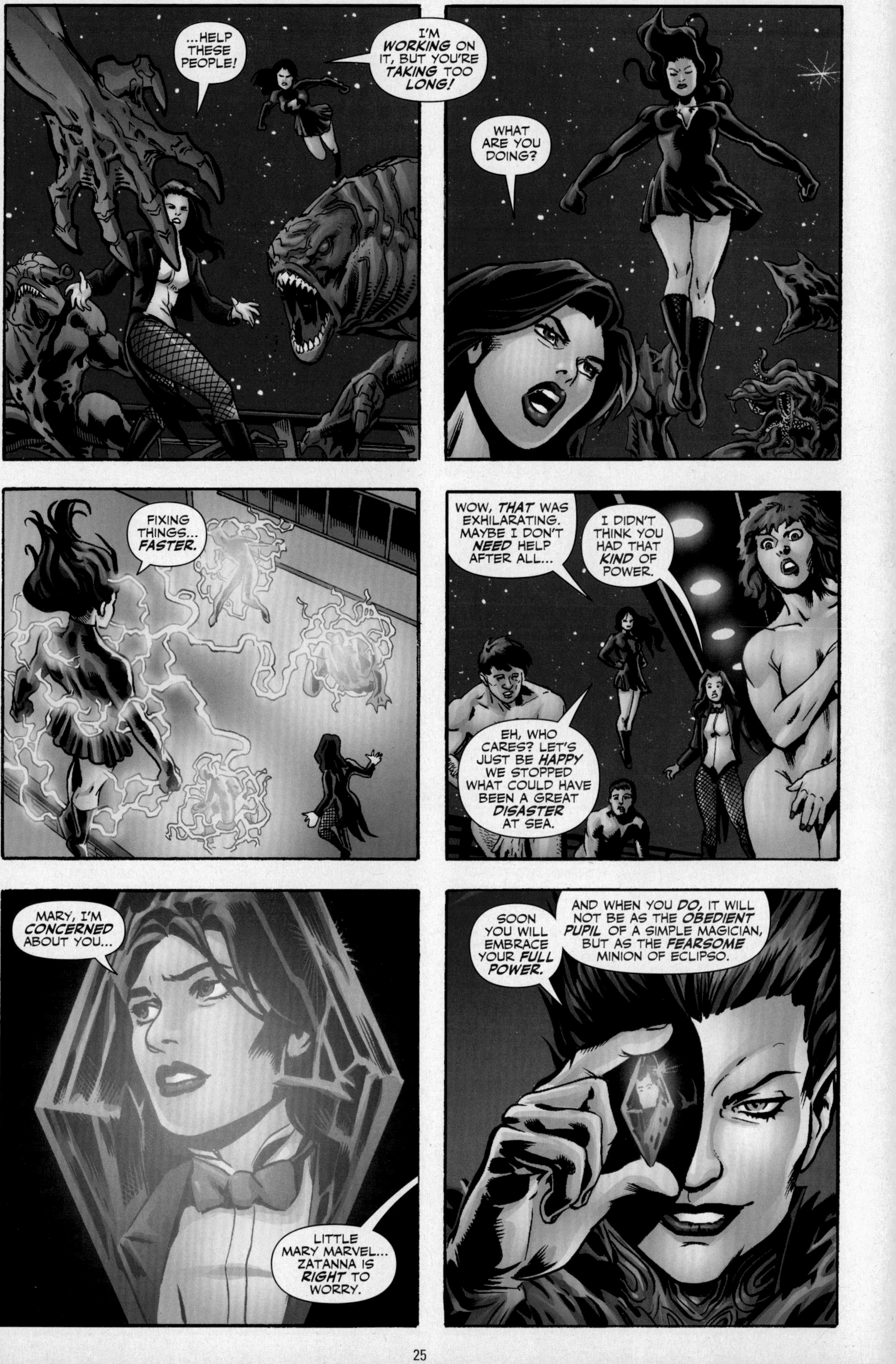
...HELP THESE PEOPLE!
I'M WORKING ON IT, BUT YOU'RE TAKING TOO LONG!
WHAT ARE YOU DOING?
FIXING THINGS... FASTER.
WOW, THAT WAS EXHILARATING. MAYBE I DON'T NEED HELP AFTER ALL...
I DIDN'T THINK YOU HAD THAT KIND OF POWER.
EH, WHO CARES? LET'S JUST BE HAPPY WE STOPPED WHAT COULD HAVE BEEN A GREAT DISASTER AT SEA.
MARY, I'M CONCERNED ABOUT YOU...
LITTLE MARY MARVEL... ZATANNA IS RIGHT TO WORRY.
SOON YOU WILL EMBRACE YOUR FULL POWER.
AND WHEN YOU DO, IT WILL NOT BE AS THE OBEDIENT PUPIL OF A SIMPLE MAGICIAN, BUT AS THE FEARSOME MINION OF ECLIPSO.

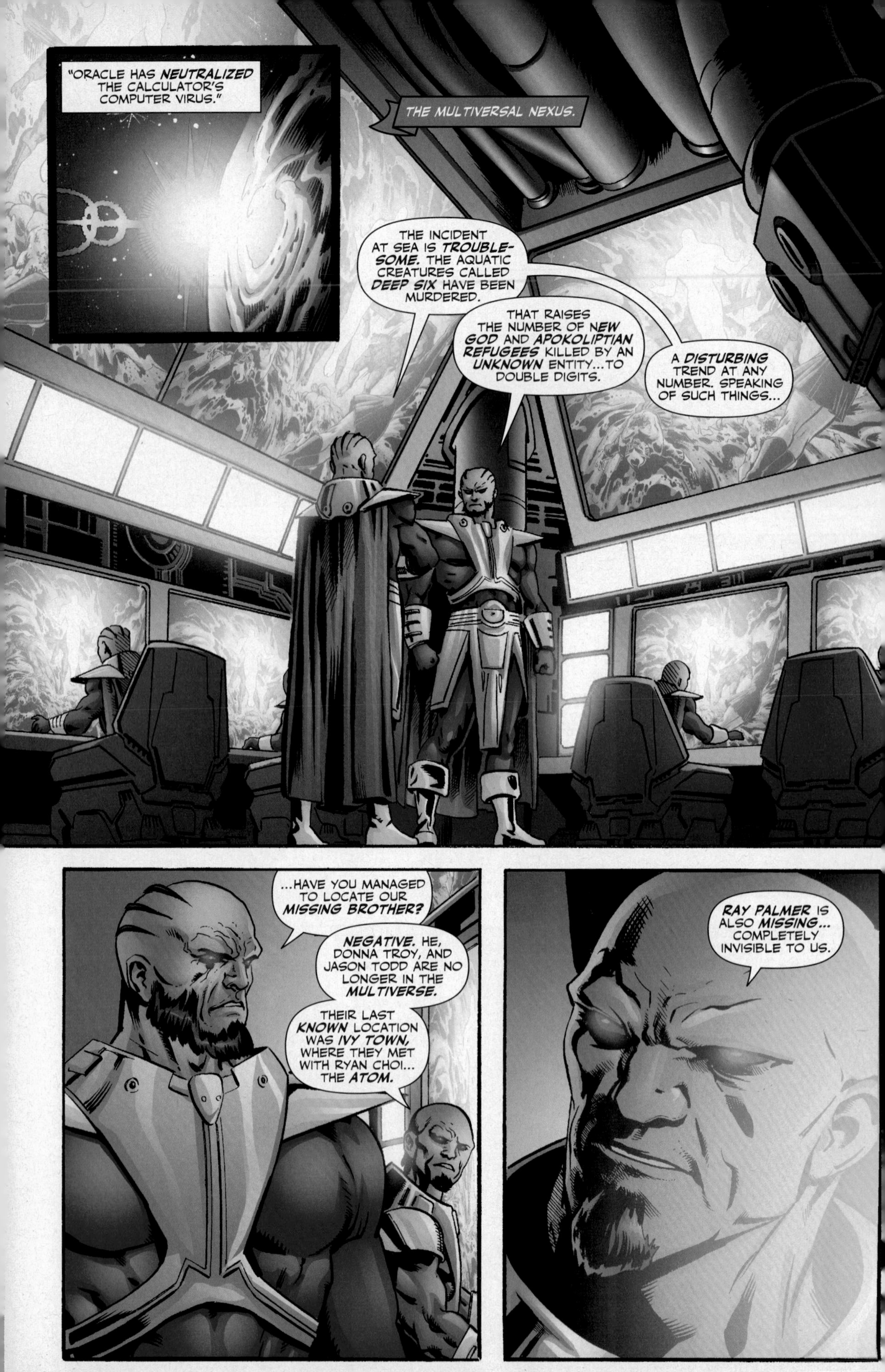
"ORACLE HAS NEUTRALIZED THE CALCULATOR'S COMPUTER VIRUS."
THE MULTIVERSAL NEXUS.
THE INCIDENT AT SEA IS TROUBLE-SOME. THE AQUATIC CREATURES CALLED DEEP SIX HAVE BEEN MURDERED.
THAT RAISES THE NUMBER OF NEW GOD AND APOKOLIPTIAN REFUGEES KILLED BY AN UNKNOWN ENTITY...TO DOUBLE DIGITS.
A DISTURBING TREND AT ANY NUMBER. SPEAKING OF SUCH THINGS...
...HAVE YOU MANAGED TO LOCATE OUR MISSING BROTHER?
NEGATIVE. HE, DONNA TROY, AND JASON TODD ARE NO LONGER IN THE MULTIVERSE.
THEIR LAST KNOWN LOCATION WAS IVY TOWN, WHERE THEY MET WITH RYAN CHOI... THE ATOM.
RAY PALMER IS ALSO MISSING... COMPLETELY INVISIBLE TO US.

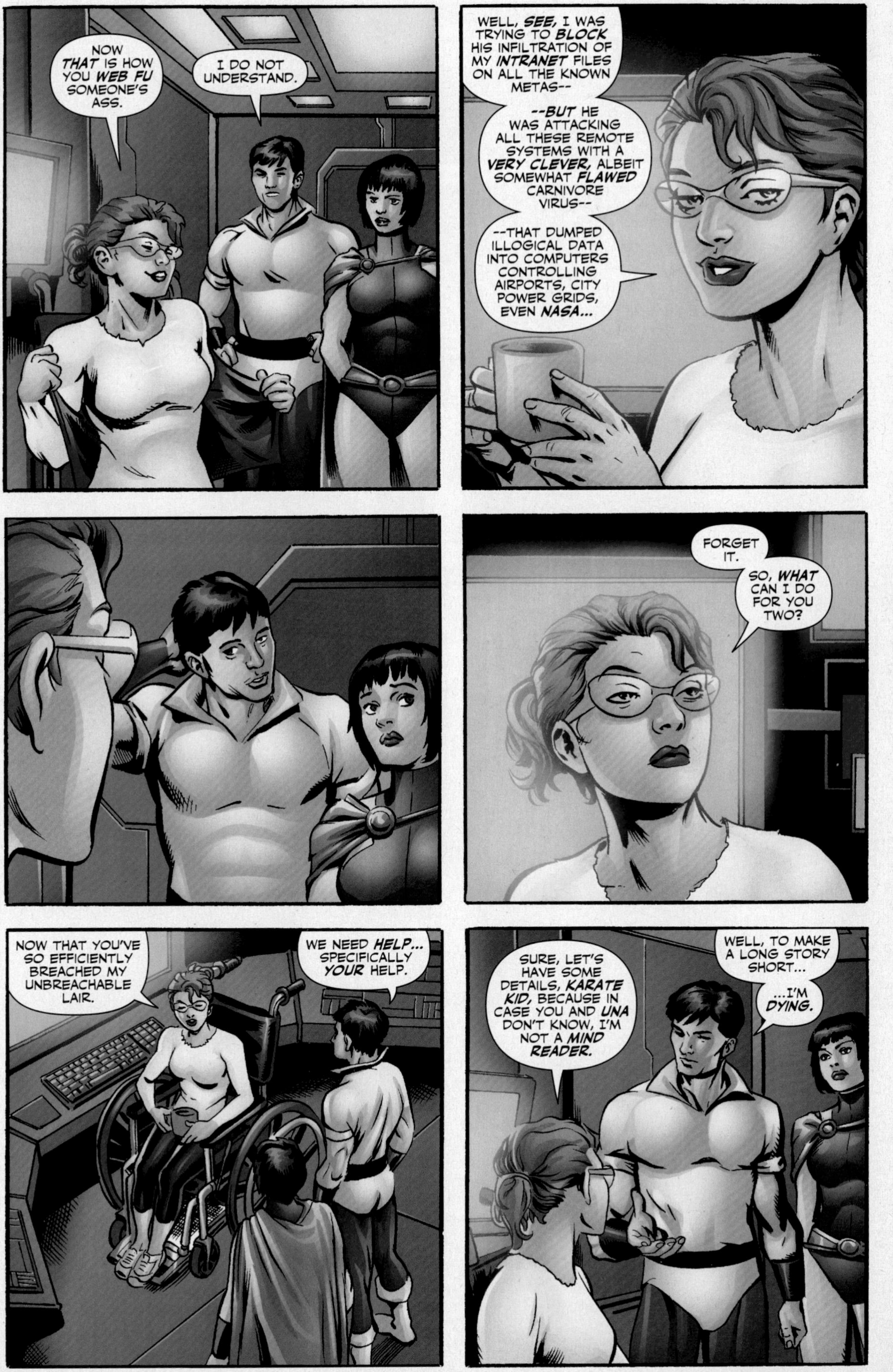
NOW THAT IS HOW YOU WEB FU SOMEONE'S ASS.
I DO NOT UNDERSTAND.
WELL, SEE, I WAS TRYING TO BLOCK HIS INFILTRATION OF MY INTRANET FILES ON ALL THE KNOWN METAS--
--BUT HE WAS ATTACKING ALL THESE REMOTE SYSTEMS WITH A VERY CLEVER, ALBEIT SOMEWHAT FLAWED CARNIVORE VIRUS--
--THAT DUMPED ILLOGICAL DATA INTO COMPUTERS CONTROLLING AIRPORTS, CITY POWER GRIDS, EVEN NASA...
FORGET IT.
SO, WHAT CAN I DO FOR YOU TWO?
NOW THAT YOU'VE SO EFFICIENTLY BREACHED MY UNBREACHABLE LAIR.
WE NEED HELP... SPECIFICALLY YOUR HELP.
SURE, LET'S HAVE SOME DETAILS, KARATE KID, BECAUSE IN CASE YOU AND UNA DON'T KNOW, I'M NOT A MIND READER.
WELL, TO MAKE A LONG STORY SHORT...
...I'M DYING.

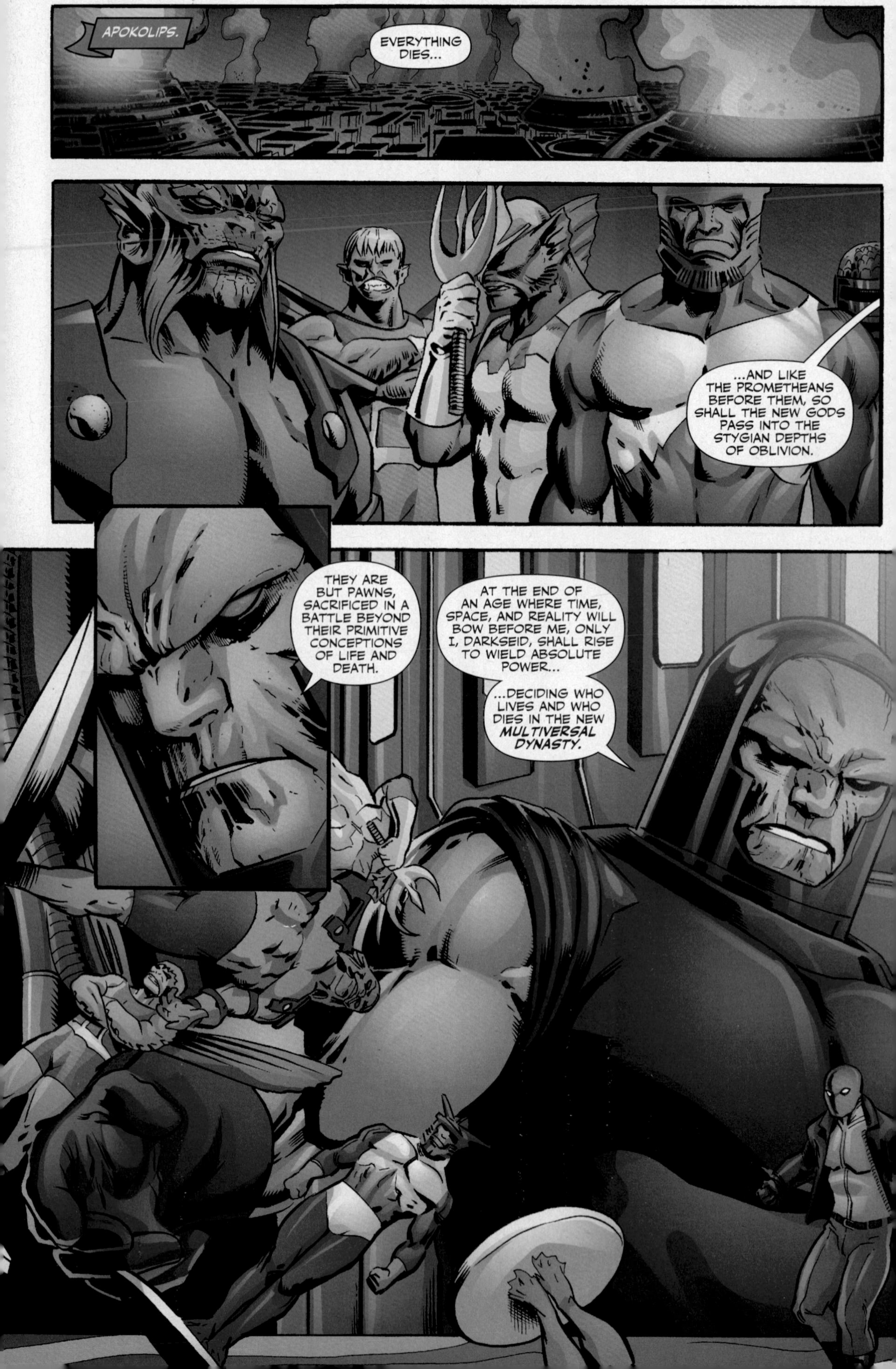
APOKOLIPS.
EVERYTHING DIES...
...AND LIKE THE PROMETHEANS BEFORE THEM, SO SHALL THE NEW GODS PASS INTO THE STYGIAN DEPTHS OF OBLIVION.
THEY ARE BUT PAWNS, SACRIFICED IN A BATTLE BEYOND THEIR PRIMITIVE CONCEPTIONS OF LIFE AND DEATH.
AT THE END OF AN AGE WHERE TIME, SPACE, AND REALITY WILL BOW BEFORE ME, ONLY I, DARKSEID, SHALL RISE TO WIELD ABSOLUTE POWER...
...DECIDING WHO LIVES AND WHO DIES IN THE NEW *MULTIVERSAL DYNASTY.*

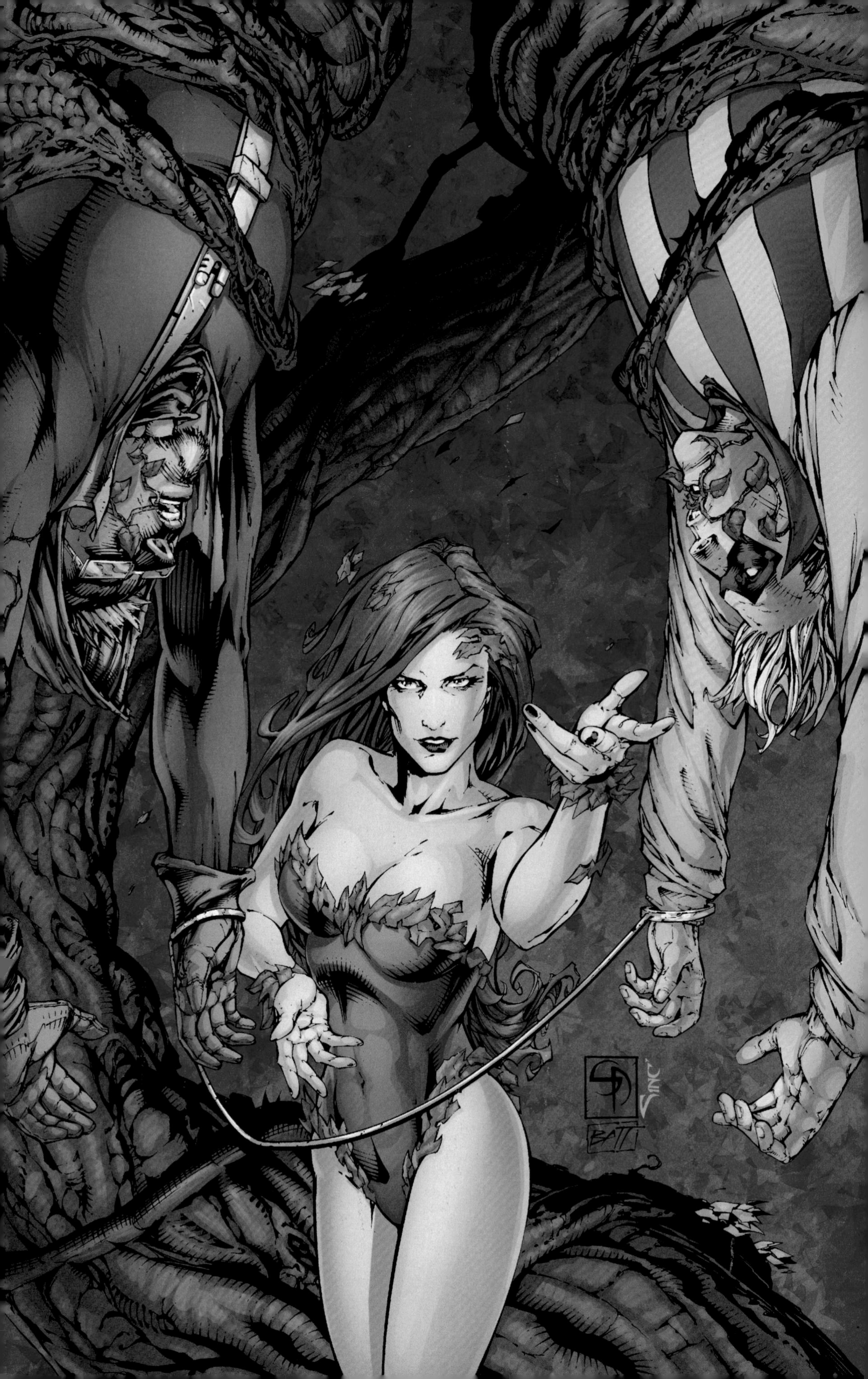

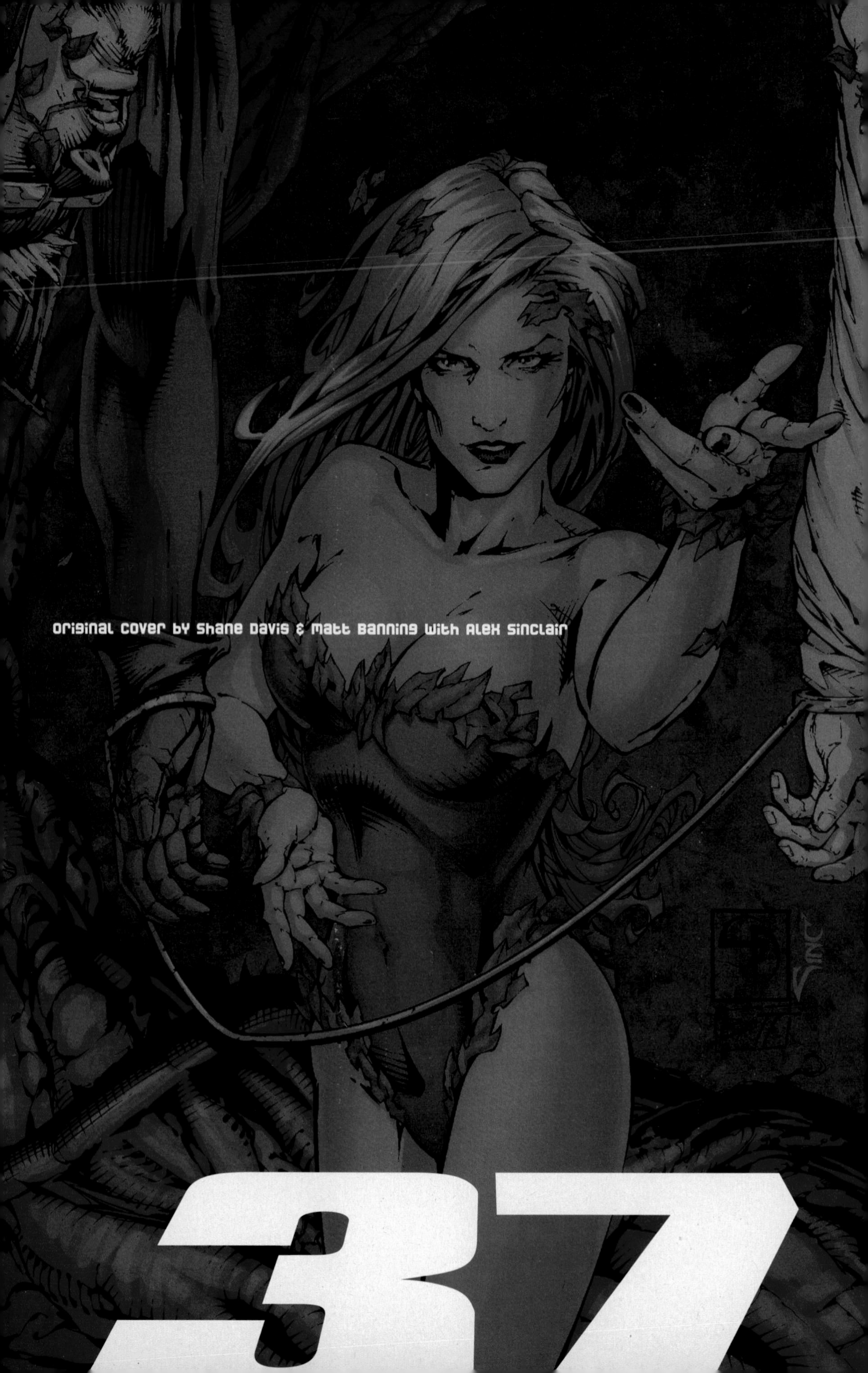

Original cover by Shane Davis & Matt Banning with Alex Sinclair

# 37

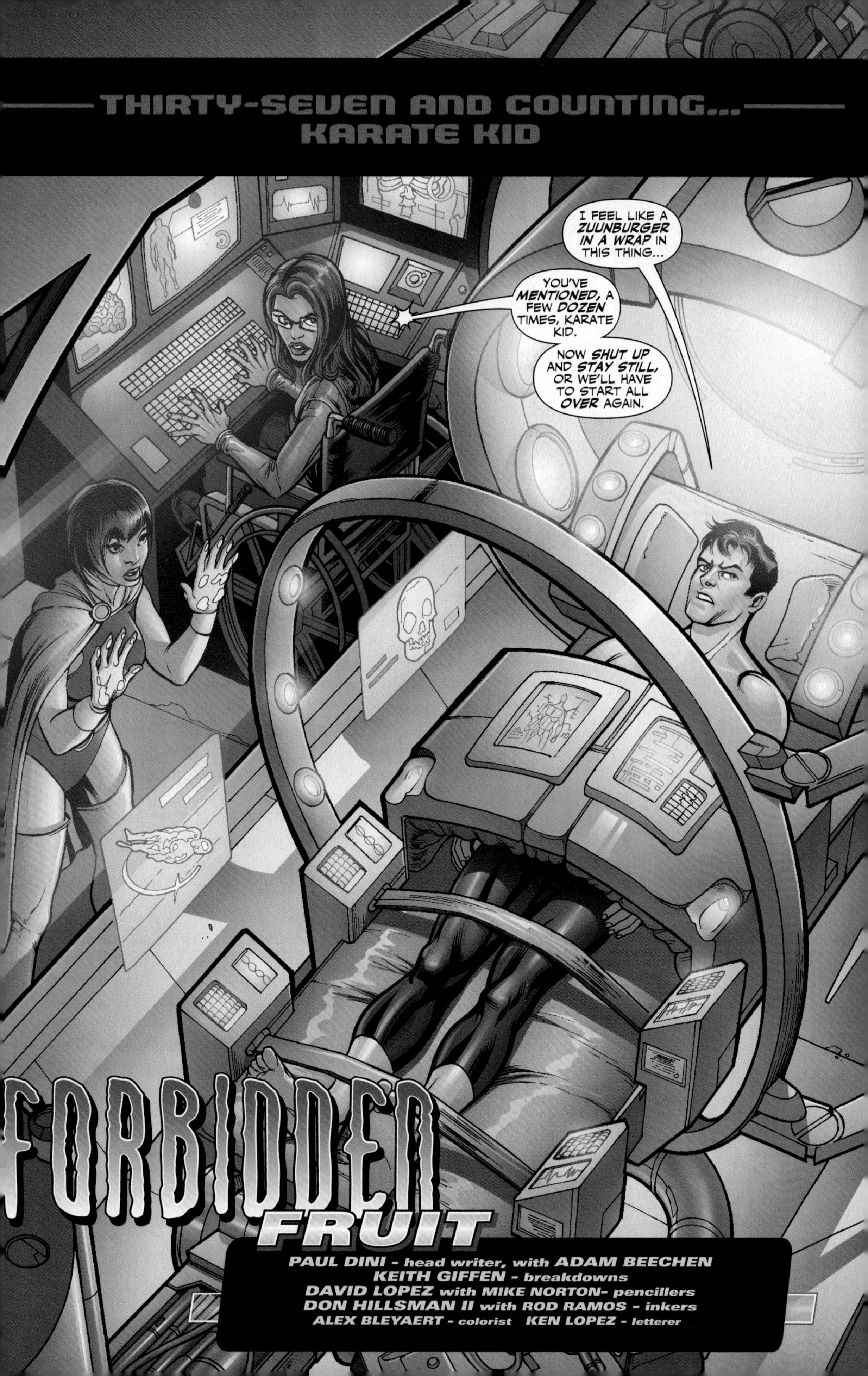
THIRTY-SEVEN AND COUNTING... KARATE KID
I FEEL LIKE A ZUUNBURGER IN A WRAP IN THIS THING...
YOU'VE MENTIONED, A FEW DOZEN TIMES, KARATE KID.
NOW SHUT UP AND STAY STILL, OR WE'LL HAVE TO START ALL OVER AGAIN.
FORBIDDEN FRUIT
PAUL DINI - head writer, with ADAM BEECHEN
KEITH GIFFEN - breakdowns
DAVID LOPEZ with MIKE NORTON- pencillers
DON HILLSMAN II with ROD RAMOS - inkers
ALEX BLEYAERT - colorist KEN LOPEZ - letterer

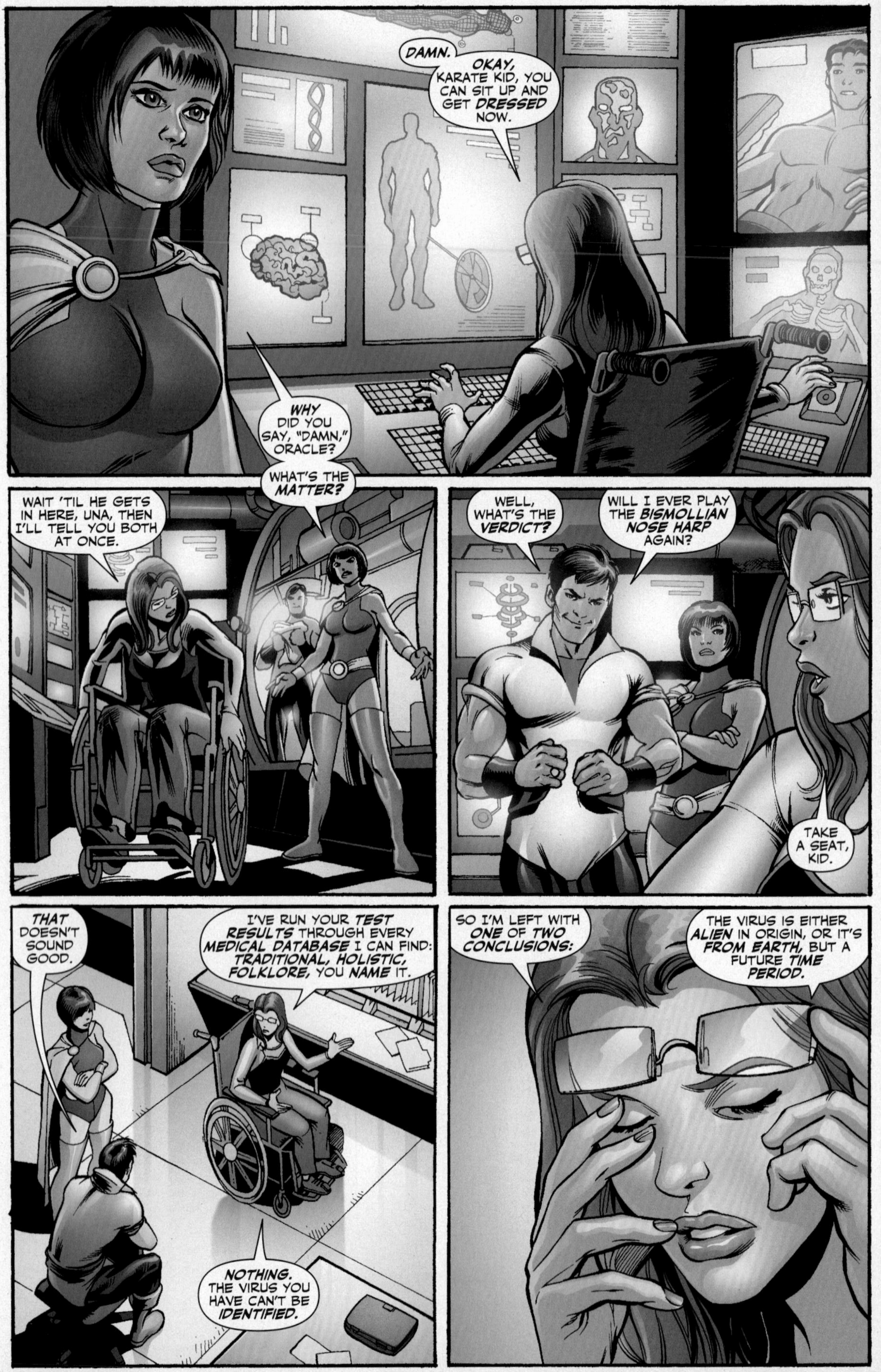
DAMN.
OKAY, KARATE KID, YOU CAN SIT UP AND GET DRESSED NOW.
WHY DID YOU SAY, "DAMN," ORACLE?
WHAT'S THE MATTER?
WAIT 'TIL HE GETS IN HERE, UNA, THEN I'LL TELL YOU BOTH AT ONCE.
WELL, WHAT'S THE VERDICT?
WILL I EVER PLAY THE BISMOLLIAN NOSE HARP AGAIN?
TAKE A SEAT, KID.
THAT DOESN'T SOUND GOOD.
I'VE RUN YOUR TEST RESULTS THROUGH EVERY MEDICAL DATABASE I CAN FIND: TRADITIONAL, HOLISTIC, FOLKLORE, YOU NAME IT.
NOTHING. THE VIRUS YOU HAVE CAN'T BE IDENTIFIED.
SO I'M LEFT WITH ONE OF TWO CONCLUSIONS:
THE VIRUS IS EITHER ALIEN IN ORIGIN, OR IT'S FROM EARTH, BUT A FUTURE TIME PERIOD.

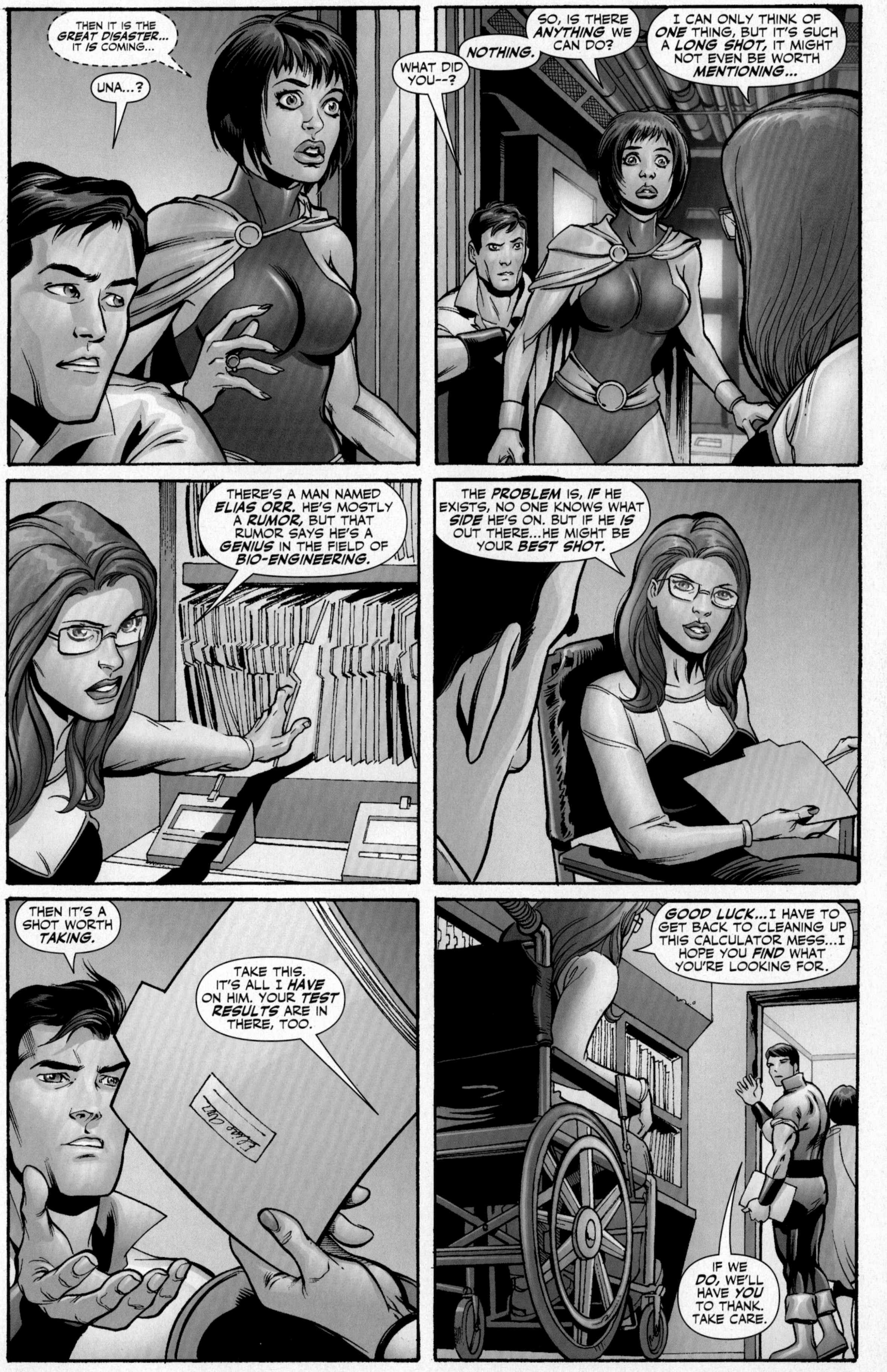
THEN IT IS THE GREAT DISASTER... IT IS COMING...
UNA...?
WHAT DID YOU--?
NOTHING.
SO, IS THERE ANYTHING WE CAN DO?
I CAN ONLY THINK OF ONE THING, BUT IT'S SUCH A LONG SHOT, IT MIGHT NOT EVEN BE WORTH MENTIONING...
THERE'S A MAN NAMED ELIAS ORR. HE'S MOSTLY A RUMOR, BUT THAT RUMOR SAYS HE'S A GENIUS IN THE FIELD OF BIO-ENGINEERING.
THE PROBLEM IS, IF HE EXISTS, NO ONE KNOWS WHAT SIDE HE'S ON. BUT IF HE IS OUT THERE...HE MIGHT BE YOUR BEST SHOT.
THEN IT'S A SHOT WORTH TAKING.
TAKE THIS. IT'S ALL I HAVE ON HIM. YOUR TEST RESULTS ARE IN THERE, TOO.
GOOD LUCK...I HAVE TO GET BACK TO CLEANING UP THIS CALCULATOR MESS...I HOPE YOU FIND WHAT YOU'RE LOOKING FOR.
IF WE DO, WE'LL HAVE YOU TO THANK. TAKE CARE.

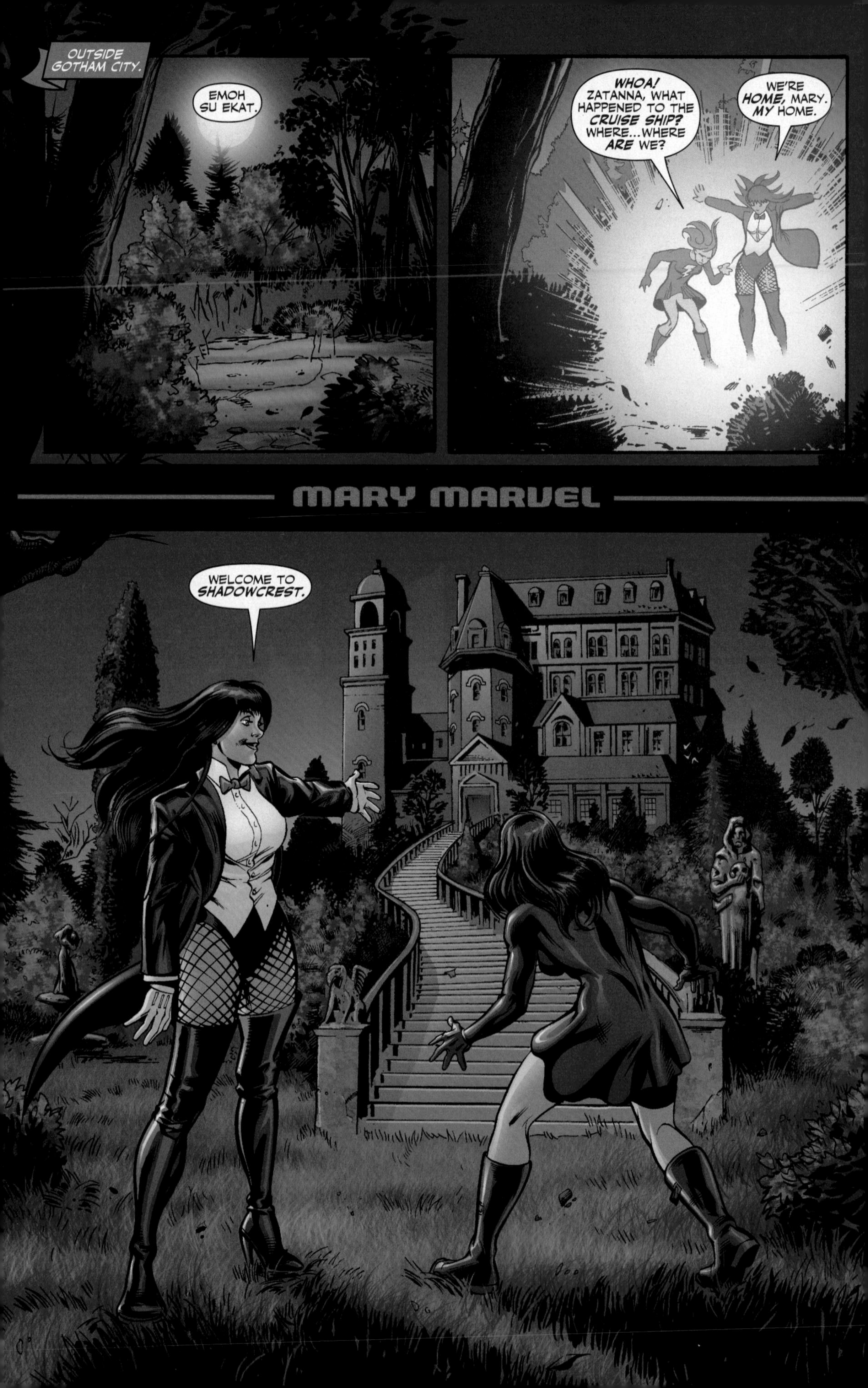
OUTSIDE GOTHAM CITY.
EMOH SU EKAT.
WHOA! ZATANNA, WHAT HAPPENED TO THE CRUISE SHIP? WHERE...WHERE ARE WE?
WE'RE HOME, MARY. MY HOME.
MARY MARVEL
WELCOME TO SHADOWCREST.

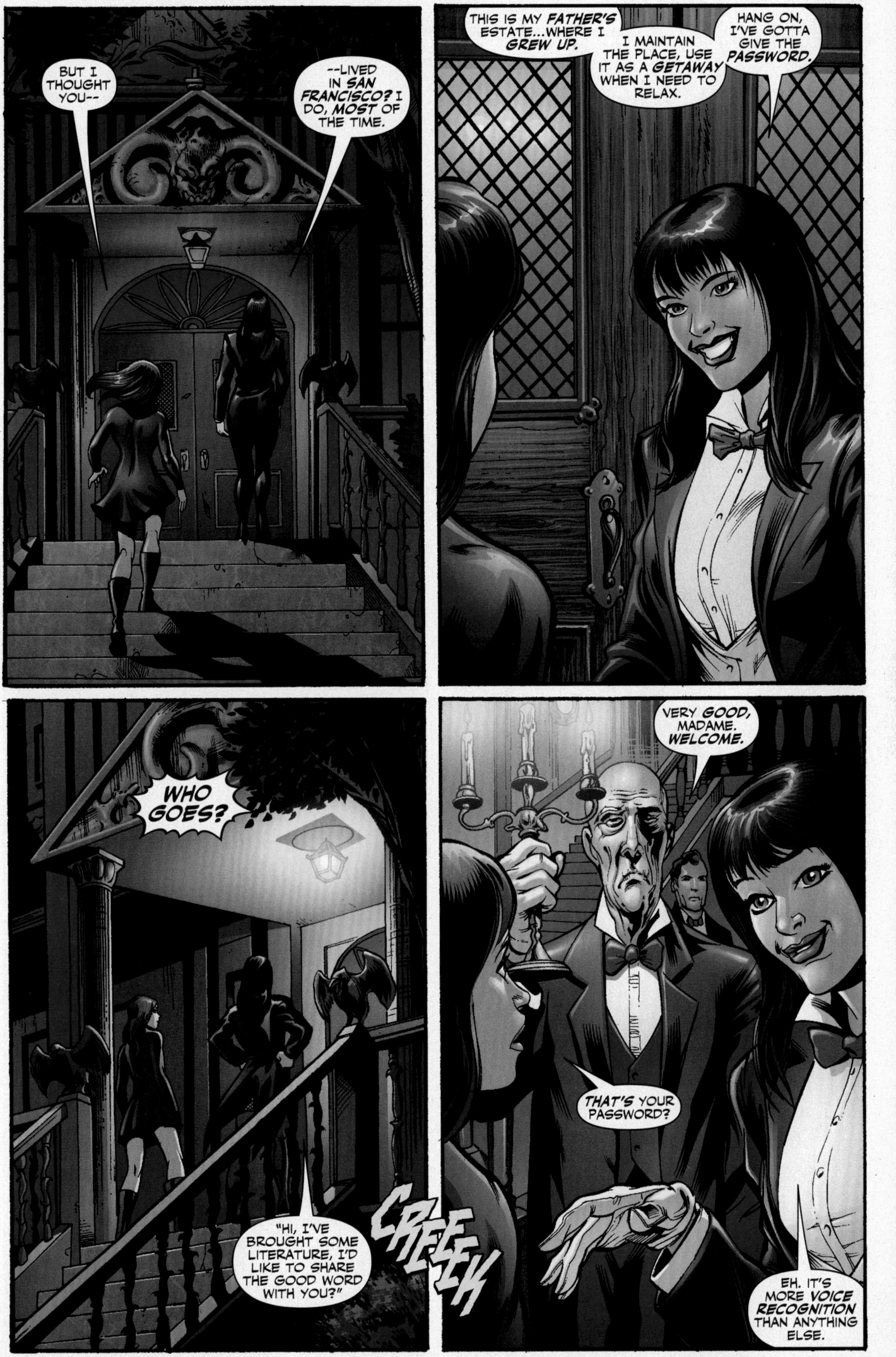

BUT I THOUGHT YOU--
--LIVED IN SAN FRANCISCO? I DO, MOST OF THE TIME.
THIS IS MY FATHER'S ESTATE...WHERE I GREW UP.
I MAINTAIN THE PLACE, USE IT AS A GETAWAY WHEN I NEED TO RELAX.
HANG ON, I'VE GOTTA GIVE THE PASSWORD.
WHO GOES?
"HI, I'VE BROUGHT SOME LITERATURE, I'D LIKE TO SHARE THE GOOD WORD WITH YOU?"
CREEEK
VERY GOOD, MADAME. WELCOME.
THAT'S YOUR PASSWORD?
EH. IT'S MORE VOICE RECOGNITION THAN ANYTHING ELSE.

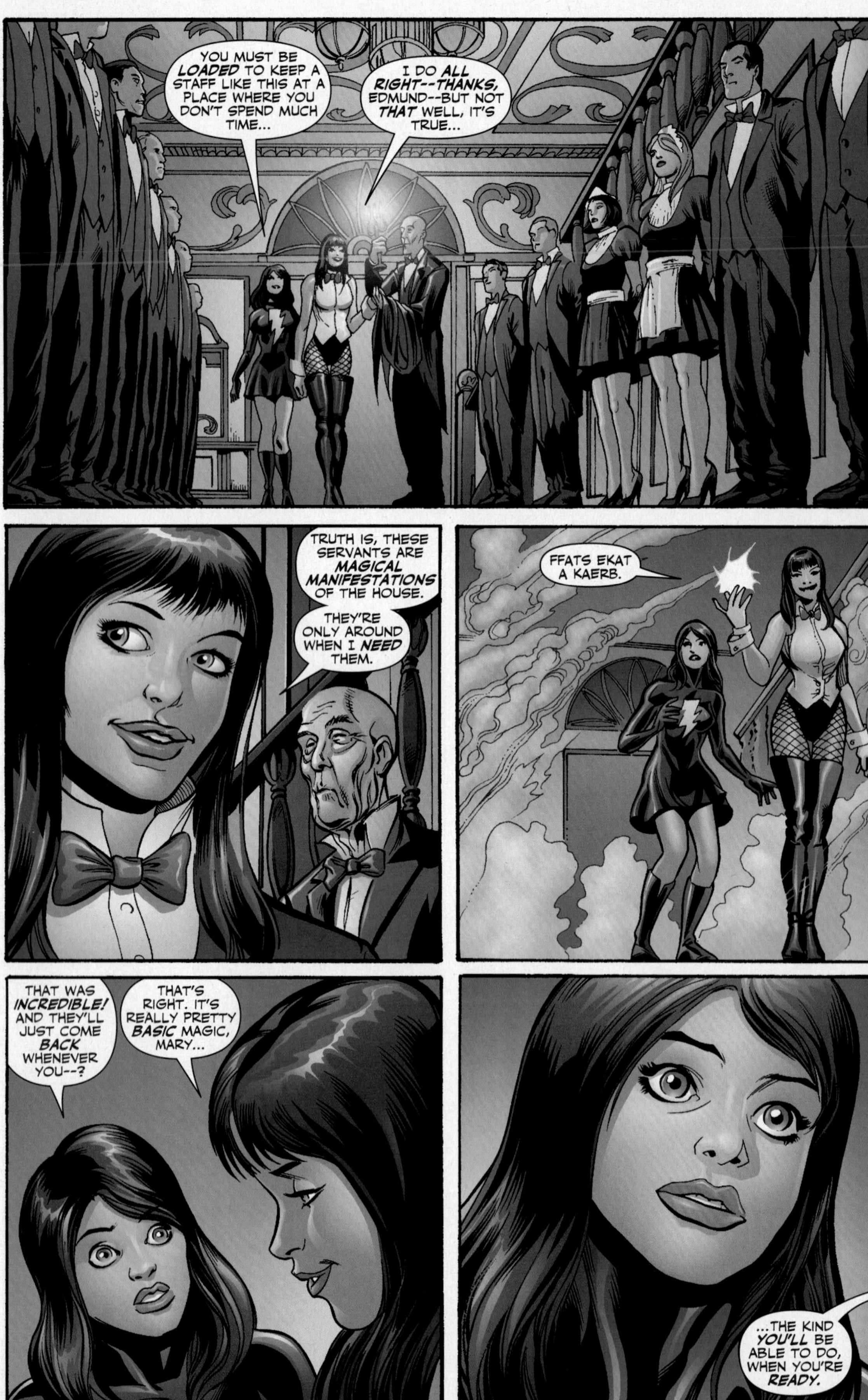
YOU MUST BE LOADED TO KEEP A STAFF LIKE THIS AT A PLACE WHERE YOU DON'T SPEND MUCH TIME...
I DO ALL RIGHT--THANKS, EDMUND--BUT NOT THAT WELL, IT'S TRUE...
TRUTH IS, THESE SERVANTS ARE MAGICAL MANIFESTATIONS OF THE HOUSE.
THEY'RE ONLY AROUND WHEN I NEED THEM.
FFATS EKAT A KAERB.
THAT WAS INCREDIBLE! AND THEY'LL JUST COME BACK WHENEVER YOU--?
THAT'S RIGHT. IT'S REALLY PRETTY BASIC MAGIC, MARY...
...THE KIND YOU'LL BE ABLE TO DO, WHEN YOU'RE READY.

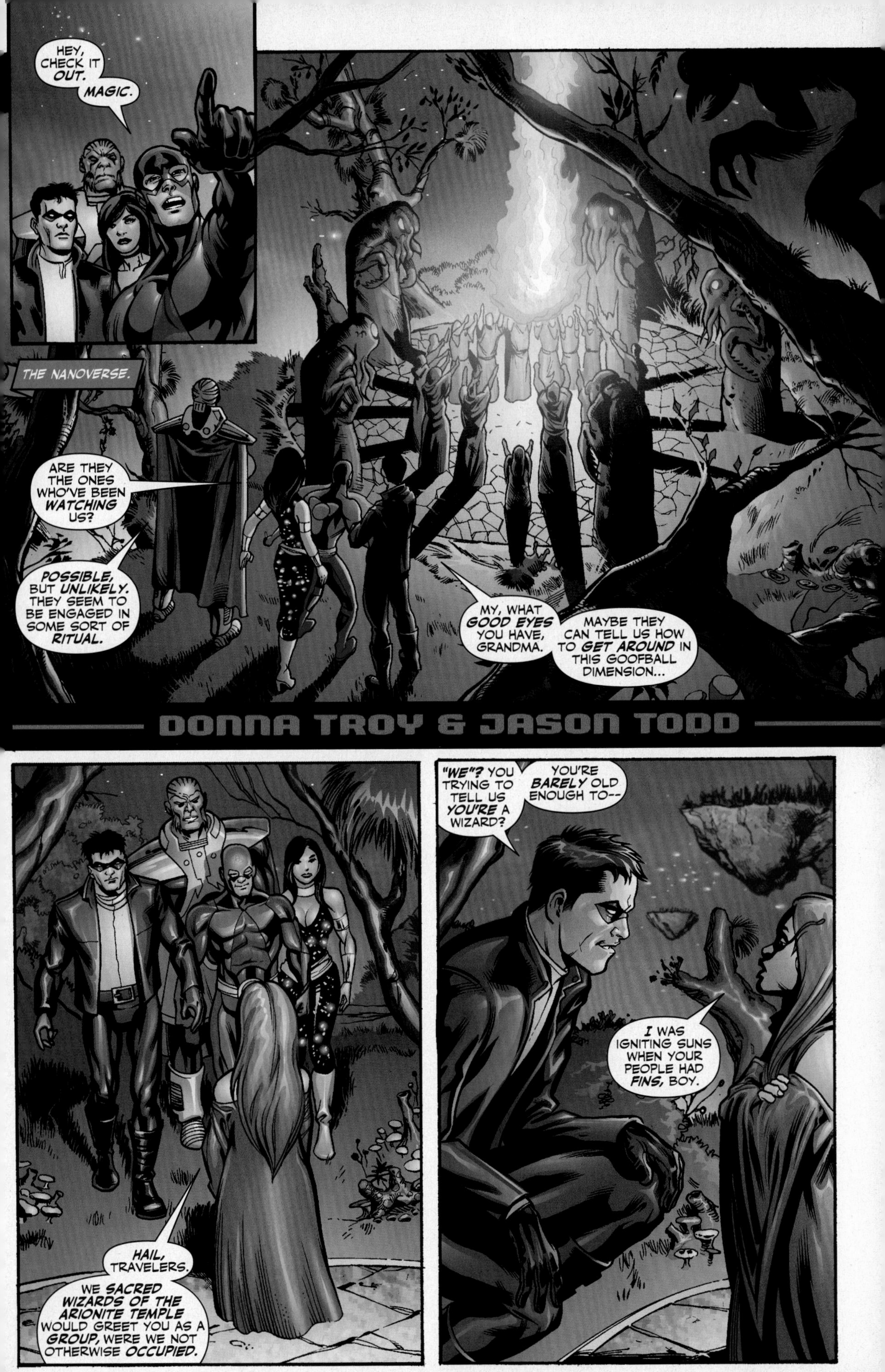
HEY, CHECK IT OUT. MAGIC.
THE NANOVERSE.
ARE THEY THE ONES WHO'VE BEEN WATCHING US?
POSSIBLE, BUT UNLIKELY. THEY SEEM TO BE ENGAGED IN SOME SORT OF RITUAL.
MY, WHAT GOOD EYES YOU HAVE, GRANDMA.
MAYBE THEY CAN TELL US HOW TO GET AROUND IN THIS GOOFBALL DIMENSION...
DONNA TROY & JASON TODD
HAIL, TRAVELERS.
WE SACRED WIZARDS OF THE ARIONITE TEMPLE WOULD GREET YOU AS A GROUP, WERE WE NOT OTHERWISE OCCUPIED.
"WE"? YOU TRYING TO TELL US YOU'RE A WIZARD?
YOU'RE BARELY OLD ENOUGH TO--
I WAS IGNITING SUNS WHEN YOUR PEOPLE HAD FINS, BOY.

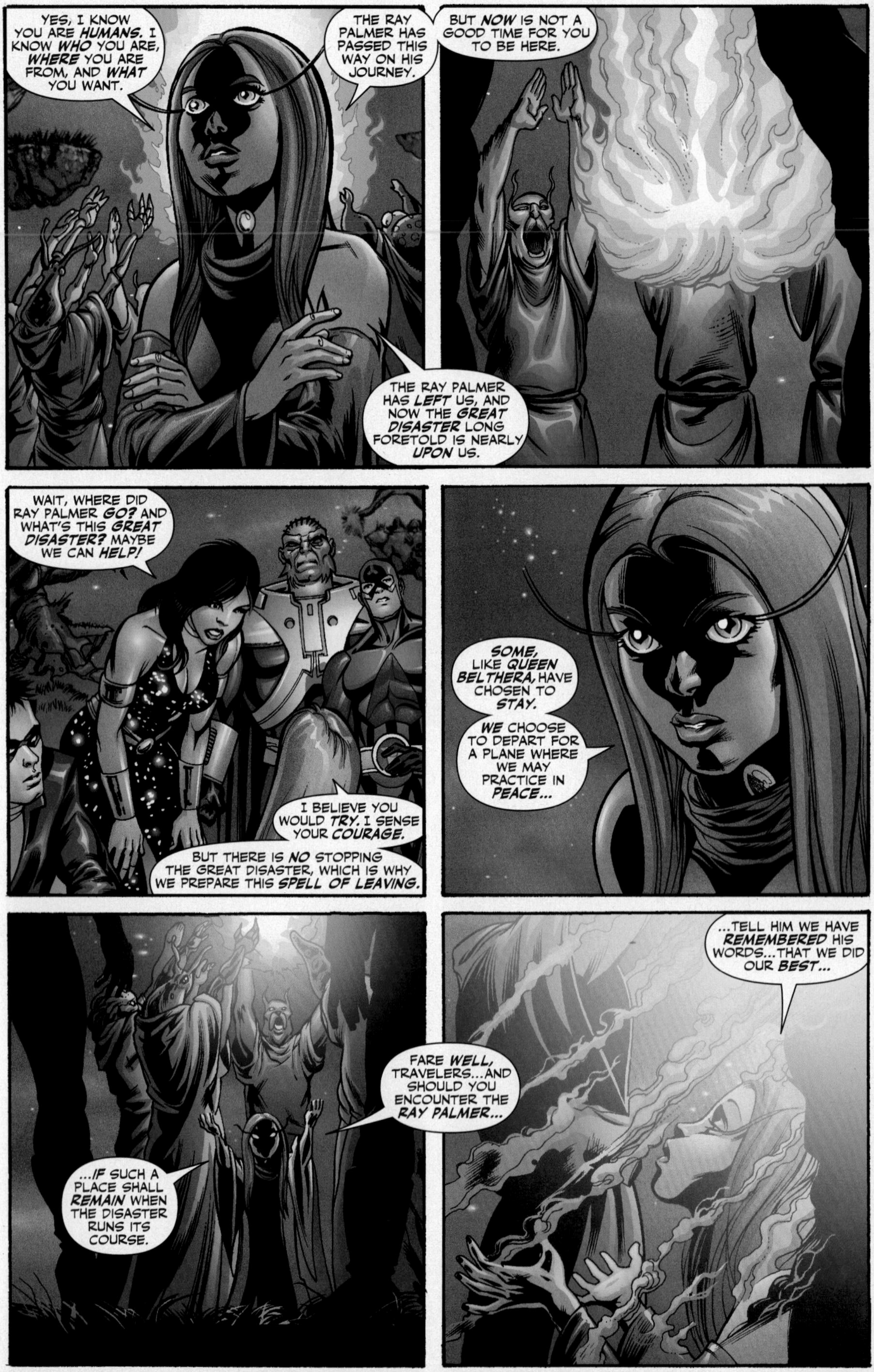
YES, I KNOW YOU ARE HUMANS. I KNOW WHO YOU ARE, WHERE YOU ARE FROM, AND WHAT YOU WANT.
THE RAY PALMER HAS PASSED THIS WAY ON HIS JOURNEY.
BUT NOW IS NOT A GOOD TIME FOR YOU TO BE HERE.
THE RAY PALMER HAS LEFT US, AND NOW THE GREAT DISASTER LONG FORETOLD IS NEARLY UPON US.
WAIT, WHERE DID RAY PALMER GO? AND WHAT'S THIS GREAT DISASTER? MAYBE WE CAN HELP!
I BELIEVE YOU WOULD TRY. I SENSE YOUR COURAGE.
BUT THERE IS NO STOPPING THE GREAT DISASTER, WHICH IS WHY WE PREPARE THIS SPELL OF LEAVING.
SOME, LIKE QUEEN BELTHERA, HAVE CHOSEN TO STAY.
WE CHOOSE TO DEPART FOR A PLANE WHERE WE MAY PRACTICE IN PEACE...
FARE WELL, TRAVELERS...AND SHOULD YOU ENCOUNTER THE RAY PALMER...
...IF SUCH A PLACE SHALL REMAIN WHEN THE DISASTER RUNS ITS COURSE.
...TELL HIM WE HAVE REMEMBERED HIS WORDS...THAT WE DID OUR BEST...

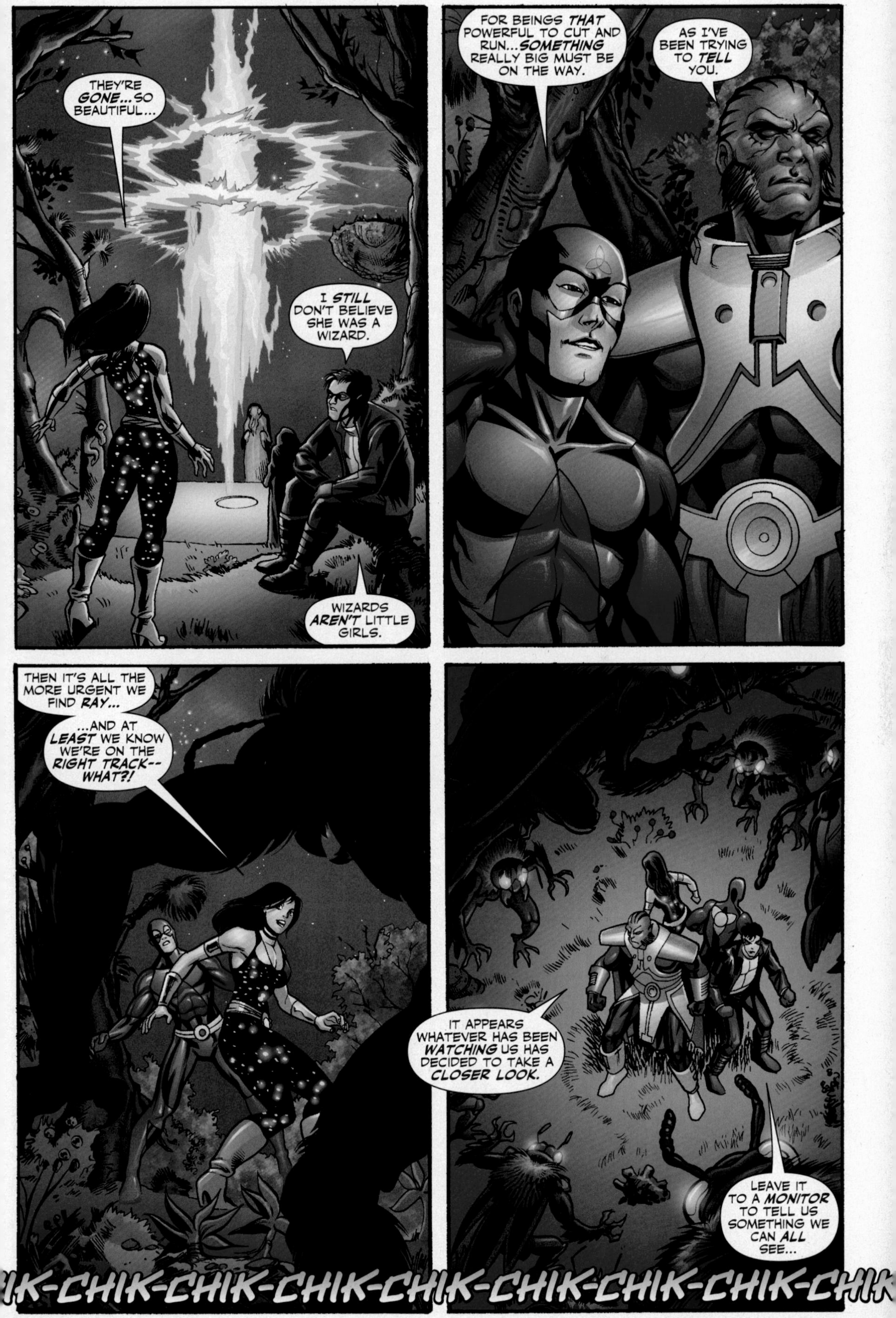
THEY'RE GONE... SO BEAUTIFUL...
I STILL DON'T BELIEVE SHE WAS A WIZARD.
WIZARDS AREN'T LITTLE GIRLS.
FOR BEINGS THAT POWERFUL TO CUT AND RUN... SOMETHING REALLY BIG MUST BE ON THE WAY.
AS I'VE BEEN TRYING TO TELL YOU.
THEN IT'S ALL THE MORE URGENT WE FIND RAY...
...AND AT LEAST WE KNOW WE'RE ON THE RIGHT TRACK-- WHAT?!
IT APPEARS WHATEVER HAS BEEN WATCHING US HAS DECIDED TO TAKE A CLOSER LOOK.
LEAVE IT TO A MONITOR TO TELL US SOMETHING WE CAN ALL SEE...
IK-CHIK-CHIK-CHIK-CHIK-CHIK-CHIK-CHIK-CHIK

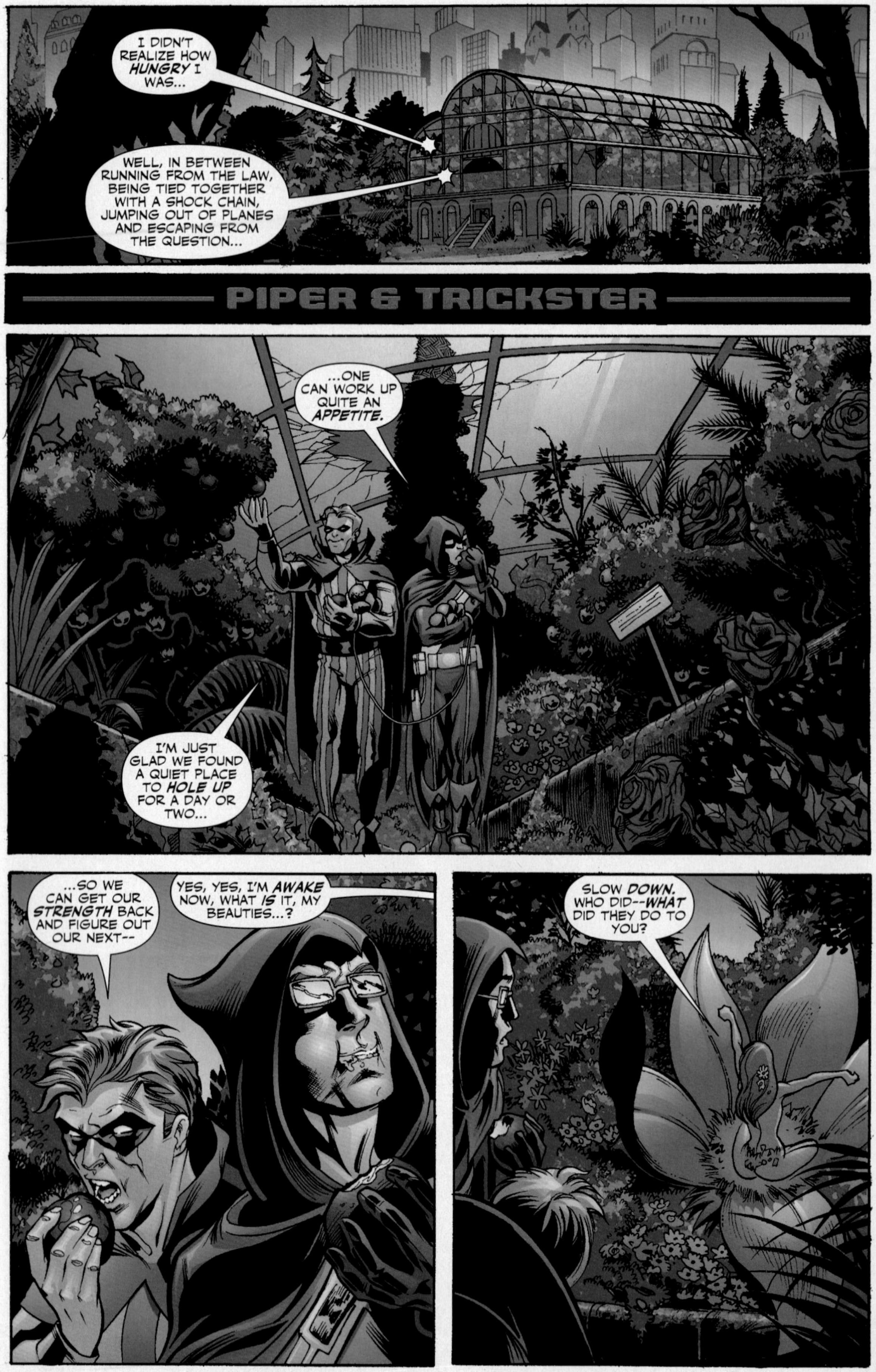
I DIDN'T REALIZE HOW HUNGRY I WAS...
WELL, IN BETWEEN RUNNING FROM THE LAW, BEING TIED TOGETHER WITH A SHOCK CHAIN, JUMPING OUT OF PLANES AND ESCAPING FROM THE QUESTION...
PIPER & TRICKSTER
...ONE CAN WORK UP QUITE AN APPETITE.
I'M JUST GLAD WE FOUND A QUIET PLACE TO HOLE UP FOR A DAY OR TWO...
...SO WE CAN GET OUR STRENGTH BACK AND FIGURE OUT OUR NEXT--
YES, YES, I'M AWAKE NOW, WHAT IS IT, MY BEAUTIES...?
SLOW DOWN. WHO DID--WHAT DID THEY DO TO YOU?

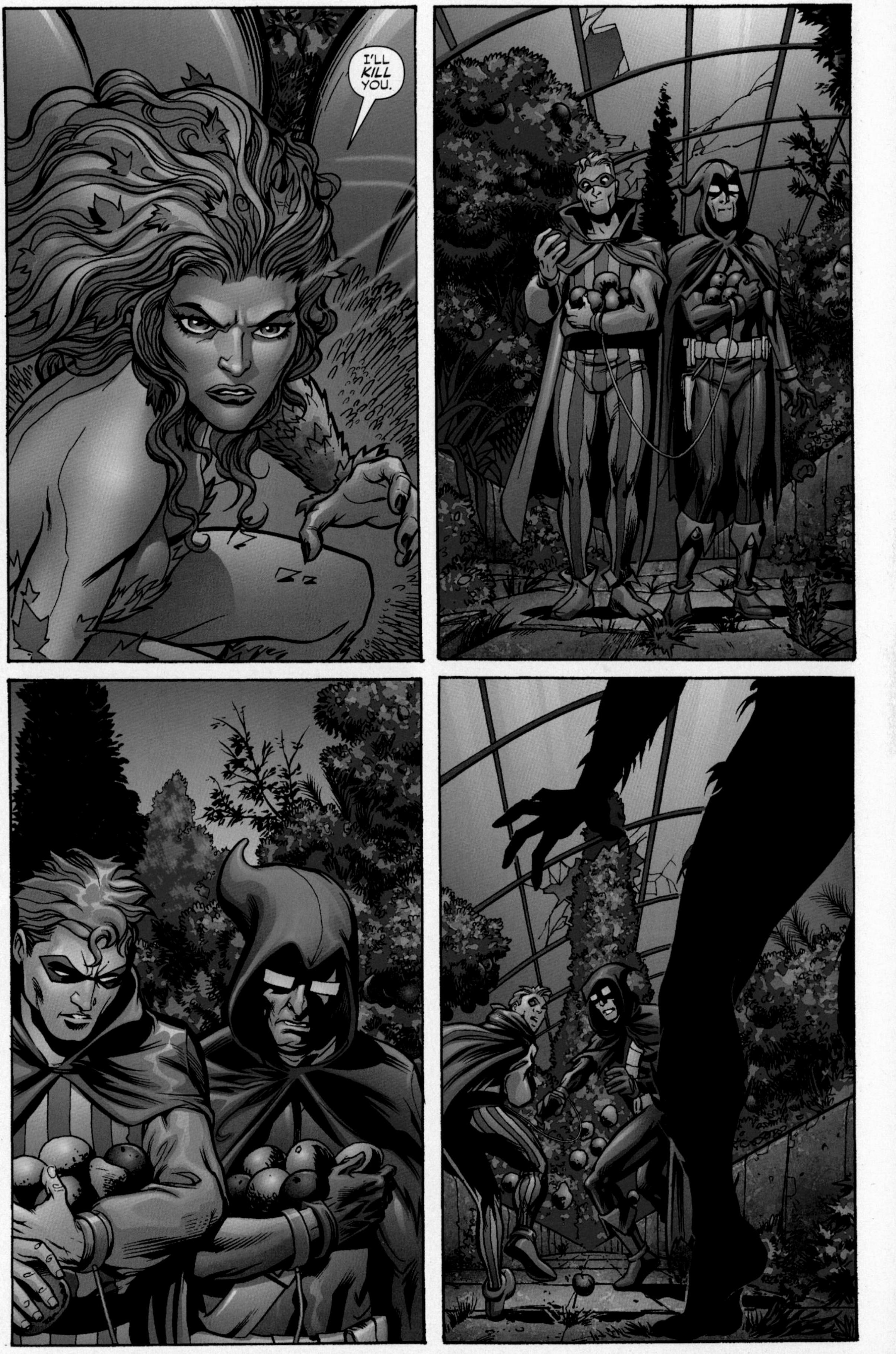
I'LL KILL YOU.

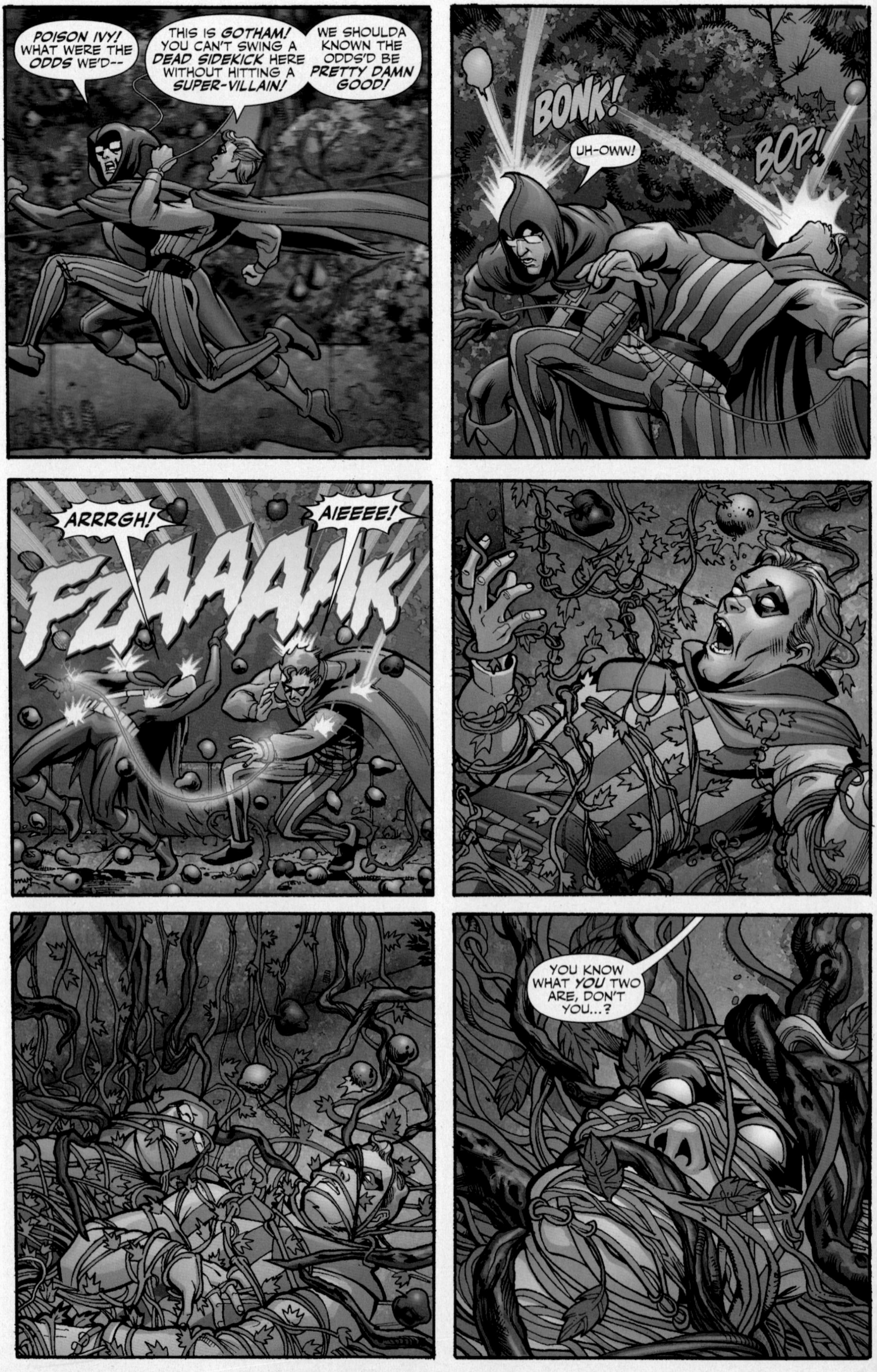
POISON IVY! WHAT WERE THE ODDS WE'D--
THIS IS GOTHAM! YOU CAN'T SWING A DEAD SIDEKICK HERE WITHOUT HITTING A SUPER-VILLAIN!
WE SHOULDA KNOWN THE ODDS'D BE PRETTY DAMN GOOD!
BONK!
UH-OWW!
BOP!
ARRRGH!
AIEEEE!
FZAAAAK
YOU KNOW WHAT YOU TWO ARE, DON'T YOU...?

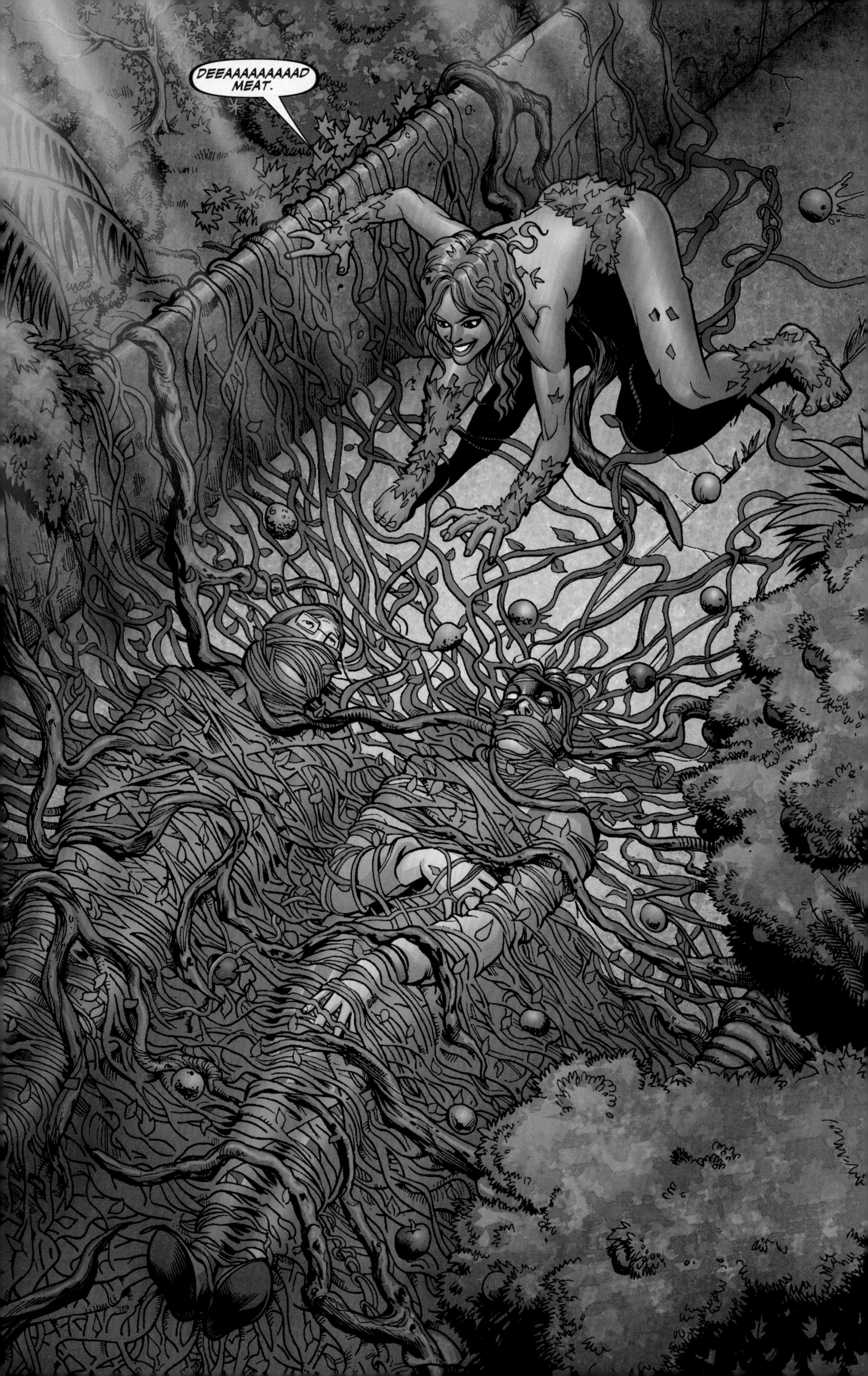
DEEAAAAAAAAAAD MEAT.

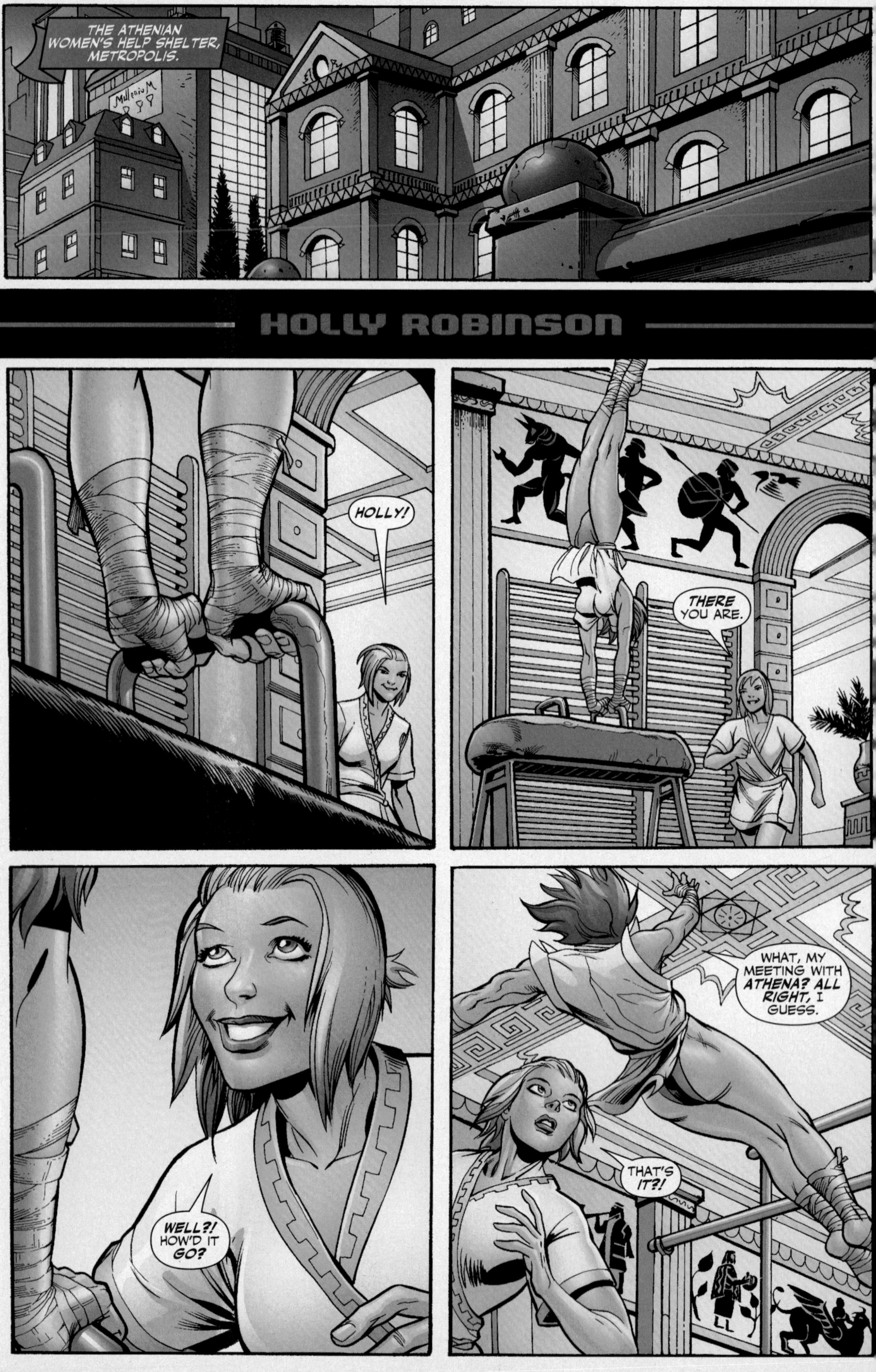
THE ATHENIAN WOMEN'S HELP SHELTER, METROPOLIS.
HOLLY ROBINSON
HOLLY!
THERE YOU ARE.
WELL?! HOW'D IT GO?
WHAT, MY MEETING WITH ATHENA? ALL RIGHT, I GUESS.
THAT'S IT?!

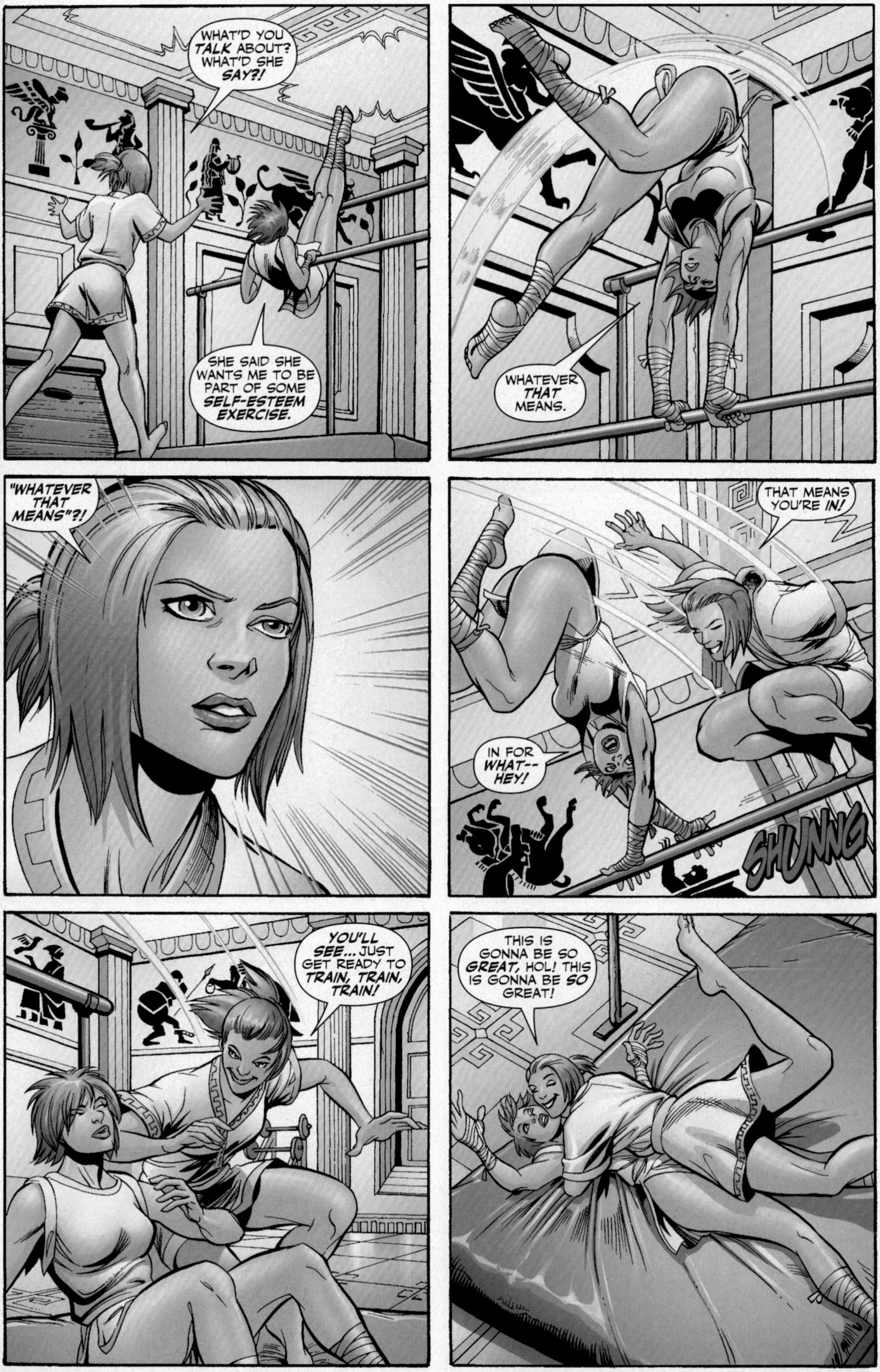
WHAT'D YOU TALK ABOUT? WHAT'D SHE SAY?!
SHE SAID SHE WANTS ME TO BE PART OF SOME SELF-ESTEEM EXERCISE.
WHATEVER THAT MEANS.
"WHATEVER THAT MEANS"?!
THAT MEANS YOU'RE IN!
IN FOR WHAT-- HEY!
SHUNNG
YOU'LL SEE... JUST GET READY TO TRAIN, TRAIN, TRAIN!
THIS IS GONNA BE SO GREAT, HOL! THIS IS GONNA BE SO GREAT!

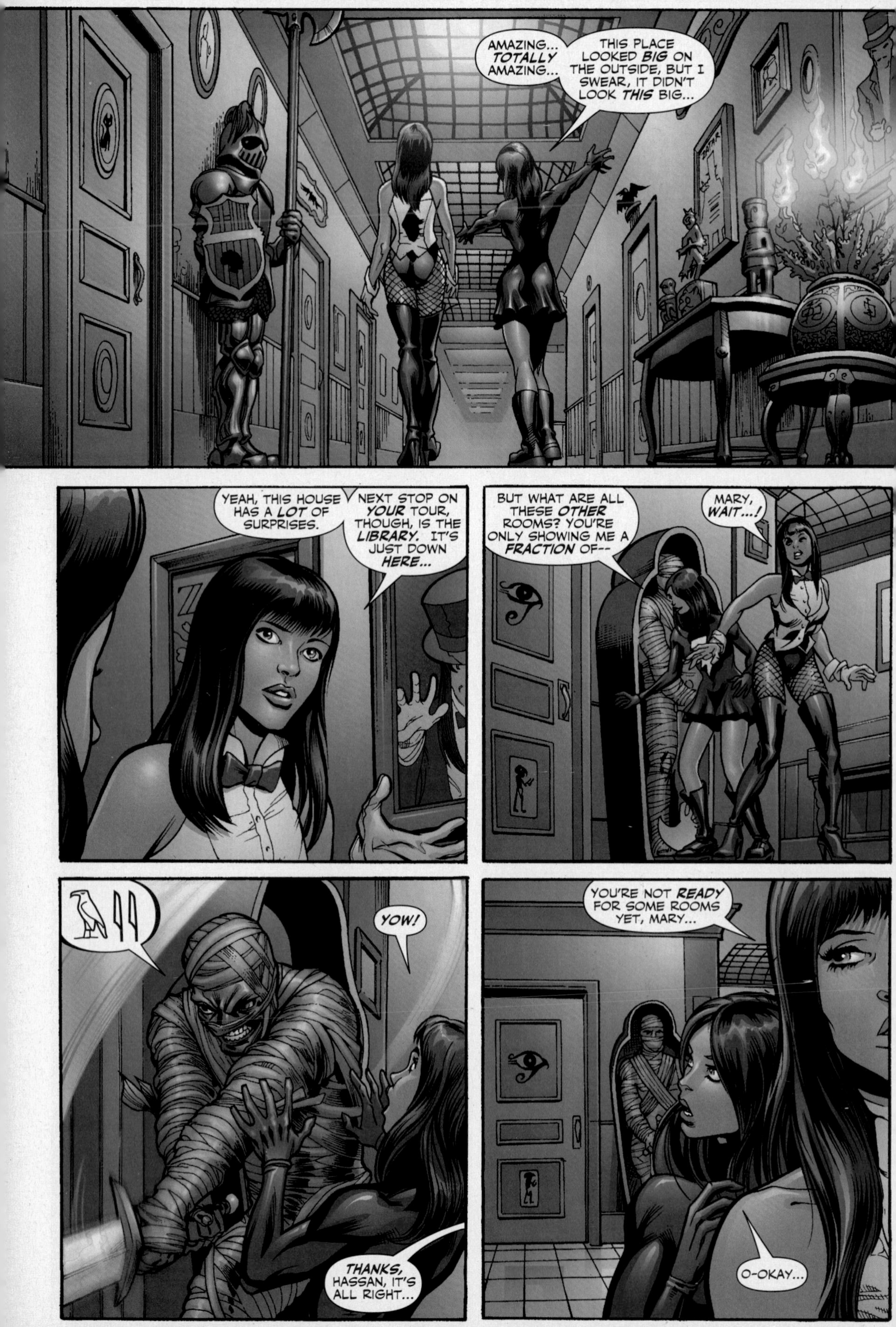
AMAZING... TOTALLY AMAZING...
THIS PLACE LOOKED BIG ON THE OUTSIDE, BUT I SWEAR, IT DIDN'T LOOK THIS BIG...
YEAH, THIS HOUSE HAS A LOT OF SURPRISES.
NEXT STOP ON YOUR TOUR, THOUGH, IS THE LIBRARY. IT'S JUST DOWN HERE...
BUT WHAT ARE ALL THESE OTHER ROOMS? YOU'RE ONLY SHOWING ME A FRACTION OF--
MARY, WAIT...!
YOW!
THANKS, HASSAN, IT'S ALL RIGHT...
YOU'RE NOT READY FOR SOME ROOMS YET, MARY...
O-OKAY...

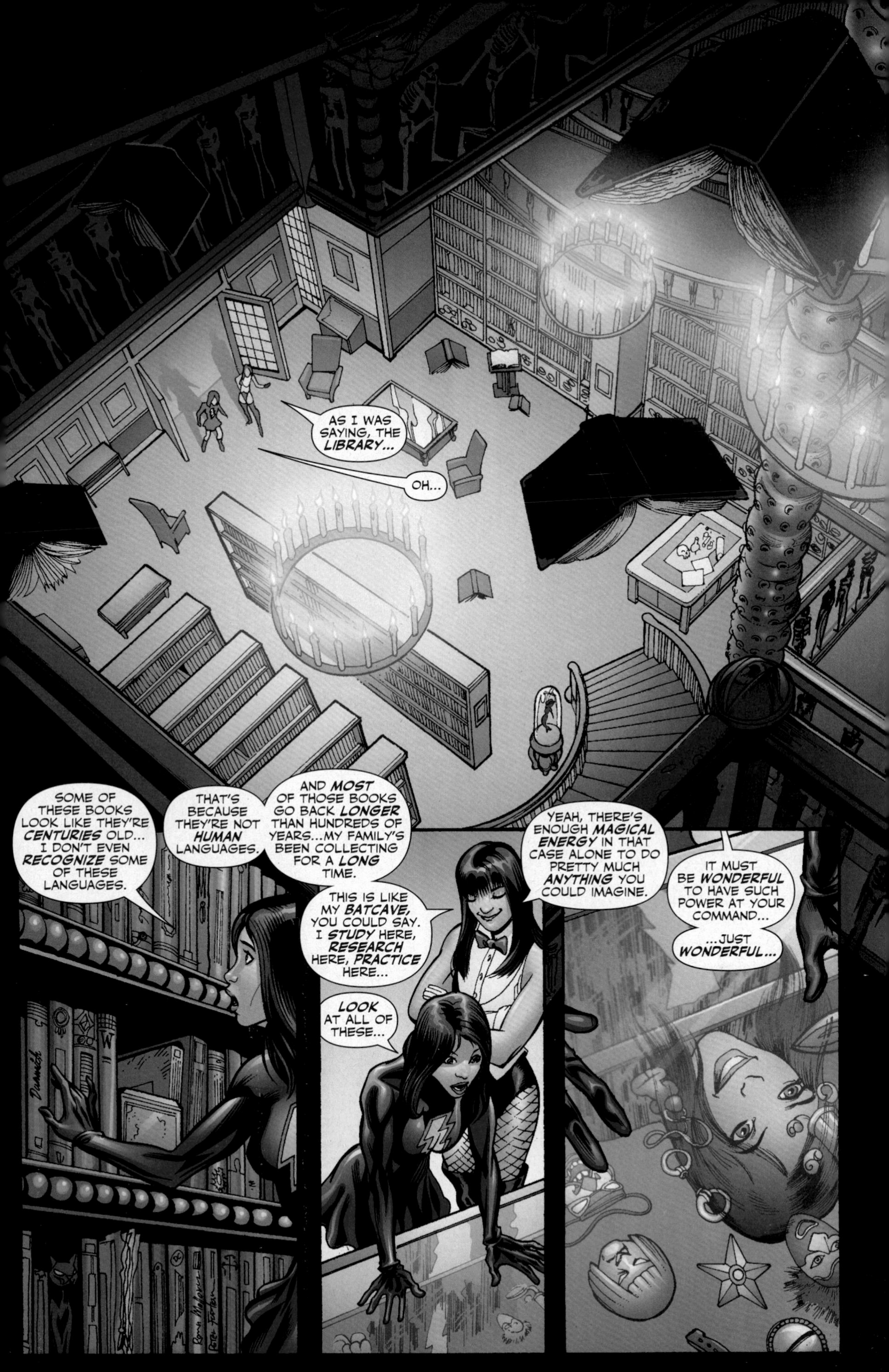
AS I WAS SAYING, THE LIBRARY...
OH...
SOME OF THESE BOOKS LOOK LIKE THEY'RE CENTURIES OLD... I DON'T EVEN RECOGNIZE SOME OF THESE LANGUAGES.
THAT'S BECAUSE THEY'RE NOT HUMAN LANGUAGES.
AND MOST OF THOSE BOOKS GO BACK LONGER THAN HUNDREDS OF YEARS...MY FAMILY'S BEEN COLLECTING FOR A LONG TIME.
THIS IS LIKE MY BATCAVE, YOU COULD SAY. I STUDY HERE, RESEARCH HERE, PRACTICE HERE...
LOOK AT ALL OF THESE...
YEAH, THERE'S ENOUGH MAGICAL ENERGY IN THAT CASE ALONE TO DO PRETTY MUCH ANYTHING YOU COULD IMAGINE.
IT MUST BE WONDERFUL TO HAVE SUCH POWER AT YOUR COMMAND...
...JUST WONDERFUL...

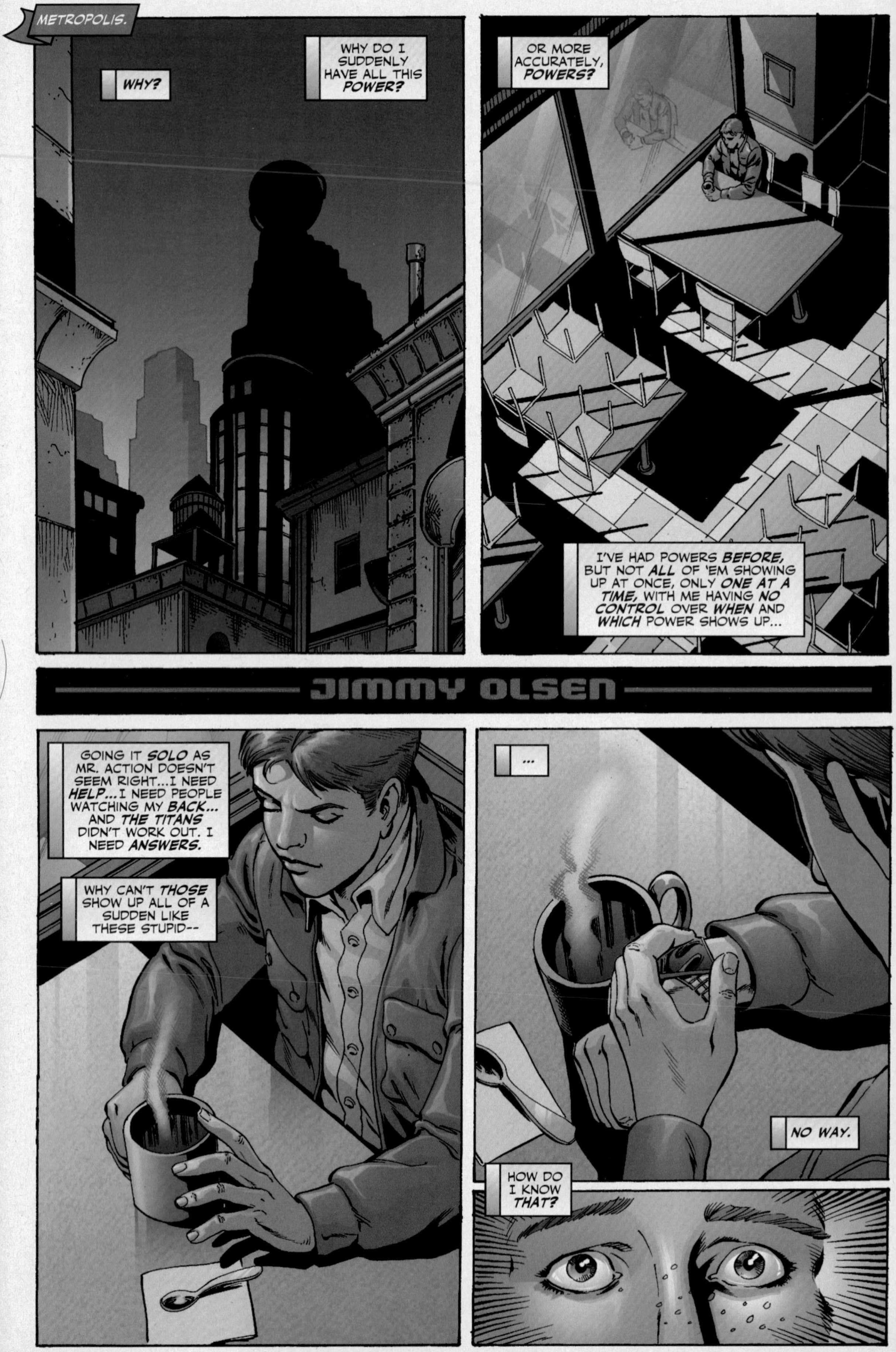
METROPOLIS.
WHY?
WHY DO I SUDDENLY HAVE ALL THIS POWER?
OR MORE ACCURATELY, POWERS?
I'VE HAD POWERS BEFORE, BUT NOT ALL OF 'EM SHOWING UP AT ONCE, ONLY ONE AT A TIME, WITH ME HAVING NO CONTROL OVER WHEN AND WHICH POWER SHOWS UP...
JIMMY OLSEN
GOING IT SOLO AS MR. ACTION DOESN'T SEEM RIGHT...I NEED HELP...I NEED PEOPLE WATCHING MY BACK... AND THE TITANS DIDN'T WORK OUT. I NEED ANSWERS.
WHY CAN'T THOSE SHOW UP ALL OF A SUDDEN LIKE THESE STUPID--
...
NO WAY.
HOW DO I KNOW THAT?

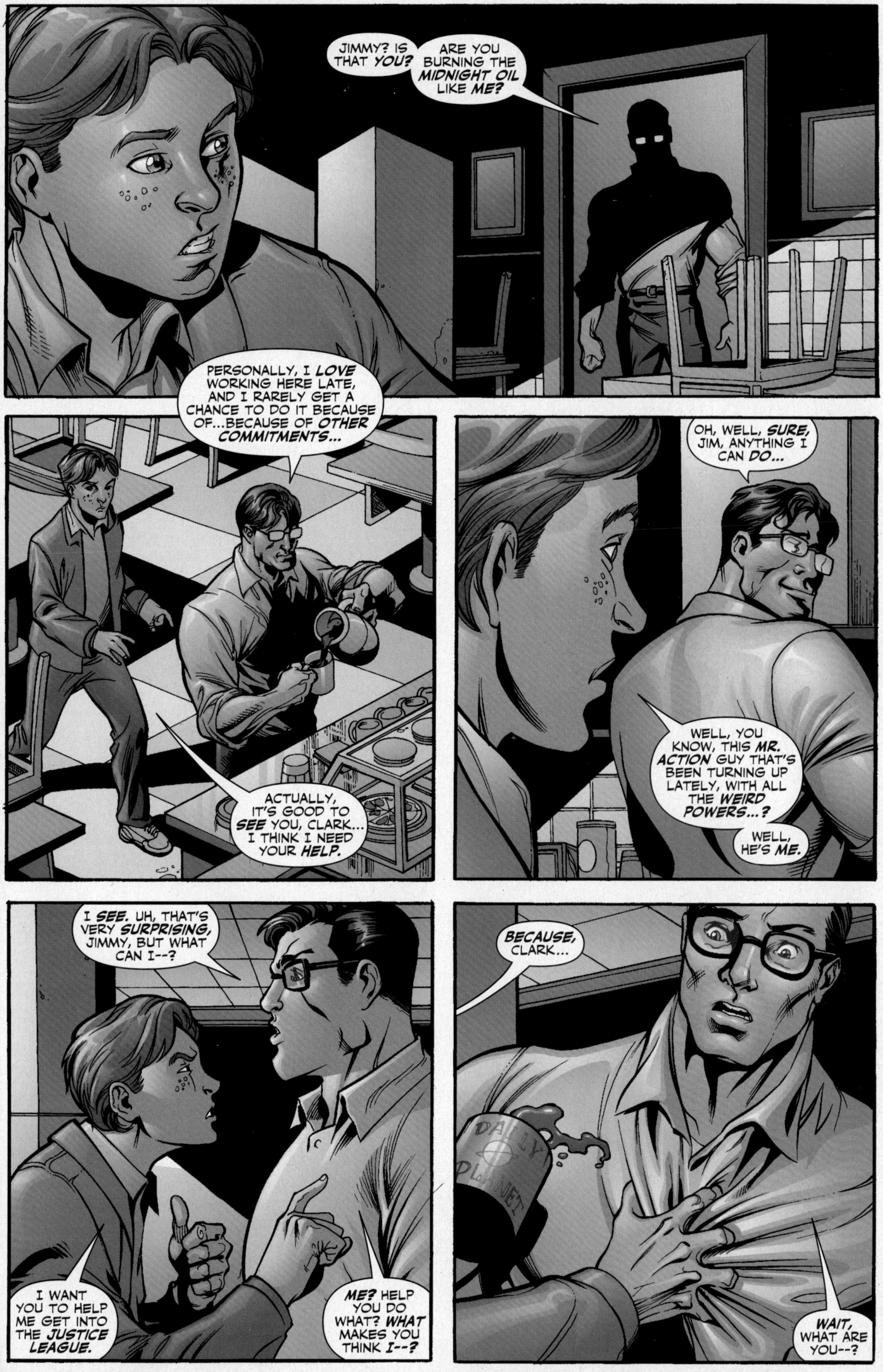
JIMMY? IS THAT YOU?
ARE YOU BURNING THE MIDNIGHT OIL LIKE ME?
PERSONALLY, I LOVE WORKING HERE LATE, AND I RARELY GET A CHANCE TO DO IT BECAUSE OF...BECAUSE OF OTHER COMMITMENTS...
ACTUALLY, IT'S GOOD TO SEE YOU, CLARK... I THINK I NEED YOUR HELP.
OH, WELL, SURE, JIM, ANYTHING I CAN DO...
WELL, YOU KNOW, THIS MR. ACTION GUY THAT'S BEEN TURNING UP LATELY, WITH ALL THE WEIRD POWERS...?
WELL, HE'S ME.
I SEE. UH, THAT'S VERY SURPRISING, JIMMY, BUT WHAT CAN I--?
I WANT YOU TO HELP ME GET INTO THE JUSTICE LEAGUE.
ME? HELP YOU DO WHAT? WHAT MAKES YOU THINK I--?
BECAUSE, CLARK...
DAILY PLANET
WAIT, WHAT ARE YOU--?

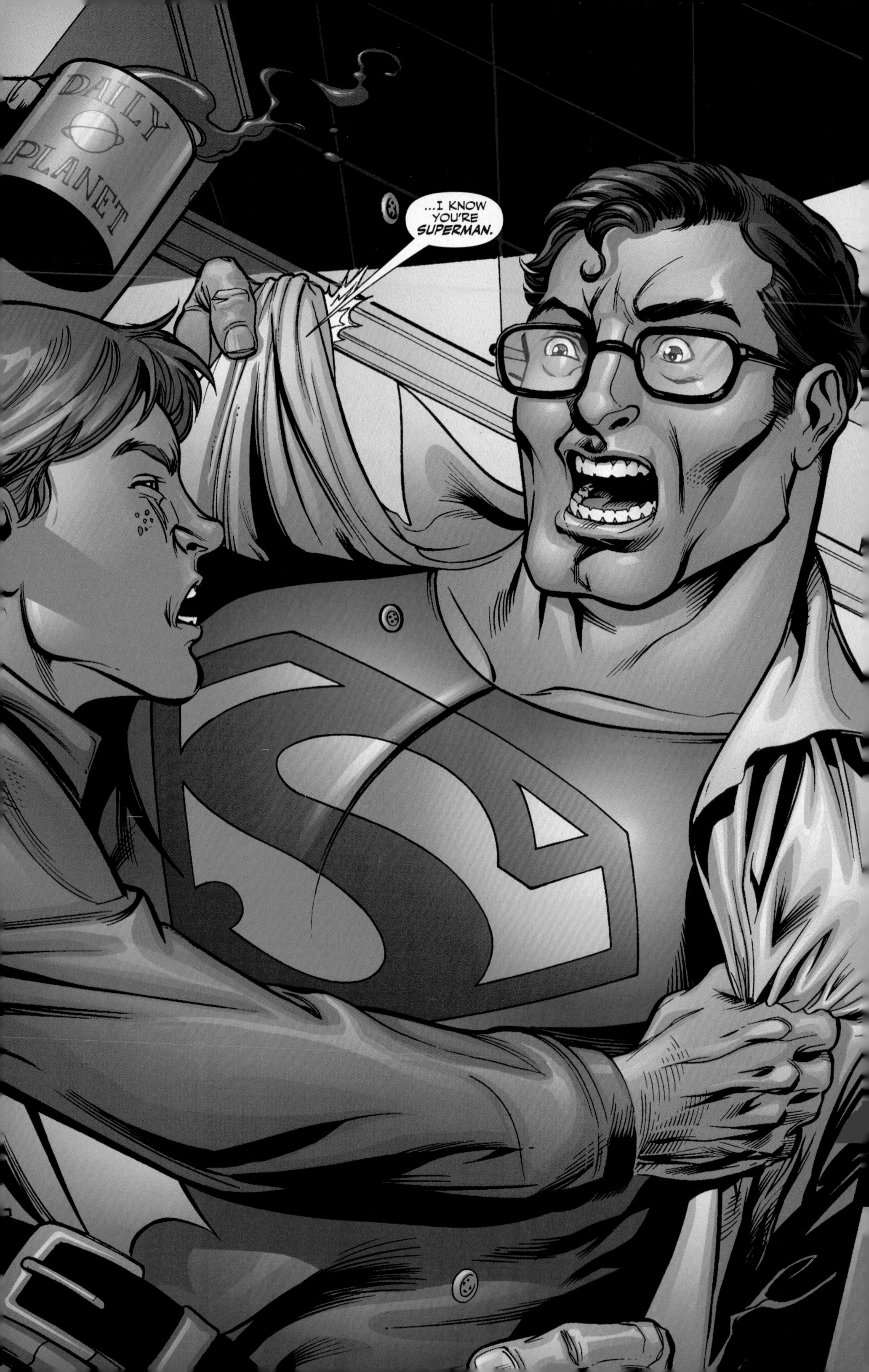

...I KNOW YOU'RE SUPERMAN.
DAILY PLANET

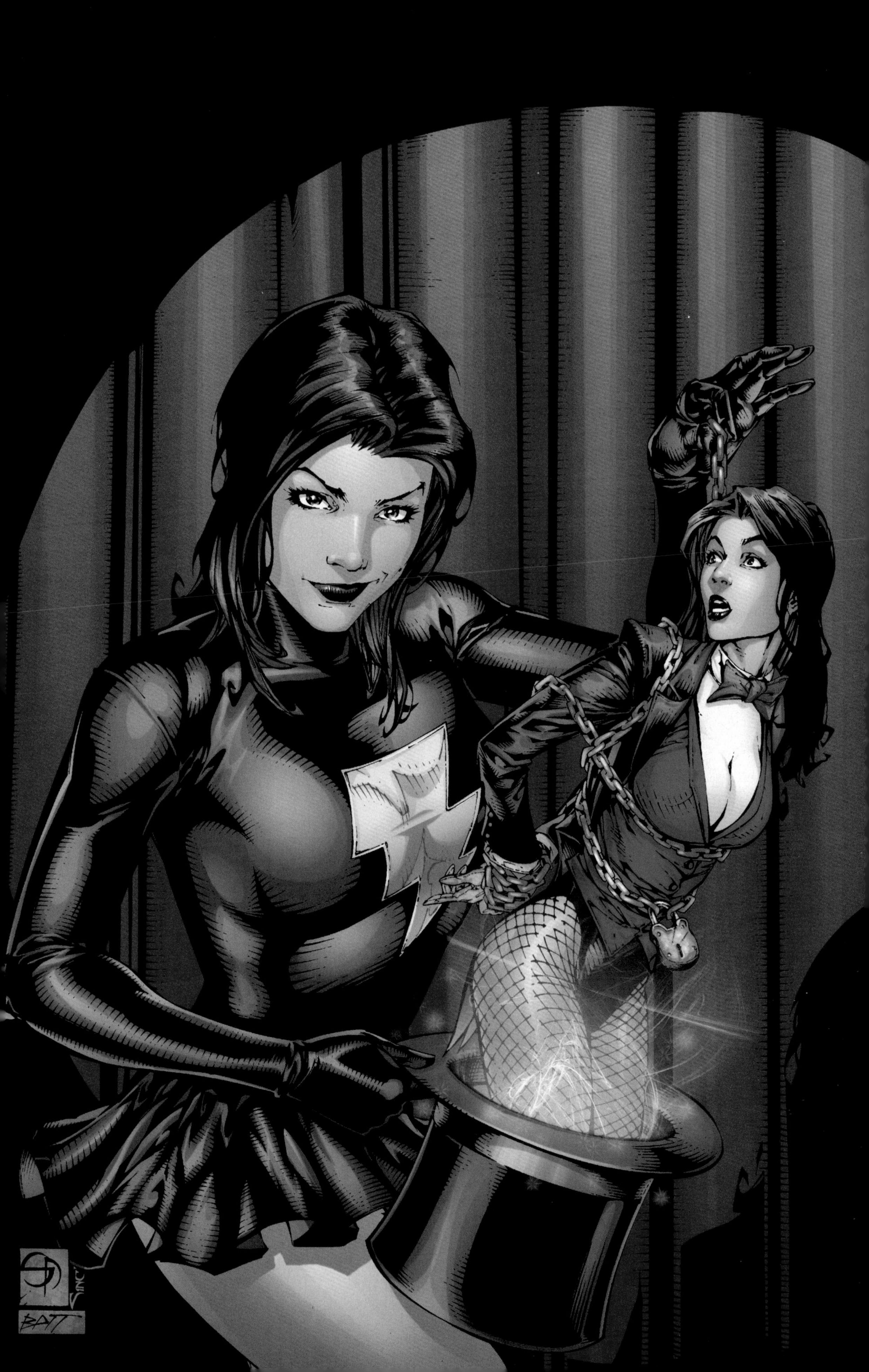

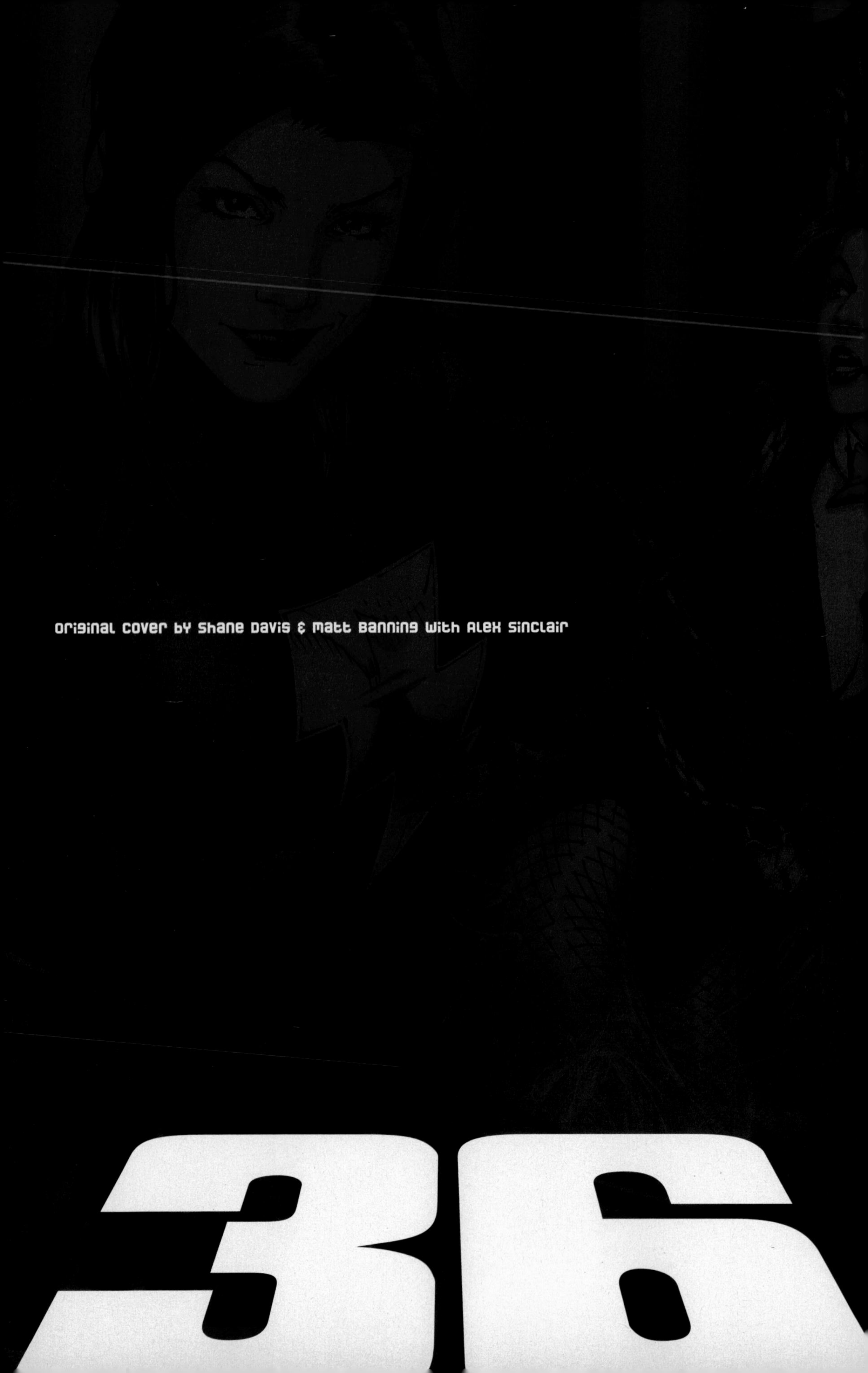

original cover by Shane Davis & Matt Banning with Alex Sinclair

# 36

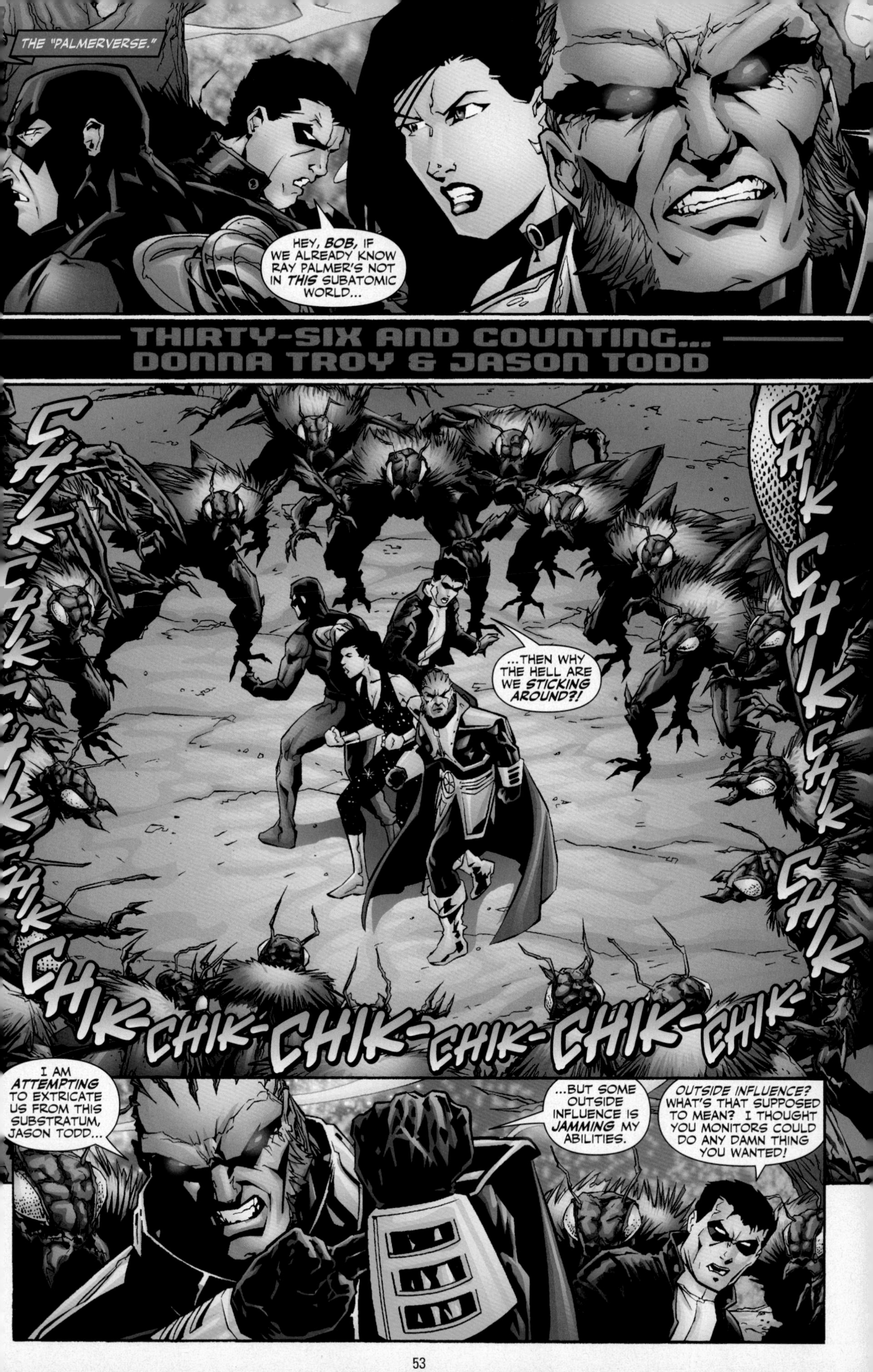
THE "PALMERVERSE."
HEY, BOB, IF WE ALREADY KNOW RAY PALMER'S NOT IN THIS SUBATOMIC WORLD...
THIRTY-SIX AND COUNTING... DONNA TROY & JASON TODD
...THEN WHY THE HELL ARE WE STICKING AROUND?!
CHIK-CHIK-CHIK-CHIK-CHIK-CHIK-CHIK-CHIK-CHIK-CHIK-CHIK-CHIK-CHIK-CHIK
I AM ATTEMPTING TO EXTRICATE US FROM THIS SUBSTRATUM, JASON TODD...
...BUT SOME OUTSIDE INFLUENCE IS JAMMING MY ABILITIES.
OUTSIDE INFLUENCE? WHAT'S THAT SUPPOSED TO MEAN? I THOUGHT YOU MONITORS COULD DO ANY DAMN THING YOU WANTED!

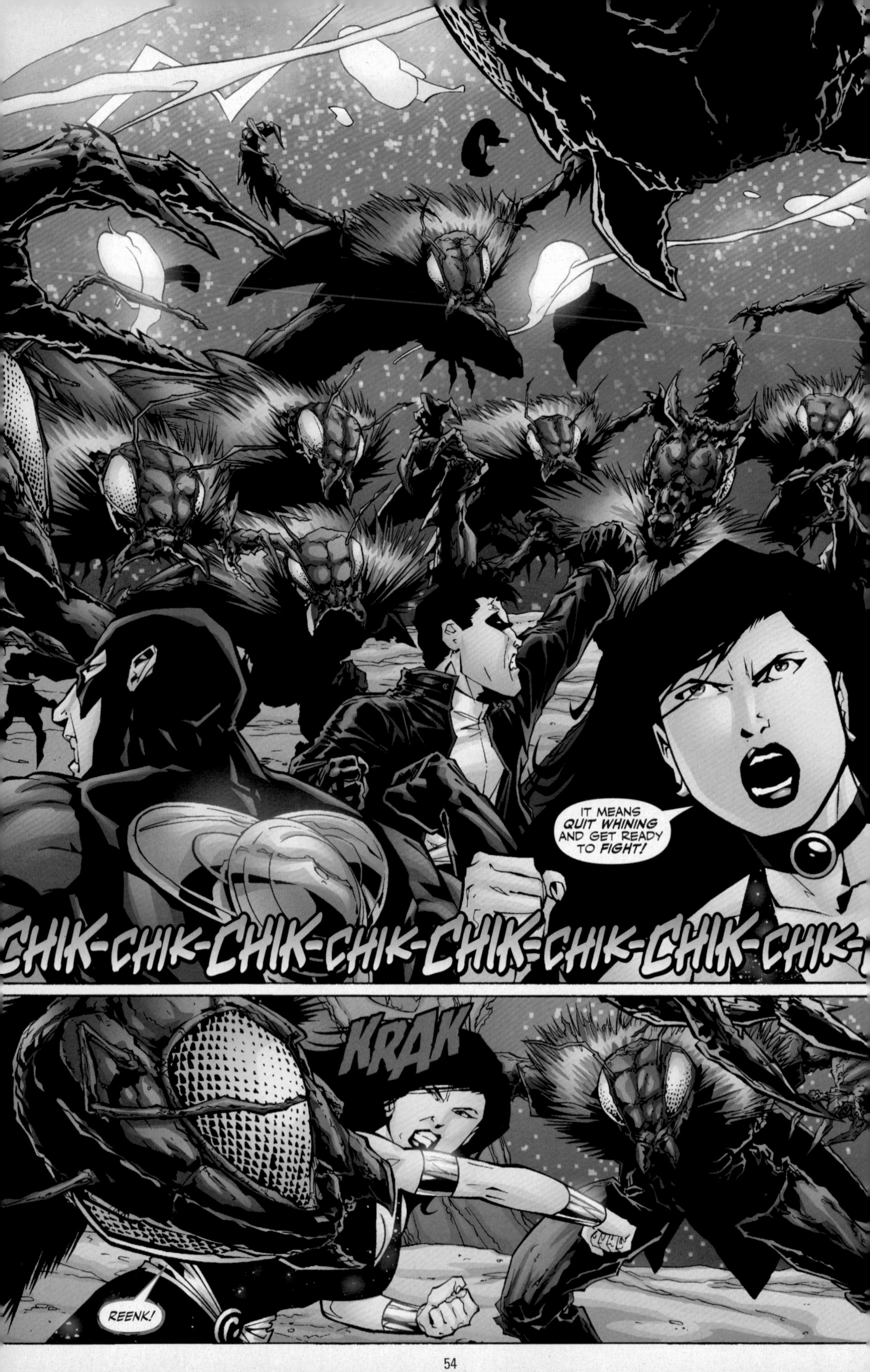
IT MEANS QUIT WHINING AND GET READY TO FIGHT!
CHIK-CHIK-CHIK-CHIK-CHIK-CHIK-CHIK-CHIK-
KRAK
REENK!

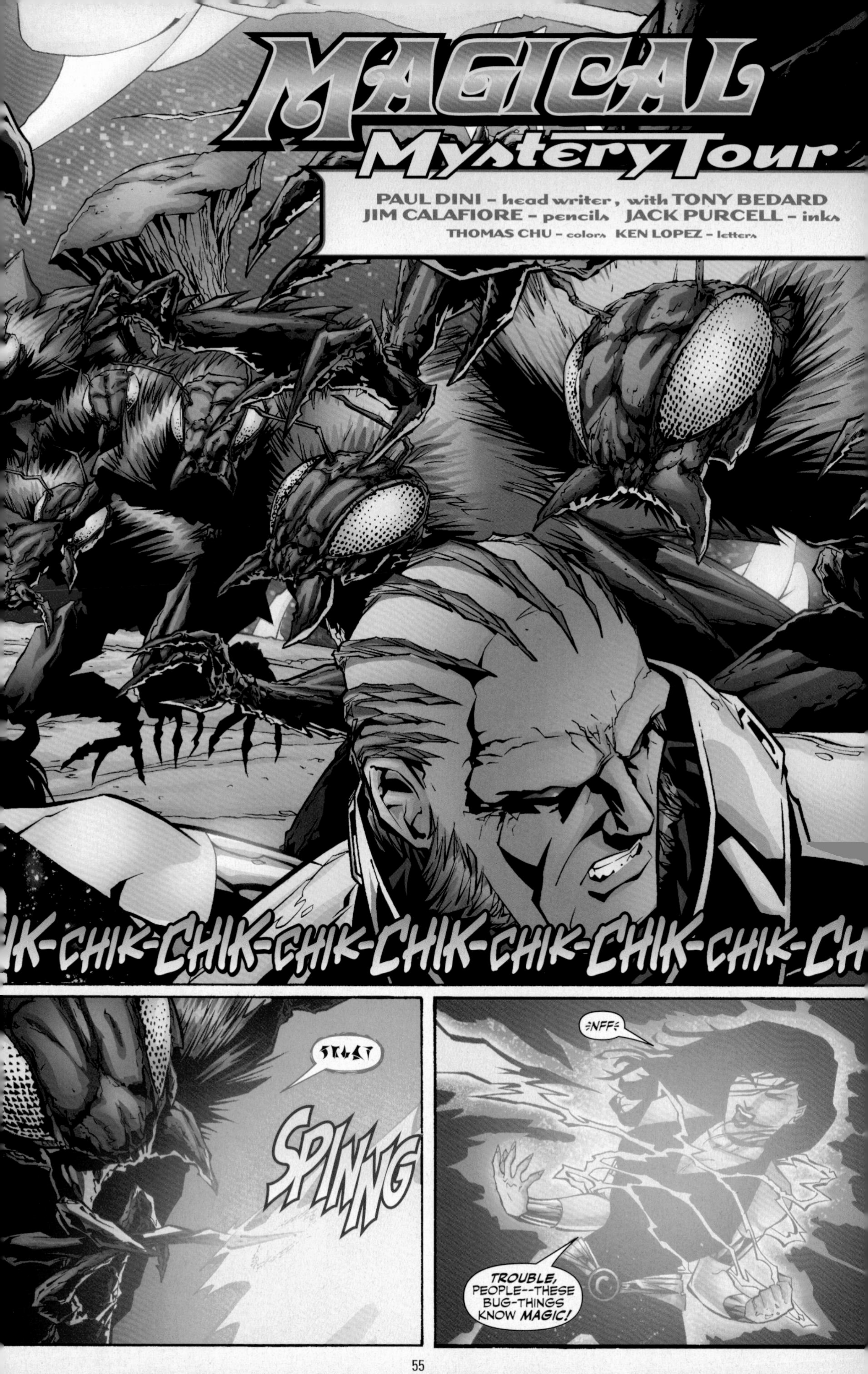
MAGICAL
Mystery Tour
PAUL DINI – head writer, with TONY BEDARD
JIM CALAFIORE – pencils JACK PURCELL – inks
THOMAS CHU – colors KEN LOPEZ – letters
K-CHIK-CHIK-CHIK-CHIK-CHIK-CHIK-CHIK-CH
SPINNG
NFF
TROUBLE, PEOPLE--THESE BUG-THINGS KNOW MAGIC!

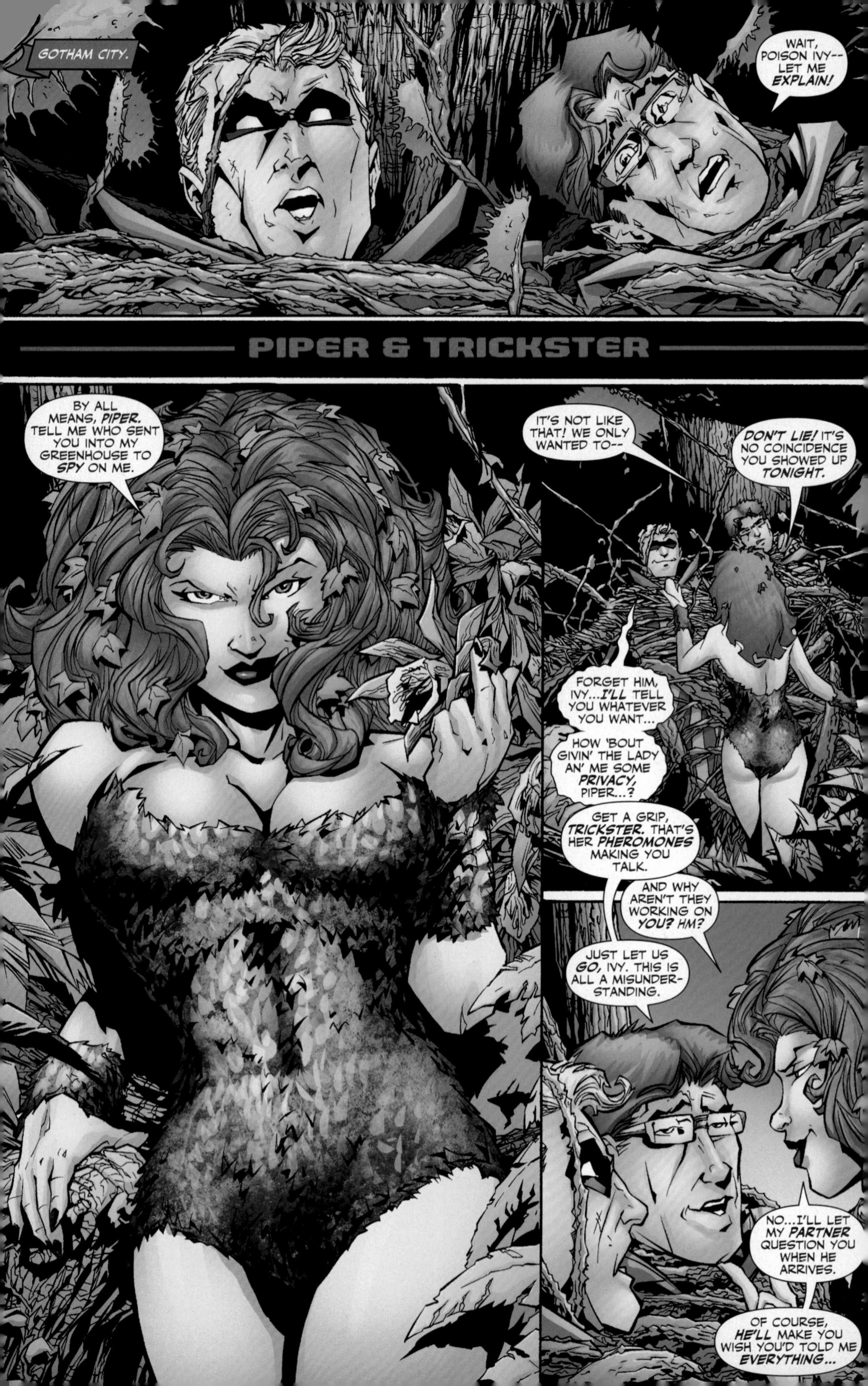
GOTHAM CITY.
WAIT, POISON IVY-- LET ME EXPLAIN!
PIPER & TRICKSTER
BY ALL MEANS, PIPER. TELL ME WHO SENT YOU INTO MY GREENHOUSE TO SPY ON ME.
IT'S NOT LIKE THAT! WE ONLY WANTED TO--
DON'T LIE! IT'S NO COINCIDENCE YOU SHOWED UP TONIGHT.
FORGET HIM, IVY...I'LL TELL YOU WHATEVER YOU WANT...
HOW 'BOUT GIVIN' THE LADY AN' ME SOME PRIVACY, PIPER...?
GET A GRIP, TRICKSTER. THAT'S HER PHEROMONES MAKING YOU TALK.
AND WHY AREN'T THEY WORKING ON YOU? HM?
JUST LET US GO, IVY. THIS IS ALL A MISUNDER-STANDING.
NO...I'LL LET MY PARTNER QUESTION YOU WHEN HE ARRIVES.
OF COURSE, HE'LL MAKE YOU WISH YOU'D TOLD ME EVERYTHING...

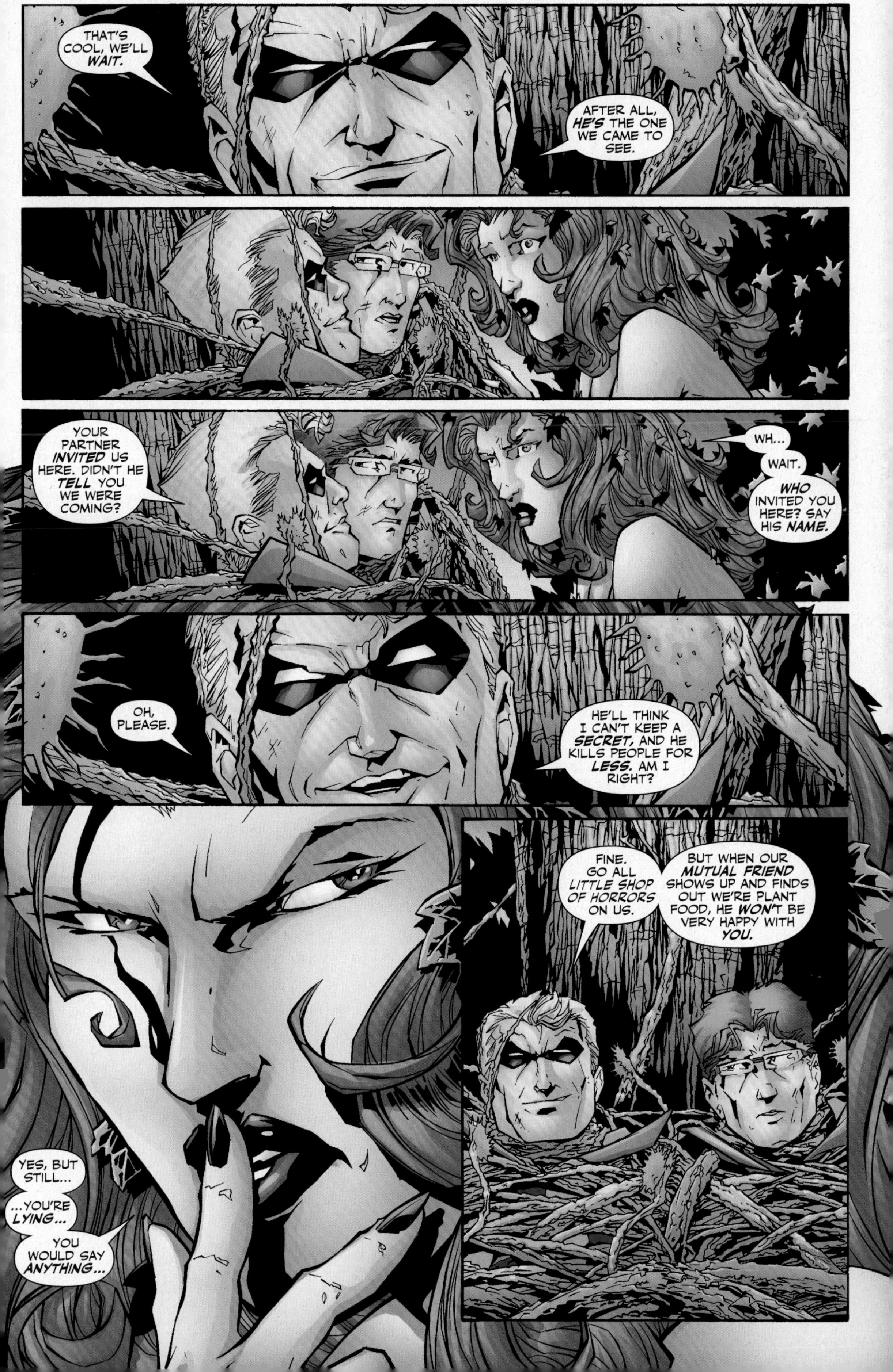
THAT'S COOL, WE'LL *WAIT.*
AFTER ALL, *HE'S* THE ONE WE CAME TO SEE.
YOUR PARTNER *INVITED* US HERE. DIDN'T HE *TELL* YOU WE WERE COMING?
WH...
WAIT.
*WHO* INVITED YOU HERE? SAY HIS *NAME.*
OH, PLEASE.
HE'LL THINK I CAN'T KEEP A *SECRET,* AND HE KILLS PEOPLE FOR *LESS.* AM I RIGHT?
YES, BUT STILL...
...YOU'RE *LYING...*
YOU WOULD SAY *ANYTHING...*
FINE. GO ALL *LITTLE SHOP OF HORRORS* ON US.
BUT WHEN OUR *MUTUAL FRIEND* SHOWS UP AND FINDS OUT WE'RE PLANT FOOD, HE *WON'T* BE VERY HAPPY WITH *YOU.*

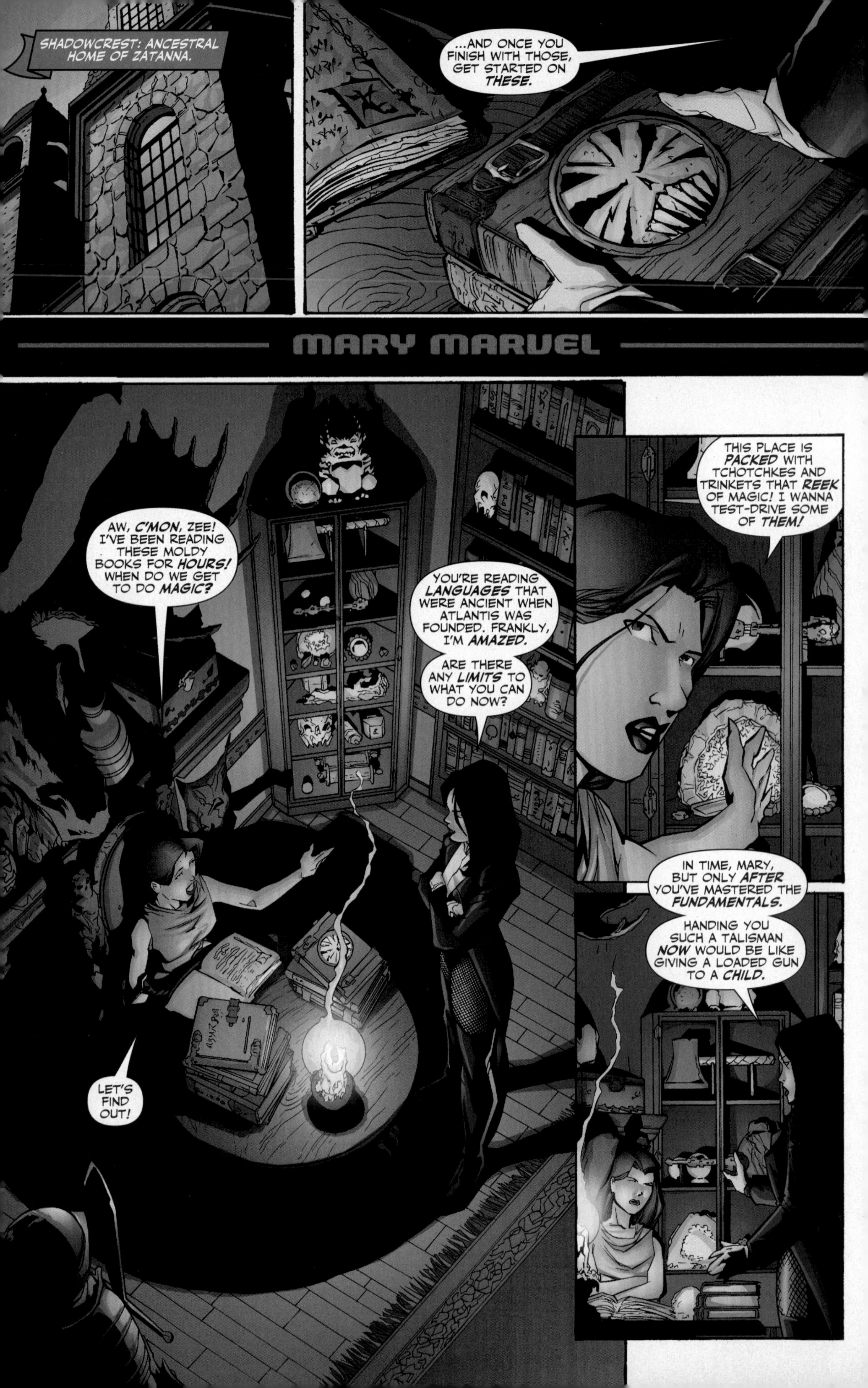
SHADOWCREST: ANCESTRAL HOME OF ZATANNA.
...AND ONCE YOU FINISH WITH THOSE, GET STARTED ON *THESE.*
MARY MARVEL
AW, *C'MON*, ZEE! I'VE BEEN READING THESE MOLDY BOOKS FOR *HOURS!* WHEN DO WE GET TO DO *MAGIC?*
YOU'RE READING *LANGUAGES* THAT WERE ANCIENT WHEN ATLANTIS WAS FOUNDED. FRANKLY, I'M *AMAZED.*
ARE THERE ANY *LIMITS* TO WHAT YOU CAN DO NOW?
LET'S FIND OUT!
THIS PLACE IS *PACKED* WITH TCHOTCHKES AND TRINKETS THAT *REEK* OF MAGIC! I WANNA TEST-DRIVE SOME OF *THEM!*
IN TIME, MARY, BUT ONLY *AFTER* YOU'VE MASTERED THE *FUNDAMENTALS.*
HANDING YOU SUCH A TALISMAN *NOW* WOULD BE LIKE GIVING A LOADED GUN TO A *CHILD.*

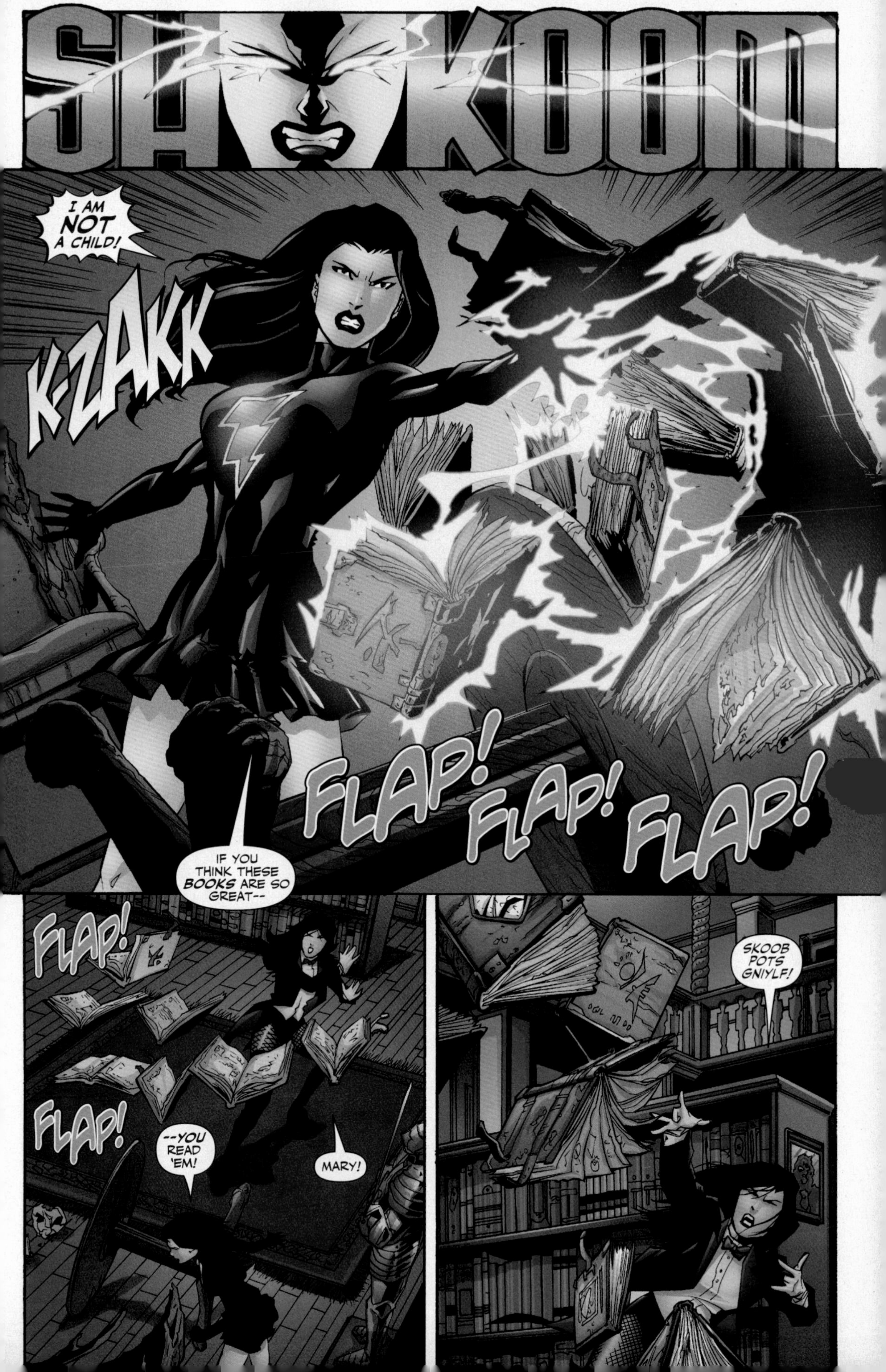
SHAKOOM
I AM NOT A CHILD!
K-ZAKK
FLAP! FLAP! FLAP!
IF YOU THINK THESE BOOKS ARE SO GREAT--
FLAP!
FLAP!
--YOU READ 'EM!
MARY!
SKOOB POTS GNIYLF!

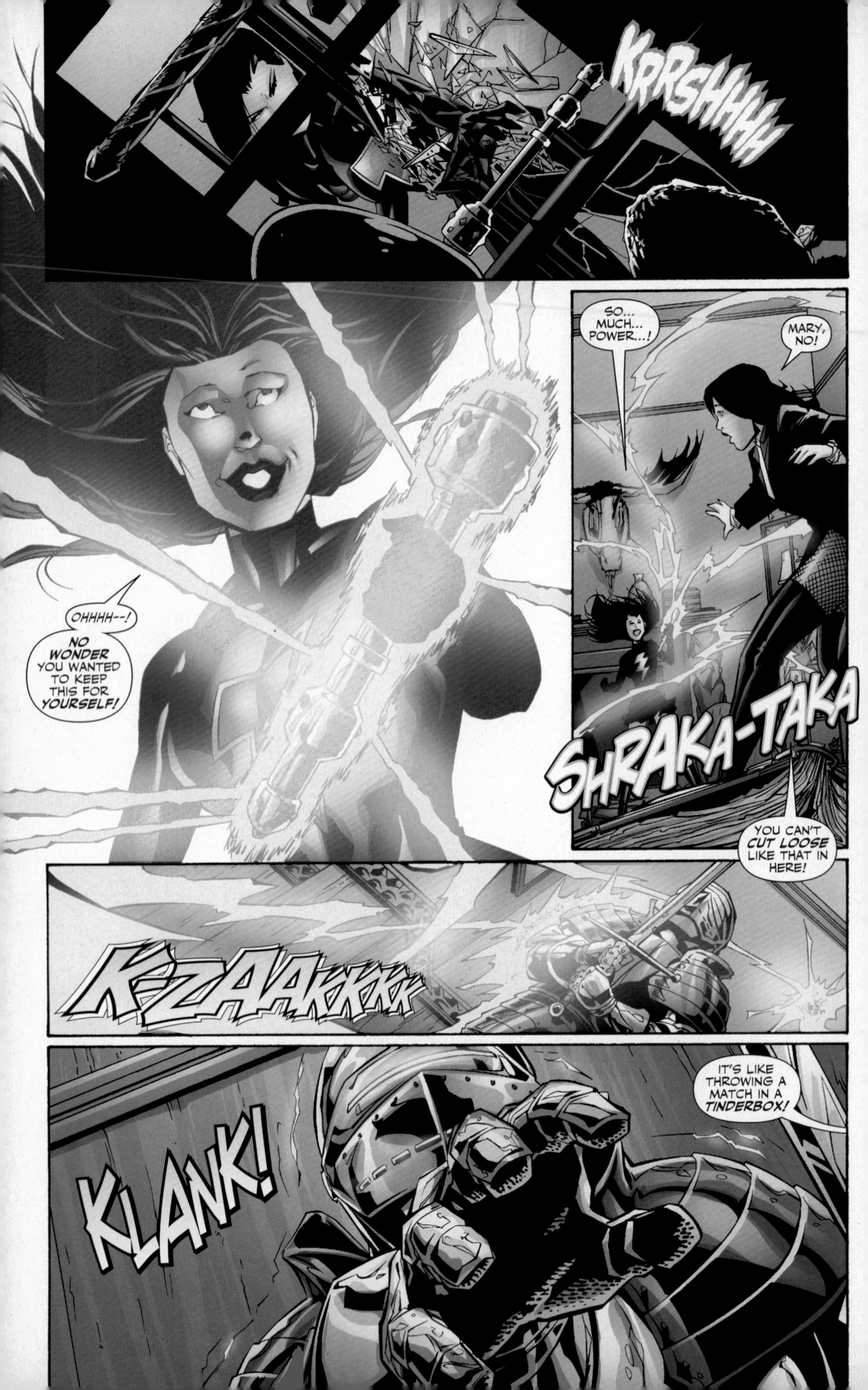
KRRSHHHH
SO... MUCH... POWER...!
MARY, NO!
OHHHH--! NO WONDER YOU WANTED TO KEEP THIS FOR YOURSELF!
SHRAKA-TAKA
YOU CAN'T CUT LOOSE LIKE THAT IN HERE!
K-ZAAKKKKK
IT'S LIKE THROWING A MATCH IN A TINDERBOX!
KLANK!

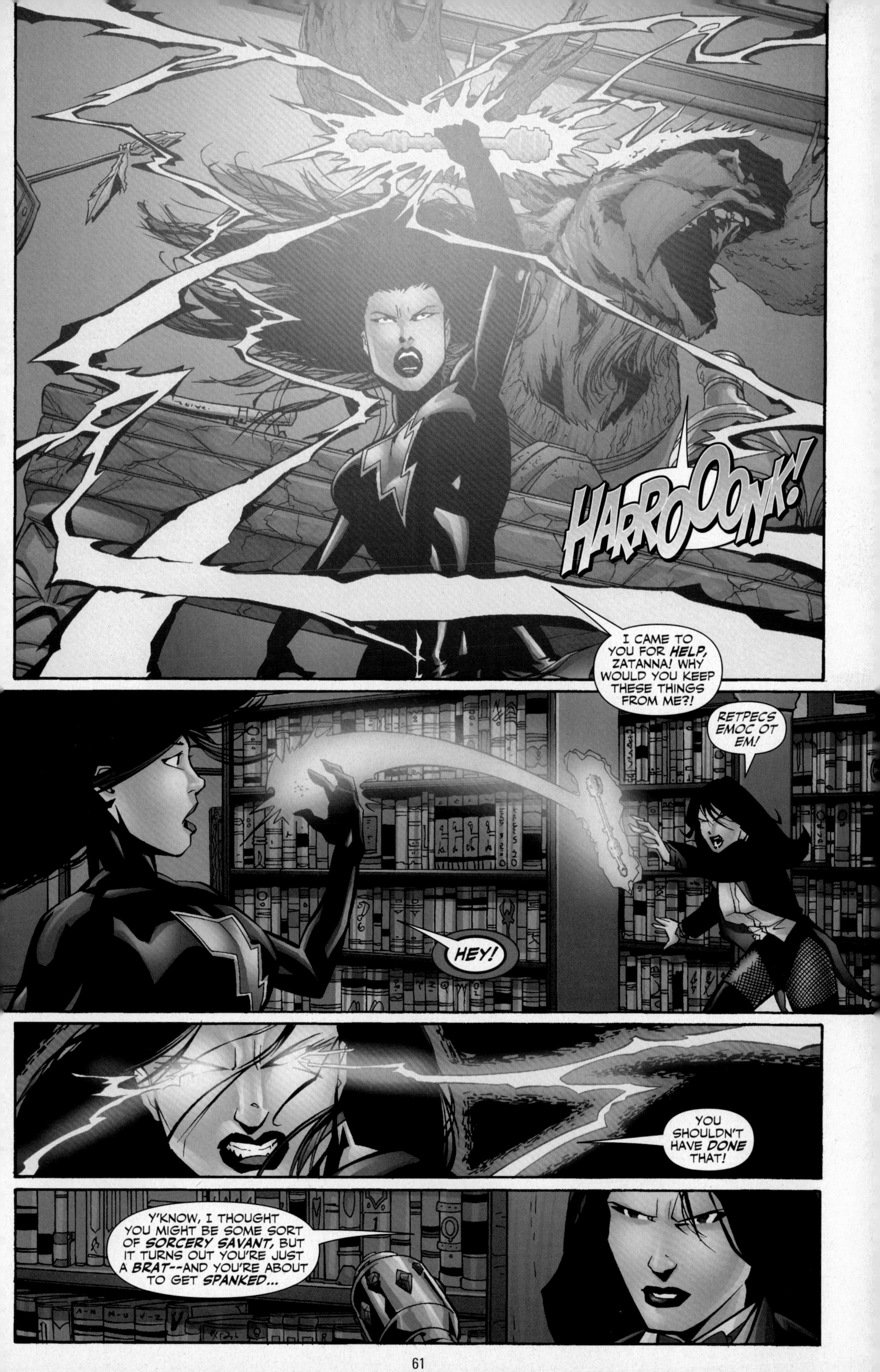
HARROOOONK!
I CAME TO YOU FOR HELP, ZATANNA! WHY WOULD YOU KEEP THESE THINGS FROM ME?!
RETPECS EMOC OT EM!
HEY!
YOU SHOULDN'T HAVE DONE THAT!
Y'KNOW, I THOUGHT YOU MIGHT BE SOME SORT OF SORCERY SAVANT, BUT IT TURNS OUT YOU'RE JUST A BRAT--AND YOU'RE ABOUT TO GET SPANKED...

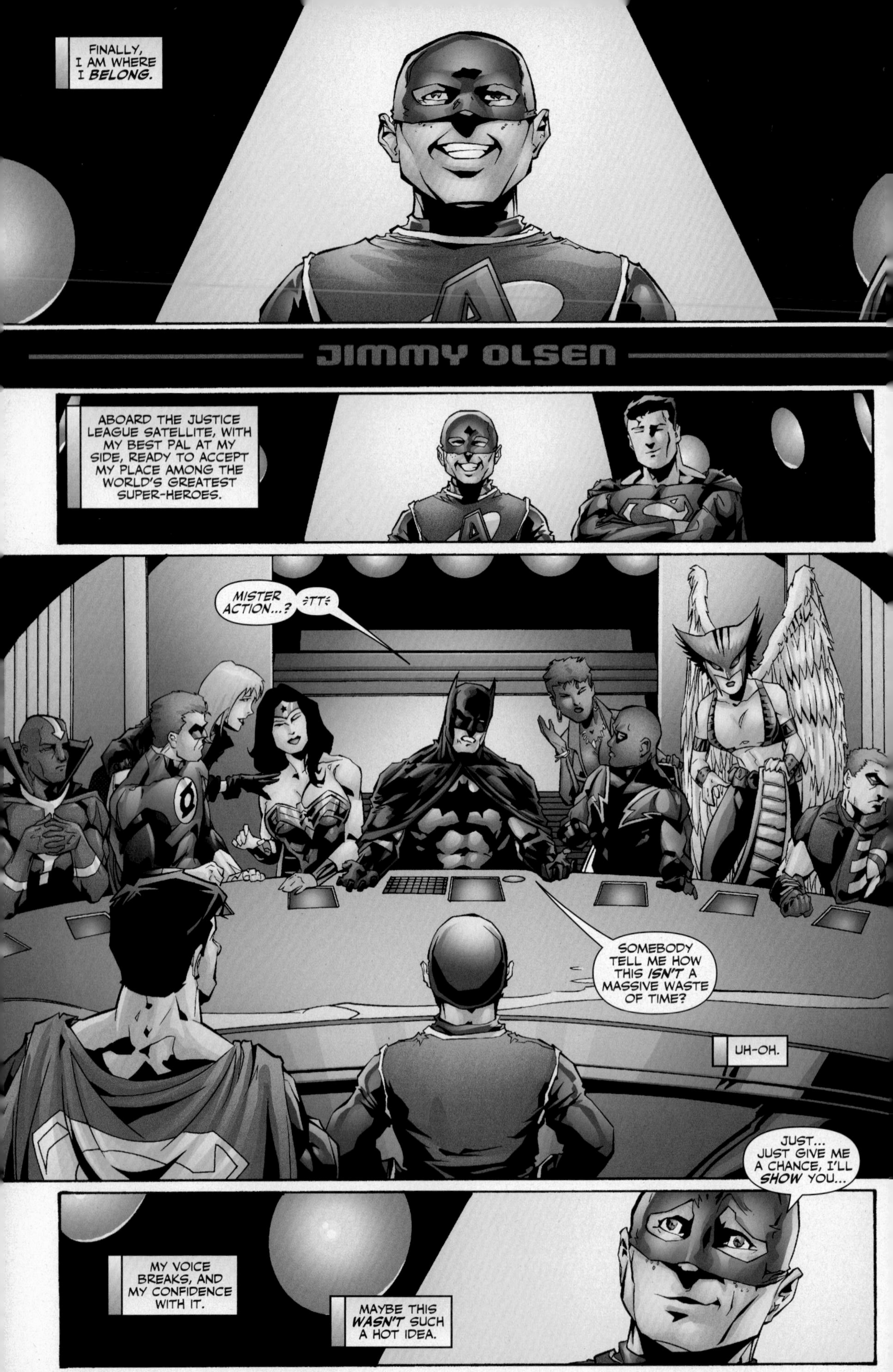
FINALLY, I AM WHERE I BELONG.
JIMMY OLSEN
ABOARD THE JUSTICE LEAGUE SATELLITE, WITH MY BEST PAL AT MY SIDE, READY TO ACCEPT MY PLACE AMONG THE WORLD'S GREATEST SUPER-HEROES.
MISTER ACTION...?
TT
SOMEBODY TELL ME HOW THIS ISN'T A MASSIVE WASTE OF TIME?
UH-OH.
JUST... JUST GIVE ME A CHANCE, I'LL SHOW YOU...
MY VOICE BREAKS, AND MY CONFIDENCE WITH IT.
MAYBE THIS WASN'T SUCH A HOT IDEA.

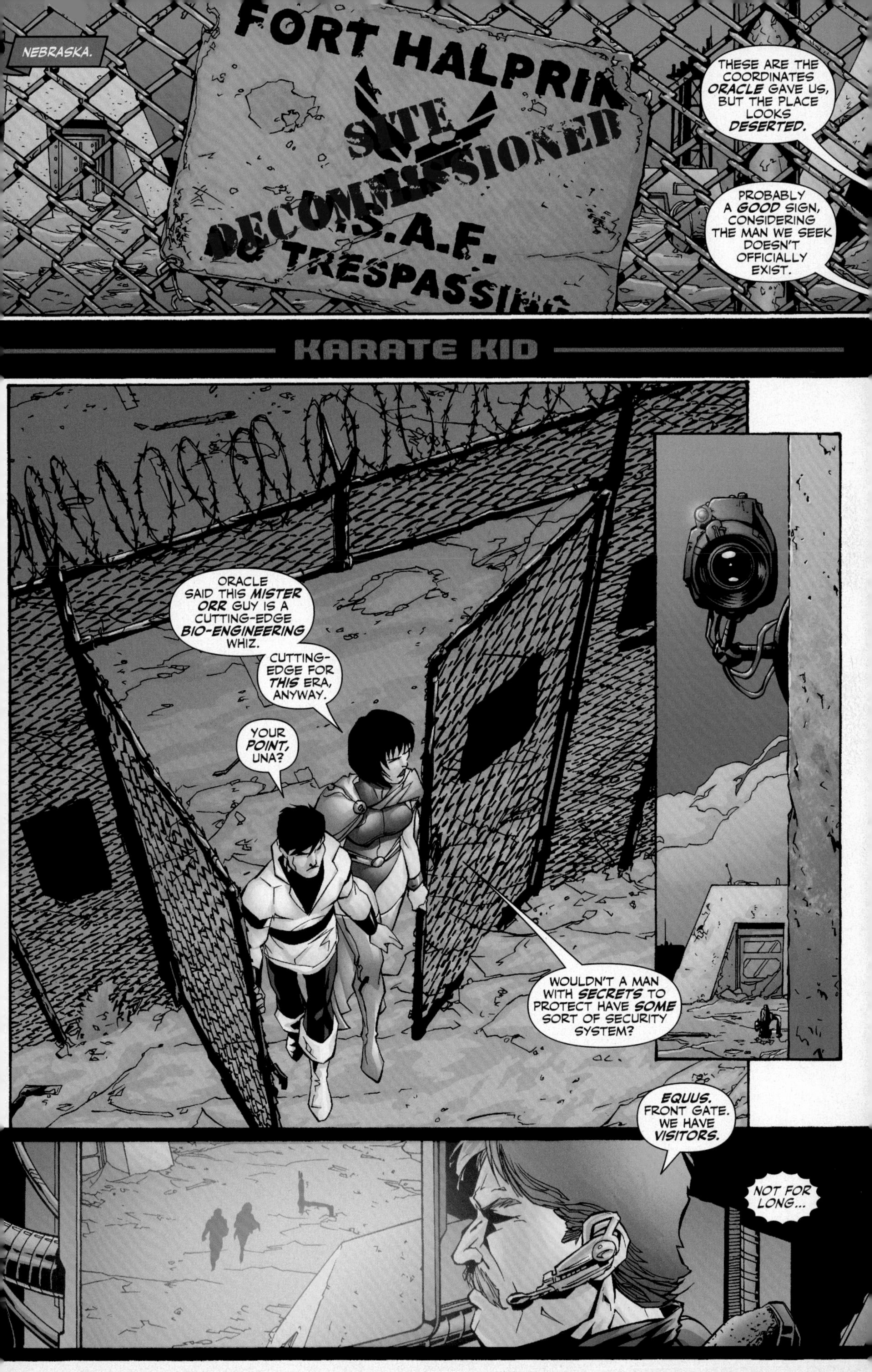
NEBRASKA.
FORT HALPRIN
SITE DECOMMISSIONED
U.S.A.F.
NO TRESPASSING
THESE ARE THE COORDINATES ORACLE GAVE US, BUT THE PLACE LOOKS DESERTED.
PROBABLY A GOOD SIGN, CONSIDERING THE MAN WE SEEK DOESN'T OFFICIALLY EXIST.
KARATE KID
ORACLE SAID THIS MISTER ORR GUY IS A CUTTING-EDGE BIO-ENGINEERING WHIZ.
CUTTING-EDGE FOR THIS ERA, ANYWAY.
YOUR POINT, UNA?
WOULDN'T A MAN WITH SECRETS TO PROTECT HAVE SOME SORT OF SECURITY SYSTEM?
EQUUS. FRONT GATE. WE HAVE VISITORS.
NOT FOR LONG...

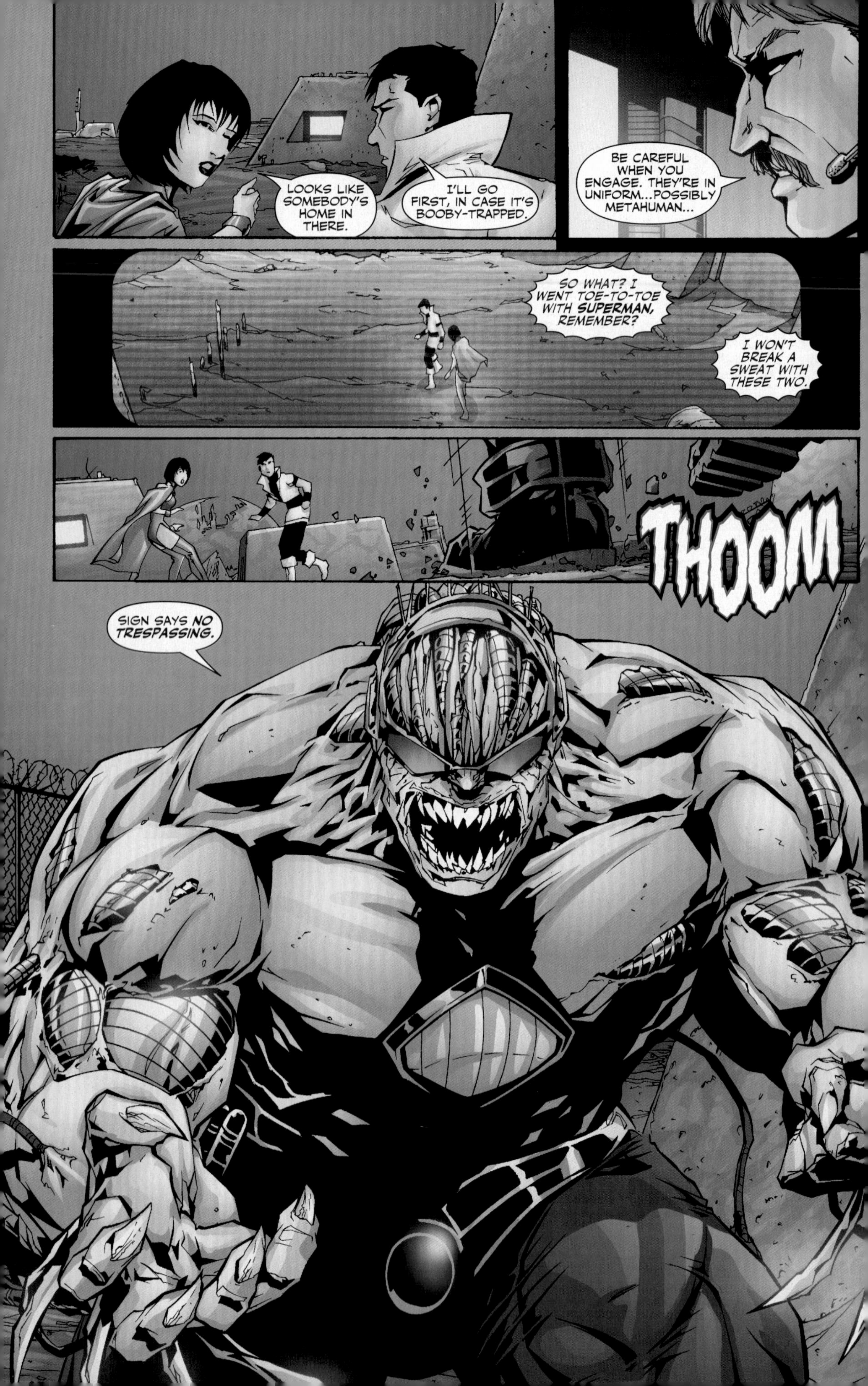

LOOKS LIKE SOMEBODY'S HOME IN THERE.
I'LL GO FIRST, IN CASE IT'S BOOBY-TRAPPED.
BE CAREFUL WHEN YOU ENGAGE. THEY'RE IN UNIFORM...POSSIBLY METAHUMAN...
SO WHAT? I WENT TOE-TO-TOE WITH SUPERMAN, REMEMBER?
I WON'T BREAK A SWEAT WITH THESE TWO.
THOOM
SIGN SAYS NO TRESPASSING.

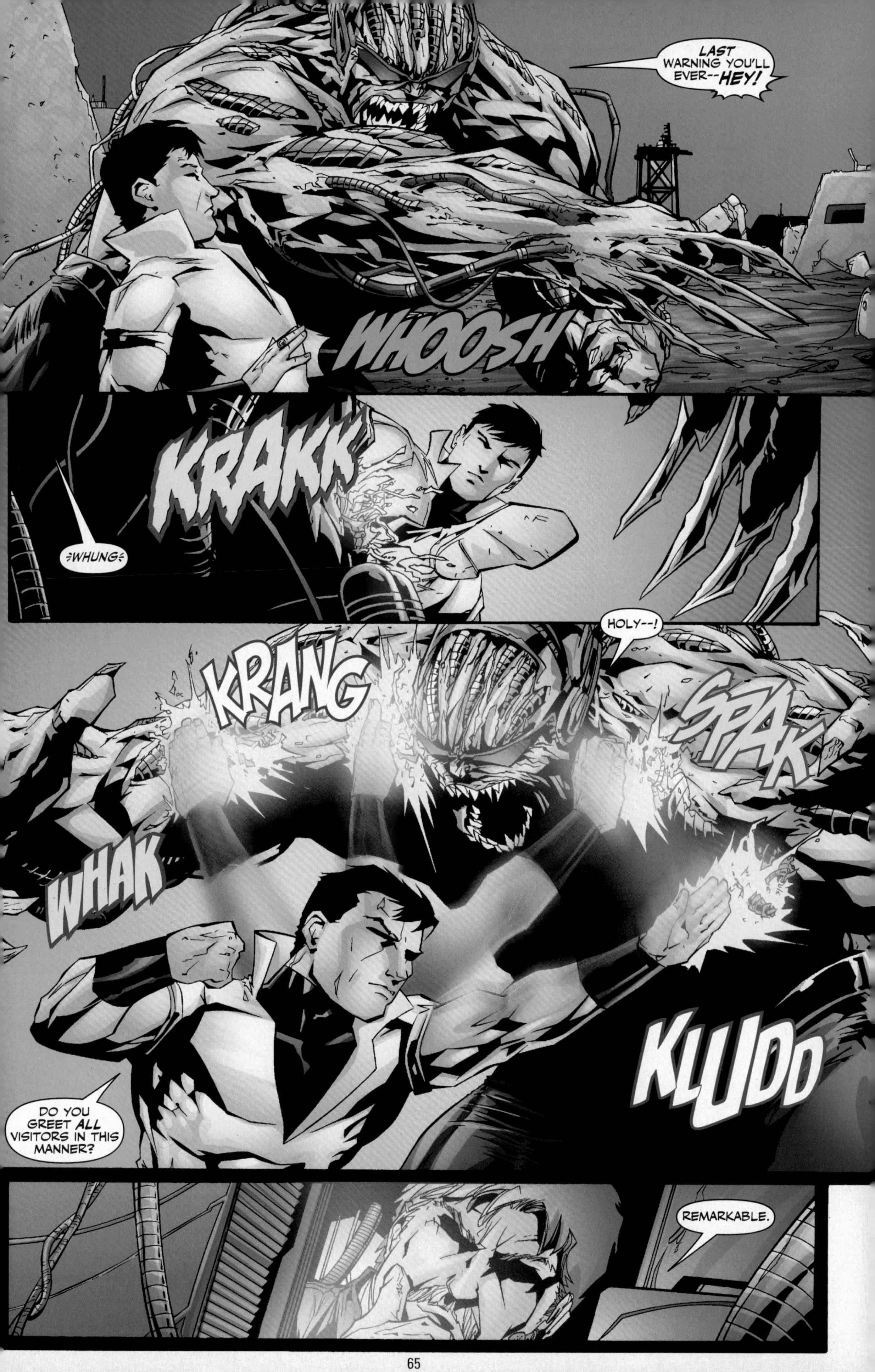
LAST WARNING YOU'LL EVER--HEY!
WHOOSH
KRAKK
WHUNG
HOLY--!
KRANG
SPAK
WHAK
KLUDD
DO YOU GREET ALL VISITORS IN THIS MANNER?
REMARKABLE.

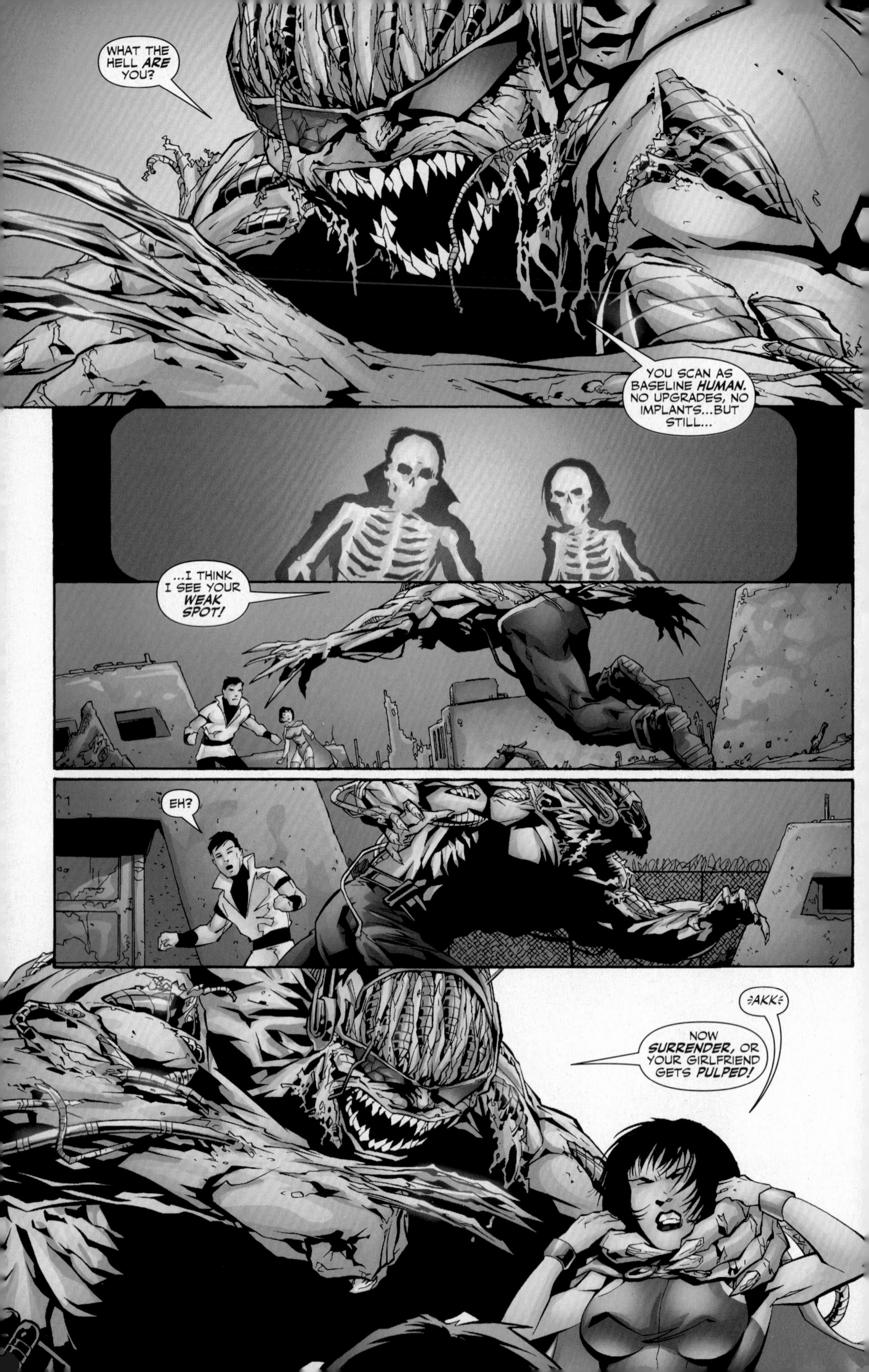
WHAT THE HELL ARE YOU?
YOU SCAN AS BASELINE HUMAN. NO UPGRADES, NO IMPLANTS...BUT STILL...
...I THINK I SEE YOUR WEAK SPOT!
EH?
AKK
NOW SURRENDER, OR YOUR GIRLFRIEND GETS PULPED!

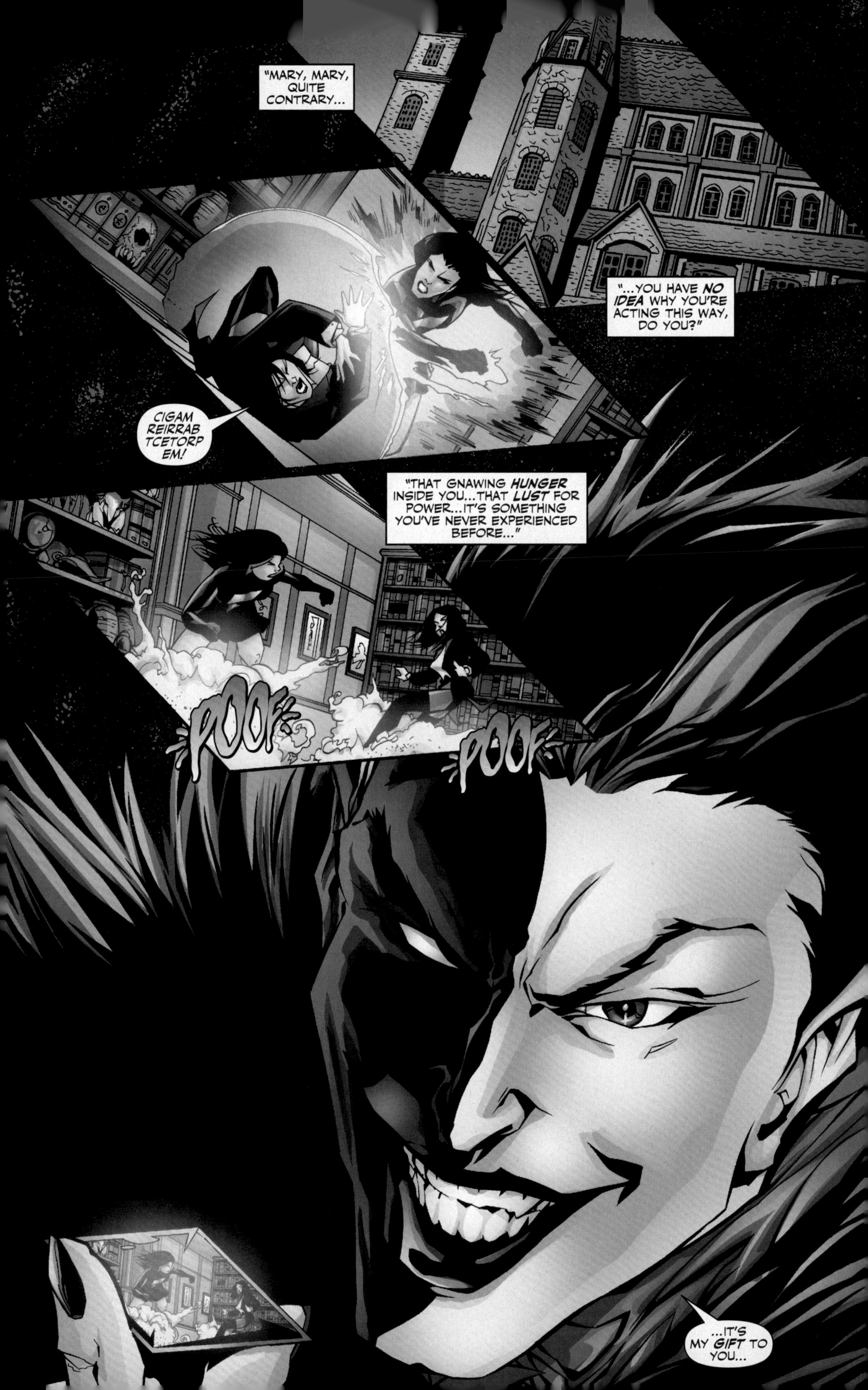
"MARY, MARY, QUITE CONTRARY...
"...YOU HAVE NO IDEA WHY YOU'RE ACTING THIS WAY, DO YOU?"
CIGAM REIRRAB TCETORP EM!
"THAT GNAWING HUNGER INSIDE YOU...THAT LUST FOR POWER...IT'S SOMETHING YOU'VE NEVER EXPERIENCED BEFORE..."
POOF
POOF
...IT'S MY GIFT TO YOU...

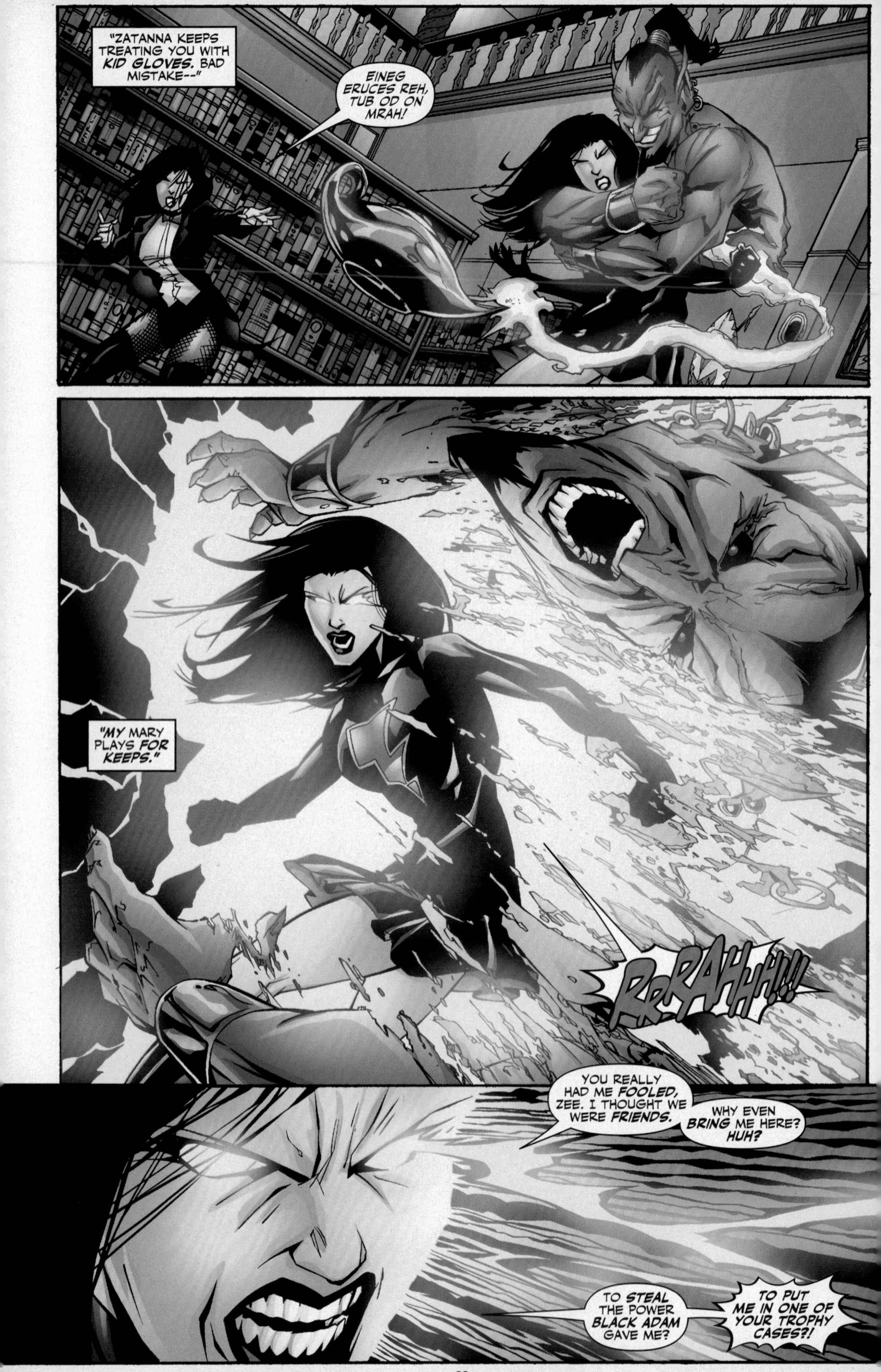
"ZATANNA KEEPS TREATING YOU WITH KID GLOVES. BAD MISTAKE--"
EINEG ERUCES REH, TUB OD ON MRAH!
"MY MARY PLAYS FOR KEEPS."
RRRAHHH!!!
YOU REALLY HAD ME FOOLED, ZEE. I THOUGHT WE WERE FRIENDS.
WHY EVEN BRING ME HERE? HUH?
TO STEAL THE POWER BLACK ADAM GAVE ME?
TO PUT ME IN ONE OF YOUR TROPHY CASES?!

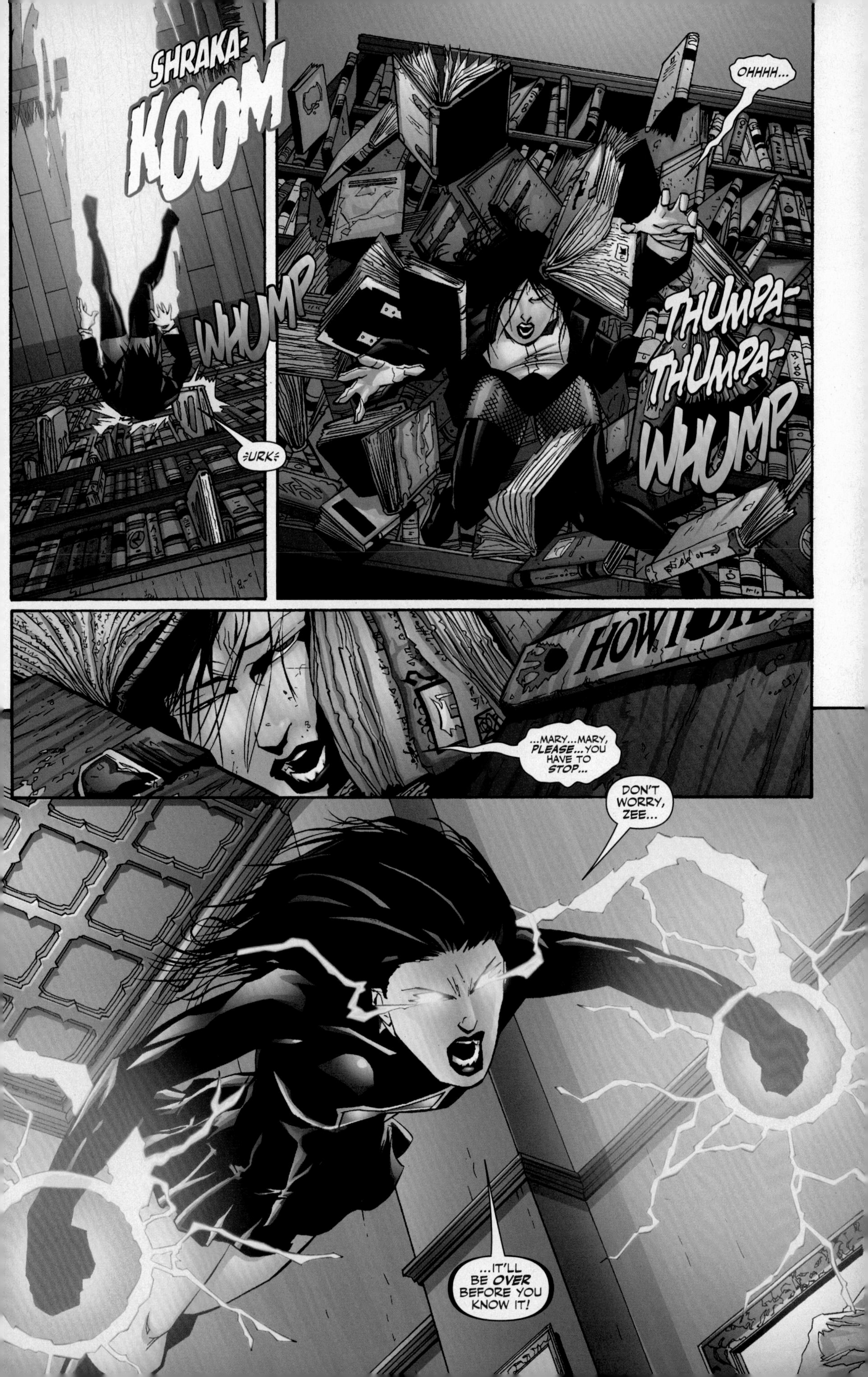
SHRAKA-
KOOM
WHUMP
URK
OHHHH...
THUMPA-
THUMPA-
WHUMP
HOW I DID
...MARY...MARY, PLEASE...YOU HAVE TO STOP...
DON'T WORRY, ZEE...
...IT'LL BE OVER BEFORE YOU KNOW IT!

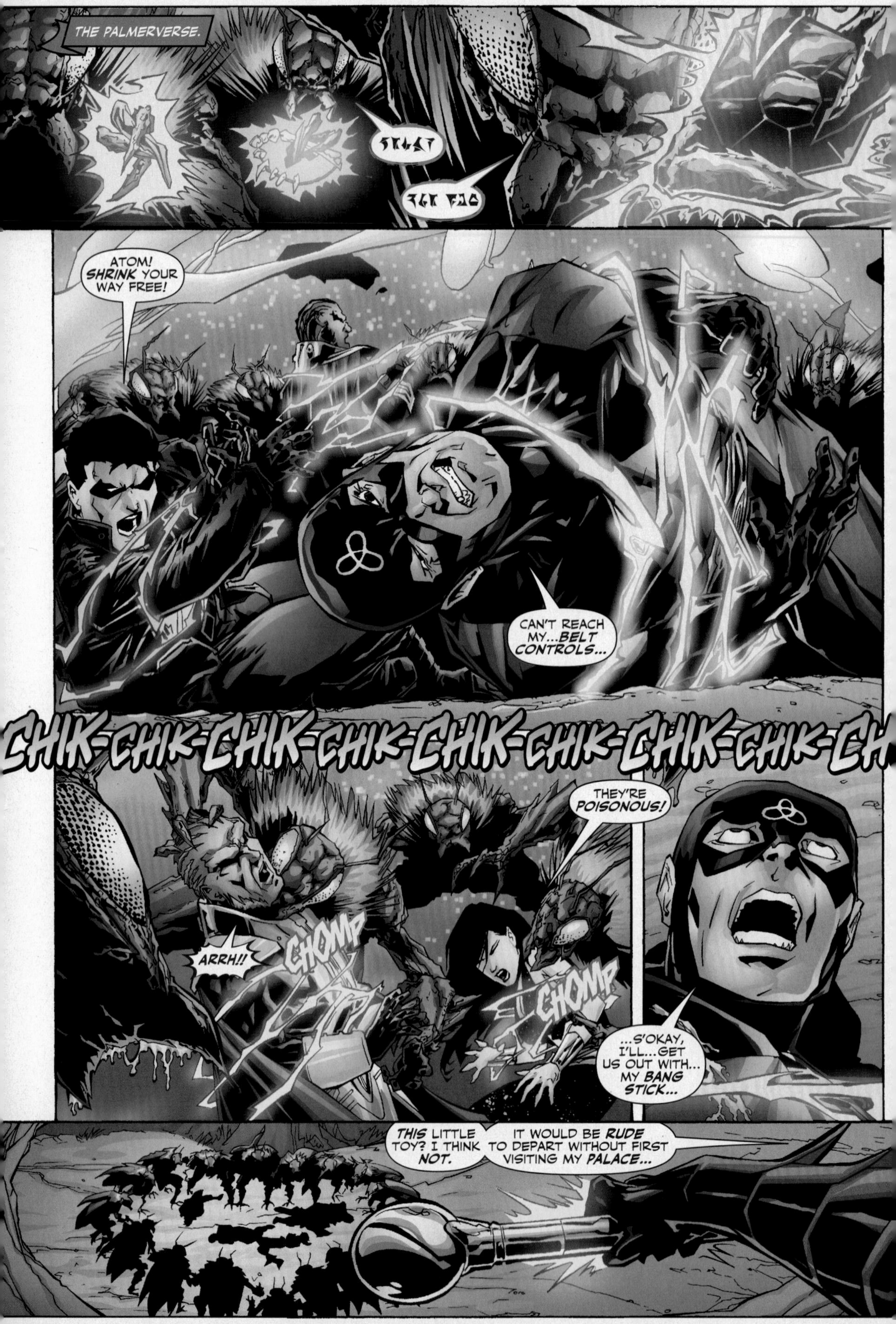
THE PALMERVERSE.
ATOM! SHRINK YOUR WAY FREE!
CAN'T REACH MY...BELT CONTROLS...
CHIK-CHIK-CHIK-CHIK-CHIK-CHIK-CHIK-CHIK-CH
ARRH!!
CHOMP
THEY'RE POISONOUS!
CHOMP
...S'OKAY, I'LL...GET US OUT WITH... MY BANG STICK...
THIS LITTLE TOY? I THINK NOT.
IT WOULD BE RUDE TO DEPART WITHOUT FIRST VISITING MY PALACE...

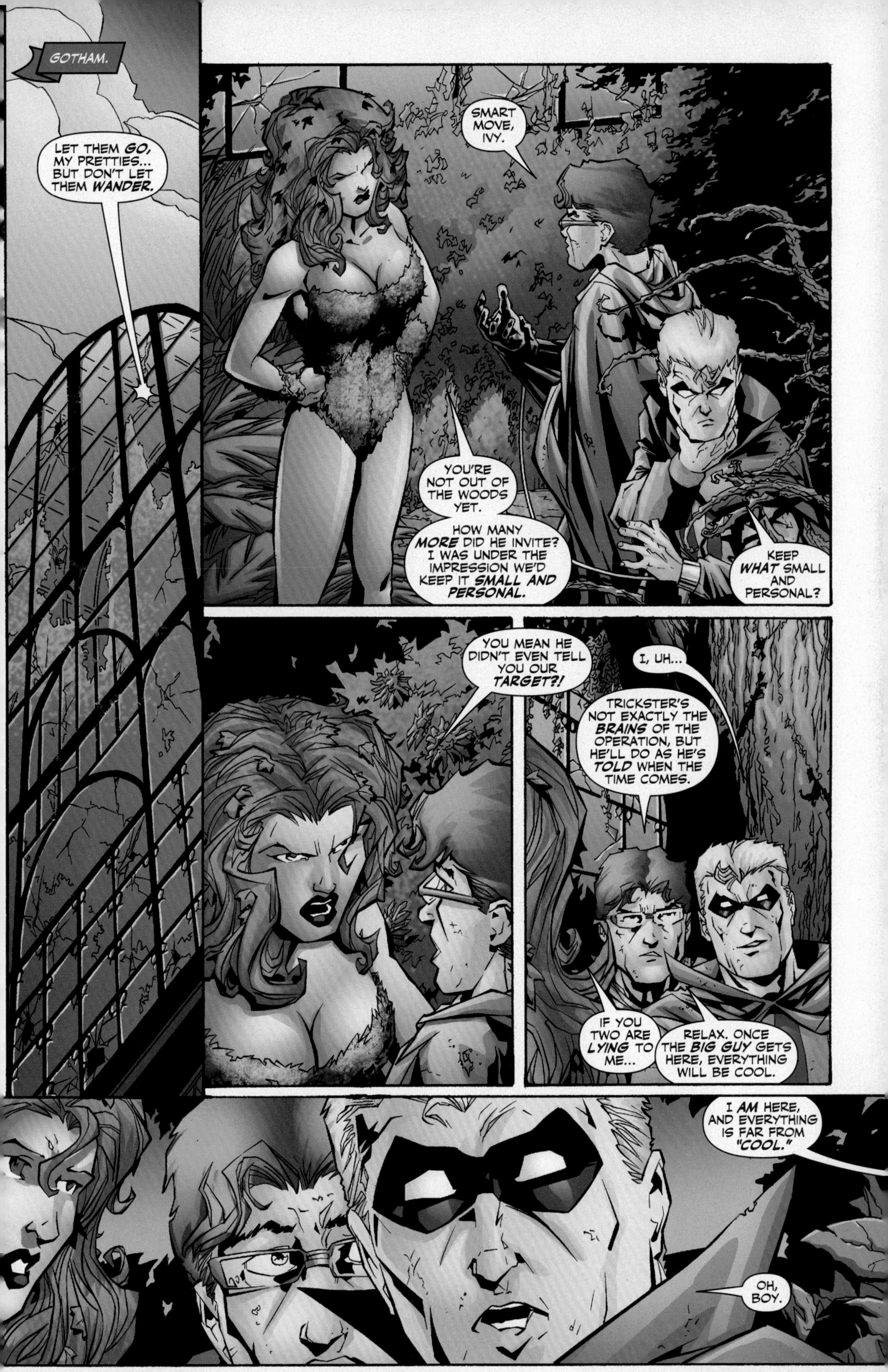
GOTHAM.
LET THEM GO, MY PRETTIES... BUT DON'T LET THEM WANDER.
SMART MOVE, IVY.
YOU'RE NOT OUT OF THE WOODS YET.
HOW MANY MORE DID HE INVITE? I WAS UNDER THE IMPRESSION WE'D KEEP IT SMALL AND PERSONAL.
KEEP WHAT SMALL AND PERSONAL?
YOU MEAN HE DIDN'T EVEN TELL YOU OUR TARGET?!
I, UH...
TRICKSTER'S NOT EXACTLY THE BRAINS OF THE OPERATION, BUT HE'LL DO AS HE'S TOLD WHEN THE TIME COMES.
IF YOU TWO ARE LYING TO ME...
RELAX. ONCE THE BIG GUY GETS HERE, EVERYTHING WILL BE COOL.
I AM HERE, AND EVERYTHING IS FAR FROM "COOL."
OH, BOY.

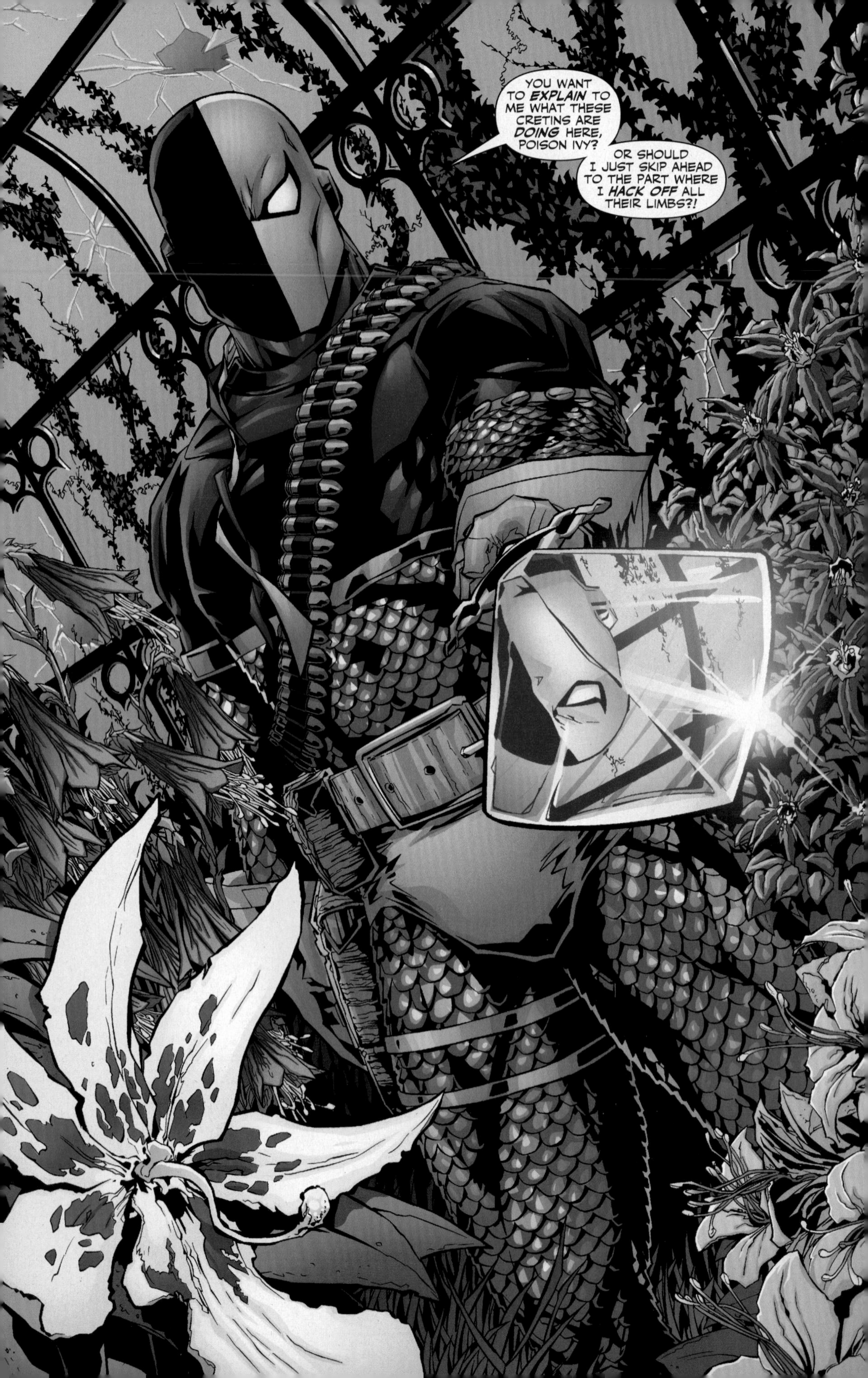
YOU WANT TO EXPLAIN TO ME WHAT THESE CRETINS ARE DOING HERE, POISON IVY?
OR SHOULD I JUST SKIP AHEAD TO THE PART WHERE I HACK OFF ALL THEIR LIMBS?!

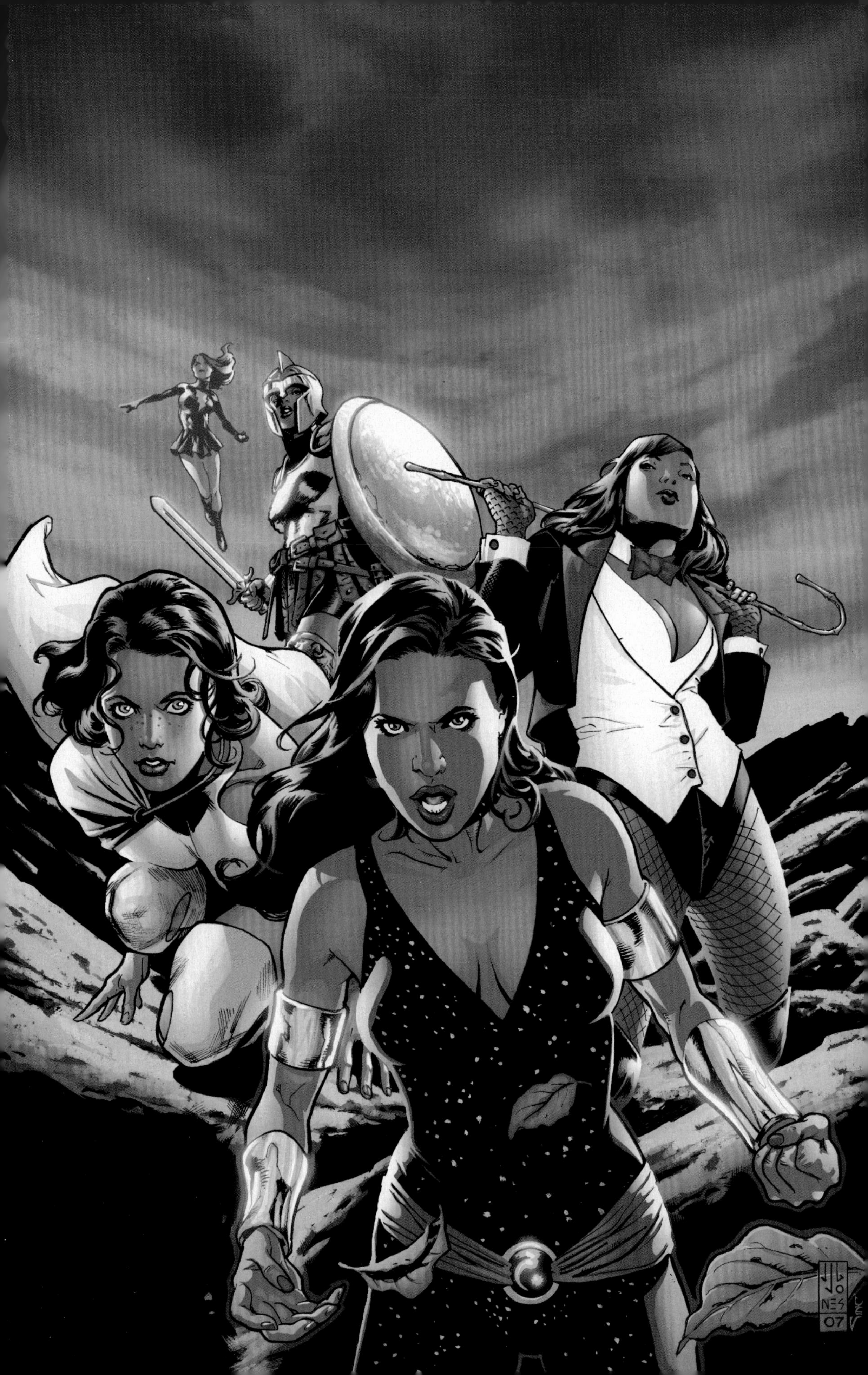

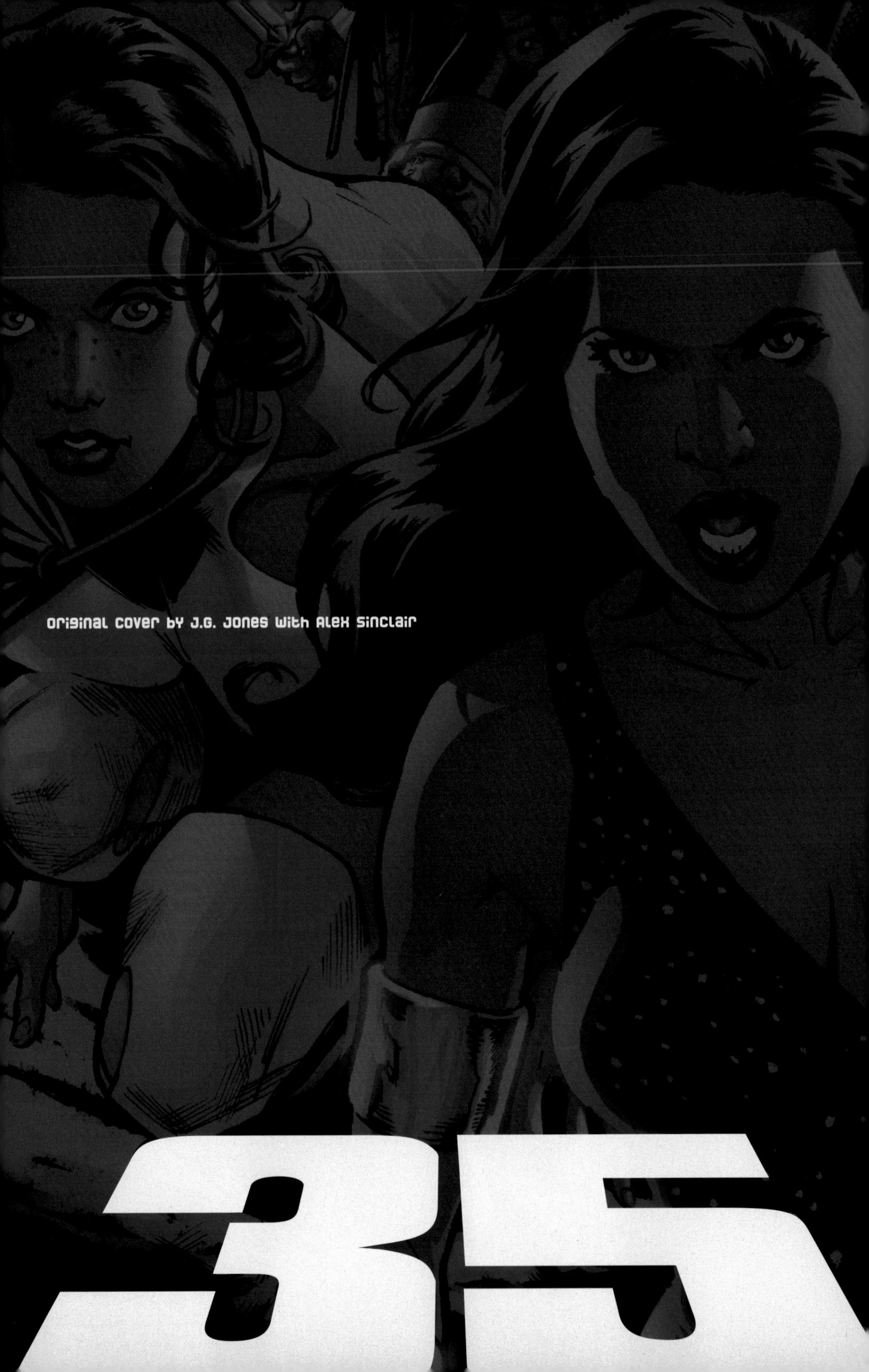
original cover by J.G. Jones with Alex Sinclair
35

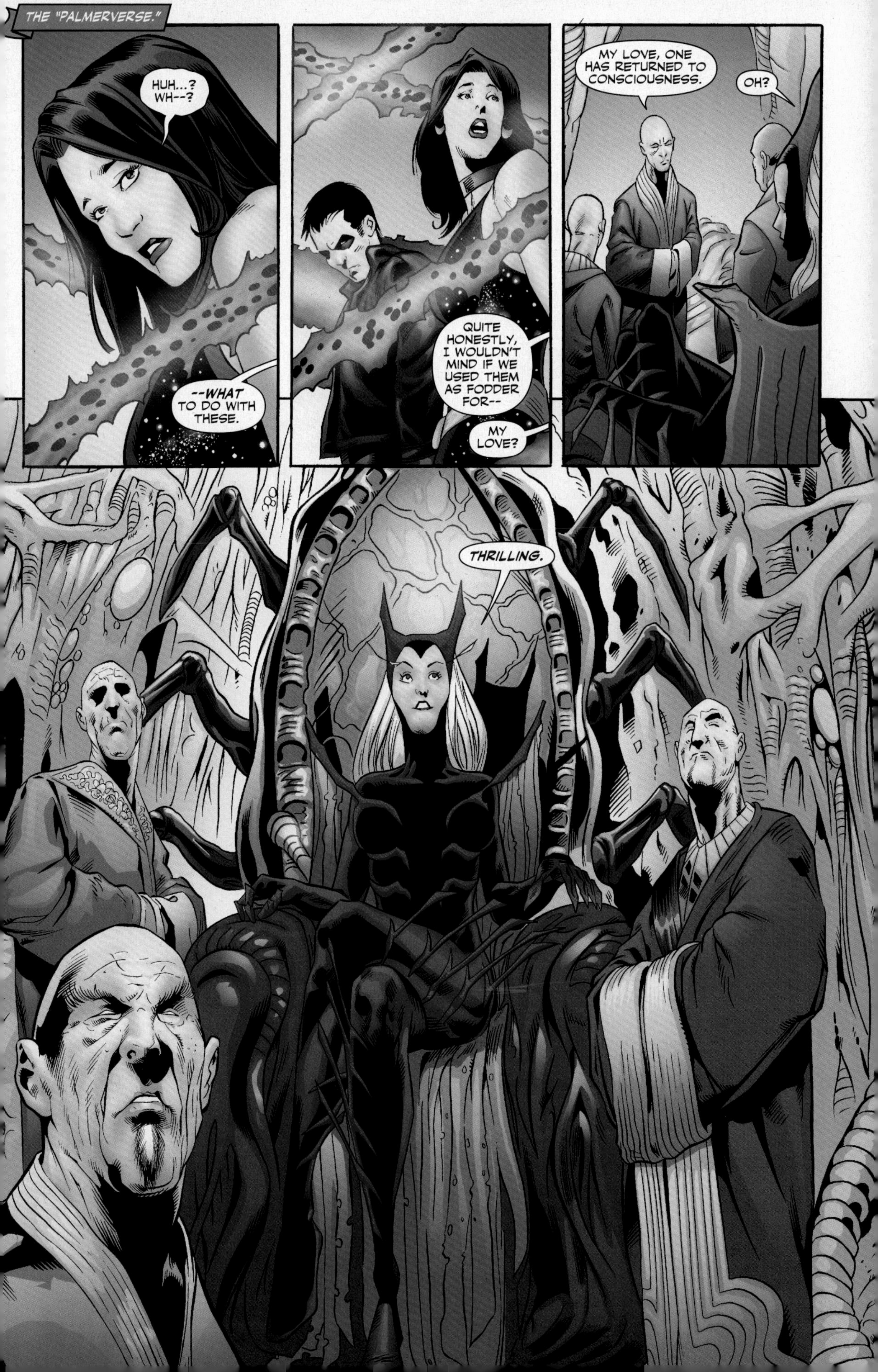
THE "PALMERVERSE."
HUH...? WH--?
--WHAT TO DO WITH THESE.
QUITE HONESTLY, I WOULDN'T MIND IF WE USED THEM AS FODDER FOR--
MY LOVE?
MY LOVE, ONE HAS RETURNED TO CONSCIOUSNESS.
OH?
THRILLING.

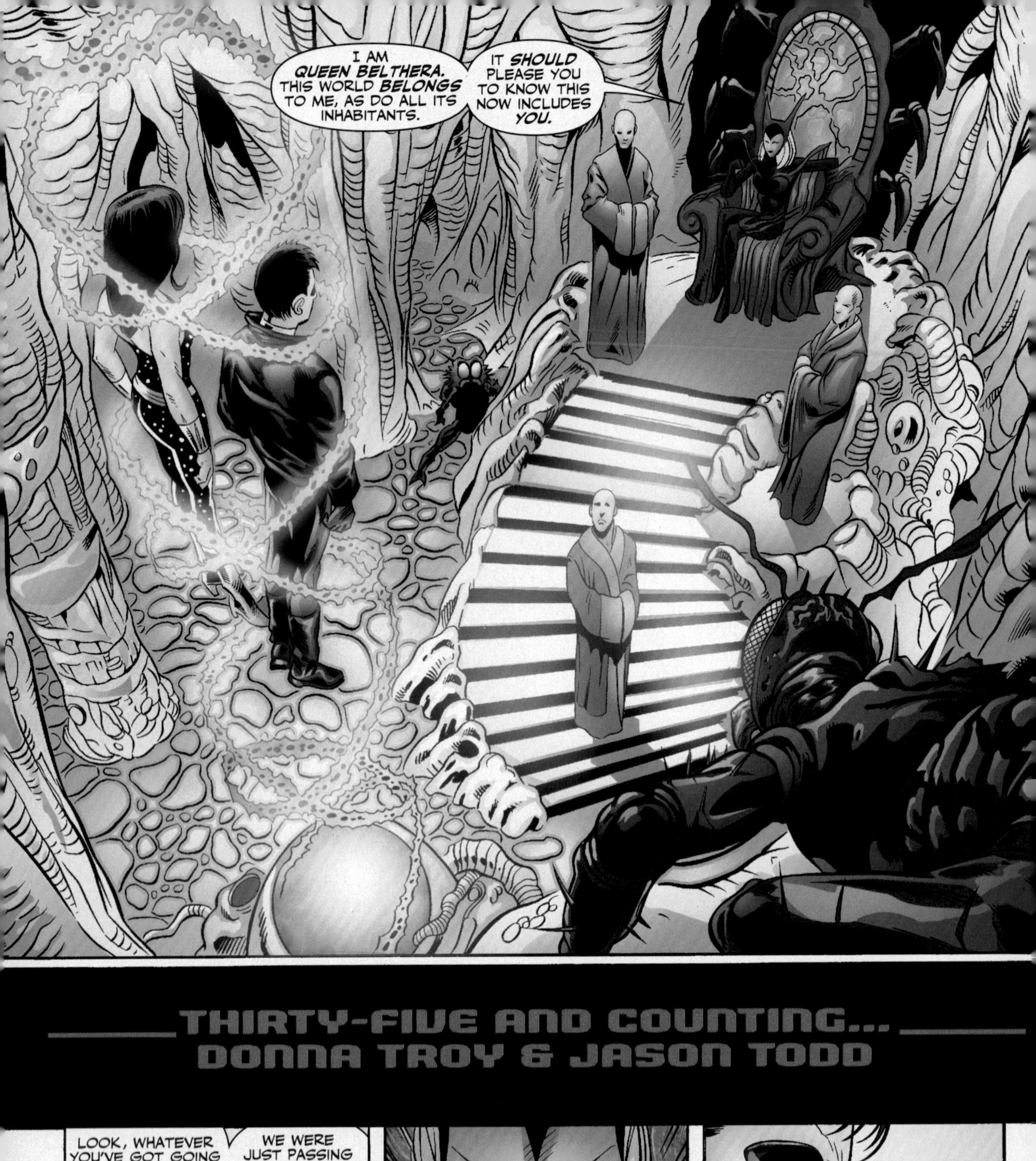
I AM *QUEEN BELTHERA.* THIS WORLD *BELONGS* TO ME, AS DO ALL ITS INHABITANTS.
IT *SHOULD* PLEASE YOU TO KNOW THIS NOW INCLUDES *YOU.*

## THIRTY-FIVE AND COUNTING... DONNA TROY & JASON TODD

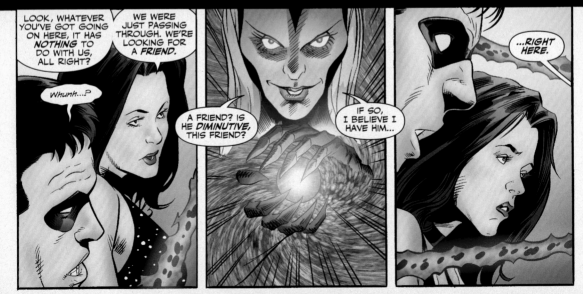

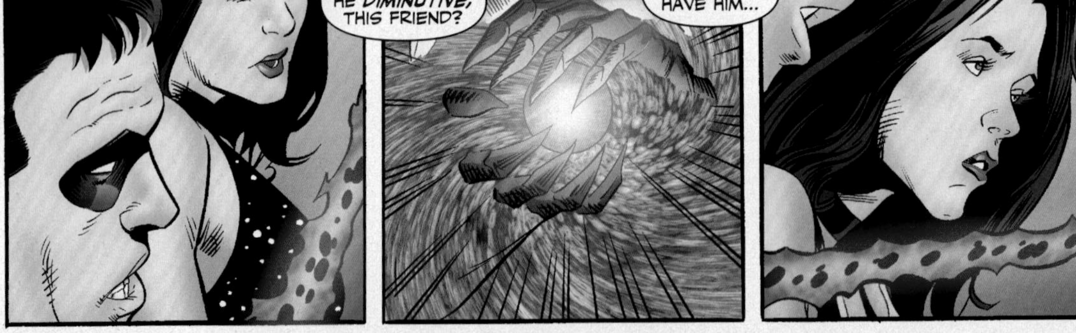
LOOK, WHATEVER YOU'VE GOT GOING ON HERE, IT HAS *NOTHING* TO DO WITH US, ALL RIGHT?
WE WERE JUST PASSING THROUGH. WE'RE LOOKING FOR A *FRIEND.*
*Whunh...?*
A FRIEND? IS HE *DIMINUTIVE,* THIS FRIEND?
IF SO, I BELIEVE I HAVE HIM...
*...RIGHT HERE.*

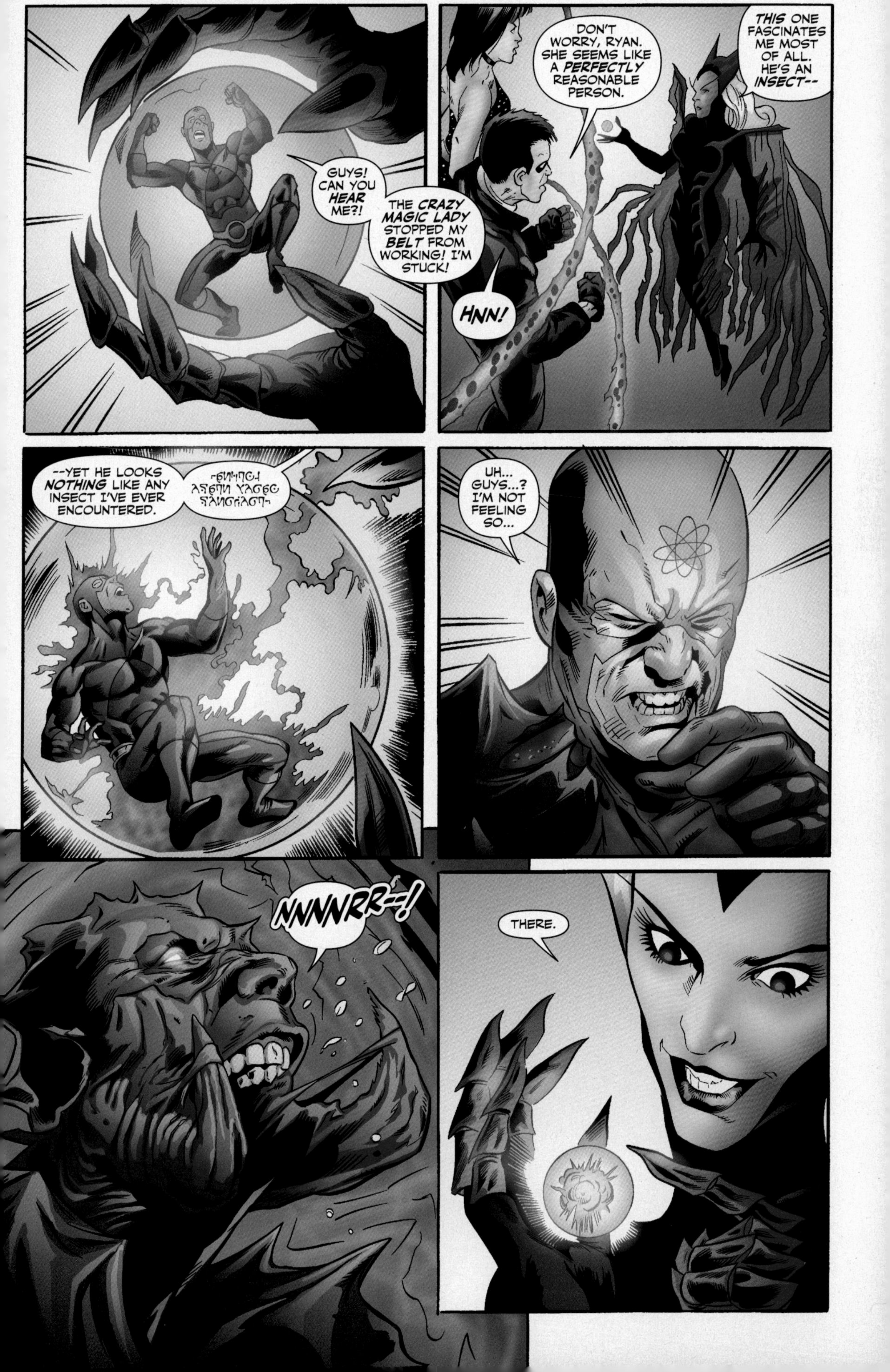
GUYS! CAN YOU HEAR ME?!
THE CRAZY MAGIC LADY STOPPED MY BELT FROM WORKING! I'M STUCK!
DON'T WORRY, RYAN. SHE SEEMS LIKE A PERFECTLY REASONABLE PERSON.
THIS ONE FASCINATES ME MOST OF ALL. HE'S AN INSECT--
HNN!
--YET HE LOOKS NOTHING LIKE ANY INSECT I'VE EVER ENCOUNTERED.
UH... GUYS...? I'M NOT FEELING SO...
NNNNRR--!
THERE.

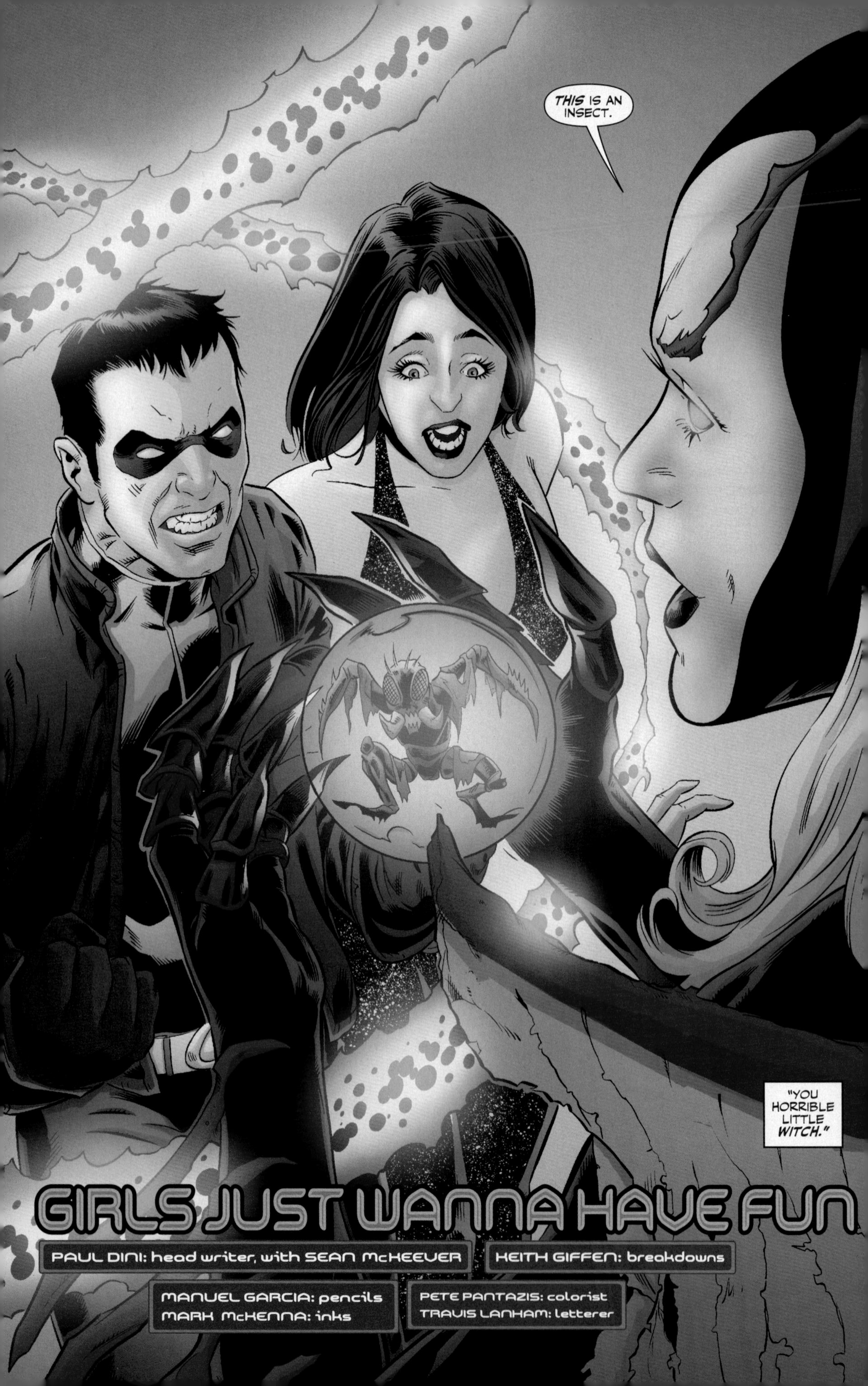
THIS IS AN INSECT.
"YOU HORRIBLE LITTLE WITCH."
GIRLS JUST WANNA HAVE FUN
PAUL DINI: head writer, with SEAN McKEEVER
KEITH GIFFEN: breakdowns
MANUEL GARCIA: pencils
MARK McKENNA: inks
PETE PANTAZIS: colorist
TRAVIS LANHAM: letterer

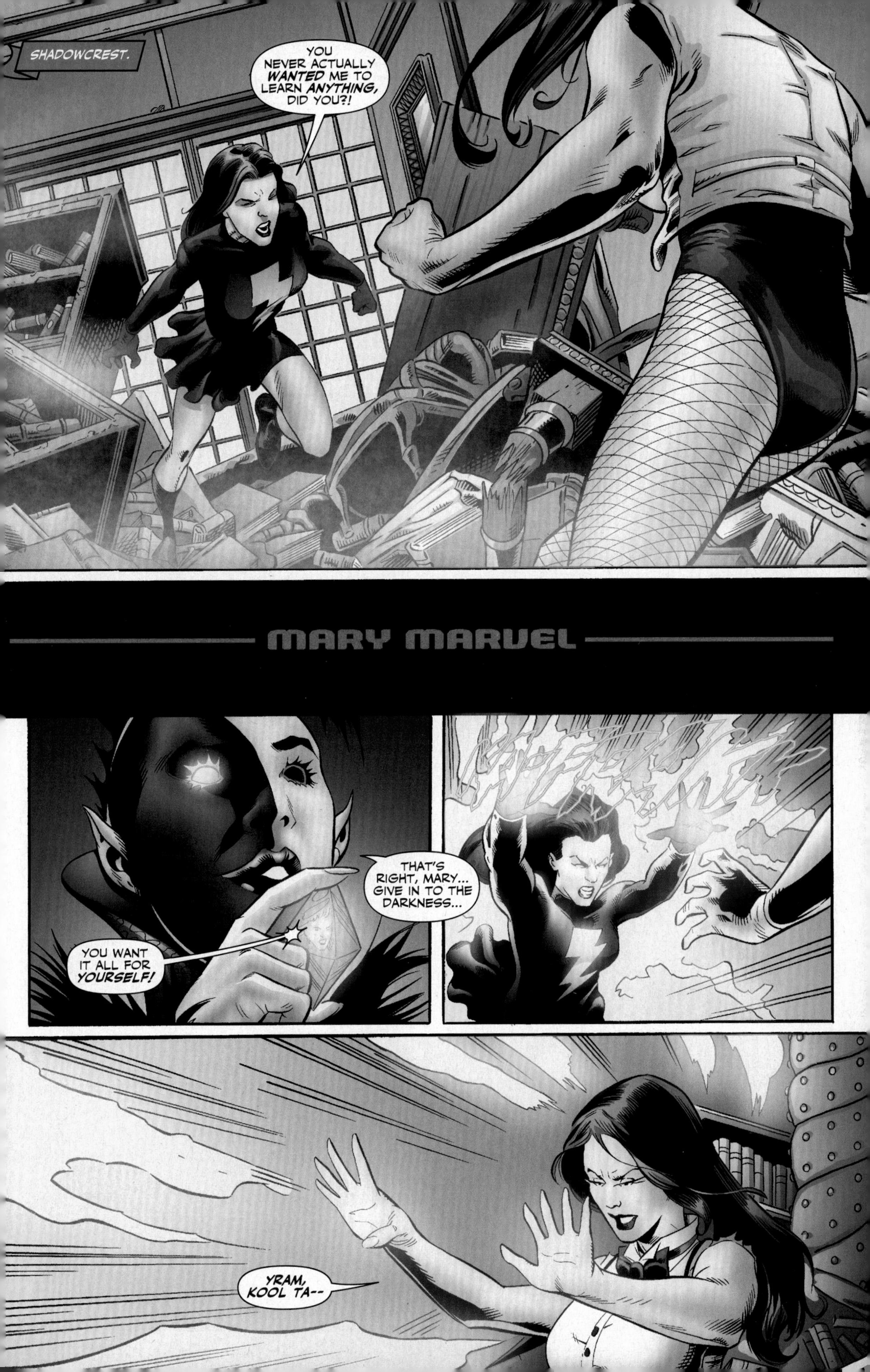
SHADOWCREST.
YOU NEVER ACTUALLY WANTED ME TO LEARN ANYTHING, DID YOU?!
MARY MARVEL
YOU WANT IT ALL FOR YOURSELF!
THAT'S RIGHT, MARY... GIVE IN TO THE DARKNESS...
YRAM, KOOL TA--

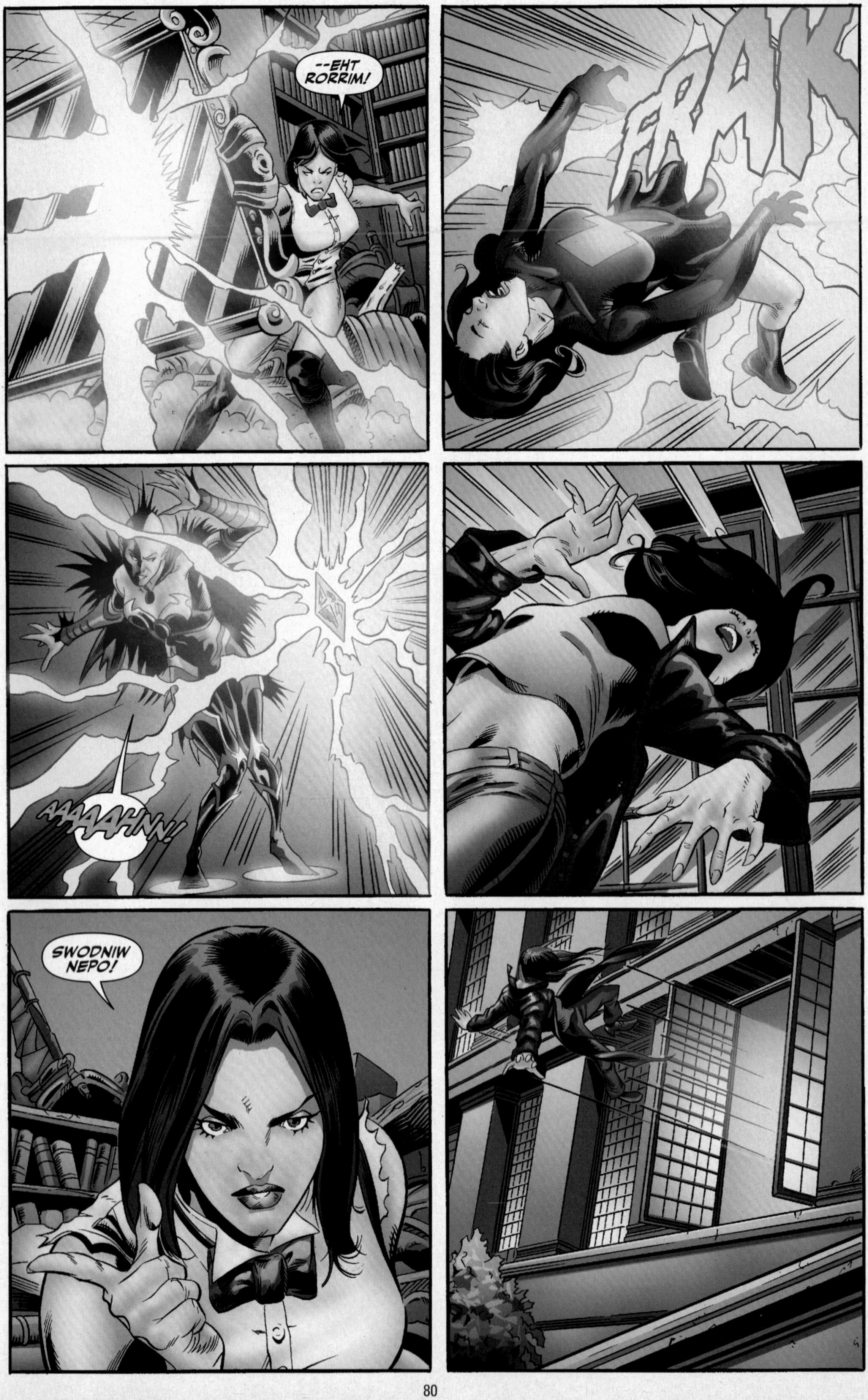
--EHT RORRIM!
FRAK
AAAAAHNN!
SWODNIW NEPO!

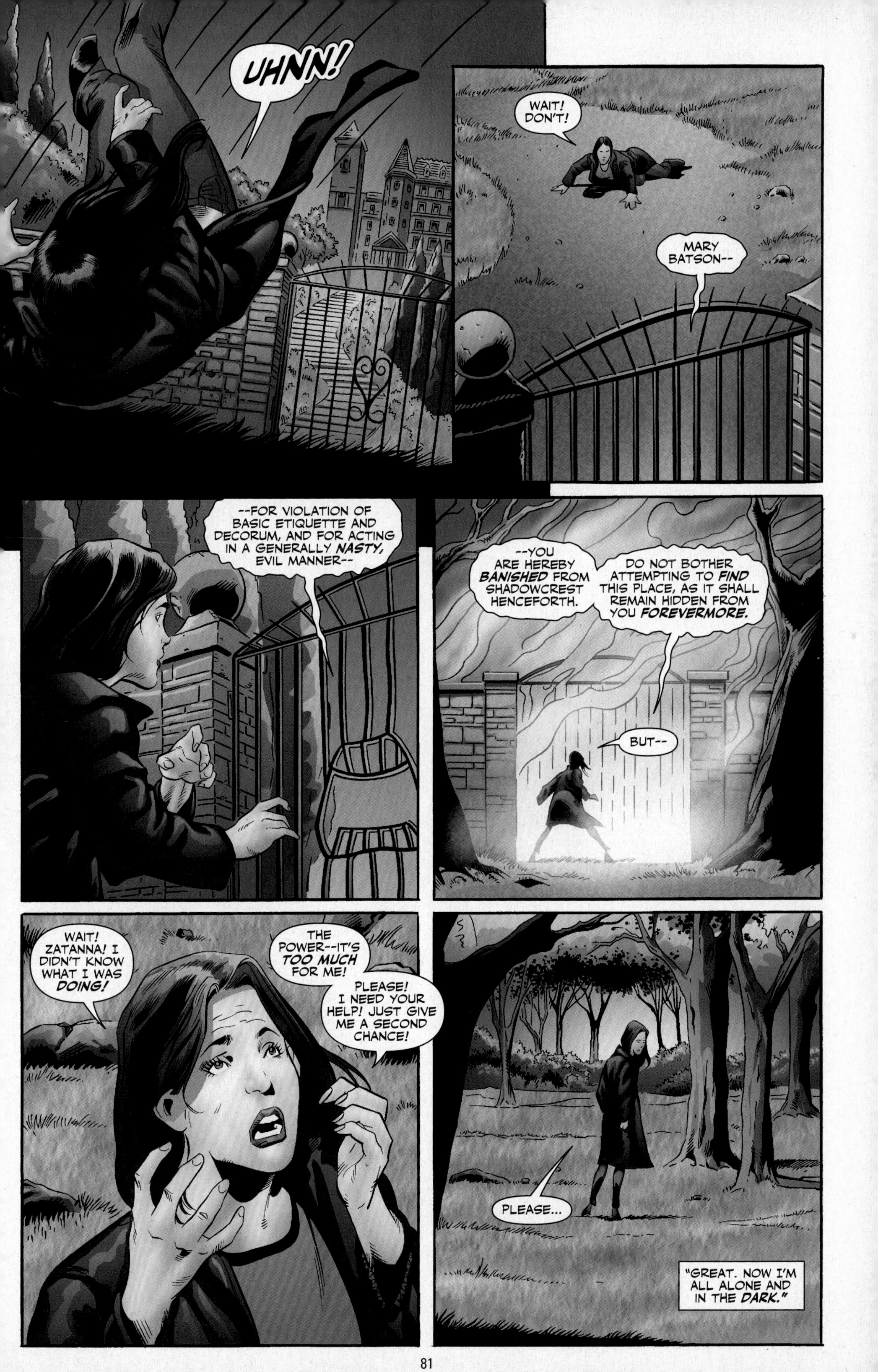
UHNN!
WAIT! DON'T!
MARY BATSON--
--FOR VIOLATION OF BASIC ETIQUETTE AND DECORUM, AND FOR ACTING IN A GENERALLY NASTY, EVIL MANNER--
--YOU ARE HEREBY BANISHED FROM SHADOWCREST HENCEFORTH.
DO NOT BOTHER ATTEMPTING TO FIND THIS PLACE, AS IT SHALL REMAIN HIDDEN FROM YOU FOREVERMORE.
BUT--
WAIT! ZATANNA! I DIDN'T KNOW WHAT I WAS DOING!
THE POWER--IT'S TOO MUCH FOR ME!
PLEASE! I NEED YOUR HELP! JUST GIVE ME A SECOND CHANCE!
PLEASE...
"GREAT. NOW I'M ALL ALONE AND IN THE DARK."

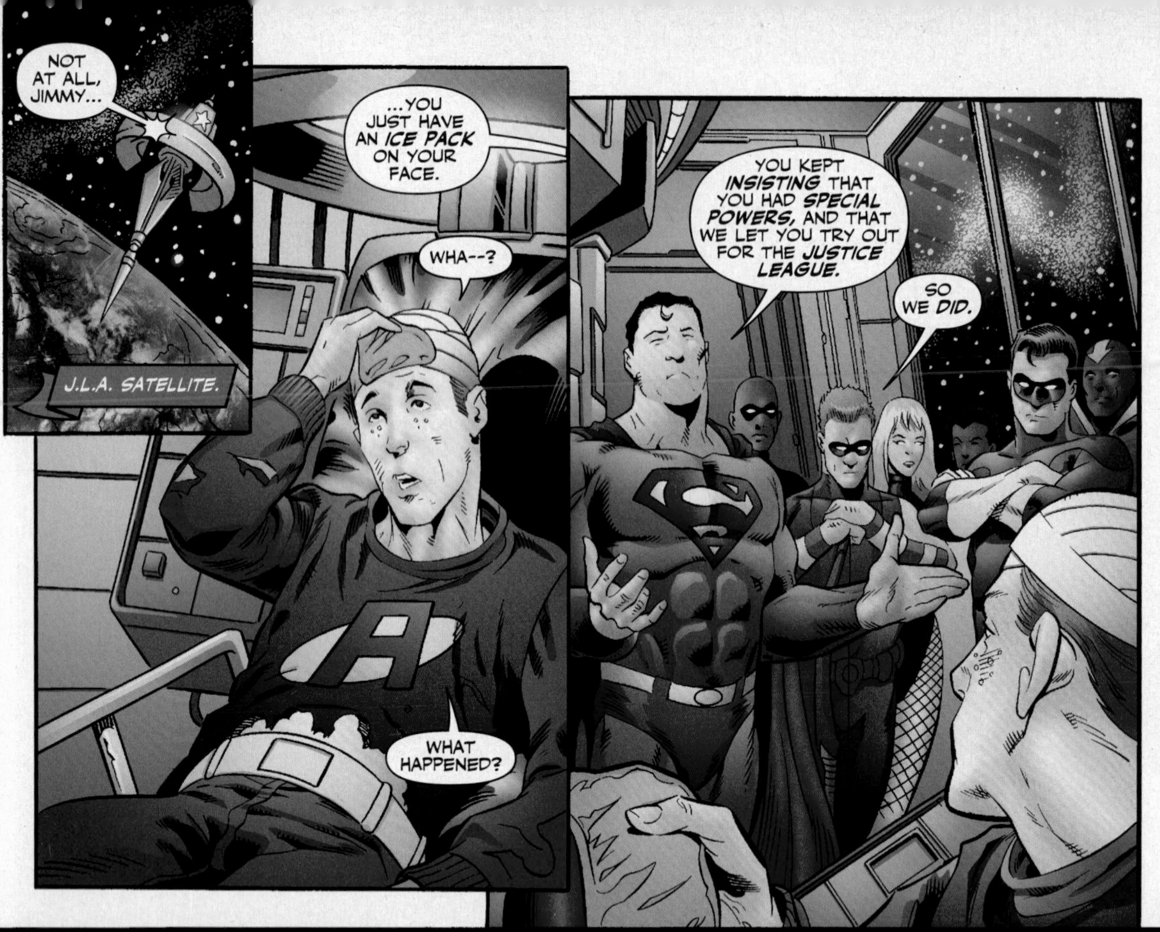
NOT AT ALL, JIMMY...
J.L.A. SATELLITE.
...YOU JUST HAVE AN ICE PACK ON YOUR FACE.
WHA--?
WHAT HAPPENED?
YOU KEPT INSISTING THAT YOU HAD SPECIAL POWERS, AND THAT WE LET YOU TRY OUT FOR THE JUSTICE LEAGUE.
SO WE DID.

# JIMMY OLSEN

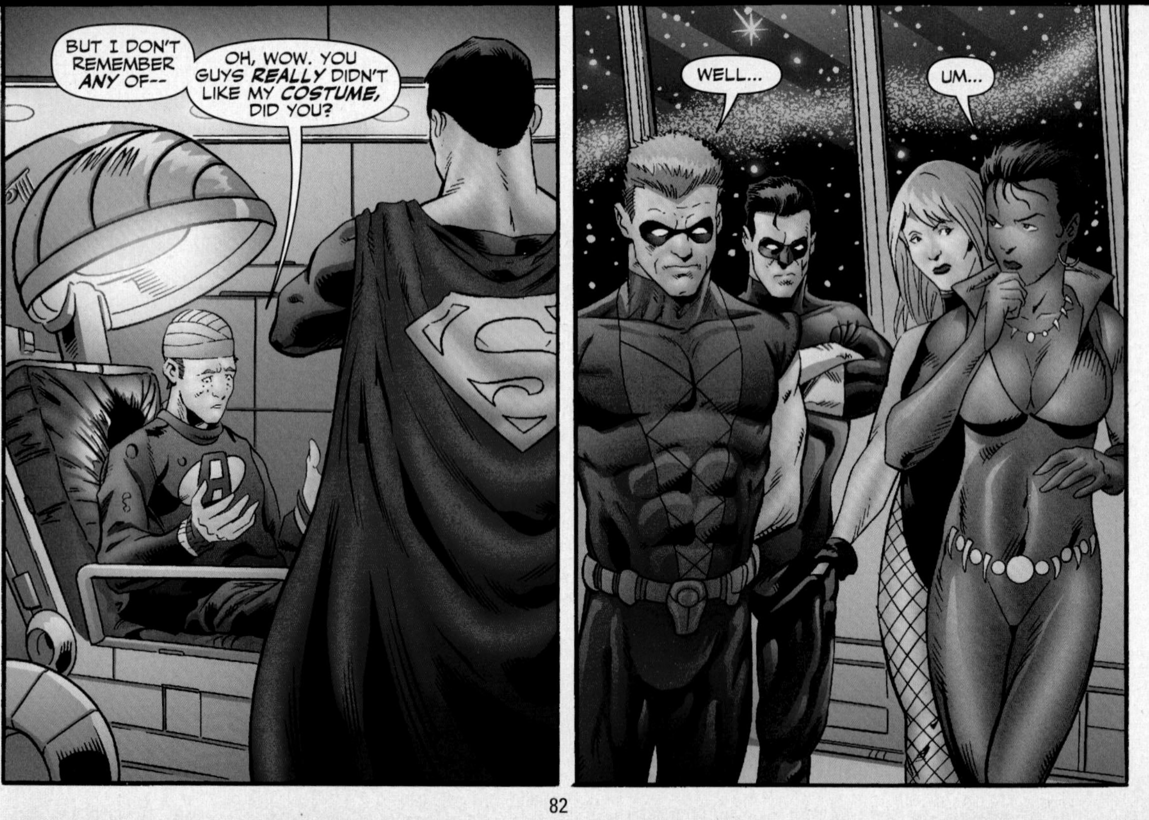
BUT I DON'T REMEMBER ANY OF--
OH, WOW. YOU GUYS REALLY DIDN'T LIKE MY COSTUME, DID YOU?
WELL...
UM...

BOP

WAK

WHOOSH

KRAK

CRRRARR!!!

ZOOM

OH. AND... WHAT'S THIS FROM?

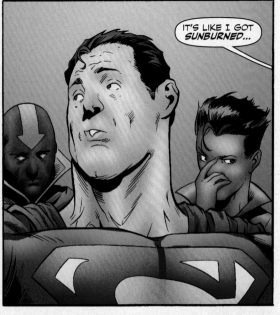

IT'S LIKE I GOT SUNBURNED...

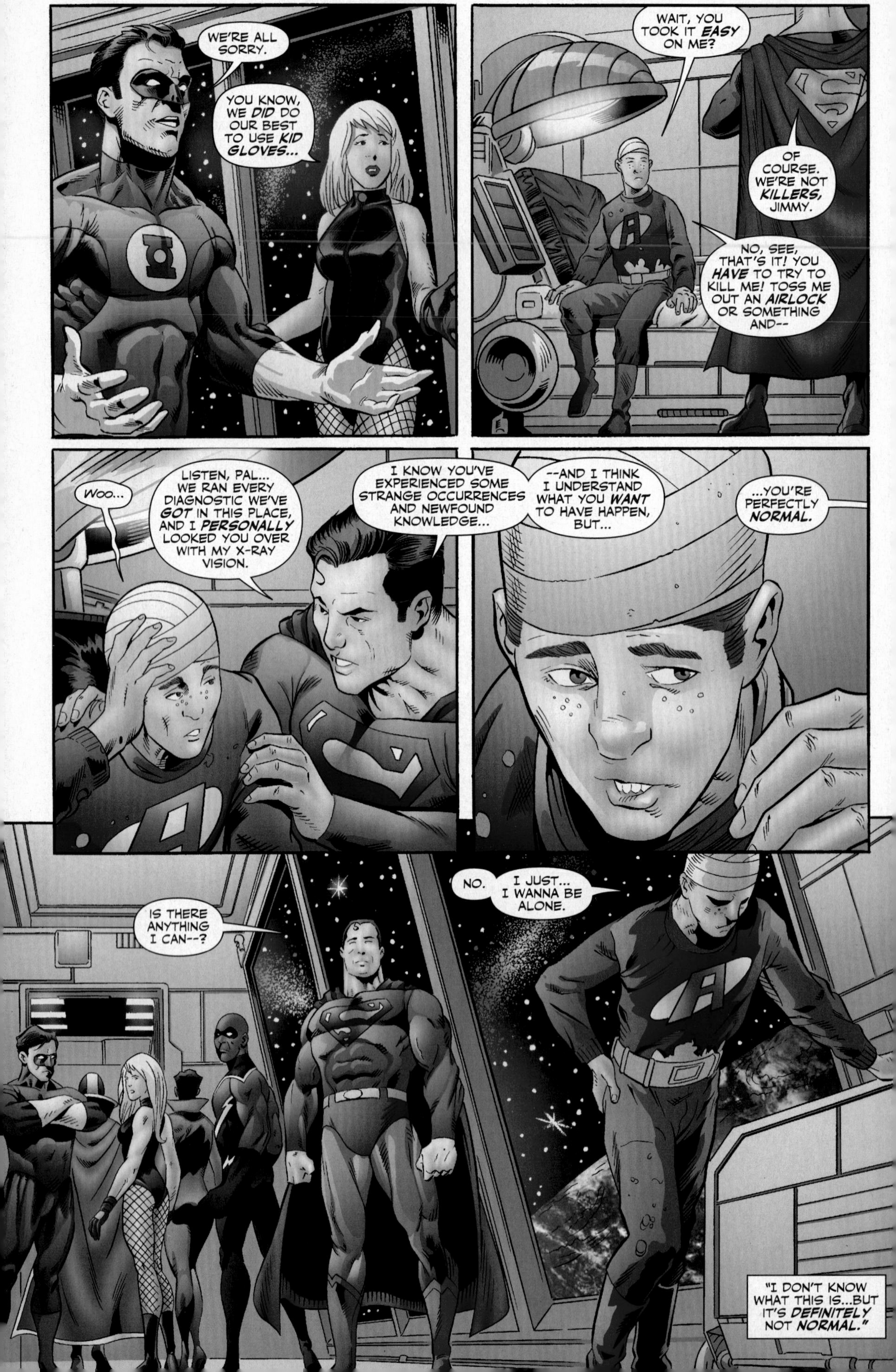
WE'RE ALL SORRY.
YOU KNOW, WE DID DO OUR BEST TO USE KID GLOVES...
WAIT, YOU TOOK IT EASY ON ME?
OF COURSE. WE'RE NOT KILLERS, JIMMY.
NO, SEE, THAT'S IT! YOU HAVE TO TRY TO KILL ME! TOSS ME OUT AN AIRLOCK OR SOMETHING AND--
WOO...
LISTEN, PAL... WE RAN EVERY DIAGNOSTIC WE'VE GOT IN THIS PLACE, AND I PERSONALLY LOOKED YOU OVER WITH MY X-RAY VISION.
I KNOW YOU'VE EXPERIENCED SOME STRANGE OCCURRENCES AND NEWFOUND KNOWLEDGE...
--AND I THINK I UNDERSTAND WHAT YOU WANT TO HAVE HAPPEN, BUT...
...YOU'RE PERFECTLY NORMAL.
IS THERE ANYTHING I CAN--?
NO.
I JUST... I WANNA BE ALONE.
"I DON'T KNOW WHAT THIS IS...BUT IT'S DEFINITELY NOT NORMAL."

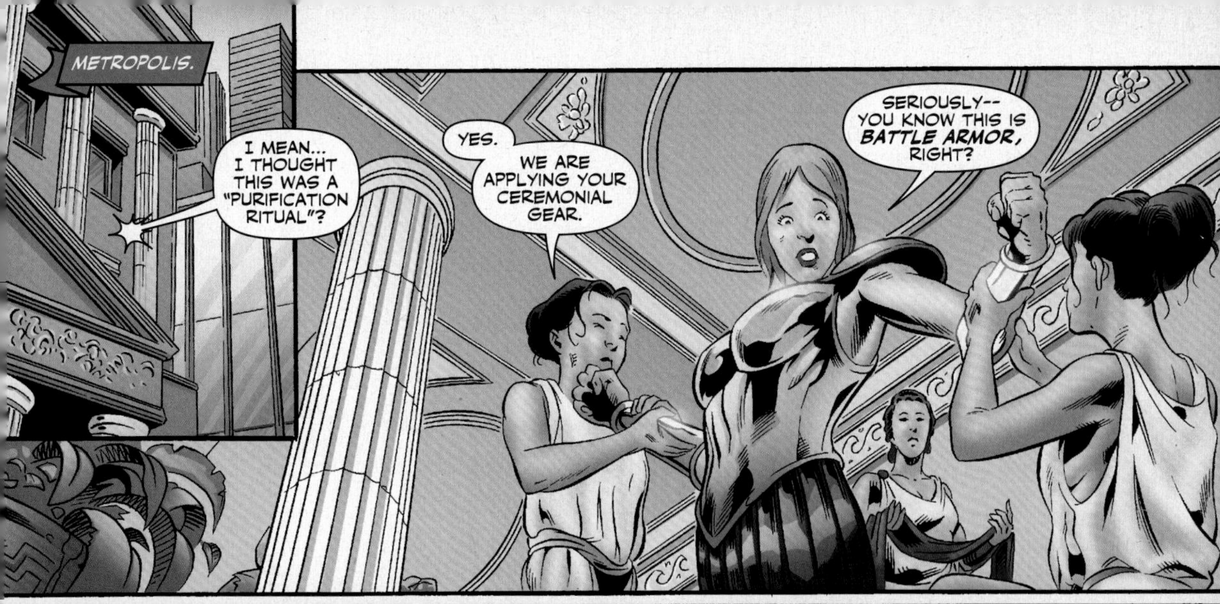
METROPOLIS.
I MEAN... I THOUGHT THIS WAS A "PURIFICATION RITUAL"?
YES.
WE ARE APPLYING YOUR CEREMONIAL GEAR.
SERIOUSLY-- YOU KNOW THIS IS *BATTLE ARMOR,* RIGHT?

# HOLLY ROBINSON

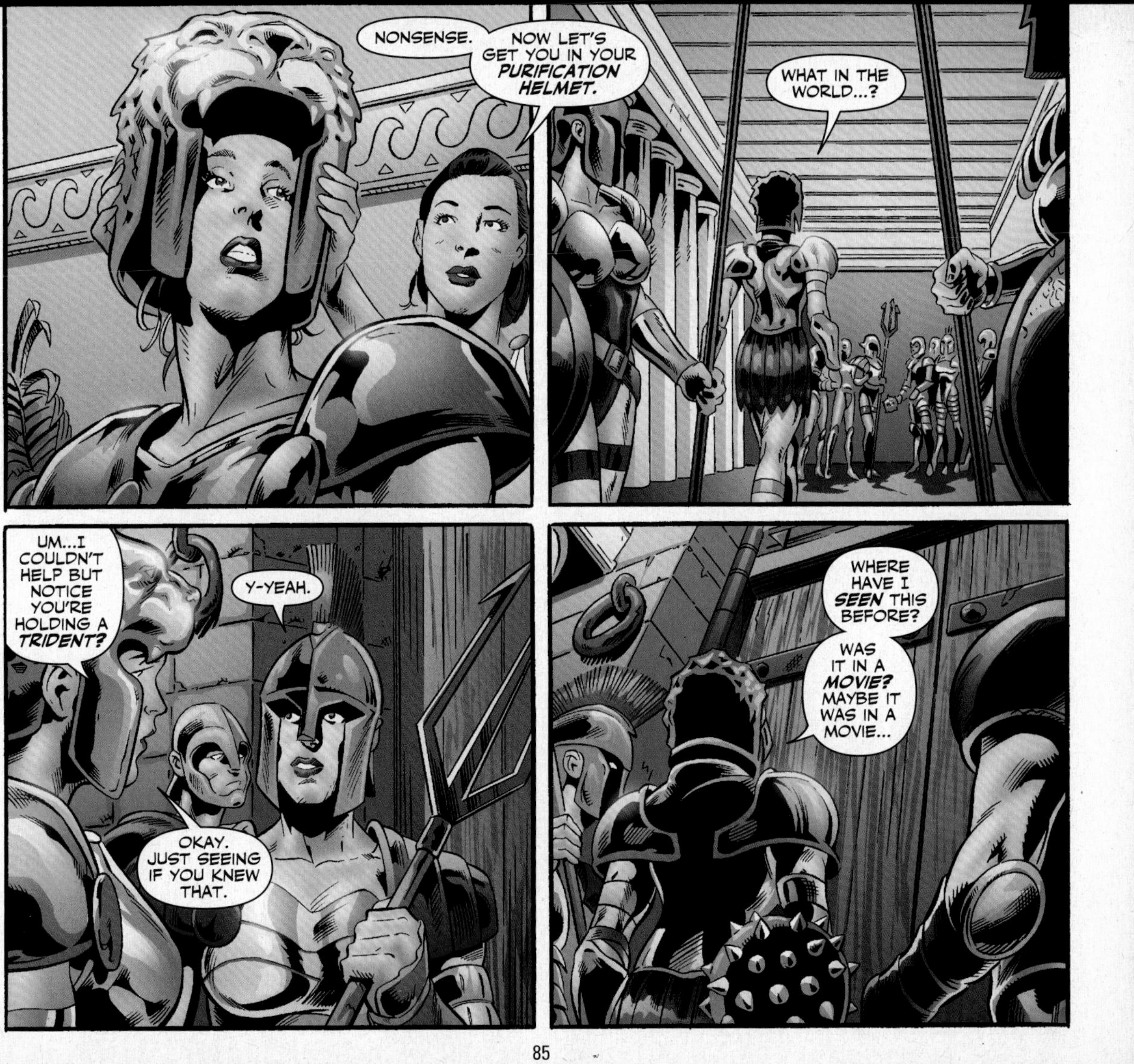
NONSENSE.
NOW LET'S GET YOU IN YOUR *PURIFICATION HELMET.*
WHAT IN THE WORLD...?
UM...I COULDN'T HELP BUT NOTICE YOU'RE HOLDING A *TRIDENT?*
Y-YEAH.
OKAY. JUST SEEING IF YOU KNEW THAT.
WHERE HAVE I *SEEN* THIS BEFORE?
WAS IT IN A *MOVIE?* MAYBE IT WAS IN A MOVIE...

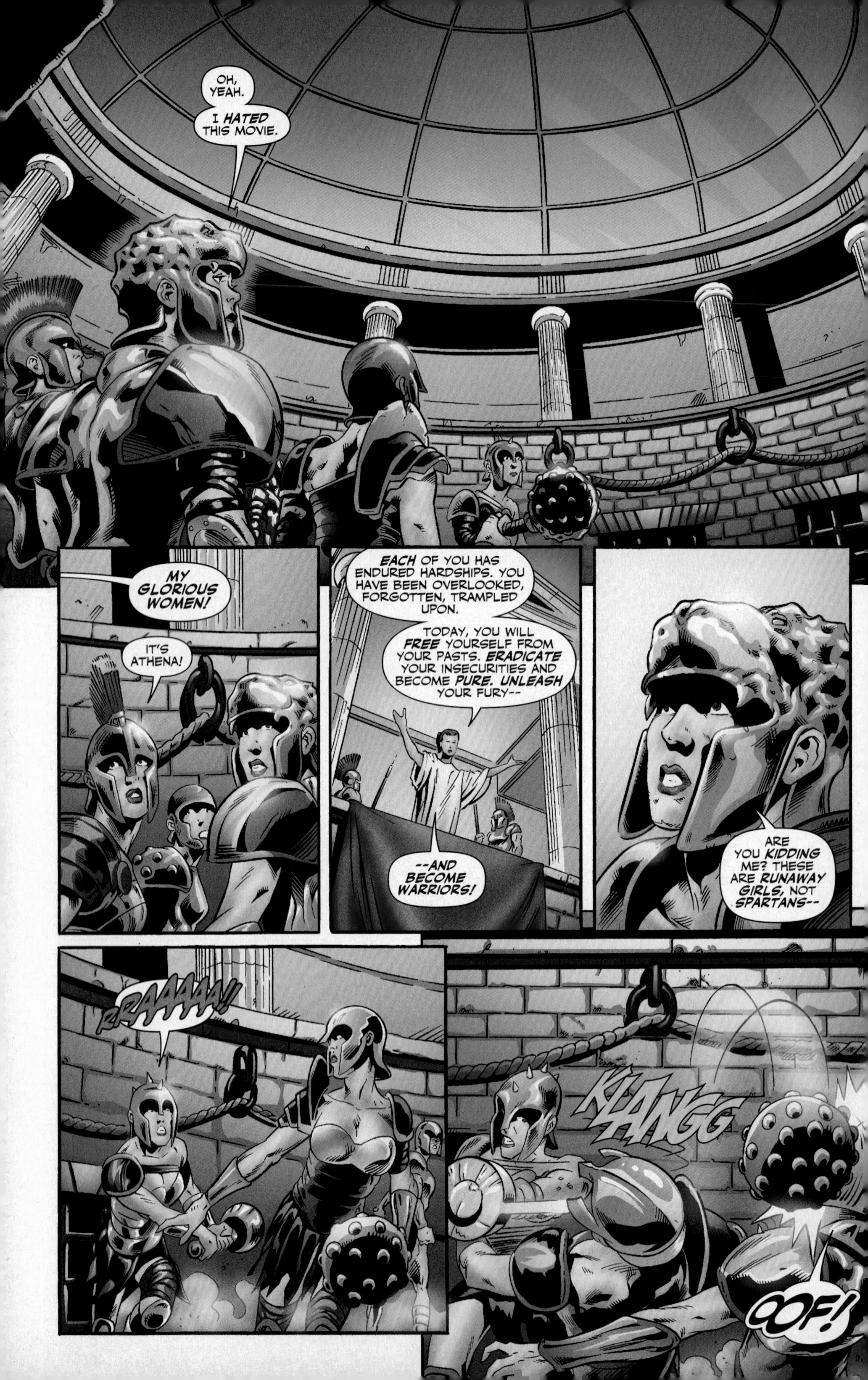

OH, YEAH.
I HATED THIS MOVIE.
MY GLORIOUS WOMEN!
IT'S ATHENA!
EACH OF YOU HAS ENDURED HARDSHIPS. YOU HAVE BEEN OVERLOOKED, FORGOTTEN, TRAMPLED UPON.
TODAY, YOU WILL FREE YOURSELF FROM YOUR PASTS. ERADICATE YOUR INSECURITIES AND BECOME PURE. UNLEASH YOUR FURY--
--AND BECOME WARRIORS!
ARE YOU KIDDING ME? THESE ARE RUNAWAY GIRLS, NOT SPARTANS--
RRAAAAA!!
KLANGG
OOF!

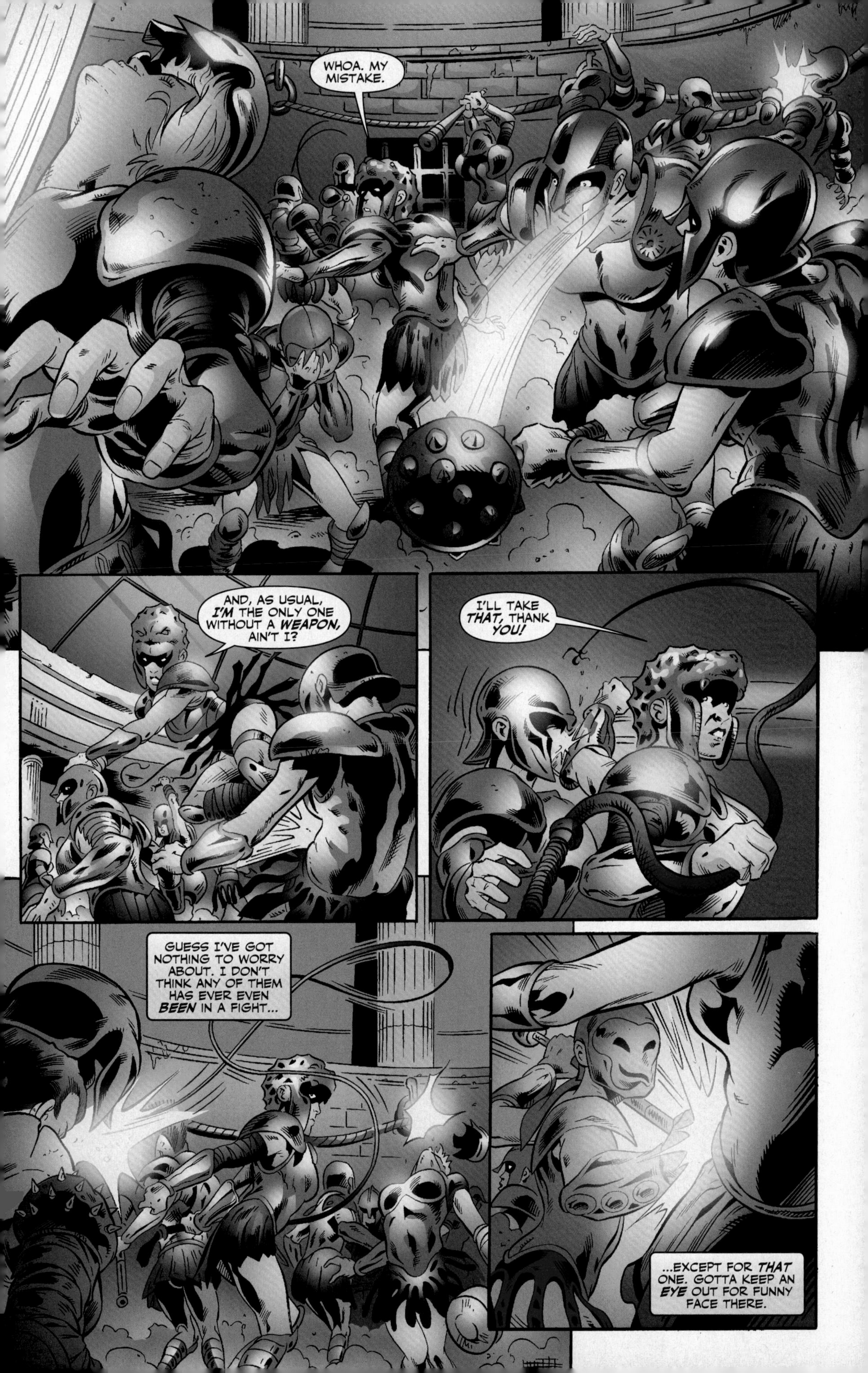
WHOA. MY MISTAKE.
AND, AS USUAL, I'M THE ONLY ONE WITHOUT A WEAPON, AIN'T I?
I'LL TAKE THAT, THANK YOU!
GUESS I'VE GOT NOTHING TO WORRY ABOUT. I DON'T THINK ANY OF THEM HAS EVER EVEN BEEN IN A FIGHT...
...EXCEPT FOR THAT ONE. GOTTA KEEP AN EYE OUT FOR FUNNY FACE THERE.

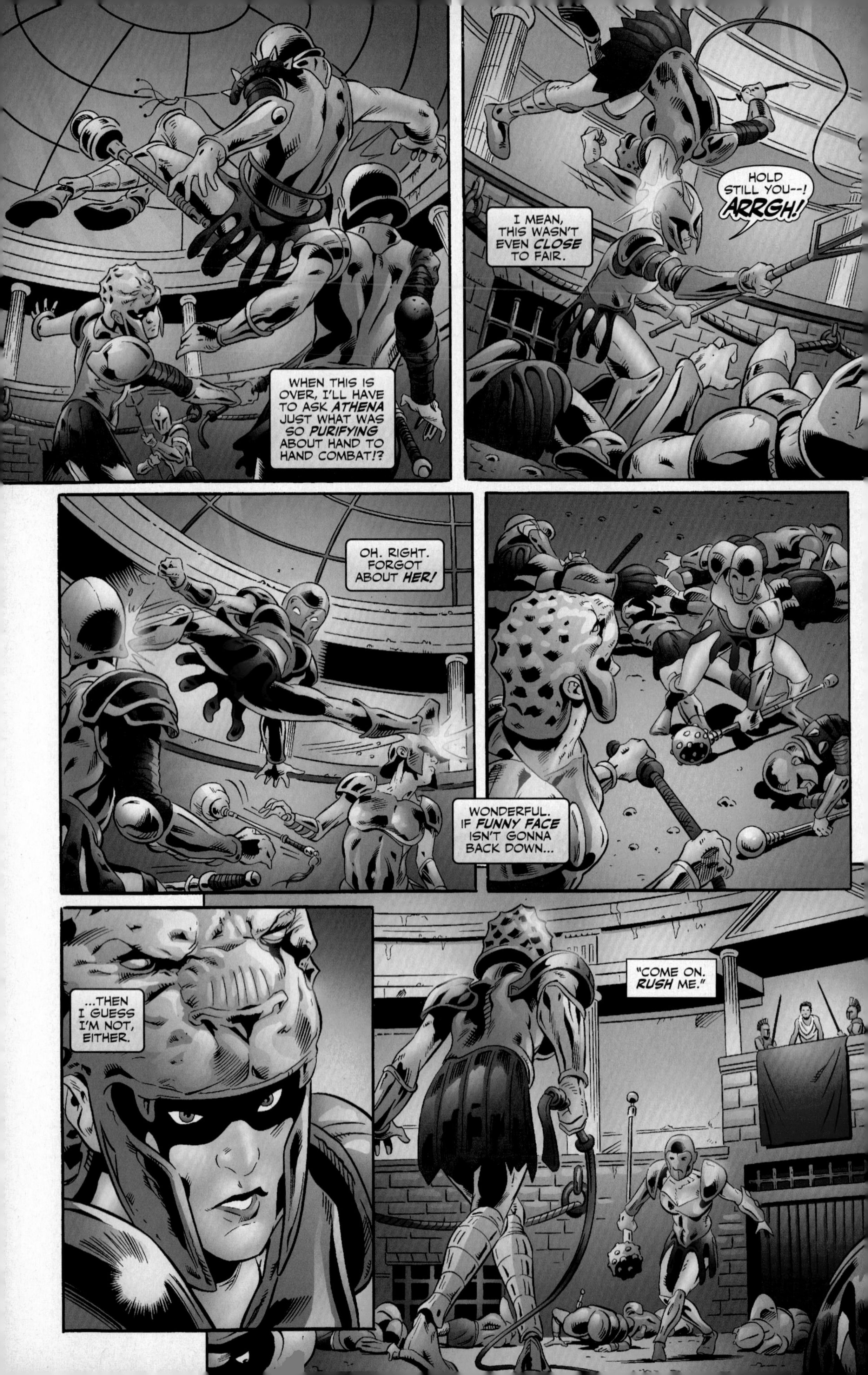
WHEN THIS IS OVER, I'LL HAVE TO ASK *ATHENA* JUST WHAT WAS SO *PURIFYING* ABOUT HAND TO HAND COMBAT!?
I MEAN, THIS WASN'T EVEN *CLOSE* TO FAIR.
HOLD STILL YOU--! *ARRGH!*
OH. RIGHT. FORGOT ABOUT *HER!*
WONDERFUL. IF *FUNNY FACE* ISN'T GONNA BACK DOWN...
...THEN I GUESS I'M NOT, EITHER.
"COME ON. *RUSH* ME."

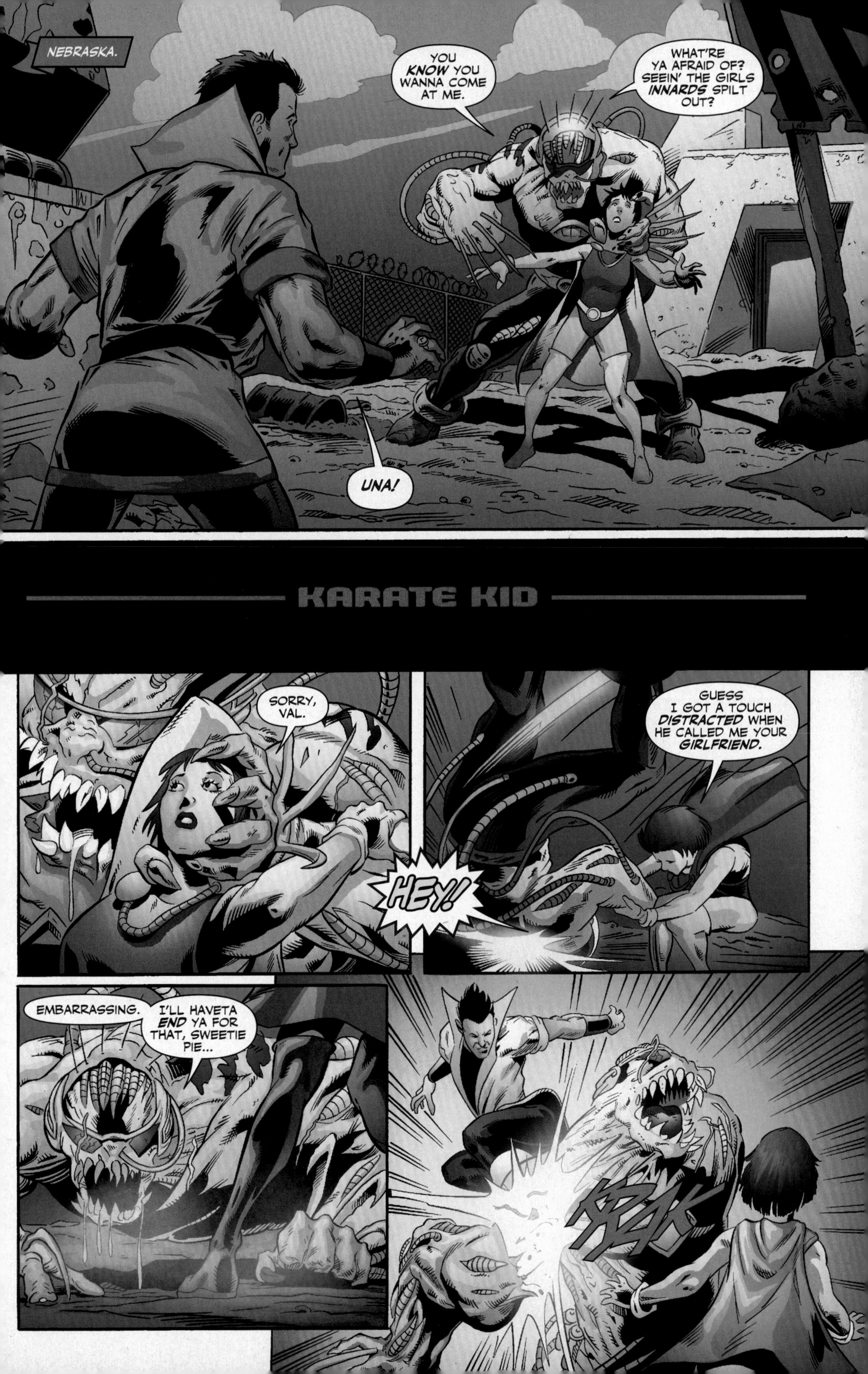
NEBRASKA.
YOU KNOW YOU WANNA COME AT ME.
WHAT'RE YA AFRAID OF? SEEIN' THE GIRLS INNARDS SPILT OUT?
UNA!
KARATE KID
SORRY, VAL.
GUESS I GOT A TOUCH DISTRACTED WHEN HE CALLED ME YOUR GIRLFRIEND.
HEY!!
EMBARRASSING.
I'LL HAVETA END YA FOR THAT, SWEETIE PIE...
KRAK

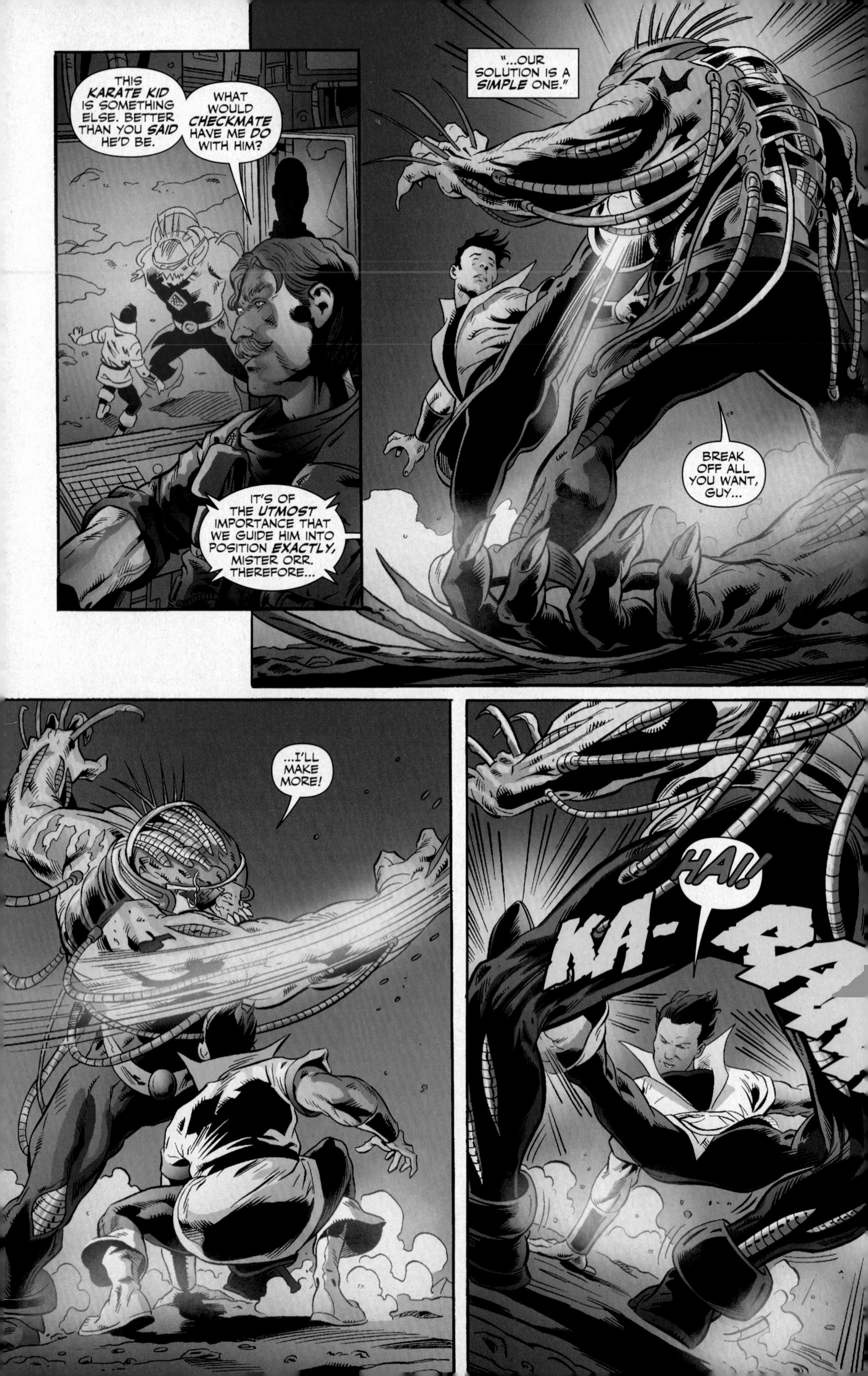
THIS KARATE KID IS SOMETHING ELSE. BETTER THAN YOU SAID HE'D BE.
WHAT WOULD CHECKMATE HAVE ME DO WITH HIM?
IT'S OF THE UTMOST IMPORTANCE THAT WE GUIDE HIM INTO POSITION EXACTLY, MISTER ORR. THEREFORE...
"...OUR SOLUTION IS A SIMPLE ONE."
BREAK OFF ALL YOU WANT, GUY...
...I'LL MAKE MORE!
HAI!
KA-

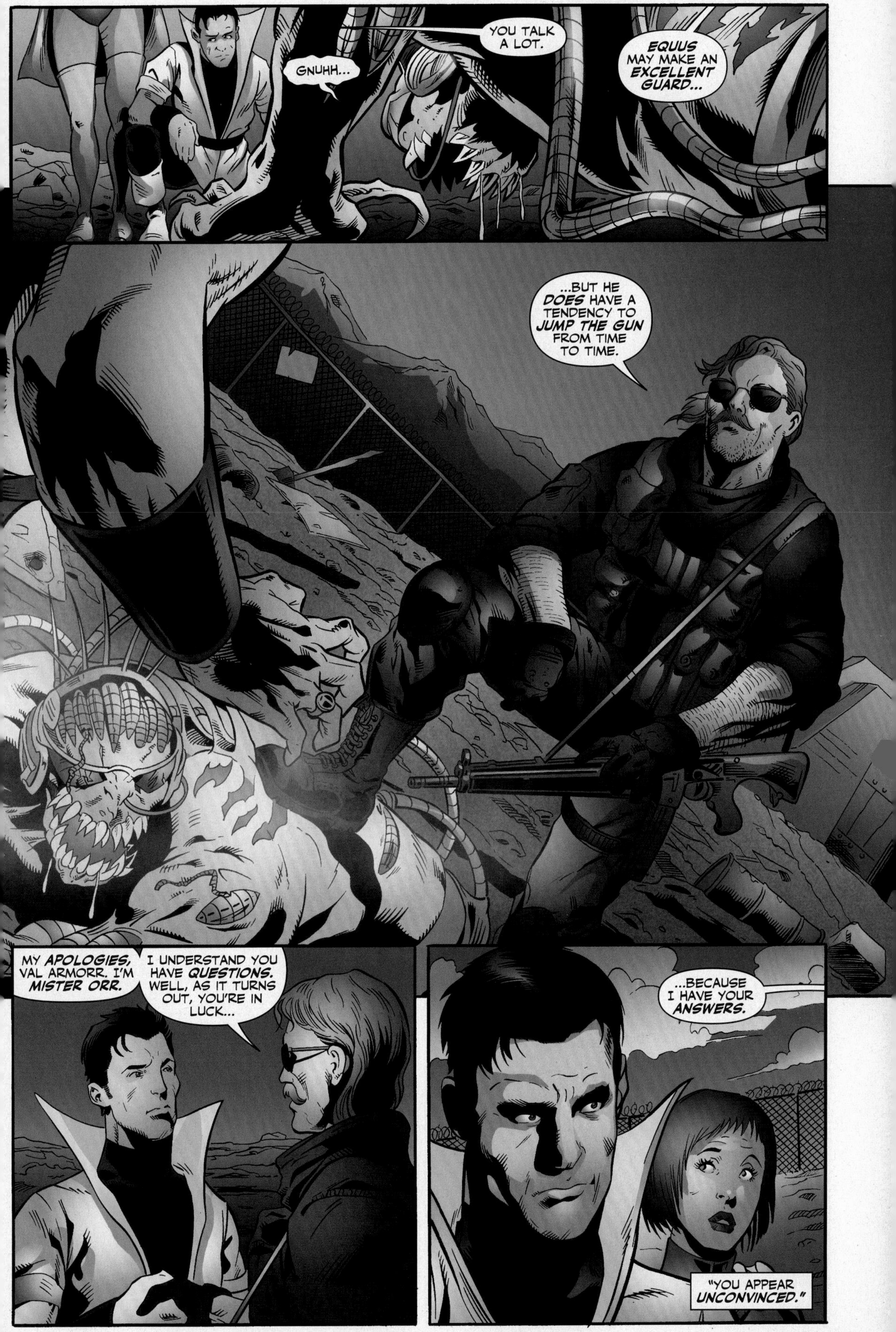
GNUHH...
YOU TALK A LOT.
EQUUS MAY MAKE AN EXCELLENT GUARD...
...BUT HE DOES HAVE A TENDENCY TO JUMP THE GUN FROM TIME TO TIME.
MY APOLOGIES, VAL ARMORR. I'M MISTER ORR.
I UNDERSTAND YOU HAVE QUESTIONS. WELL, AS IT TURNS OUT, YOU'RE IN LUCK...
...BECAUSE I HAVE YOUR ANSWERS.
"YOU APPEAR UNCONVINCED."

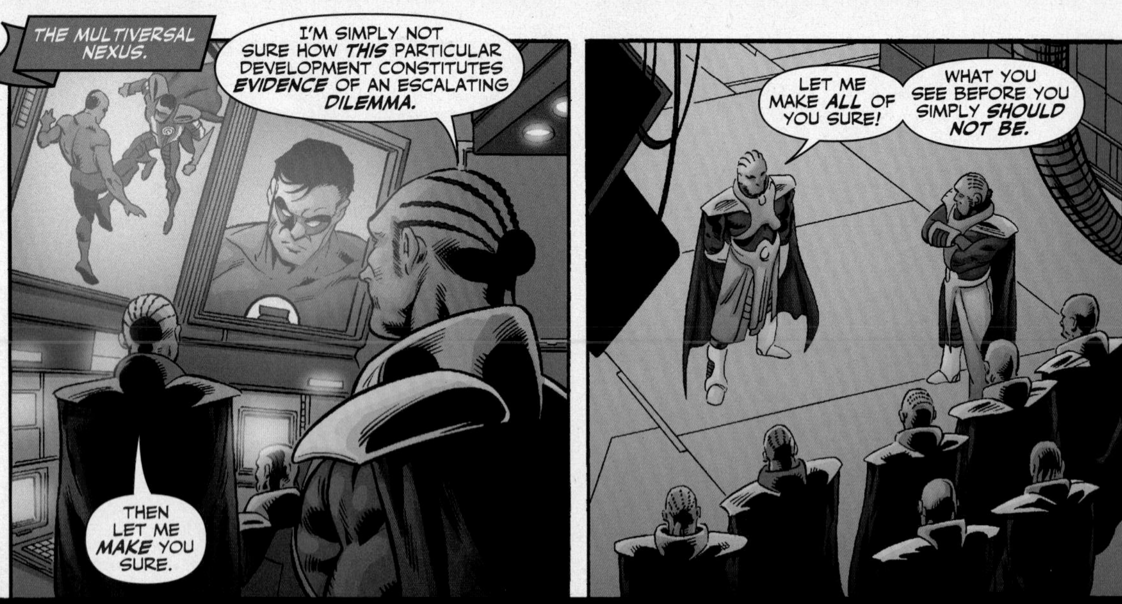
THE MULTIVERSAL NEXUS.
I'M SIMPLY NOT SURE HOW THIS PARTICULAR DEVELOPMENT CONSTITUTES EVIDENCE OF AN ESCALATING DILEMMA.
THEN LET ME MAKE YOU SURE.
LET ME MAKE ALL OF YOU SURE!
WHAT YOU SEE BEFORE YOU SIMPLY SHOULD NOT BE.

# THE MONITORS

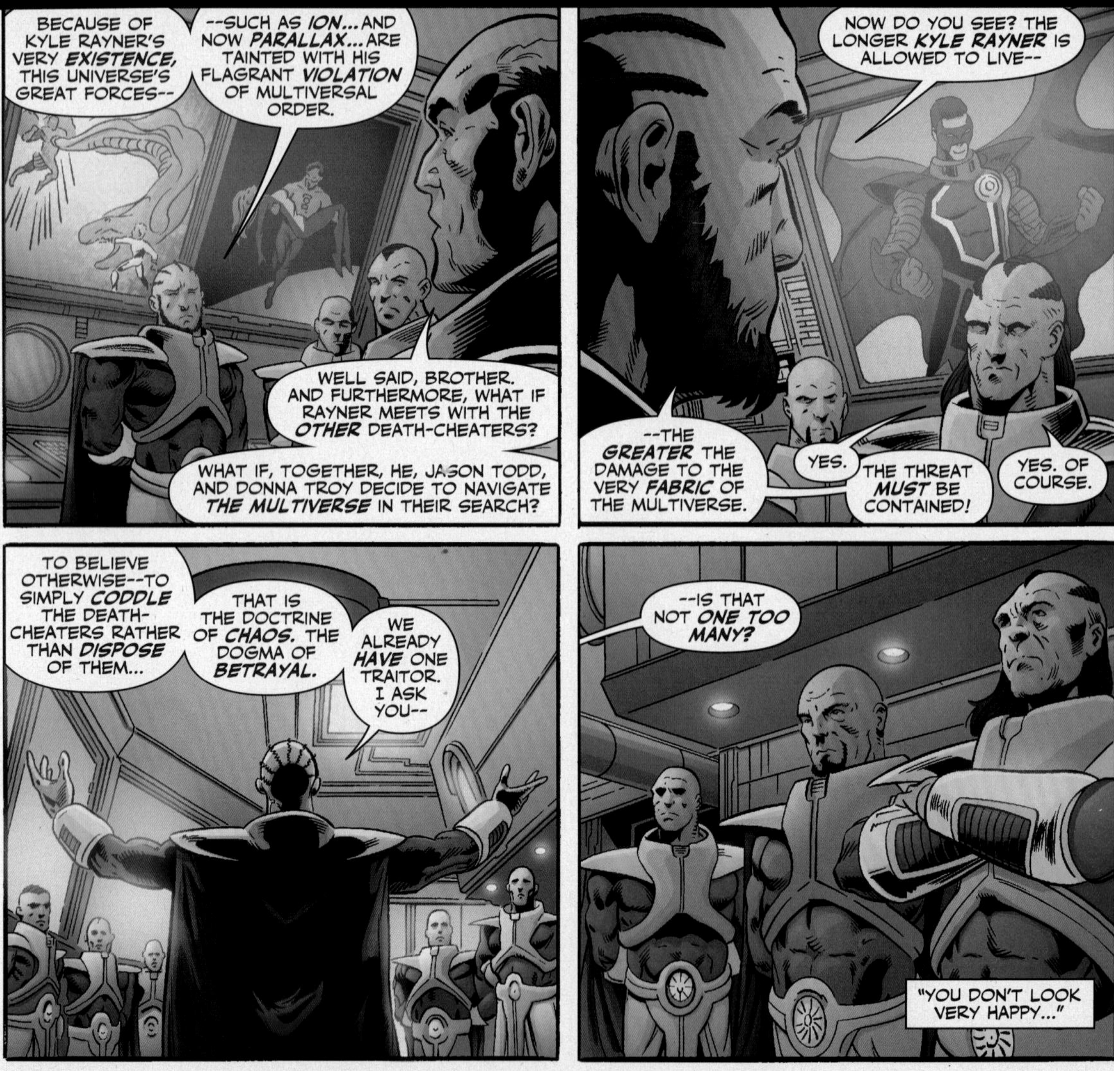
BECAUSE OF KYLE RAYNER'S VERY EXISTENCE, THIS UNIVERSE'S GREAT FORCES--
--SUCH AS ION... AND NOW PARALLAX... ARE TAINTED WITH HIS FLAGRANT VIOLATION OF MULTIVERSAL ORDER.
WELL SAID, BROTHER. AND FURTHERMORE, WHAT IF RAYNER MEETS WITH THE OTHER DEATH-CHEATERS?
WHAT IF, TOGETHER, HE, JASON TODD, AND DONNA TROY DECIDE TO NAVIGATE THE MULTIVERSE IN THEIR SEARCH?
NOW DO YOU SEE? THE LONGER KYLE RAYNER IS ALLOWED TO LIVE--
--THE GREATER THE DAMAGE TO THE VERY FABRIC OF THE MULTIVERSE.
YES.
THE THREAT MUST BE CONTAINED!
YES. OF COURSE.
TO BELIEVE OTHERWISE--TO SIMPLY CODDLE THE DEATH-CHEATERS RATHER THAN DISPOSE OF THEM...
THAT IS THE DOCTRINE OF CHAOS. THE DOGMA OF BETRAYAL.
WE ALREADY HAVE ONE TRAITOR. I ASK YOU--
--IS THAT NOT ONE TOO MANY?
"YOU DON'T LOOK VERY HAPPY..."

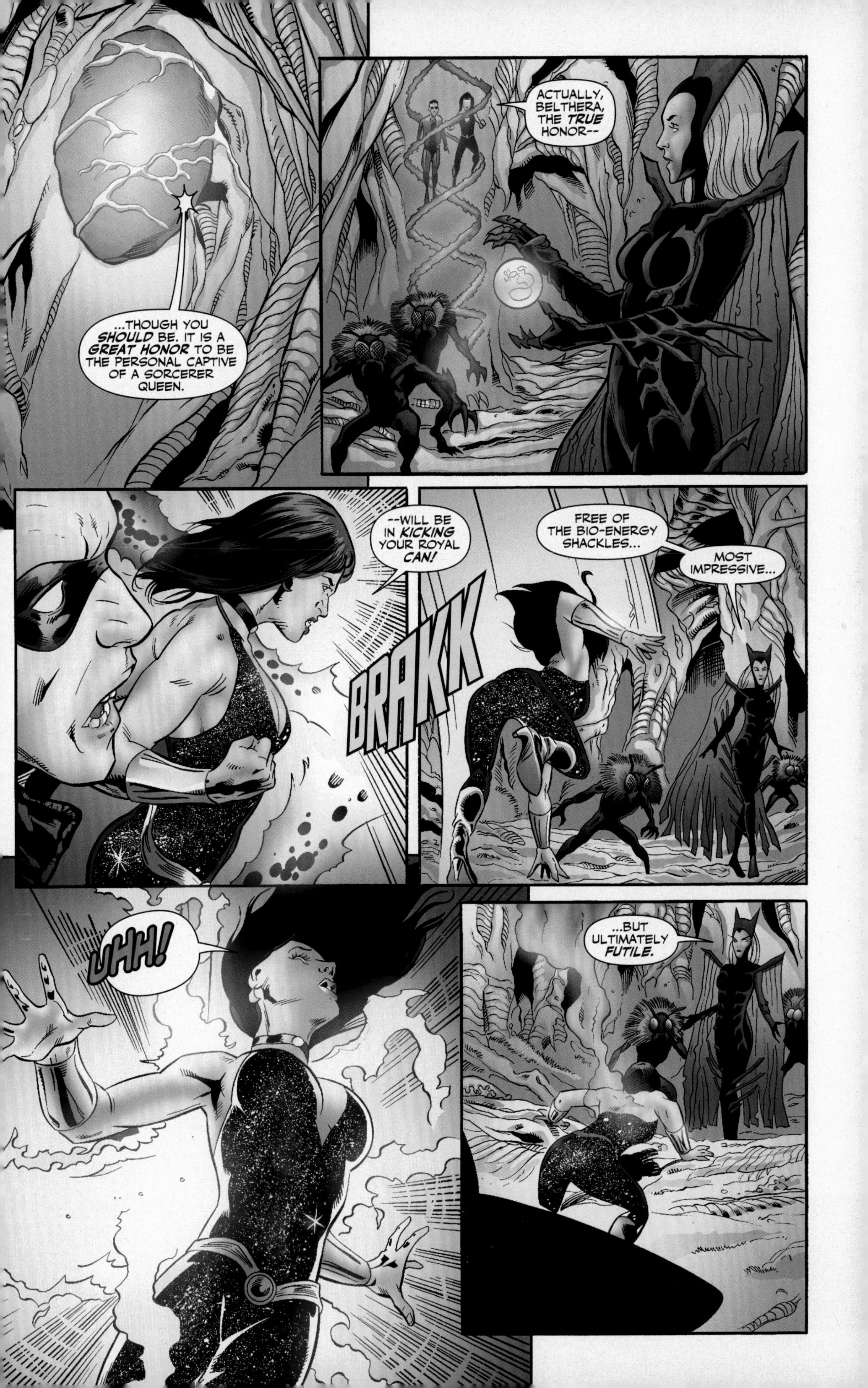
...THOUGH YOU SHOULD BE. IT IS A GREAT HONOR TO BE THE PERSONAL CAPTIVE OF A SORCERER QUEEN.
ACTUALLY, BELTHERA, THE TRUE HONOR--
--WILL BE IN KICKING YOUR ROYAL CAN!
BRAKK
FREE OF THE BIO-ENERGY SHACKLES...
MOST IMPRESSIVE...
UHH!
...BUT ULTIMATELY FUTILE.

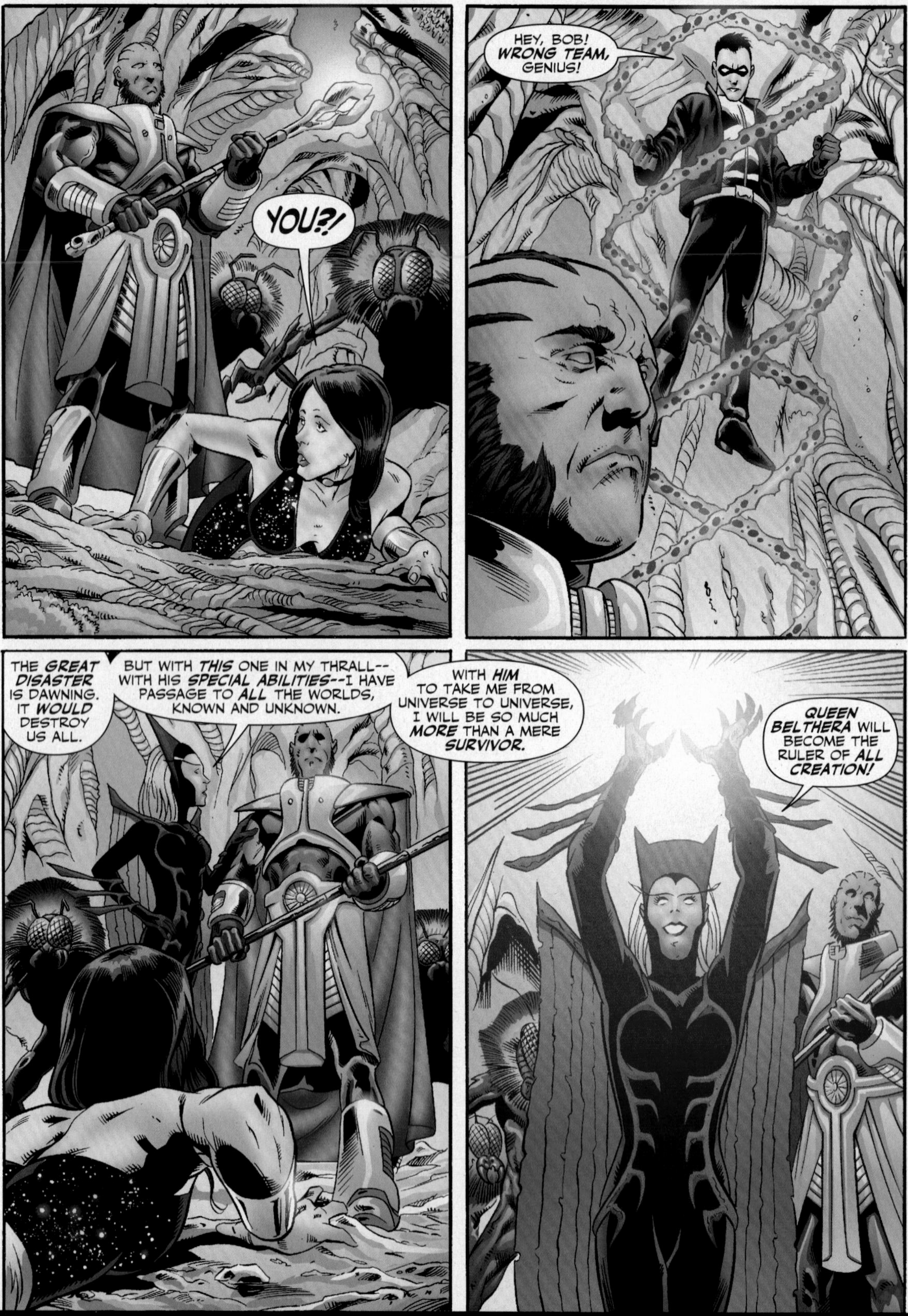
YOU?!
HEY, BOB! WRONG TEAM, GENIUS!
THE GREAT DISASTER IS DAWNING. IT WOULD DESTROY US ALL.
BUT WITH THIS ONE IN MY THRALL-- WITH HIS SPECIAL ABILITIES--I HAVE PASSAGE TO ALL THE WORLDS, KNOWN AND UNKNOWN.
WITH HIM TO TAKE ME FROM UNIVERSE TO UNIVERSE, I WILL BE SO MUCH MORE THAN A MERE SURVIVOR.
QUEEN BELTHERA WILL BECOME THE RULER OF ALL CREATION!

[redacted]

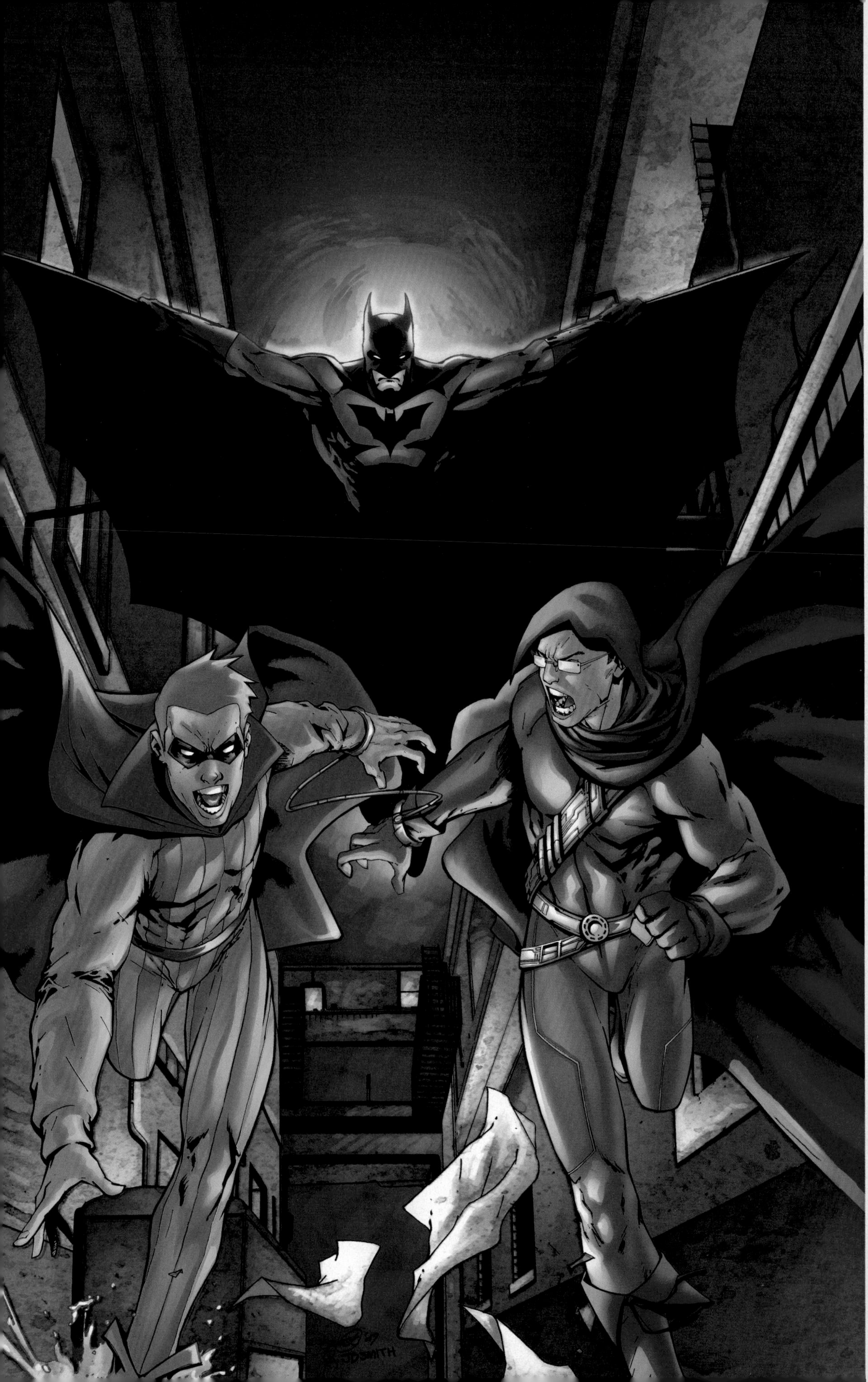

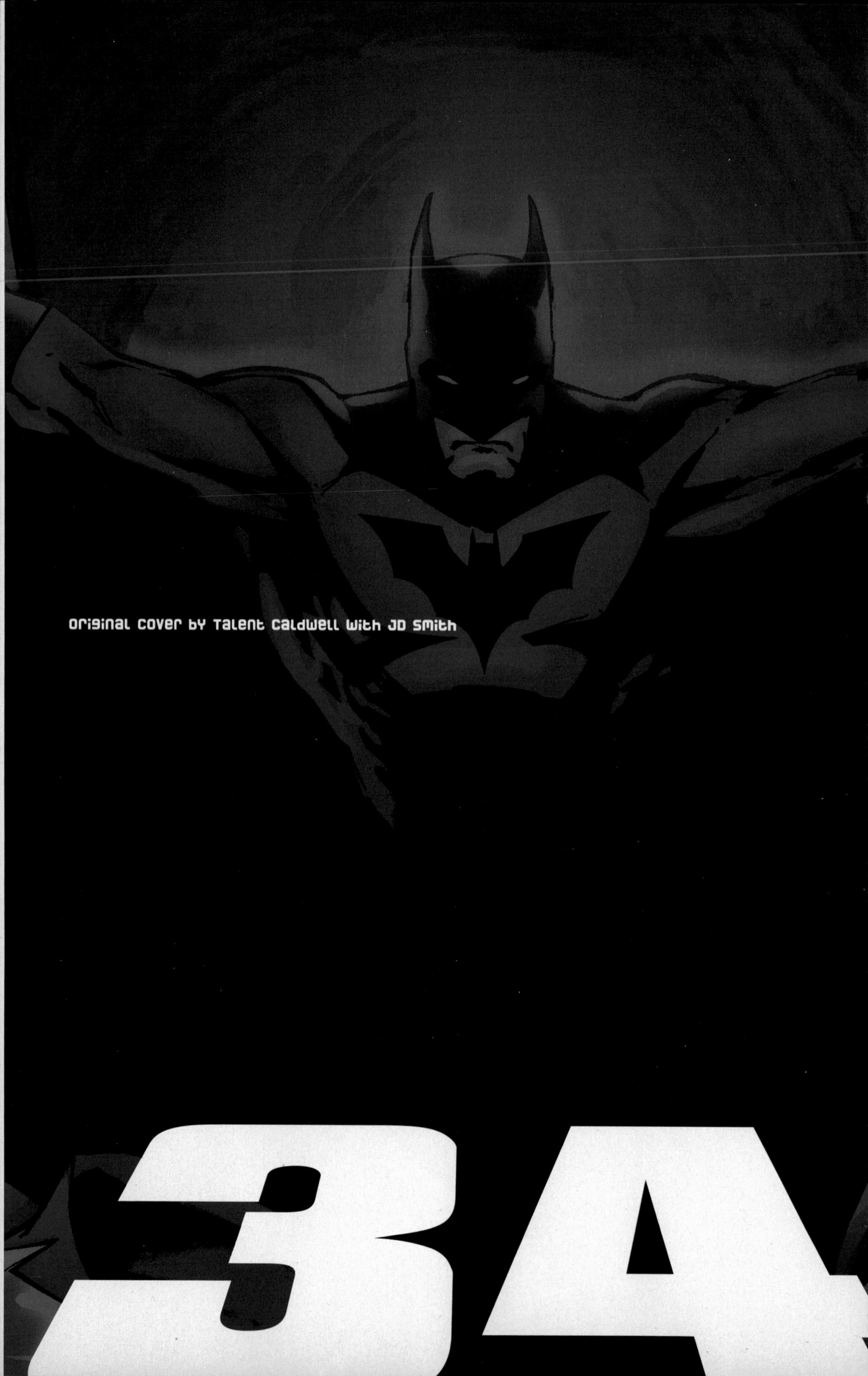
34
Original cover by Talent Caldwell with JD Smith

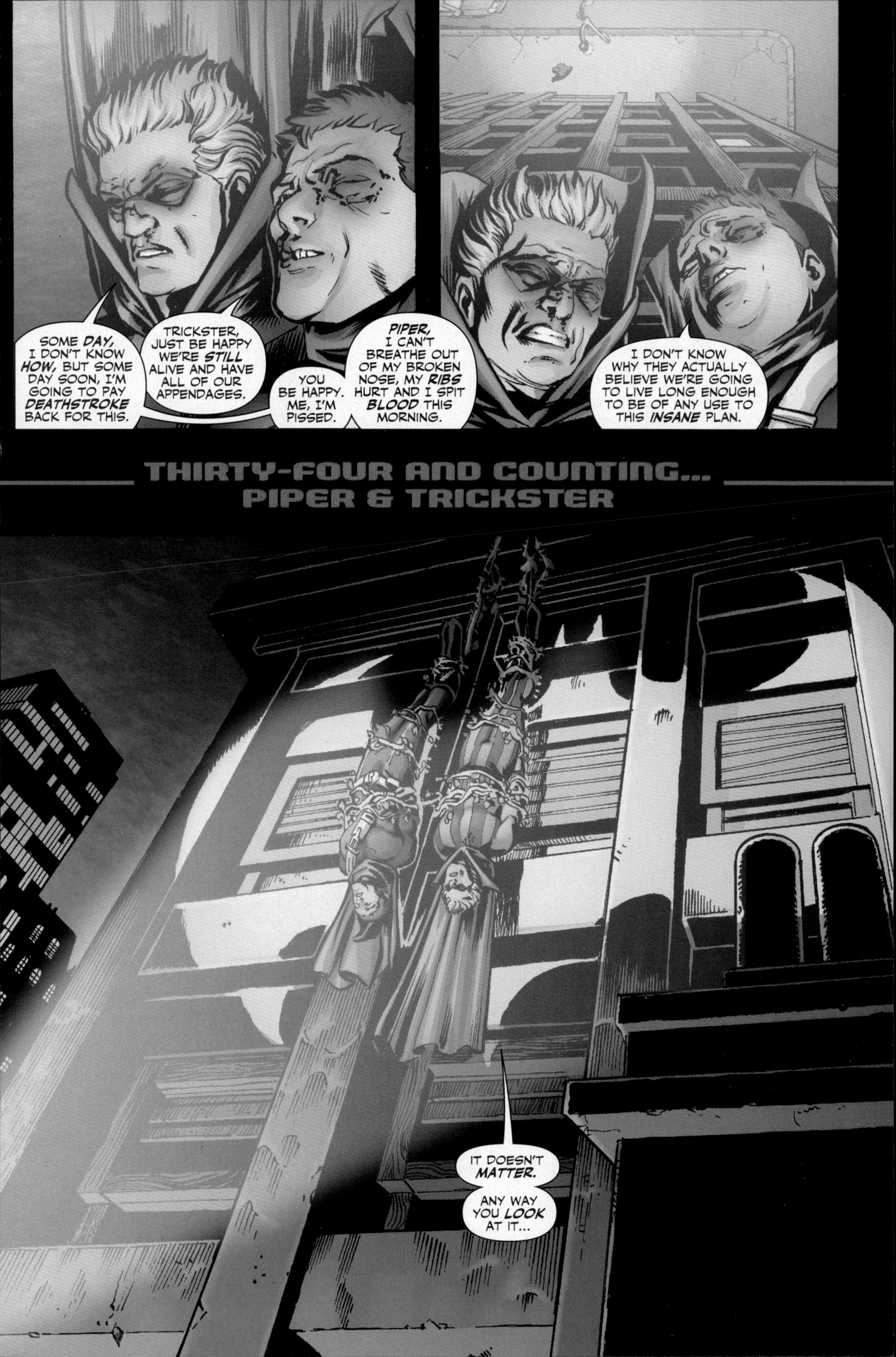
SOME DAY, I DON'T KNOW HOW, BUT SOME DAY SOON, I'M GOING TO PAY DEATHSTROKE BACK FOR THIS.
TRICKSTER, JUST BE HAPPY WE'RE STILL ALIVE AND HAVE ALL OF OUR APPENDAGES.
YOU BE HAPPY. ME, I'M PISSED.
PIPER, I CAN'T BREATHE OUT OF MY BROKEN NOSE, MY RIBS HURT AND I SPIT BLOOD THIS MORNING.
I DON'T KNOW WHY THEY ACTUALLY BELIEVE WE'RE GOING TO LIVE LONG ENOUGH TO BE OF ANY USE TO THIS INSANE PLAN.
THIRTY-FOUR AND COUNTING... PIPER & TRICKSTER
IT DOESN'T MATTER.
ANY WAY YOU LOOK AT IT...

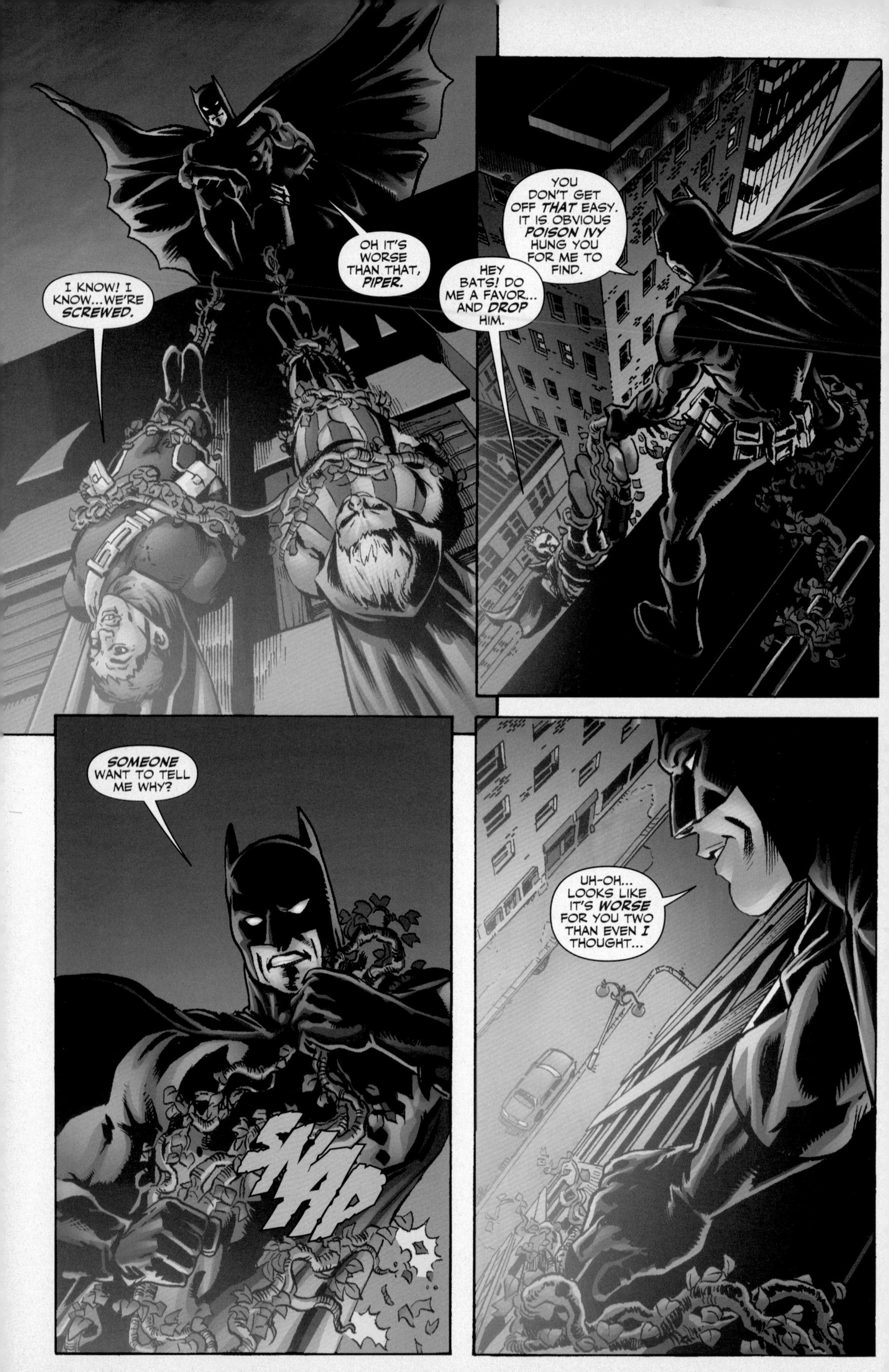
I KNOW! I KNOW...WE'RE SCREWED.
OH IT'S WORSE THAN THAT, PIPER.
HEY BATS! DO ME A FAVOR... AND DROP HIM.
YOU DON'T GET OFF THAT EASY. IT IS OBVIOUS POISON IVY HUNG YOU FOR ME TO FIND.
SOMEONE WANT TO TELL ME WHY?
SNAP
UH-OH... LOOKS LIKE IT'S WORSE FOR YOU TWO THAN EVEN I THOUGHT...

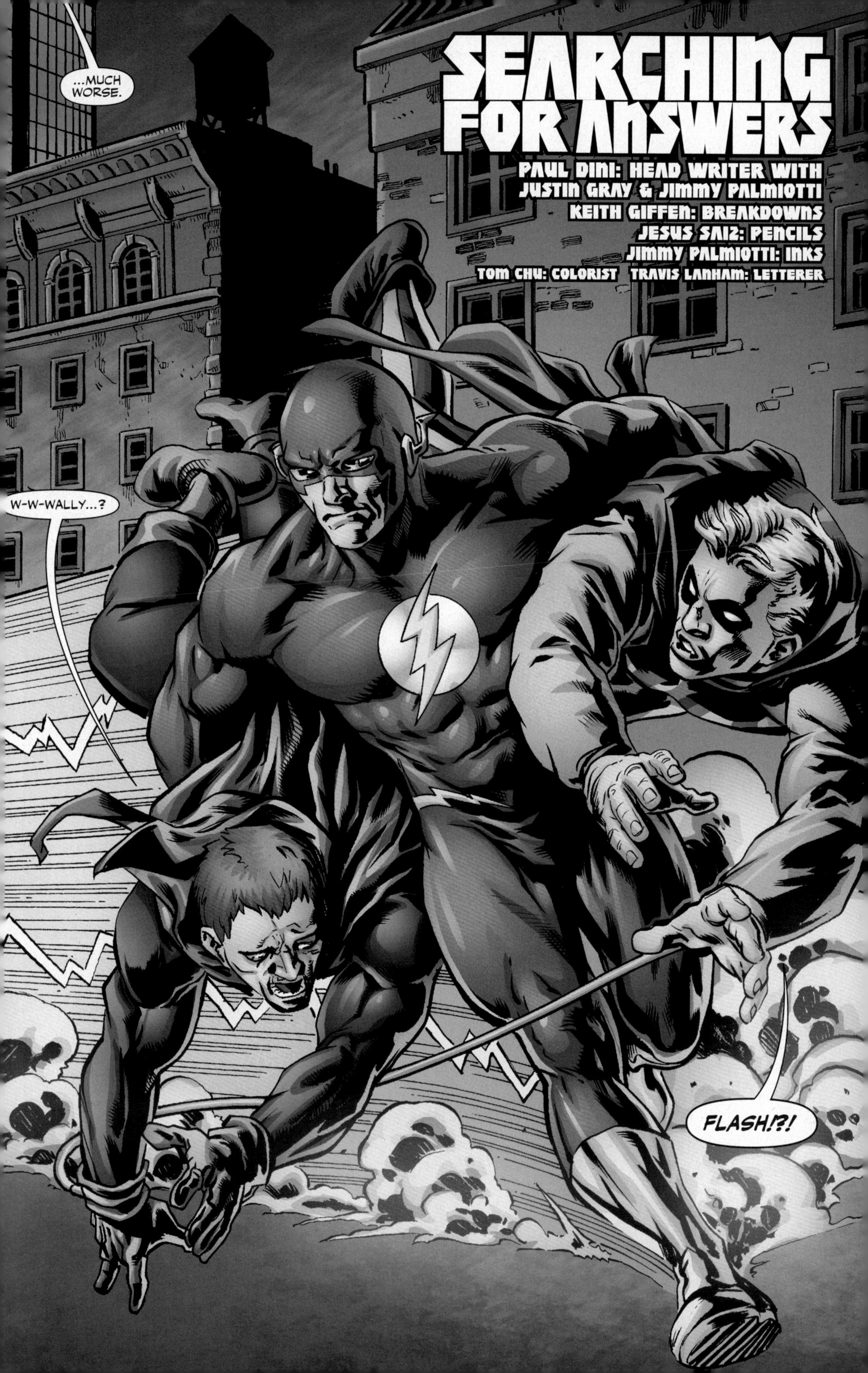
...MUCH WORSE.
SEARCHING FOR ANSWERS
PAUL DINI: HEAD WRITER WITH
JUSTIN GRAY & JIMMY PALMIOTTI
KEITH GIFFEN: BREAKDOWNS
JESUS SAIZ: PENCILS
JIMMY PALMIOTTI: INKS
TOM CHU: COLORIST TRAVIS LANHAM: LETTERER
W-W-WALLY...?
FLASH!?!

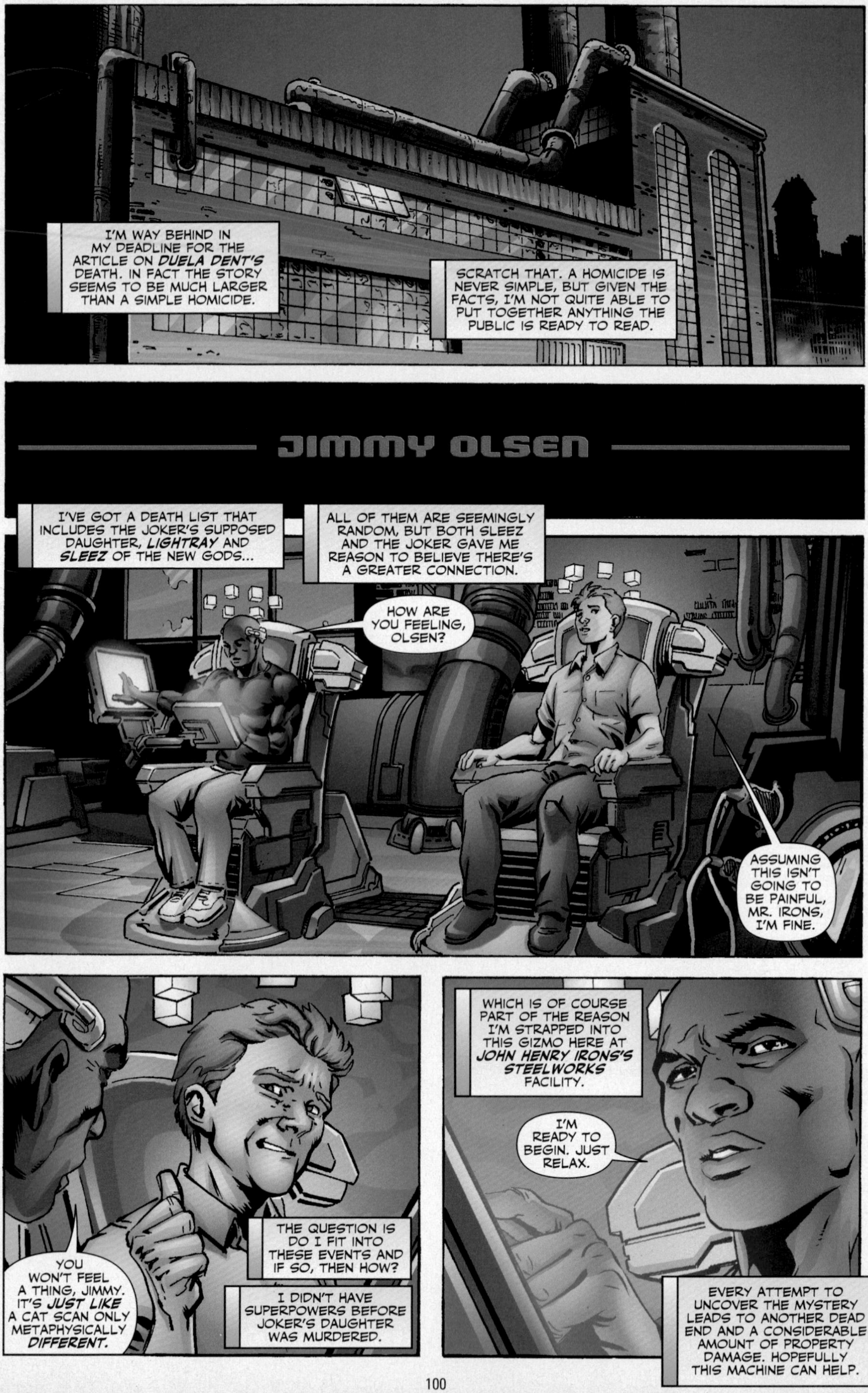

I'M WAY BEHIND IN MY DEADLINE FOR THE ARTICLE ON DUELA DENT'S DEATH. IN FACT THE STORY SEEMS TO BE MUCH LARGER THAN A SIMPLE HOMICIDE.
SCRATCH THAT. A HOMICIDE IS NEVER SIMPLE, BUT GIVEN THE FACTS, I'M NOT QUITE ABLE TO PUT TOGETHER ANYTHING THE PUBLIC IS READY TO READ.
JIMMY OLSEN
I'VE GOT A DEATH LIST THAT INCLUDES THE JOKER'S SUPPOSED DAUGHTER, LIGHTRAY AND SLEEZ OF THE NEW GODS...
ALL OF THEM ARE SEEMINGLY RANDOM, BUT BOTH SLEEZ AND THE JOKER GAVE ME REASON TO BELIEVE THERE'S A GREATER CONNECTION.
HOW ARE YOU FEELING, OLSEN?
ASSUMING THIS ISN'T GOING TO BE PAINFUL, MR. IRONS, I'M FINE.
THE QUESTION IS DO I FIT INTO THESE EVENTS AND IF SO, THEN HOW?
YOU WON'T FEEL A THING, JIMMY. IT'S JUST LIKE A CAT SCAN ONLY METAPHYSICALLY DIFFERENT.
I DIDN'T HAVE SUPERPOWERS BEFORE JOKER'S DAUGHTER WAS MURDERED.
WHICH IS OF COURSE PART OF THE REASON I'M STRAPPED INTO THIS GIZMO HERE AT JOHN HENRY IRONS'S STEELWORKS FACILITY.
I'M READY TO BEGIN. JUST RELAX.
EVERY ATTEMPT TO UNCOVER THE MYSTERY LEADS TO ANOTHER DEAD END AND A CONSIDERABLE AMOUNT OF PROPERTY DAMAGE. HOPEFULLY THIS MACHINE CAN HELP.

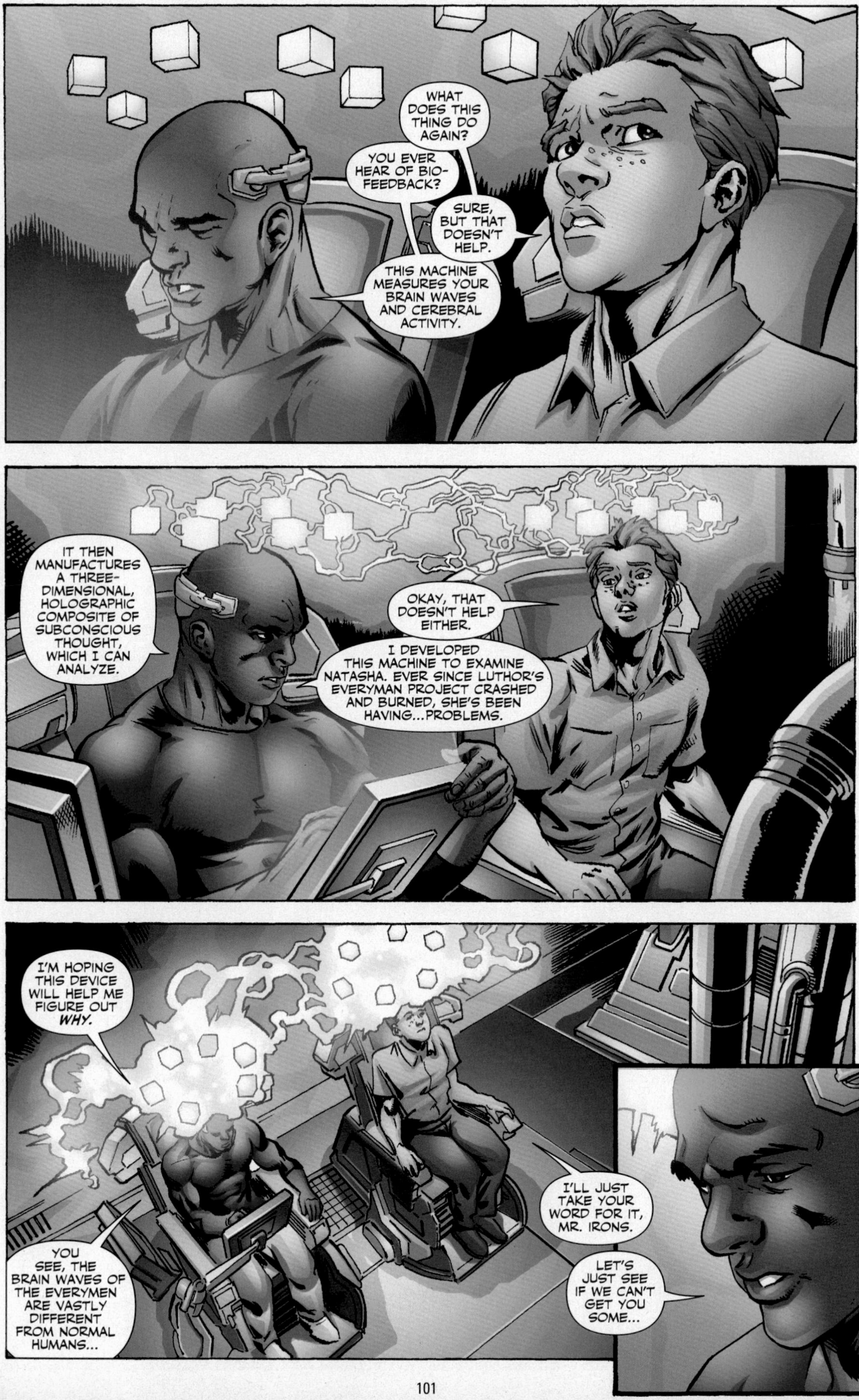
WHAT DOES THIS THING DO AGAIN?
YOU EVER HEAR OF BIO-FEEDBACK?
SURE, BUT THAT DOESN'T HELP.
THIS MACHINE MEASURES YOUR BRAIN WAVES AND CEREBRAL ACTIVITY.
IT THEN MANUFACTURES A THREE-DIMENSIONAL, HOLOGRAPHIC COMPOSITE OF SUBCONSCIOUS THOUGHT, WHICH I CAN ANALYZE.
OKAY, THAT DOESN'T HELP EITHER.
I DEVELOPED THIS MACHINE TO EXAMINE NATASHA. EVER SINCE LUTHOR'S EVERYMAN PROJECT CRASHED AND BURNED, SHE'S BEEN HAVING...PROBLEMS.
I'M HOPING THIS DEVICE WILL HELP ME FIGURE OUT *WHY.*
YOU SEE, THE BRAIN WAVES OF THE EVERYMEN ARE VASTLY DIFFERENT FROM NORMAL HUMANS...
I'LL JUST TAKE YOUR WORD FOR IT, MR. IRONS.
LET'S JUST SEE IF WE CAN'T GET YOU SOME...

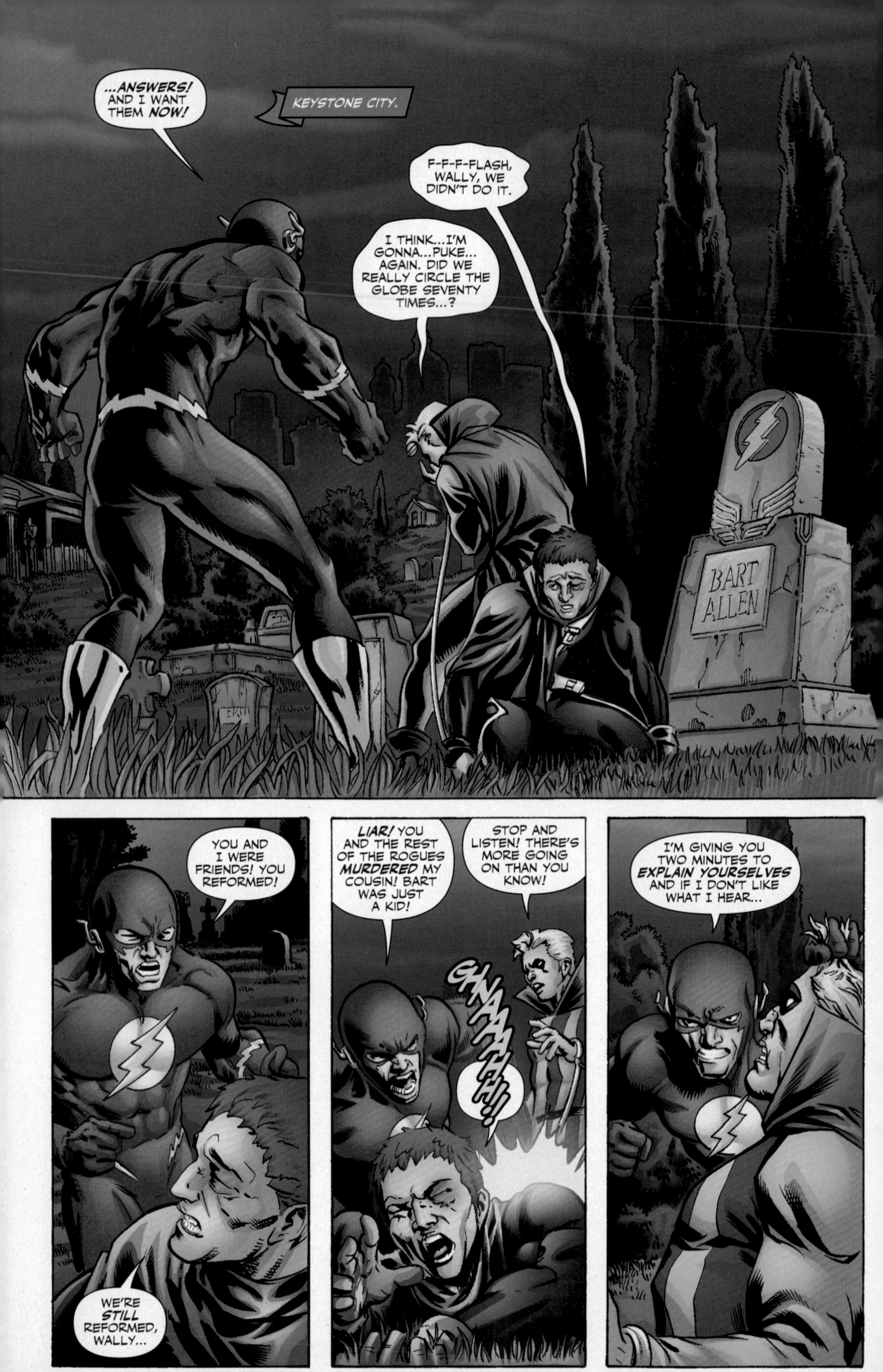
...ANSWERS! AND I WANT THEM NOW!
KEYSTONE CITY.
F-F-F-FLASH, WALLY, WE DIDN'T DO IT.
I THINK...I'M GONNA...PUKE... AGAIN. DID WE REALLY CIRCLE THE GLOBE SEVENTY TIMES...?
BART ALLEN
YOU AND I WERE FRIENDS! YOU REFORMED!
WE'RE STILL REFORMED, WALLY...
LIAR! YOU AND THE REST OF THE ROGUES MURDERED MY COUSIN! BART WAS JUST A KID!
STOP AND LISTEN! THERE'S MORE GOING ON THAN YOU KNOW!
GHNAAAHH!!
I'M GIVING YOU TWO MINUTES TO EXPLAIN YOURSELVES AND IF I DON'T LIKE WHAT I HEAR...

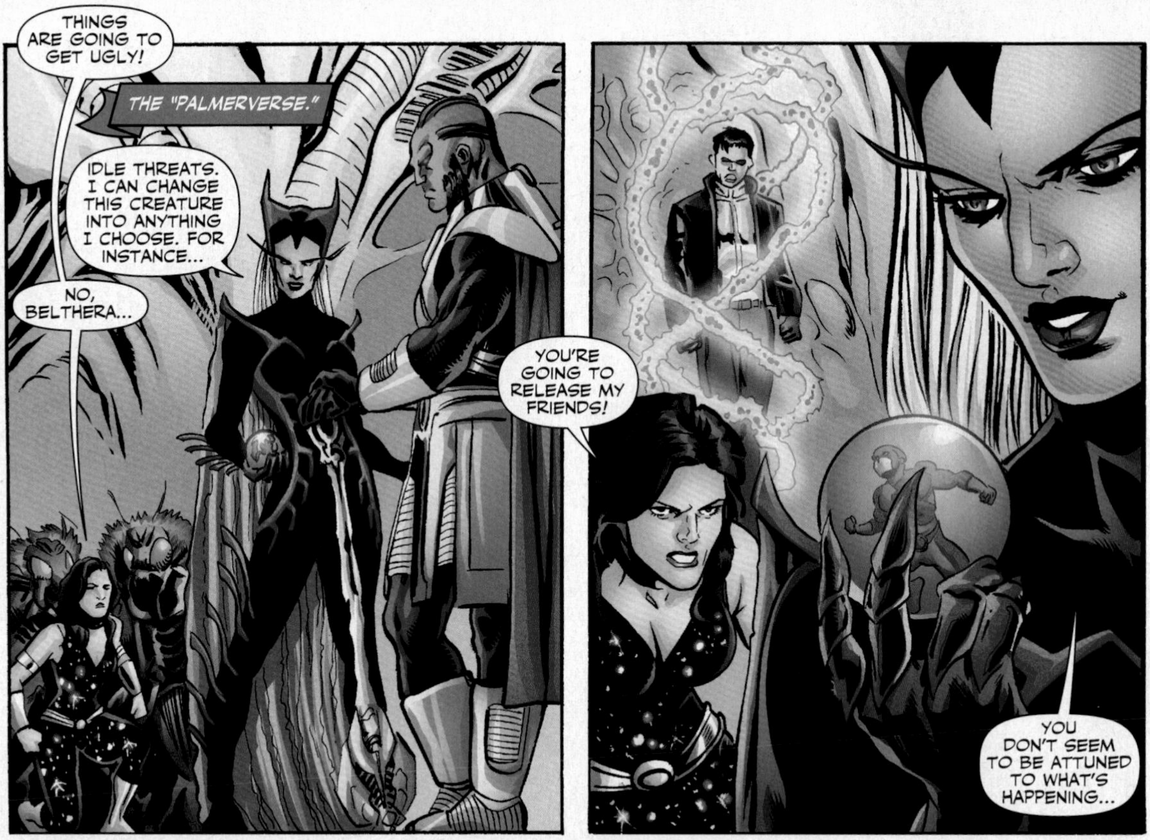
THINGS ARE GOING TO GET UGLY!
THE "PALMERVERSE."
IDLE THREATS. I CAN CHANGE THIS CREATURE INTO ANYTHING I CHOOSE. FOR INSTANCE...
NO, BELTHERA...
YOU'RE GOING TO RELEASE MY FRIENDS!
YOU DON'T SEEM TO BE ATTUNED TO WHAT'S HAPPENING...

DONNA TROY & JASON TODD

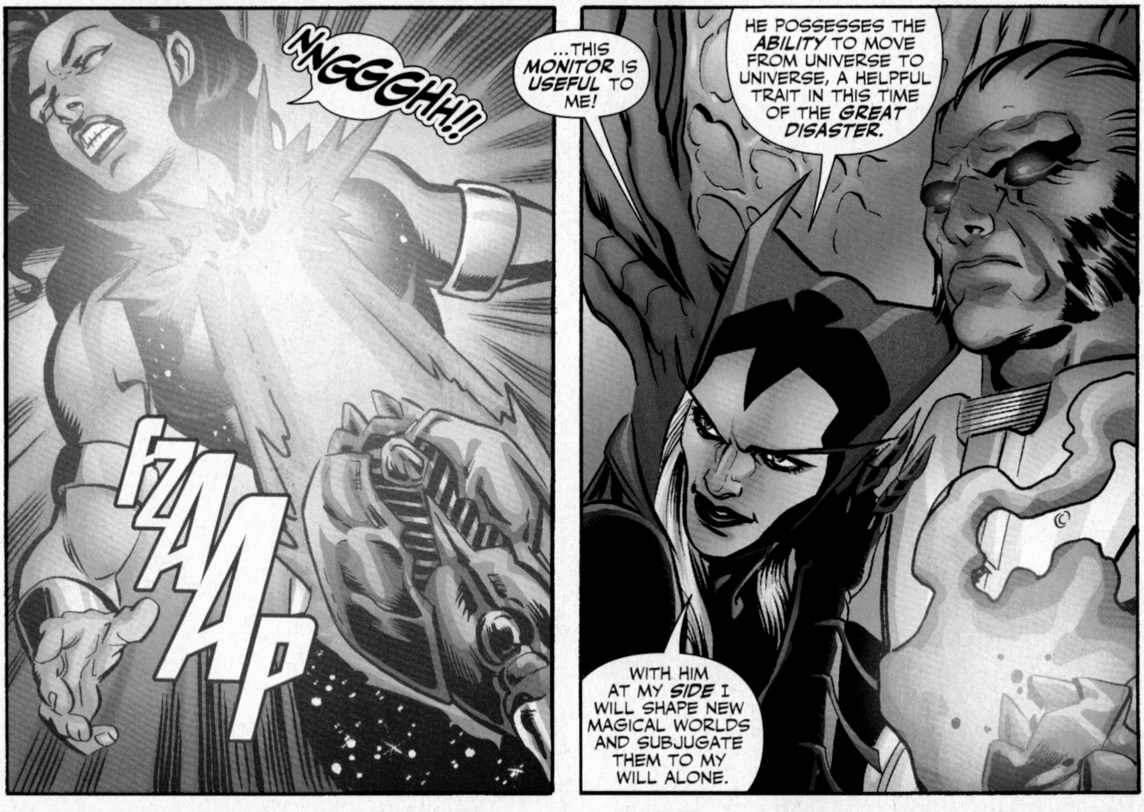
NNGGGHH!!
FZAAAP
...THIS MONITOR IS USEFUL TO ME!
HE POSSESSES THE ABILITY TO MOVE FROM UNIVERSE TO UNIVERSE, A HELPFUL TRAIT IN THIS TIME OF THE GREAT DISASTER.
WITH HIM AT MY SIDE I WILL SHAPE NEW MAGICAL WORLDS AND SUBJUGATE THEM TO MY WILL ALONE.

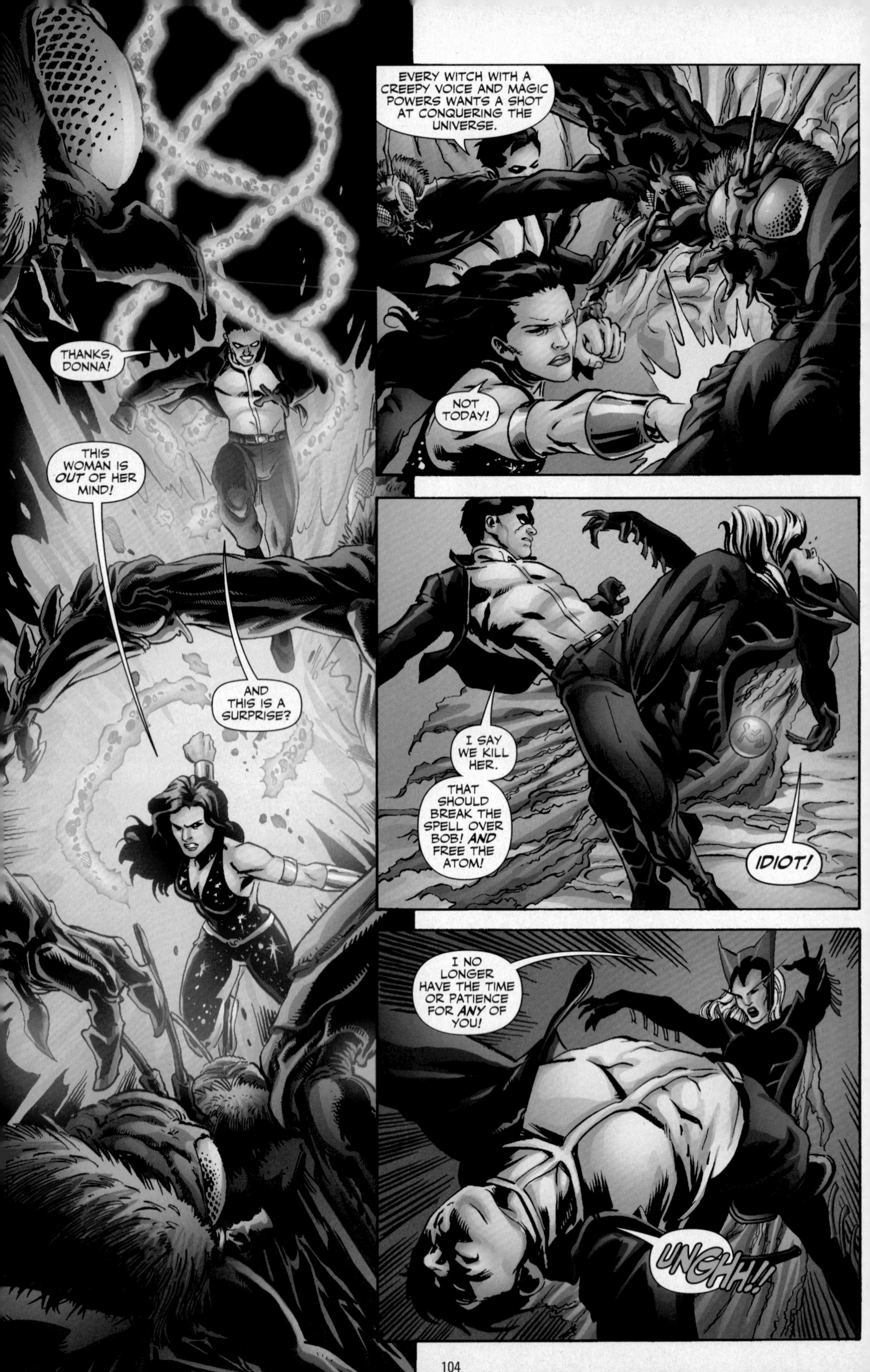
THANKS, DONNA!
THIS WOMAN IS OUT OF HER MIND!
AND THIS IS A SURPRISE?
EVERY WITCH WITH A CREEPY VOICE AND MAGIC POWERS WANTS A SHOT AT CONQUERING THE UNIVERSE.
NOT TODAY!
I SAY WE KILL HER.
THAT SHOULD BREAK THE SPELL OVER BOB! AND FREE THE ATOM!
IDIOT!
I NO LONGER HAVE THE TIME OR PATIENCE FOR ANY OF YOU!
UNGHH!!

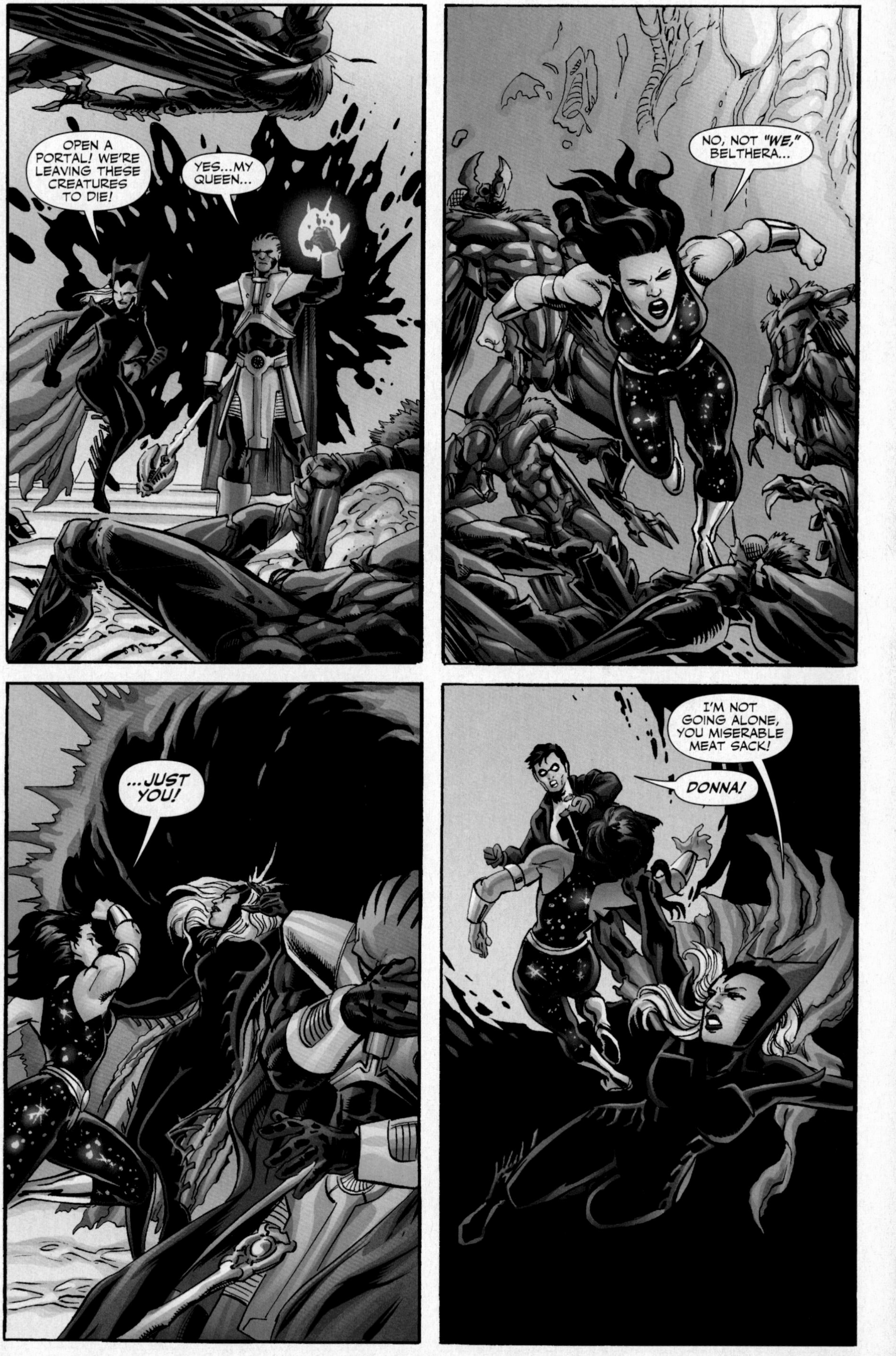
OPEN A PORTAL! WE'RE LEAVING THESE CREATURES TO DIE!
YES...MY QUEEN...
NO, NOT "WE," BELTHERA...
...JUST YOU!
I'M NOT GOING ALONE, YOU MISERABLE MEAT SACK!
DONNA!

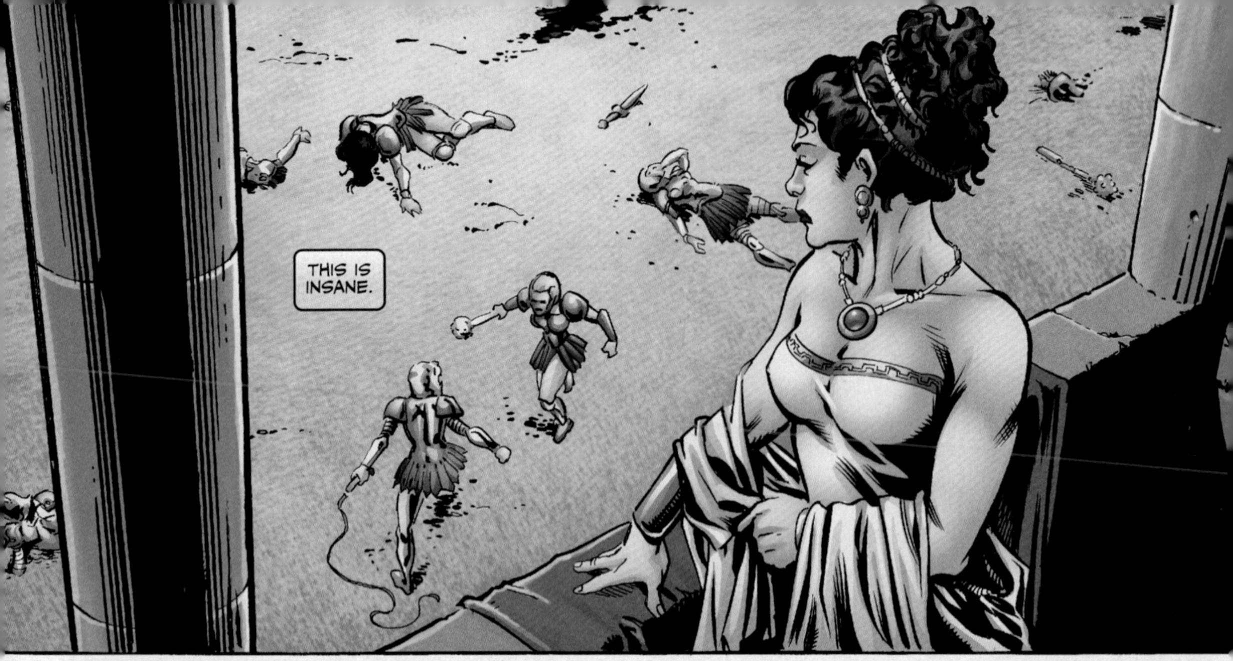
THIS IS INSANE.

## HOLLY ROBINSON

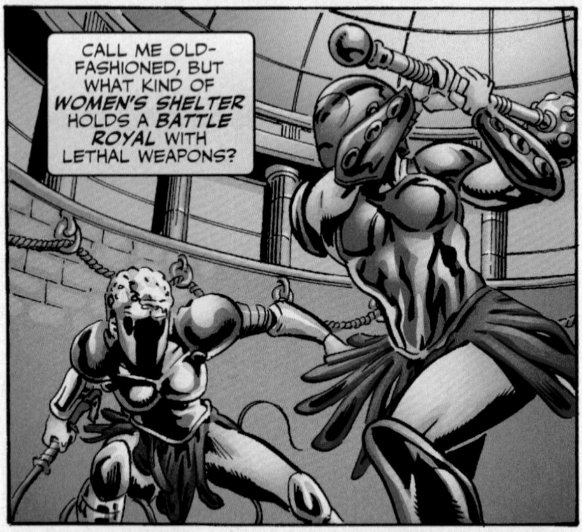
CALL ME OLD-FASHIONED, BUT WHAT KIND OF WOMEN'S SHELTER HOLDS A BATTLE ROYAL WITH LETHAL WEAPONS?

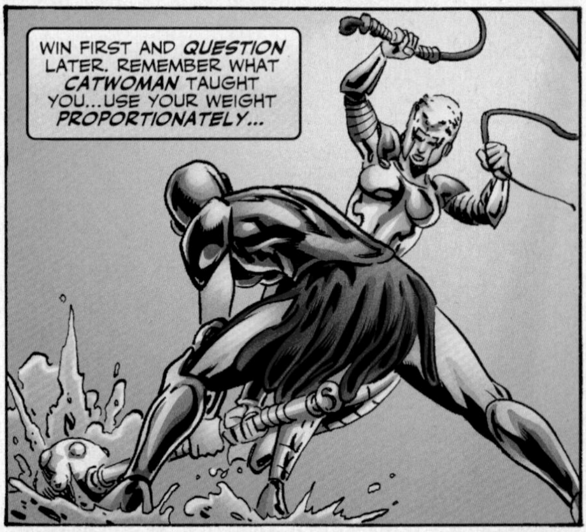
WIN FIRST AND QUESTION LATER. REMEMBER WHAT CATWOMAN TAUGHT YOU...USE YOUR WEIGHT PROPORTIONATELY...

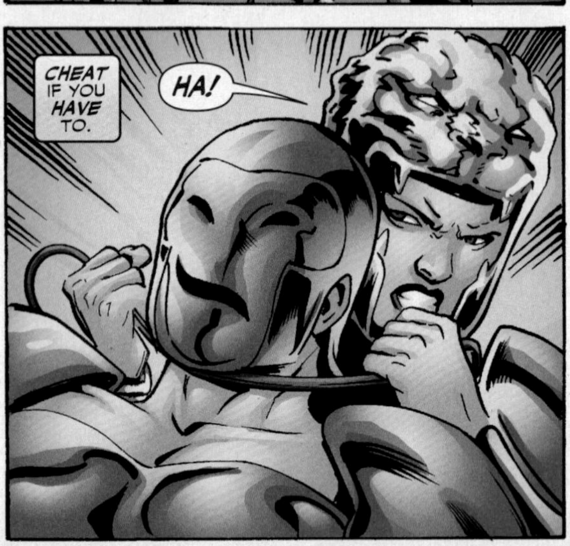
CHEAT IF YOU HAVE TO.
HA!

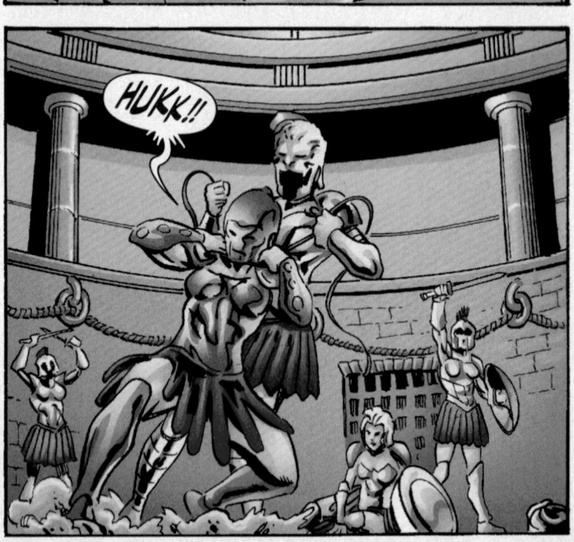
HUKK!!

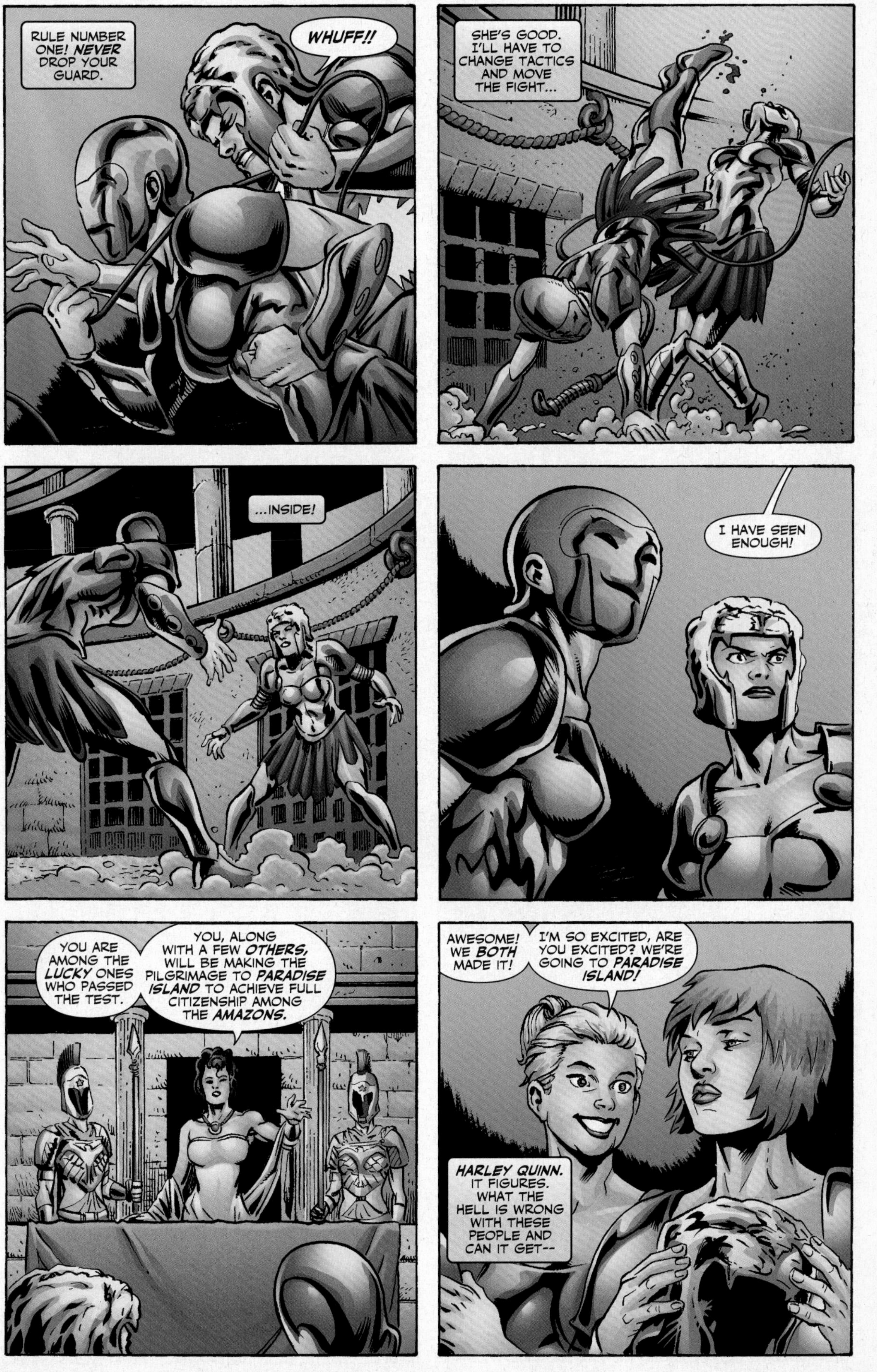
RULE NUMBER ONE! NEVER DROP YOUR GUARD.
WHUFF!!
SHE'S GOOD. I'LL HAVE TO CHANGE TACTICS AND MOVE THE FIGHT...
...INSIDE!
I HAVE SEEN ENOUGH!
YOU ARE AMONG THE LUCKY ONES WHO PASSED THE TEST.
YOU, ALONG WITH A FEW OTHERS, WILL BE MAKING THE PILGRIMAGE TO PARADISE ISLAND TO ACHIEVE FULL CITIZENSHIP AMONG THE AMAZONS.
AWESOME! WE BOTH MADE IT!
I'M SO EXCITED, ARE YOU EXCITED? WE'RE GOING TO PARADISE ISLAND!
HARLEY QUINN. IT FIGURES. WHAT THE HELL IS WRONG WITH THESE PEOPLE AND CAN IT GET--

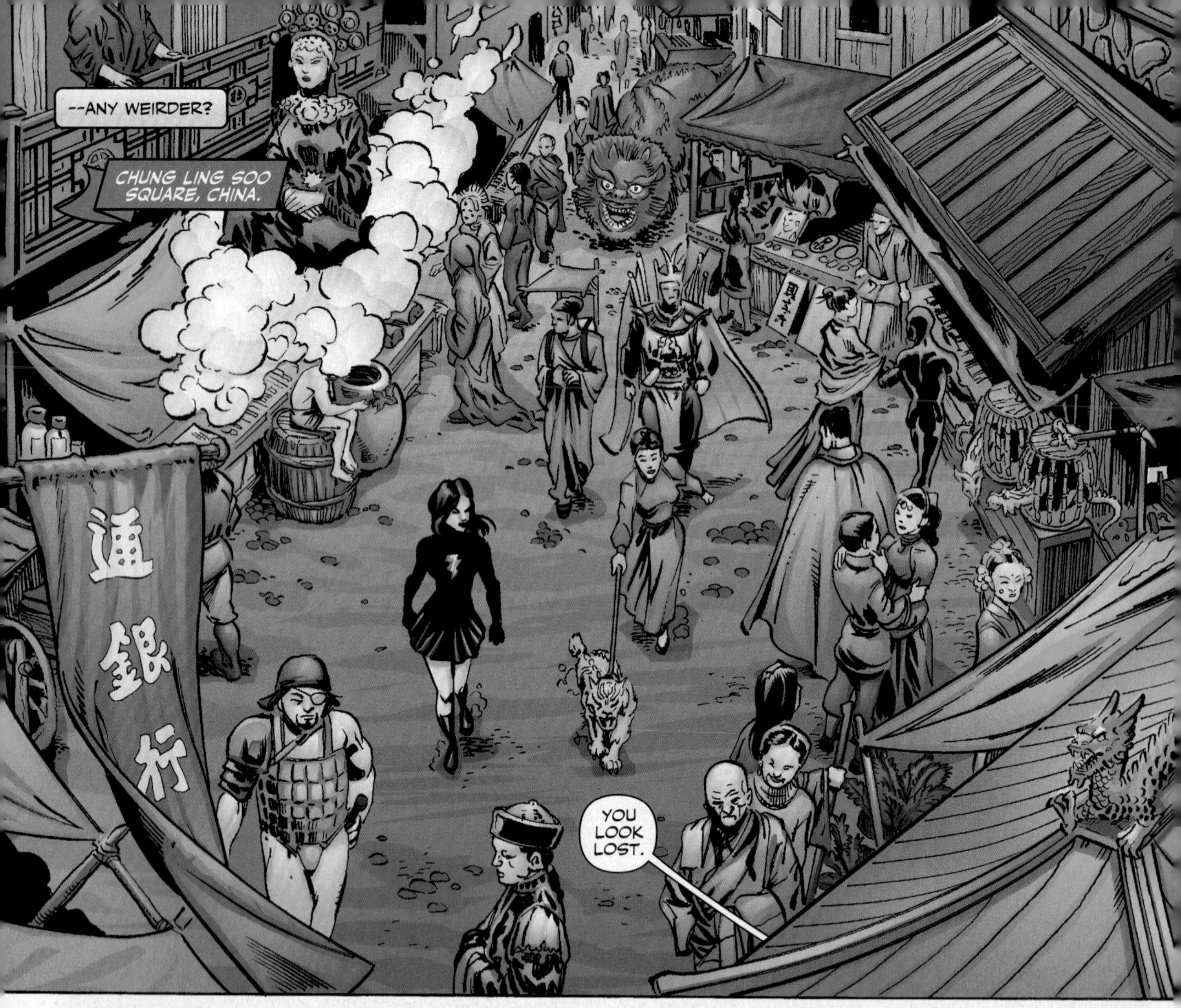
--ANY WEIRDER?
CHUNG LING SOO SQUARE, CHINA.
通銀行
YOU LOOK LOST.

# MARY MARVEL

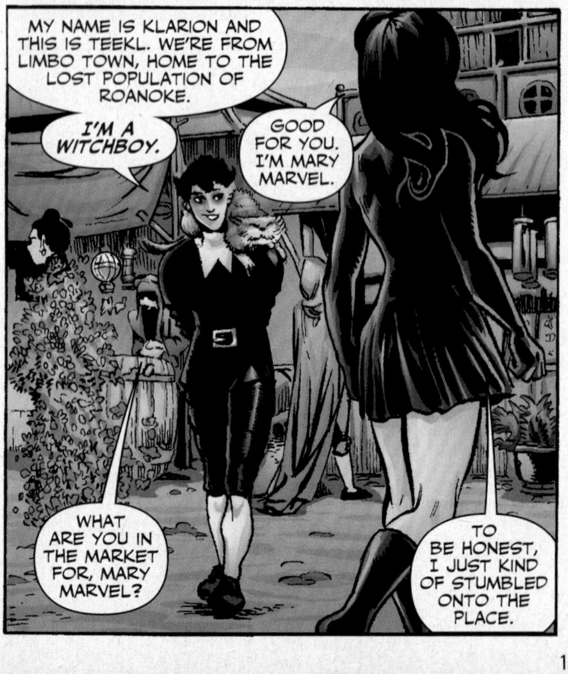
MY NAME IS KLARION AND THIS IS TEEKL. WE'RE FROM LIMBO TOWN, HOME TO THE LOST POPULATION OF ROANOKE.
I'M A WITCHBOY.
GOOD FOR YOU. I'M MARY MARVEL.
WHAT ARE YOU IN THE MARKET FOR, MARY MARVEL?
TO BE HONEST, I JUST KIND OF STUMBLED ONTO THE PLACE.

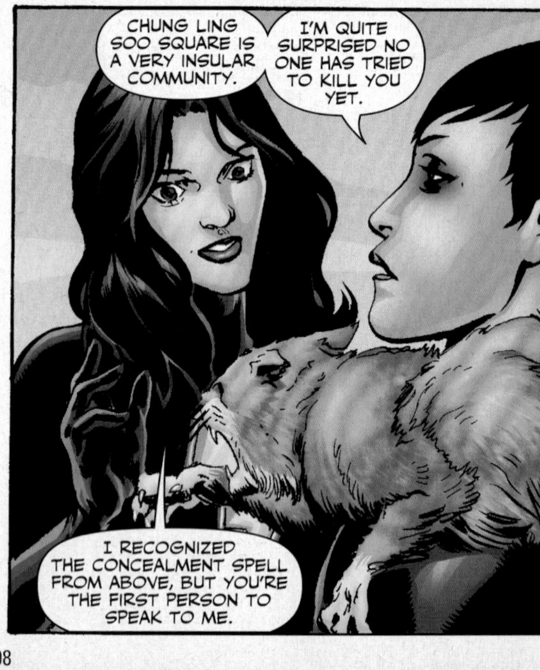
CHUNG LING SOO SQUARE IS A VERY INSULAR COMMUNITY.
I'M QUITE SURPRISED NO ONE HAS TRIED TO KILL YOU YET.
I RECOGNIZED THE CONCEALMENT SPELL FROM ABOVE, BUT YOU'RE THE FIRST PERSON TO SPEAK TO ME.

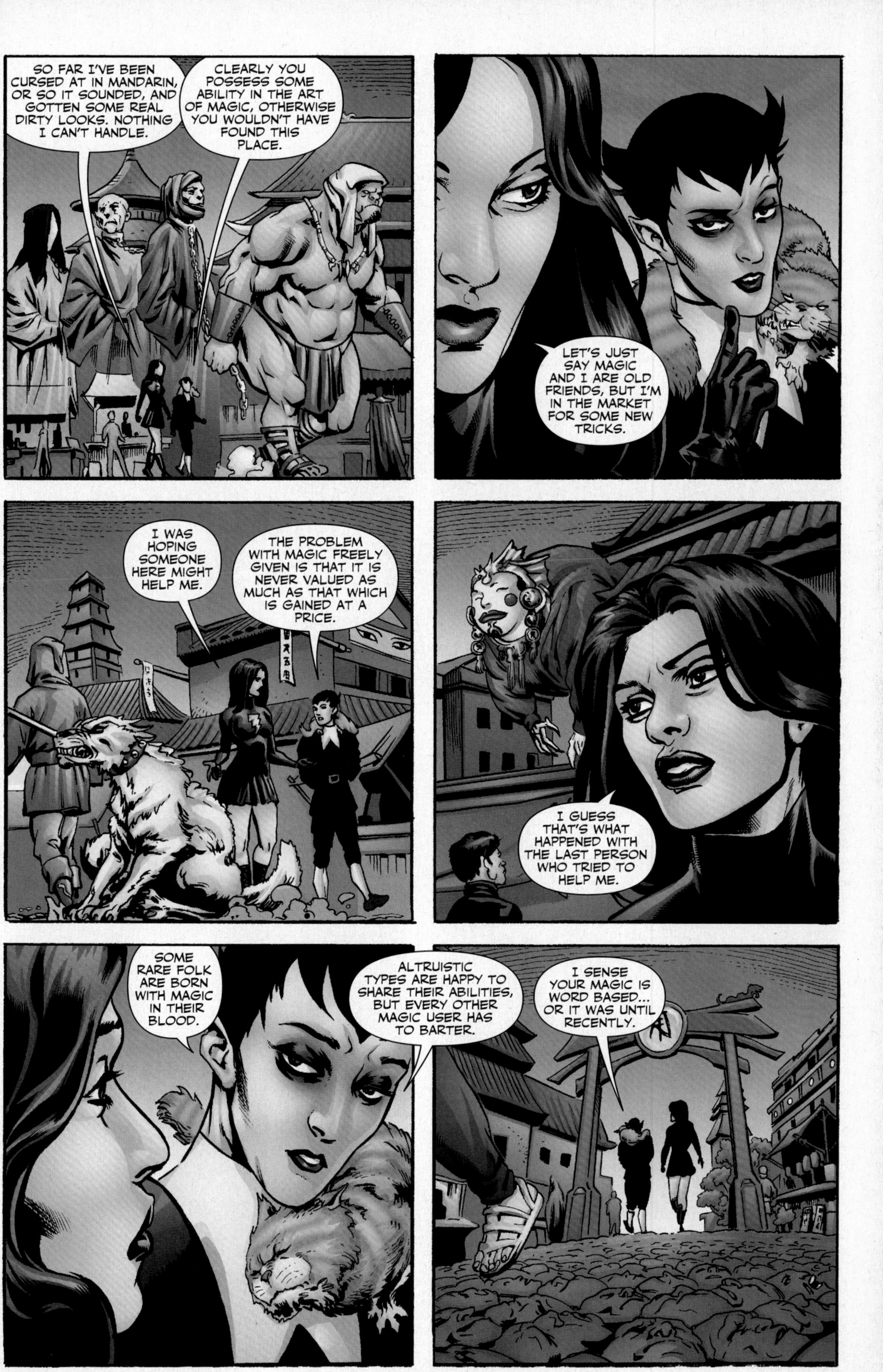
SO FAR I'VE BEEN CURSED AT IN MANDARIN, OR SO IT SOUNDED, AND GOTTEN SOME REAL DIRTY LOOKS. NOTHING I CAN'T HANDLE.
CLEARLY YOU POSSESS SOME ABILITY IN THE ART OF MAGIC, OTHERWISE YOU WOULDN'T HAVE FOUND THIS PLACE.
LET'S JUST SAY MAGIC AND I ARE OLD FRIENDS, BUT I'M IN THE MARKET FOR SOME NEW TRICKS.
I WAS HOPING SOMEONE HERE MIGHT HELP ME.
THE PROBLEM WITH MAGIC FREELY GIVEN IS THAT IT IS NEVER VALUED AS MUCH AS THAT WHICH IS GAINED AT A PRICE.
I GUESS THAT'S WHAT HAPPENED WITH THE LAST PERSON WHO TRIED TO HELP ME.
SOME RARE FOLK ARE BORN WITH MAGIC IN THEIR BLOOD.
ALTRUISTIC TYPES ARE HAPPY TO SHARE THEIR ABILITIES, BUT EVERY OTHER MAGIC USER HAS TO BARTER.
I SENSE YOUR MAGIC IS WORD BASED... OR IT WAS UNTIL RECENTLY.

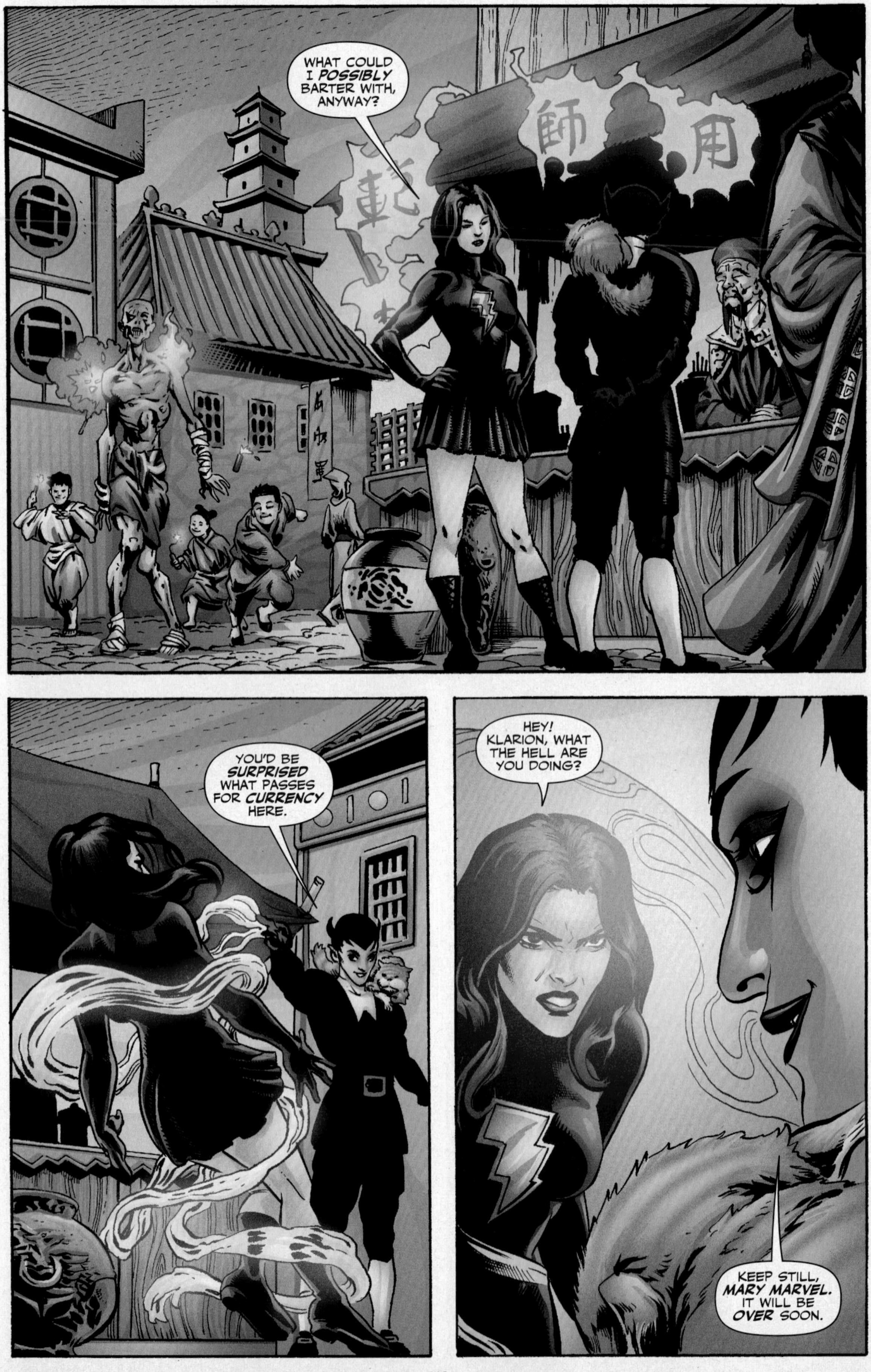
WHAT COULD I *POSSIBLY* BARTER WITH, ANYWAY?
YOU'D BE *SURPRISED* WHAT PASSES FOR *CURRENCY* HERE.
HEY! KLARION, WHAT THE HELL ARE YOU DOING?
KEEP STILL, *MARY MARVEL.* IT WILL BE *OVER* SOON.

NEBRASKA.

ARE YOU FAMILIAR WITH *O.M.A.C.?*

# KARATE KID

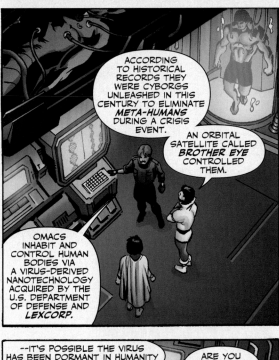

ACCORDING TO HISTORICAL RECORDS THEY WERE CYBORGS UNLEASHED IN THIS CENTURY TO ELIMINATE *META-HUMANS* DURING A CRISIS EVENT.

AN ORBITAL SATELLITE CALLED *BROTHER EYE* CONTROLLED THEM.

OMACS INHABIT AND CONTROL HUMAN BODIES VIA A VIRUS-DERIVED NANOTECHNOLOGY ACQUIRED BY THE U.S. DEPARTMENT OF DEFENSE AND *LEXCORP.*

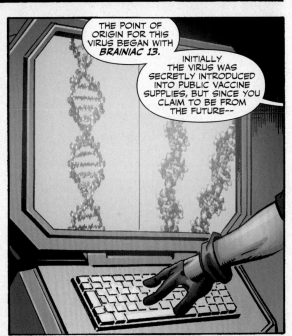

THE POINT OF ORIGIN FOR THIS VIRUS BEGAN WITH *BRAINIAC 13.*

INITIALLY THE VIRUS WAS SECRETLY INTRODUCED INTO PUBLIC VACCINE SUPPLIES, BUT SINCE YOU CLAIM TO BE FROM THE FUTURE--

--IT'S POSSIBLE THE VIRUS HAS BEEN DORMANT IN HUMANITY FOR A QUITE A LONG TIME.

ARE YOU SAYING VAL IS TURNING INTO SOME KIND OF MACHINE?

I'M MERELY STATING THAT THE VIRAL INFECTION HAS MANY SIMILARITIES TO THE ORIGINAL OMAC VIRUS. LIKE ALL LIVING THINGS, IT MAY HAVE EVOLVED.

THE ONLY WAY TO CONFIRM MY SUSPICIONS IS TO CONTACT *BUDDY BLANK,* A RESEARCH SCIENTIST WORKING FOR *PSEUDO-PEOPLE,* INC.

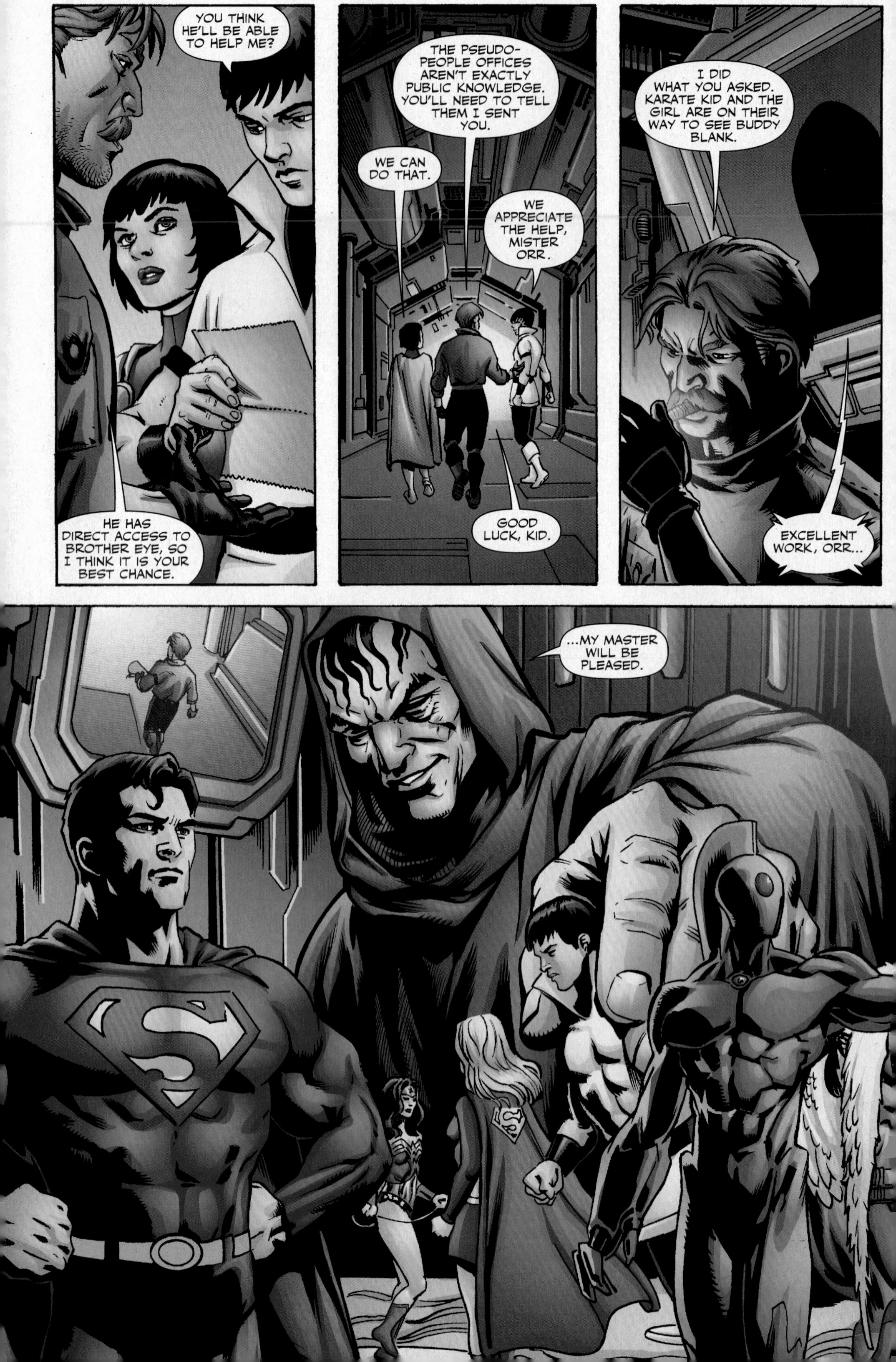
YOU THINK HE'LL BE ABLE TO HELP ME?
HE HAS DIRECT ACCESS TO BROTHER EYE, SO I THINK IT IS YOUR BEST CHANCE.
THE PSEUDO-PEOPLE OFFICES AREN'T EXACTLY PUBLIC KNOWLEDGE. YOU'LL NEED TO TELL THEM I SENT YOU.
WE CAN DO THAT.
WE APPRECIATE THE HELP, MISTER ORR.
GOOD LUCK, KID.
I DID WHAT YOU ASKED. KARATE KID AND THE GIRL ARE ON THEIR WAY TO SEE BUDDY BLANK.
EXCELLENT WORK, ORR...
...MY MASTER WILL BE PLEASED.

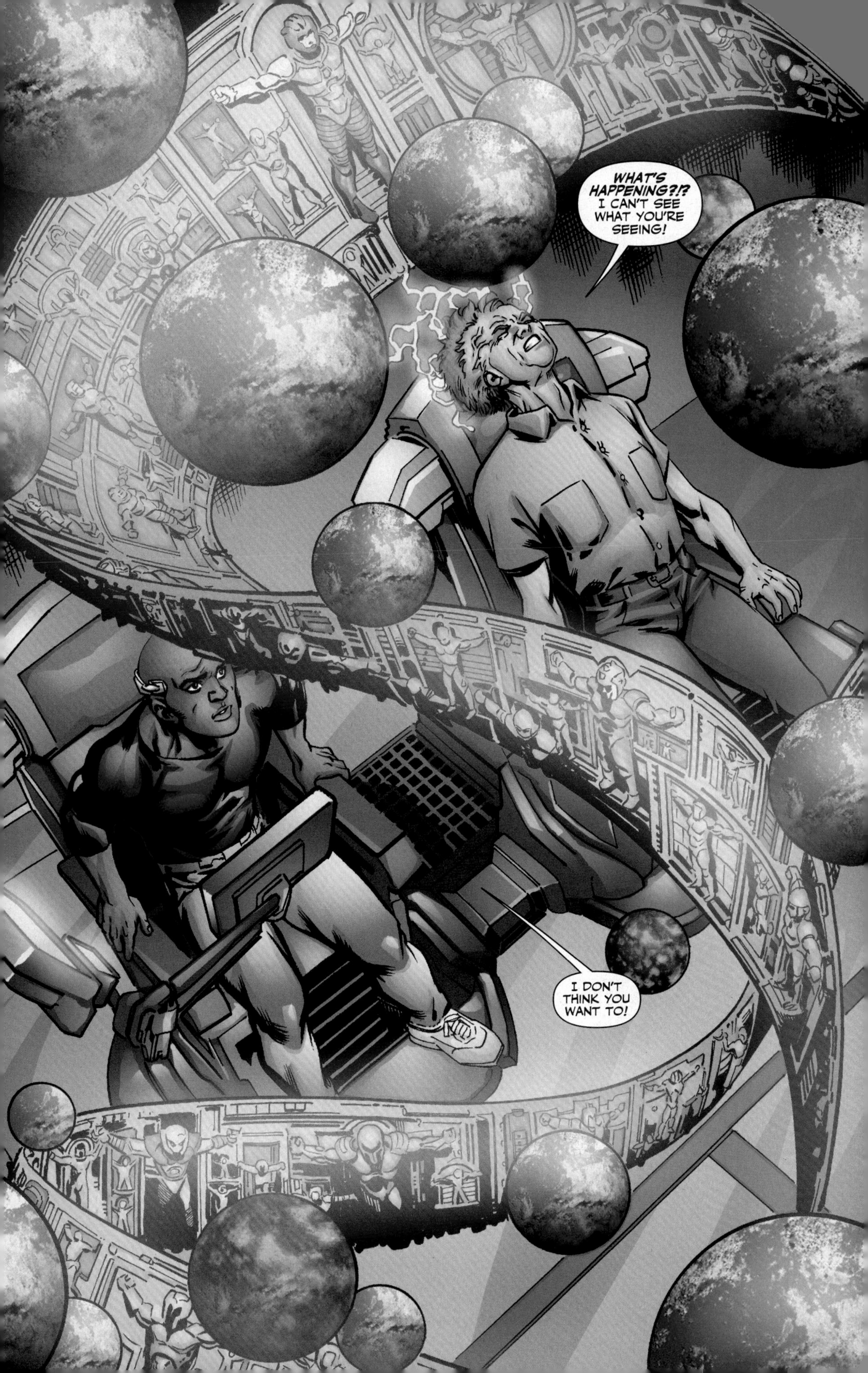
WHAT'S HAPPENING?!? I CAN'T SEE WHAT YOU'RE SEEING!
I DON'T THINK YOU WANT TO!

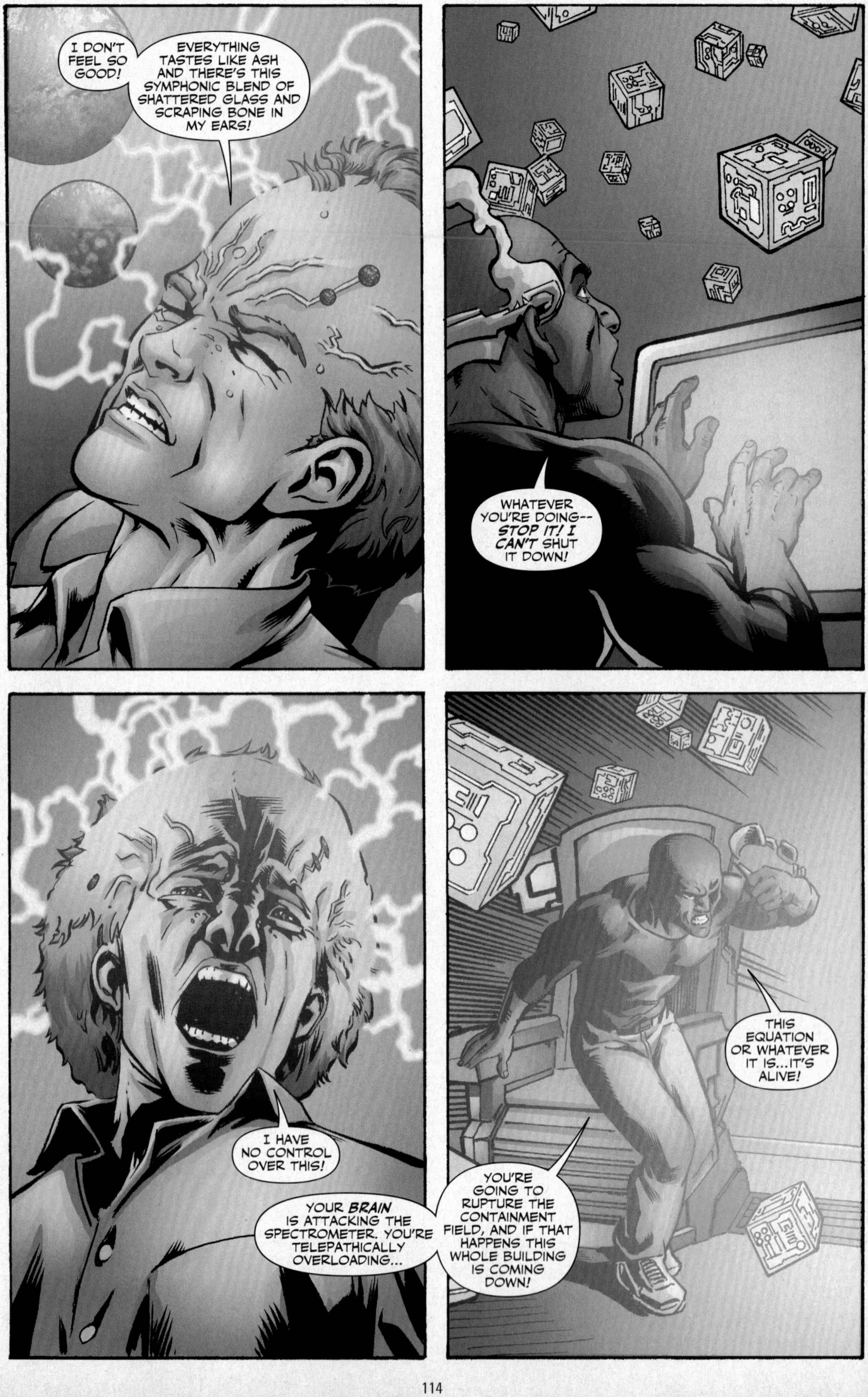
I DON'T FEEL SO GOOD!
EVERYTHING TASTES LIKE ASH AND THERE'S THIS SYMPHONIC BLEND OF SHATTERED GLASS AND SCRAPING BONE IN MY EARS!
WHATEVER YOU'RE DOING-- STOP IT! I CAN'T SHUT IT DOWN!
I HAVE NO CONTROL OVER THIS!
YOUR BRAIN IS ATTACKING THE SPECTROMETER. YOU'RE TELEPATHICALLY OVERLOADING...
THIS EQUATION OR WHATEVER IT IS...IT'S ALIVE!
YOU'RE GOING TO RUPTURE THE CONTAINMENT FIELD, AND IF THAT HAPPENS THIS WHOLE BUILDING IS COMING DOWN!

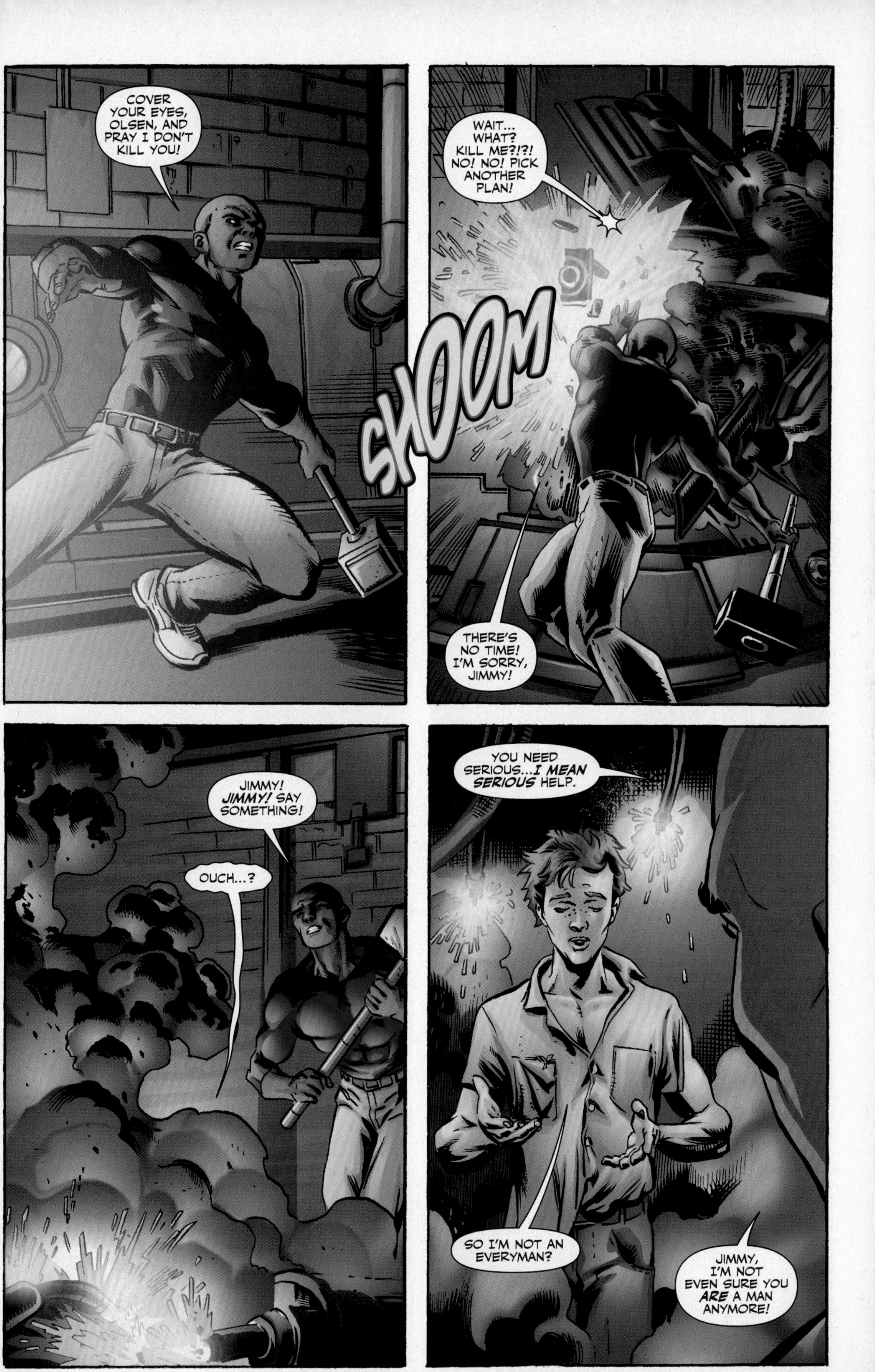
COVER YOUR EYES, OLSEN, AND PRAY I DON'T KILL YOU!
WAIT... WHAT? KILL ME?!?! NO! NO! PICK ANOTHER PLAN!
SHOOM
THERE'S NO TIME! I'M SORRY, JIMMY!
JIMMY! *JIMMY!* SAY SOMETHING!
OUCH...?
YOU NEED SERIOUS...*I MEAN SERIOUS* HELP.
SO I'M NOT AN EVERYMAN?
JIMMY, I'M NOT EVEN SURE YOU *ARE* A MAN ANYMORE!

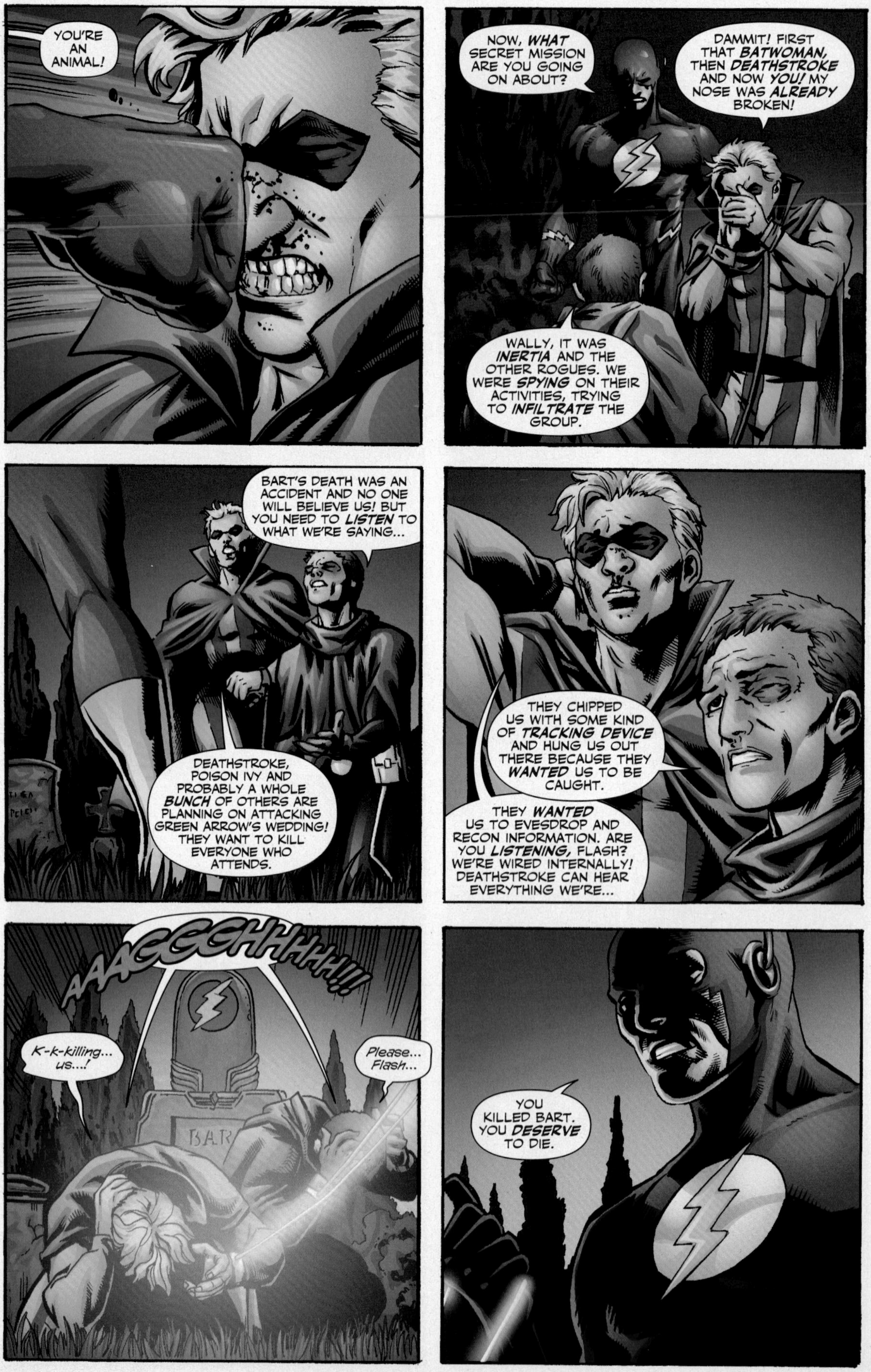
YOU'RE AN ANIMAL!
NOW, WHAT SECRET MISSION ARE YOU GOING ON ABOUT?
DAMMIT! FIRST THAT BATWOMAN, THEN DEATHSTROKE AND NOW YOU! MY NOSE WAS ALREADY BROKEN!
WALLY, IT WAS INERTIA AND THE OTHER ROGUES. WE WERE SPYING ON THEIR ACTIVITIES, TRYING TO INFILTRATE THE GROUP.
BART'S DEATH WAS AN ACCIDENT AND NO ONE WILL BELIEVE US! BUT YOU NEED TO LISTEN TO WHAT WE'RE SAYING...
DEATHSTROKE, POISON IVY AND PROBABLY A WHOLE BUNCH OF OTHERS ARE PLANNING ON ATTACKING GREEN ARROW'S WEDDING! THEY WANT TO KILL EVERYONE WHO ATTENDS.
THEY CHIPPED US WITH SOME KIND OF TRACKING DEVICE AND HUNG US OUT THERE BECAUSE THEY WANTED US TO BE CAUGHT.
THEY WANTED US TO EVESDROP AND RECON INFORMATION. ARE YOU LISTENING, FLASH? WE'RE WIRED INTERNALLY! DEATHSTROKE CAN HEAR EVERYTHING WE'RE...
AAAGGGHHHHH!!!
K-k-killing... us...!
Please... Flash...
BAR
YOU KILLED BART. YOU DESERVE TO DIE.

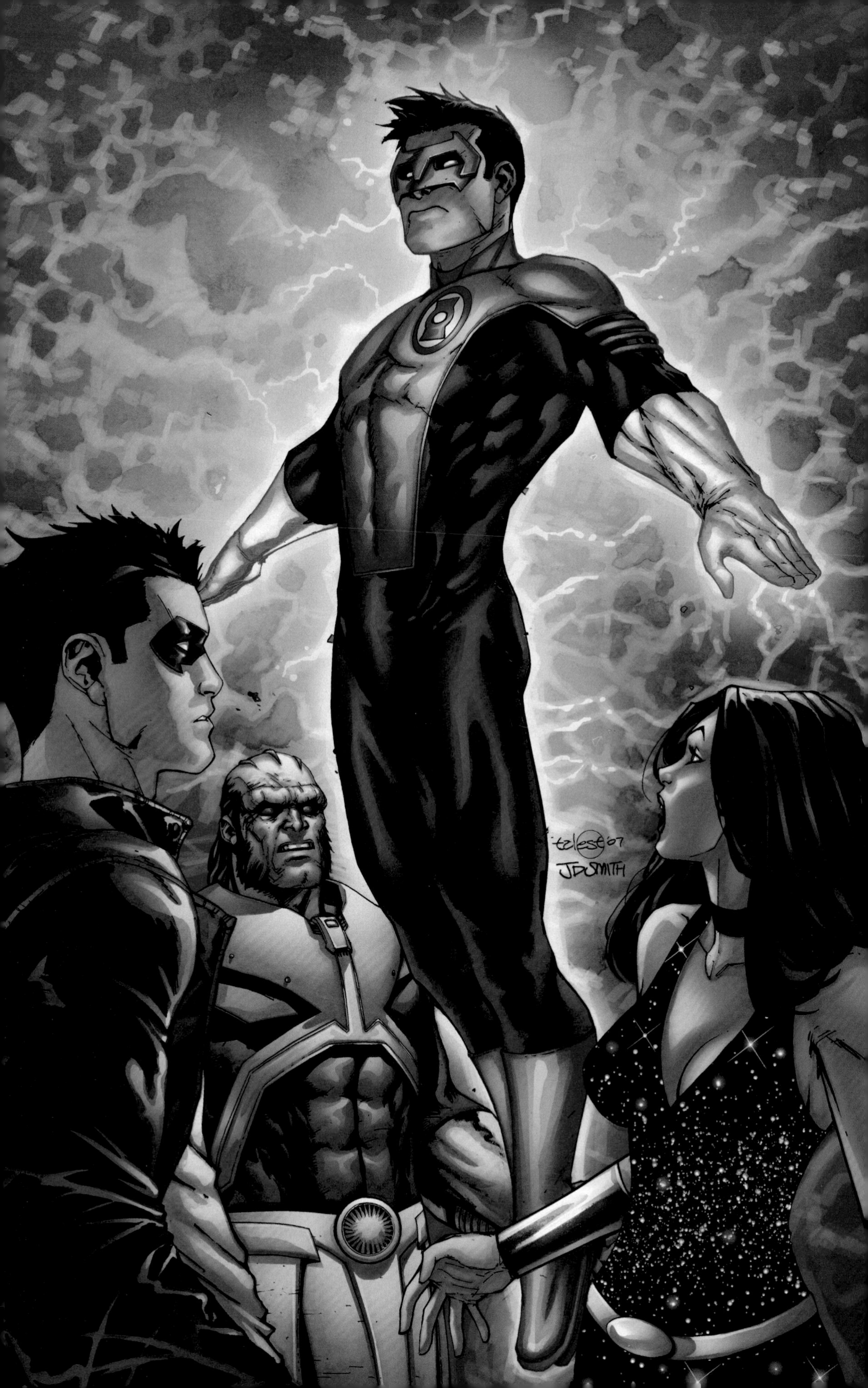
JDSMITH

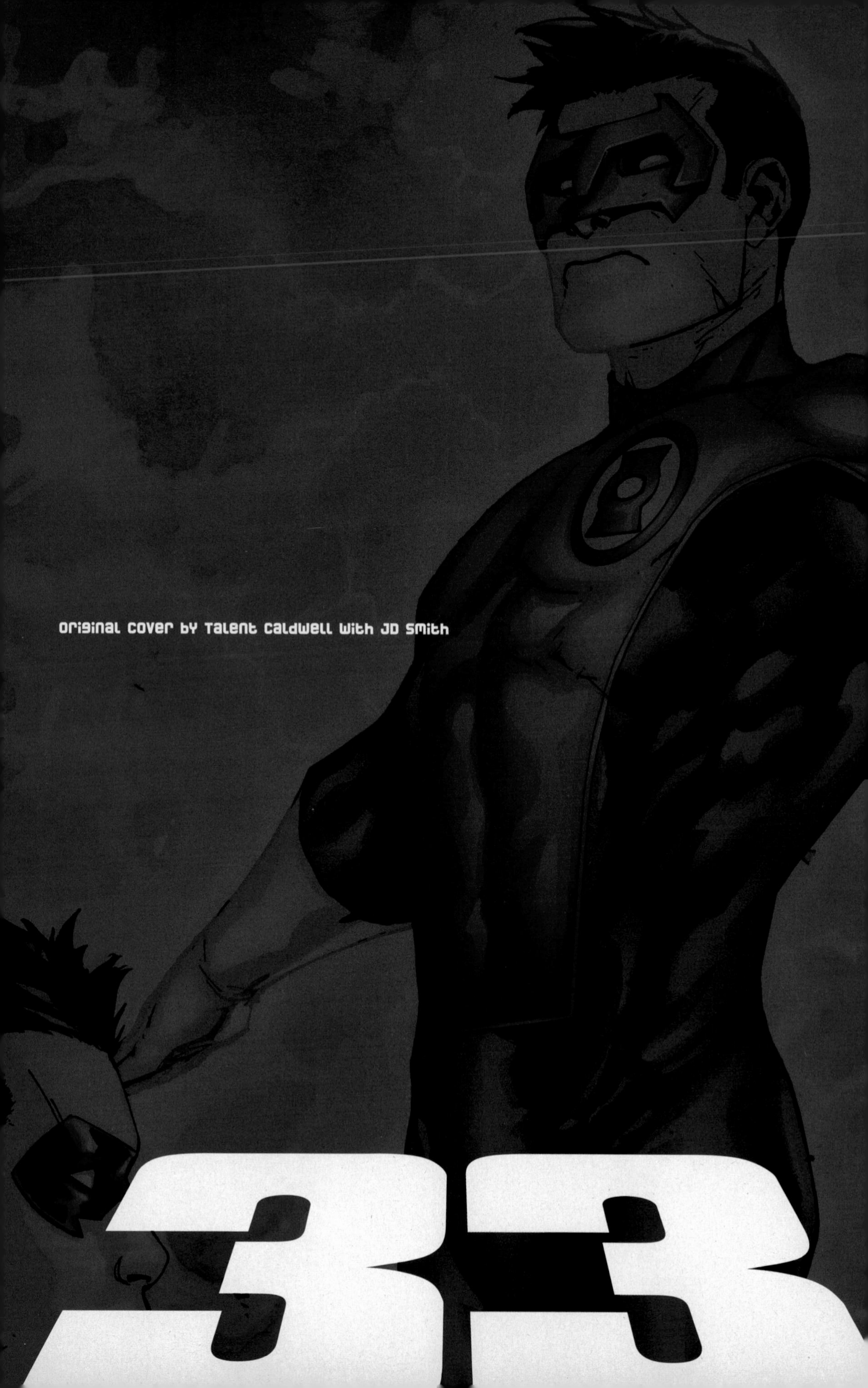
33

Original cover by Talent Caldwell with JD Smith

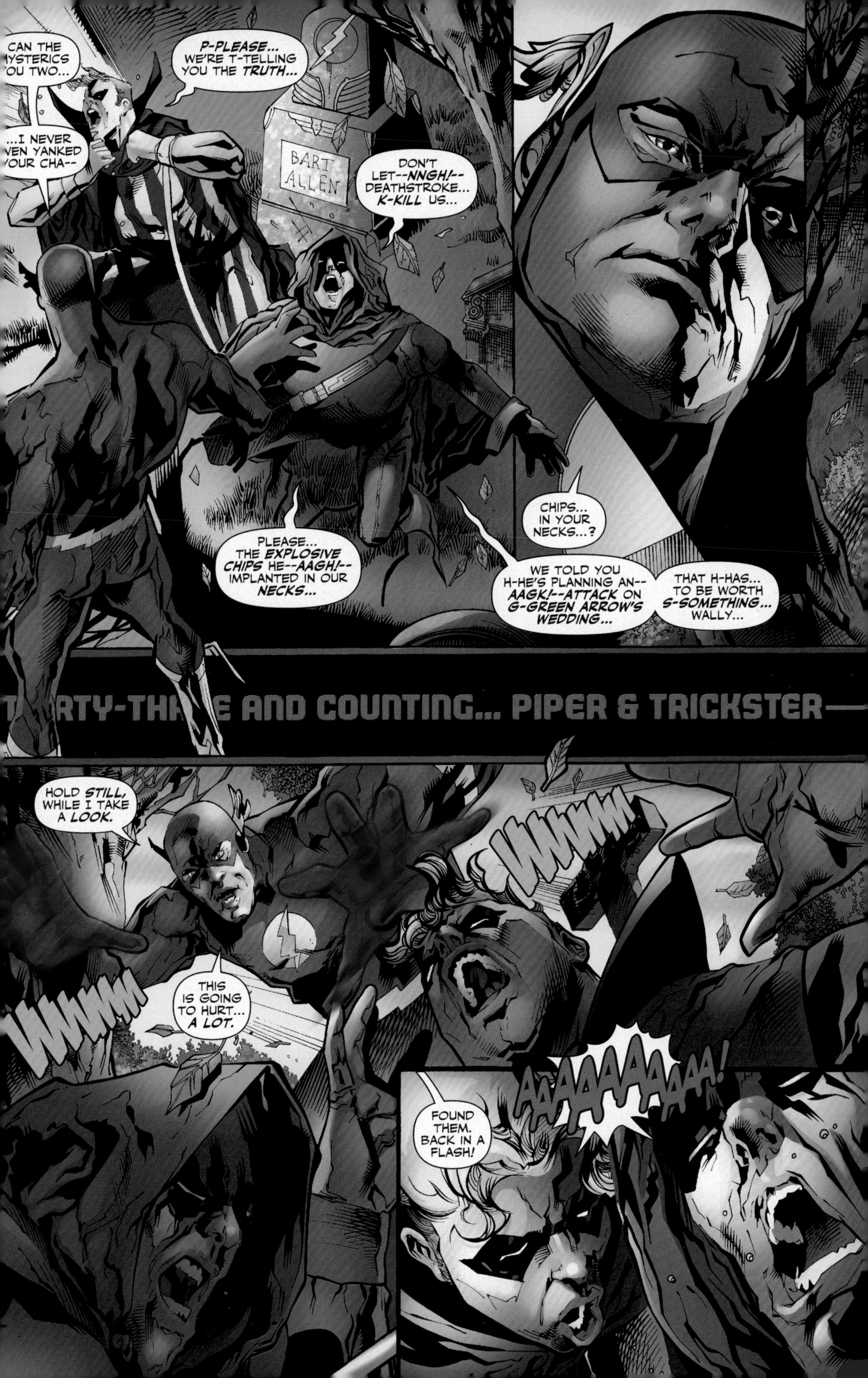
CAN THE
YSTERICS
OU TWO...
...I NEVER
VEN YANKED
OUR CHA--
P-PLEASE... WE'RE T-TELLING YOU THE TRUTH...
DON'T LET--NNGH!--DEATHSTROKE... K-KILL US...
BART ALLEN
PLEASE... THE EXPLOSIVE CHIPS HE--AAGH!--IMPLANTED IN OUR NECKS...
WE TOLD YOU H-HE'S PLANNING AN--AAGK!--ATTACK ON G-GREEN ARROW'S WEDDING...
CHIPS... IN YOUR NECKS...?
THAT H-HAS... TO BE WORTH S-SOMETHING... WALLY...
RTY-THR E AND COUNTING... PIPER & TRICKSTER—
HOLD STILL, WHILE I TAKE A LOOK.
THIS IS GOING TO HURT... A LOT.
WWWWW
WWWWWW
AAAAAAAAAA!
FOUND THEM. BACK IN A FLASH!

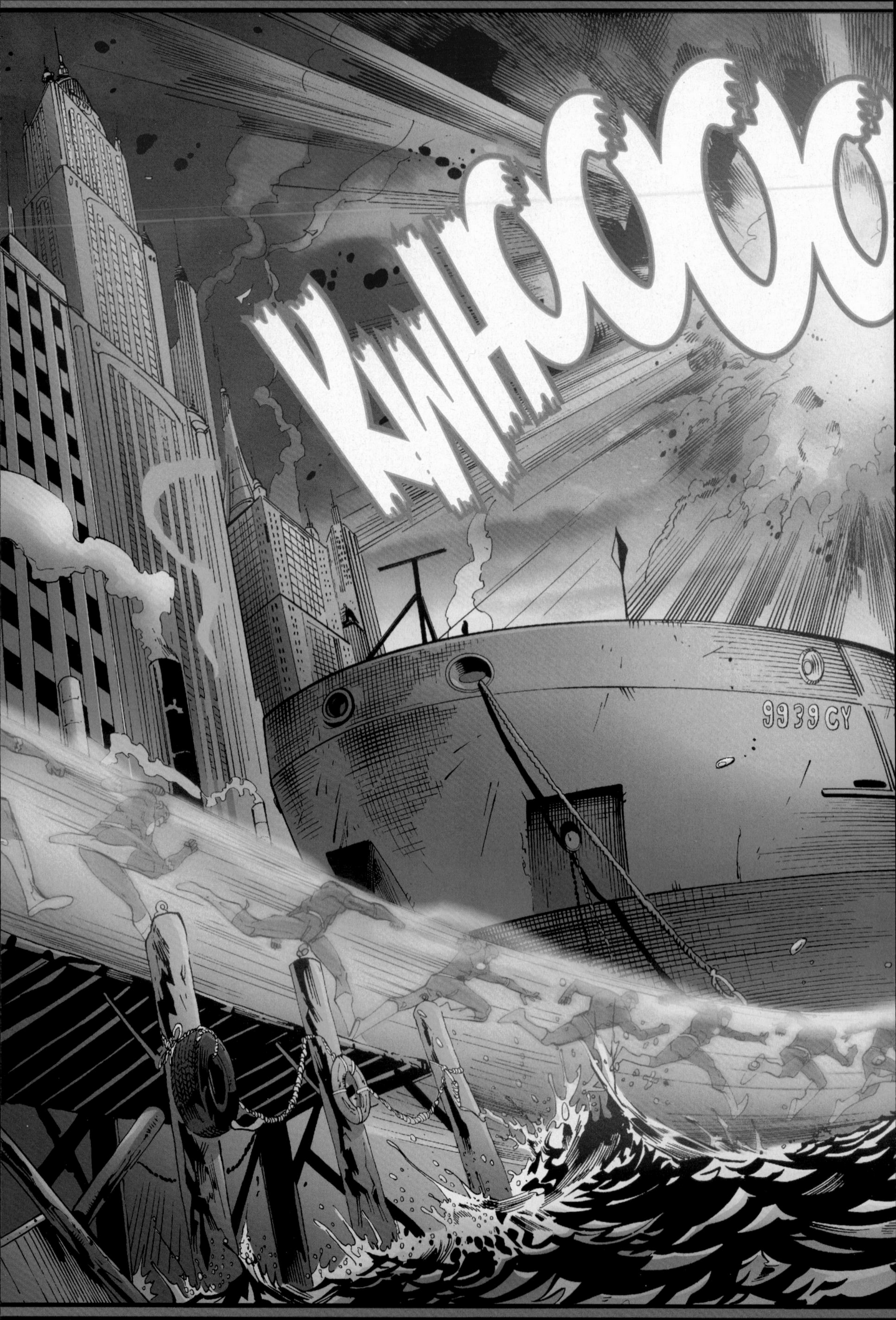
KWHOOO
9939 CY

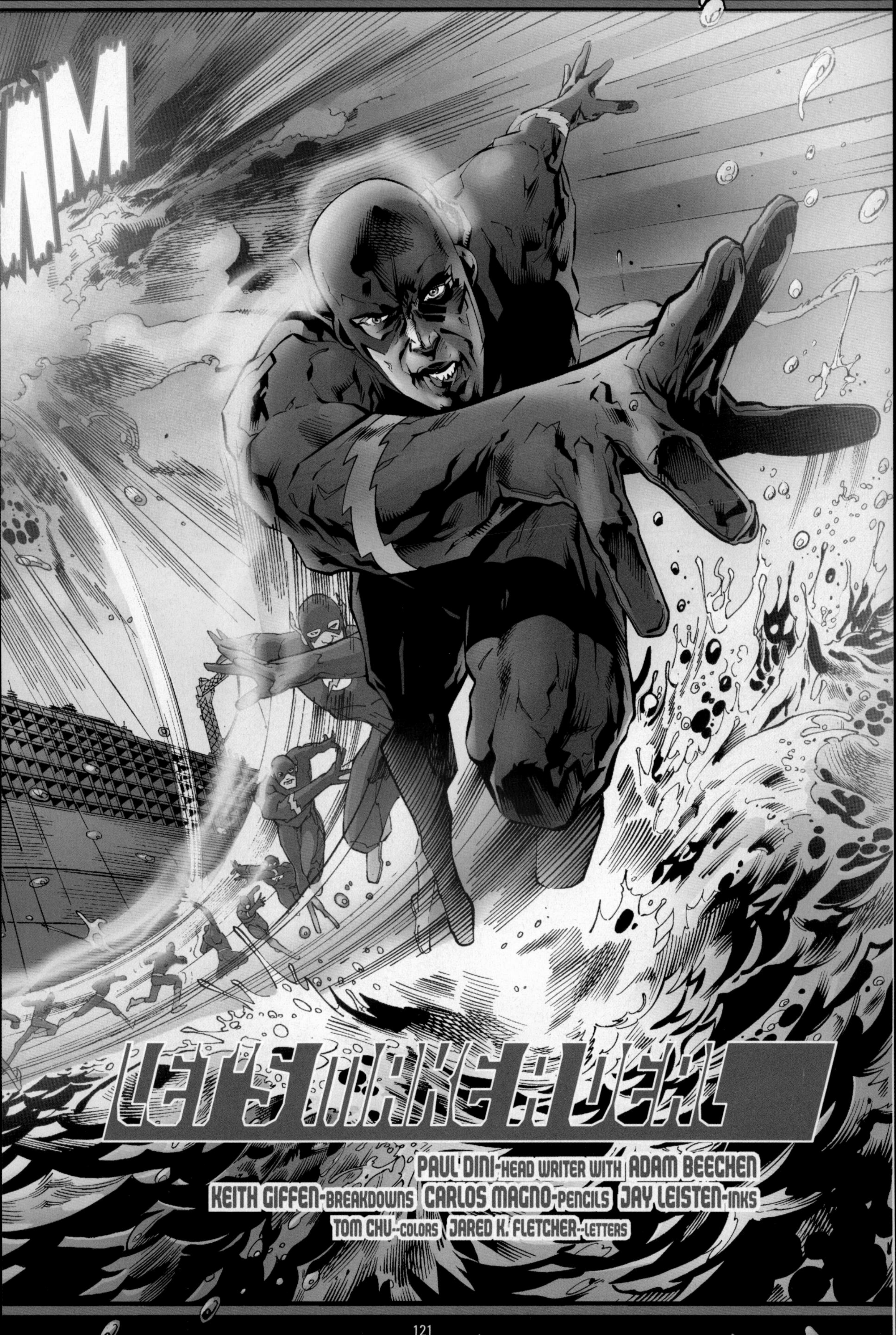
MM
LET'S MAKE A DEAL
PAUL DINI-HEAD WRITER WITH ADAM BEECHEN
KEITH GIFFEN-BREAKDOWNS CARLOS MAGNO-PENCILS JAY LEISTEN-INKS
TOM CHU--COLORS JARED K. FLETCHER--LETTERS

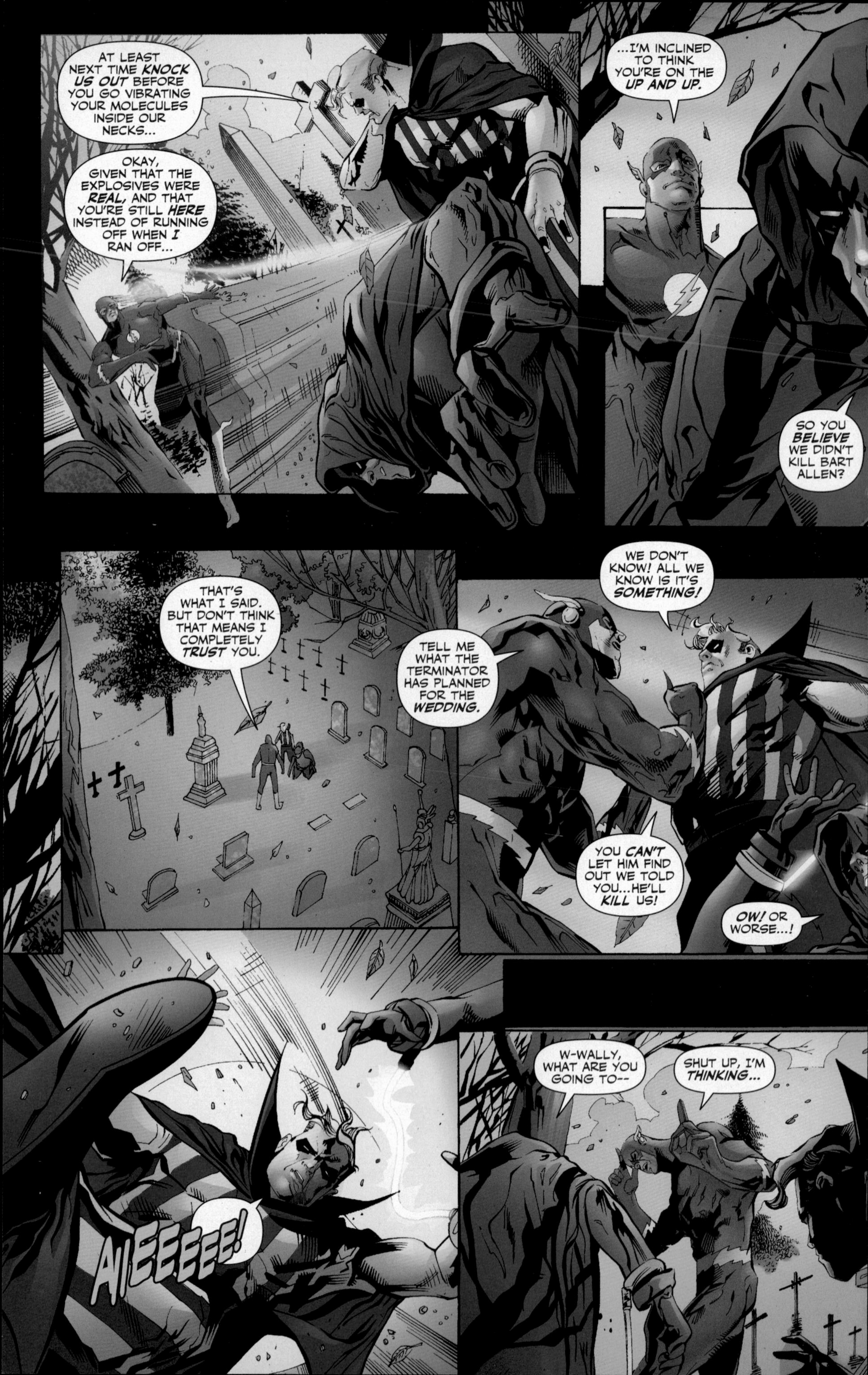
AT LEAST NEXT TIME KNOCK US OUT BEFORE YOU GO VIBRATING YOUR MOLECULES INSIDE OUR NECKS...
OKAY, GIVEN THAT THE EXPLOSIVES WERE REAL, AND THAT YOU'RE STILL HERE INSTEAD OF RUNNING OFF WHEN I RAN OFF...
...I'M INCLINED TO THINK YOU'RE ON THE UP AND UP.
SO YOU BELIEVE WE DIDN'T KILL BART ALLEN?
THAT'S WHAT I SAID. BUT DON'T THINK THAT MEANS I COMPLETELY TRUST YOU.
TELL ME WHAT THE TERMINATOR HAS PLANNED FOR THE WEDDING.
WE DON'T KNOW! ALL WE KNOW IS IT'S SOMETHING!
YOU CAN'T LET HIM FIND OUT WE TOLD YOU...HE'LL KILL US!
OW! OR WORSE...!
AIEEEEEE!
W-WALLY, WHAT ARE YOU GOING TO--
SHUT UP, I'M THINKING...

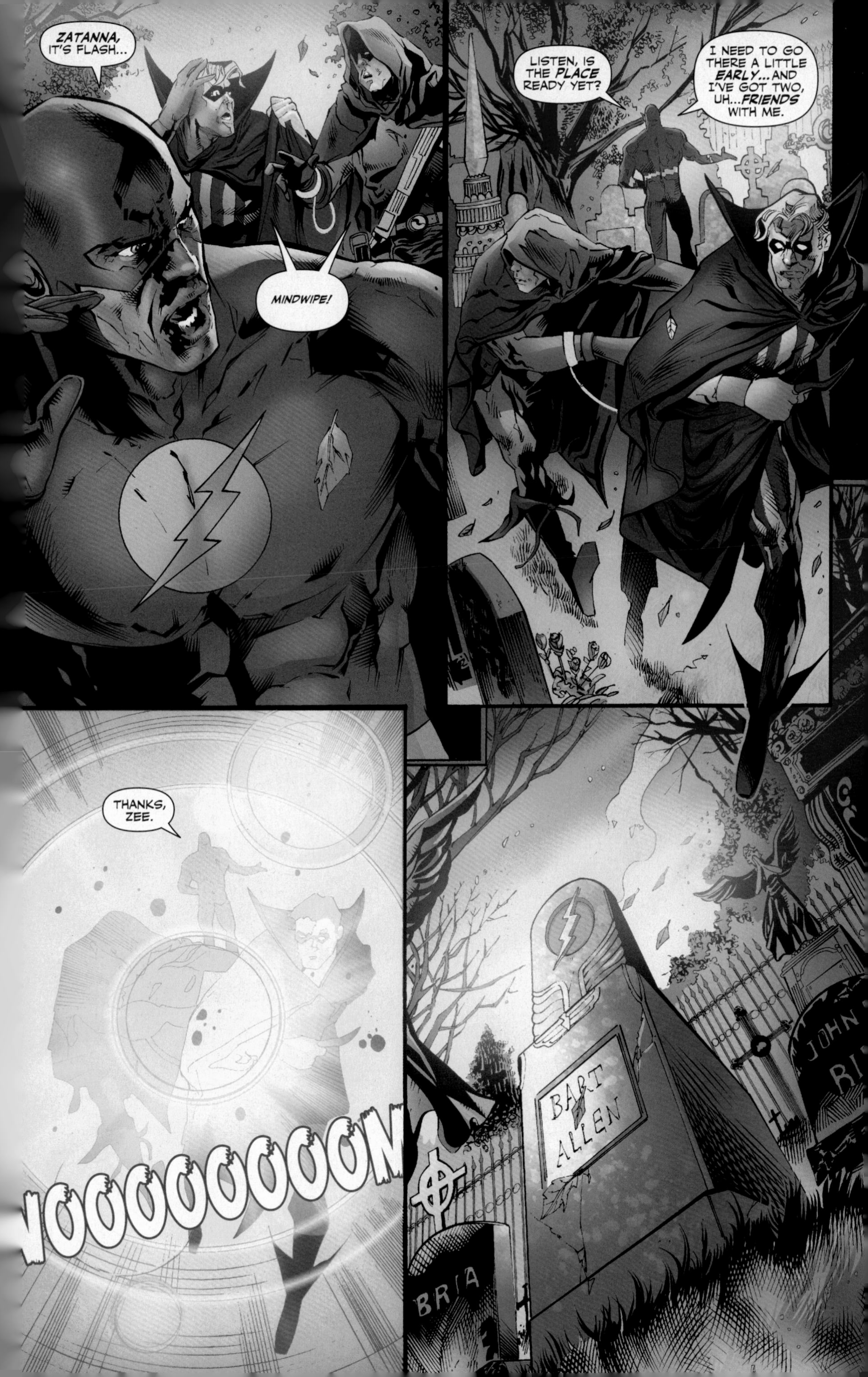
ZATANNA, IT'S FLASH...
MINDWIPE!
LISTEN, IS THE PLACE READY YET?
I NEED TO GO THERE A LITTLE EARLY... AND I'VE GOT TWO, UH... FRIENDS WITH ME.
THANKS, ZEE.
WOOOOOOOOOM
BART ALLEN
JOHN
BRIA

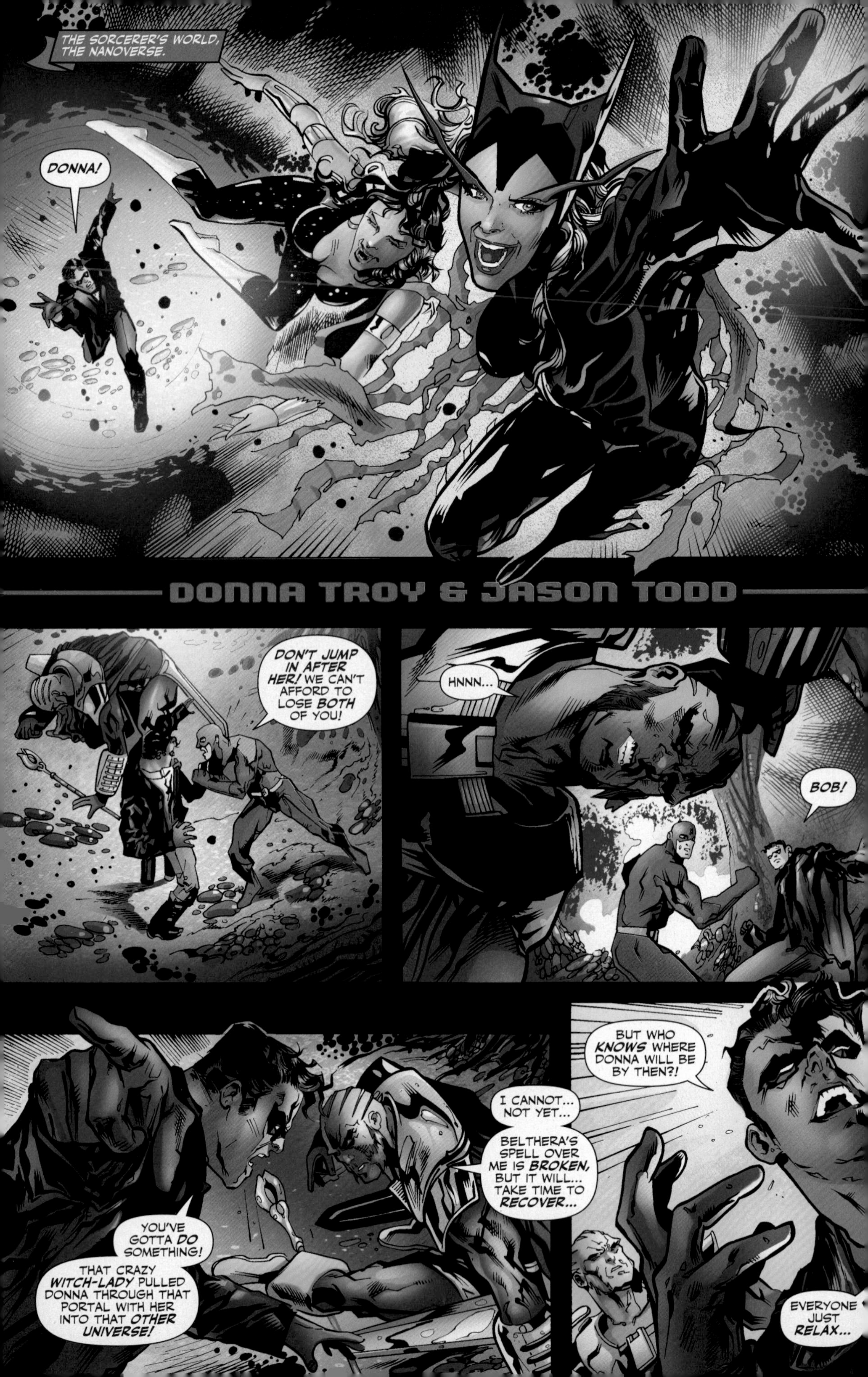
THE SORCERER'S WORLD, THE NANOVERSE.
DONNA!
DONNA TROY & JASON TODD
DON'T JUMP IN AFTER HER! WE CAN'T AFFORD TO LOSE BOTH OF YOU!
HNNN...
BOB!
YOU'VE GOTTA DO SOMETHING!
THAT CRAZY WITCH-LADY PULLED DONNA THROUGH THAT PORTAL WITH HER INTO THAT OTHER UNIVERSE!
I CANNOT... NOT YET...
BELTHERA'S SPELL OVER ME IS BROKEN, BUT IT WILL... TAKE TIME TO RECOVER...
BUT WHO KNOWS WHERE DONNA WILL BE BY THEN?!
EVERYONE JUST RELAX...

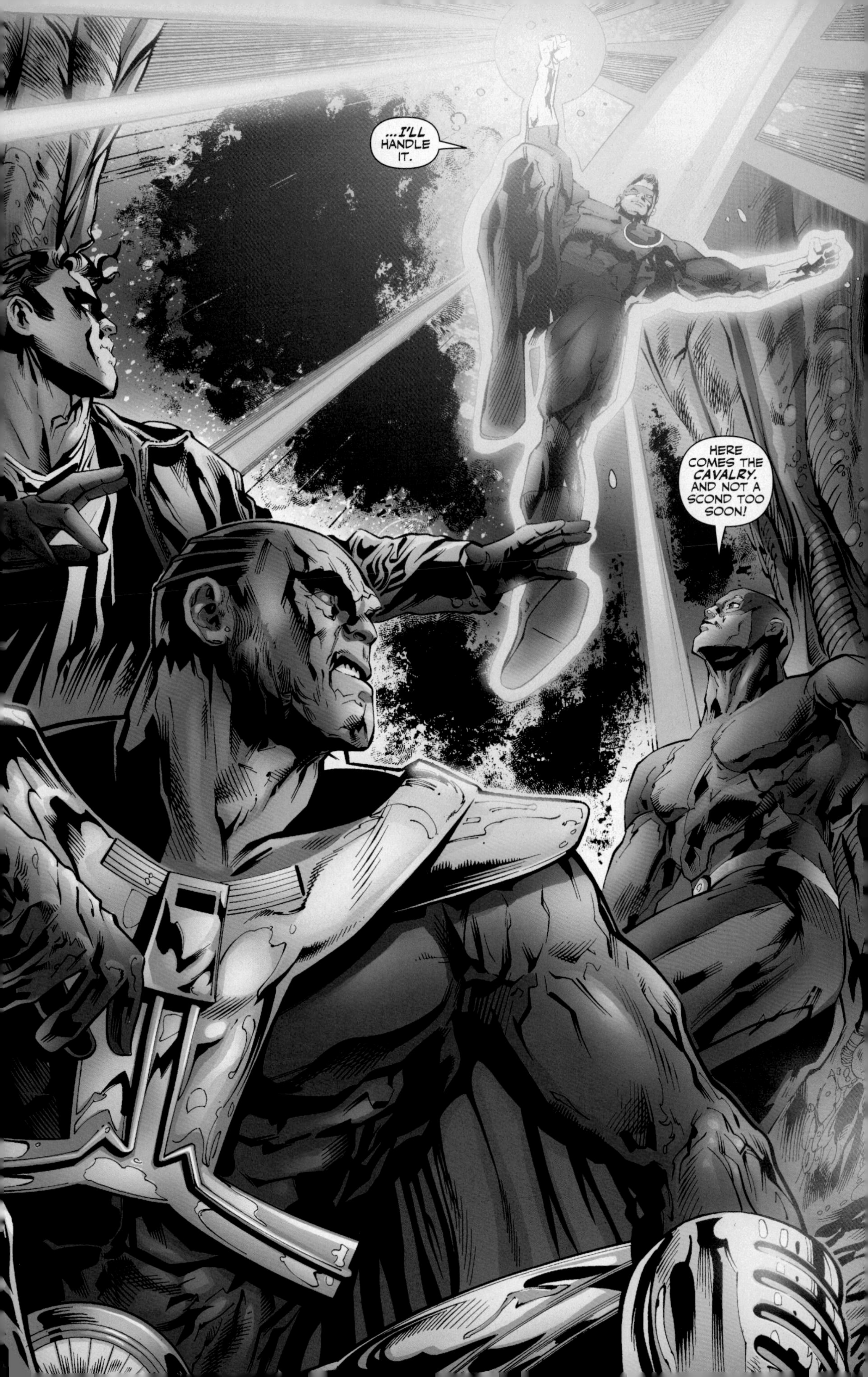
...I'LL HANDLE IT.
HERE COMES THE CAVALRY. AND NOT A SCOND TOO SOON!

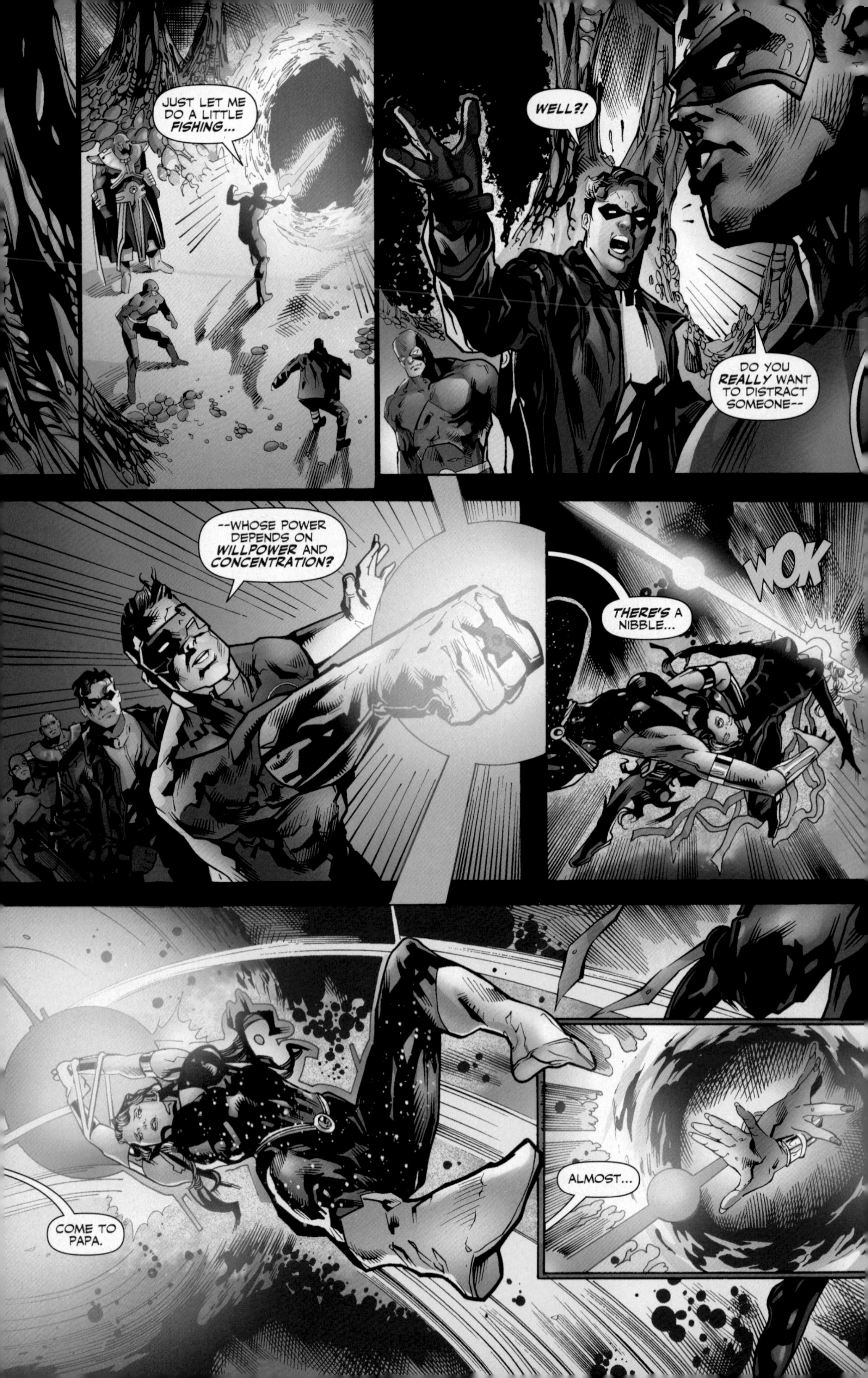
JUST LET ME DO A LITTLE FISHING...
WELL?!
DO YOU REALLY WANT TO DISTRACT SOMEONE--
--WHOSE POWER DEPENDS ON WILLPOWER AND CONCENTRATION?
WOK
THERE'S A NIBBLE...
COME TO PAPA.
ALMOST...

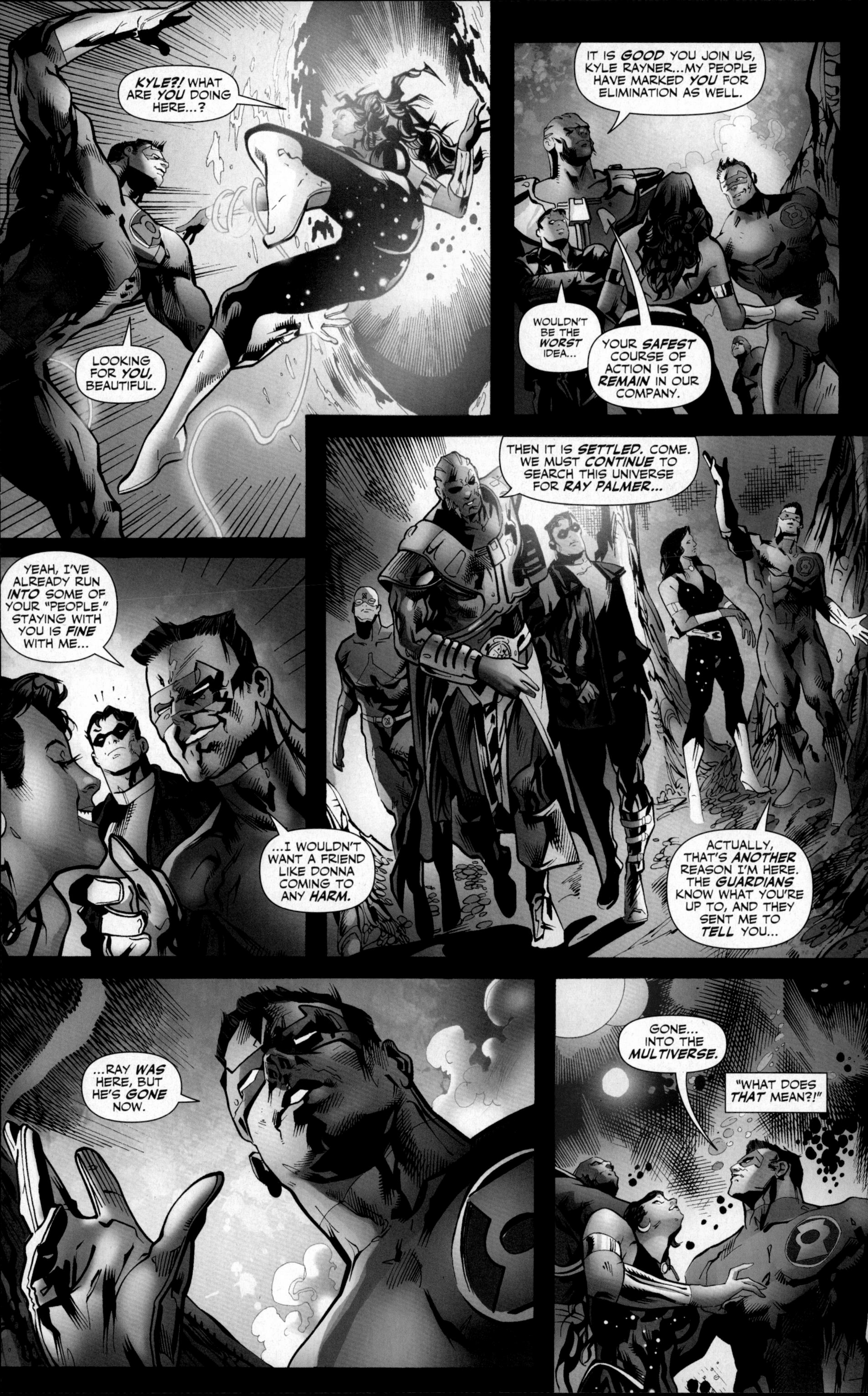
KYLE?! WHAT ARE YOU DOING HERE...?
LOOKING FOR YOU, BEAUTIFUL.
IT IS GOOD YOU JOIN US, KYLE RAYNER...MY PEOPLE HAVE MARKED YOU FOR ELIMINATION AS WELL.
WOULDN'T BE THE WORST IDEA...
YOUR SAFEST COURSE OF ACTION IS TO REMAIN IN OUR COMPANY.
YEAH, I'VE ALREADY RUN INTO SOME OF YOUR "PEOPLE." STAYING WITH YOU IS FINE WITH ME...
...I WOULDN'T WANT A FRIEND LIKE DONNA COMING TO ANY HARM.
THEN IT IS SETTLED. COME. WE MUST CONTINUE TO SEARCH THIS UNIVERSE FOR RAY PALMER...
ACTUALLY, THAT'S ANOTHER REASON I'M HERE. THE GUARDIANS KNOW WHAT YOU'RE UP TO, AND THEY SENT ME TO TELL YOU...
...RAY WAS HERE, BUT HE'S GONE NOW.
GONE... INTO THE MULTIVERSE.
"WHAT DOES THAT MEAN?!"

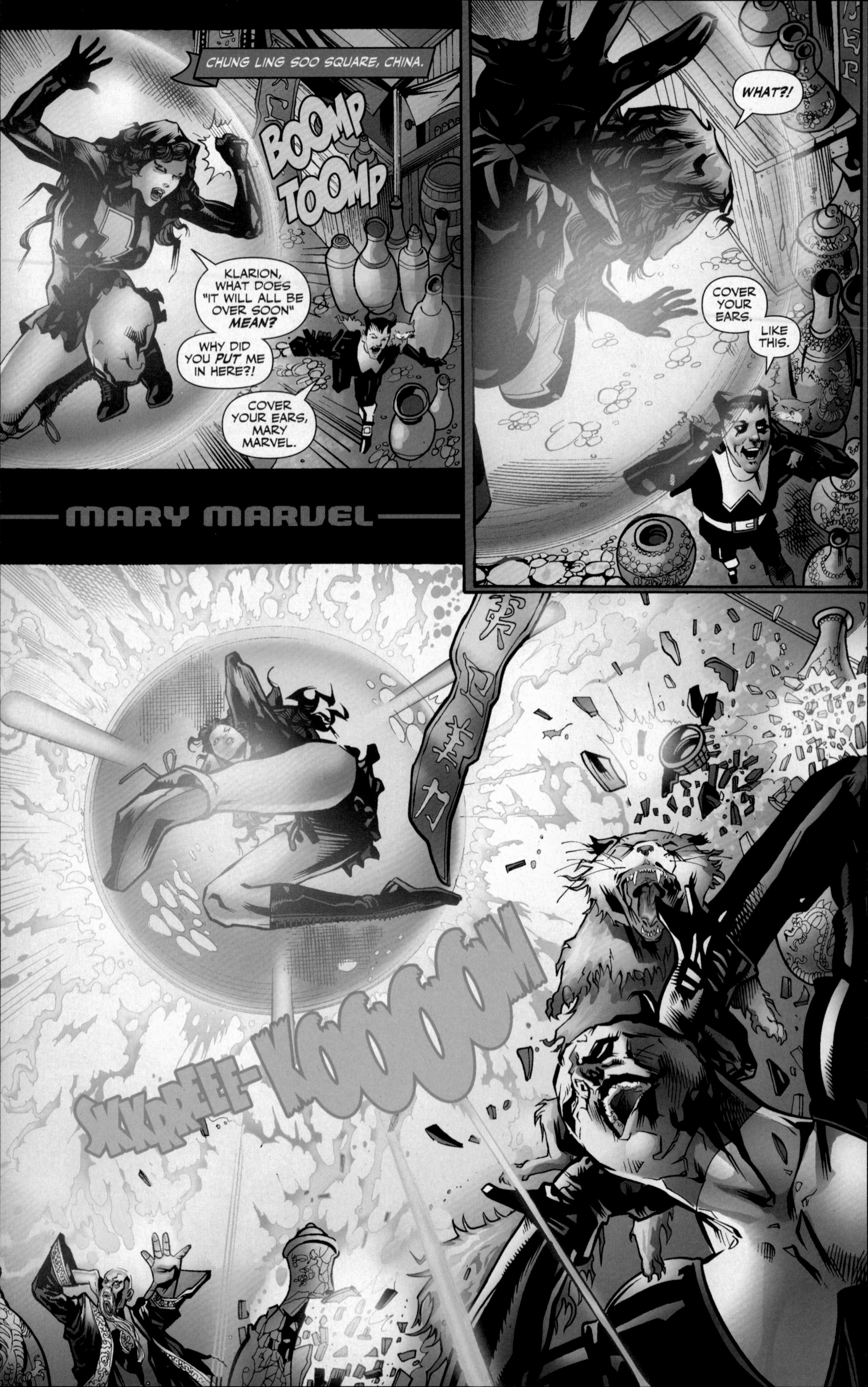
CHUNG LING SOO SQUARE, CHINA.
BOOMP
TOOMP
KLARION, WHAT DOES "IT WILL ALL BE OVER SOON" MEAN?
WHY DID YOU PUT ME IN HERE?!
COVER YOUR EARS, MARY MARVEL.
MARY MARVEL
WHAT?!
COVER YOUR EARS.
LIKE THIS.
SKKREEE-KOOOOOM

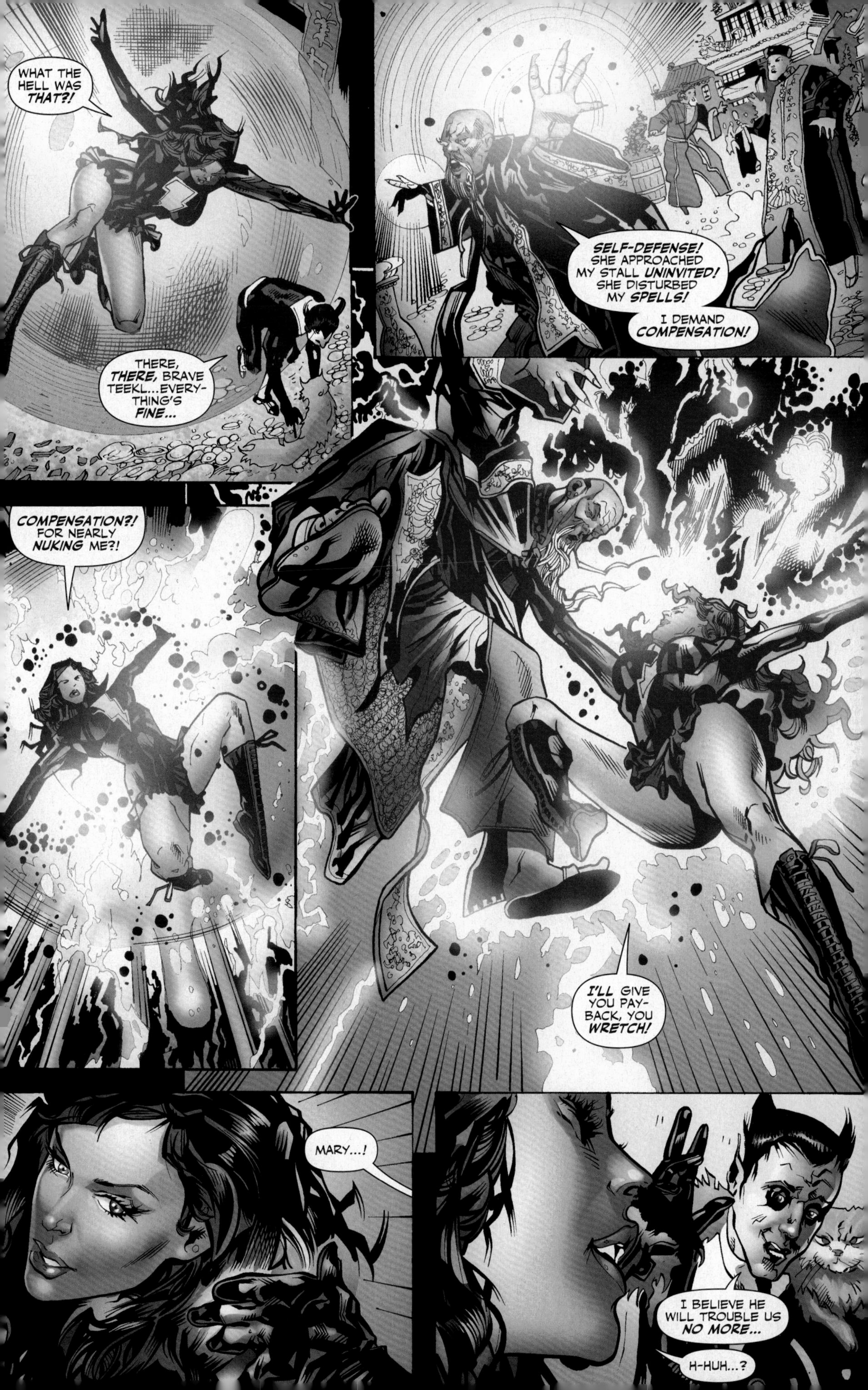
WHAT THE HELL WAS THAT?!
THERE, THERE, BRAVE TEEKL...EVERY-THING'S FINE...
SELF-DEFENSE! SHE APPROACHED MY STALL UNINVITED! SHE DISTURBED MY SPELLS!
I DEMAND COMPENSATION!
COMPENSATION?! FOR NEARLY NUKING ME?!
I'LL GIVE YOU PAY-BACK, YOU WRETCH!
MARY...!
I BELIEVE HE WILL TROUBLE US NO MORE...
H-HUH...?

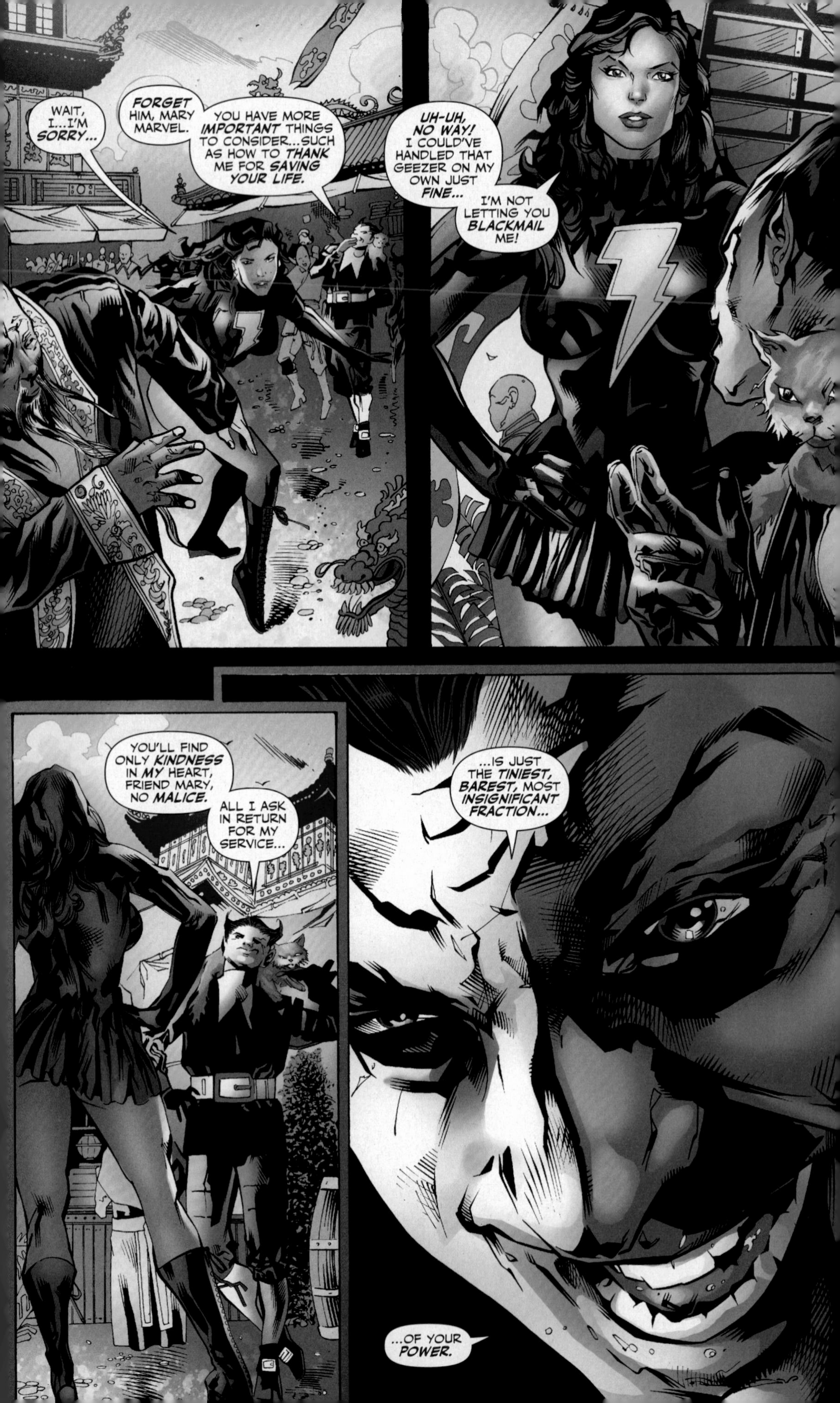
WAIT, I...I'M SORRY...
FORGET HIM, MARY MARVEL.
YOU HAVE MORE IMPORTANT THINGS TO CONSIDER...SUCH AS HOW TO THANK ME FOR SAVING YOUR LIFE.
UH-UH, NO WAY! I COULD'VE HANDLED THAT GEEZER ON MY OWN JUST FINE...
I'M NOT LETTING YOU BLACKMAIL ME!
YOU'LL FIND ONLY KINDNESS IN MY HEART, FRIEND MARY, NO MALICE.
ALL I ASK IN RETURN FOR MY SERVICE...
...IS JUST THE TINIEST, BAREST, MOST INSIGNIFICANT FRACTION...
...OF YOUR POWER.

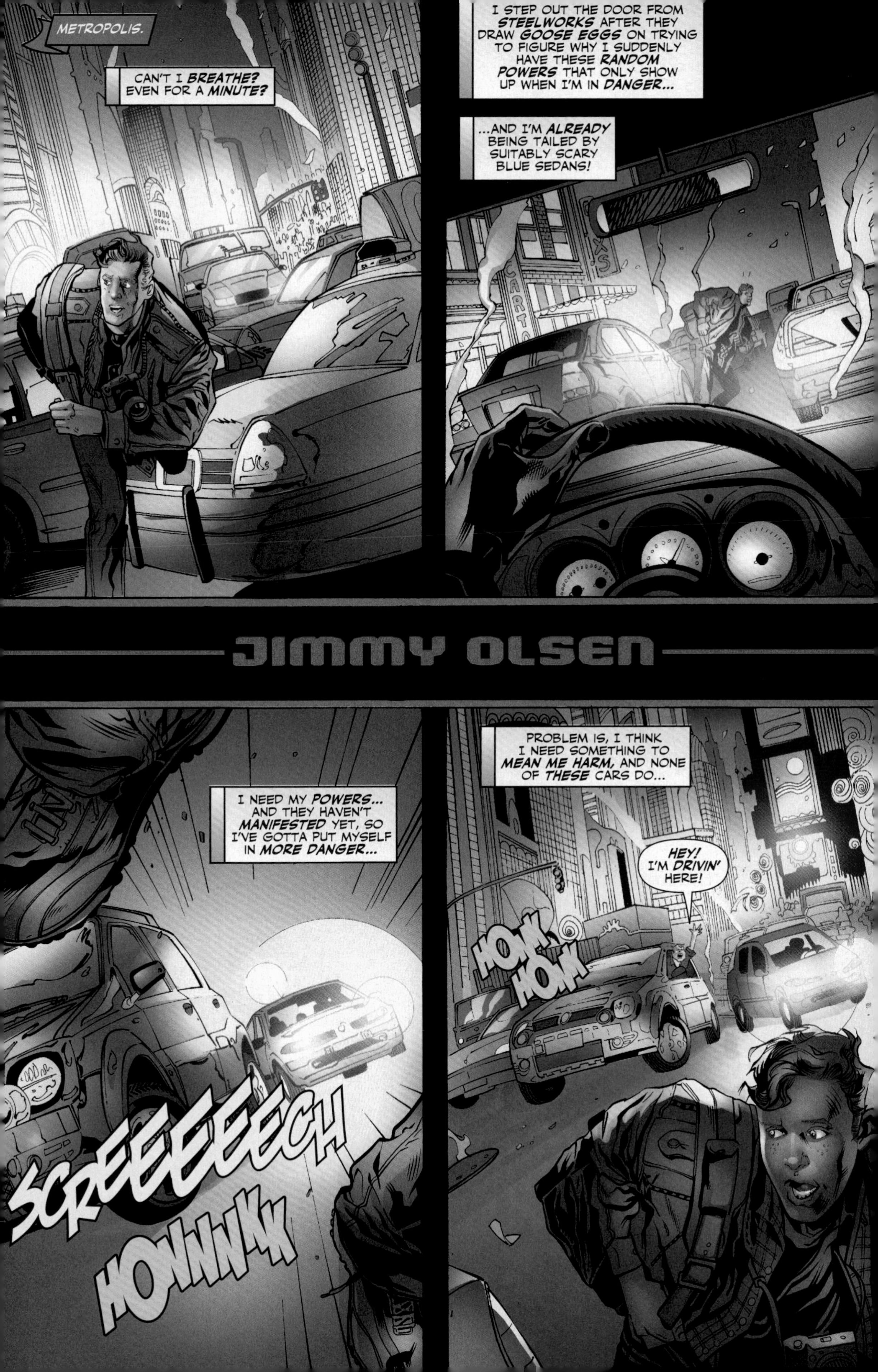

METROPOLIS.
CAN'T I BREATHE? EVEN FOR A MINUTE?
I STEP OUT THE DOOR FROM STEELWORKS AFTER THEY DRAW GOOSE EGGS ON TRYING TO FIGURE WHY I SUDDENLY HAVE THESE RANDOM POWERS THAT ONLY SHOW UP WHEN I'M IN DANGER...
...AND I'M ALREADY BEING TAILED BY SUITABLY SCARY BLUE SEDANS!
JIMMY OLSEN
I NEED MY POWERS... AND THEY HAVEN'T MANIFESTED YET, SO I'VE GOTTA PUT MYSELF IN MORE DANGER...
SCREEEEECH
HONNNKK
PROBLEM IS, I THINK I NEED SOMETHING TO MEAN ME HARM, AND NONE OF THESE CARS DO...
HEY! I'M DRIVIN' HERE!
HONK HONK

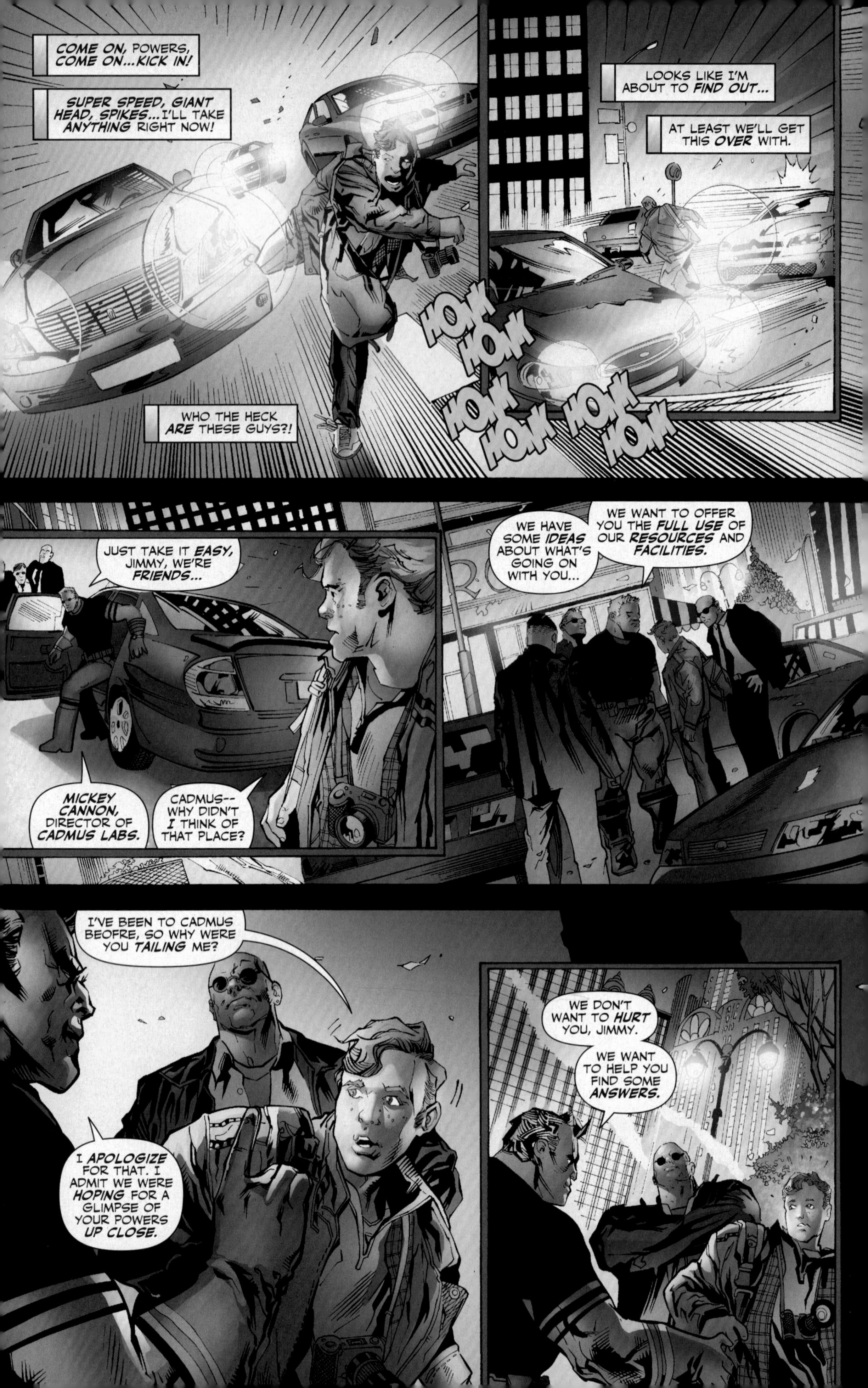
COME ON, POWERS, COME ON...KICK IN!
SUPER SPEED, GIANT HEAD, SPIKES...I'LL TAKE ANYTHING RIGHT NOW!
WHO THE HECK ARE THESE GUYS?!
LOOKS LIKE I'M ABOUT TO FIND OUT...
AT LEAST WE'LL GET THIS OVER WITH.
HONK HONK HONK HONK HONK HONK
JUST TAKE IT EASY, JIMMY, WE'RE FRIENDS...
MICKEY CANNON, DIRECTOR OF CADMUS LABS.
CADMUS-- WHY DIDN'T I THINK OF THAT PLACE?
WE HAVE SOME IDEAS ABOUT WHAT'S GOING ON WITH YOU...
WE WANT TO OFFER YOU THE FULL USE OF OUR RESOURCES AND FACILITIES.
I'VE BEEN TO CADMUS BEOFRE, SO WHY WERE YOU TAILING ME?
I APOLOGIZE FOR THAT. I ADMIT WE WERE HOPING FOR A GLIMPSE OF YOUR POWERS UP CLOSE.
WE DON'T WANT TO HURT YOU, JIMMY.
WE WANT TO HELP YOU FIND SOME ANSWERS.

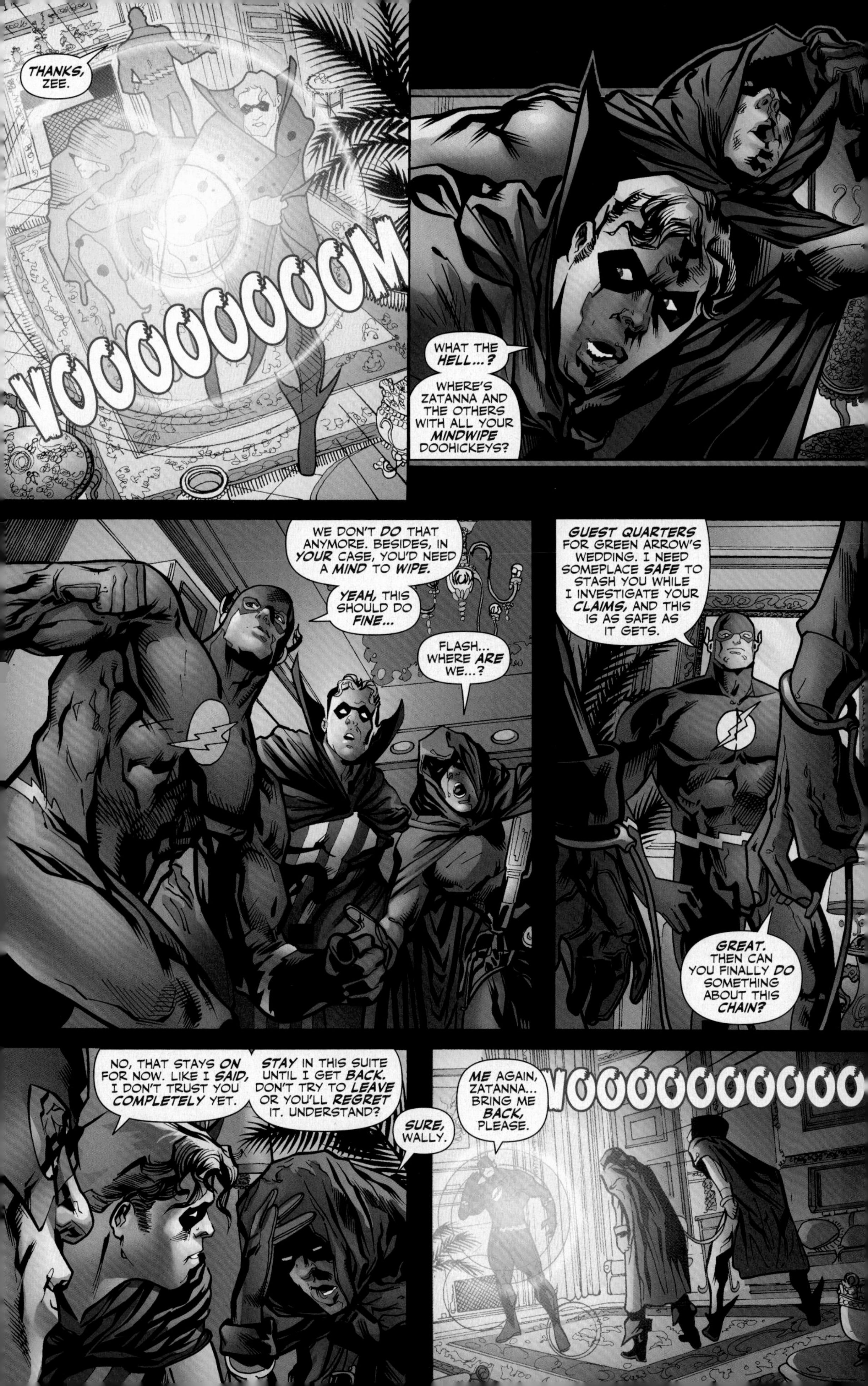
THANKS, ZEE.
VOOOOOOOOM
WHAT THE HELL...?
WHERE'S ZATANNA AND THE OTHERS WITH ALL YOUR MINDWIPE DOOHICKEYS?
WE DON'T DO THAT ANYMORE. BESIDES, IN YOUR CASE, YOU'D NEED A MIND TO WIPE.
YEAH, THIS SHOULD DO FINE...
FLASH... WHERE ARE WE...?
GUEST QUARTERS FOR GREEN ARROW'S WEDDING. I NEED SOMEPLACE SAFE TO STASH YOU WHILE I INVESTIGATE YOUR CLAIMS, AND THIS IS AS SAFE AS IT GETS.
GREAT. THEN CAN YOU FINALLY DO SOMETHING ABOUT THIS CHAIN?
NO, THAT STAYS ON FOR NOW. LIKE I SAID, I DON'T TRUST YOU COMPLETELY YET.
STAY IN THIS SUITE UNTIL I GET BACK. DON'T TRY TO LEAVE OR YOU'LL REGRET IT. UNDERSTAND?
SURE, WALLY.
ME AGAIN, ZATANNA... BRING ME BACK, PLEASE.
VOOOOOOOOOO

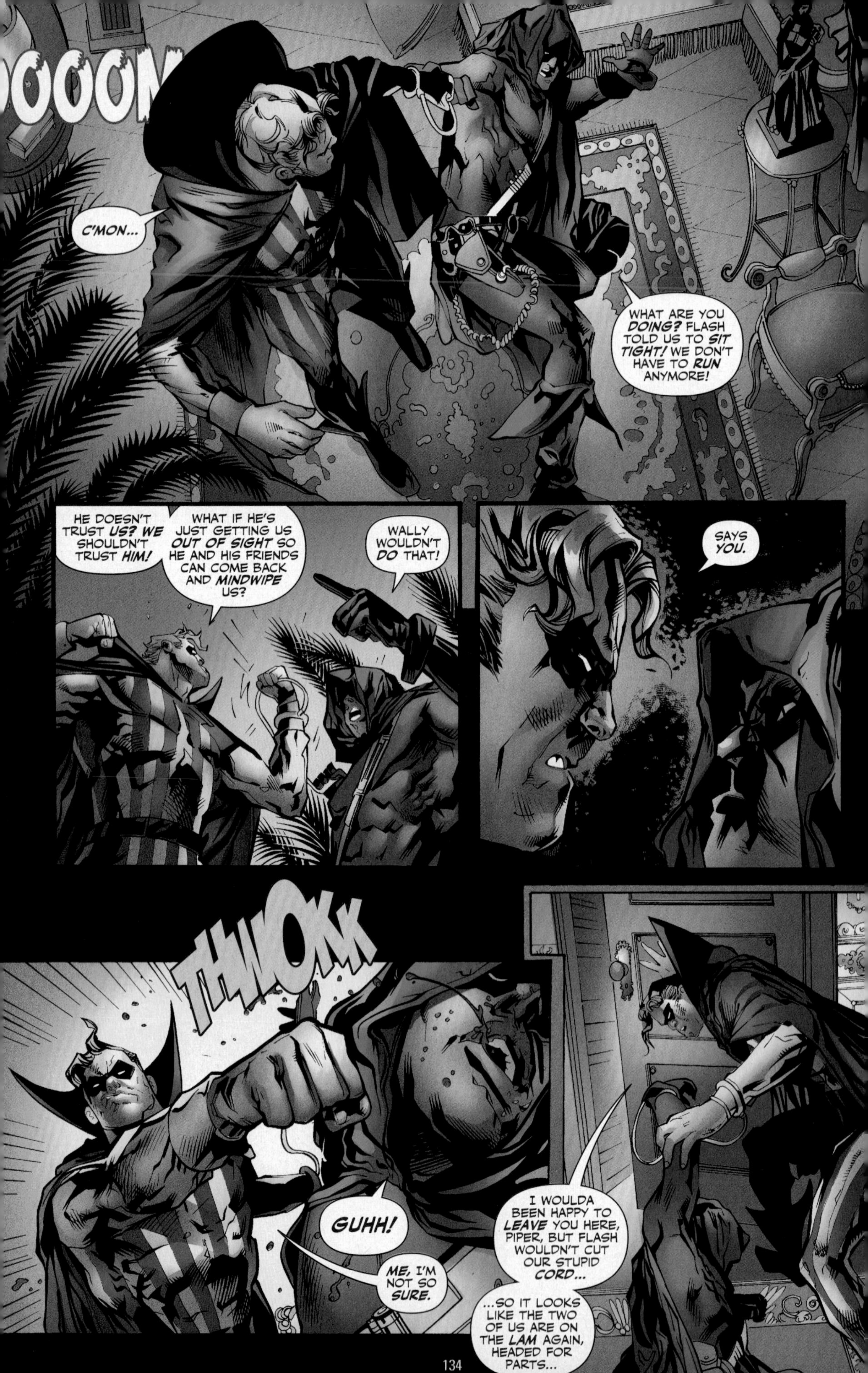

OOOOM
C'MON...
WHAT ARE YOU DOING? FLASH TOLD US TO SIT TIGHT! WE DON'T HAVE TO RUN ANYMORE!
HE DOESN'T TRUST US? WE SHOULDN'T TRUST HIM!
WHAT IF HE'S JUST GETTING US OUT OF SIGHT SO HE AND HIS FRIENDS CAN COME BACK AND MINDWIPE US?
WALLY WOULDN'T DO THAT!
SAYS YOU.
THWOKK
GUHH!
ME, I'M NOT SO SURE.
I WOULDA BEEN HAPPY TO LEAVE YOU HERE, PIPER, BUT FLASH WOULDN'T CUT OUR STUPID CORD...
...SO IT LOOKS LIKE THE TWO OF US ARE ON THE LAM AGAIN, HEADED FOR PARTS...

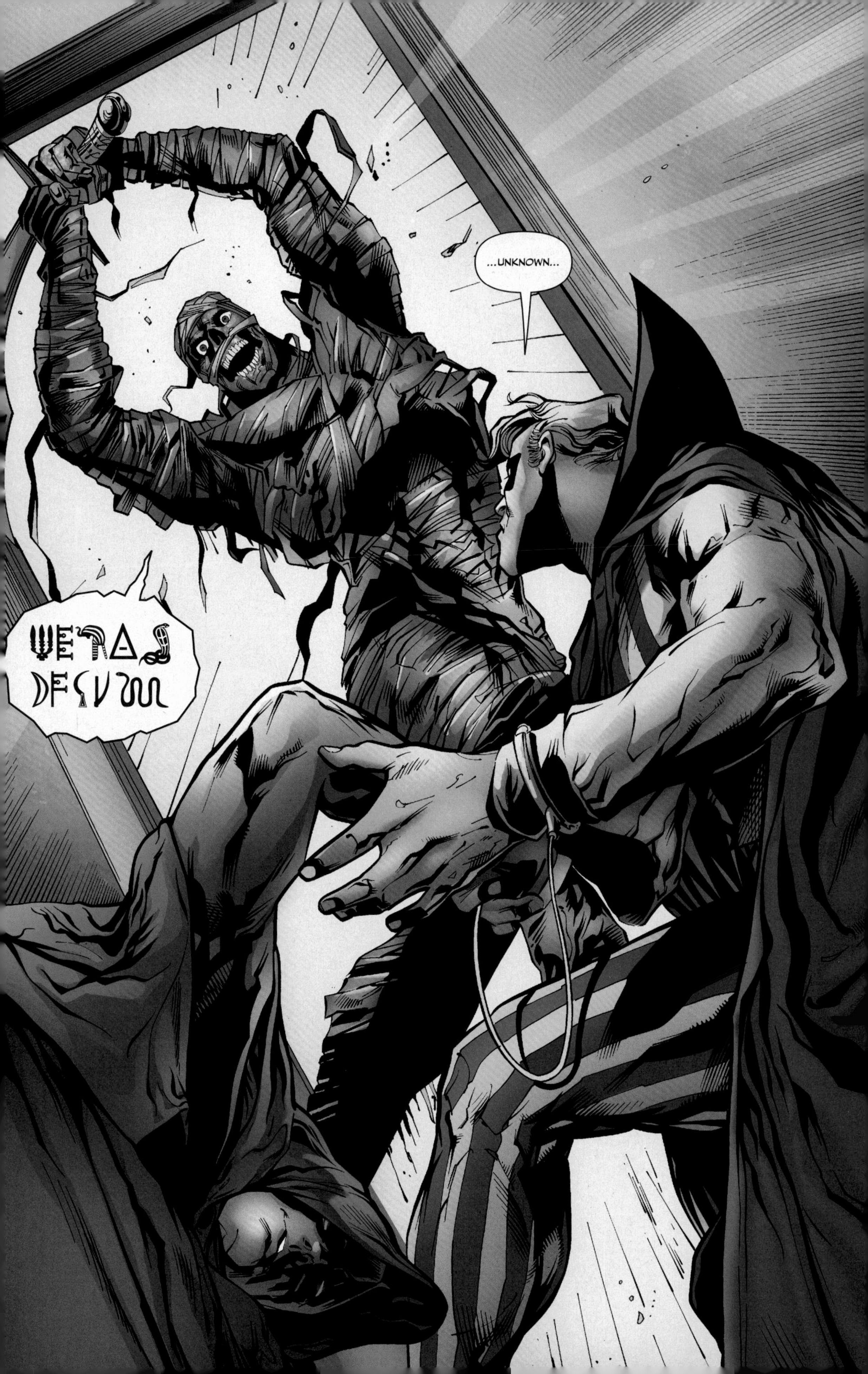
...UNKNOWN...

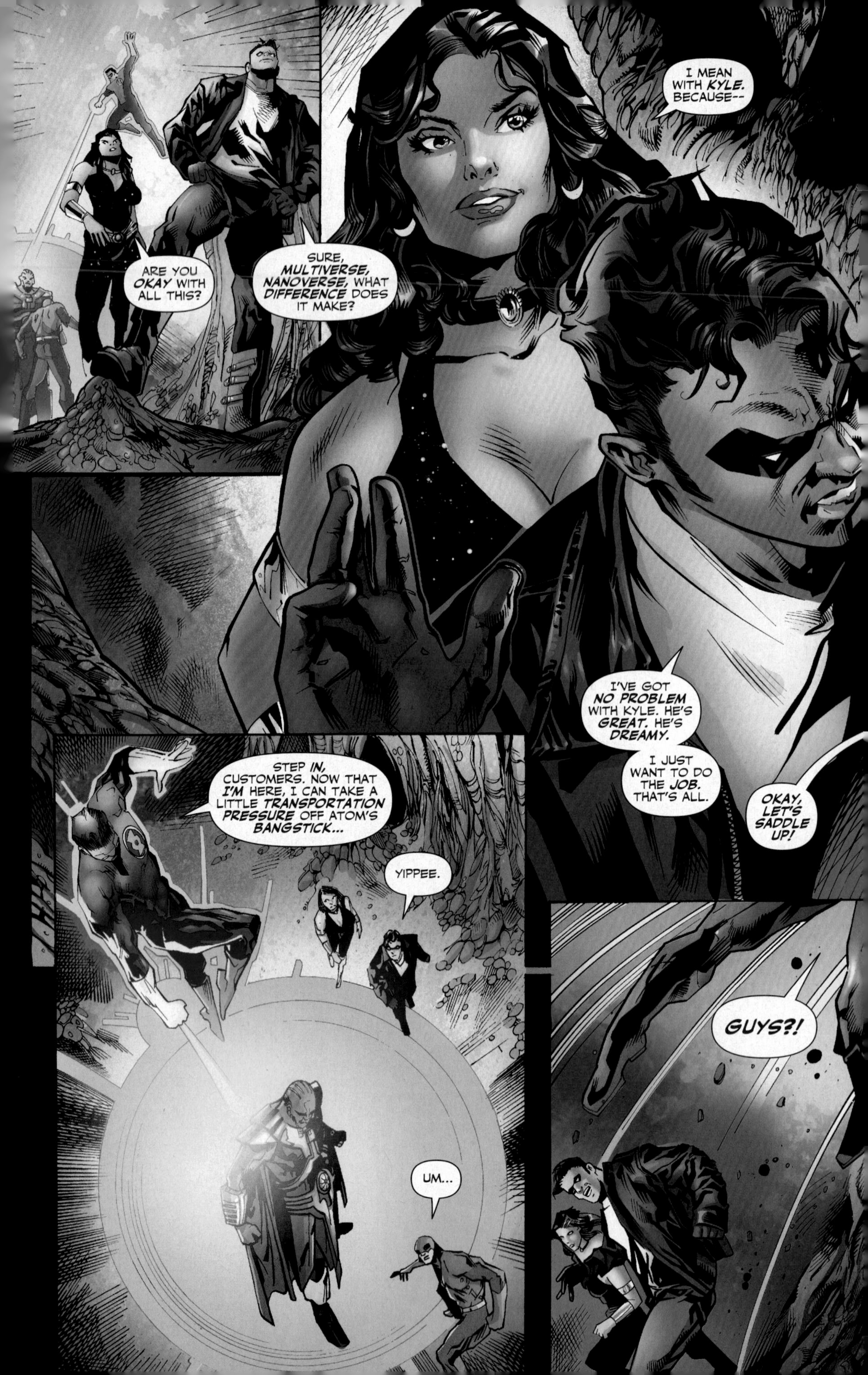
ARE YOU OKAY WITH ALL THIS?
SURE, MULTIVERSE, NANOVERSE, WHAT DIFFERENCE DOES IT MAKE?
I MEAN WITH KYLE. BECAUSE--
I'VE GOT NO PROBLEM WITH KYLE. HE'S GREAT. HE'S DREAMY.
I JUST WANT TO DO THE JOB. THAT'S ALL.
OKAY, LET'S SADDLE UP!
STEP IN, CUSTOMERS. NOW THAT I'M HERE, I CAN TAKE A LITTLE TRANSPORTATION PRESSURE OFF ATOM'S BANGSTICK...
YIPPEE.
UM...
GUYS?!

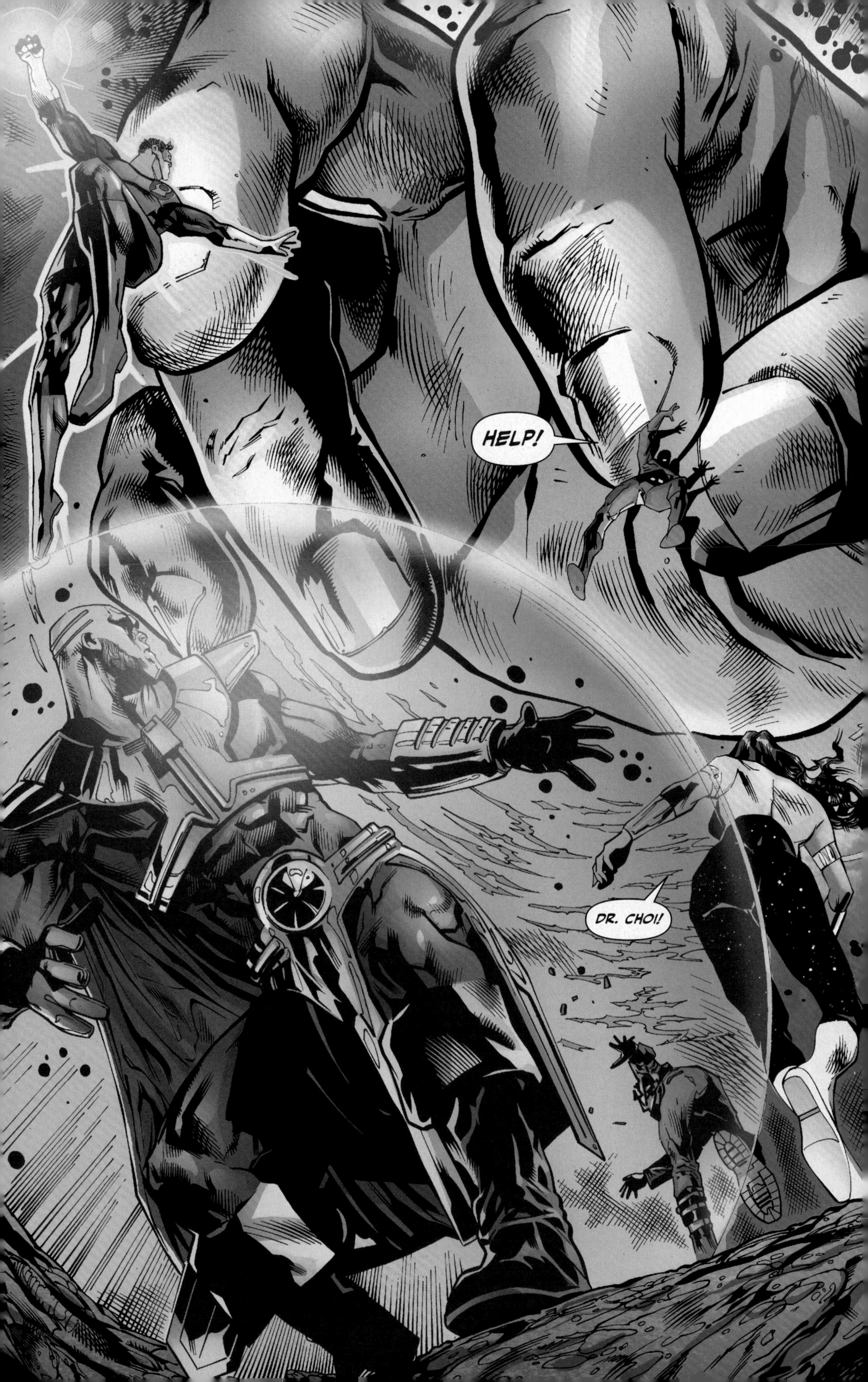
HELP!
DR. CHOI!

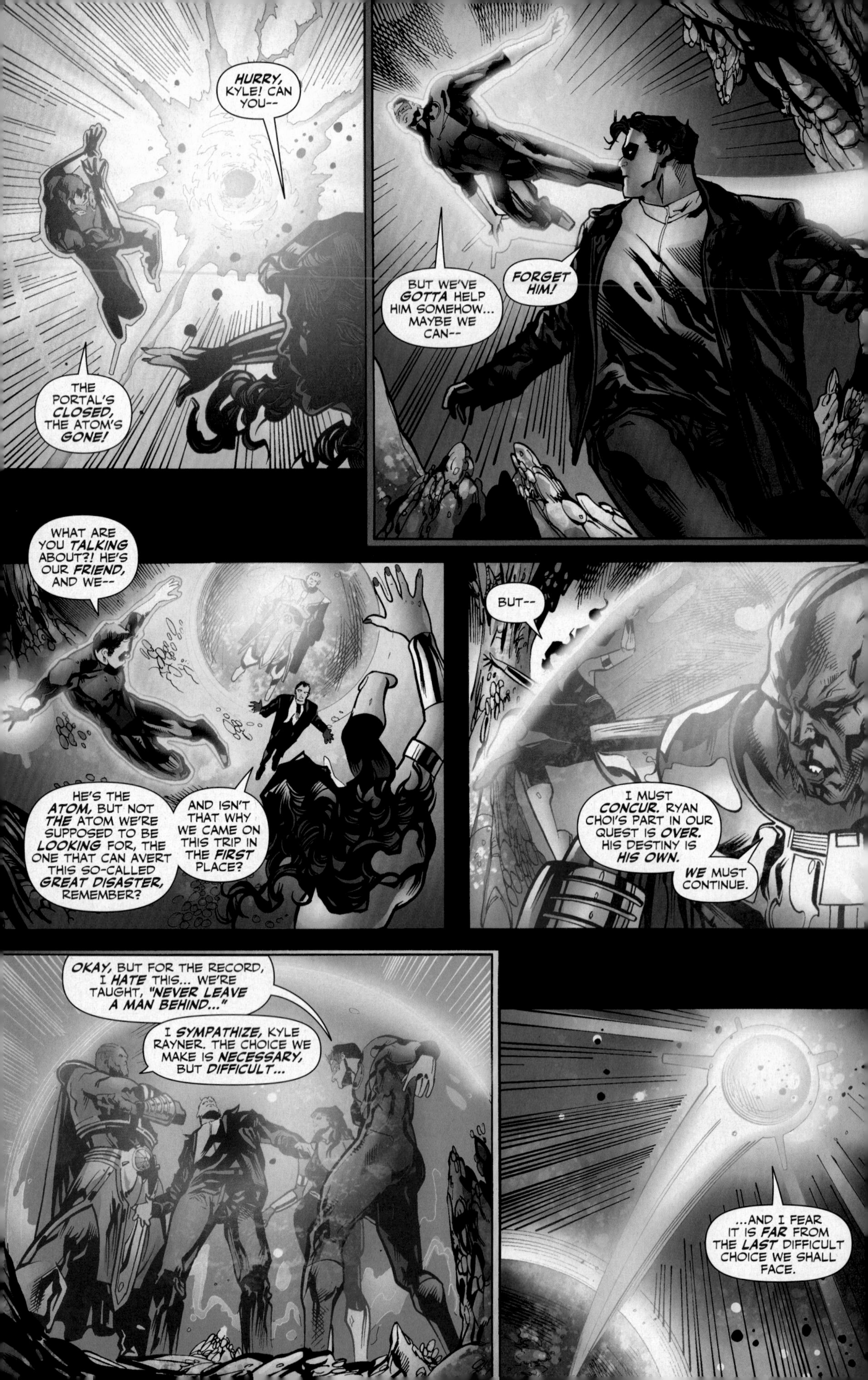
HURRY, KYLE! CAN YOU--
THE PORTAL'S CLOSED, THE ATOM'S GONE!
BUT WE'VE GOTTA HELP HIM SOMEHOW... MAYBE WE CAN--
FORGET HIM!
WHAT ARE YOU TALKING ABOUT?! HE'S OUR FRIEND, AND WE--
HE'S THE ATOM, BUT NOT THE ATOM WE'RE SUPPOSED TO BE LOOKING FOR, THE ONE THAT CAN AVERT THIS SO-CALLED GREAT DISASTER, REMEMBER?
AND ISN'T THAT WHY WE CAME ON THIS TRIP IN THE FIRST PLACE?
BUT--
I MUST CONCUR. RYAN CHOI'S PART IN OUR QUEST IS OVER. HIS DESTINY IS HIS OWN.
WE MUST CONTINUE.
OKAY, BUT FOR THE RECORD, I HATE THIS... WE'RE TAUGHT, "NEVER LEAVE A MAN BEHIND..."
I SYMPATHIZE, KYLE RAYNER. THE CHOICE WE MAKE IS NECESSARY, BUT DIFFICULT...
...AND I FEAR IT IS FAR FROM THE LAST DIFFICULT CHOICE WE SHALL FACE.

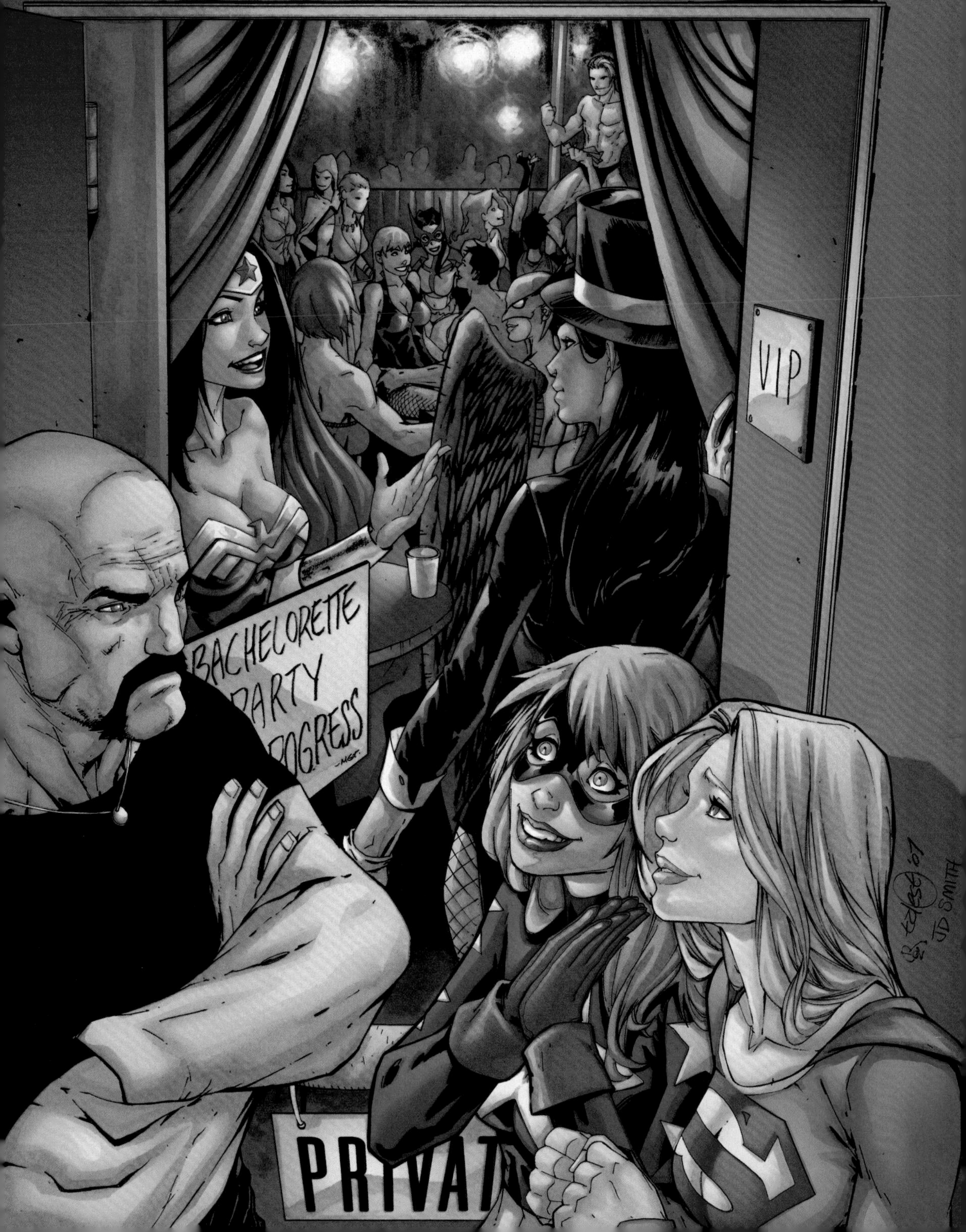
VIP
BACHELORETTE PARTY ...PROGRESS
PRIVAT

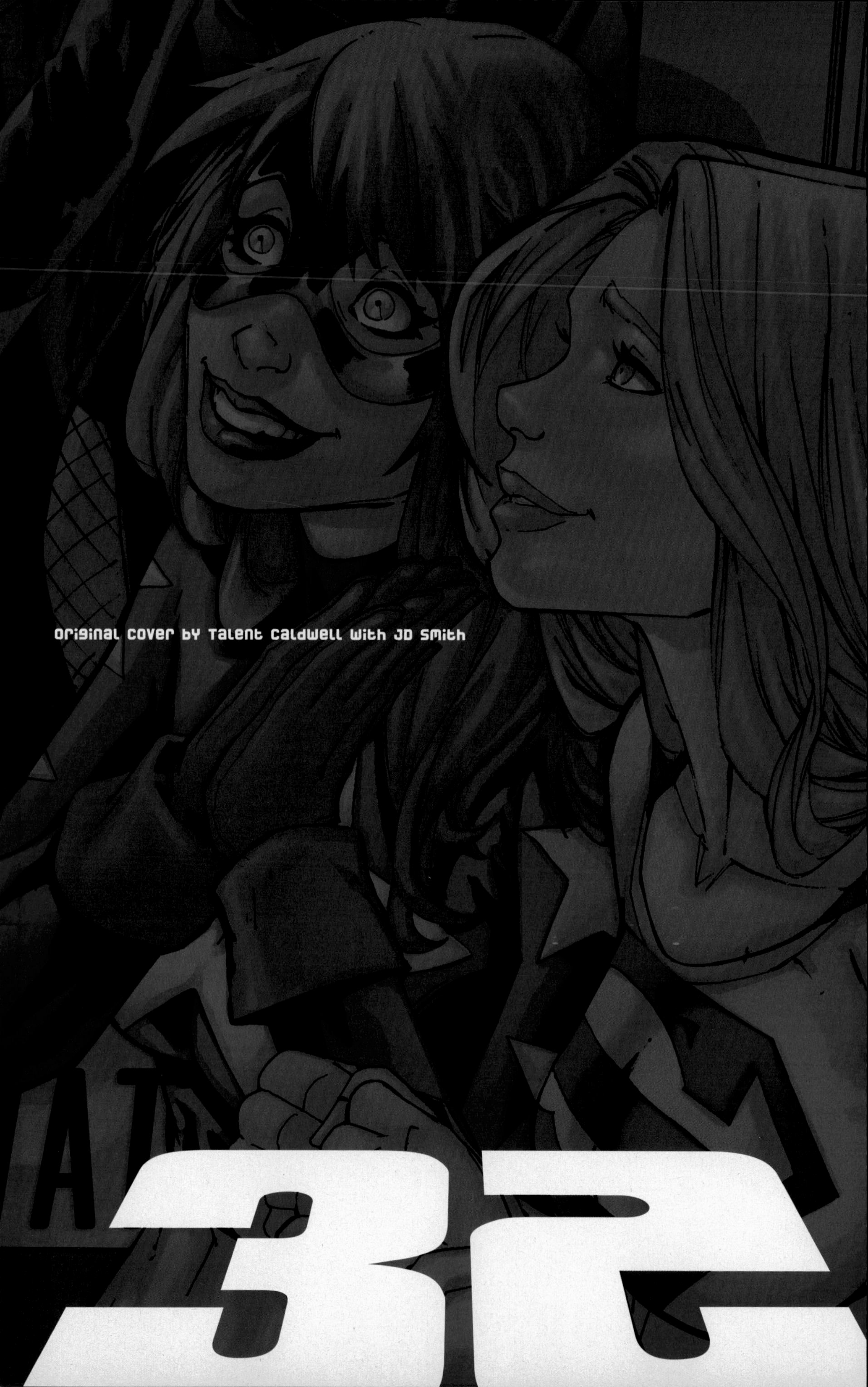
32

Original cover by Talent Caldwell with JD Smith

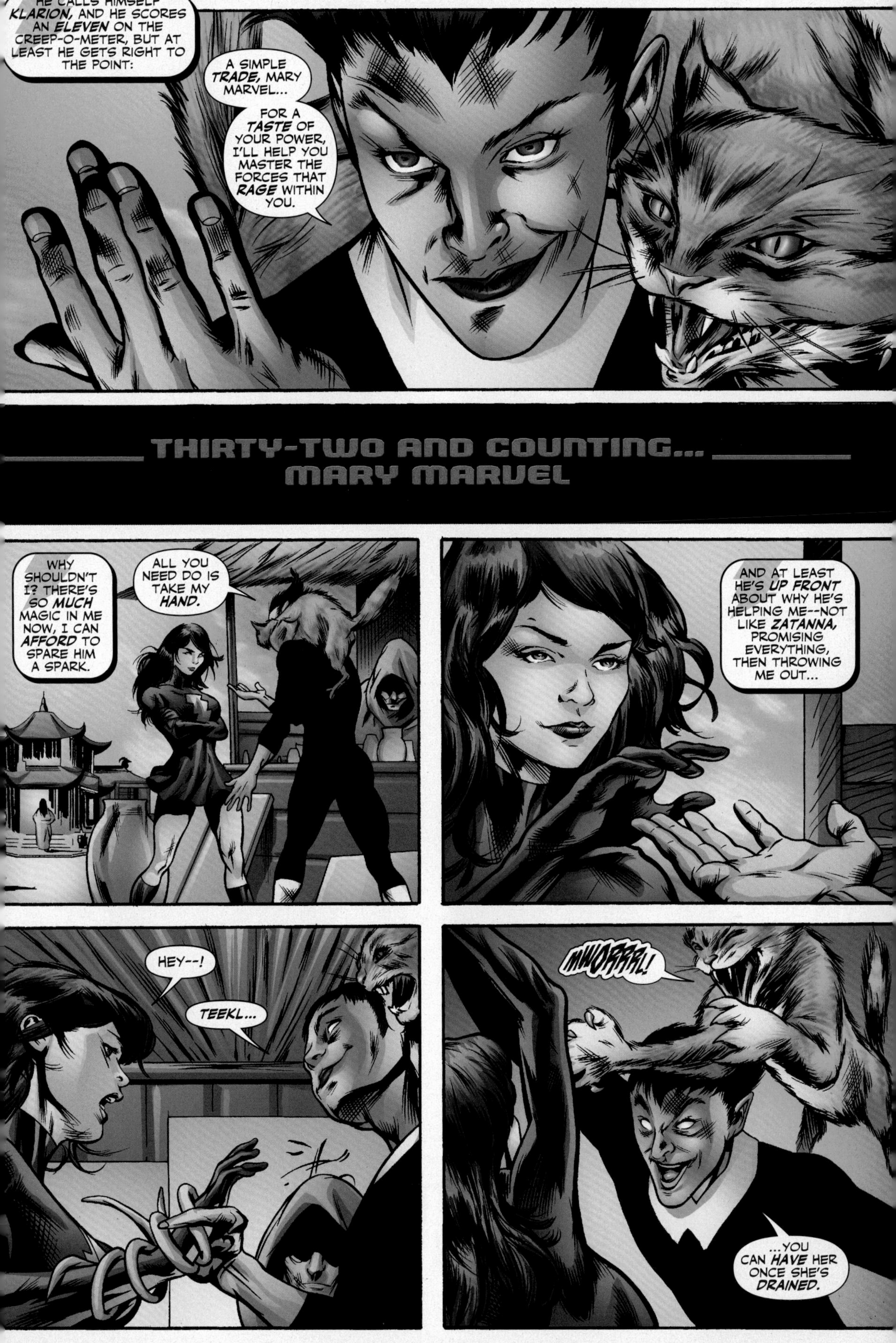
HE CALLS HIMSELF KLARION, AND HE SCORES AN ELEVEN ON THE CREEP-O-METER, BUT AT LEAST HE GETS RIGHT TO THE POINT:
A SIMPLE TRADE, MARY MARVEL...
FOR A TASTE OF YOUR POWER, I'LL HELP YOU MASTER THE FORCES THAT RAGE WITHIN YOU.
THIRTY-TWO AND COUNTING... MARY MARVEL
WHY SHOULDN'T I? THERE'S SO MUCH MAGIC IN ME NOW, I CAN AFFORD TO SPARE HIM A SPARK.
ALL YOU NEED DO IS TAKE MY HAND.
AND AT LEAST HE'S UP FRONT ABOUT WHY HE'S HELPING ME--NOT LIKE ZATANNA, PROMISING EVERYTHING, THEN THROWING ME OUT...
HEY--!
TEEKL...
MWORRRL!
...YOU CAN HAVE HER ONCE SHE'S DRAINED.

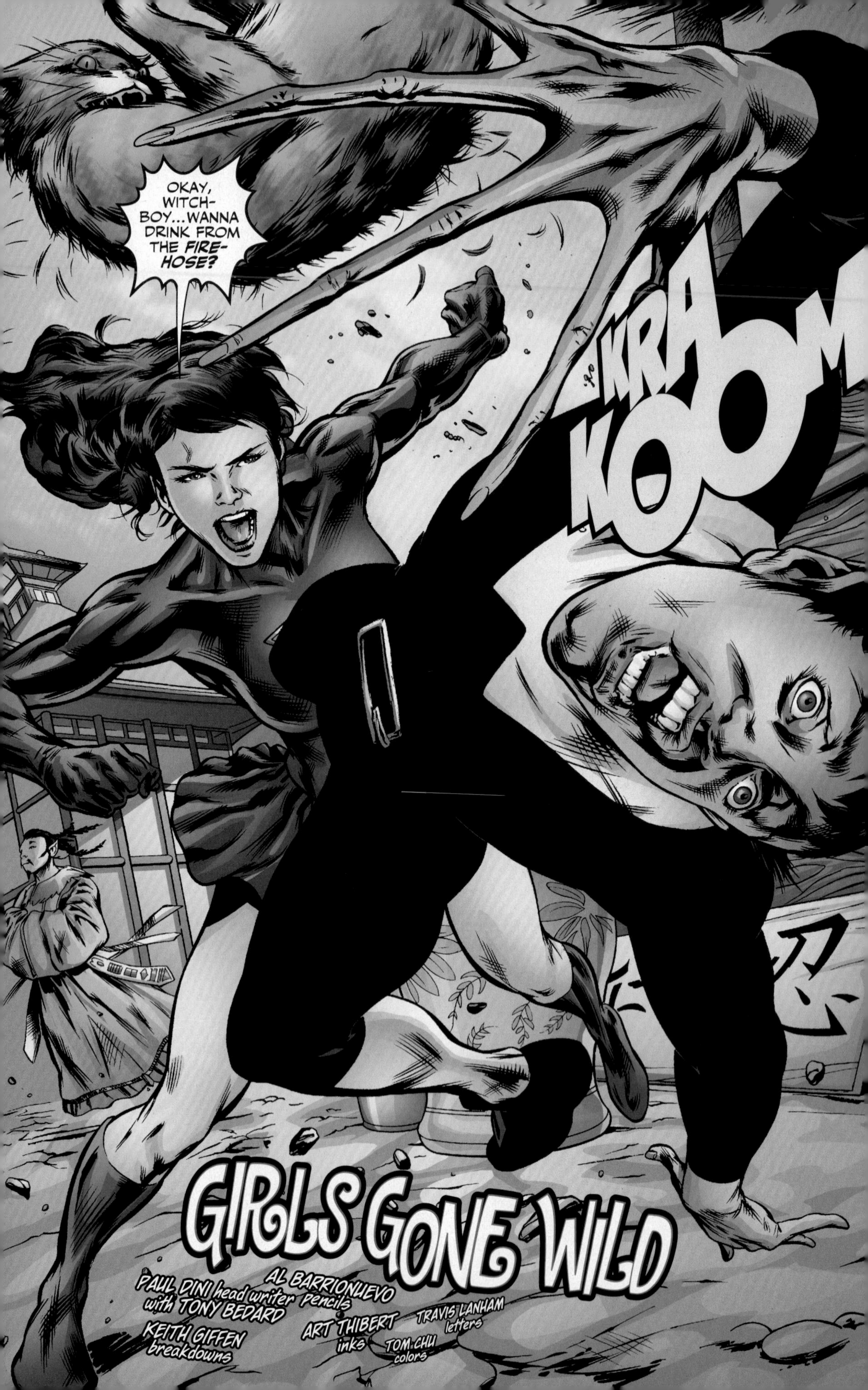

OKAY, WITCH-BOY...WANNA DRINK FROM THE FIRE-HOSE?
KRAKOOM
GIRLS GONE WILD
PAUL DINI head writer
with TONY BEDARD
AL BARRIONUEVO pencils
KEITH GIFFEN breakdowns
ART THIBERT inks
TRAVIS LANHAM letters
TOM CHU colors

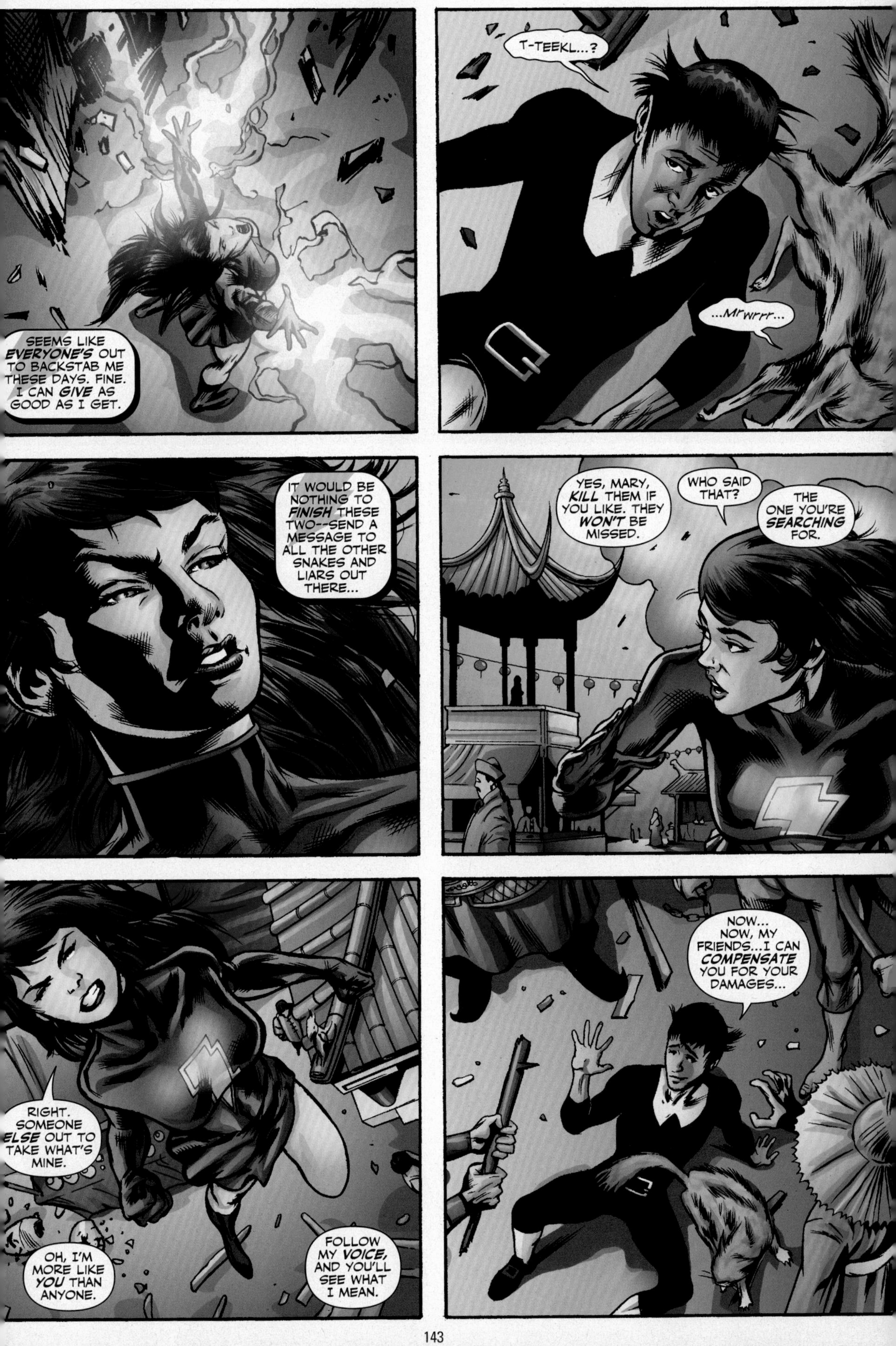
SEEMS LIKE EVERYONE'S OUT TO BACKSTAB ME THESE DAYS. FINE. I CAN GIVE AS GOOD AS I GET.
T-TEEKL...?
...Mrwrrr...
IT WOULD BE NOTHING TO FINISH THESE TWO--SEND A MESSAGE TO ALL THE OTHER SNAKES AND LIARS OUT THERE...
YES, MARY, KILL THEM IF YOU LIKE. THEY WON'T BE MISSED.
WHO SAID THAT?
THE ONE YOU'RE SEARCHING FOR.
RIGHT. SOMEONE ELSE OUT TO TAKE WHAT'S MINE.
OH, I'M MORE LIKE YOU THAN ANYONE.
FOLLOW MY VOICE, AND YOU'LL SEE WHAT I MEAN.
NOW... NOW, MY FRIENDS...I CAN COMPENSATE YOU FOR YOUR DAMAGES...

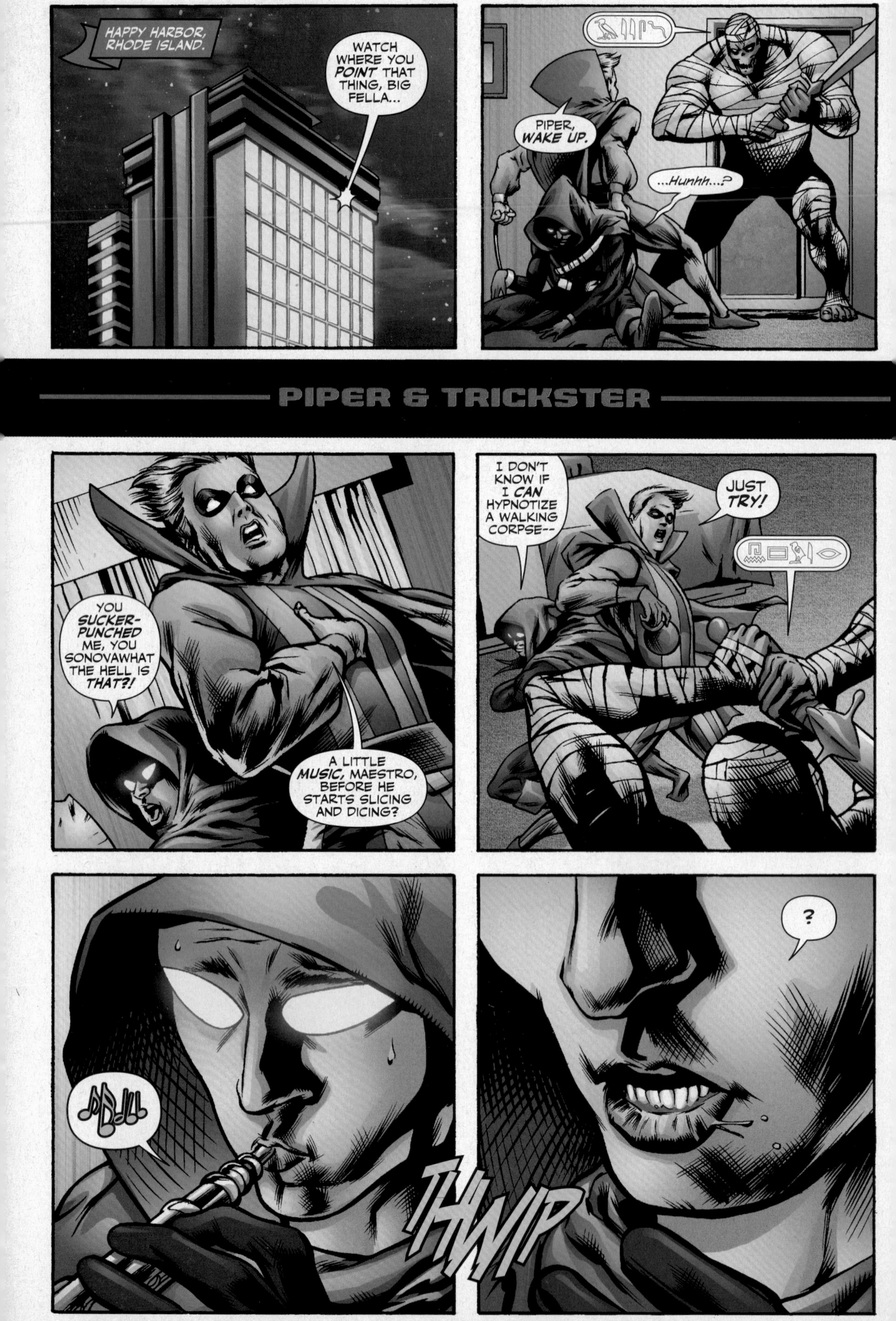
HAPPY HARBOR, RHODE ISLAND.
WATCH WHERE YOU POINT THAT THING, BIG FELLA...
PIPER, WAKE UP.
...Hunhh...?
PIPER & TRICKSTER
YOU SUCKER-PUNCHED ME, YOU SONOVAWHAT THE HELL IS THAT?!
A LITTLE MUSIC, MAESTRO, BEFORE HE STARTS SLICING AND DICING?
I DON'T KNOW IF I CAN HYPNOTIZE A WALKING CORPSE--
JUST TRY!
?
THWIP

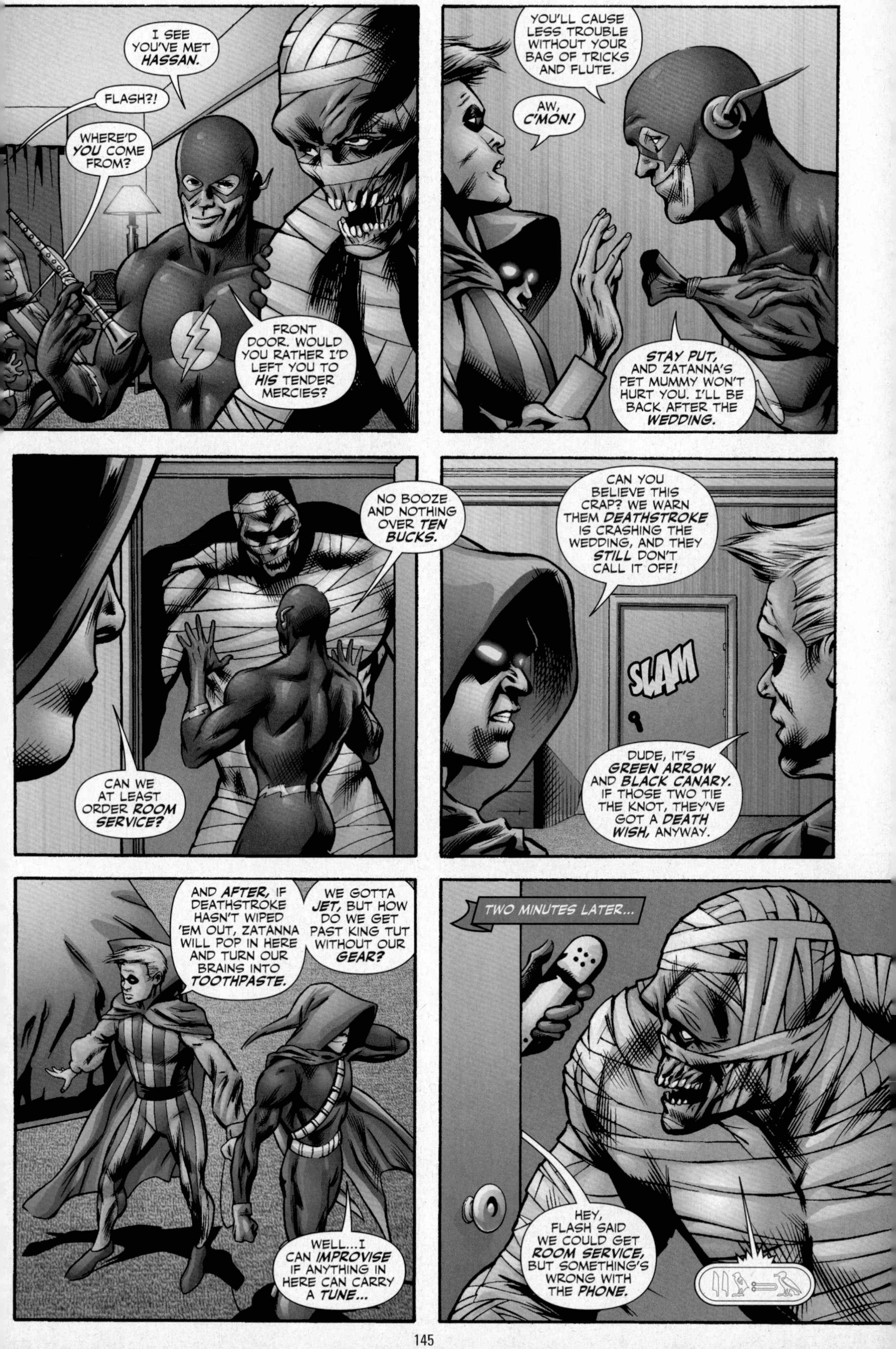
I SEE YOU'VE MET HASSAN.
FLASH?!
WHERE'D YOU COME FROM?
FRONT DOOR. WOULD YOU RATHER I'D LEFT YOU TO HIS TENDER MERCIES?
YOU'LL CAUSE LESS TROUBLE WITHOUT YOUR BAG OF TRICKS AND FLUTE.
AW, C'MON!
STAY PUT, AND ZATANNA'S PET MUMMY WON'T HURT YOU. I'LL BE BACK AFTER THE WEDDING.
NO BOOZE AND NOTHING OVER TEN BUCKS.
CAN WE AT LEAST ORDER ROOM SERVICE?
CAN YOU BELIEVE THIS CRAP? WE WARN THEM DEATHSTROKE IS CRASHING THE WEDDING, AND THEY STILL DON'T CALL IT OFF!
SLAM
DUDE, IT'S GREEN ARROW AND BLACK CANARY. IF THOSE TWO TIE THE KNOT, THEY'VE GOT A DEATH WISH, ANYWAY.
AND AFTER, IF DEATHSTROKE HASN'T WIPED 'EM OUT, ZATANNA WILL POP IN HERE AND TURN OUR BRAINS INTO TOOTHPASTE.
WE GOTTA JET, BUT HOW DO WE GET PAST KING TUT WITHOUT OUR GEAR?
WELL...I CAN IMPROVISE IF ANYTHING IN HERE CAN CARRY A TUNE...
TWO MINUTES LATER...
HEY, FLASH SAID WE COULD GET ROOM SERVICE, BUT SOMETHING'S WRONG WITH THE PHONE.

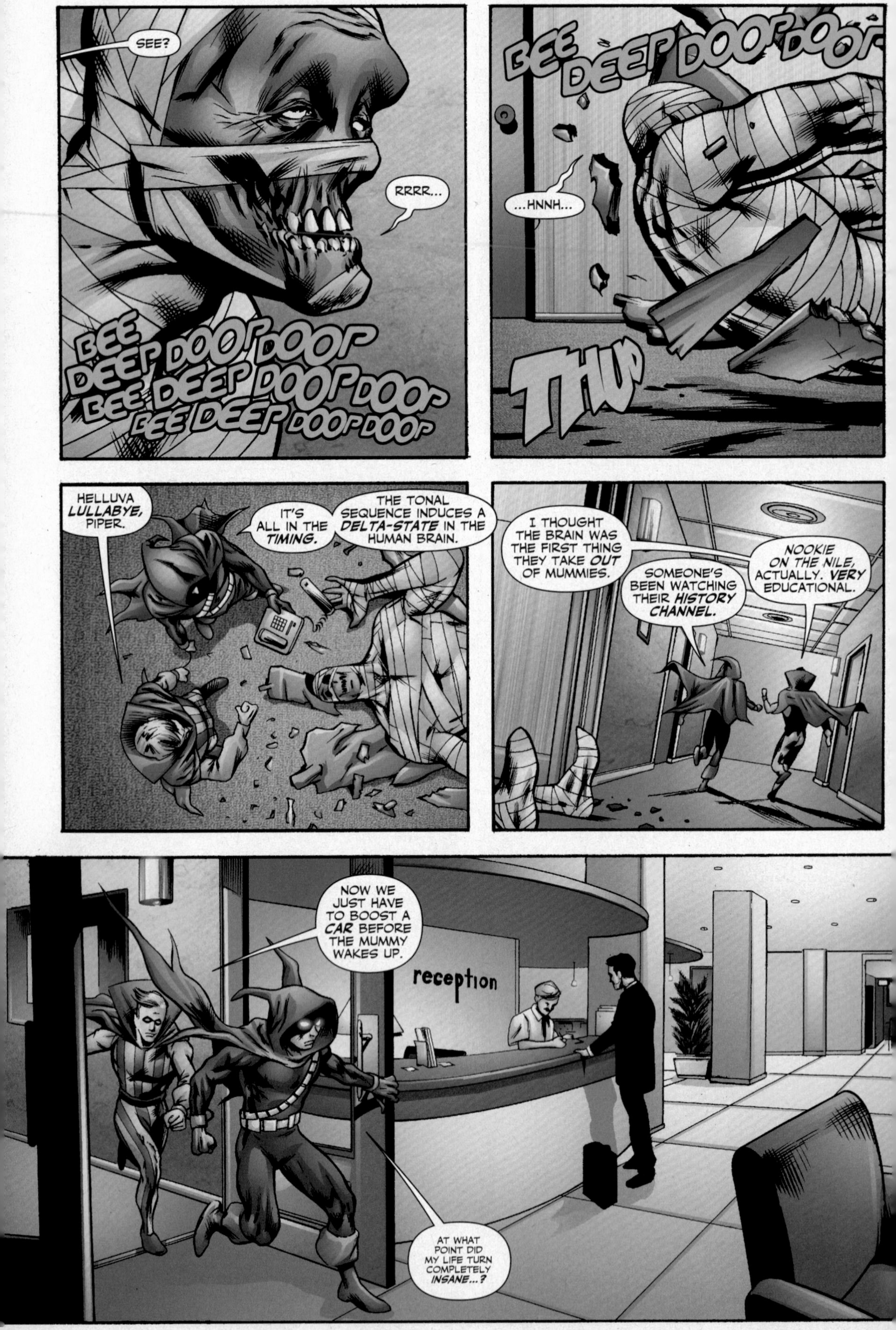

SEE?
RRRR...
BEE DEEP DOOP DOOP BEE DEEP DOOP DOOP BEE DEEP DOOP DOOP
BEE DEEP DOOP DOOP
...HNNH...
THUD
HELLUVA *LULLABYE,* PIPER.
IT'S ALL IN THE *TIMING.*
THE TONAL SEQUENCE INDUCES A *DELTA-STATE* IN THE HUMAN BRAIN.
I THOUGHT THE BRAIN WAS THE FIRST THING THEY TAKE *OUT* OF MUMMIES.
SOMEONE'S BEEN WATCHING THEIR *HISTORY CHANNEL.*
*NOOKIE ON THE NILE,* ACTUALLY. *VERY* EDUCATIONAL.
NOW WE JUST HAVE TO BOOST A *CAR* BEFORE THE MUMMY WAKES UP.
reception
AT WHAT POINT DID MY LIFE TURN COMPLETELY *INSANE...?*

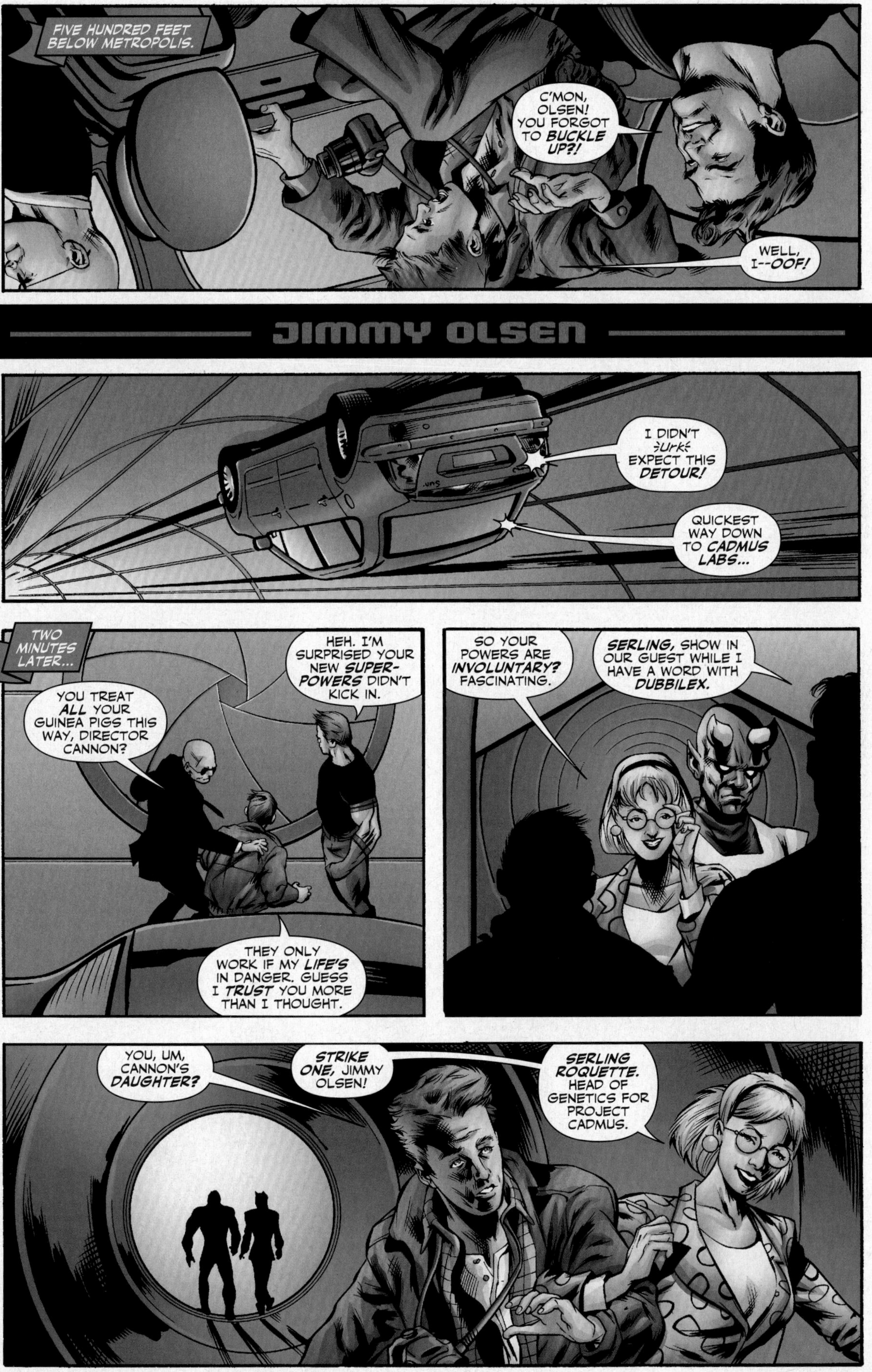
FIVE HUNDRED FEET BELOW METROPOLIS.
C'MON, OLSEN! YOU FORGOT TO BUCKLE UP?!
WELL, I--OOF!
JIMMY OLSEN
I DIDN'T *URK* EXPECT THIS DETOUR!
QUICKEST WAY DOWN TO CADMUS LABS...
TWO MINUTES LATER...
HEH. I'M SURPRISED YOUR NEW SUPER-POWERS DIDN'T KICK IN.
YOU TREAT ALL YOUR GUINEA PIGS THIS WAY, DIRECTOR CANNON?
THEY ONLY WORK IF MY LIFE'S IN DANGER. GUESS I TRUST YOU MORE THAN I THOUGHT.
SO YOUR POWERS ARE INVOLUNTARY? FASCINATING.
SERLING, SHOW IN OUR GUEST WHILE I HAVE A WORD WITH DUBBILEX.
YOU, UM, CANNON'S DAUGHTER?
STRIKE ONE, JIMMY OLSEN!
SERLING ROQUETTE. HEAD OF GENETICS FOR PROJECT CADMUS.

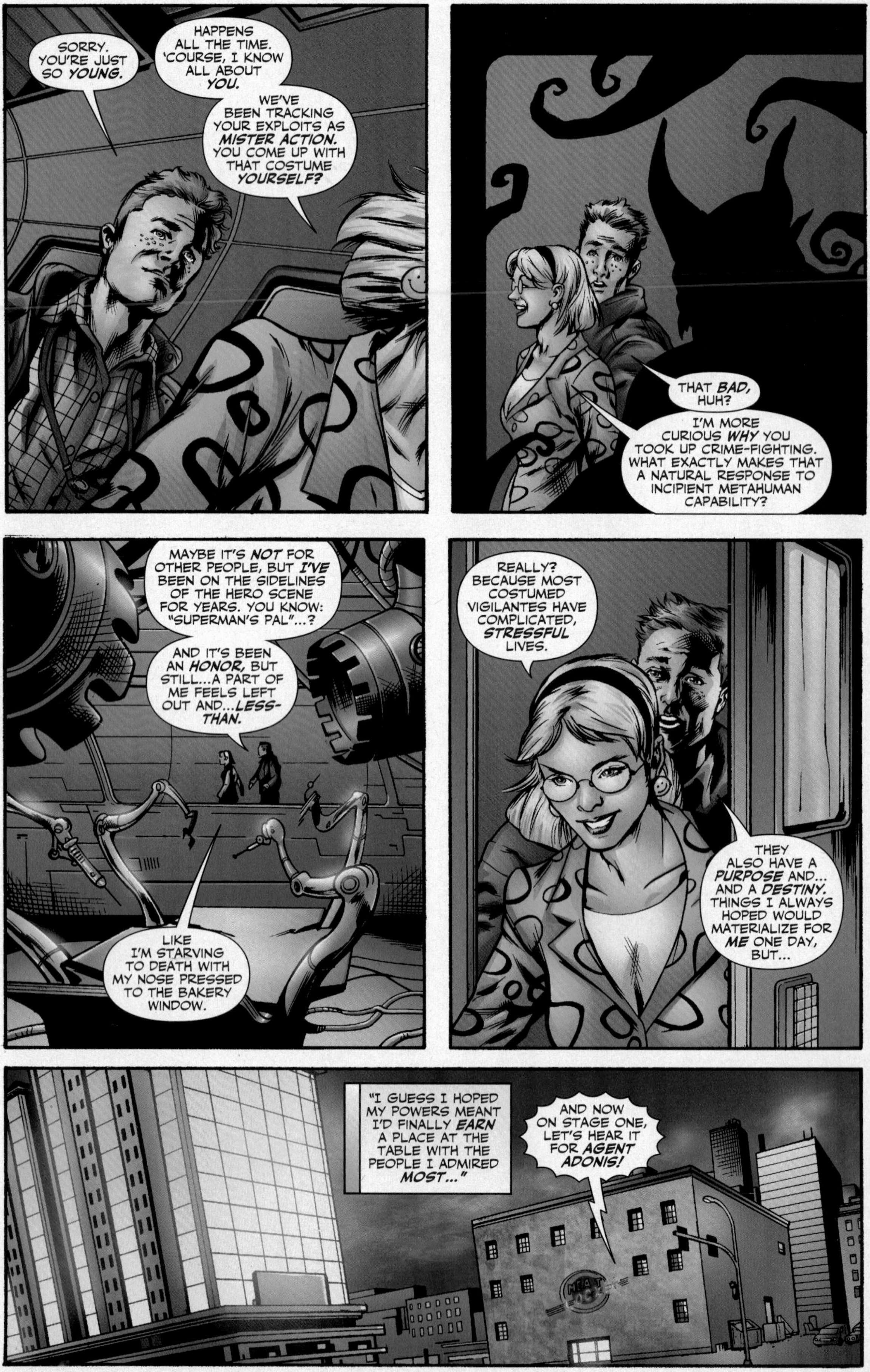
SORRY. YOU'RE JUST SO *YOUNG.*
HAPPENS ALL THE TIME. 'COURSE, I KNOW ALL ABOUT *YOU.*
WE'VE BEEN TRACKING YOUR EXPLOITS AS *MISTER ACTION.* YOU COME UP WITH THAT COSTUME *YOURSELF?*
THAT *BAD,* HUH?
I'M MORE CURIOUS *WHY* YOU TOOK UP CRIME-FIGHTING. WHAT EXACTLY MAKES THAT A NATURAL RESPONSE TO INCIPIENT METAHUMAN CAPABILITY?
MAYBE IT'S *NOT* FOR OTHER PEOPLE, BUT *I'VE* BEEN ON THE SIDELINES OF THE HERO SCENE FOR YEARS. YOU KNOW: "SUPERMAN'S PAL"...?
AND IT'S BEEN AN *HONOR,* BUT STILL...A PART OF ME FEELS LEFT OUT AND...*LESS-THAN.*
LIKE I'M STARVING TO DEATH WITH MY NOSE PRESSED TO THE BAKERY WINDOW.
REALLY? BECAUSE MOST COSTUMED VIGILANTES HAVE COMPLICATED, *STRESSFUL* LIVES.
THEY ALSO HAVE A *PURPOSE* AND... AND A *DESTINY.* THINGS I ALWAYS HOPED WOULD MATERIALIZE FOR *ME* ONE DAY, BUT...
"I GUESS I HOPED MY POWERS MEANT I'D FINALLY *EARN* A PLACE AT THE TABLE WITH THE PEOPLE I ADMIRED *MOST...*"
AND NOW ON STAGE ONE, LET'S HEAR IT FOR *AGENT ADONIS!*

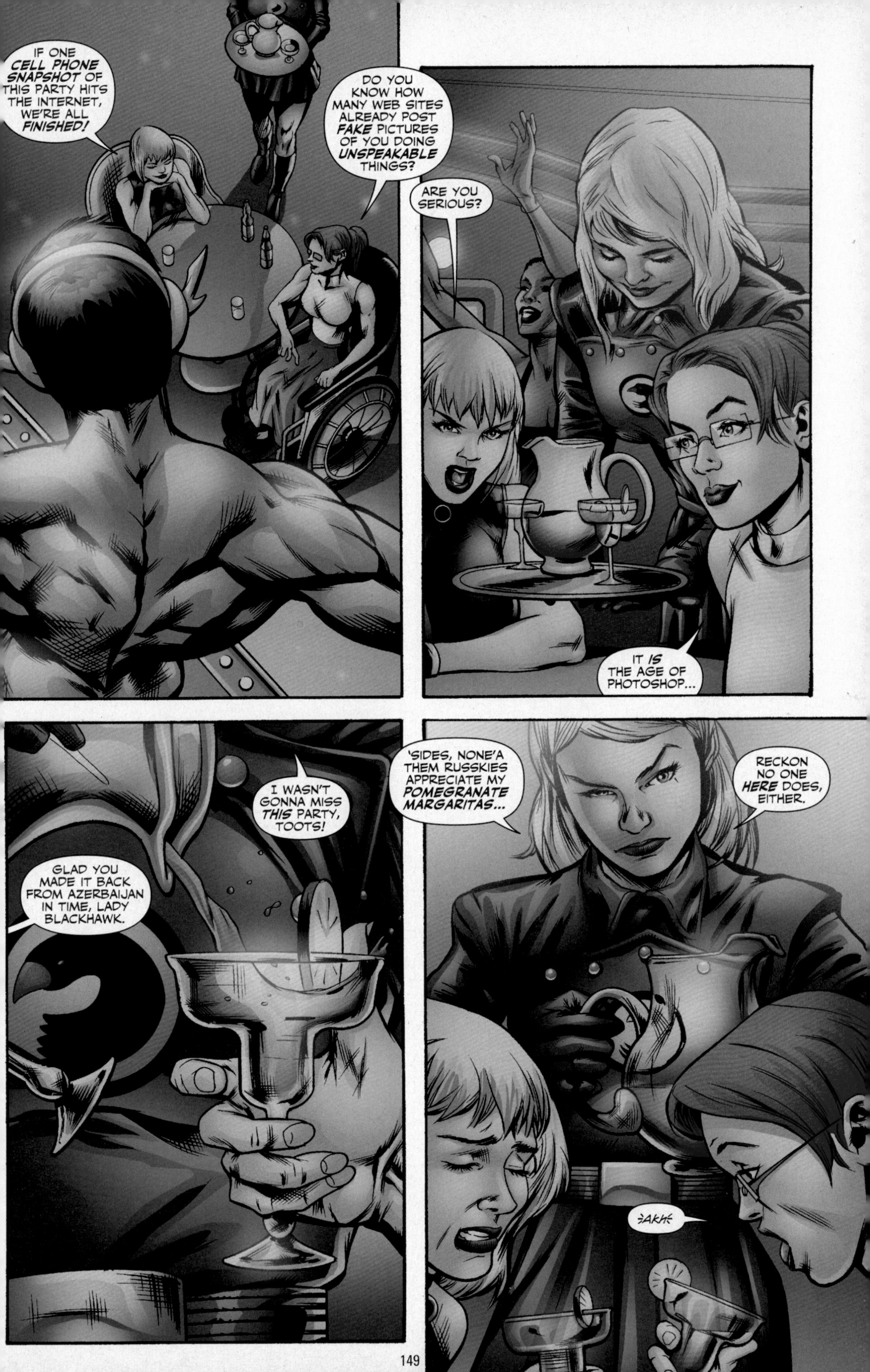

IF ONE *CELL PHONE SNAPSHOT* OF THIS PARTY HITS THE INTERNET, WE'RE ALL *FINISHED!*
DO YOU KNOW HOW MANY WEB SITES ALREADY POST *FAKE* PICTURES OF YOU DOING *UNSPEAKABLE* THINGS?
ARE YOU SERIOUS?
IT *IS* THE AGE OF PHOTOSHOP...
I WASN'T GONNA MISS *THIS* PARTY, TOOTS!
GLAD YOU MADE IT BACK FROM AZERBAIJAN IN TIME, LADY BLACKHAWK.
'SIDES, NONE'A THEM RUSSKIES APPRECIATE MY *POMEGRANATE MARGARITAS...*
RECKON NO ONE *HERE* DOES, EITHER.
AKH

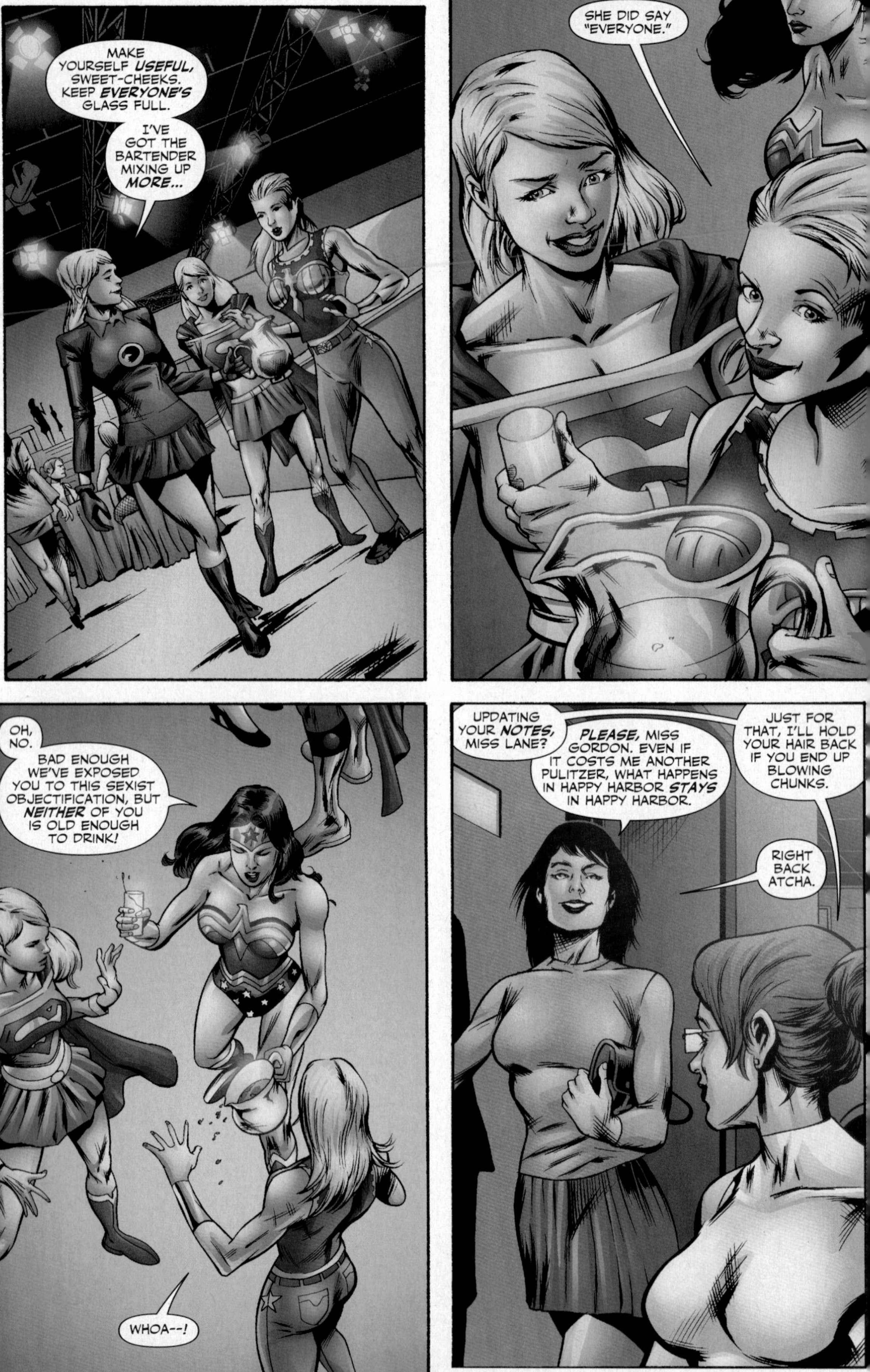
MAKE YOURSELF USEFUL, SWEET-CHEEKS. KEEP EVERYONE'S GLASS FULL.
I'VE GOT THE BARTENDER MIXING UP MORE...
SHE DID SAY "EVERYONE."
OH, NO.
BAD ENOUGH WE'VE EXPOSED YOU TO THIS SEXIST OBJECTIFICATION, BUT NEITHER OF YOU IS OLD ENOUGH TO DRINK!
WHOA--!
UPDATING YOUR NOTES, MISS LANE?
PLEASE, MISS GORDON. EVEN IF IT COSTS ME ANOTHER PULITZER, WHAT HAPPENS IN HAPPY HARBOR STAYS IN HAPPY HARBOR.
JUST FOR THAT, I'LL HOLD YOUR HAIR BACK IF YOU END UP BLOWING CHUNKS.
RIGHT BACK ATCHA.

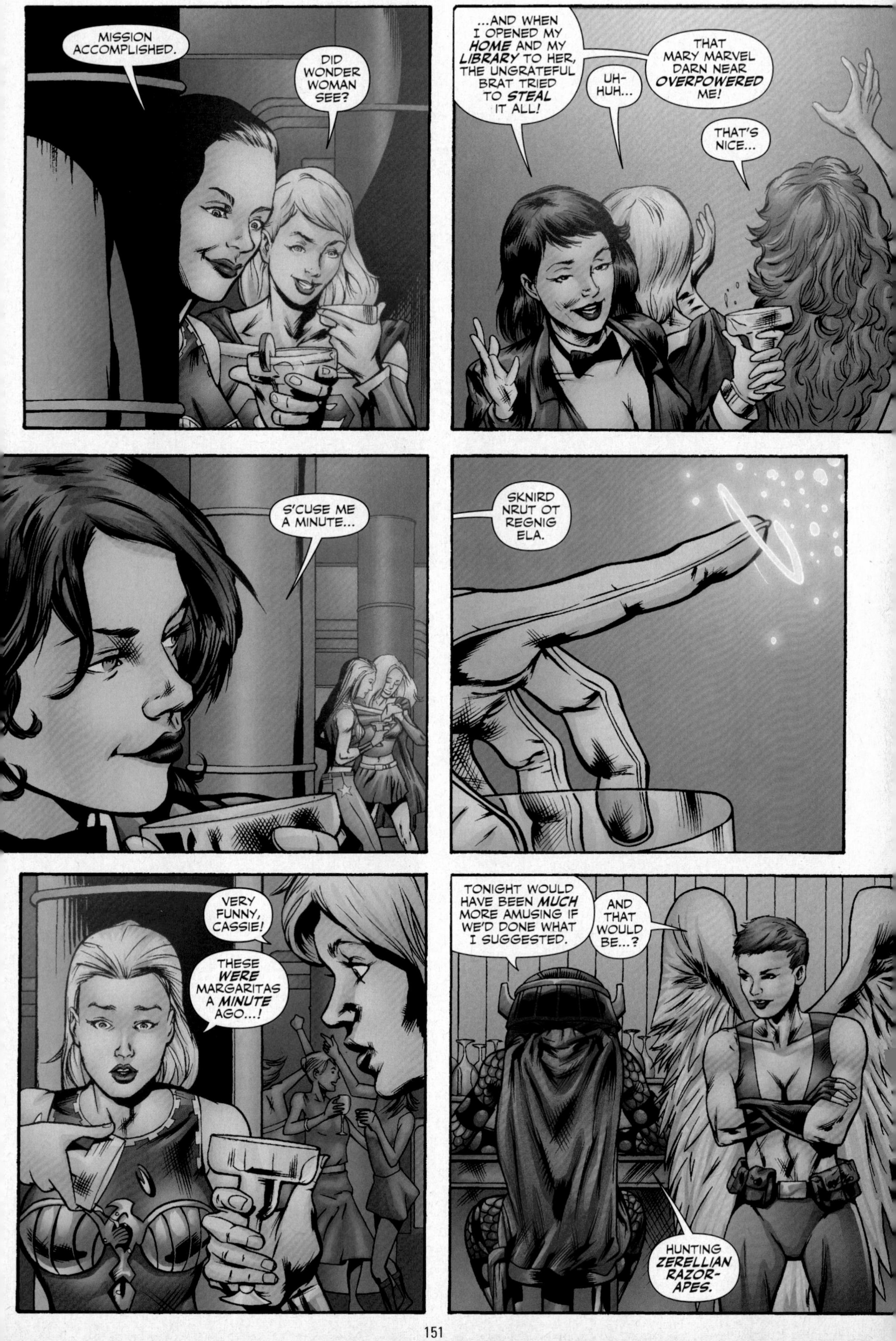
MISSION ACCOMPLISHED.
DID WONDER WOMAN SEE?
...AND WHEN I OPENED MY **HOME** AND MY **LIBRARY** TO HER, THE UNGRATEFUL BRAT TRIED TO **STEAL** IT ALL!
UH-HUH...
THAT MARY MARVEL DARN NEAR **OVERPOWERED** ME!
THAT'S NICE...
S'CUSE ME A MINUTE...
SKNIRD NRUT OT REGNIG ELA.
VERY FUNNY, CASSIE!
THESE **WERE** MARGARITAS A **MINUTE** AGO...!
TONIGHT WOULD HAVE BEEN **MUCH** MORE AMUSING IF WE'D DONE WHAT I SUGGESTED.
AND THAT WOULD BE...?
HUNTING **ZERELLIAN RAZOR-APES.**

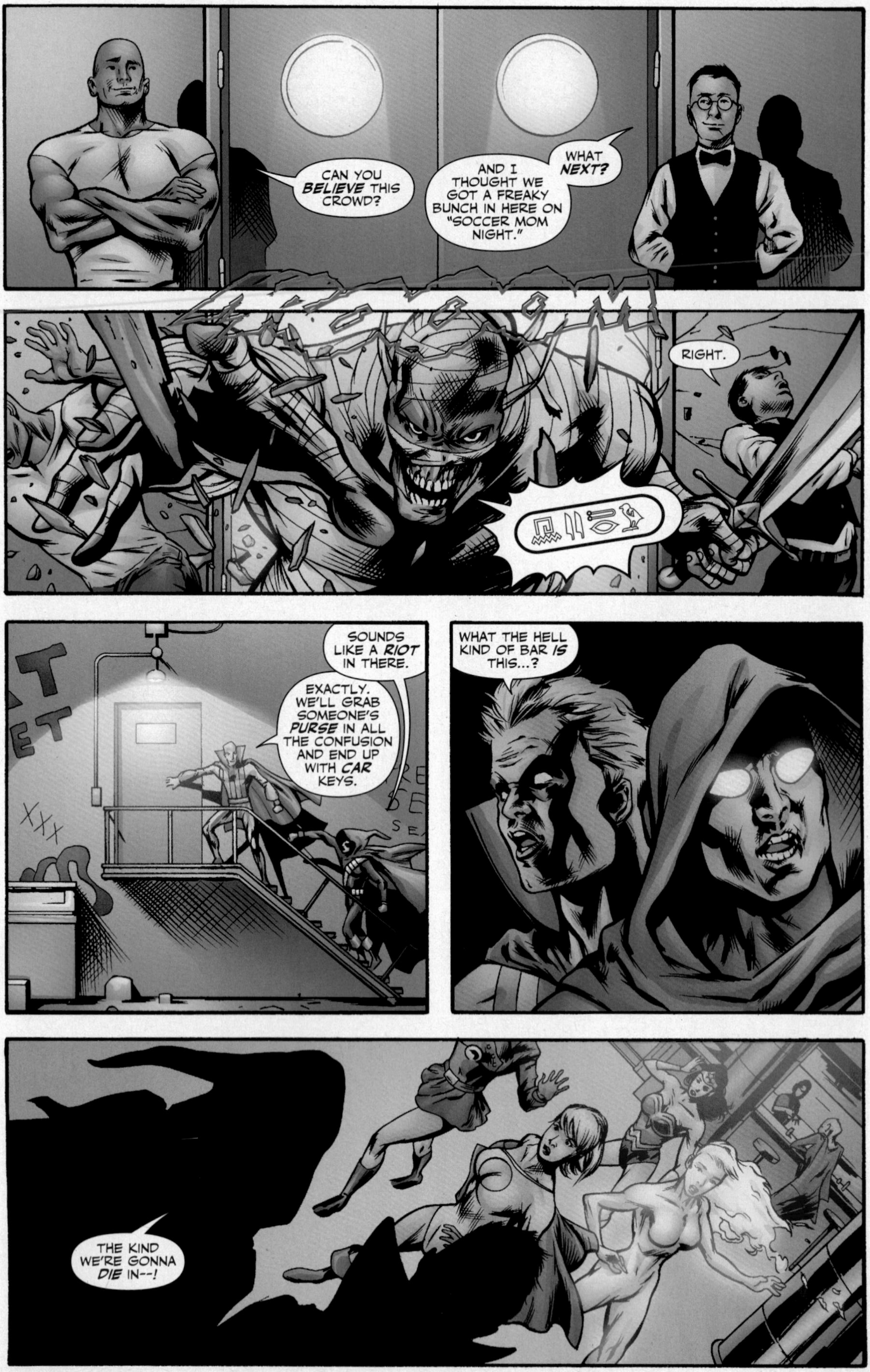
CAN YOU BELIEVE THIS CROWD?
AND I THOUGHT WE GOT A FREAKY BUNCH IN HERE ON "SOCCER MOM NIGHT."
WHAT NEXT?
RIGHT.
SOUNDS LIKE A RIOT IN THERE.
EXACTLY. WE'LL GRAB SOMEONE'S PURSE IN ALL THE CONFUSION AND END UP WITH CAR KEYS.
WHAT THE HELL KIND OF BAR IS THIS...?
THE KIND WE'RE GONNA DIE IN--!

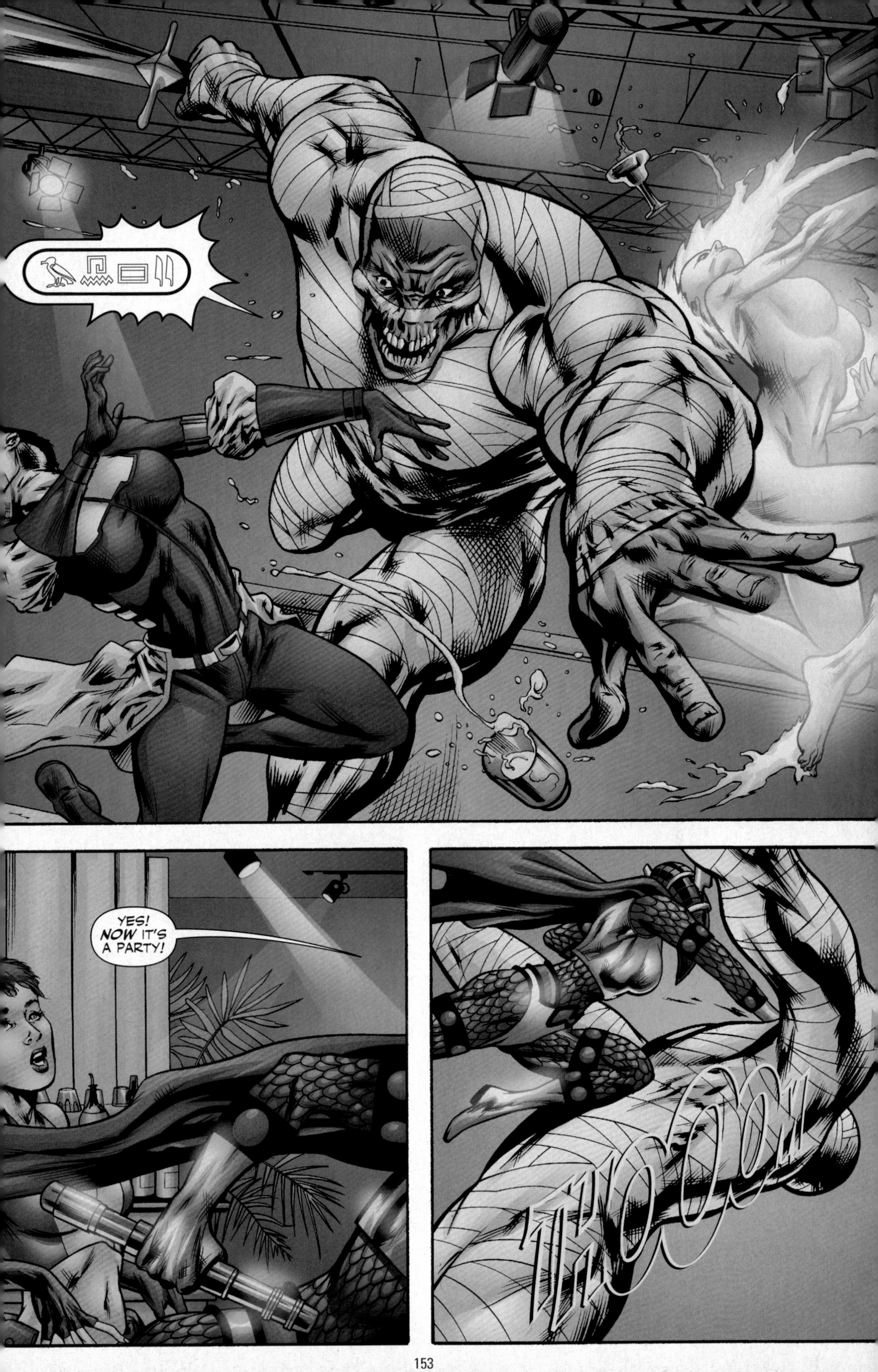
YES! NOW IT'S A PARTY!
THOOOM

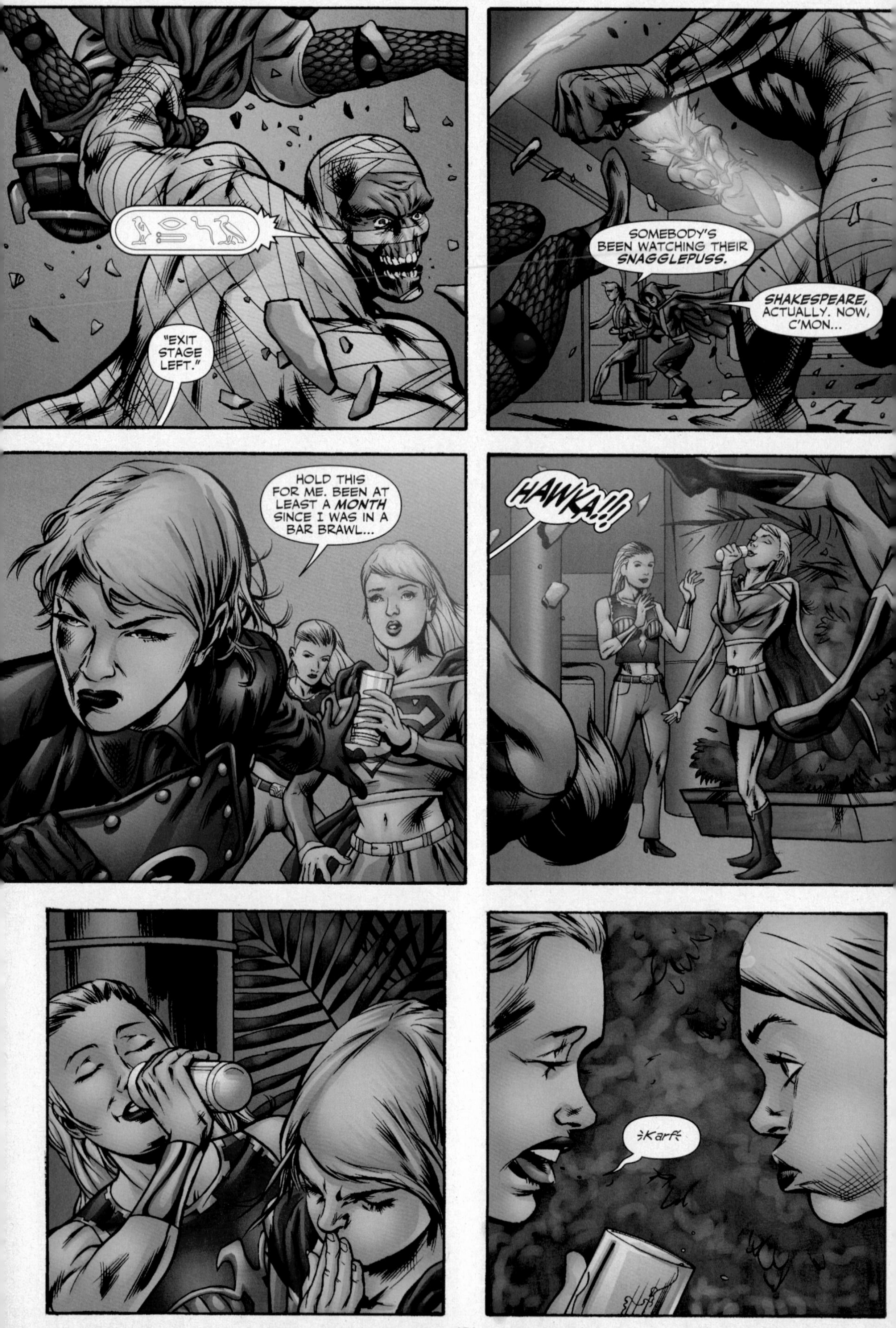
"EXIT STAGE LEFT."
SOMEBODY'S BEEN WATCHING THEIR SNAGGLEPUSS.
SHAKESPEARE, ACTUALLY. NOW, C'MON...
HOLD THIS FOR ME. BEEN AT LEAST A MONTH SINCE I WAS IN A BAR BRAWL...
HAWKA!!!
Karf

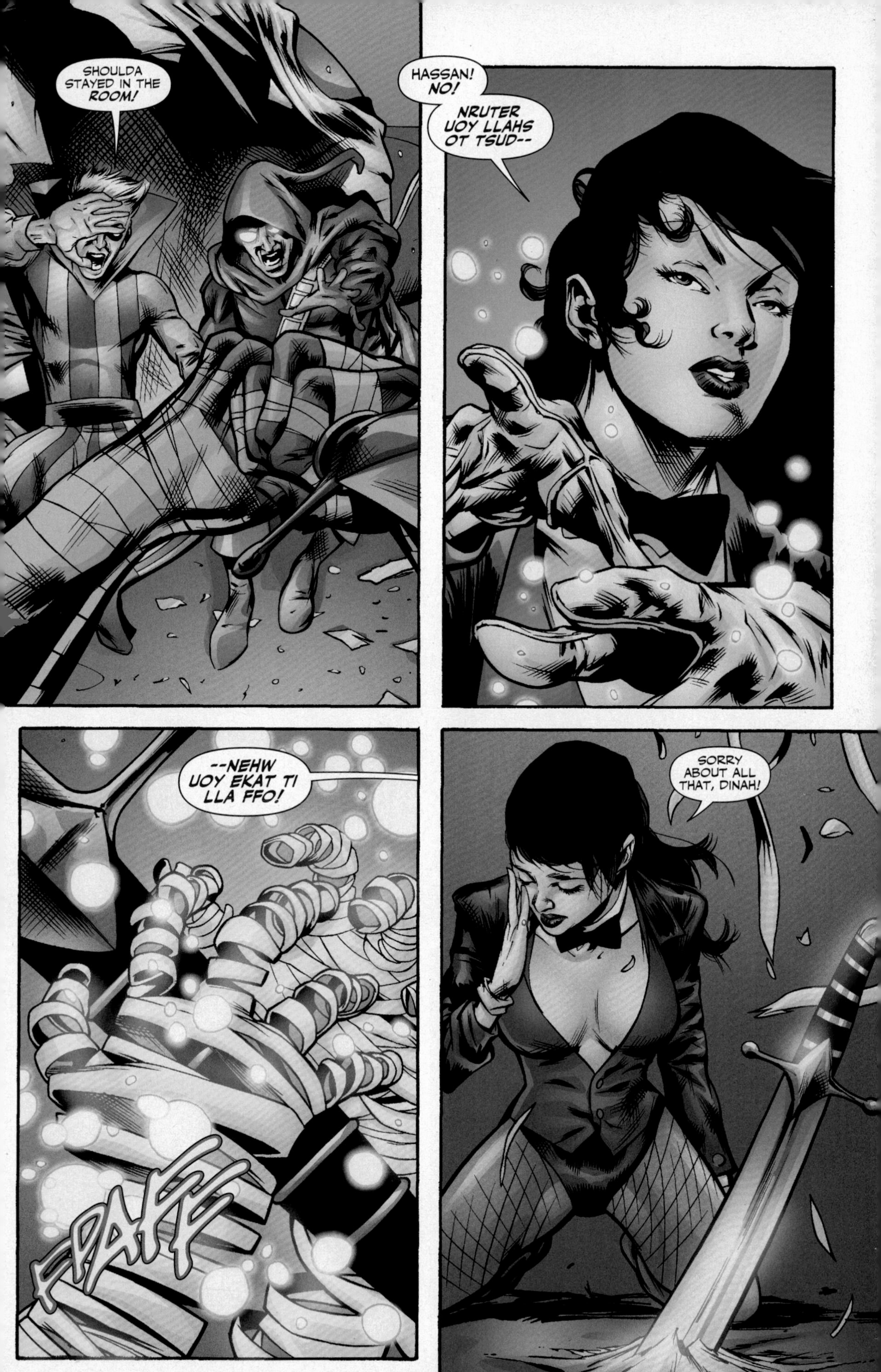
SHOULDA STAYED IN THE ROOM!
HASSAN! NO!
NRUTER UOY LLAHS OT TSUD--
--NEHW UOY EKAT TI LLA FFO!
FPAFF
SORRY ABOUT ALL THAT, DINAH!

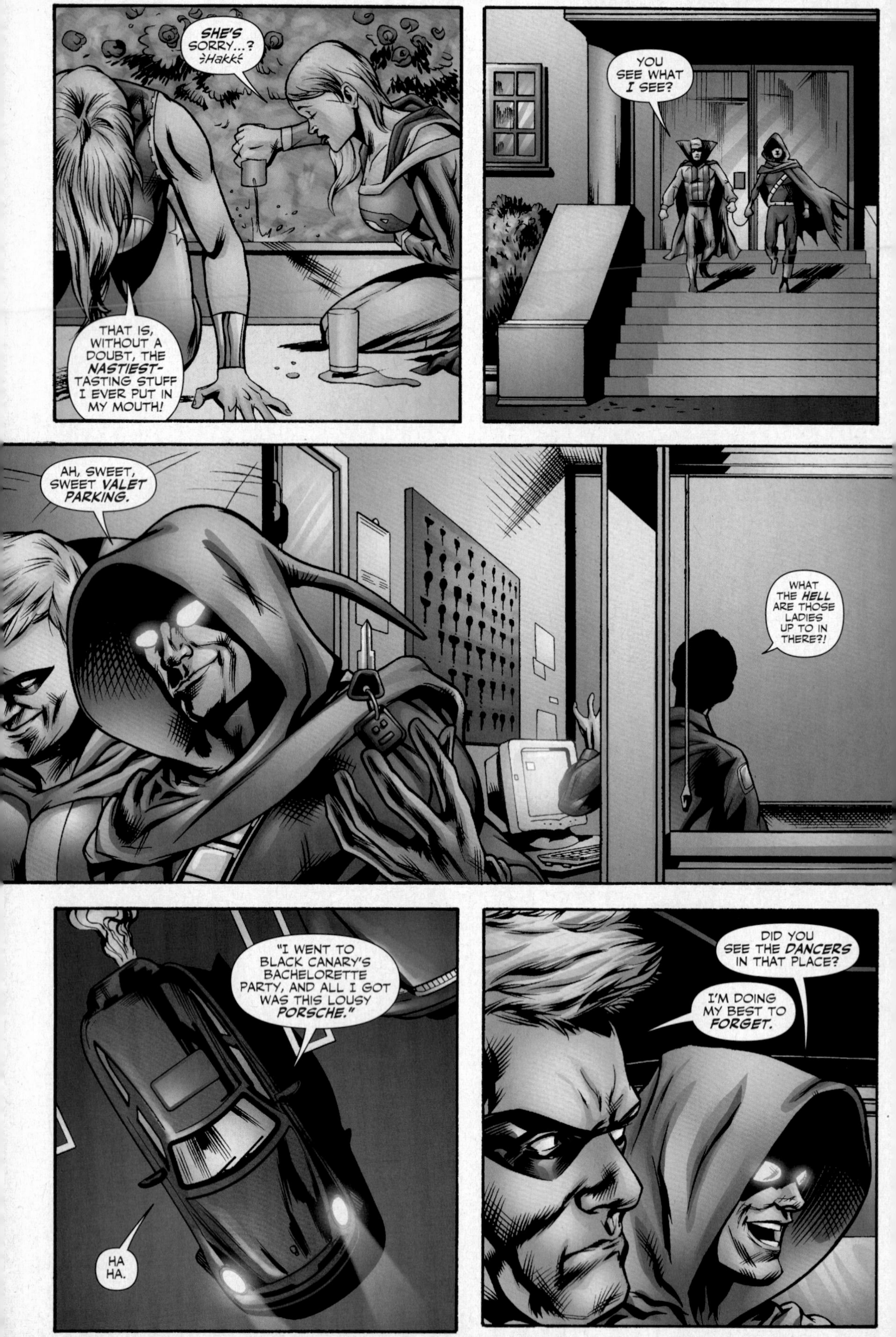
SHE'S SORRY...? *Hakk*
THAT IS, WITHOUT A DOUBT, THE NASTIEST-TASTING STUFF I EVER PUT IN MY MOUTH!
YOU SEE WHAT I SEE?
AH, SWEET, SWEET VALET PARKING.
WHAT THE HELL ARE THOSE LADIES UP TO IN THERE?!
"I WENT TO BLACK CANARY'S BACHELORETTE PARTY, AND ALL I GOT WAS THIS LOUSY PORSCHE."
HA HA.
DID YOU SEE THE DANCERS IN THAT PLACE?
I'M DOING MY BEST TO FORGET.

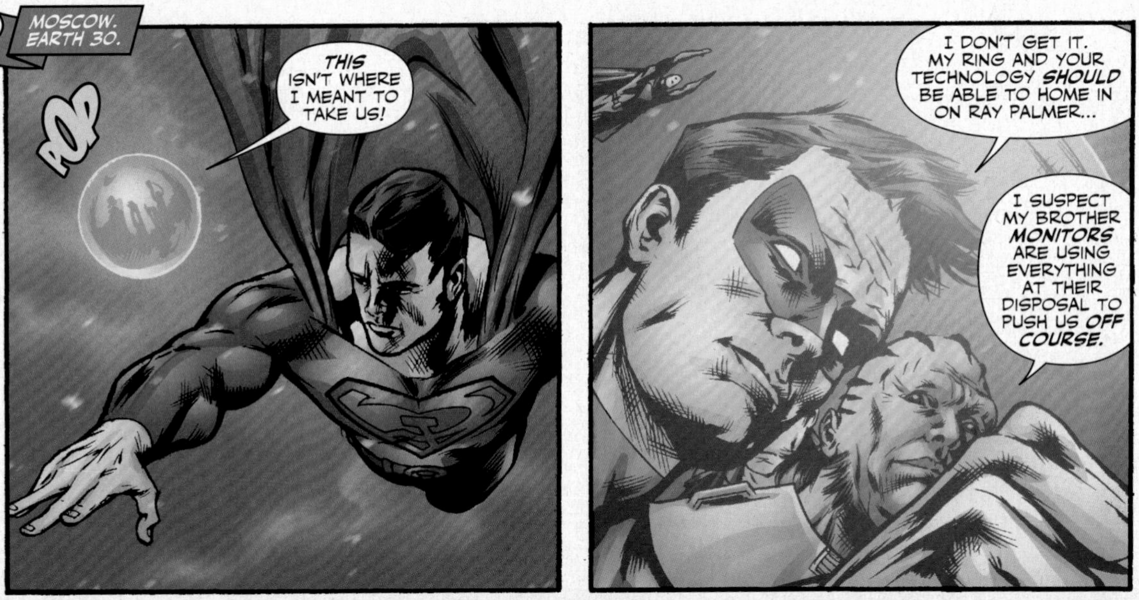
MOSCOW. EARTH 30.
POP
THIS ISN'T WHERE I MEANT TO TAKE US!
I DON'T GET IT. MY RING AND YOUR TECHNOLOGY SHOULD BE ABLE TO HOME IN ON RAY PALMER...
I SUSPECT MY BROTHER MONITORS ARE USING EVERYTHING AT THEIR DISPOSAL TO PUSH US OFF COURSE.

## DONNA TROY & JASON TODD

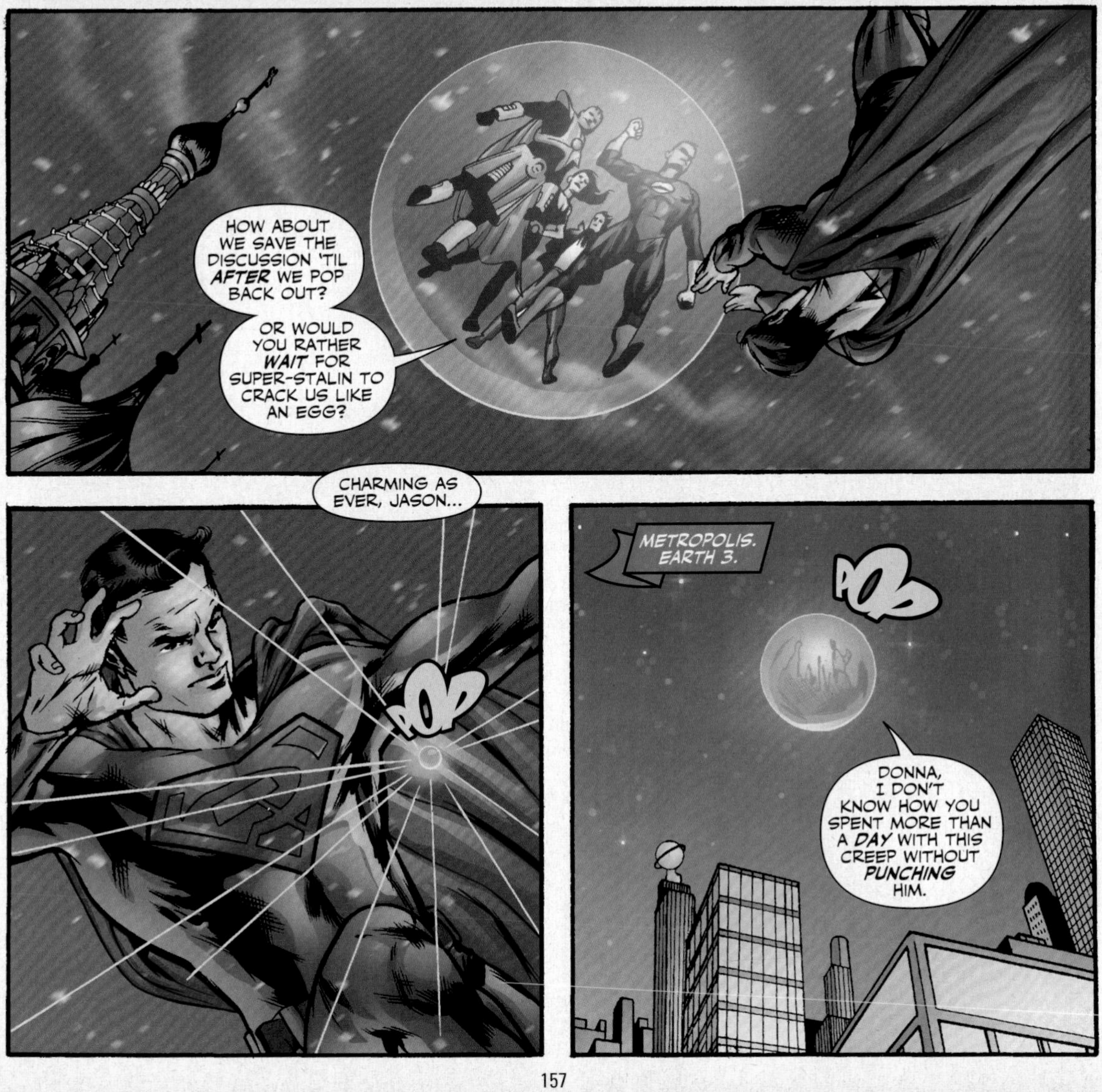
HOW ABOUT WE SAVE THE DISCUSSION 'TIL AFTER WE POP BACK OUT?
OR WOULD YOU RATHER WAIT FOR SUPER-STALIN TO CRACK US LIKE AN EGG?
CHARMING AS EVER, JASON...
POP
METROPOLIS. EARTH 3.
POP
DONNA, I DON'T KNOW HOW YOU SPENT MORE THAN A DAY WITH THIS CREEP WITHOUT PUNCHING HIM.

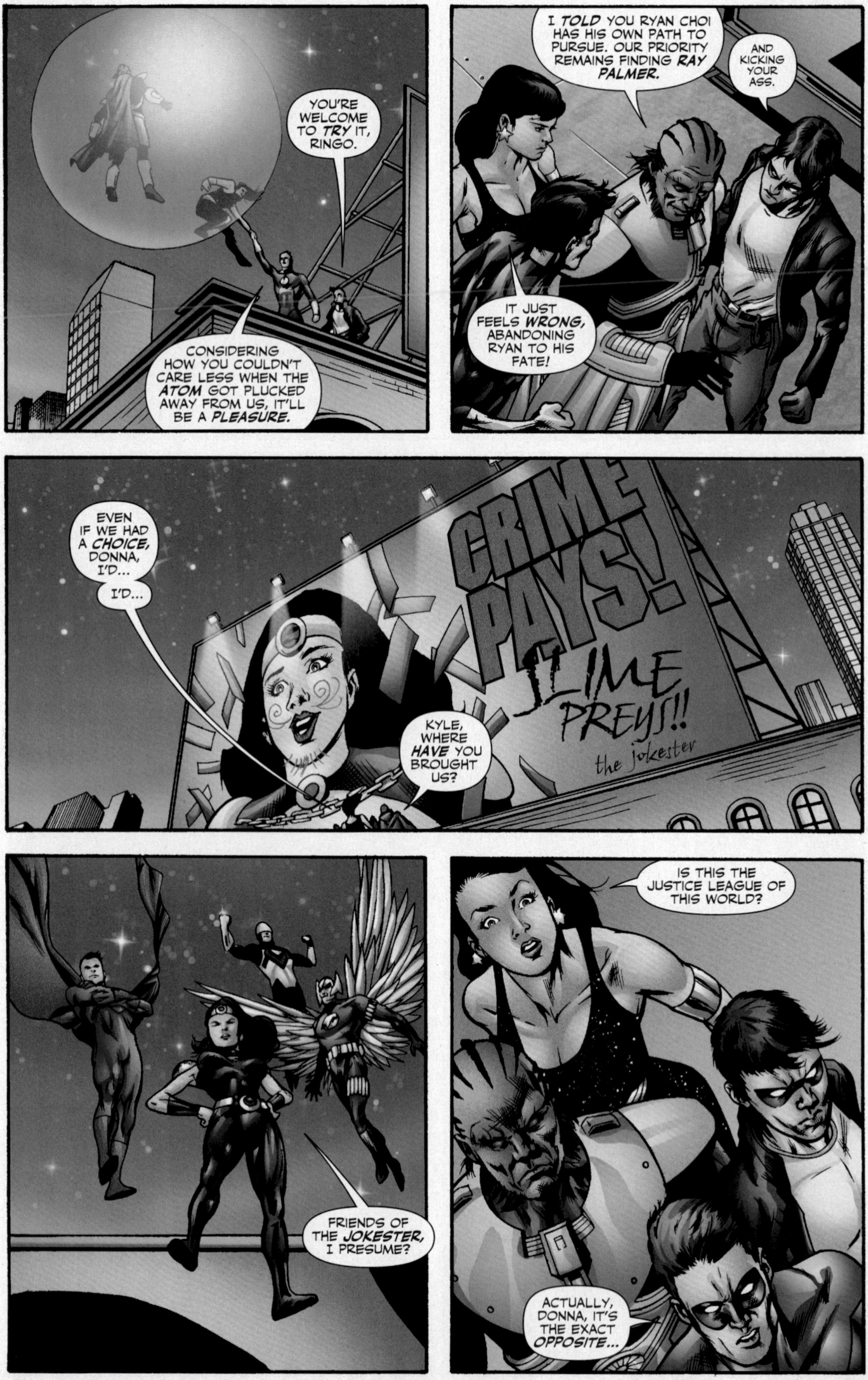
YOU'RE WELCOME TO TRY IT, RINGO.
CONSIDERING HOW YOU COULDN'T CARE LESS WHEN THE ATOM GOT PLUCKED AWAY FROM US, IT'LL BE A PLEASURE.
I TOLD YOU RYAN CHOI HAS HIS OWN PATH TO PURSUE. OUR PRIORITY REMAINS FINDING RAY PALMER.
AND KICKING YOUR ASS.
IT JUST FEELS WRONG, ABANDONING RYAN TO HIS FATE!
EVEN IF WE HAD A CHOICE, DONNA, I'D...
I'D...
CRIME PAYS!
SLIME PREYS!!
the Jokester
KYLE, WHERE HAVE YOU BROUGHT US?
FRIENDS OF THE JOKESTER, I PRESUME?
IS THIS THE JUSTICE LEAGUE OF THIS WORLD?
ACTUALLY, DONNA, IT'S THE EXACT OPPOSITE...

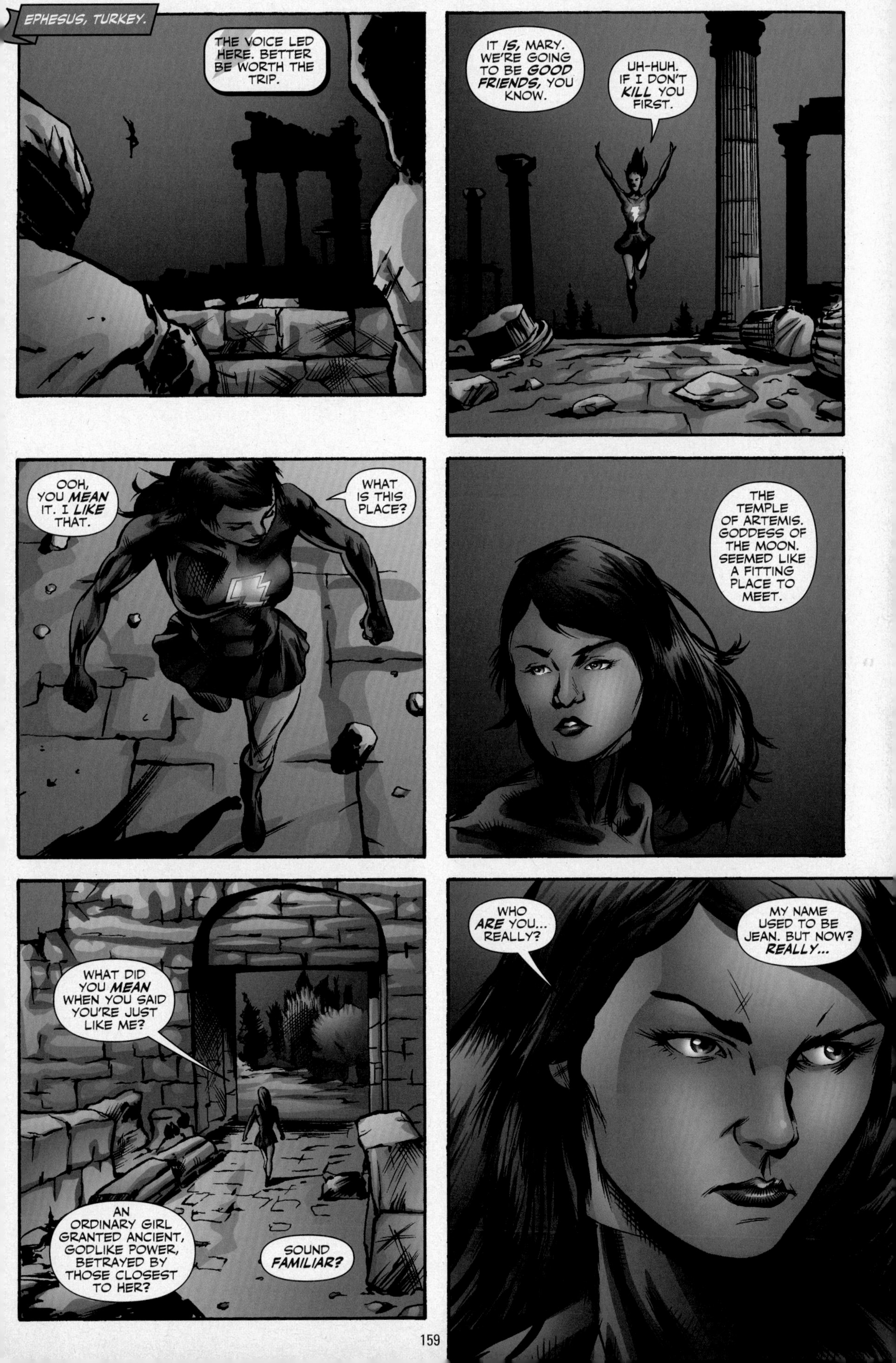
EPHESUS, TURKEY.
THE VOICE LED HERE. BETTER BE WORTH THE TRIP.
IT IS, MARY. WE'RE GOING TO BE GOOD FRIENDS, YOU KNOW.
UH-HUH. IF I DON'T KILL YOU FIRST.
OOH, YOU MEAN IT. I LIKE THAT.
WHAT IS THIS PLACE?
THE TEMPLE OF ARTEMIS. GODDESS OF THE MOON. SEEMED LIKE A FITTING PLACE TO MEET.
WHAT DID YOU MEAN WHEN YOU SAID YOU'RE JUST LIKE ME?
AN ORDINARY GIRL GRANTED ANCIENT, GODLIKE POWER, BETRAYED BY THOSE CLOSEST TO HER?
SOUND FAMILIAR?
WHO ARE YOU... REALLY?
MY NAME USED TO BE JEAN. BUT NOW? REALLY...

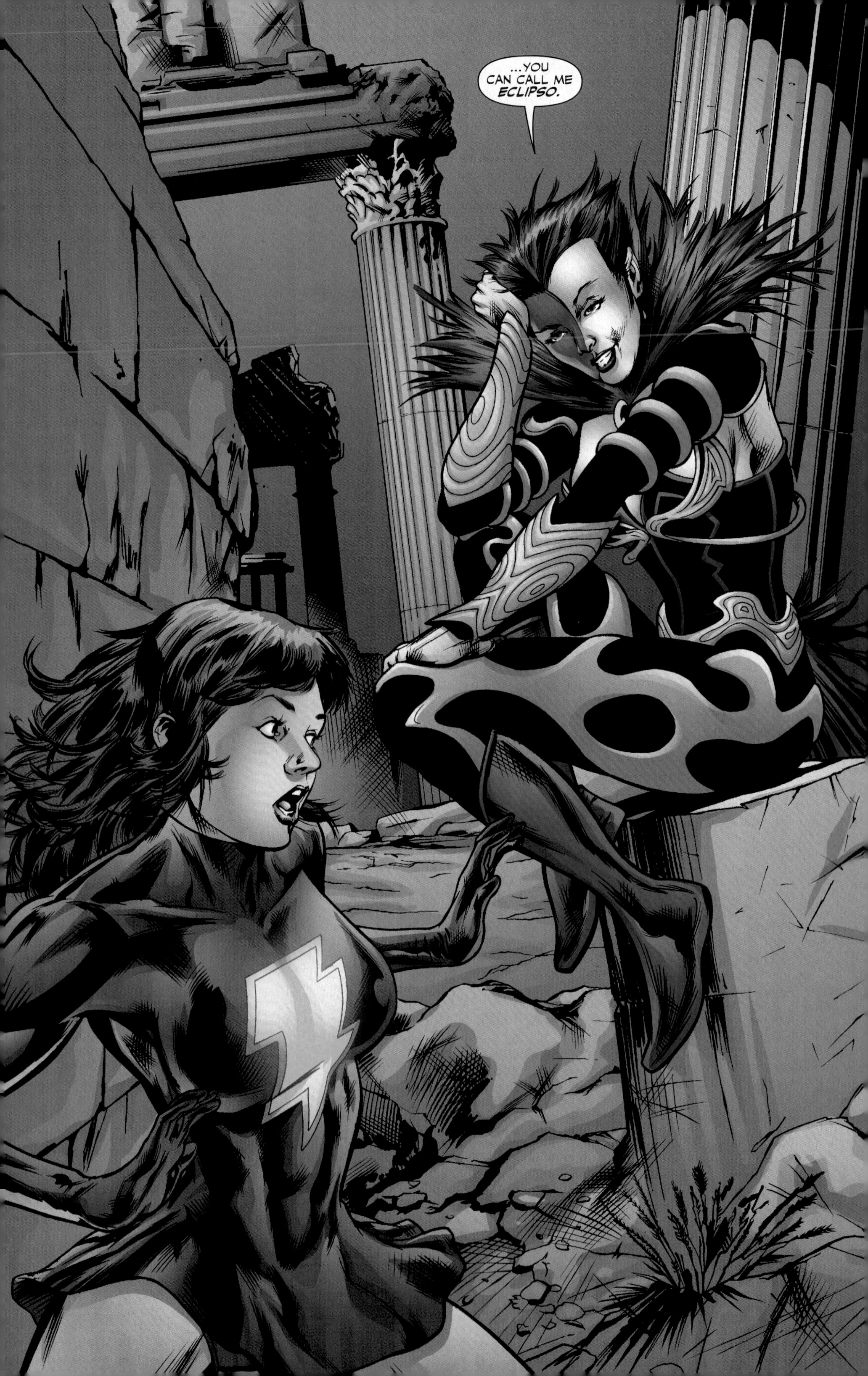
...YOU CAN CALL ME ECLIPSO.

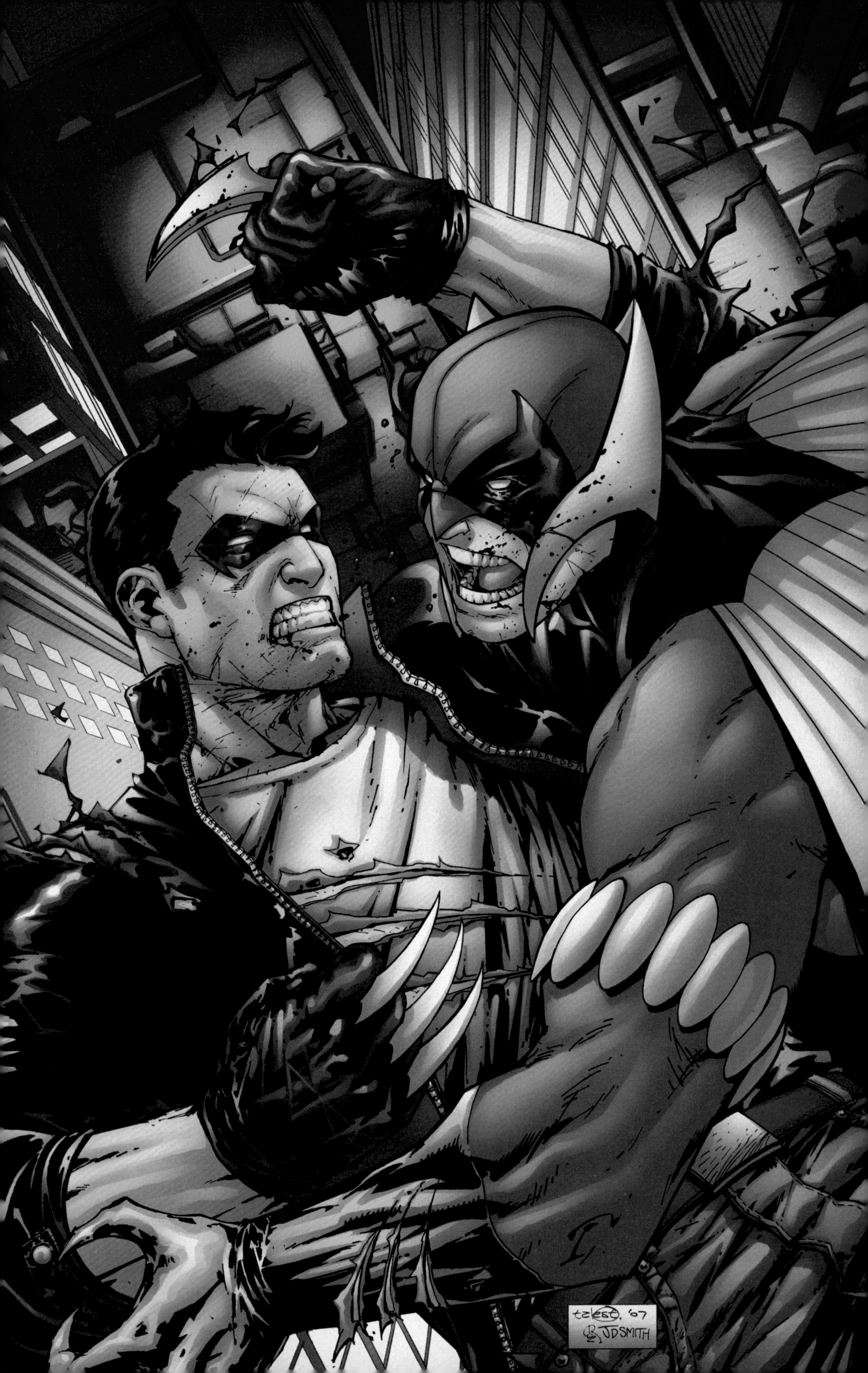

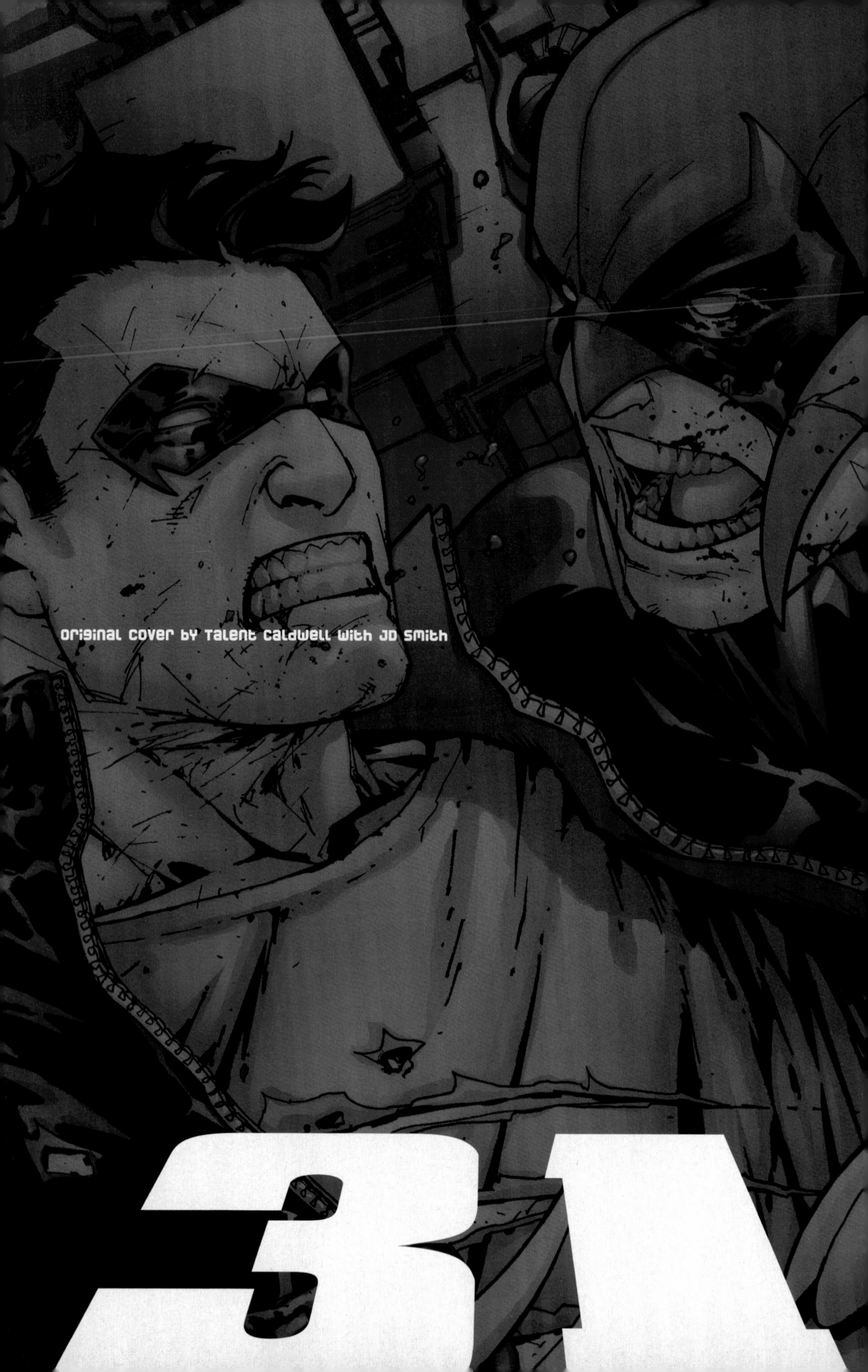
31

Original cover by Talent Caldwell with JD Smith

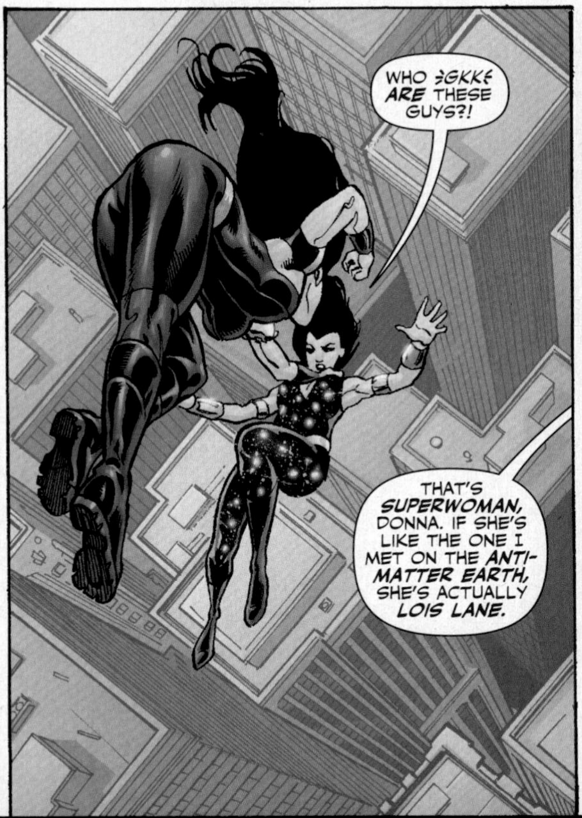
WHO ƎGKK€ *ARE* THESE GUYS?!
THAT'S *SUPERWOMAN*, DONNA. IF SHE'S LIKE THE ONE I MET ON THE *ANTI-MATTER EARTH,* SHE'S ACTUALLY *LOIS LANE.*

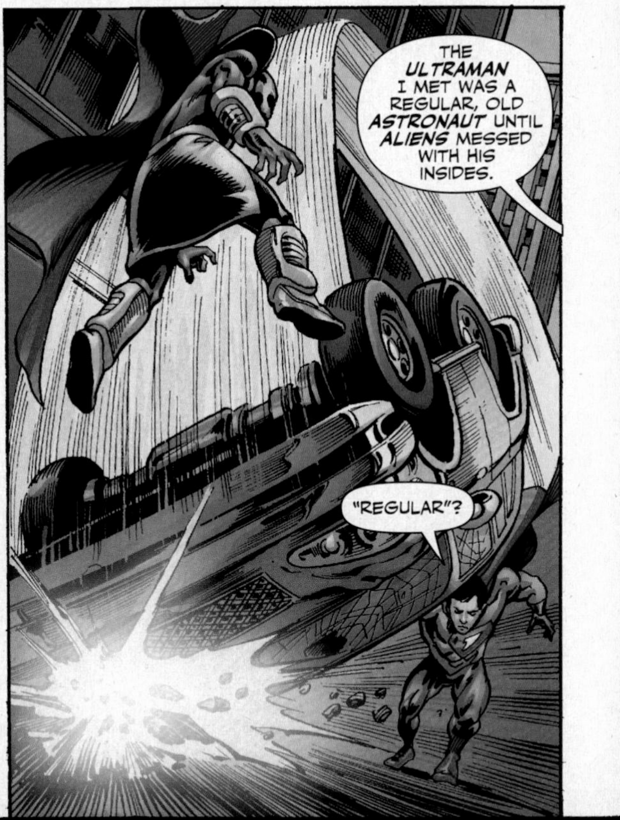
THE *ULTRAMAN* I MET WAS A REGULAR, OLD *ASTRONAUT* UNTIL *ALIENS* MESSED WITH HIS INSIDES.
"REGULAR"?

THIRTY-ONE AND COUNTING... THE CHALLENGERS

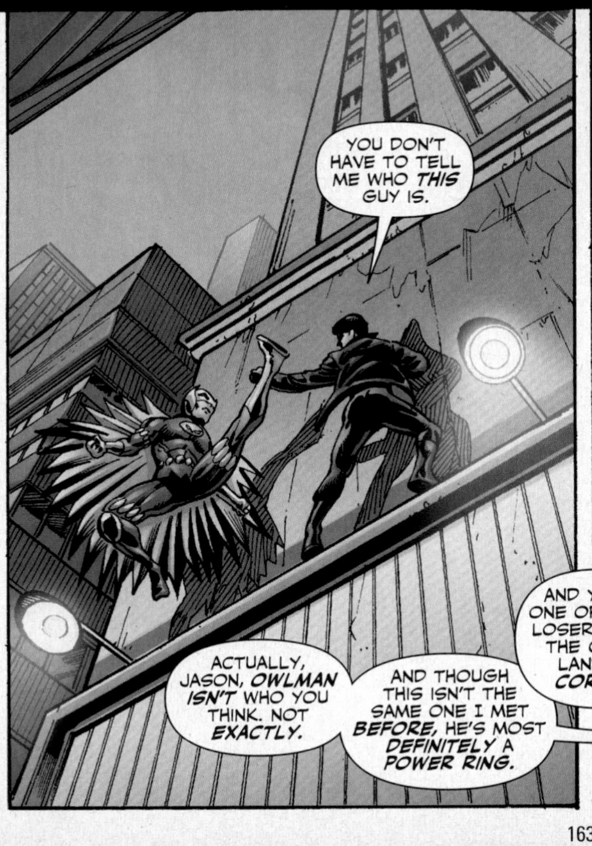
YOU DON'T HAVE TO TELL ME WHO *THIS* GUY IS.
AND YOU'RE ONE OF THOSE LOSERS FROM THE GREEN LANTERN *CORPSE!*
ACTUALLY, JASON, *OWLMAN ISN'T* WHO YOU THINK. NOT *EXACTLY.*
AND THOUGH THIS ISN'T THE SAME ONE I MET *BEFORE,* HE'S MOST *DEFINITELY* A *POWER RING.*

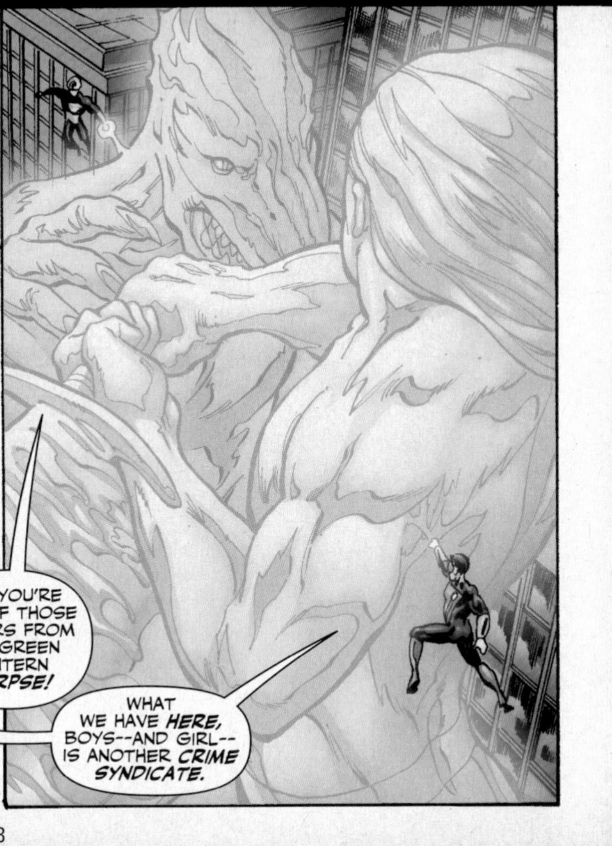
WHAT WE HAVE *HERE,* BOYS--AND GIRL--IS ANOTHER *CRIME SYNDICATE.*

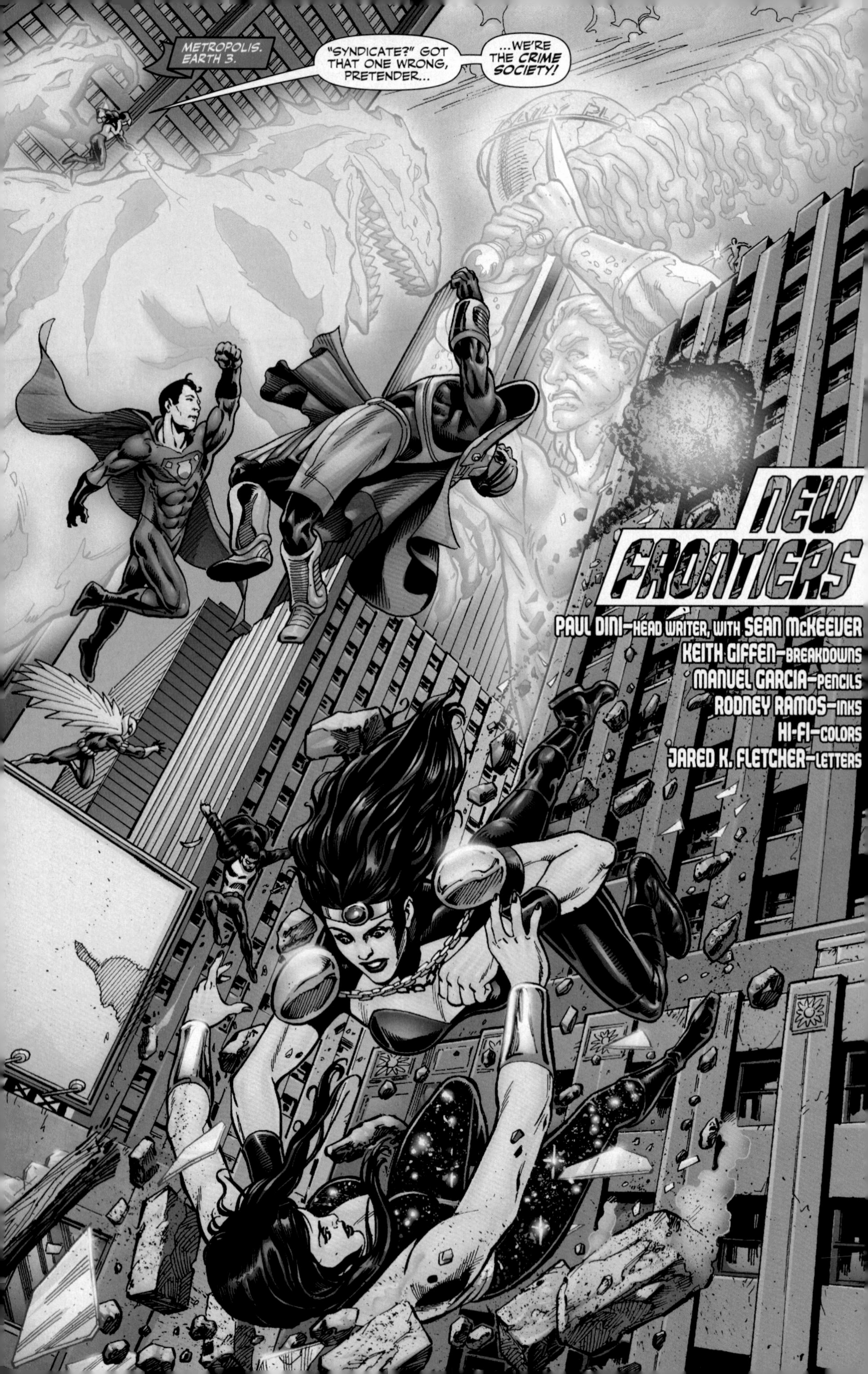

METROPOLIS. EARTH 3.
"SYNDICATE?" GOT THAT ONE WRONG, PRETENDER...
...WE'RE THE CRIME SOCIETY!
NEW FRONTIERS
PAUL DINI–HEAD WRITER, WITH SEAN McKEEVER
KEITH GIFFEN–BREAKDOWNS
MANUEL GARCIA–PENCILS
RODNEY RAMOS–INKS
HI-FI–COLORS
JARED K. FLETCHER–LETTERS

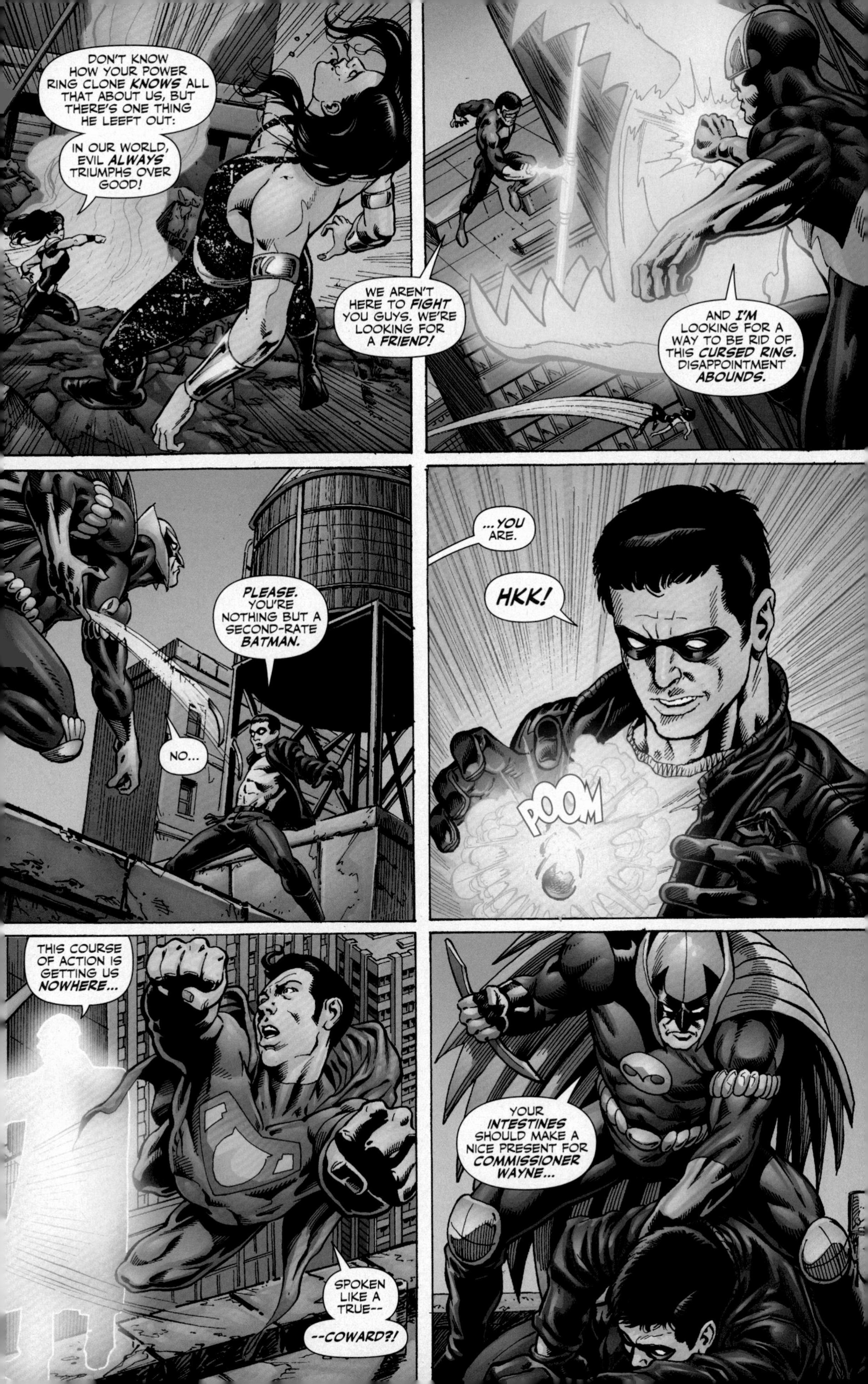
DON'T KNOW HOW YOUR POWER RING CLONE KNOWS ALL THAT ABOUT US, BUT THERE'S ONE THING HE LEEFT OUT:
IN OUR WORLD, EVIL ALWAYS TRIUMPHS OVER GOOD!
WE AREN'T HERE TO FIGHT YOU GUYS. WE'RE LOOKING FOR A FRIEND!
AND I'M LOOKING FOR A WAY TO BE RID OF THIS CURSED RING. DISAPPOINTMENT ABOUNDS.
PLEASE. YOU'RE NOTHING BUT A SECOND-RATE BATMAN.
NO...
...YOU ARE.
HKK!
POOM
THIS COURSE OF ACTION IS GETTING US NOWHERE...
SPOKEN LIKE A TRUE--
--COWARD?!
YOUR INTESTINES SHOULD MAKE A NICE PRESENT FOR COMMISSIONER WAYNE...

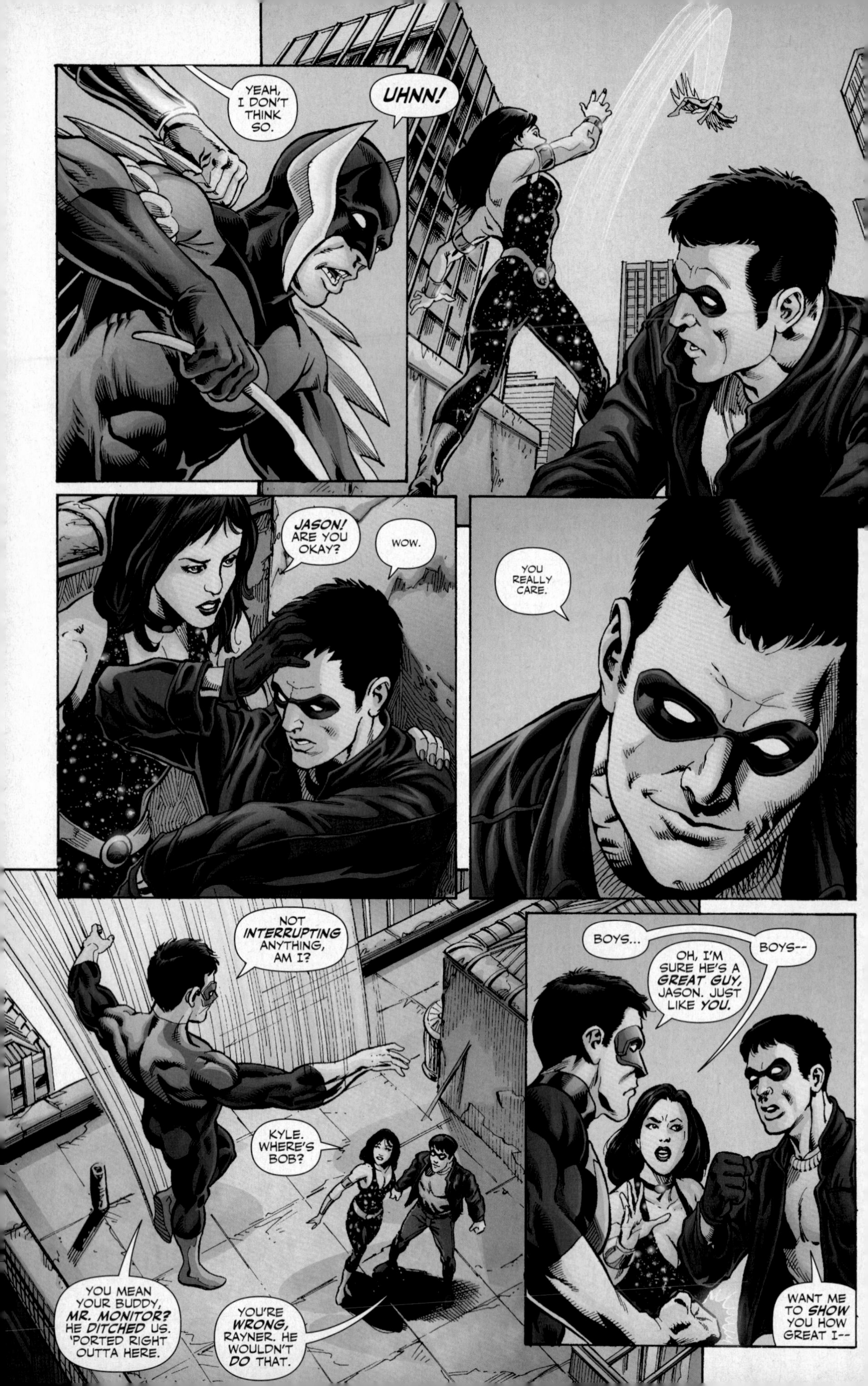
YEAH, I DON'T THINK SO.
UHNN!
JASON! ARE YOU OKAY?
WOW.
YOU REALLY CARE.
NOT INTERRUPTING ANYTHING, AM I?
KYLE. WHERE'S BOB?
YOU MEAN YOUR BUDDY, MR. MONITOR? HE DITCHED US. 'PORTED RIGHT OUTTA HERE.
YOU'RE WRONG, RAYNER. HE WOULDN'T DO THAT.
BOYS...
OH, I'M SURE HE'S A GREAT GUY, JASON. JUST LIKE YOU.
BOYS--
WANT ME TO SHOW YOU HOW GREAT I--

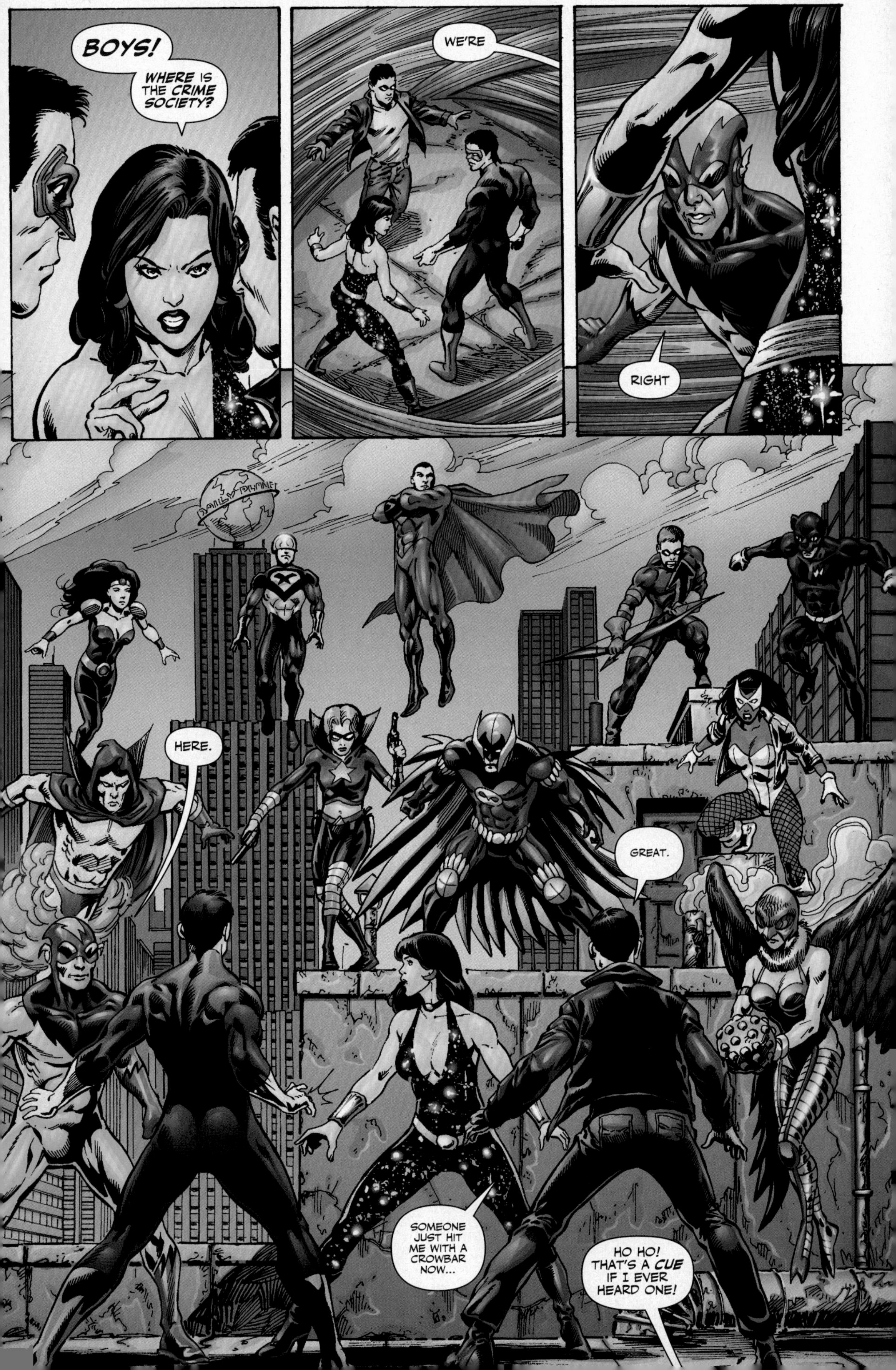
BOYS!
WHERE IS THE CRIME SOCIETY?
WE'RE
RIGHT
HERE.
GREAT.
SOMEONE JUST HIT ME WITH A CROWBAR NOW...
HO HO! THAT'S A CUE IF I EVER HEARD ONE!

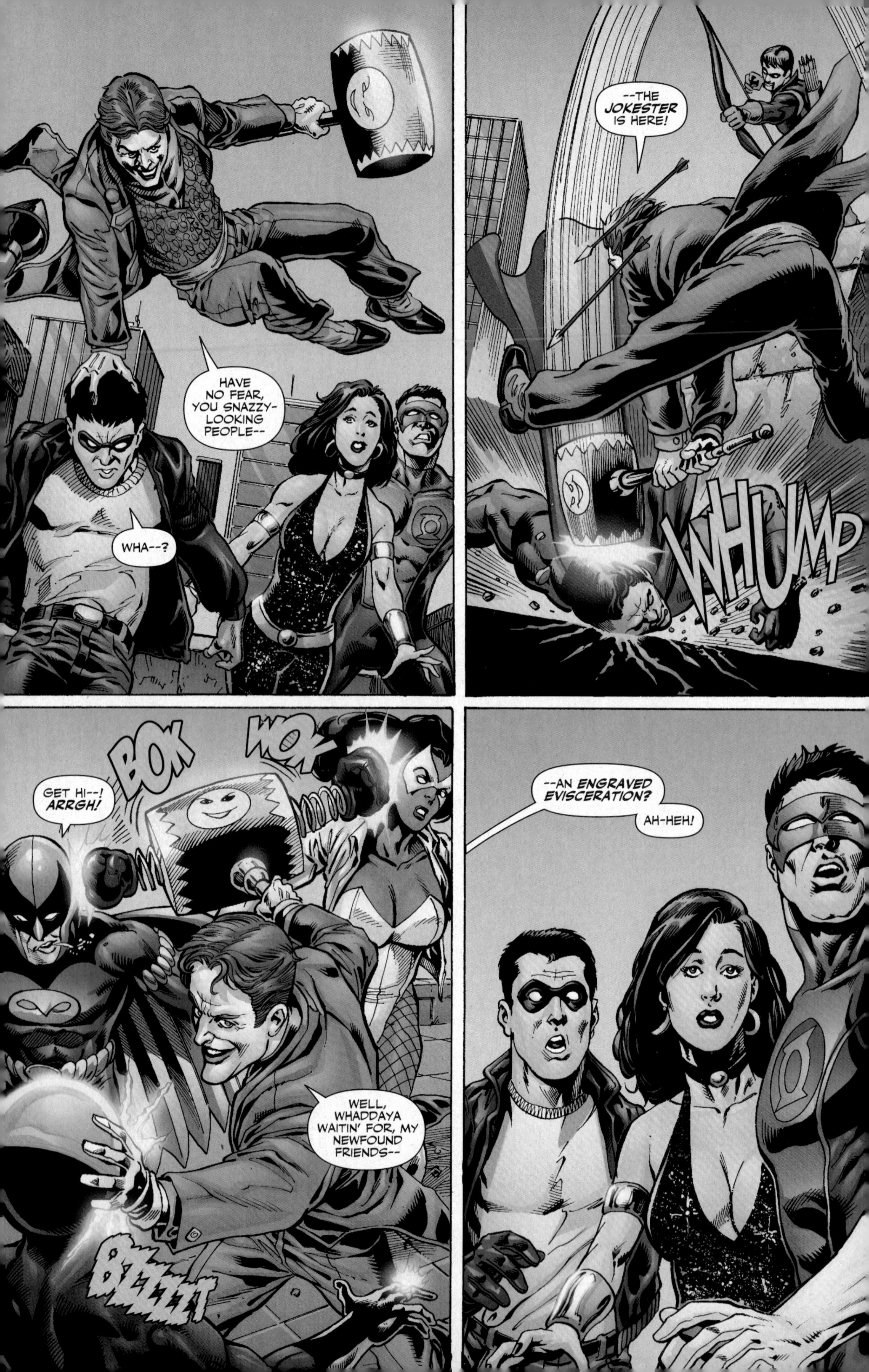
HAVE NO FEAR, YOU SNAZZY-LOOKING PEOPLE--
WHA--?
--THE JOKESTER IS HERE!
WHUMP
GET HI--! ARRGH!
BOK
WOK
WELL, WHADDAYA WAITIN' FOR, MY NEWFOUND FRIENDS--
BZZZZT
--AN ENGRAVED EVISCERATION?
AH-HEH!

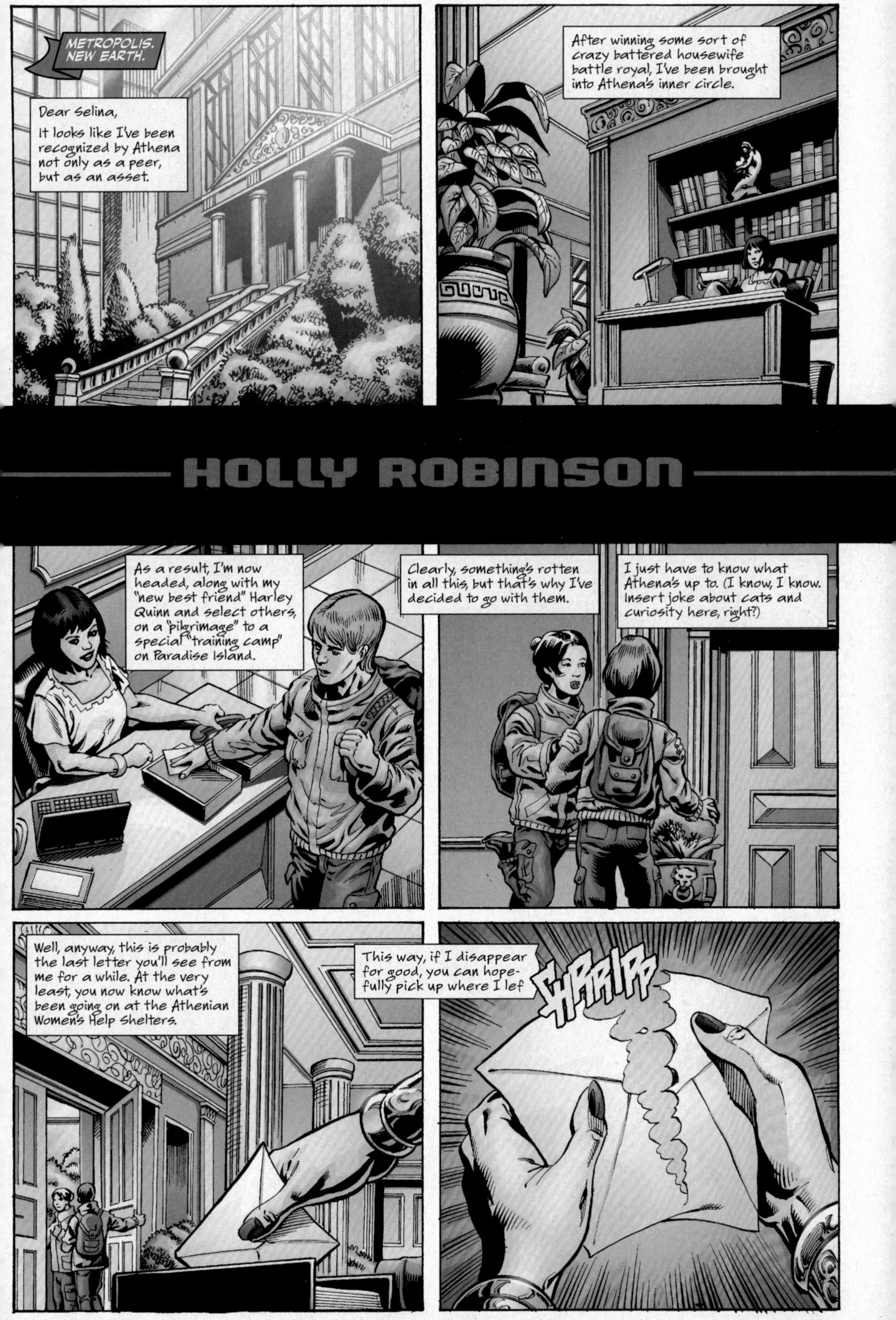

METROPOLIS. NEW EARTH.
Dear Selina,
It looks like I've been recognized by Athena not only as a peer, but as an asset.
After winning some sort of crazy battered housewife battle royal, I've been brought into Athena's inner circle.
HOLLY ROBINSON
As a result, I'm now headed, along with my "new best friend" Harley Quinn and select others, on a "pilgrimage" to a special "training camp" on Paradise Island.
Clearly, something's rotten in all this, but that's why I've decided to go with them.
I just have to know what Athena's up to. (I know, I know. Insert joke about cats and curiosity here, right?)
Well, anyway, this is probably the last letter you'll see from me for a while. At the very least, you now know what's been going on at the Athenian Women's Help Shelters.
This way, if I disappear for good, you can hope-fully pick up where I lef
SHRRIPP

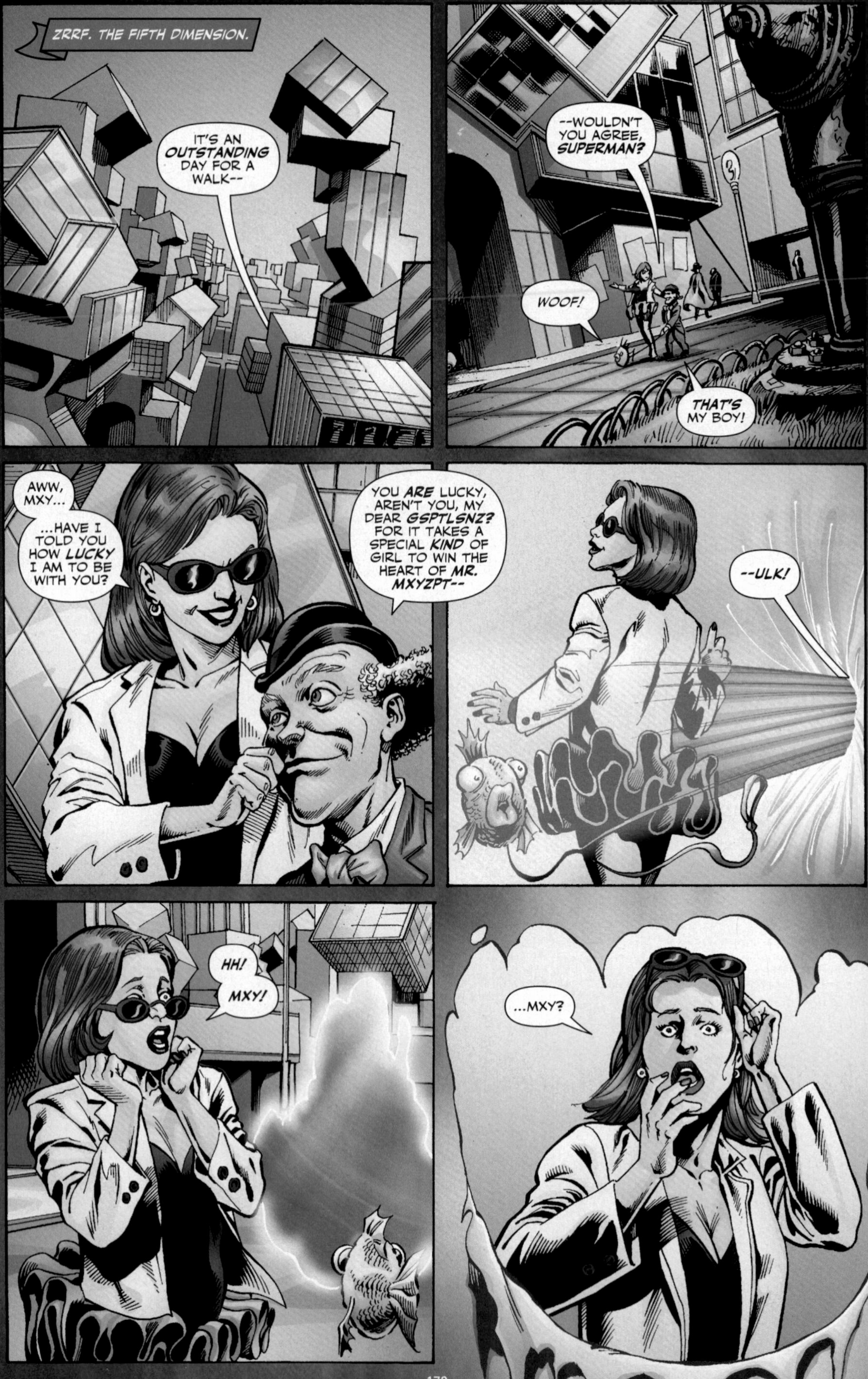
ZRRF. THE FIFTH DIMENSION.
IT'S AN OUTSTANDING DAY FOR A WALK--
--WOULDN'T YOU AGREE, SUPERMAN?
WOOF!
THAT'S MY BOY!
AWW, MXY...
...HAVE I TOLD YOU HOW LUCKY I AM TO BE WITH YOU?
YOU ARE LUCKY, AREN'T YOU, MY DEAR GSPTLSNZ? FOR IT TAKES A SPECIAL KIND OF GIRL TO WIN THE HEART OF MR. MXYZPT--
--ULK!
HH!
MXY!
...MXY?

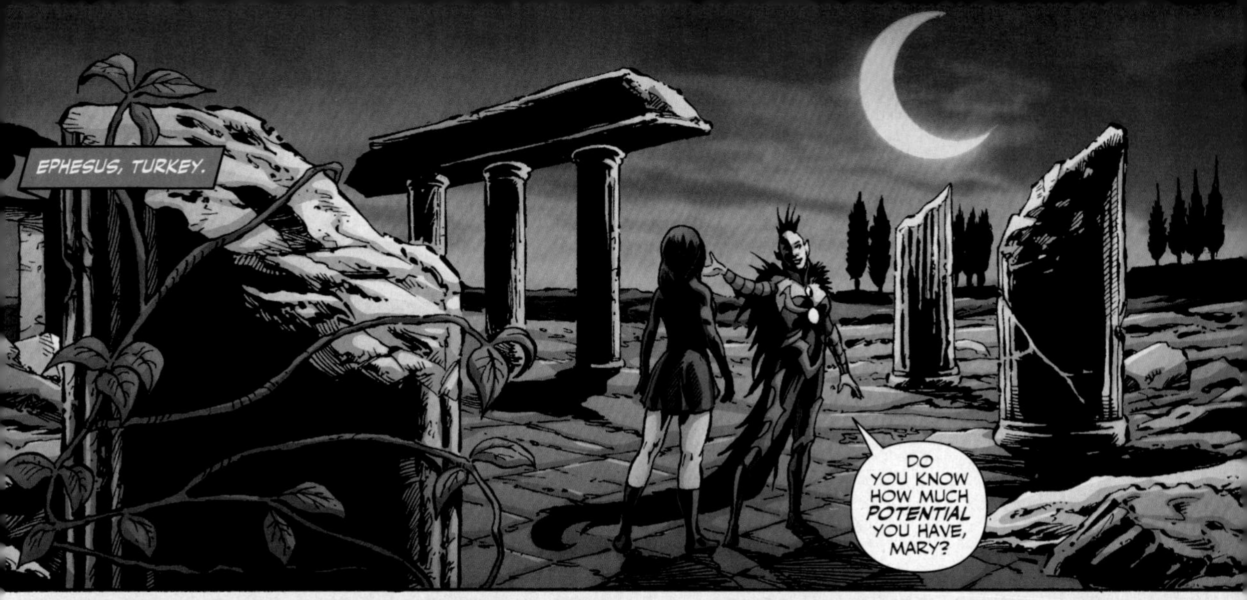
EPHESUS, TURKEY.
DO YOU KNOW HOW MUCH POTENTIAL YOU HAVE, MARY?

# MARY MARVEL

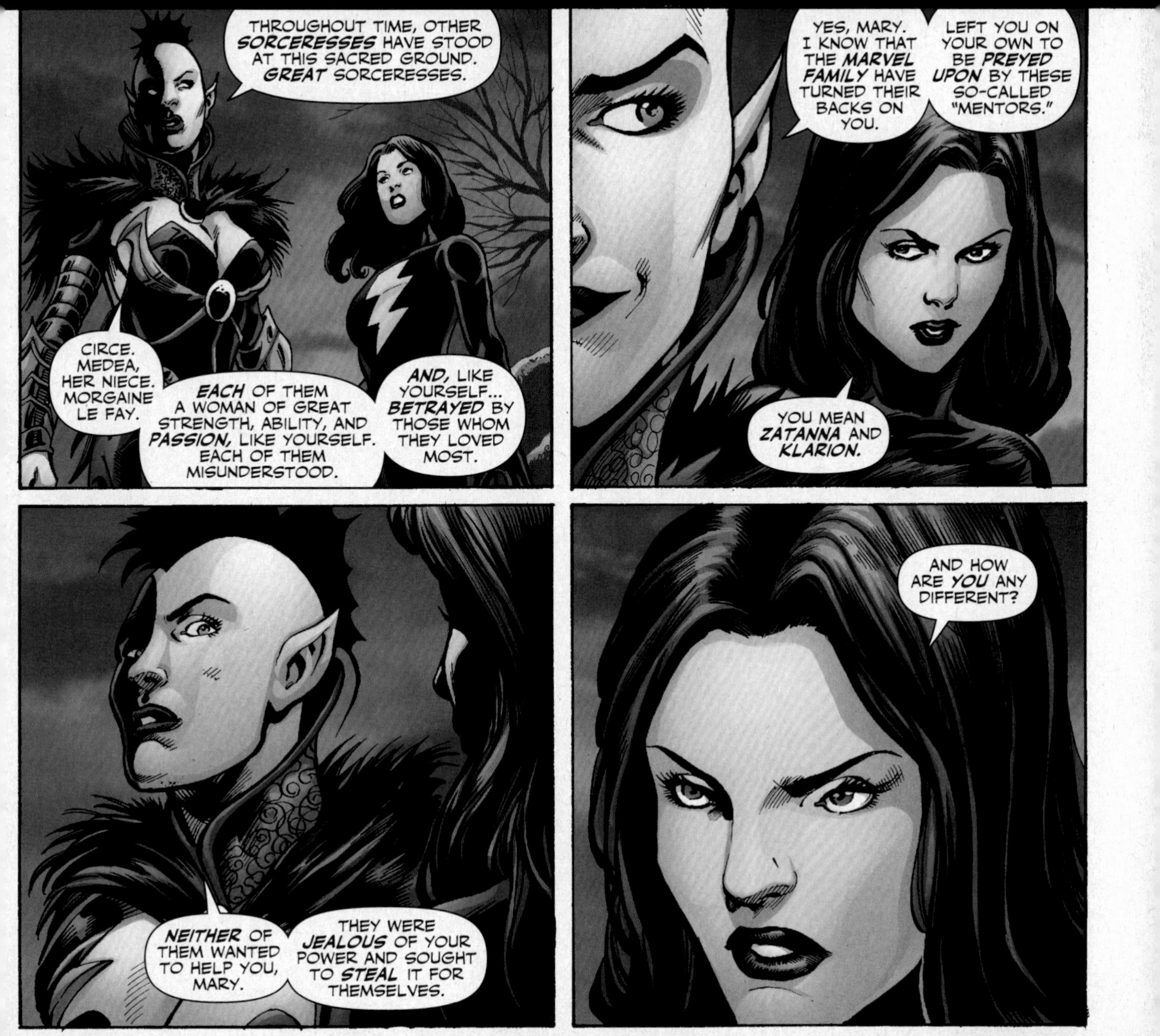
THROUGHOUT TIME, OTHER SORCERESSES HAVE STOOD AT THIS SACRED GROUND. GREAT SORCERESSES.
CIRCE. MEDEA, HER NIECE. MORGAINE LE FAY.
EACH OF THEM A WOMAN OF GREAT STRENGTH, ABILITY, AND PASSION, LIKE YOURSELF. EACH OF THEM MISUNDERSTOOD.
AND, LIKE YOURSELF... BETRAYED BY THOSE WHOM THEY LOVED MOST.
YES, MARY. I KNOW THAT THE MARVEL FAMILY HAVE TURNED THEIR BACKS ON YOU.
LEFT YOU ON YOUR OWN TO BE PREYED UPON BY THESE SO-CALLED "MENTORS."
YOU MEAN ZATANNA AND KLARION.
NEITHER OF THEM WANTED TO HELP YOU, MARY.
THEY WERE JEALOUS OF YOUR POWER AND SOUGHT TO STEAL IT FOR THEMSELVES.
AND HOW ARE YOU ANY DIFFERENT?

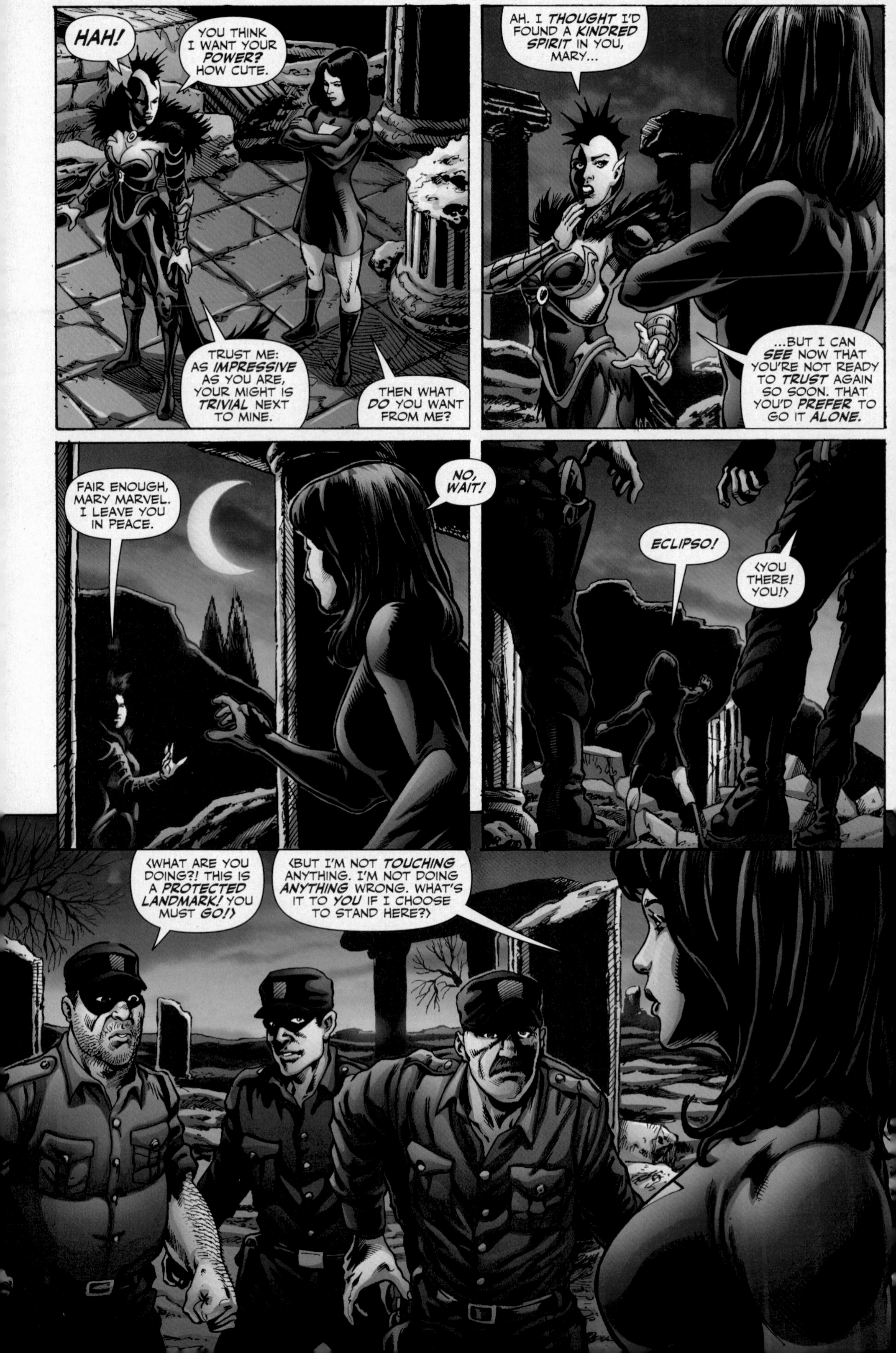
HAH!
YOU THINK I WANT YOUR POWER? HOW CUTE.
TRUST ME: AS IMPRESSIVE AS YOU ARE, YOUR MIGHT IS TRIVIAL NEXT TO MINE.
THEN WHAT DO YOU WANT FROM ME?
AH. I THOUGHT I'D FOUND A KINDRED SPIRIT IN YOU, MARY...
...BUT I CAN SEE NOW THAT YOU'RE NOT READY TO TRUST AGAIN SO SOON. THAT YOU'D PREFER TO GO IT ALONE.
FAIR ENOUGH, MARY MARVEL. I LEAVE YOU IN PEACE.
NO, WAIT!
ECLIPSO!
‹YOU THERE! YOU!›
‹WHAT ARE YOU DOING?! THIS IS A PROTECTED LANDMARK! YOU MUST GO!›
‹BUT I'M NOT TOUCHING ANYTHING. I'M NOT DOING ANYTHING WRONG. WHAT'S IT TO YOU IF I CHOOSE TO STAND HERE?›

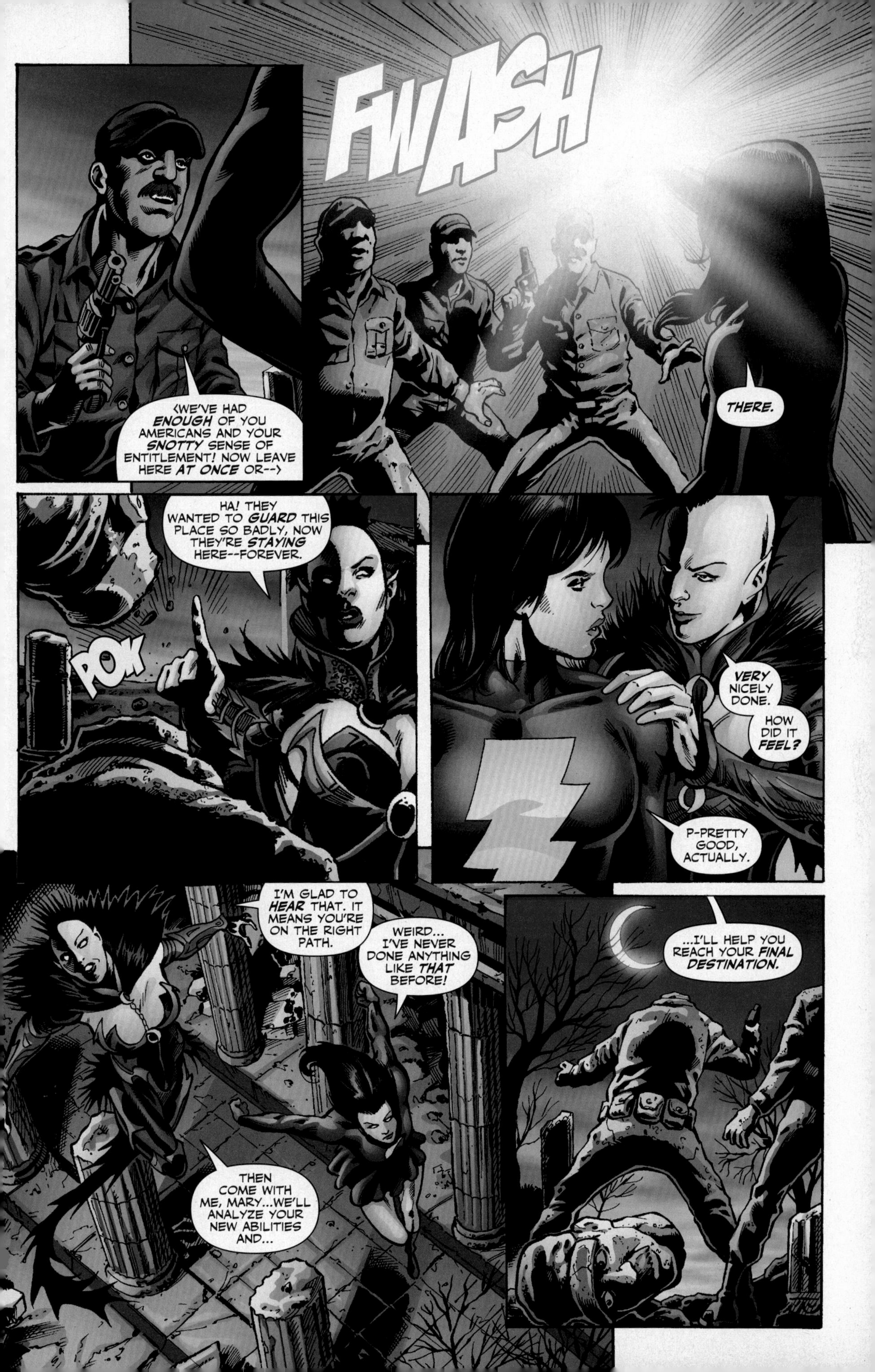

FWASH
<WE'VE HAD ENOUGH OF YOU AMERICANS AND YOUR SNOTTY SENSE OF ENTITLEMENT! NOW LEAVE HERE AT ONCE OR-->
THERE.
HA! THEY WANTED TO GUARD THIS PLACE SO BADLY, NOW THEY'RE STAYING HERE--FOREVER.
POK
VERY NICELY DONE.
HOW DID IT FEEL?
P-PRETTY GOOD, ACTUALLY.
I'M GLAD TO HEAR THAT. IT MEANS YOU'RE ON THE RIGHT PATH.
WEIRD... I'VE NEVER DONE ANYTHING LIKE THAT BEFORE!
THEN COME WITH ME, MARY...WE'LL ANALYZE YOUR NEW ABILITIES AND...
...I'LL HELP YOU REACH YOUR FINAL DESTINATION.

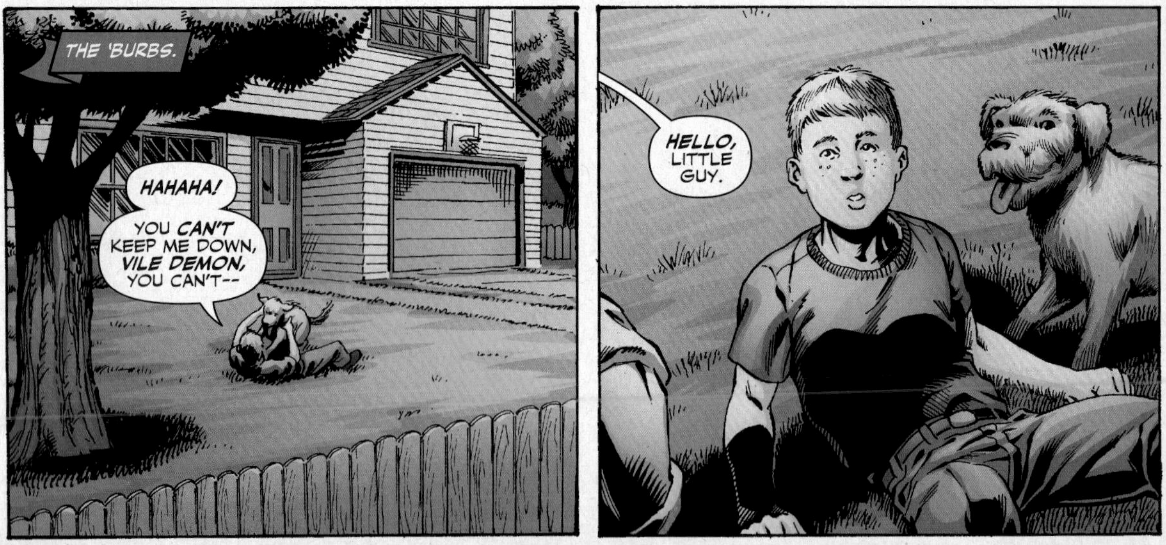
THE 'BURBS.
HAHAHA!
YOU CAN'T KEEP ME DOWN, VILE DEMON, YOU CAN'T--
HELLO, LITTLE GUY.

# KARATE KID

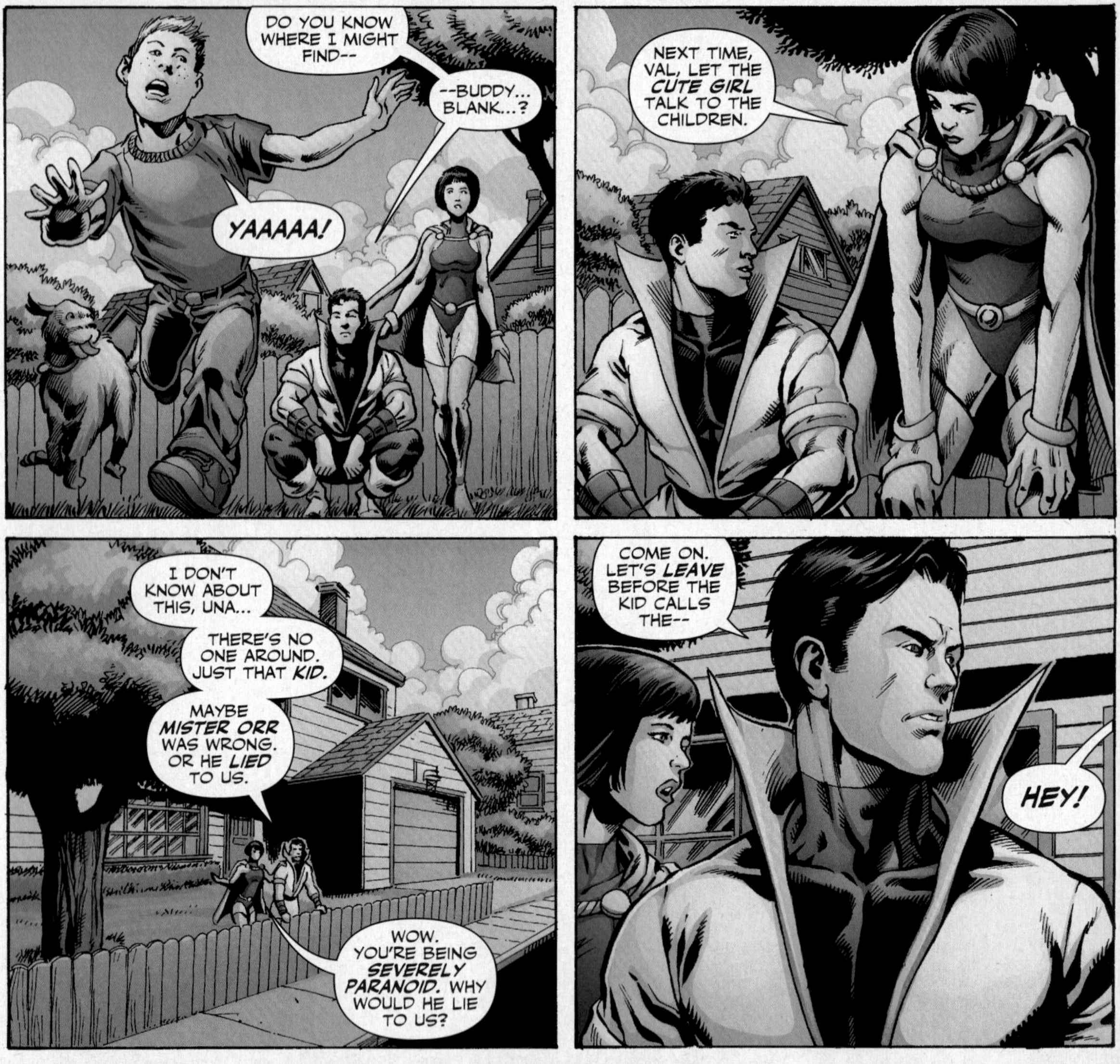
DO YOU KNOW WHERE I MIGHT FIND--
--BUDDY... BLANK...?
YAAAAA!
NEXT TIME, VAL, LET THE CUTE GIRL TALK TO THE CHILDREN.
I DON'T KNOW ABOUT THIS, UNA...
THERE'S NO ONE AROUND. JUST THAT KID.
MAYBE MISTER ORR WAS WRONG. OR HE LIED TO US.
WOW. YOU'RE BEING SEVERELY PARANOID. WHY WOULD HE LIE TO US?
COME ON. LET'S LEAVE BEFORE THE KID CALLS THE--
HEY!

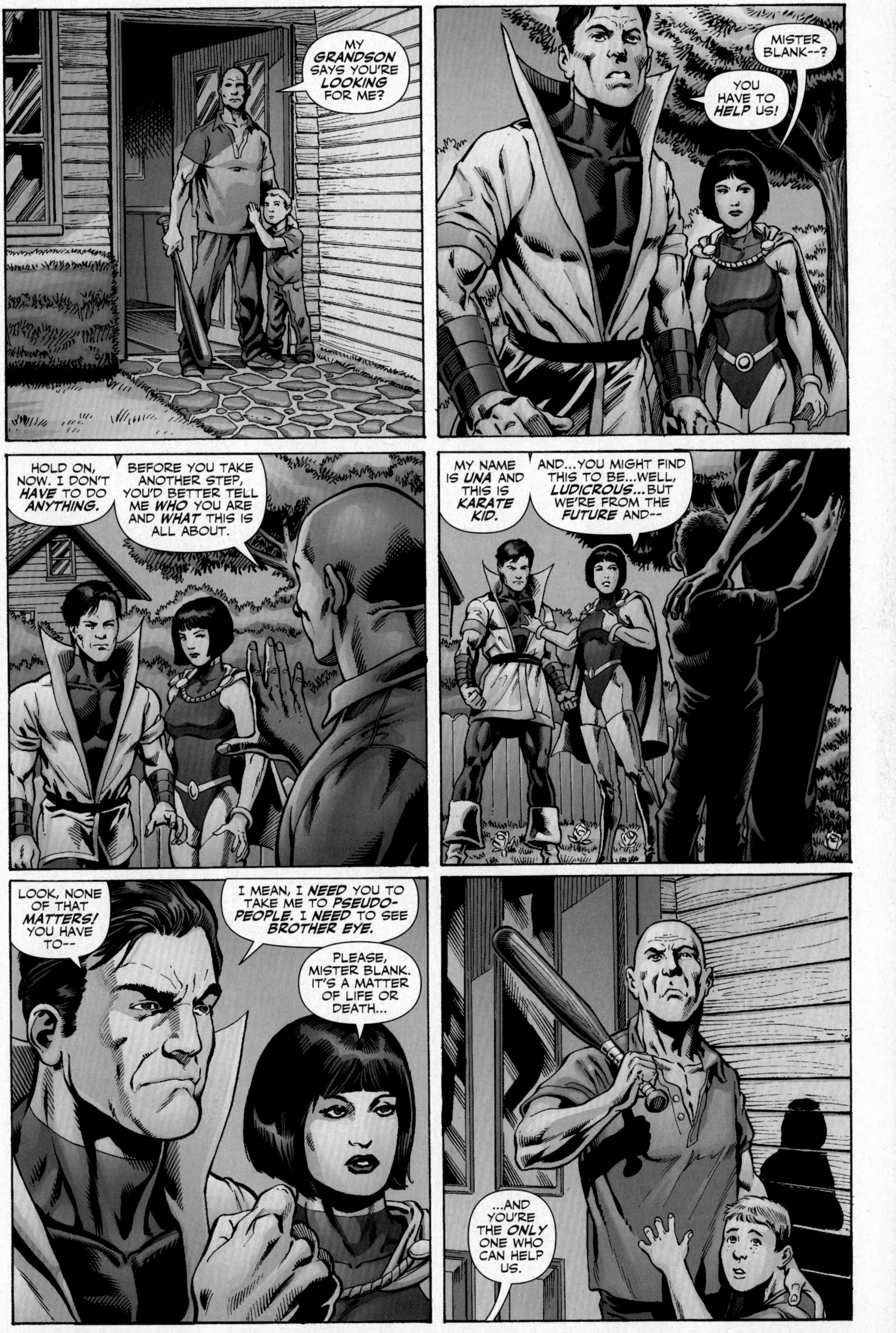

MY *GRANDSON* SAYS YOU'RE *LOOKING* FOR ME?
MISTER BLANK--?
YOU HAVE TO *HELP* US!
HOLD ON, NOW. I DON'T *HAVE* TO DO *ANYTHING.*
BEFORE YOU TAKE ANOTHER STEP, YOU'D BETTER TELL ME *WHO* YOU ARE AND *WHAT* THIS IS ALL ABOUT.
MY NAME IS *UNA* AND THIS IS *KARATE KID.*
AND...YOU MIGHT FIND THIS TO BE...WELL, *LUDICROUS*...BUT WE'RE FROM THE *FUTURE* AND--
LOOK, NONE OF THAT *MATTERS!* YOU HAVE TO--
I MEAN, I *NEED* YOU TO TAKE ME TO *PSEUDO-PEOPLE.* I *NEED* TO SEE *BROTHER EYE.*
PLEASE, MISTER BLANK. IT'S A MATTER OF LIFE OR DEATH...
...AND YOU'RE THE *ONLY* ONE WHO CAN HELP US.

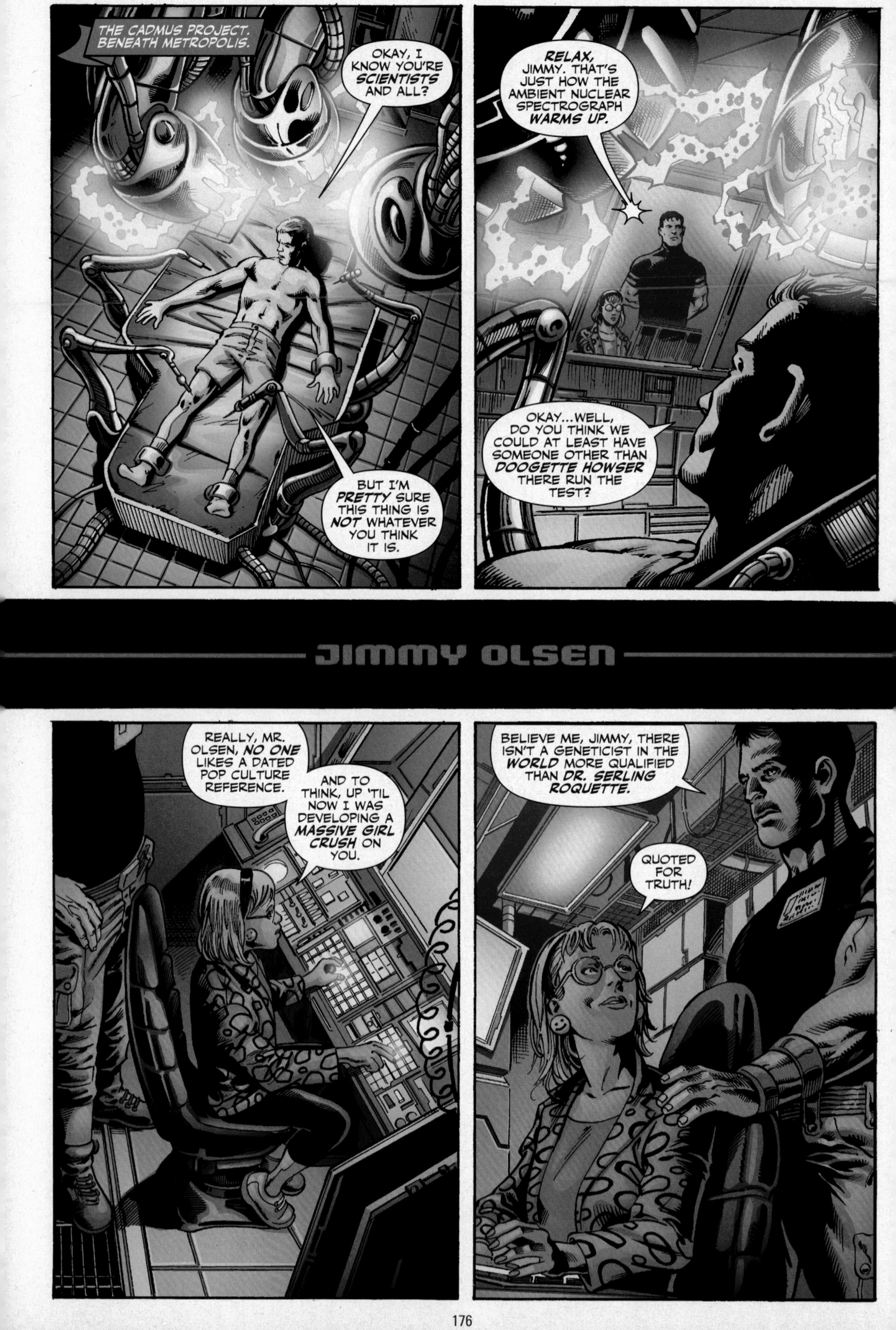
THE CADMUS PROJECT. BENEATH METROPOLIS.
OKAY, I KNOW YOU'RE SCIENTISTS AND ALL?
BUT I'M PRETTY SURE THIS THING IS NOT WHATEVER YOU THINK IT IS.
RELAX, JIMMY. THAT'S JUST HOW THE AMBIENT NUCLEAR SPECTROGRAPH WARMS UP.
OKAY...WELL, DO YOU THINK WE COULD AT LEAST HAVE SOMEONE OTHER THAN DOOGETTE HOWSER THERE RUN THE TEST?
JIMMY OLSEN
REALLY, MR. OLSEN, NO ONE LIKES A DATED POP CULTURE REFERENCE.
AND TO THINK, UP 'TIL NOW I WAS DEVELOPING A MASSIVE GIRL CRUSH ON YOU.
BELIEVE ME, JIMMY, THERE ISN'T A GENETICIST IN THE WORLD MORE QUALIFIED THAN DR. SERLING ROQUETTE.
QUOTED FOR TRUTH!

JUST KICK BACK AND, AS **MR. CANNON** HERE SO ELOQUENTLY PUT IT, **RELAX.**

LET THE **AMBIENT NUCLEAR ULTRA-SPECTROGRAPH** DO ITS THING.

WHY DON'T YOU JUST USE AN **ACRONYM?**

YOU THINK ABOUT THAT.

VMMMMMMMM

OKAY, WE'RE UP AND RUNNING AND EVERYTHING LOOKS-- OH-TO-THE-CRAP.

WHAT IS IT?

UH... GUYS?

IMMMMMMMMMM MMMMMMMMMMM

STOP IT!

I CAN'T!

W-WUH... WHAT'S...?

IMMMMMMMMM MMMMMMMMMMM MMMMMMMMMM

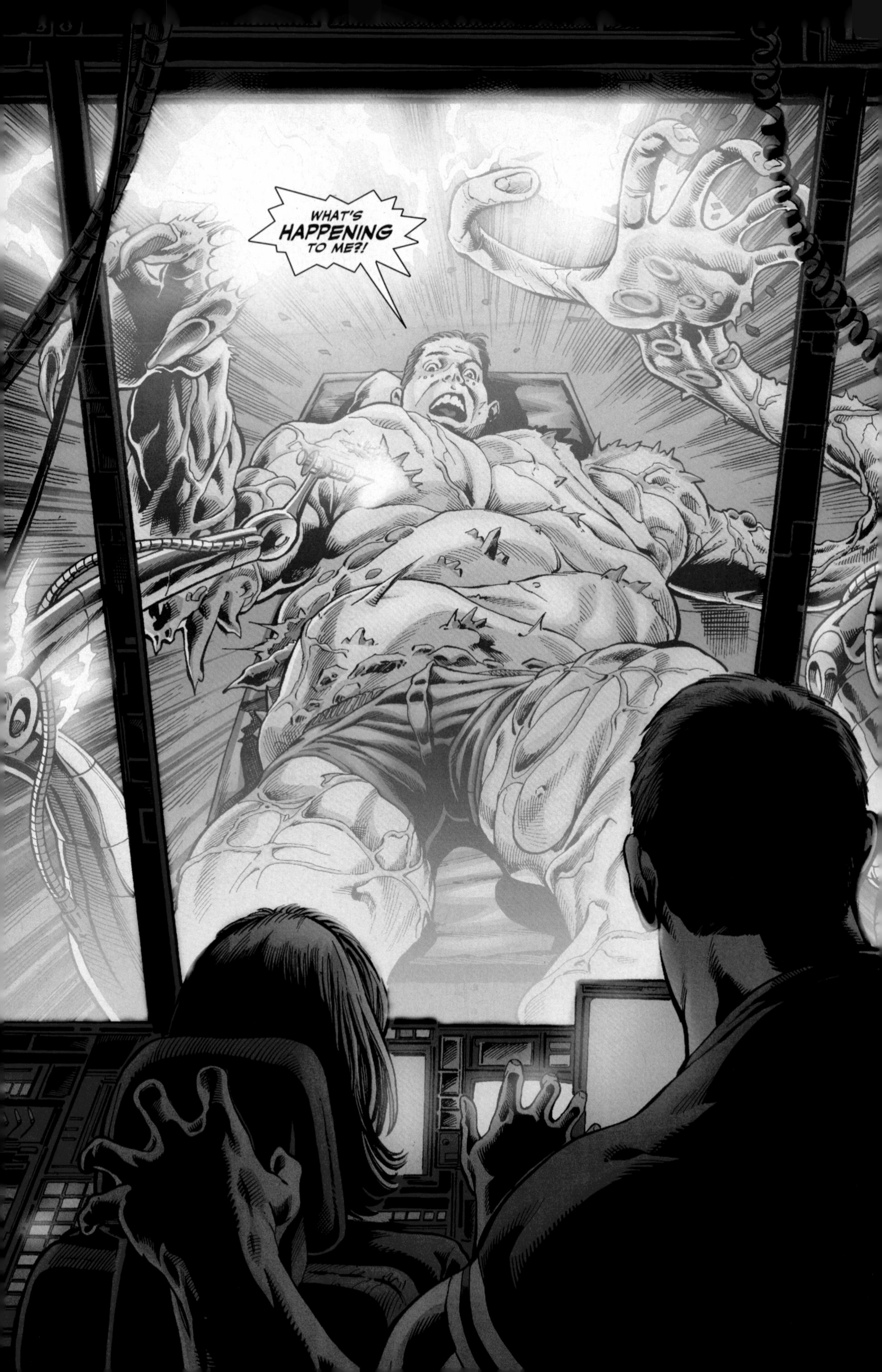
WHAT'S HAPPENING TO ME?!

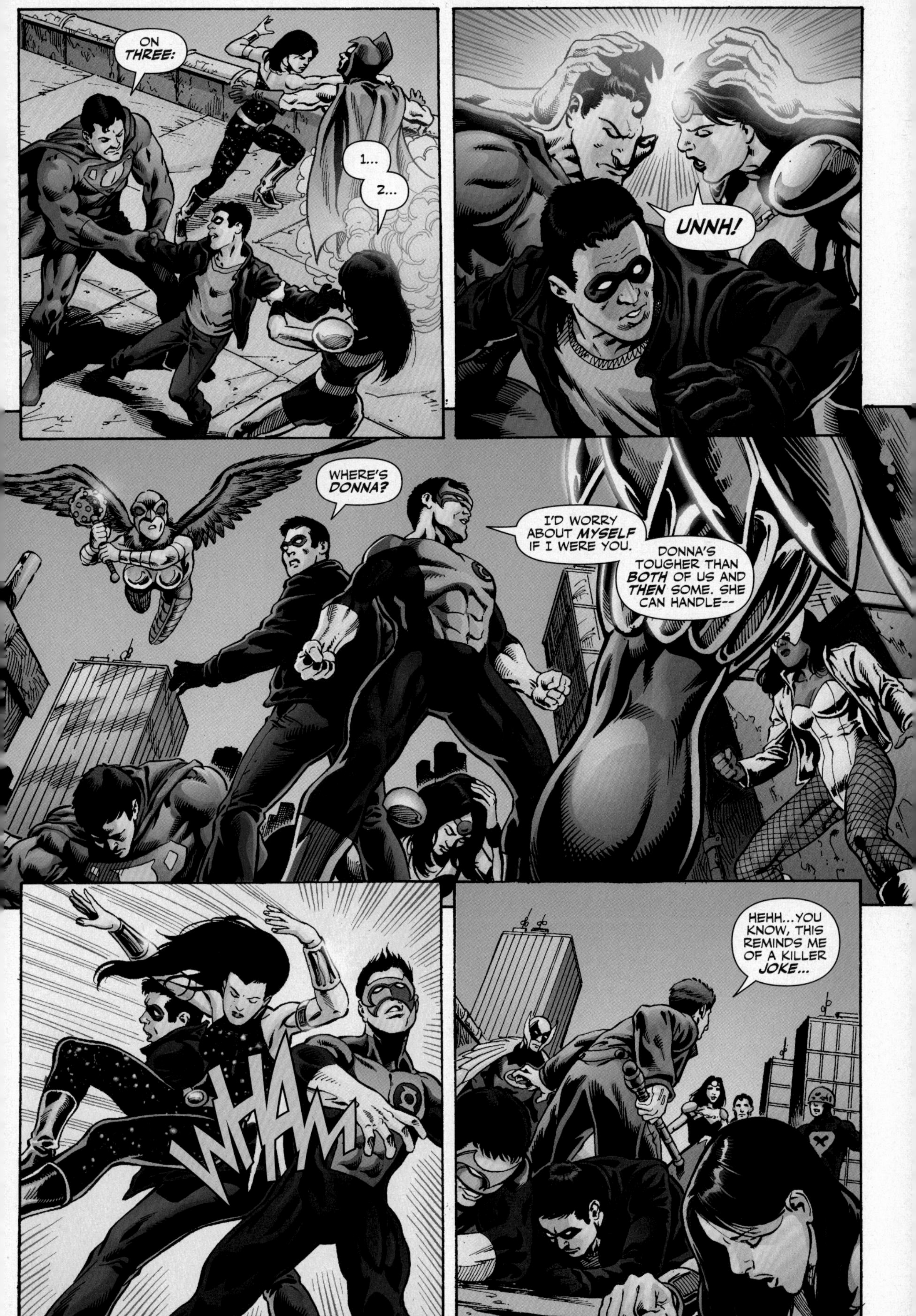
ON THREE:
1...
2...
UNNH!
WHERE'S DONNA?
I'D WORRY ABOUT MYSELF IF I WERE YOU.
DONNA'S TOUGHER THAN BOTH OF US AND THEN SOME. SHE CAN HANDLE--
WHAM
HEHH...YOU KNOW, THIS REMINDS ME OF A KILLER JOKE...

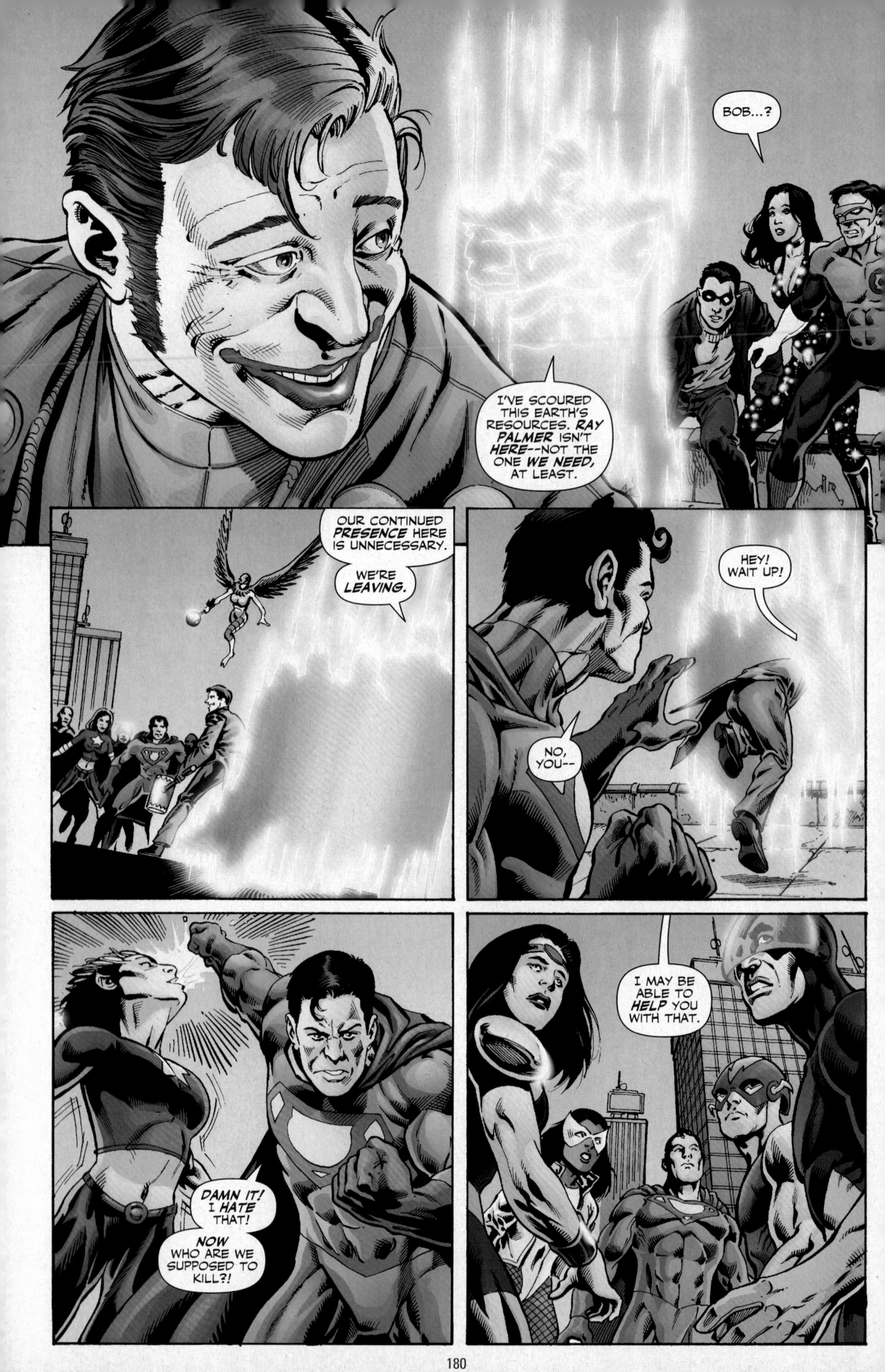
BOB...?
I'VE SCOURED THIS EARTH'S RESOURCES. RAY PALMER ISN'T HERE--NOT THE ONE WE NEED, AT LEAST.
OUR CONTINUED PRESENCE HERE IS UNNECESSARY.
WE'RE LEAVING.
HEY! WAIT UP!
NO, YOU--
DAMN IT! I HATE THAT!
NOW WHO ARE WE SUPPOSED TO KILL?!
I MAY BE ABLE TO HELP YOU WITH THAT.

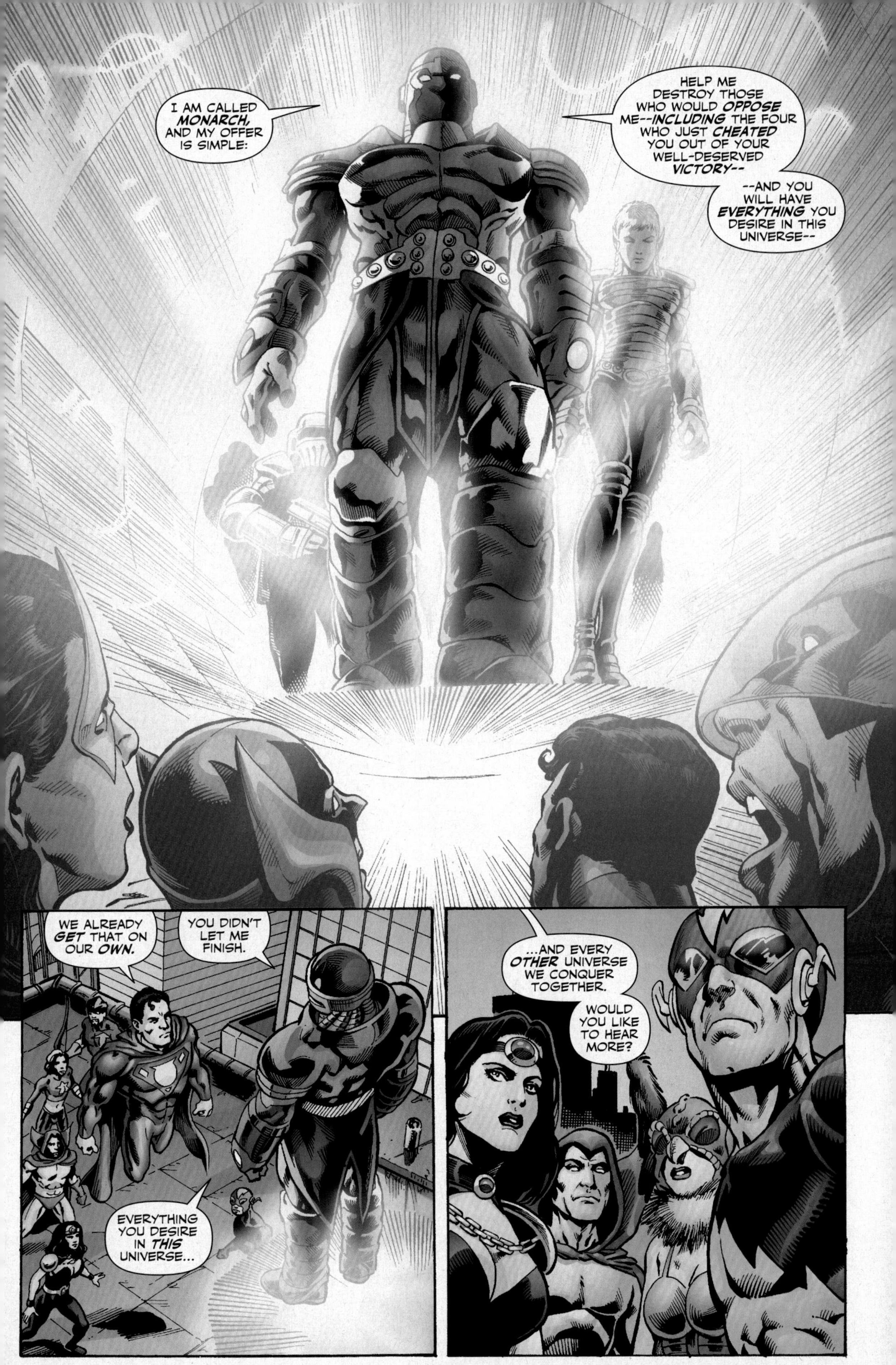
I AM CALLED MONARCH, AND MY OFFER IS SIMPLE:
HELP ME DESTROY THOSE WHO WOULD OPPOSE ME--INCLUDING THE FOUR WHO JUST CHEATED YOU OUT OF YOUR WELL-DESERVED VICTORY--
--AND YOU WILL HAVE EVERYTHING YOU DESIRE IN THIS UNIVERSE--
WE ALREADY GET THAT ON OUR OWN.
YOU DIDN'T LET ME FINISH.
EVERYTHING YOU DESIRE IN THIS UNIVERSE...
...AND EVERY OTHER UNIVERSE WE CONQUER TOGETHER.
WOULD YOU LIKE TO HEAR MORE?

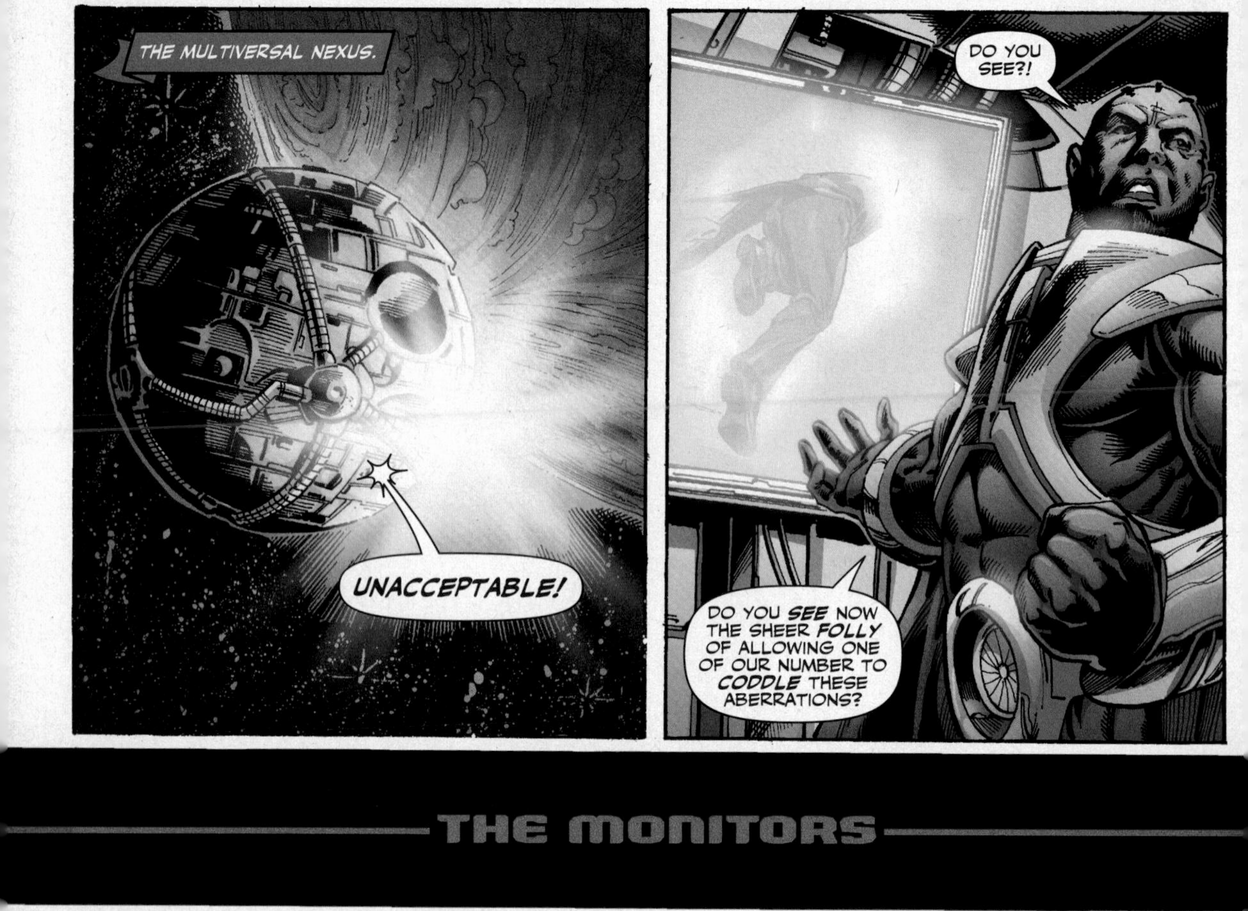
THE MULTIVERSAL NEXUS.
UNACCEPTABLE!
DO YOU SEE?!
DO YOU SEE NOW THE SHEER FOLLY OF ALLOWING ONE OF OUR NUMBER TO CODDLE THESE ABERRATIONS?

## THE MONITORS

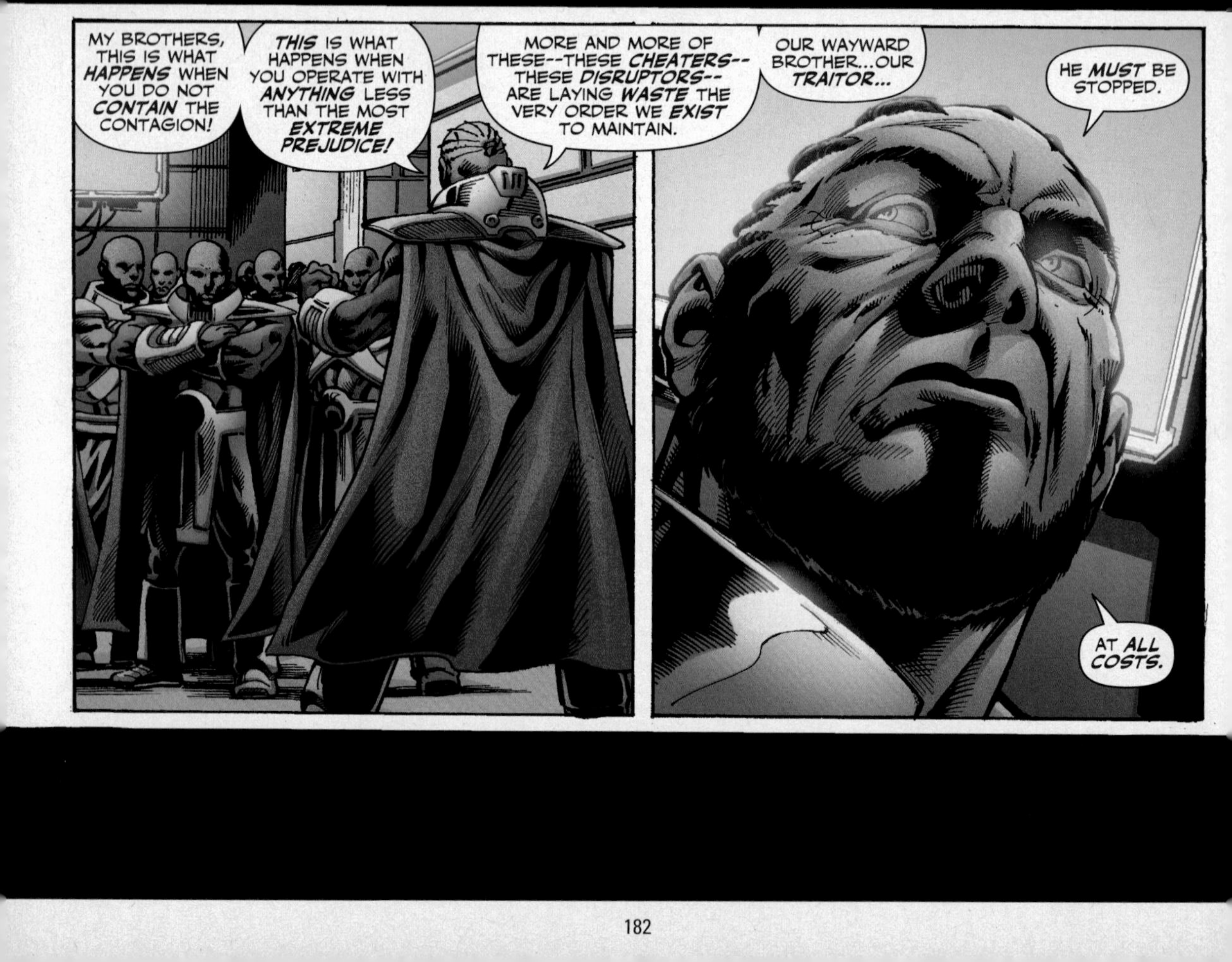
MY BROTHERS, THIS IS WHAT HAPPENS WHEN YOU DO NOT CONTAIN THE CONTAGION!
THIS IS WHAT HAPPENS WHEN YOU OPERATE WITH ANYTHING LESS THAN THE MOST EXTREME PREJUDICE!
MORE AND MORE OF THESE--THESE CHEATERS--THESE DISRUPTORS--ARE LAYING WASTE THE VERY ORDER WE EXIST TO MAINTAIN.
OUR WAYWARD BROTHER...OUR TRAITOR...
HE MUST BE STOPPED.
AT ALL COSTS.

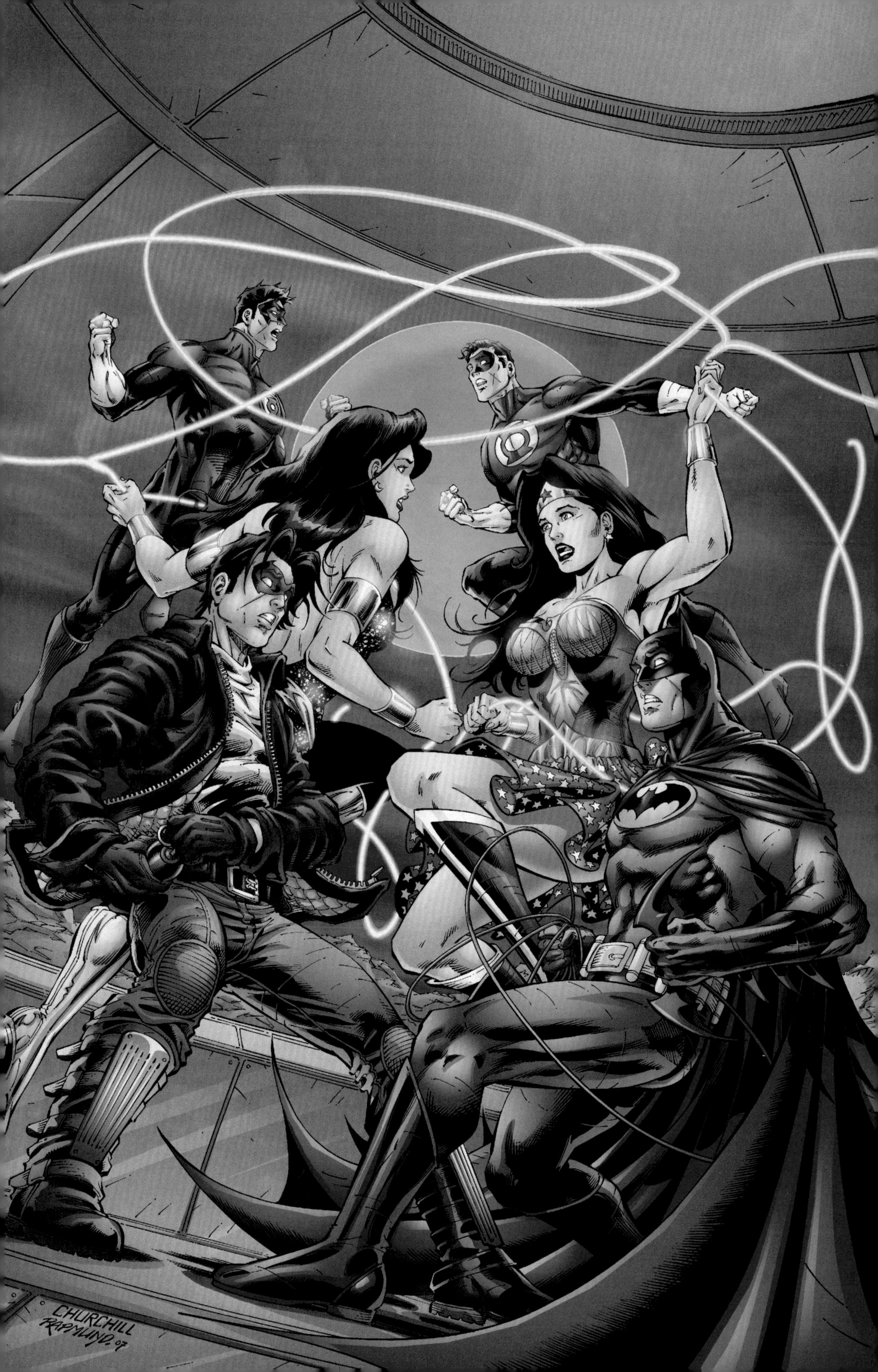
CHURCHILL
RAPMUND '07

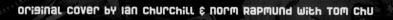

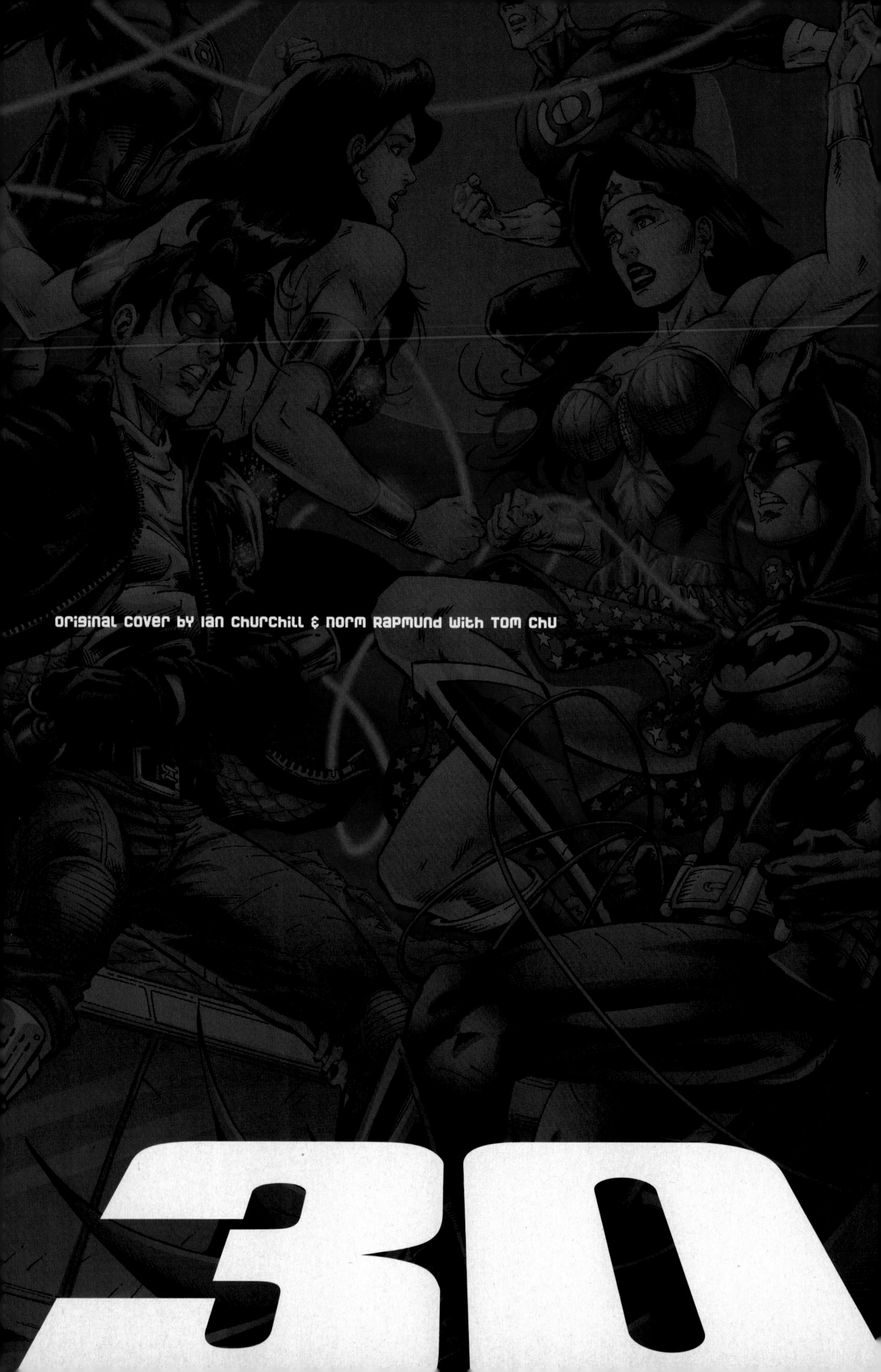

ORIGINAL COVER BY IAN CHURCHILL & NORM RAPMUND WITH TOM CHU

3D

WHO IS THERE?

HELLO, BROTHER EYE, IT'S ME, BUDDY.

HELLO PROFESSOR BLANK.

## THIRTY AND COUNTING... KARATE KID

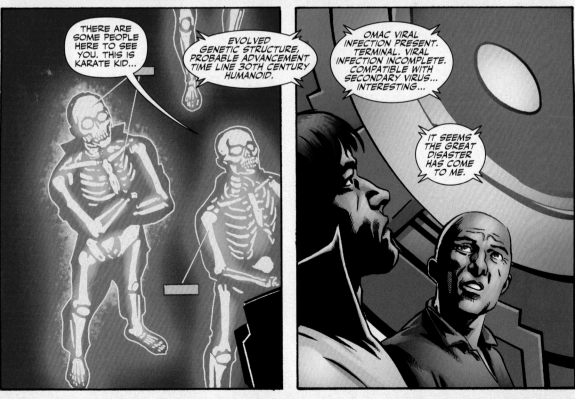

THERE ARE SOME PEOPLE HERE TO SEE YOU. THIS IS KARATE KID...

EVOLVED GENETIC STRUCTURE, PROBABLE ADVANCEMENT TIME LINE 30TH CENTURY HUMANOID.

OMAC VIRAL INFECTION PRESENT. TERMINAL. VIRAL INFECTION INCOMPLETE. COMPATIBLE WITH SECONDARY VIRUS... INTERESTING...

IT SEEMS THE GREAT DISASTER HAS COME TO ME.

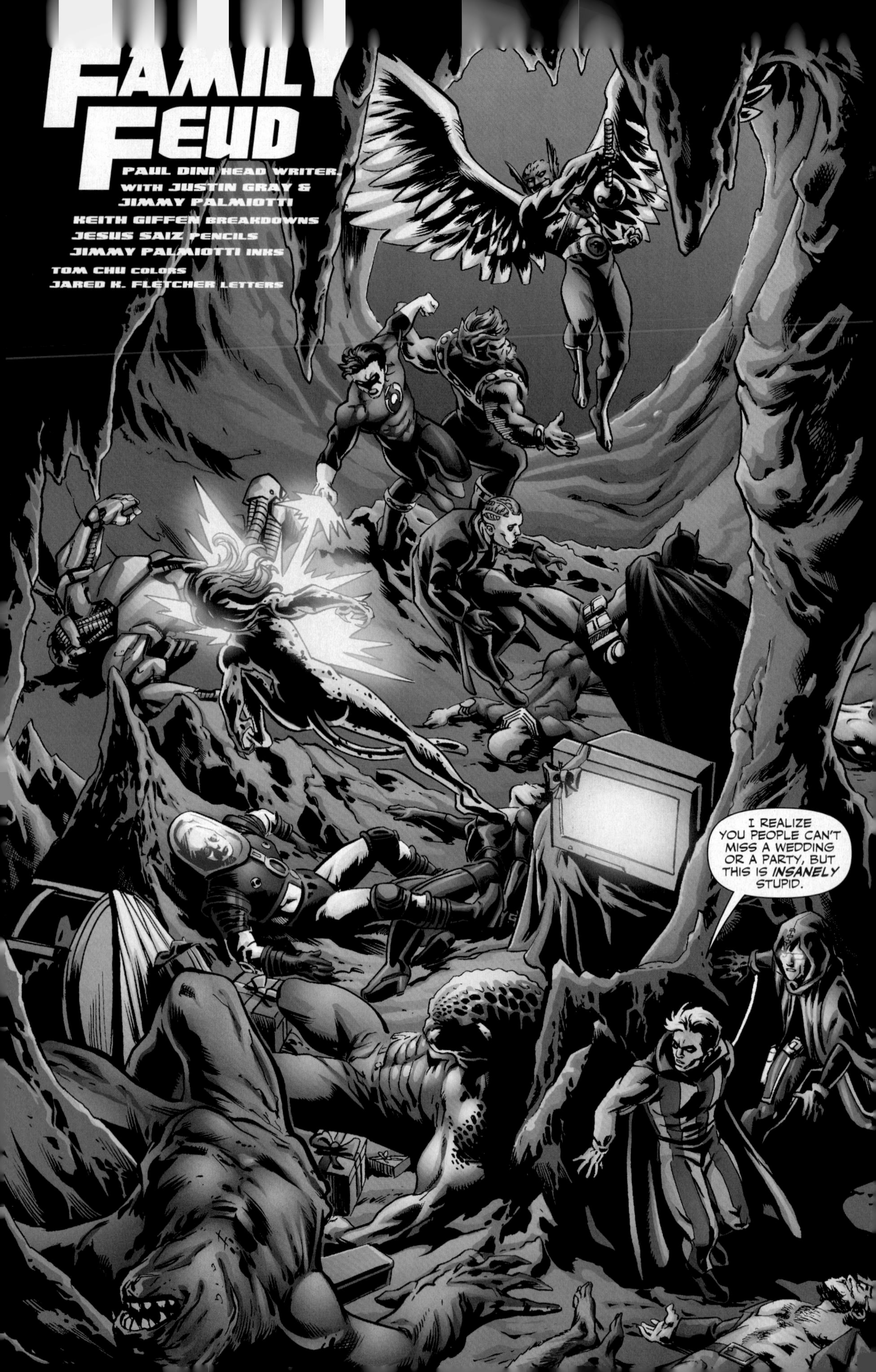
FAMILY FEUD
PAUL DINI HEAD WRITER, WITH JUSTIN GRAY & JIMMY PALMIOTTI
KEITH GIFFEN BREAKDOWNS
JESUS SAIZ PENCILS
JIMMY PALMIOTTI INKS
TOM CHU COLORS
JARED K. FLETCHER LETTERS
I REALIZE YOU PEOPLE CAN'T MISS A WEDDING OR A PARTY, BUT THIS IS INSANELY STUPID.

# PIPER & TRICKSTER

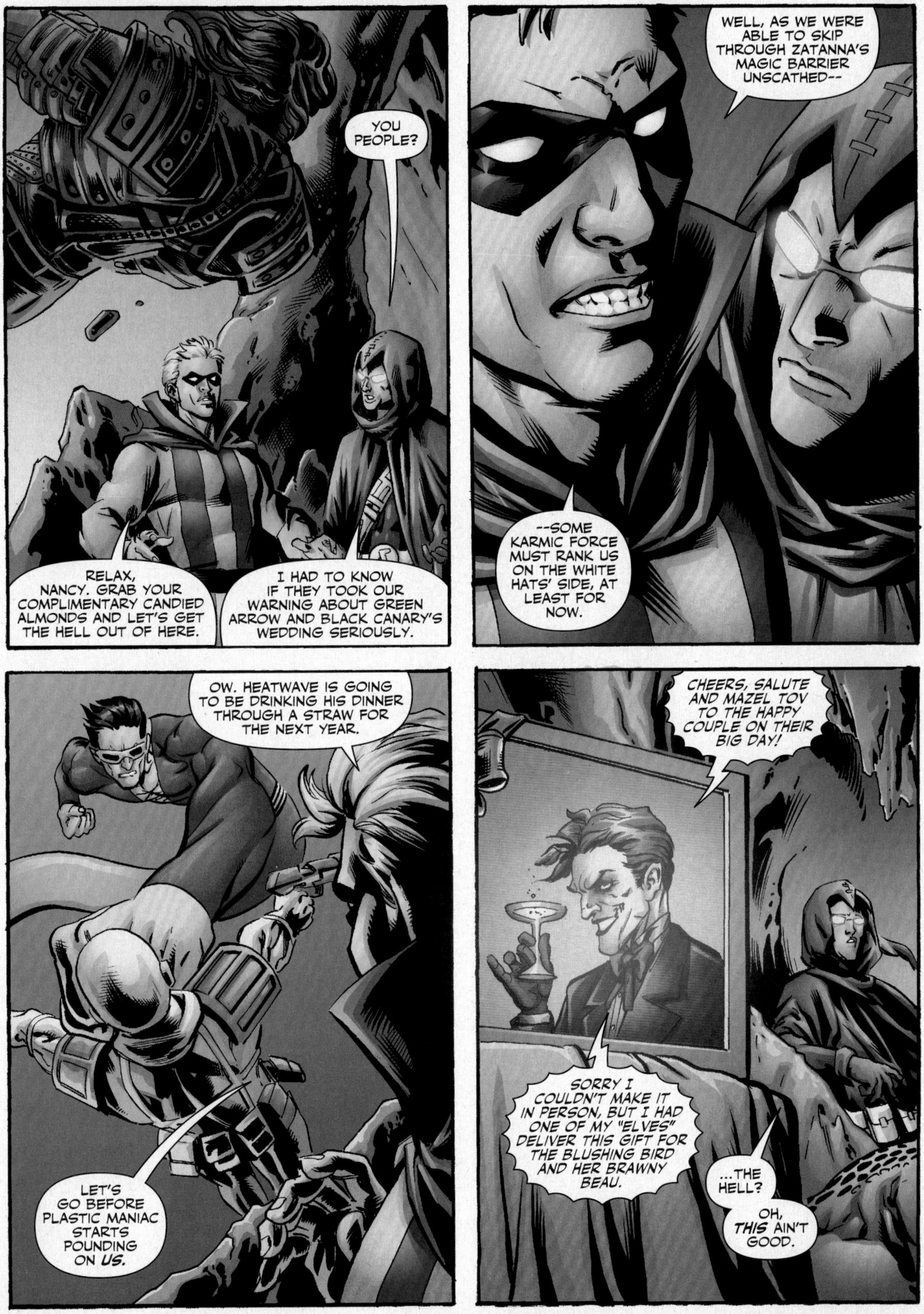
YOU PEOPLE?
RELAX, NANCY. GRAB YOUR COMPLIMENTARY CANDIED ALMONDS AND LET'S GET THE HELL OUT OF HERE.
I HAD TO KNOW IF THEY TOOK OUR WARNING ABOUT GREEN ARROW AND BLACK CANARY'S WEDDING SERIOUSLY.
WELL, AS WE WERE ABLE TO SKIP THROUGH ZATANNA'S MAGIC BARRIER UNSCATHED--
--SOME KARMIC FORCE MUST RANK US ON THE WHITE HATS' SIDE, AT LEAST FOR NOW.
OW. HEATWAVE IS GOING TO BE DRINKING HIS DINNER THROUGH A STRAW FOR THE NEXT YEAR.
LET'S GO BEFORE PLASTIC MANIAC STARTS POUNDING ON *US.*
CHEERS, SALUTE AND MAZEL TOV TO THE HAPPY COUPLE ON THEIR BIG DAY!
SORRY I COULDN'T MAKE IT IN PERSON, BUT I HAD ONE OF MY "ELVES" DELIVER THIS GIFT FOR THE BLUSHING BIRD AND HER BRAWNY BEAU.
...THE HELL?
OH, *THIS* AIN'T GOOD.

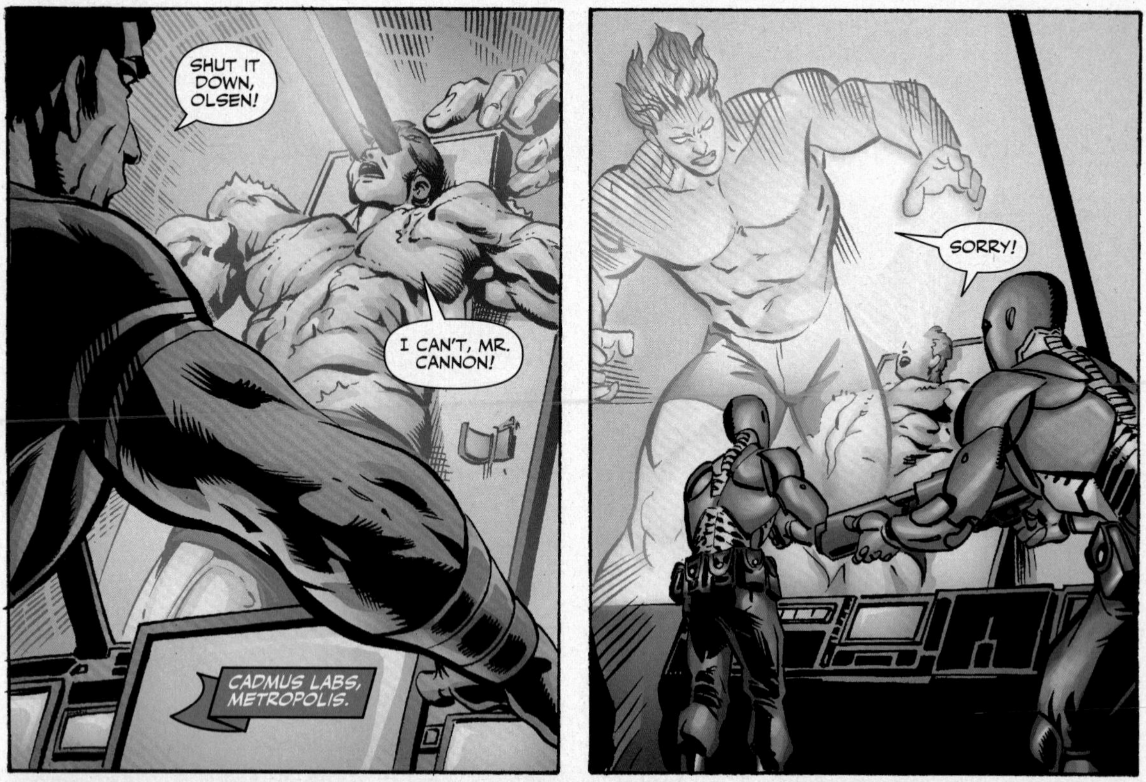
SHUT IT DOWN, OLSEN!
I CAN'T, MR. CANNON!
CADMUS LABS, METROPOLIS.
SORRY!

# JIMMY OLSEN

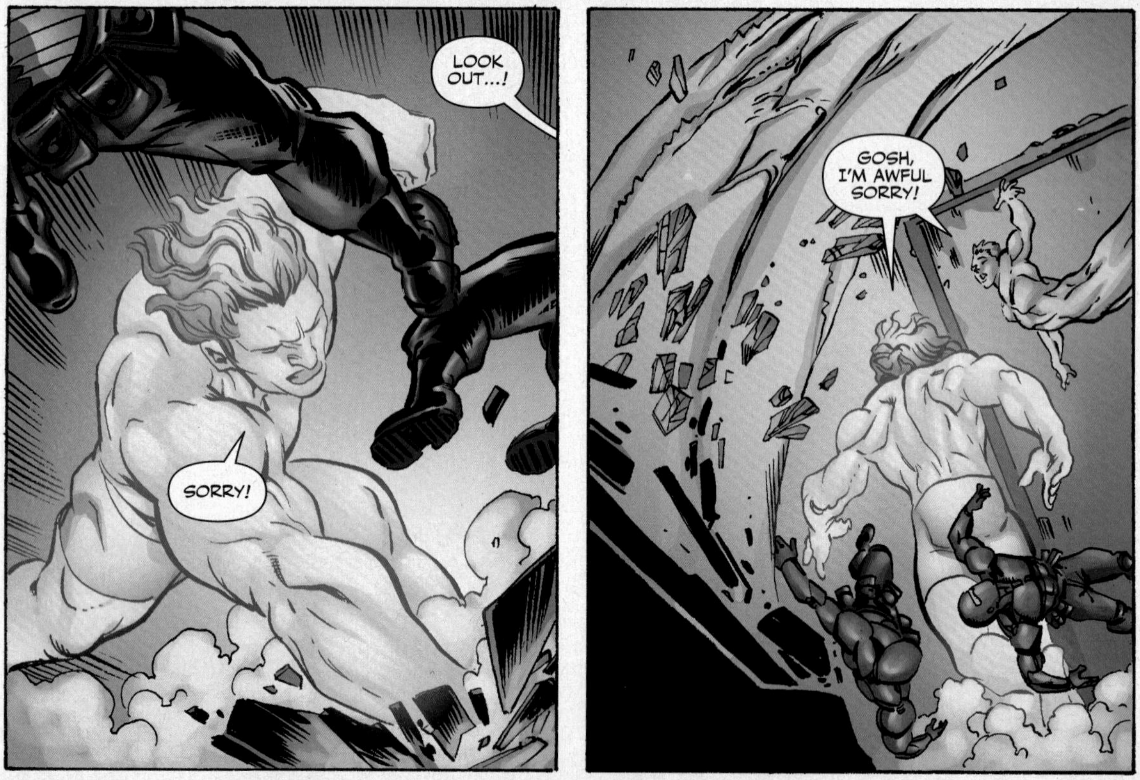
LOOK OUT...!
SORRY!
GOSH, I'M AWFUL SORRY!

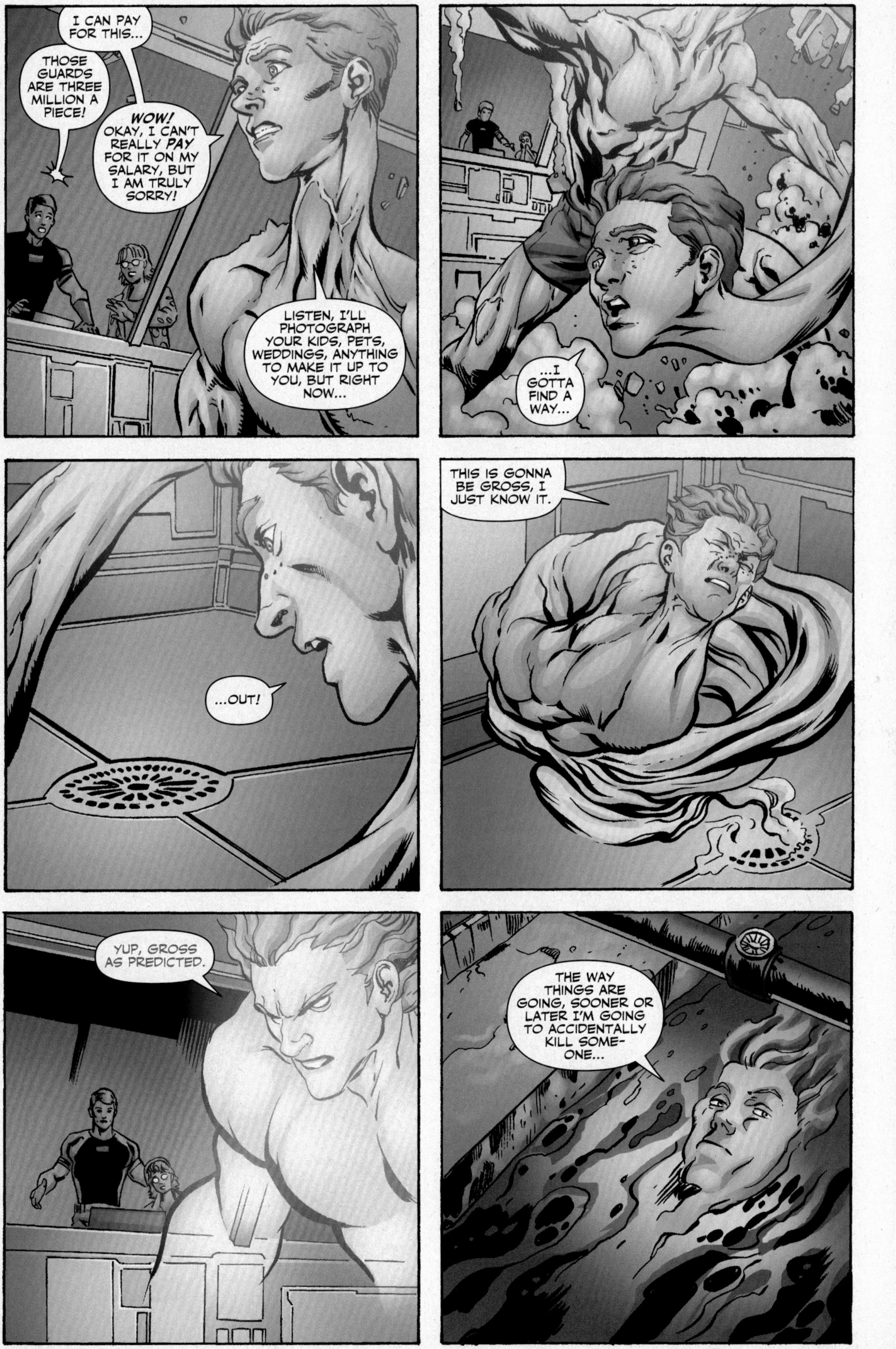
I CAN PAY FOR THIS...
THOSE GUARDS ARE THREE MILLION A PIECE!
WOW! OKAY, I CAN'T REALLY PAY FOR IT ON MY SALARY, BUT I AM TRULY SORRY!
LISTEN, I'LL PHOTOGRAPH YOUR KIDS, PETS, WEDDINGS, ANYTHING TO MAKE IT UP TO YOU, BUT RIGHT NOW...
...I GOTTA FIND A WAY...
...OUT!
THIS IS GONNA BE GROSS, I JUST KNOW IT.
YUP, GROSS AS PREDICTED.
THE WAY THINGS ARE GOING, SOONER OR LATER I'M GOING TO ACCIDENTALLY KILL SOME-ONE...

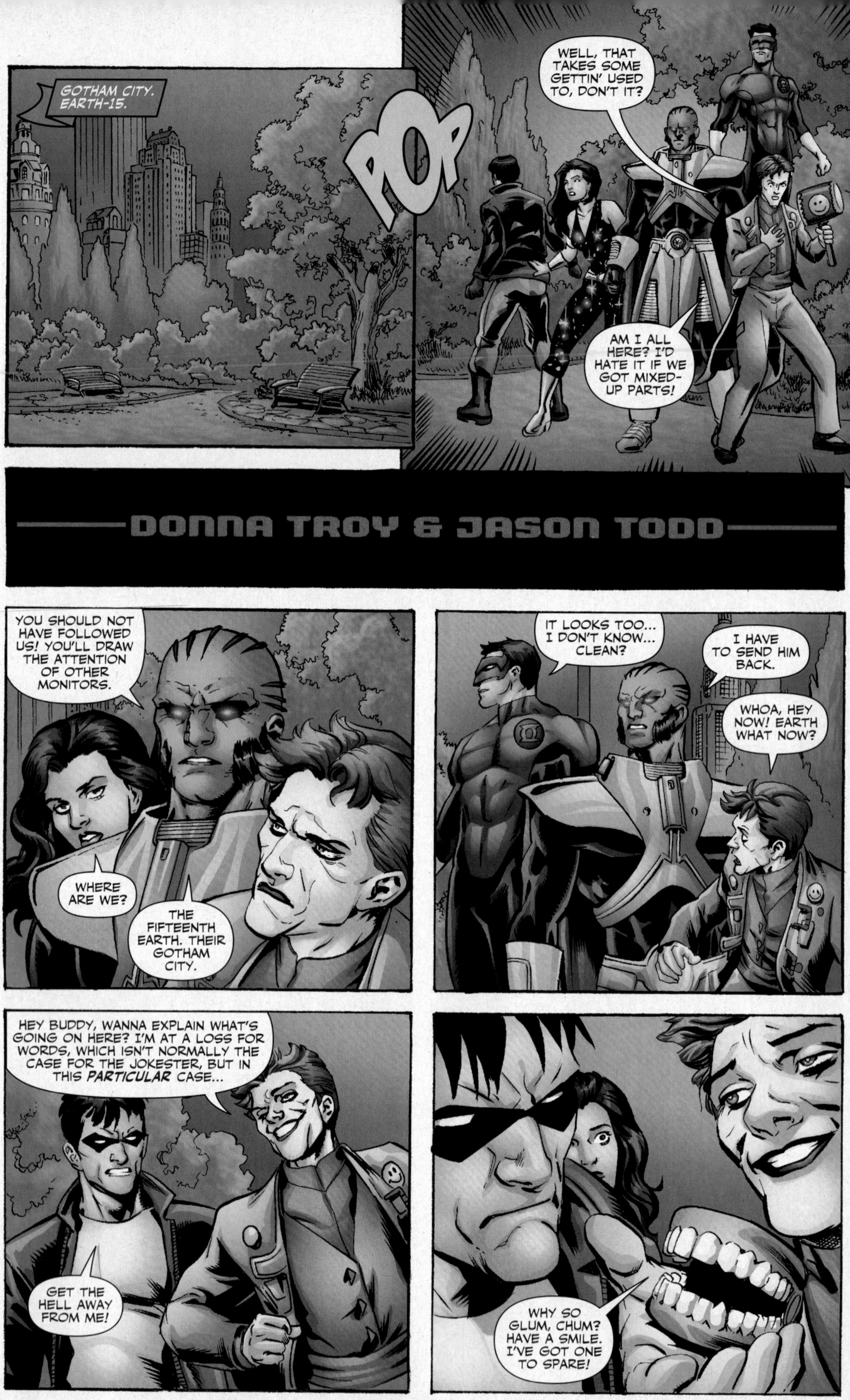
GOTHAM CITY. EARTH-15.
POP
WELL, THAT TAKES SOME GETTIN' USED TO, DON'T IT?
AM I ALL HERE? I'D HATE IT IF WE GOT MIXED-UP PARTS!
DONNA TROY & JASON TODD
YOU SHOULD NOT HAVE FOLLOWED US! YOU'LL DRAW THE ATTENTION OF OTHER MONITORS.
WHERE ARE WE?
THE FIFTEENTH EARTH. THEIR GOTHAM CITY.
IT LOOKS TOO... I DON'T KNOW... CLEAN?
I HAVE TO SEND HIM BACK.
WHOA, HEY NOW! EARTH WHAT NOW?
HEY BUDDY, WANNA EXPLAIN WHAT'S GOING ON HERE? I'M AT A LOSS FOR WORDS, WHICH ISN'T NORMALLY THE CASE FOR THE JOKESTER, BUT IN THIS *PARTICULAR* CASE...
GET THE HELL AWAY FROM ME!
WHY SO GLUM, CHUM? HAVE A SMILE. I'VE GOT ONE TO SPARE!

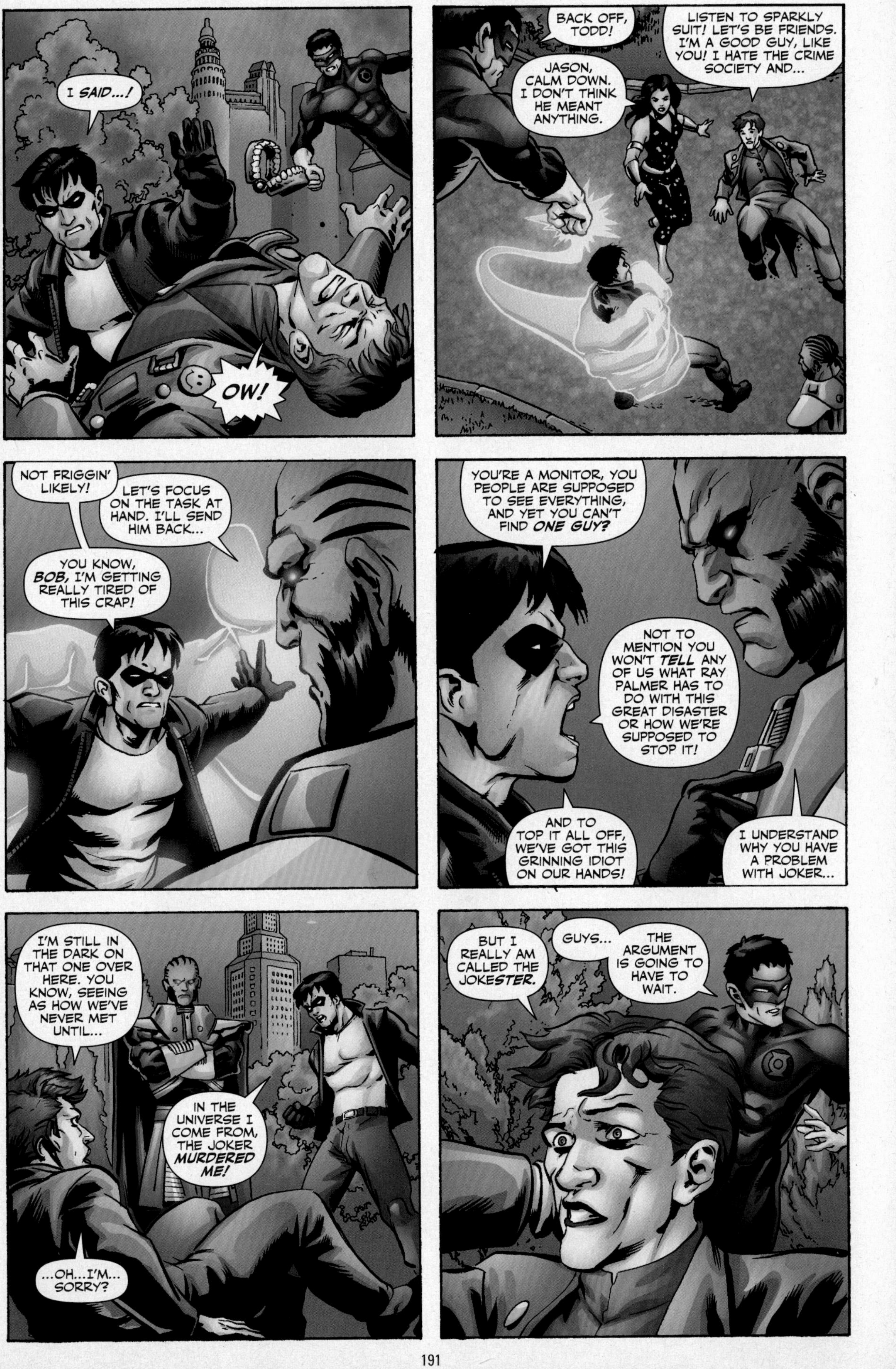
I SAID...!
OW!
BACK OFF, TODD!
LISTEN TO SPARKLY SUIT! LET'S BE FRIENDS. I'M A GOOD GUY, LIKE YOU! I HATE THE CRIME SOCIETY AND...
JASON, CALM DOWN. I DON'T THINK HE MEANT ANYTHING.
NOT FRIGGIN' LIKELY!
LET'S FOCUS ON THE TASK AT HAND. I'LL SEND HIM BACK...
YOU KNOW, BOB, I'M GETTING REALLY TIRED OF THIS CRAP!
YOU'RE A MONITOR, YOU PEOPLE ARE SUPPOSED TO SEE EVERYTHING, AND YET YOU CAN'T FIND ONE GUY?
NOT TO MENTION YOU WON'T TELL ANY OF US WHAT RAY PALMER HAS TO DO WITH THIS GREAT DISASTER OR HOW WE'RE SUPPOSED TO STOP IT!
AND TO TOP IT ALL OFF, WE'VE GOT THIS GRINNING IDIOT ON OUR HANDS!
I UNDERSTAND WHY YOU HAVE A PROBLEM WITH JOKER...
I'M STILL IN THE DARK ON THAT ONE OVER HERE. YOU KNOW, SEEING AS HOW WE'VE NEVER MET UNTIL...
IN THE UNIVERSE I COME FROM, THE JOKER MURDERED ME!
...OH...I'M... SORRY?
BUT I REALLY AM CALLED THE JOKESTER.
GUYS...
THE ARGUMENT IS GOING TO HAVE TO WAIT.

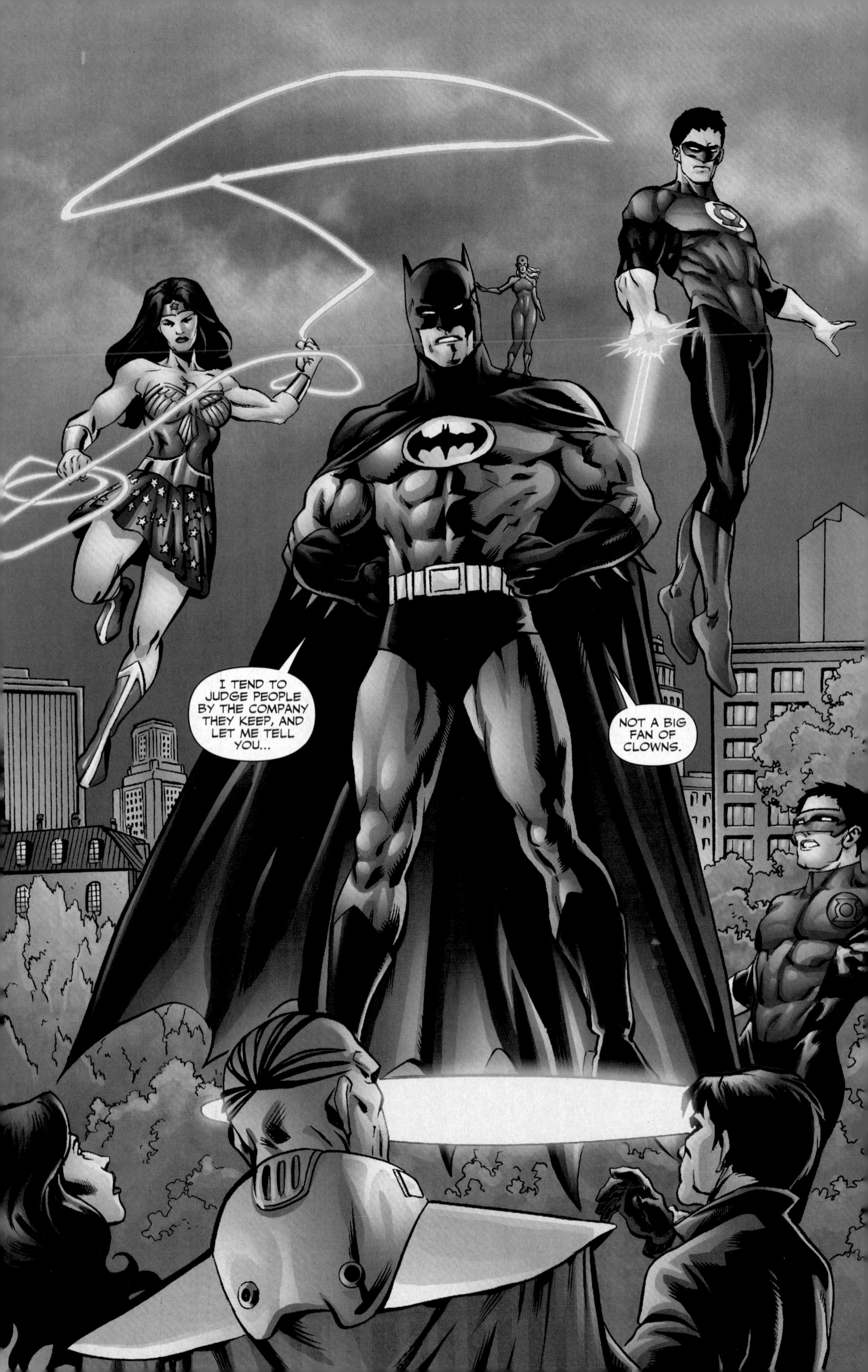
I TEND TO JUDGE PEOPLE BY THE COMPANY THEY KEEP, AND LET ME TELL YOU...
NOT A BIG FAN OF CLOWNS.

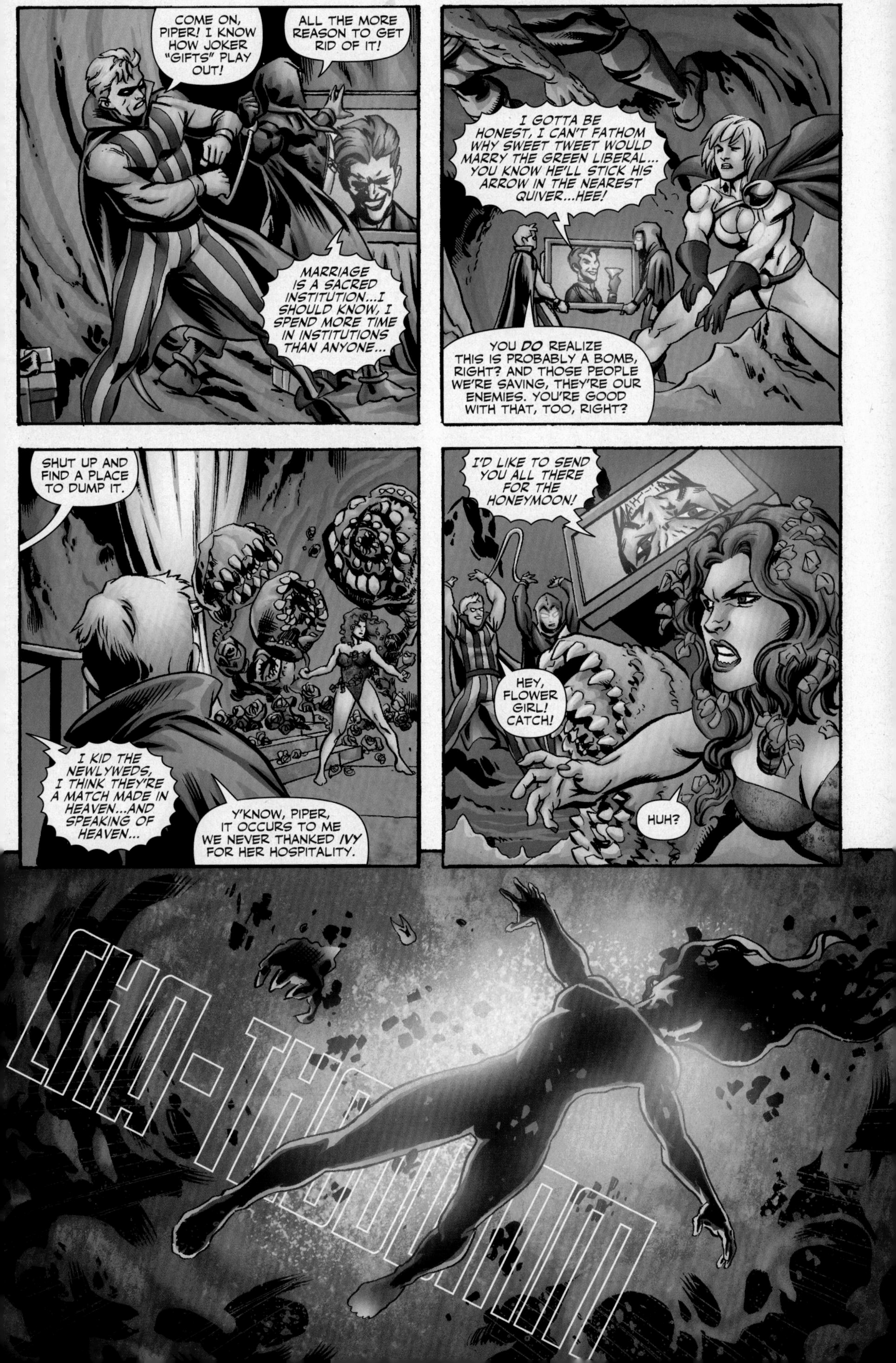

COME ON, PIPER! I KNOW HOW JOKER "GIFTS" PLAY OUT!
ALL THE MORE REASON TO GET RID OF IT!
MARRIAGE IS A SACRED INSTITUTION...I SHOULD KNOW, I SPEND MORE TIME IN INSTITUTIONS THAN ANYONE...
I GOTTA BE HONEST, I CAN'T FATHOM WHY SWEET TWEET WOULD MARRY THE GREEN LIBERAL... YOU KNOW HE'LL STICK HIS ARROW IN THE NEAREST QUIVER...HEE!
YOU DO REALIZE THIS IS PROBABLY A BOMB, RIGHT? AND THOSE PEOPLE WE'RE SAVING, THEY'RE OUR ENEMIES. YOU'RE GOOD WITH THAT, TOO, RIGHT?
SHUT UP AND FIND A PLACE TO DUMP IT.
I KID THE NEWLYWEDS, I THINK THEY'RE A MATCH MADE IN HEAVEN...AND SPEAKING OF HEAVEN...
Y'KNOW, PIPER, IT OCCURS TO ME WE NEVER THANKED IVY FOR HER HOSPITALITY.
I'D LIKE TO SEND YOU ALL THERE FOR THE HONEYMOON!
HEY, FLOWER GIRL! CATCH!
HUH?

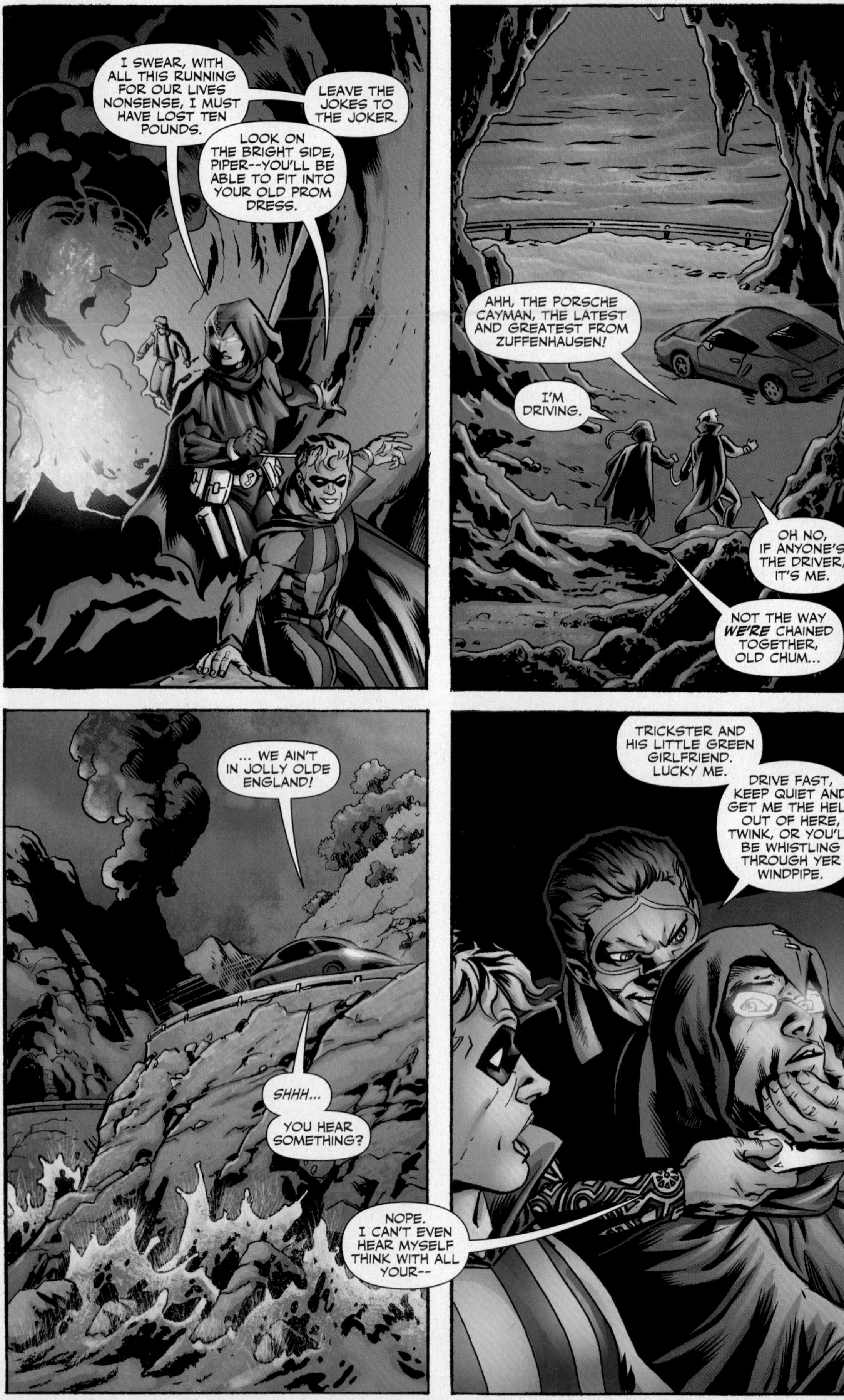
I SWEAR, WITH ALL THIS RUNNING FOR OUR LIVES NONSENSE, I MUST HAVE LOST TEN POUNDS.
LEAVE THE JOKES TO THE JOKER.
LOOK ON THE BRIGHT SIDE, PIPER--YOU'LL BE ABLE TO FIT INTO YOUR OLD PROM DRESS.
AHH, THE PORSCHE CAYMAN, THE LATEST AND GREATEST FROM ZUFFENHAUSEN!
I'M DRIVING.
OH NO, IF ANYONE'S THE DRIVER, IT'S ME.
NOT THE WAY *WE'RE* CHAINED TOGETHER, OLD CHUM...
... WE AIN'T IN JOLLY OLDE ENGLAND!
*SHHH...*
YOU HEAR SOMETHING?
NOPE. I CAN'T EVEN HEAR MYSELF THINK WITH ALL YOUR--
TRICKSTER AND HIS LITTLE GREEN GIRLFRIEND. LUCKY ME.
DRIVE FAST, KEEP QUIET AND GET ME THE HELL OUT OF HERE, TWINK, OR YOU'LL BE WHISTLING THROUGH YER WINDPIPE.

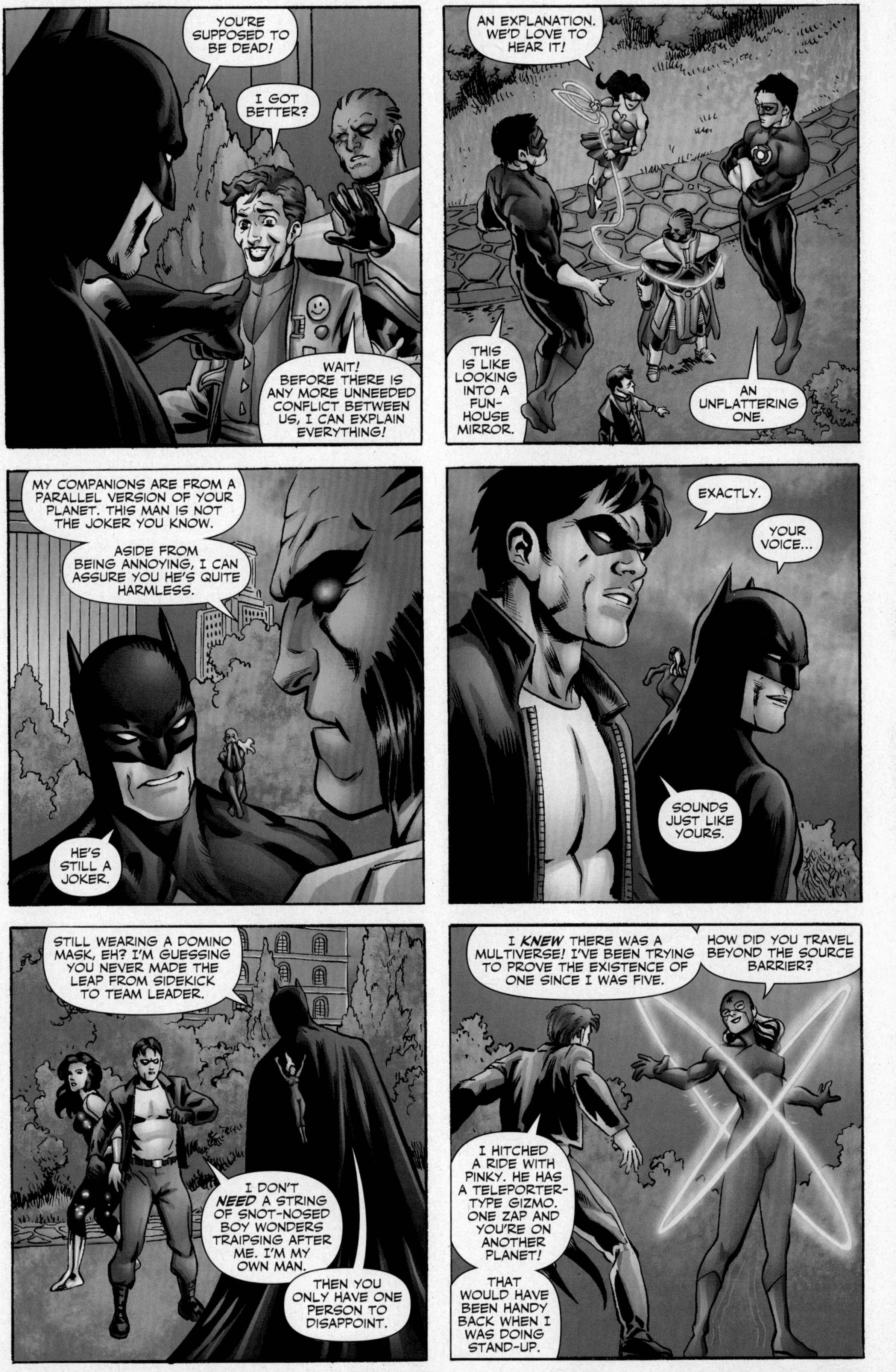
YOU'RE SUPPOSED TO BE DEAD!
I GOT BETTER?
WAIT! BEFORE THERE IS ANY MORE UNNEEDED CONFLICT BETWEEN US, I CAN EXPLAIN EVERYTHING!
AN EXPLANATION. WE'D LOVE TO HEAR IT!
THIS IS LIKE LOOKING INTO A FUN-HOUSE MIRROR.
AN UNFLATTERING ONE.
MY COMPANIONS ARE FROM A PARALLEL VERSION OF YOUR PLANET. THIS MAN IS NOT THE JOKER YOU KNOW.
ASIDE FROM BEING ANNOYING, I CAN ASSURE YOU HE'S QUITE HARMLESS.
HE'S STILL A JOKER.
EXACTLY.
YOUR VOICE...
SOUNDS JUST LIKE YOURS.
STILL WEARING A DOMINO MASK, EH? I'M GUESSING YOU NEVER MADE THE LEAP FROM SIDEKICK TO TEAM LEADER.
I DON'T NEED A STRING OF SNOT-NOSED BOY WONDERS TRAIPSING AFTER ME. I'M MY OWN MAN.
THEN YOU ONLY HAVE ONE PERSON TO DISAPPOINT.
I KNEW THERE WAS A MULTIVERSE! I'VE BEEN TRYING TO PROVE THE EXISTENCE OF ONE SINCE I WAS FIVE.
HOW DID YOU TRAVEL BEYOND THE SOURCE BARRIER?
I HITCHED A RIDE WITH PINKY. HE HAS A TELEPORTER-TYPE GIZMO. ONE ZAP AND YOU'RE ON ANOTHER PLANET!
THAT WOULD HAVE BEEN HANDY BACK WHEN I WAS DOING STAND-UP.

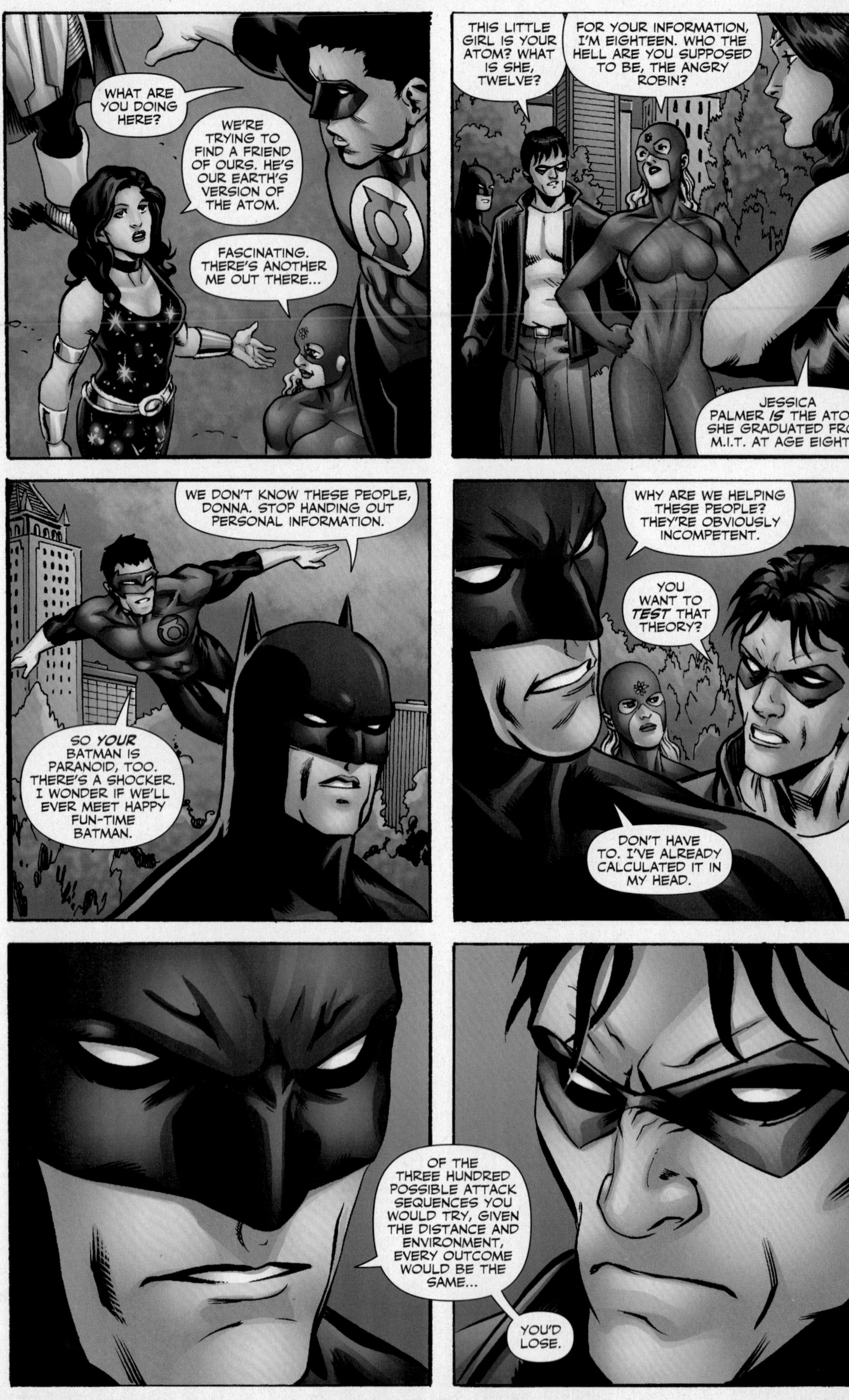
WHAT ARE YOU DOING HERE?
WE'RE TRYING TO FIND A FRIEND OF OURS. HE'S OUR EARTH'S VERSION OF THE ATOM.
FASCINATING. THERE'S ANOTHER ME OUT THERE...
THIS LITTLE GIRL IS YOUR ATOM? WHAT IS SHE, TWELVE?
FOR YOUR INFORMATION, I'M EIGHTEEN. WHO THE HELL ARE YOU SUPPOSED TO BE, THE ANGRY ROBIN?
JESSICA PALMER *IS* THE ATOM. SHE GRADUATED FROM M.I.T. AT AGE EIGHT...
WE DON'T KNOW THESE PEOPLE, DONNA. STOP HANDING OUT PERSONAL INFORMATION.
SO *YOUR* BATMAN IS PARANOID, TOO. THERE'S A SHOCKER. I WONDER IF WE'LL EVER MEET HAPPY FUN-TIME BATMAN.
WHY ARE WE HELPING THESE PEOPLE? THEY'RE OBVIOUSLY INCOMPETENT.
YOU WANT TO *TEST* THAT THEORY?
DON'T HAVE TO. I'VE ALREADY CALCULATED IT IN MY HEAD.
OF THE THREE HUNDRED POSSIBLE ATTACK SEQUENCES YOU WOULD TRY, GIVEN THE DISTANCE AND ENVIRONMENT, EVERY OUTCOME WOULD BE THE SAME...
YOU'D LOSE.

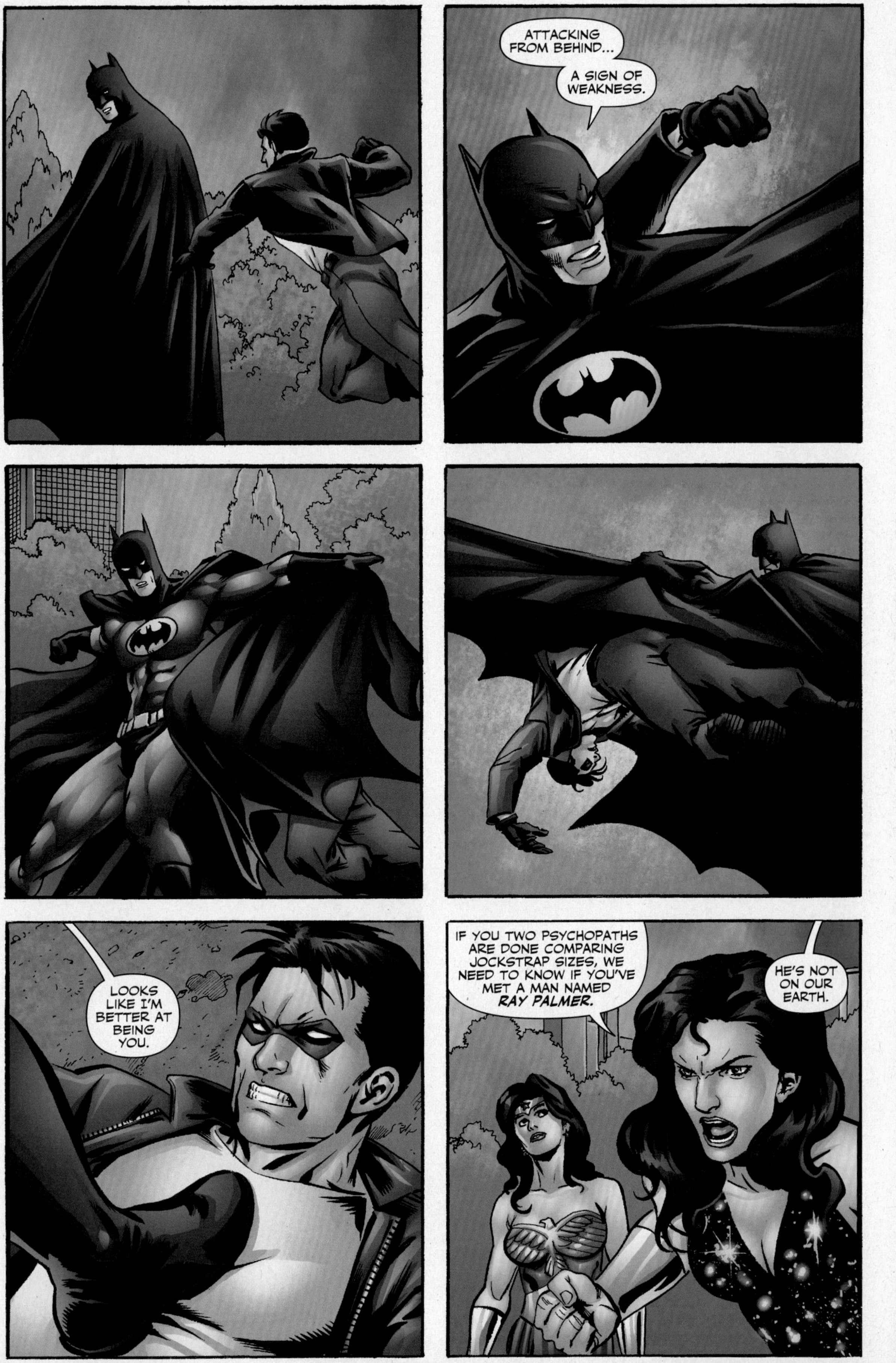
ATTACKING FROM BEHIND...
A SIGN OF WEAKNESS.
LOOKS LIKE I'M BETTER AT BEING YOU.
IF YOU TWO PSYCHOPATHS ARE DONE COMPARING JOCKSTRAP SIZES, WE NEED TO KNOW IF YOU'VE MET A MAN NAMED *RAY PALMER.*
HE'S NOT ON OUR EARTH.

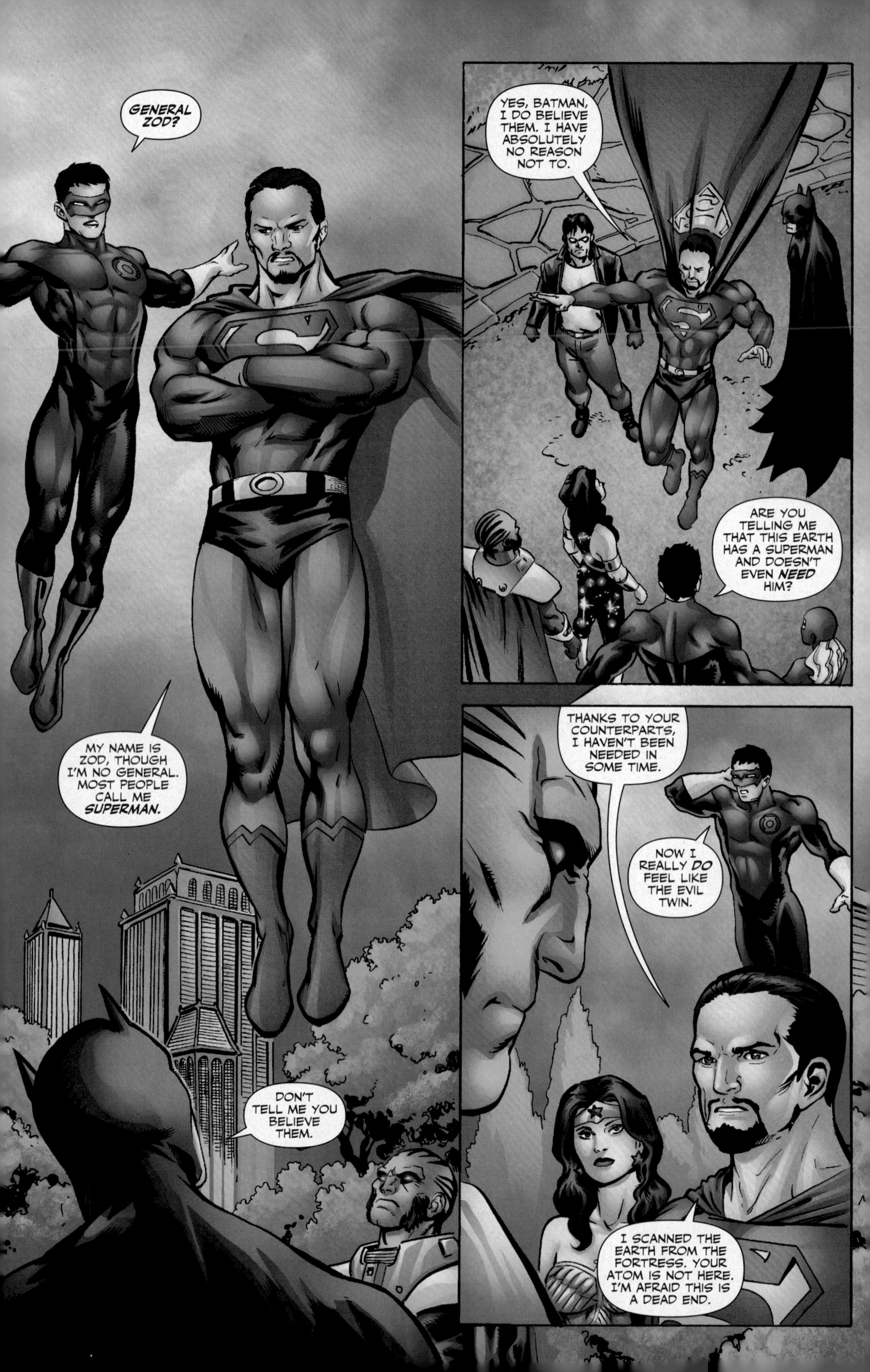
GENERAL ZOD?
MY NAME IS ZOD, THOUGH I'M NO GENERAL. MOST PEOPLE CALL ME SUPERMAN.
DON'T TELL ME YOU BELIEVE THEM.
YES, BATMAN, I DO BELIEVE THEM. I HAVE ABSOLUTELY NO REASON NOT TO.
ARE YOU TELLING ME THAT THIS EARTH HAS A SUPERMAN AND DOESN'T EVEN NEED HIM?
THANKS TO YOUR COUNTERPARTS, I HAVEN'T BEEN NEEDED IN SOME TIME.
NOW I REALLY DO FEEL LIKE THE EVIL TWIN.
I SCANNED THE EARTH FROM THE FORTRESS. YOUR ATOM IS NOT HERE. I'M AFRAID THIS IS A DEAD END.

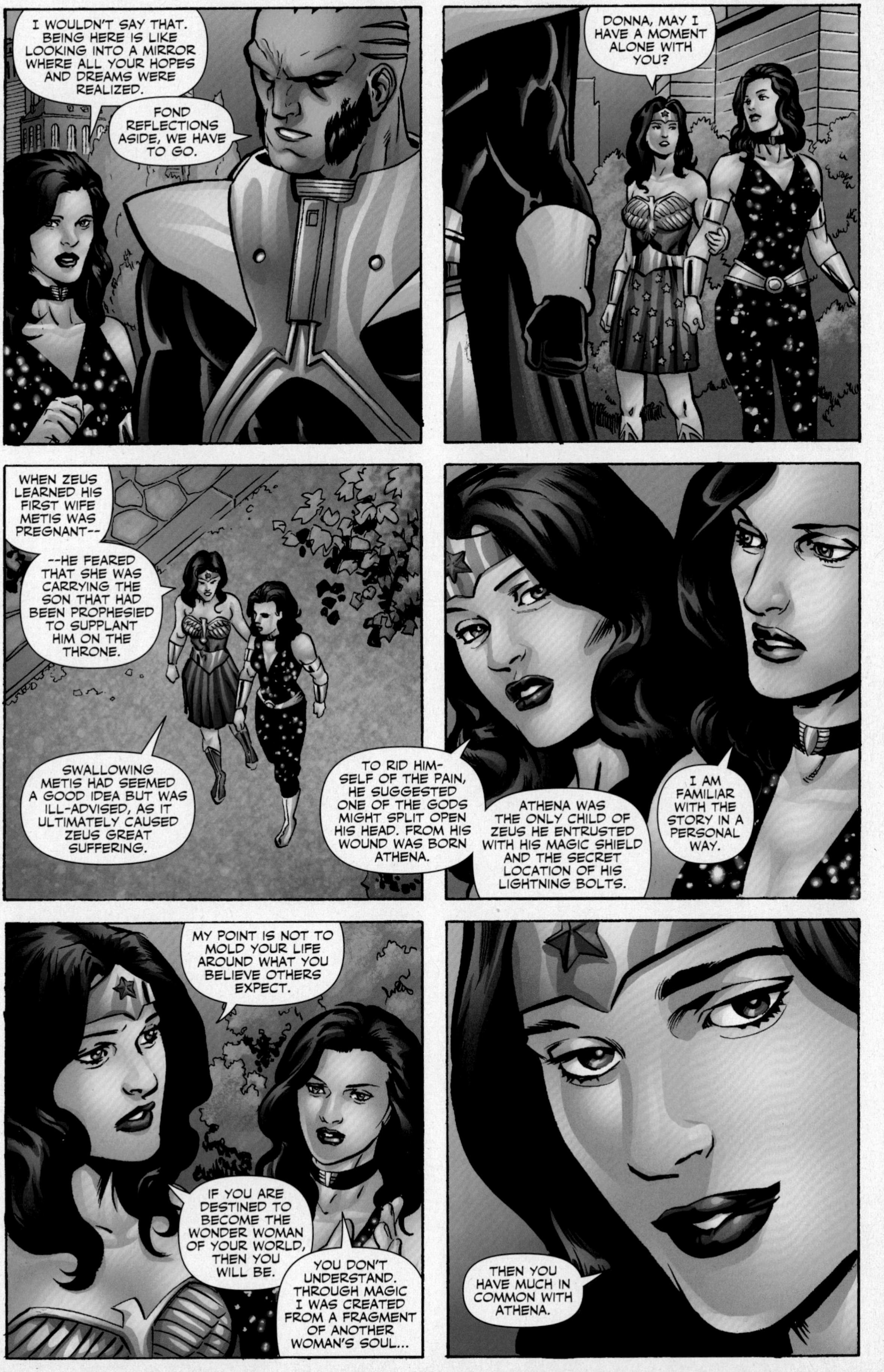
I WOULDN'T SAY THAT. BEING HERE IS LIKE LOOKING INTO A MIRROR WHERE ALL YOUR HOPES AND DREAMS WERE REALIZED.
FOND REFLECTIONS ASIDE, WE HAVE TO GO.
DONNA, MAY I HAVE A MOMENT ALONE WITH YOU?
WHEN ZEUS LEARNED HIS FIRST WIFE METIS WAS PREGNANT--
--HE FEARED THAT SHE WAS CARRYING THE SON THAT HAD BEEN PROPHESIED TO SUPPLANT HIM ON THE THRONE.
SWALLOWING METIS HAD SEEMED A GOOD IDEA BUT WAS ILL-ADVISED, AS IT ULTIMATELY CAUSED ZEUS GREAT SUFFERING.
TO RID HIMSELF OF THE PAIN, HE SUGGESTED ONE OF THE GODS MIGHT SPLIT OPEN HIS HEAD. FROM HIS WOUND WAS BORN ATHENA.
ATHENA WAS THE ONLY CHILD OF ZEUS HE ENTRUSTED WITH HIS MAGIC SHIELD AND THE SECRET LOCATION OF HIS LIGHTNING BOLTS.
I AM FAMILIAR WITH THE STORY IN A PERSONAL WAY.
MY POINT IS NOT TO MOLD YOUR LIFE AROUND WHAT YOU BELIEVE OTHERS EXPECT.
IF YOU ARE DESTINED TO BECOME THE WONDER WOMAN OF YOUR WORLD, THEN YOU WILL BE.
YOU DON'T UNDERSTAND. THROUGH MAGIC I WAS CREATED FROM A FRAGMENT OF ANOTHER WOMAN'S SOUL...
THEN YOU HAVE MUCH IN COMMON WITH ATHENA.

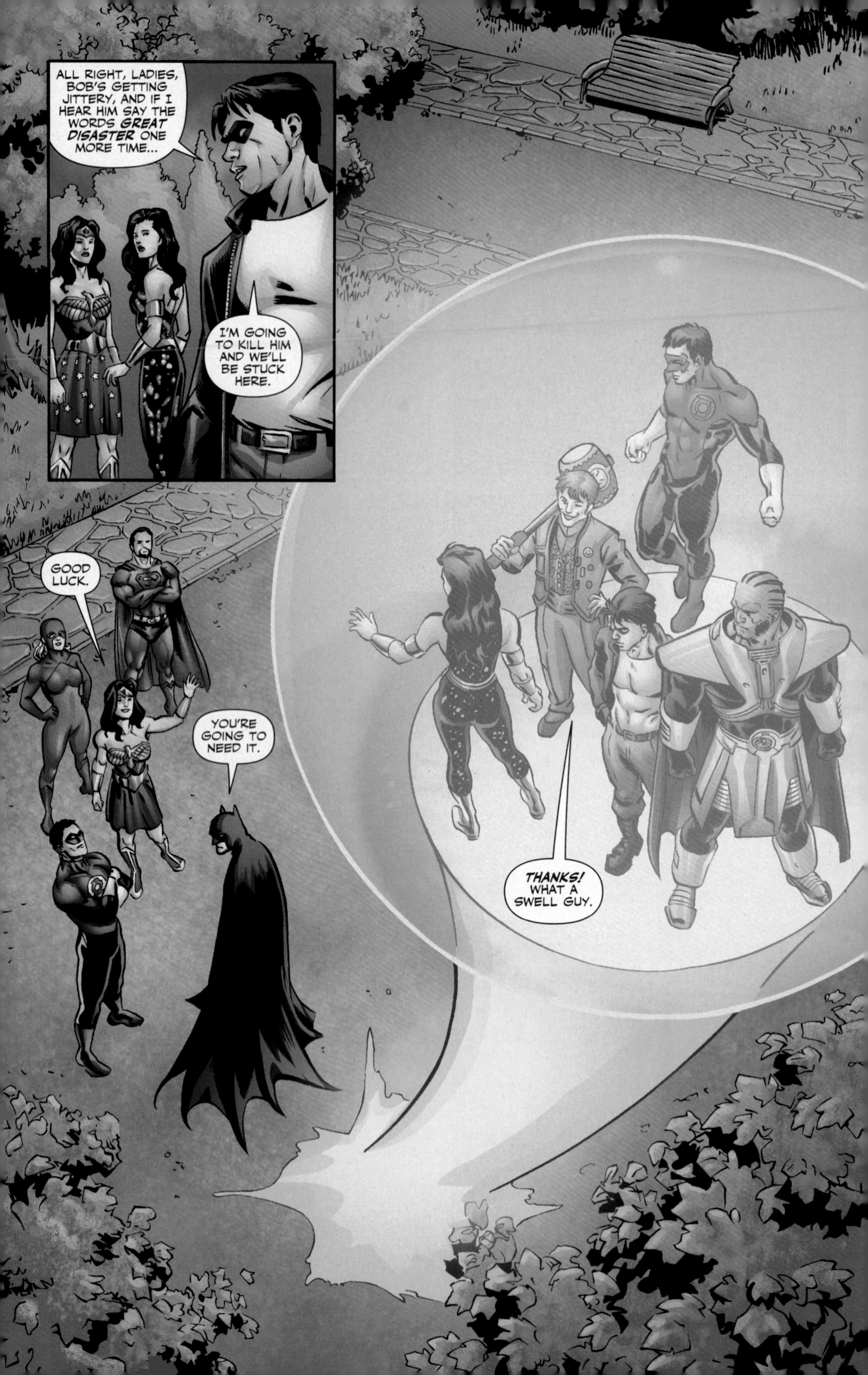
ALL RIGHT, LADIES, BOB'S GETTING JITTERY, AND IF I HEAR HIM SAY THE WORDS GREAT DISASTER ONE MORE TIME...
I'M GOING TO KILL HIM AND WE'LL BE STUCK HERE.
GOOD LUCK.
YOU'RE GOING TO NEED IT.
THANKS! WHAT A SWELL GUY.

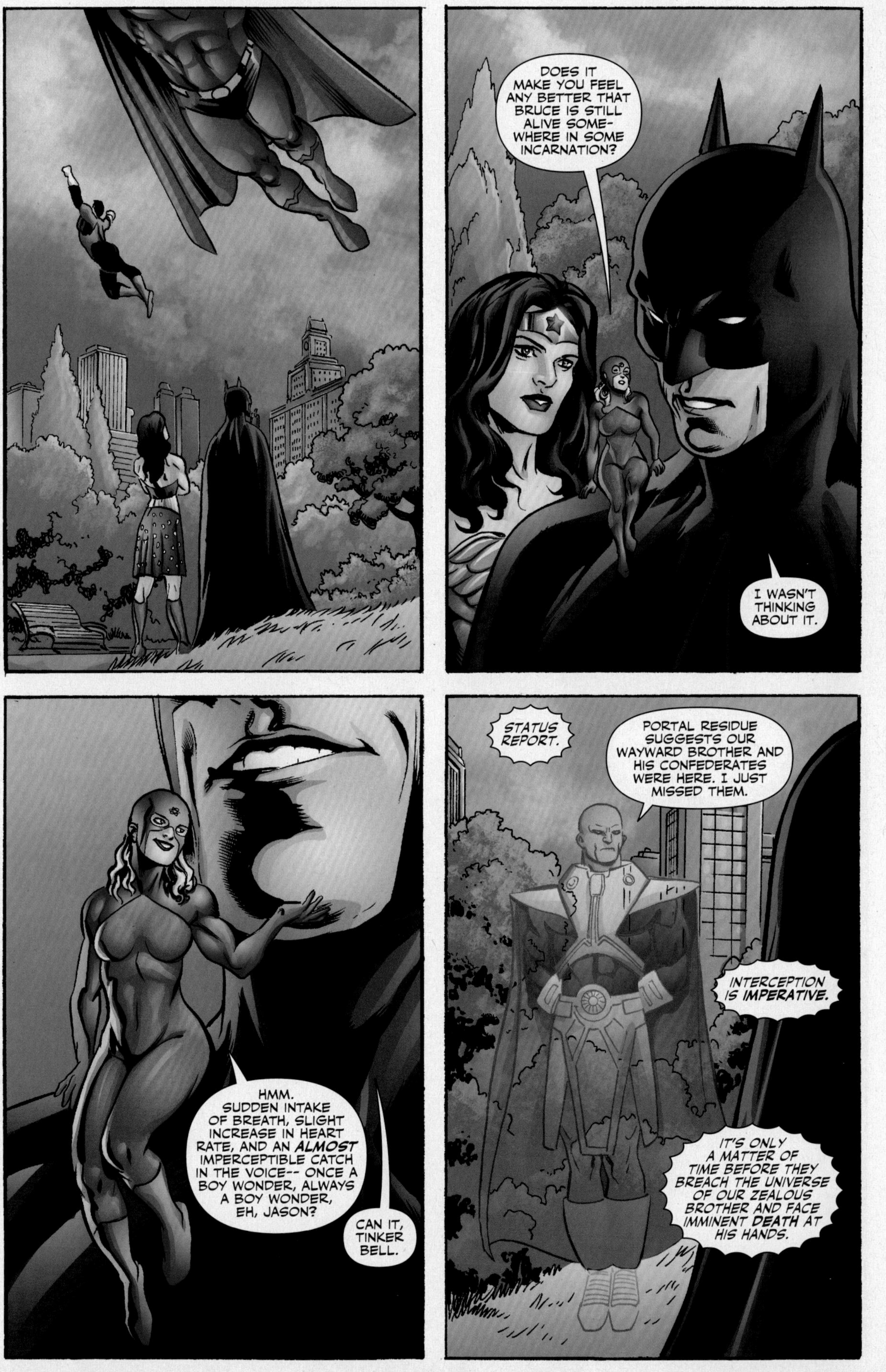
DOES IT MAKE YOU FEEL ANY BETTER THAT BRUCE IS STILL ALIVE SOME-WHERE IN SOME INCARNATION?
I WASN'T THINKING ABOUT IT.
HMM. SUDDEN INTAKE OF BREATH, SLIGHT INCREASE IN HEART RATE, AND AN ***ALMOST*** IMPERCEPTIBLE CATCH IN THE VOICE-- ONCE A BOY WONDER, ALWAYS A BOY WONDER, EH, JASON?
CAN IT, TINKER BELL.
*STATUS REPORT.*
PORTAL RESIDUE SUGGESTS OUR WAYWARD BROTHER AND HIS CONFEDERATES WERE HERE. I JUST MISSED THEM.
INTERCEPTION IS ***IMPERATIVE.***
*IT'S ONLY A MATTER OF TIME BEFORE THEY BREACH THE UNIVERSE OF OUR ZEALOUS BROTHER AND FACE IMMINENT **DEATH** AT HIS HANDS.*

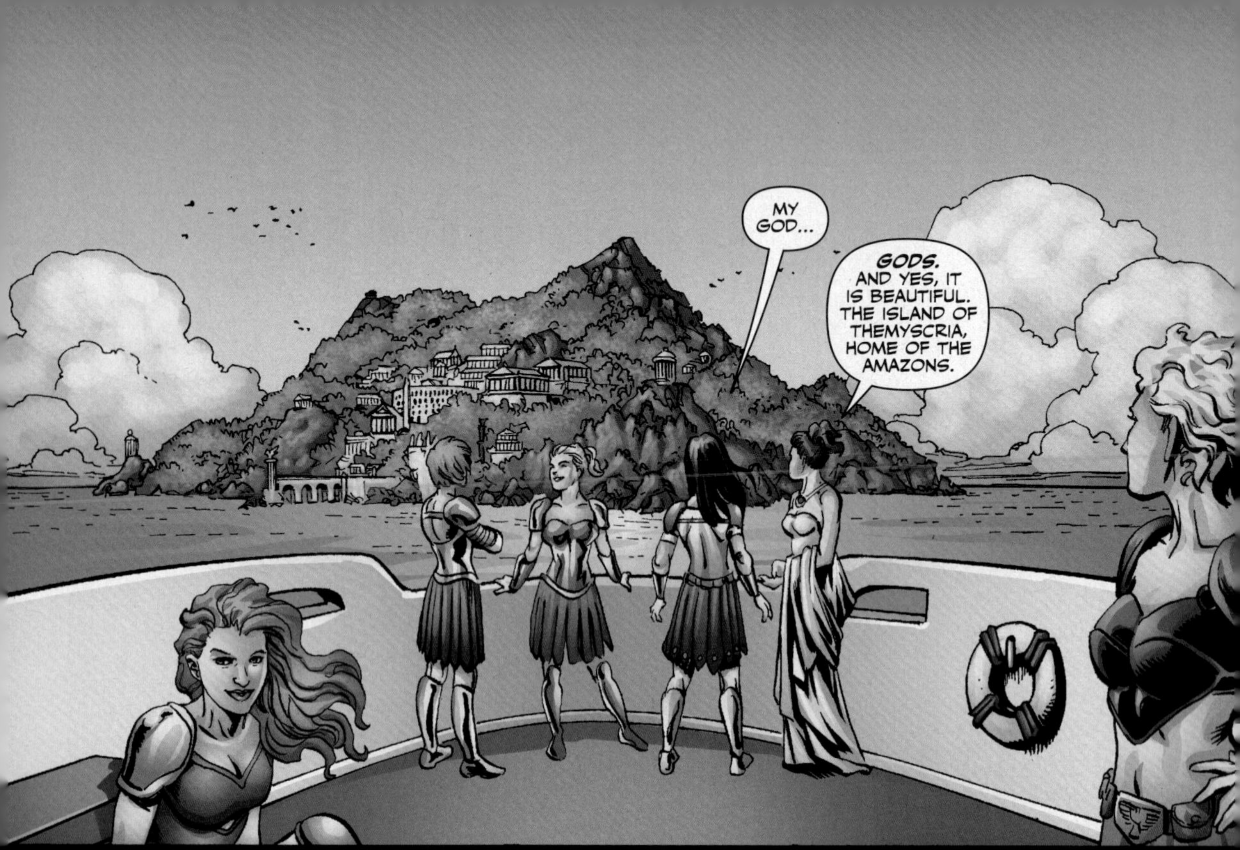
MY GOD...
GODS. AND YES, IT IS BEAUTIFUL. THE ISLAND OF THEMYSCRIA, HOME OF THE AMAZONS.

## HOLLY ROBINSON

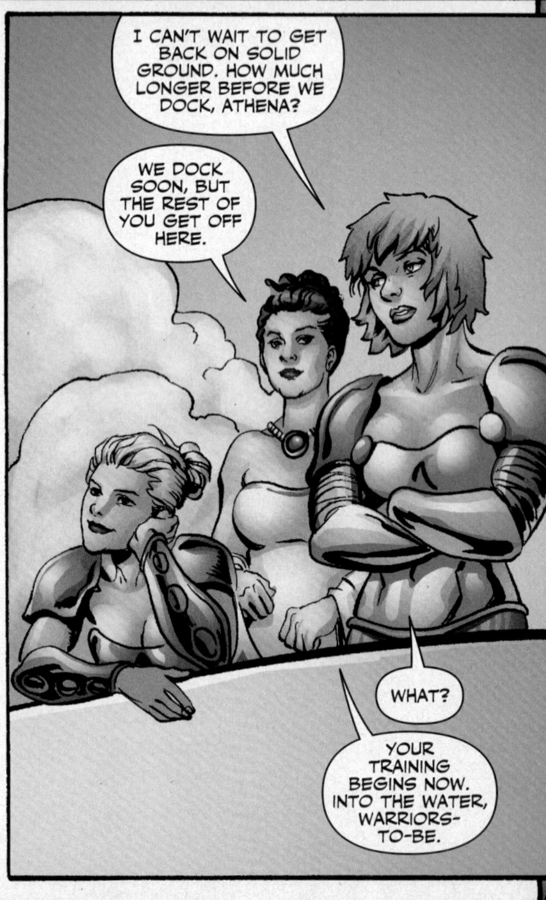
I CAN'T WAIT TO GET BACK ON SOLID GROUND. HOW MUCH LONGER BEFORE WE DOCK, ATHENA?
WE DOCK SOON, BUT THE REST OF YOU GET OFF HERE.
WHAT?
YOUR TRAINING BEGINS NOW. INTO THE WATER, WARRIORS-TO-BE.

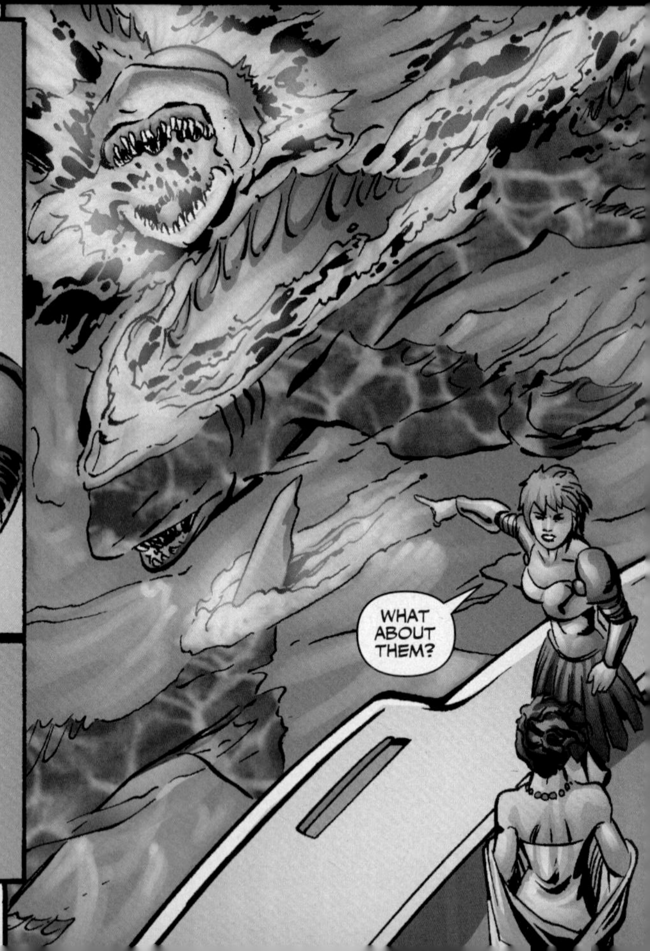
WHAT ABOUT THEM?

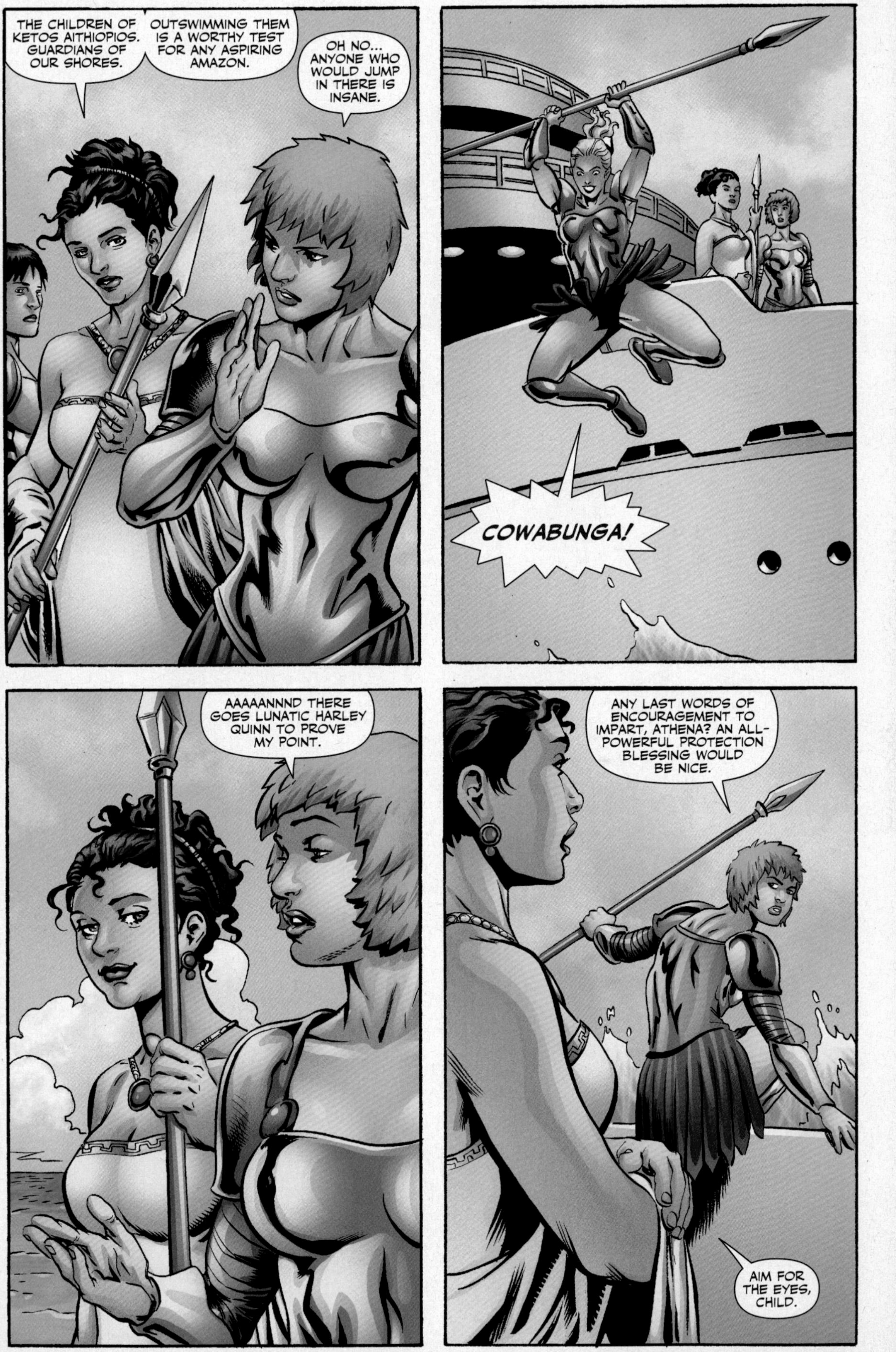
THE CHILDREN OF KETOS AITHIOPIOS. GUARDIANS OF OUR SHORES.
OUTSWIMMING THEM IS A WORTHY TEST FOR ANY ASPIRING AMAZON.
OH NO... ANYONE WHO WOULD JUMP IN THERE IS INSANE.
COWABUNGA!
AAAAANNND THERE GOES LUNATIC HARLEY QUINN TO PROVE MY POINT.
ANY LAST WORDS OF ENCOURAGEMENT TO IMPART, ATHENA? AN ALL-POWERFUL PROTECTION BLESSING WOULD BE NICE.
AIM FOR THE EYES, CHILD.

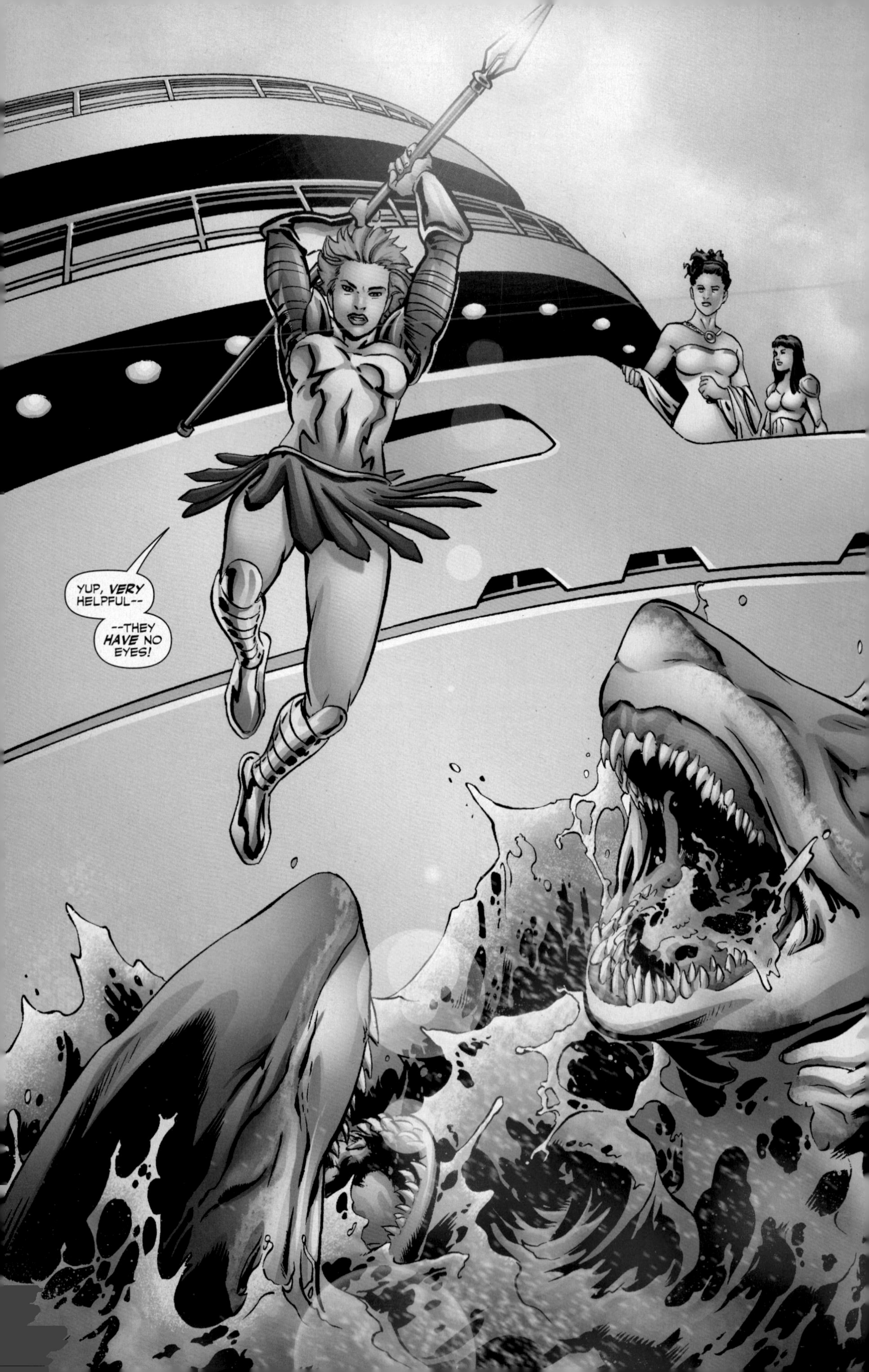
YUP, VERY HELPFUL--
--THEY HAVE NO EYES!

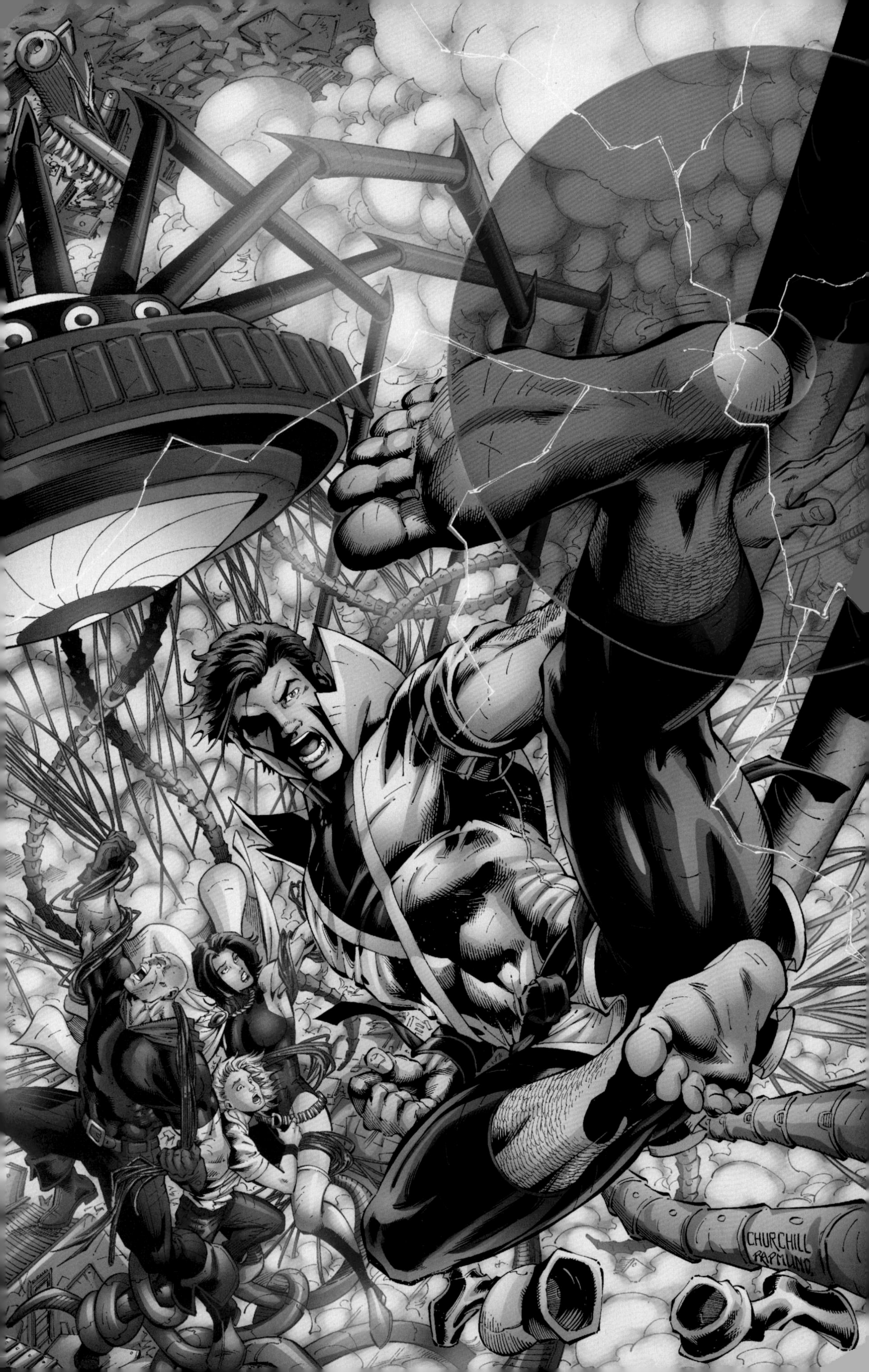
CHURCHILL
RAPMUND.

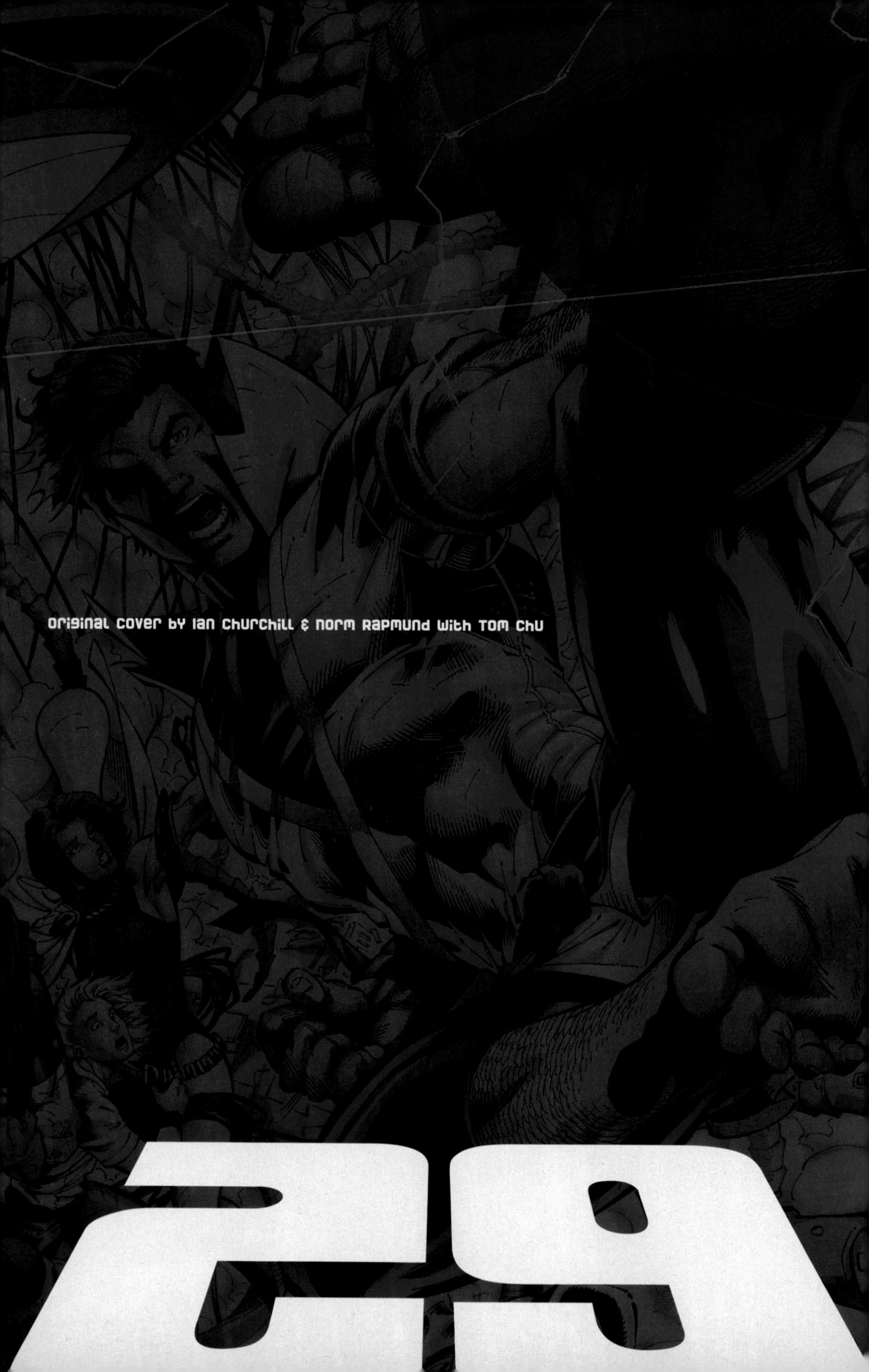
original cover by Ian Churchill & Norm Rapmund with Tom Chu
29

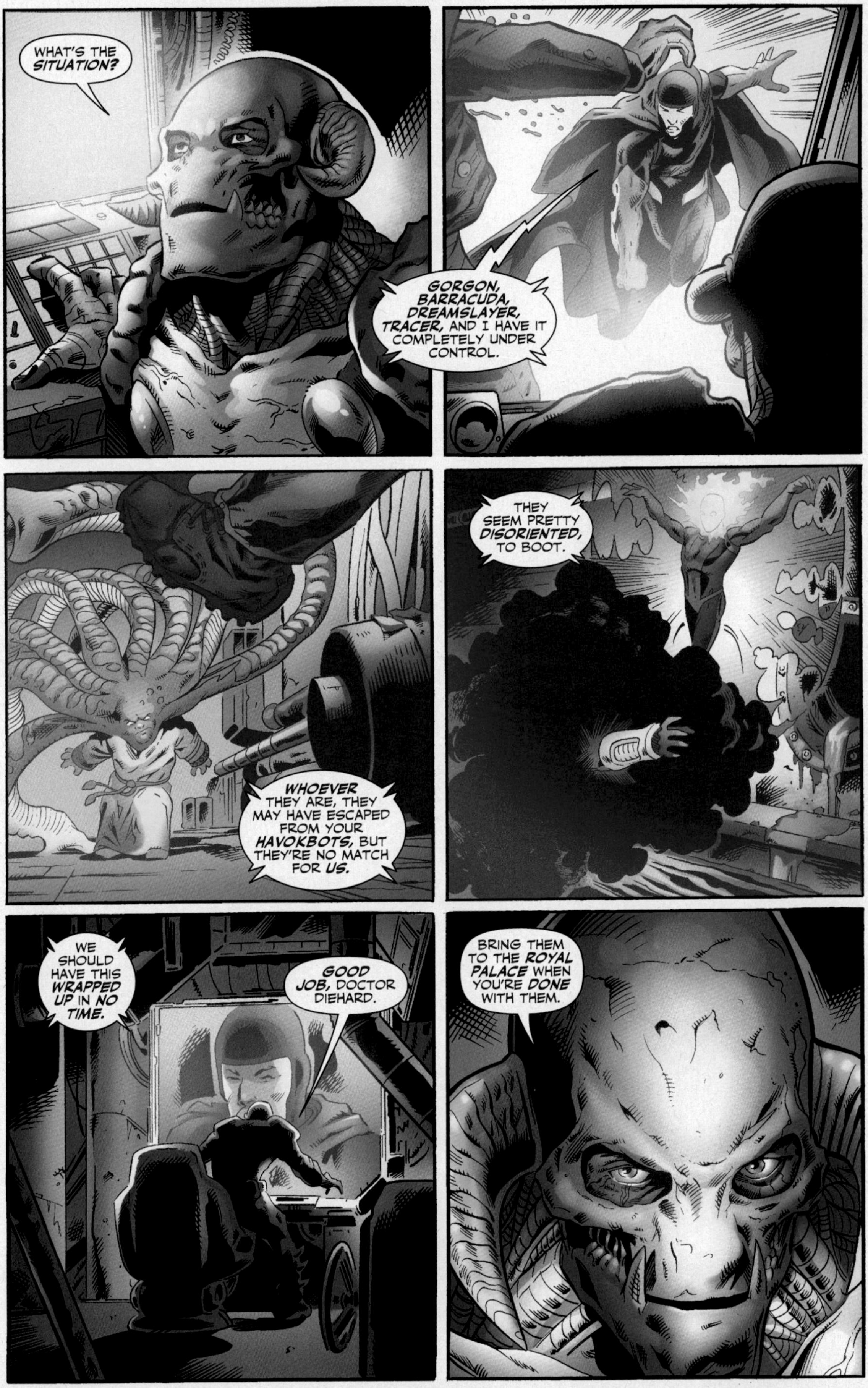

WHAT'S THE SITUATION?
GORGON, BARRACUDA, DREAMSLAYER, TRACER, AND I HAVE IT COMPLETELY UNDER CONTROL.
WHOEVER THEY ARE, THEY MAY HAVE ESCAPED FROM YOUR HAVOKBOTS, BUT THEY'RE NO MATCH FOR US.
THEY SEEM PRETTY DISORIENTED, TO BOOT.
WE SHOULD HAVE THIS WRAPPED UP IN NO TIME.
GOOD JOB, DOCTOR DIEHARD.
BRING THEM TO THE ROYAL PALACE WHEN YOU'RE DONE WITH THEM.

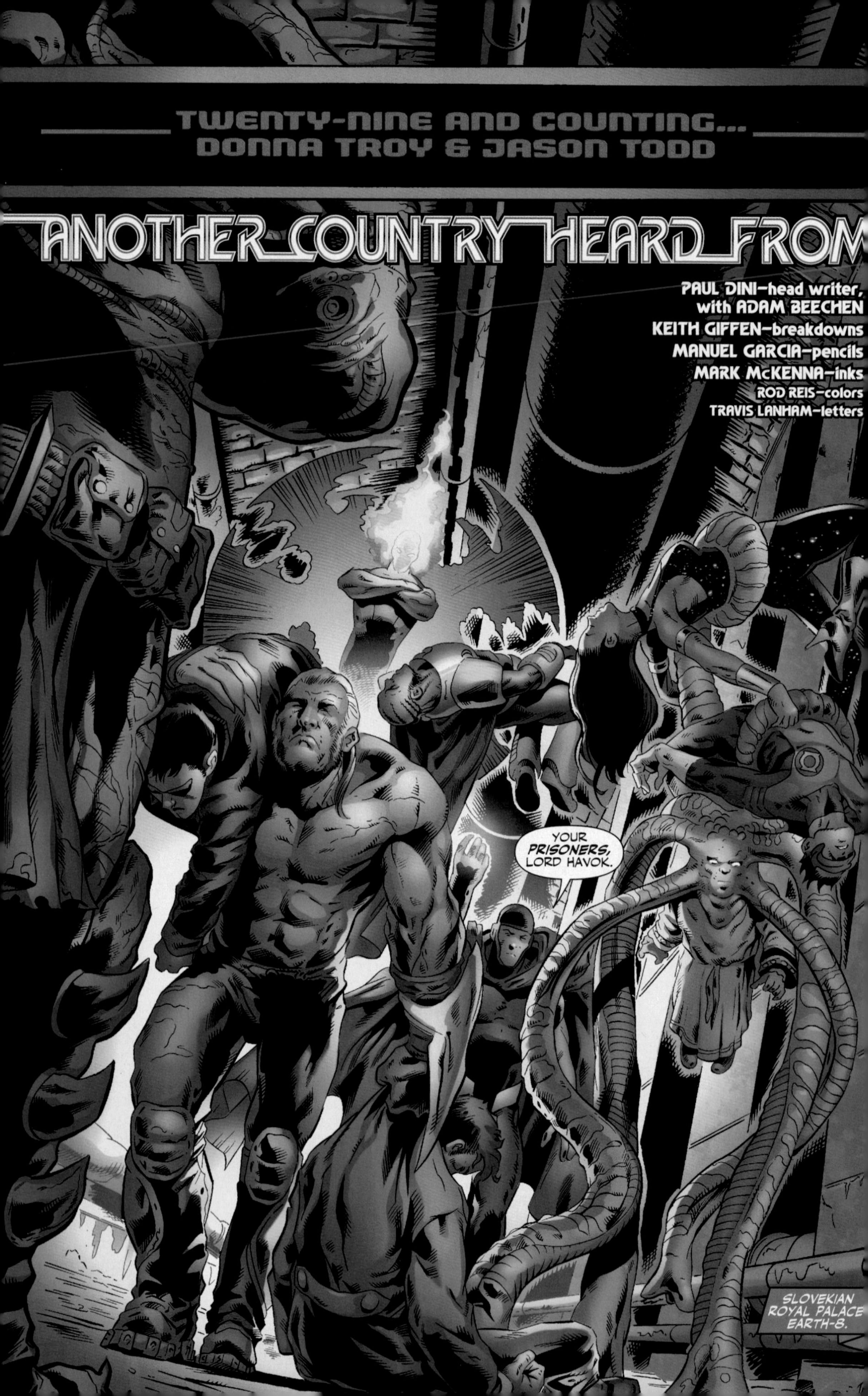
TWENTY-NINE AND COUNTING...
DONNA TROY & JASON TODD
ANOTHER COUNTRY HEARD FROM
PAUL DINI—head writer, with ADAM BEECHEN
KEITH GIFFEN—breakdowns
MANUEL GARCIA—pencils
MARK McKENNA—inks
ROD REIS—colors
TRAVIS LANHAM—letters
YOUR PRISONERS, LORD HAVOK.
SLOVEKIAN ROYAL PALACE EARTH-8.

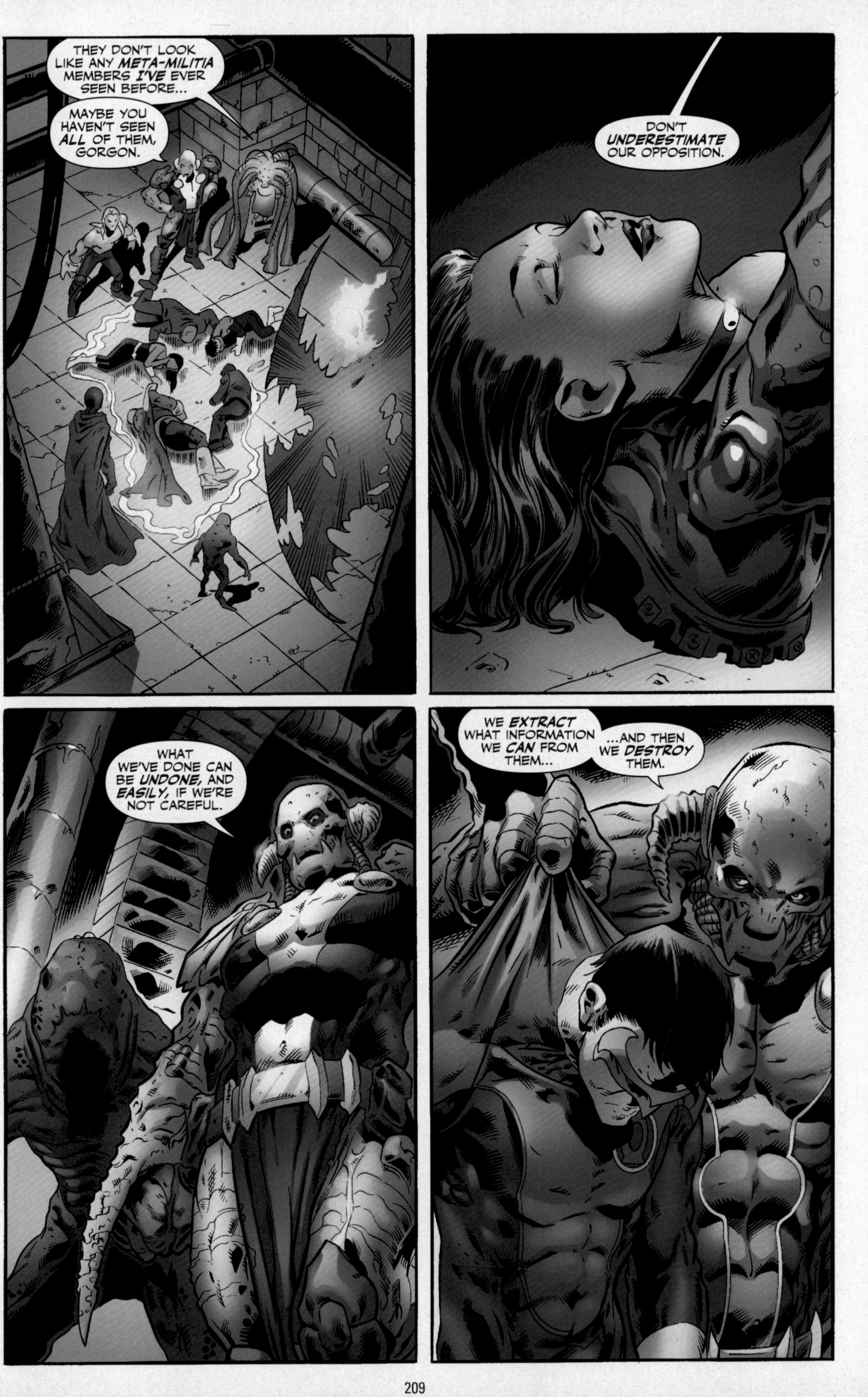
THEY DON'T LOOK LIKE ANY META-MILITIA MEMBERS I'VE EVER SEEN BEFORE...
MAYBE YOU HAVEN'T SEEN ALL OF THEM, GORGON.
DON'T UNDERESTIMATE OUR OPPOSITION.
WHAT WE'VE DONE CAN BE UNDONE, AND EASILY, IF WE'RE NOT CAREFUL.
WE EXTRACT WHAT INFORMATION WE CAN FROM THEM...
...AND THEN WE DESTROY THEM.

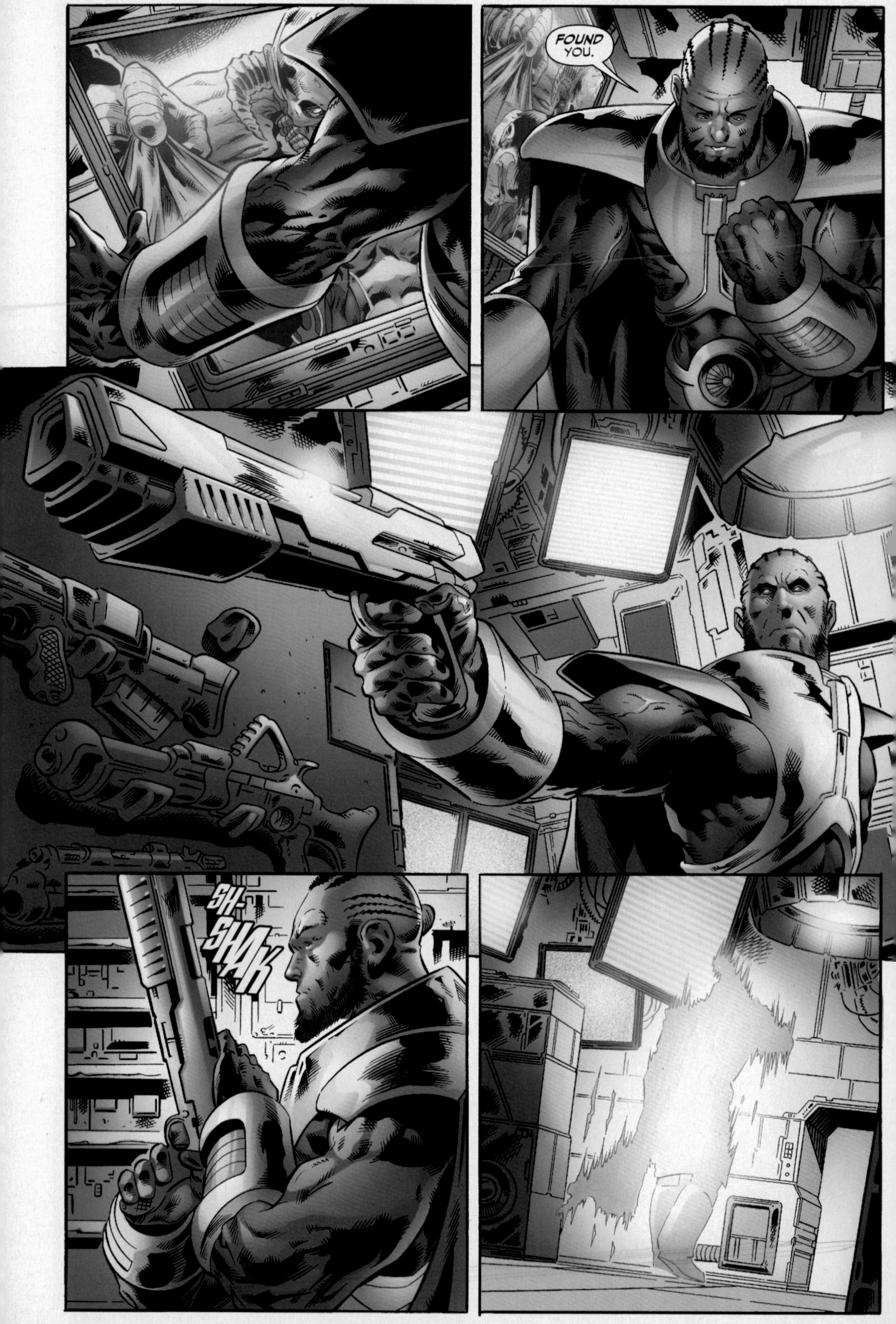
FOUND YOU.
SH-SHAK

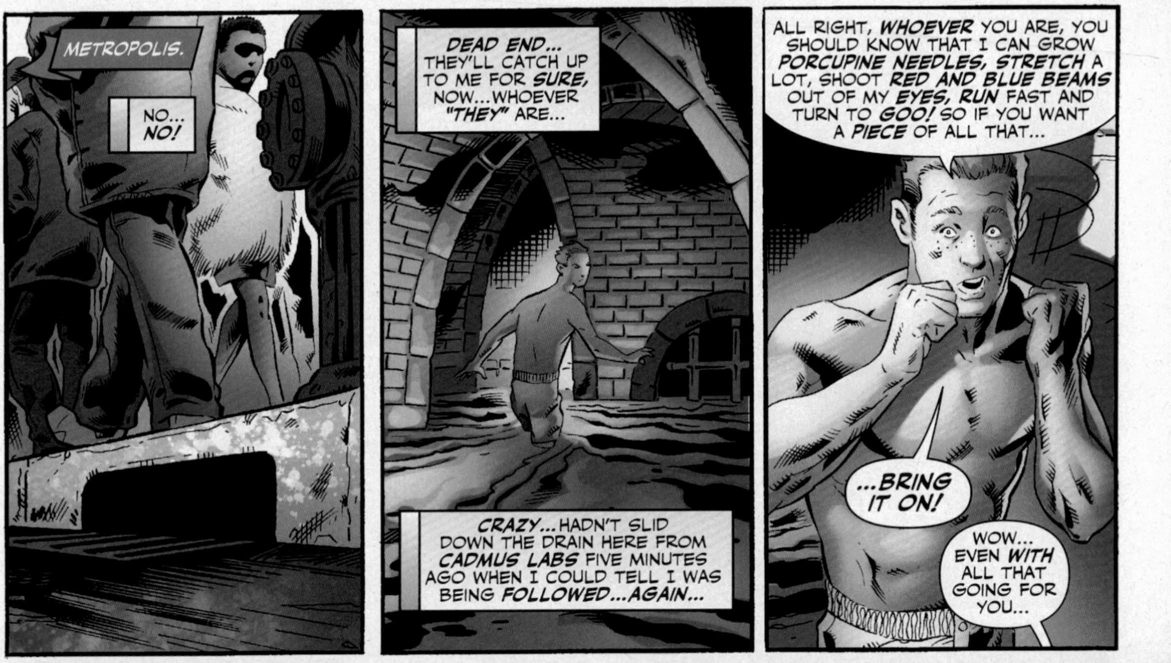
METROPOLIS.
NO... NO!
DEAD END... THEY'LL CATCH UP TO ME FOR SURE, NOW... WHOEVER "THEY" ARE...
CRAZY... HADN'T SLID DOWN THE DRAIN HERE FROM CADMUS LABS FIVE MINUTES AGO WHEN I COULD TELL I WAS BEING FOLLOWED... AGAIN...
ALL RIGHT, WHOEVER YOU ARE, YOU SHOULD KNOW THAT I CAN GROW PORCUPINE NEEDLES, STRETCH A LOT, SHOOT RED AND BLUE BEAMS OUT OF MY EYES, RUN FAST AND TURN TO GOO! SO IF YOU WANT A PIECE OF ALL THAT...
...BRING IT ON!
WOW... EVEN WITH ALL THAT GOING FOR YOU...

JIMMY OLSEN

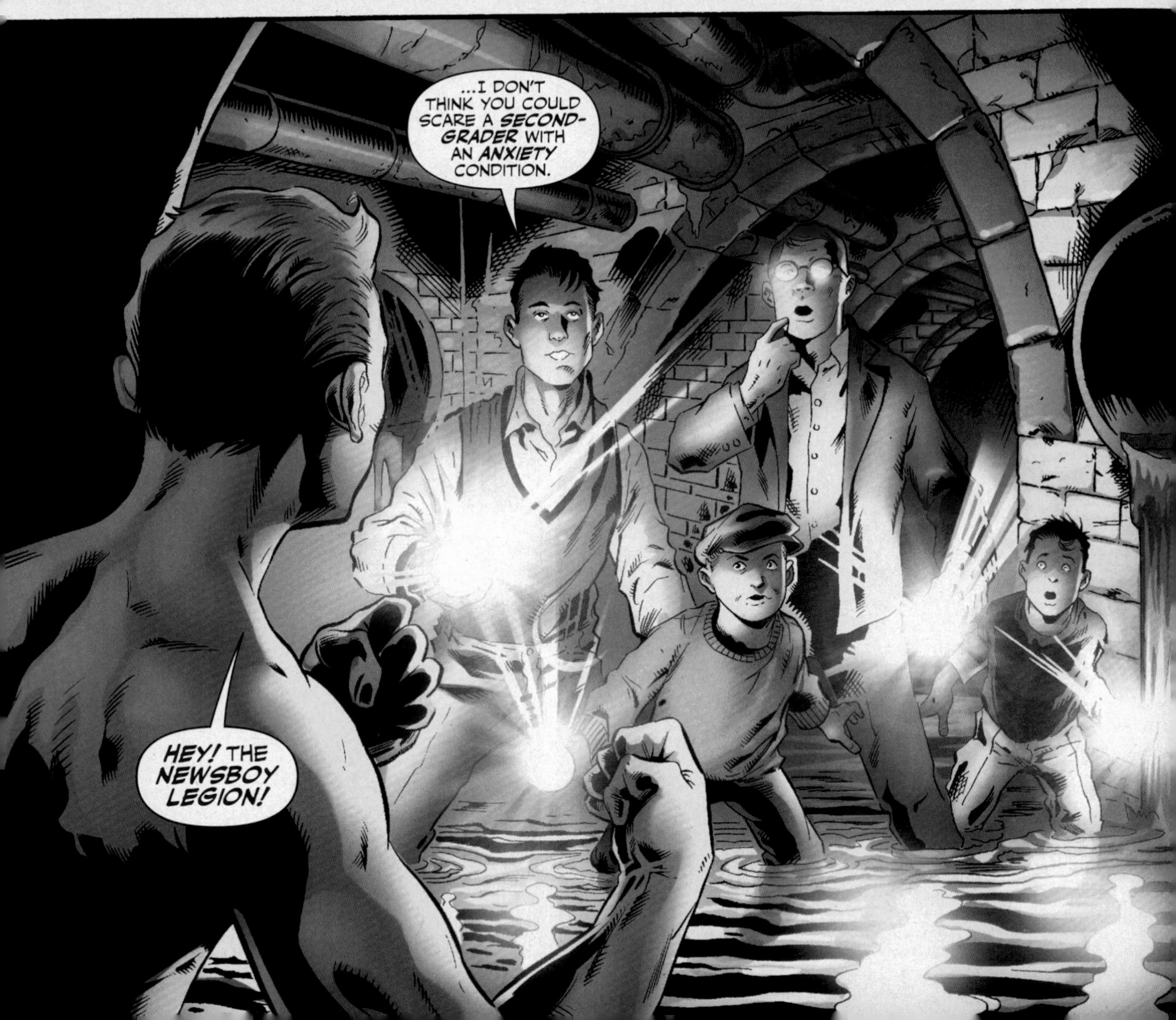
...I DON'T THINK YOU COULD SCARE A SECOND-GRADER WITH AN ANXIETY CONDITION.
HEY! THE NEWSBOY LEGION!

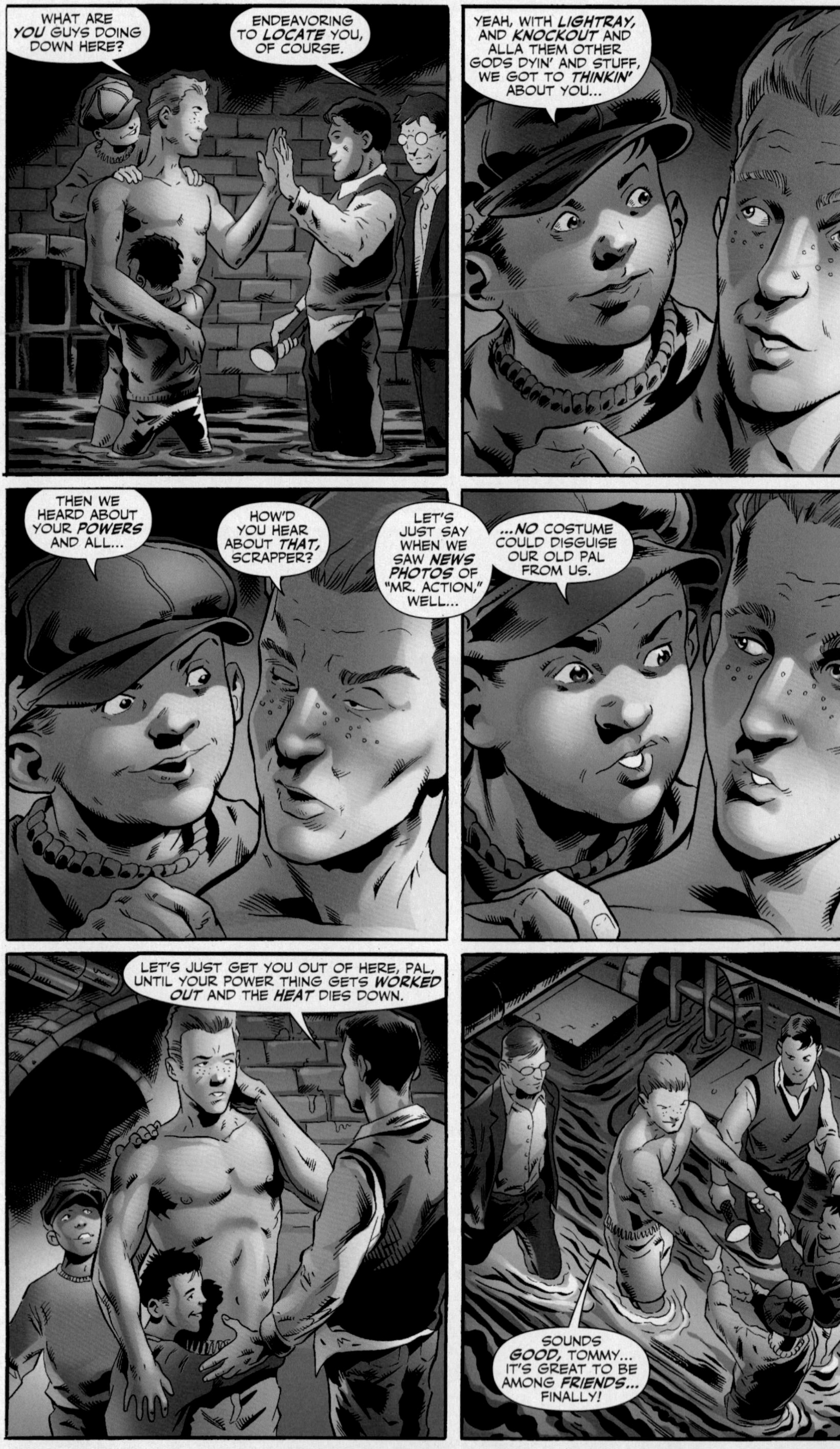
WHAT ARE YOU GUYS DOING DOWN HERE?
ENDEAVORING TO LOCATE YOU, OF COURSE.
YEAH, WITH LIGHTRAY, AND KNOCKOUT AND ALLA THEM OTHER GODS DYIN' AND STUFF, WE GOT TO THINKIN' ABOUT YOU...
THEN WE HEARD ABOUT YOUR POWERS AND ALL...
HOW'D YOU HEAR ABOUT THAT, SCRAPPER?
LET'S JUST SAY WHEN WE SAW NEWS PHOTOS OF "MR. ACTION," WELL...
...NO COSTUME COULD DISGUISE OUR OLD PAL FROM US.
LET'S JUST GET YOU OUT OF HERE, PAL, UNTIL YOUR POWER THING GETS WORKED OUT AND THE HEAT DIES DOWN.
SOUNDS GOOD, TOMMY... IT'S GREAT TO BE AMONG FRIENDS... FINALLY!

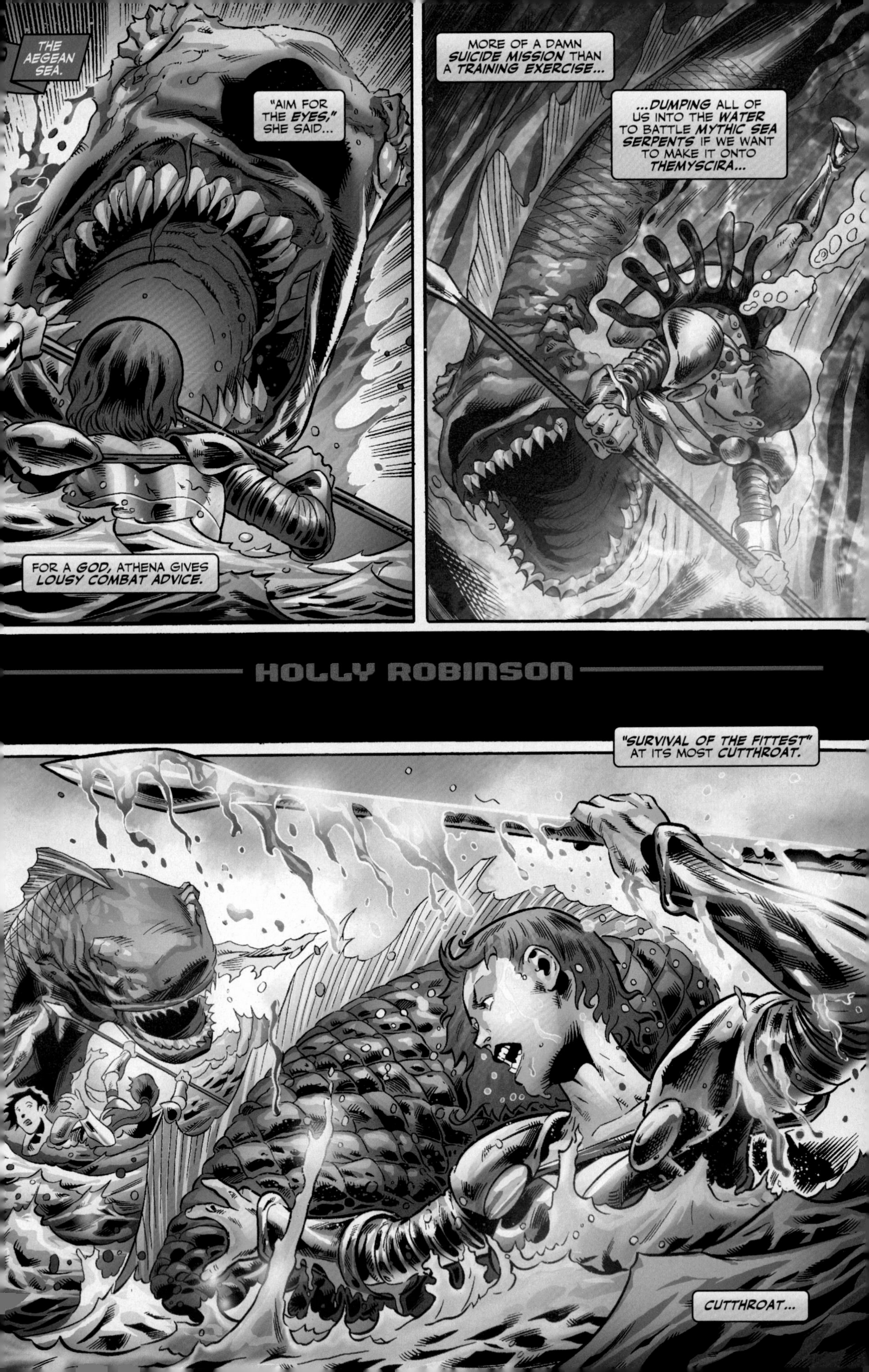
THE AEGEAN SEA.
"AIM FOR THE EYES," SHE SAID...
FOR A GOD, ATHENA GIVES LOUSY COMBAT ADVICE.
MORE OF A DAMN SUICIDE MISSION THAN A TRAINING EXERCISE...
...DUMPING ALL OF US INTO THE WATER TO BATTLE MYTHIC SEA SERPENTS IF WE WANT TO MAKE IT ONTO THEMYSCIRA...
HOLLY ROBINSON
"SURVIVAL OF THE FITTEST" AT ITS MOST CUTTHROAT.
CUTTHROAT...

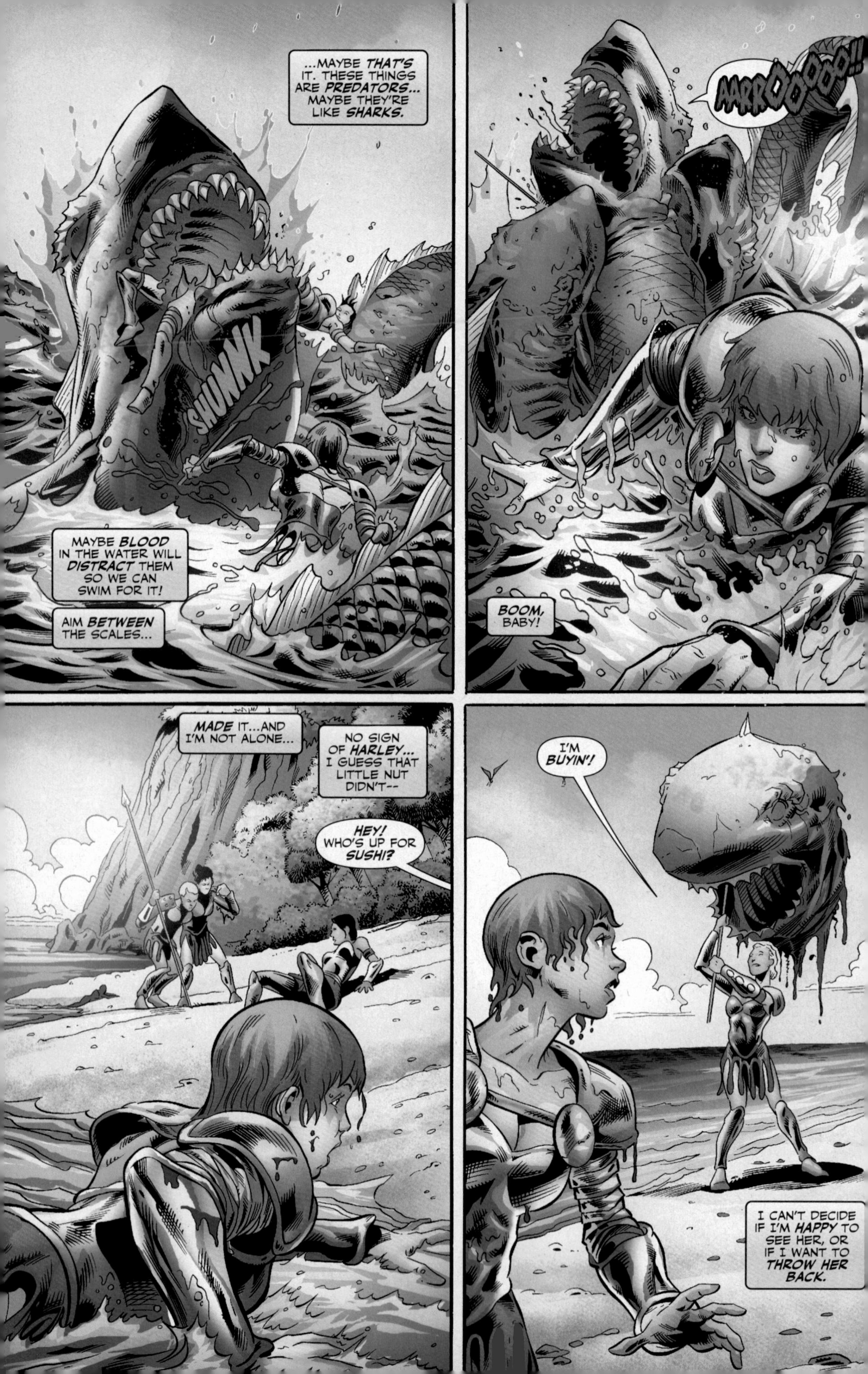
...MAYBE *THAT'S* IT. THESE THINGS ARE *PREDATORS*... MAYBE THEY'RE LIKE *SHARKS.*
SHUNKK
MAYBE *BLOOD* IN THE WATER WILL *DISTRACT* THEM SO WE CAN SWIM FOR IT!
AIM *BETWEEN* THE SCALES...
AARROOOOO!!
*BOOM,* BABY!
*MADE* IT...AND I'M NOT ALONE...
NO SIGN OF *HARLEY*... I GUESS THAT LITTLE NUT DIDN'T--
*HEY!* WHO'S UP FOR *SUSHI?*
I'M *BUYIN'!*
I CAN'T DECIDE IF I'M *HAPPY* TO SEE HER, OR IF I WANT TO *THROW HER BACK.*

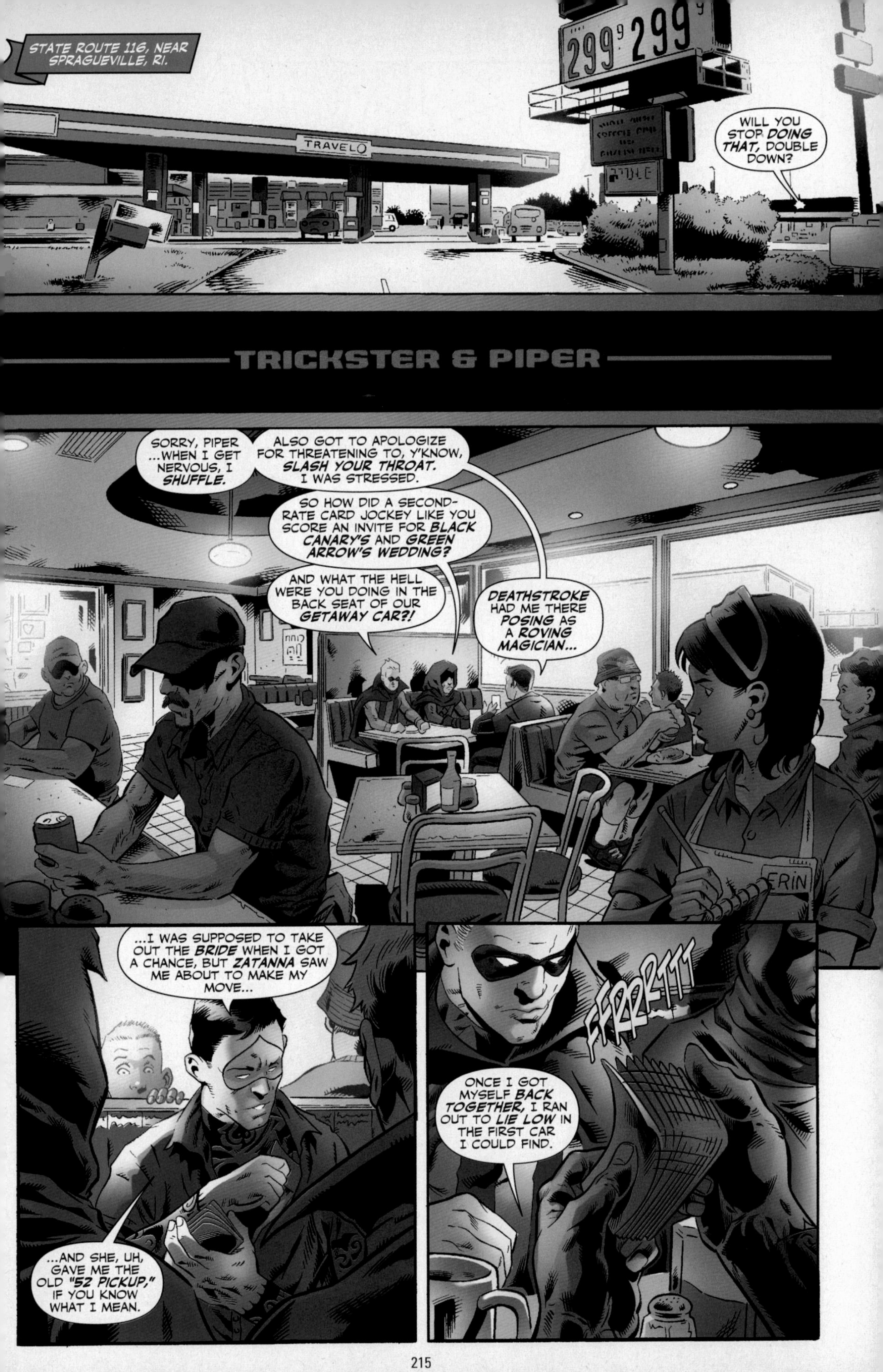
STATE ROUTE 116, NEAR SPRAGUEVILLE, RI.
299 9 299 9
TRAVELO
WILL YOU STOP DOING THAT, DOUBLE DOWN?
TRICKSTER & PIPER
SORRY, PIPER ...WHEN I GET NERVOUS, I SHUFFLE.
ALSO GOT TO APOLOGIZE FOR THREATENING TO, Y'KNOW, SLASH YOUR THROAT. I WAS STRESSED.
SO HOW DID A SECOND-RATE CARD JOCKEY LIKE YOU SCORE AN INVITE FOR BLACK CANARY'S AND GREEN ARROW'S WEDDING?
AND WHAT THE HELL WERE YOU DOING IN THE BACK SEAT OF OUR GETAWAY CAR?!
DEATHSTROKE HAD ME THERE POSING AS A ROVING MAGICIAN...
ERIN
...I WAS SUPPOSED TO TAKE OUT THE BRIDE WHEN I GOT A CHANCE, BUT ZATANNA SAW ME ABOUT TO MAKE MY MOVE...
...AND SHE, UH, GAVE ME THE OLD "52 PICKUP," IF YOU KNOW WHAT I MEAN.
FFRRRTTT
ONCE I GOT MYSELF BACK TOGETHER, I RAN OUT TO LIE LOW IN THE FIRST CAR I COULD FIND.

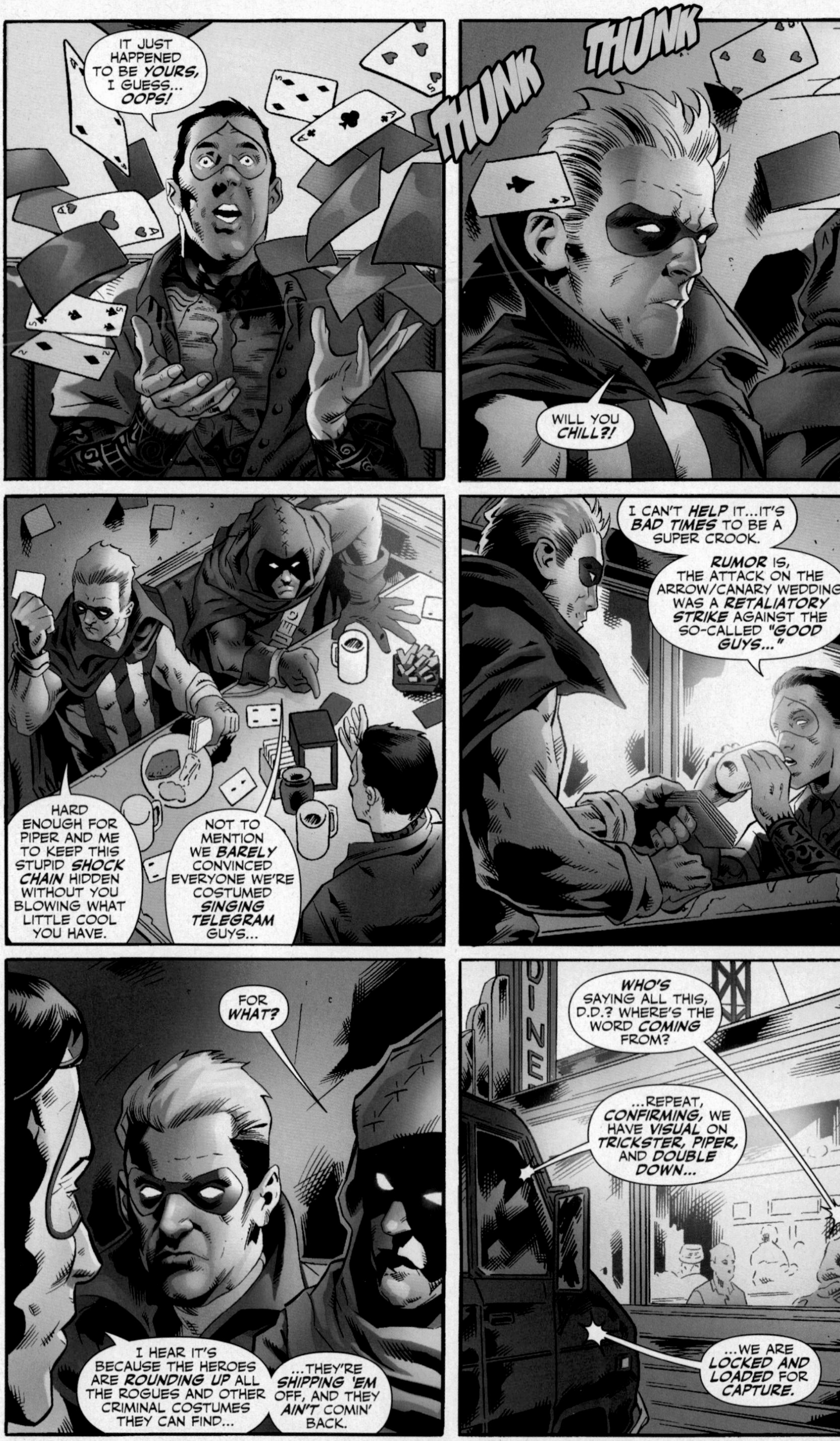

IT JUST HAPPENED TO BE YOURS, I GUESS... OOPS!
THUNK
THUNK
WILL YOU CHILL?!
HARD ENOUGH FOR PIPER AND ME TO KEEP THIS STUPID SHOCK CHAIN HIDDEN WITHOUT YOU BLOWING WHAT LITTLE COOL YOU HAVE.
NOT TO MENTION WE BARELY CONVINCED EVERYONE WE'RE COSTUMED SINGING TELEGRAM GUYS...
I CAN'T HELP IT...IT'S BAD TIMES TO BE A SUPER CROOK.
RUMOR IS, THE ATTACK ON THE ARROW/CANARY WEDDING WAS A RETALIATORY STRIKE AGAINST THE SO-CALLED "GOOD GUYS..."
FOR WHAT?
I HEAR IT'S BECAUSE THE HEROES ARE ROUNDING UP ALL THE ROGUES AND OTHER CRIMINAL COSTUMES THEY CAN FIND...
...THEY'RE SHIPPING 'EM OFF, AND THEY AIN'T COMIN' BACK.
WHO'S SAYING ALL THIS, D.D.? WHERE'S THE WORD COMING FROM?
...REPEAT, CONFIRMING, WE HAVE VISUAL ON TRICKSTER, PIPER, AND DOUBLE DOWN...
...WE ARE LOCKED AND LOADED FOR CAPTURE.

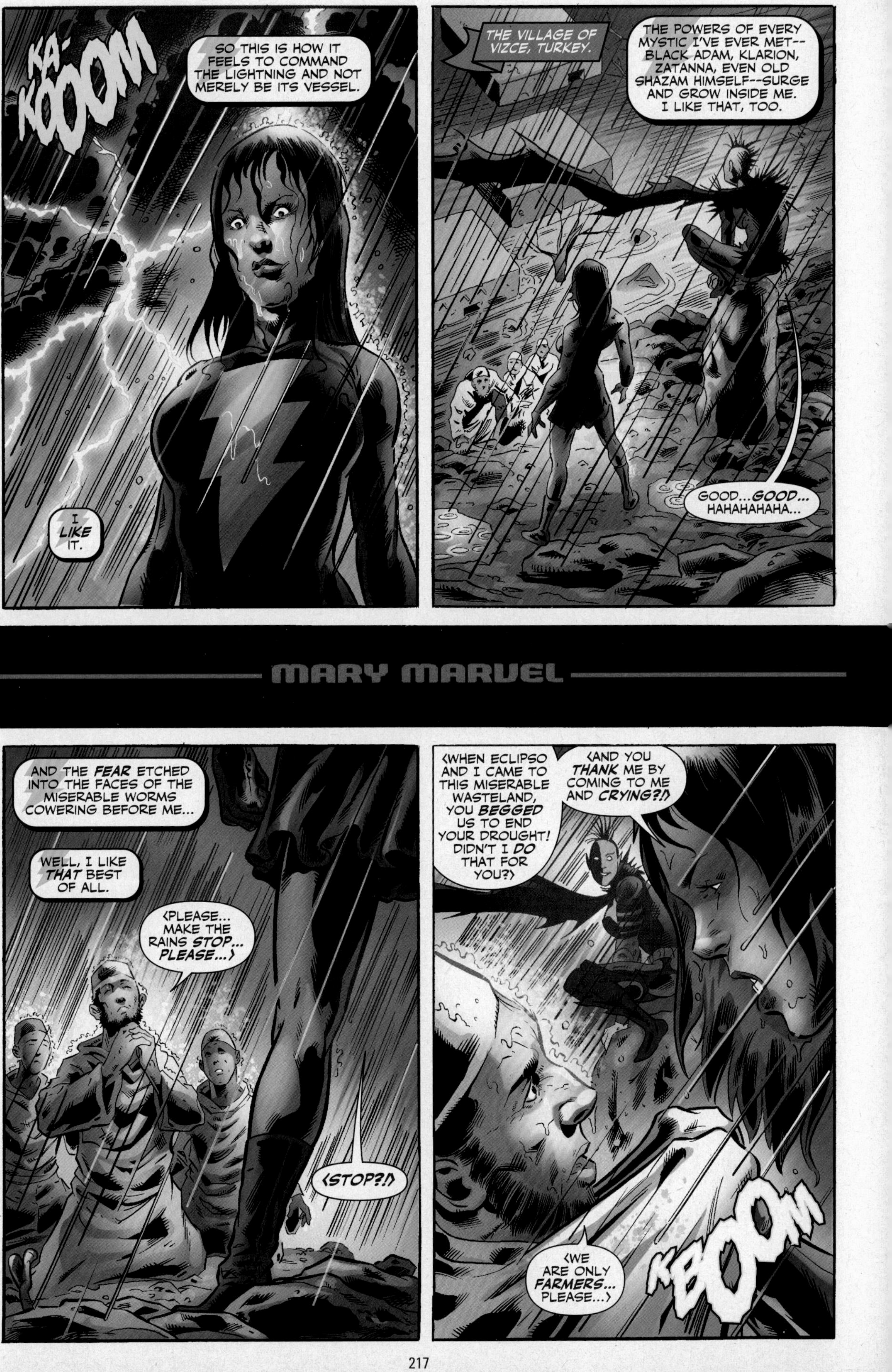
KA-KOOOM
SO THIS IS HOW IT FEELS TO COMMAND THE LIGHTNING AND NOT MERELY BE ITS VESSEL.
I LIKE IT.
THE VILLAGE OF VIZCE, TURKEY.
THE POWERS OF EVERY MYSTIC I'VE EVER MET-- BLACK ADAM, KLARION, ZATANNA, EVEN OLD SHAZAM HIMSELF--SURGE AND GROW INSIDE ME. I LIKE THAT, TOO.
GOOD...GOOD... HAHAHAHAHA...
MARY MARVEL
AND THE FEAR ETCHED INTO THE FACES OF THE MISERABLE WORMS COWERING BEFORE ME...
WELL, I LIKE THAT BEST OF ALL.
‹PLEASE... MAKE THE RAINS STOP... PLEASE...›
‹STOP?!›
‹WHEN ECLIPSO AND I CAME TO THIS MISERABLE WASTELAND, YOU BEGGED US TO END YOUR DROUGHT! DIDN'T I DO THAT FOR YOU?›
‹AND YOU THANK ME BY COMING TO ME AND CRYING?!›
‹WE ARE ONLY FARMERS... PLEASE...›
KBOOM

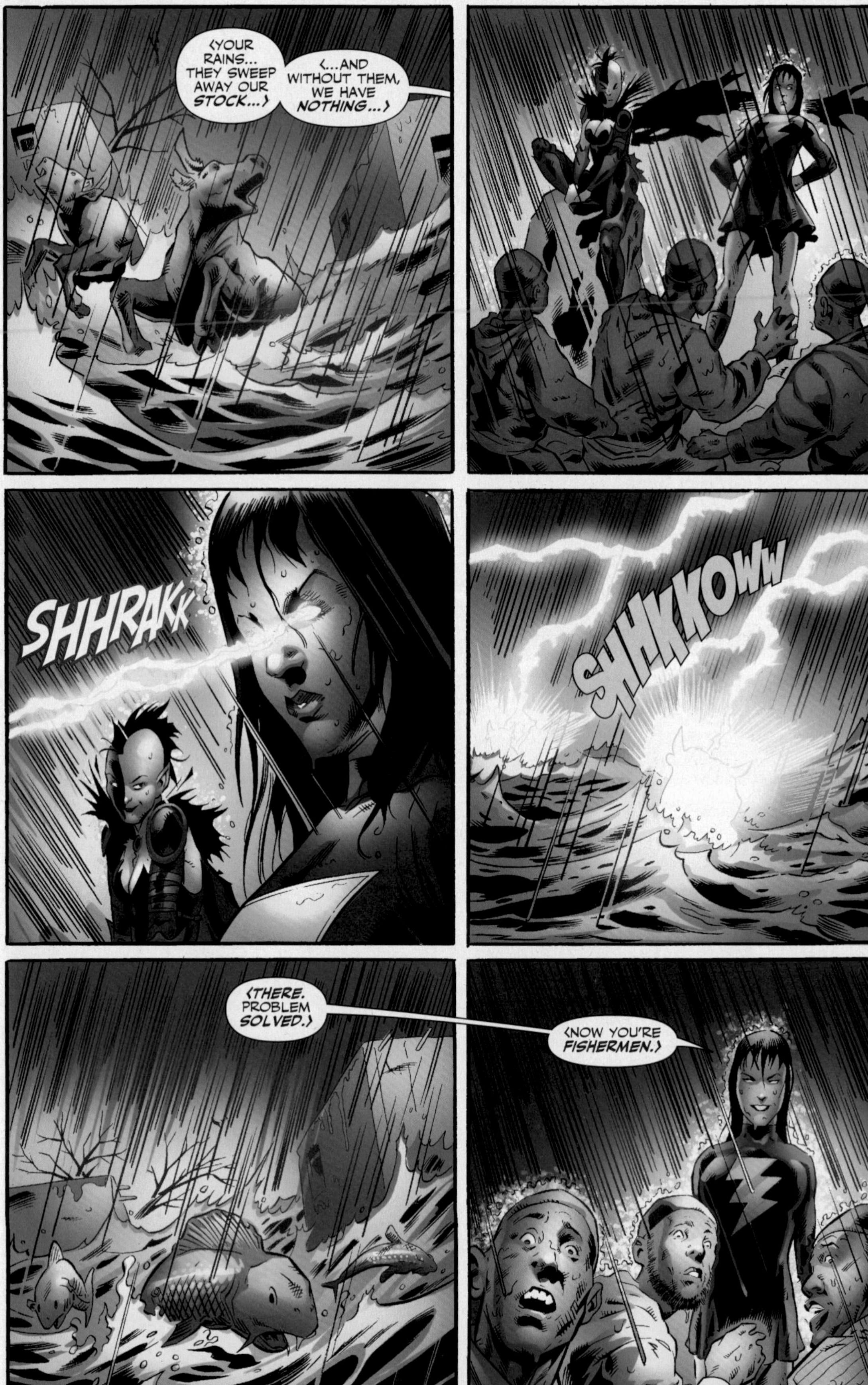
‹YOUR RAINS... THEY SWEEP AWAY OUR STOCK...›
‹...AND WITHOUT THEM, WE HAVE NOTHING...›
SHHRAKK
SHHKKOWW
‹THERE. PROBLEM SOLVED.›
‹NOW YOU'RE FISHERMEN.›

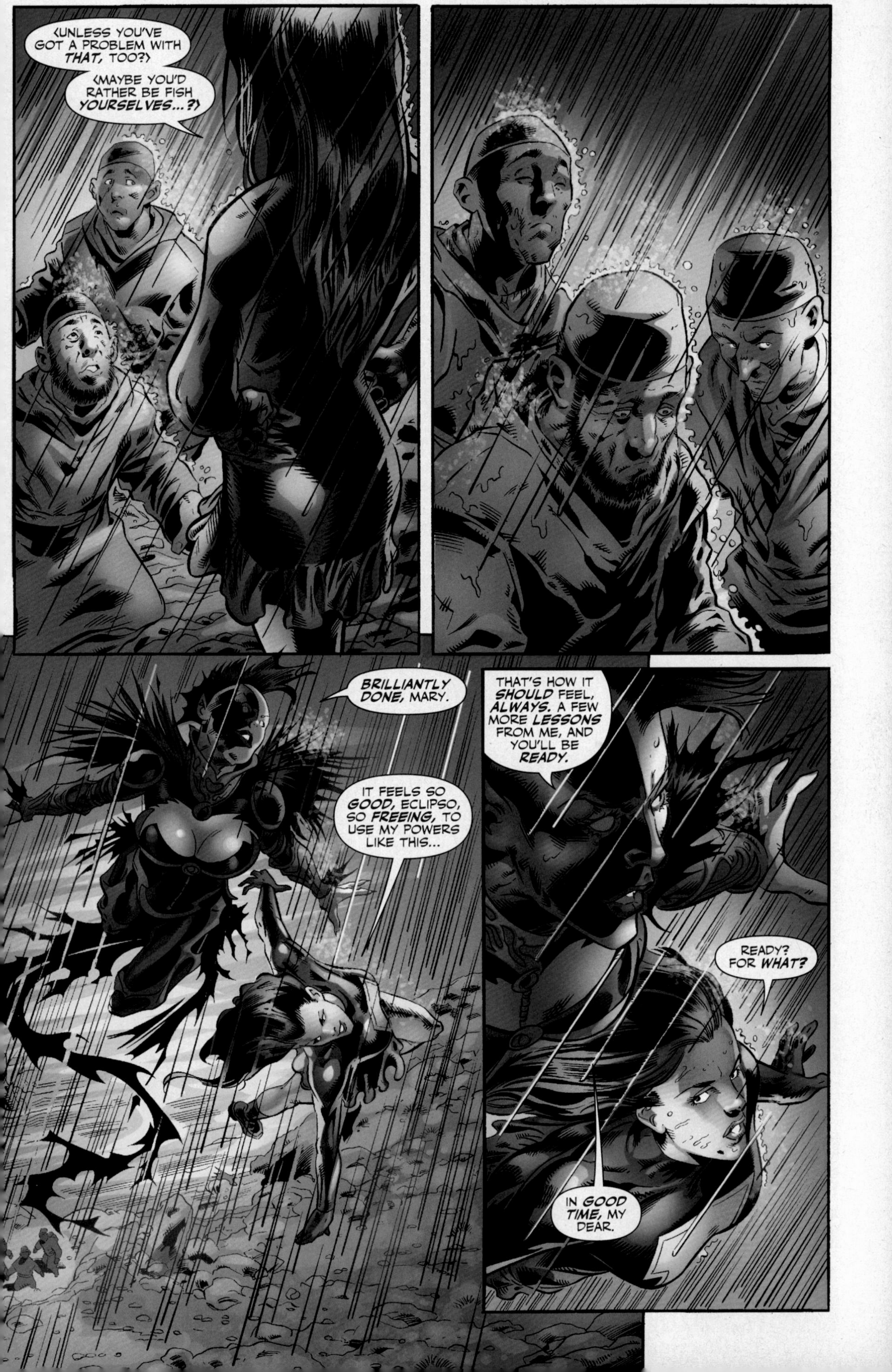
<UNLESS YOU'VE GOT A PROBLEM WITH THAT, TOO?>
<MAYBE YOU'D RATHER BE FISH YOURSELVES...?>
BRILLIANTLY DONE, MARY.
IT FEELS SO GOOD, ECLIPSO, SO FREEING, TO USE MY POWERS LIKE THIS...
THAT'S HOW IT SHOULD FEEL, ALWAYS. A FEW MORE LESSONS FROM ME, AND YOU'LL BE READY.
READY? FOR WHAT?
IN GOOD TIME, MY DEAR.

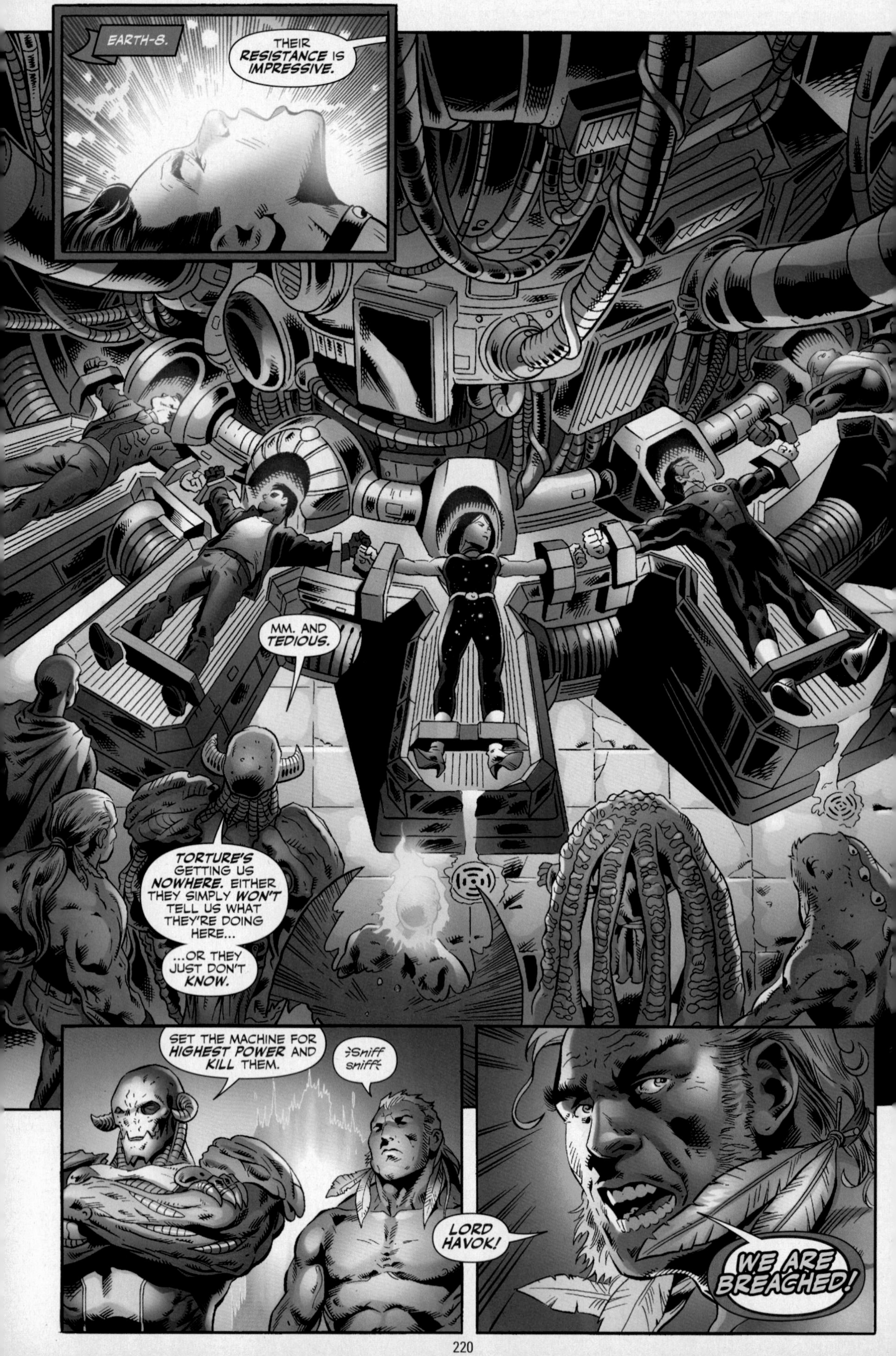
EARTH-8.
THEIR RESISTANCE IS IMPRESSIVE.
MM. AND TEDIOUS.
TORTURE'S GETTING US NOWHERE. EITHER THEY SIMPLY WON'T TELL US WHAT THEY'RE DOING HERE...
...OR THEY JUST DON'T KNOW.
SET THE MACHINE FOR HIGHEST POWER AND KILL THEM.
Sniff sniff
LORD HAVOK!
WE ARE BREACHED!

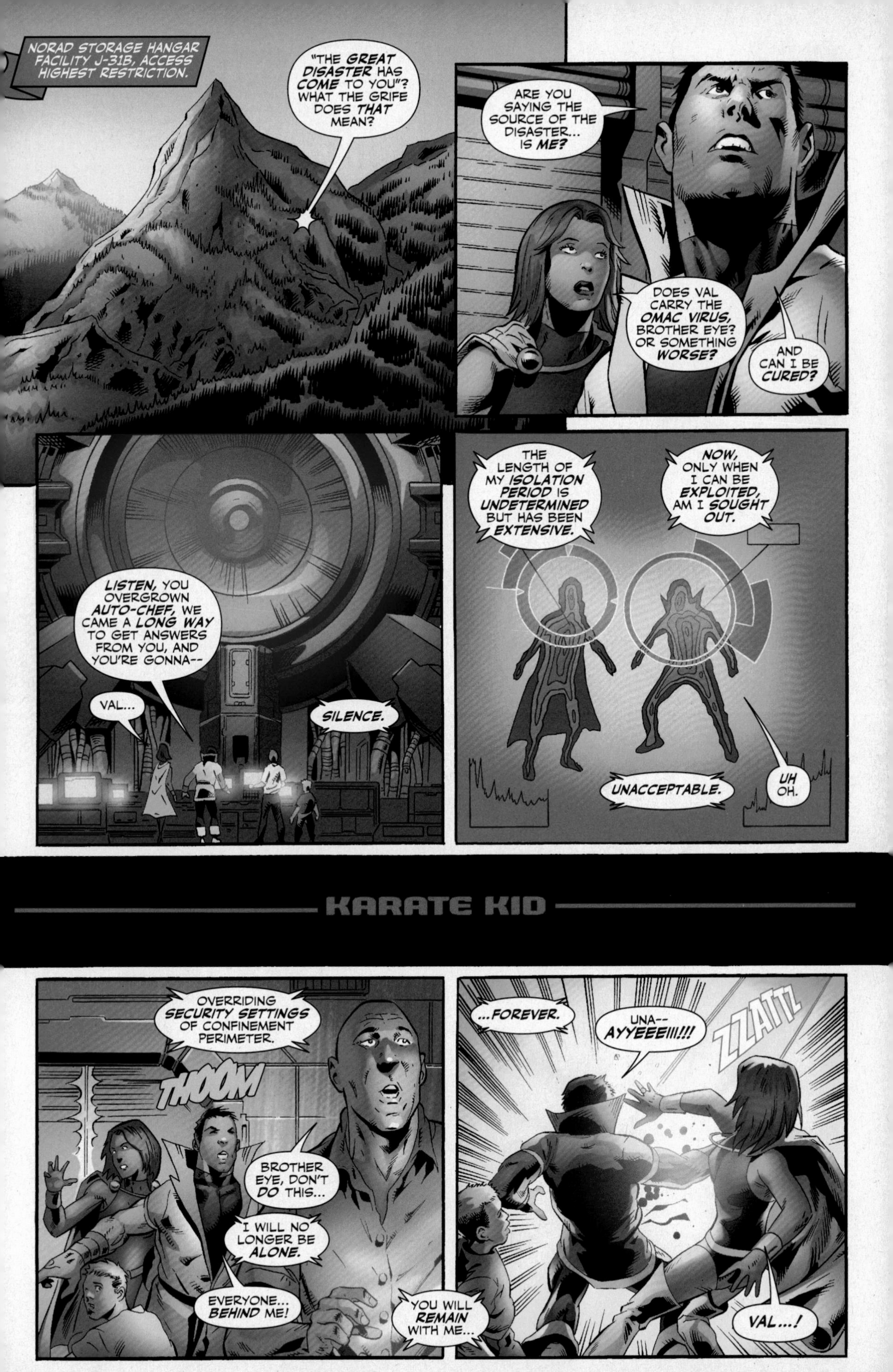
NORAD STORAGE HANGAR FACILITY J-31B, ACCESS HIGHEST RESTRICTION.
"THE GREAT DISASTER HAS COME TO YOU"? WHAT THE GRIFE DOES THAT MEAN?
ARE YOU SAYING THE SOURCE OF THE DISASTER... IS ME?
DOES VAL CARRY THE OMAC VIRUS, BROTHER EYE? OR SOMETHING WORSE?
AND CAN I BE CURED?
LISTEN, YOU OVERGROWN AUTO-CHEF, WE CAME A LONG WAY TO GET ANSWERS FROM YOU, AND YOU'RE GONNA--
VAL...
SILENCE.
THE LENGTH OF MY ISOLATION PERIOD IS UNDETERMINED BUT HAS BEEN EXTENSIVE.
NOW, ONLY WHEN I CAN BE EXPLOITED, AM I SOUGHT OUT.
UNACCEPTABLE.
UH OH.
KARATE KID
OVERRIDING SECURITY SETTINGS OF CONFINEMENT PERIMETER.
THOOM
BROTHER EYE, DON'T DO THIS...
I WILL NO LONGER BE ALONE.
EVERYONE... BEHIND ME!
YOU WILL REMAIN WITH ME...
...FOREVER.
UNA-- AYYEEEIII!!!
ZZATTZ
VAL...!

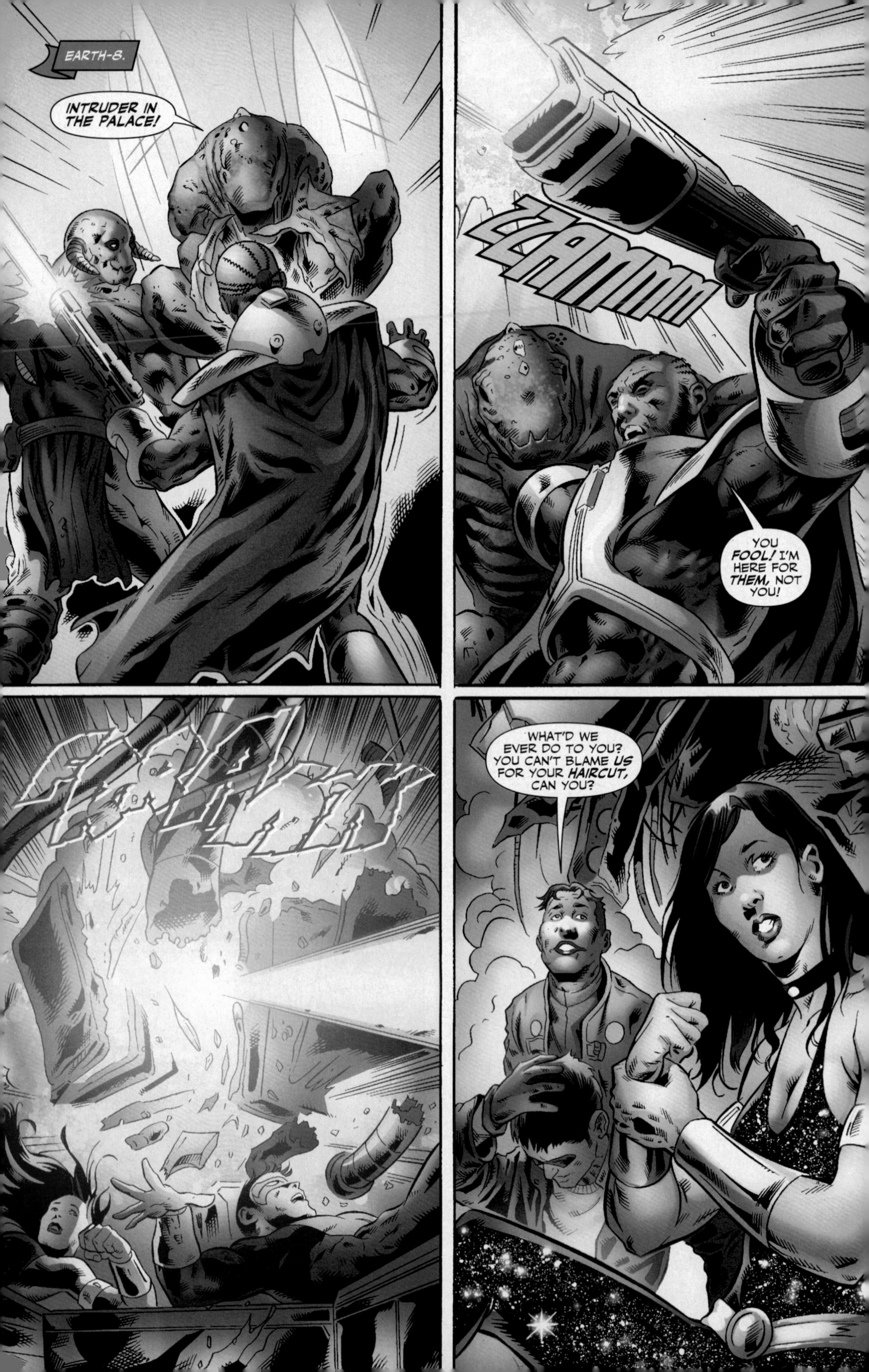
EARTH-8.
INTRUDER IN THE PALACE!
ZZAMMM
YOU FOOL! I'M HERE FOR THEM, NOT YOU!
WHAT'D WE EVER DO TO YOU? YOU CAN'T BLAME US FOR YOUR HAIRCUT, CAN YOU?

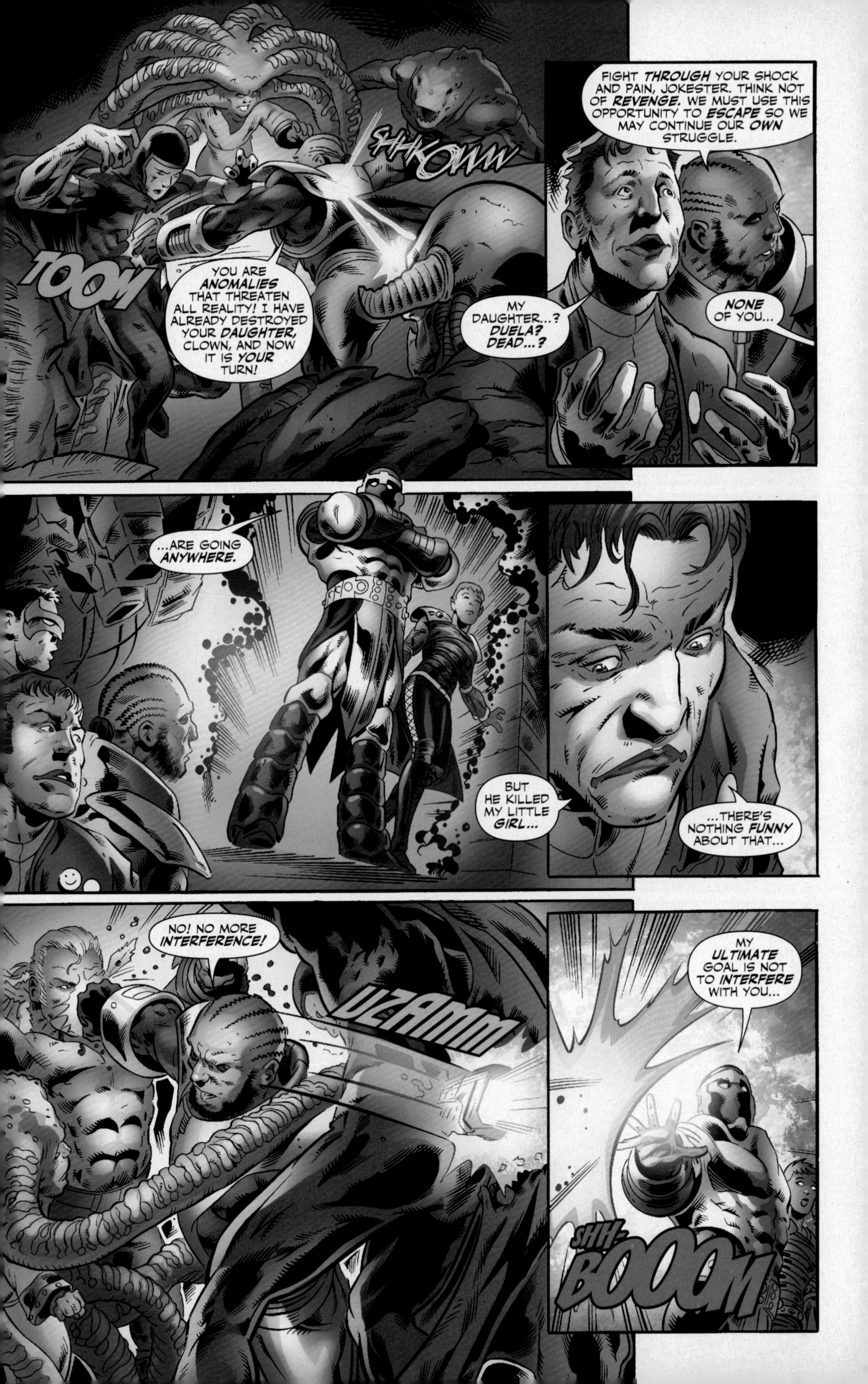
SHHKOWW
TOOM
YOU ARE ANOMALIES THAT THREATEN ALL REALITY! I HAVE ALREADY DESTROYED YOUR DAUGHTER, CLOWN, AND NOW IT IS YOUR TURN!
FIGHT THROUGH YOUR SHOCK AND PAIN, JOKESTER. THINK NOT OF REVENGE. WE MUST USE THIS OPPORTUNITY TO ESCAPE SO WE MAY CONTINUE OUR OWN STRUGGLE.
MY DAUGHTER...? DUELA? DEAD...?
NONE OF YOU...
...ARE GOING ANYWHERE.
BUT HE KILLED MY LITTLE GIRL...
...THERE'S NOTHING FUNNY ABOUT THAT...
NO! NO MORE INTERFERENCE!
UZAMM
MY ULTIMATE GOAL IS NOT TO INTERFERE WITH YOU...
SHH-BOOOM

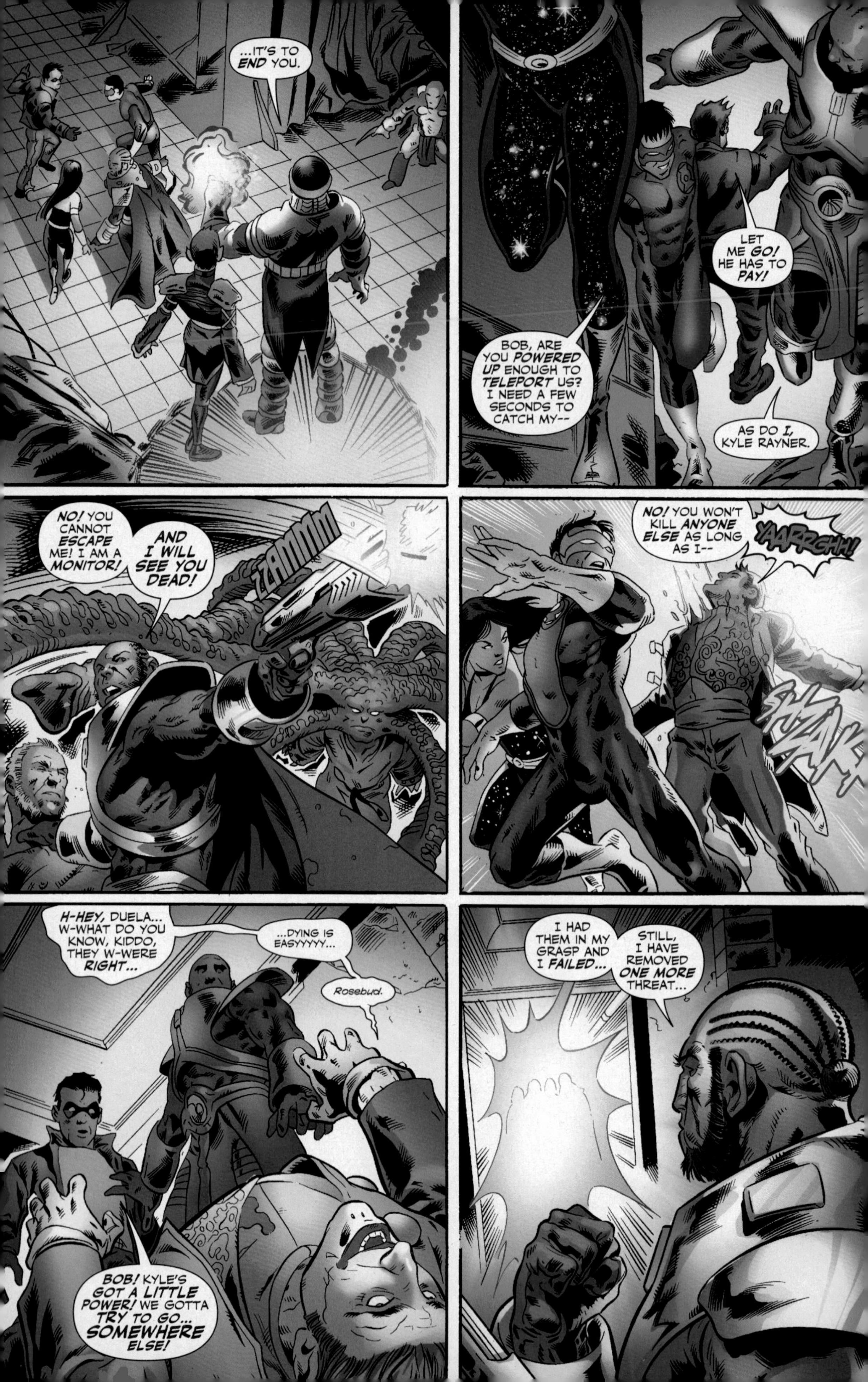

...IT'S TO END YOU.
LET ME GO! HE HAS TO PAY!
BOB, ARE YOU POWERED UP ENOUGH TO TELEPORT US? I NEED A FEW SECONDS TO CATCH MY--
AS DO I, KYLE RAYNER.
NO! YOU CANNOT ESCAPE ME! I AM A MONITOR!
AND I WILL SEE YOU DEAD!
ZZAMMM
NO! YOU WON'T KILL ANYONE ELSE AS LONG AS I--
YAARRGHH!
SHAKK
H-HEY, DUELA... W-WHAT DO YOU KNOW, KIDDO, THEY W-WERE RIGHT...
...DYING IS EASYYYYY...
Rosebud.
BOB! KYLE'S GOT A LITTLE POWER! WE GOTTA TRY TO GO... SOMEWHERE ELSE!
I HAD THEM IN MY GRASP AND I FAILED...
STILL, I HAVE REMOVED ONE MORE THREAT...

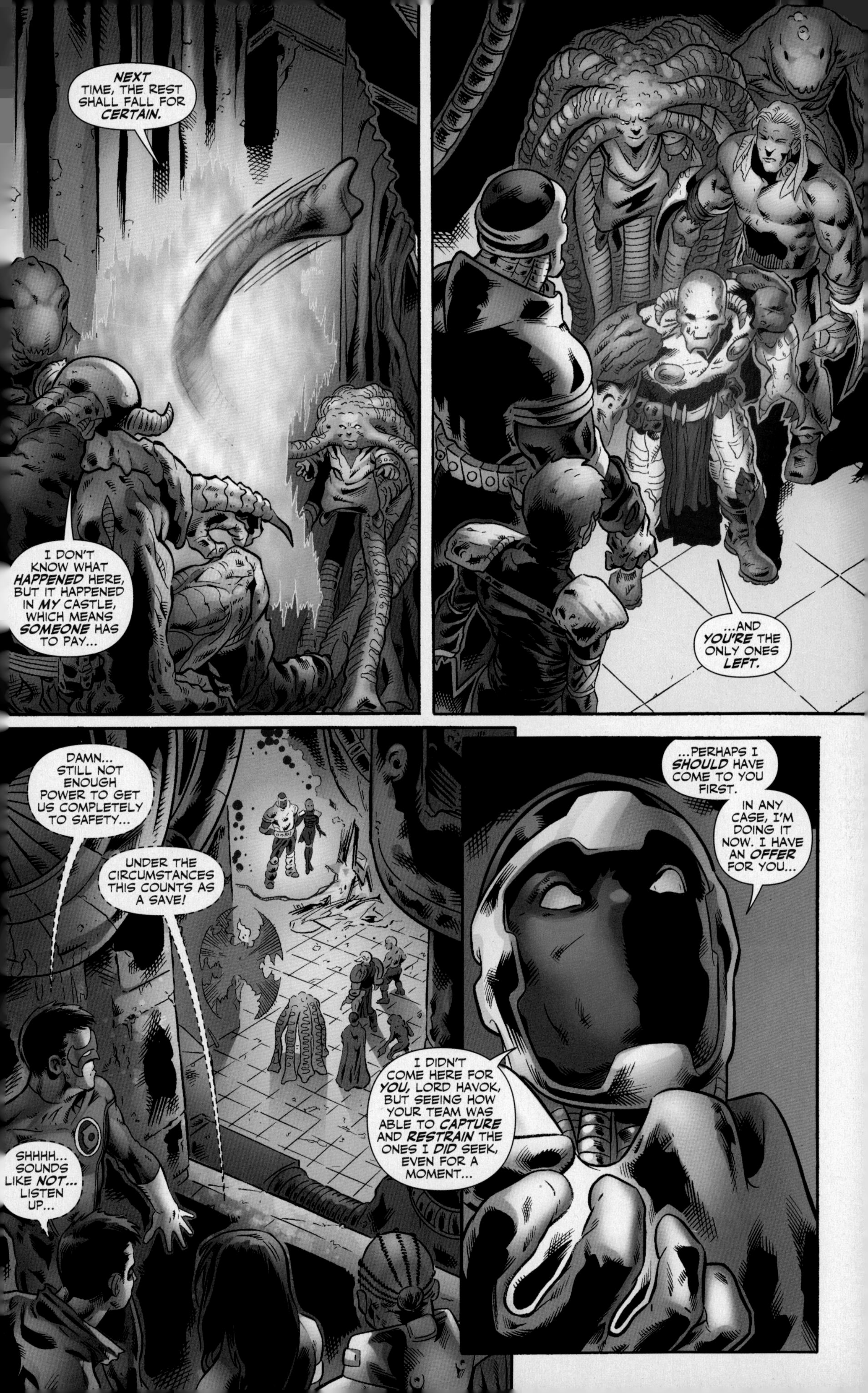
NEXT TIME, THE REST SHALL FALL FOR CERTAIN.
I DON'T KNOW WHAT HAPPENED HERE, BUT IT HAPPENED IN MY CASTLE, WHICH MEANS SOMEONE HAS TO PAY...
...AND YOU'RE THE ONLY ONES LEFT.
DAMN... STILL NOT ENOUGH POWER TO GET US COMPLETELY TO SAFETY...
UNDER THE CIRCUMSTANCES THIS COUNTS AS A SAVE!
SHHHH... SOUNDS LIKE NOT... LISTEN UP...
I DIDN'T COME HERE FOR YOU, LORD HAVOK, BUT SEEING HOW YOUR TEAM WAS ABLE TO CAPTURE AND RESTRAIN THE ONES I DID SEEK, EVEN FOR A MOMENT...
...PERHAPS I SHOULD HAVE COME TO YOU FIRST.
IN ANY CASE, I'M DOING IT NOW. I HAVE AN OFFER FOR YOU...

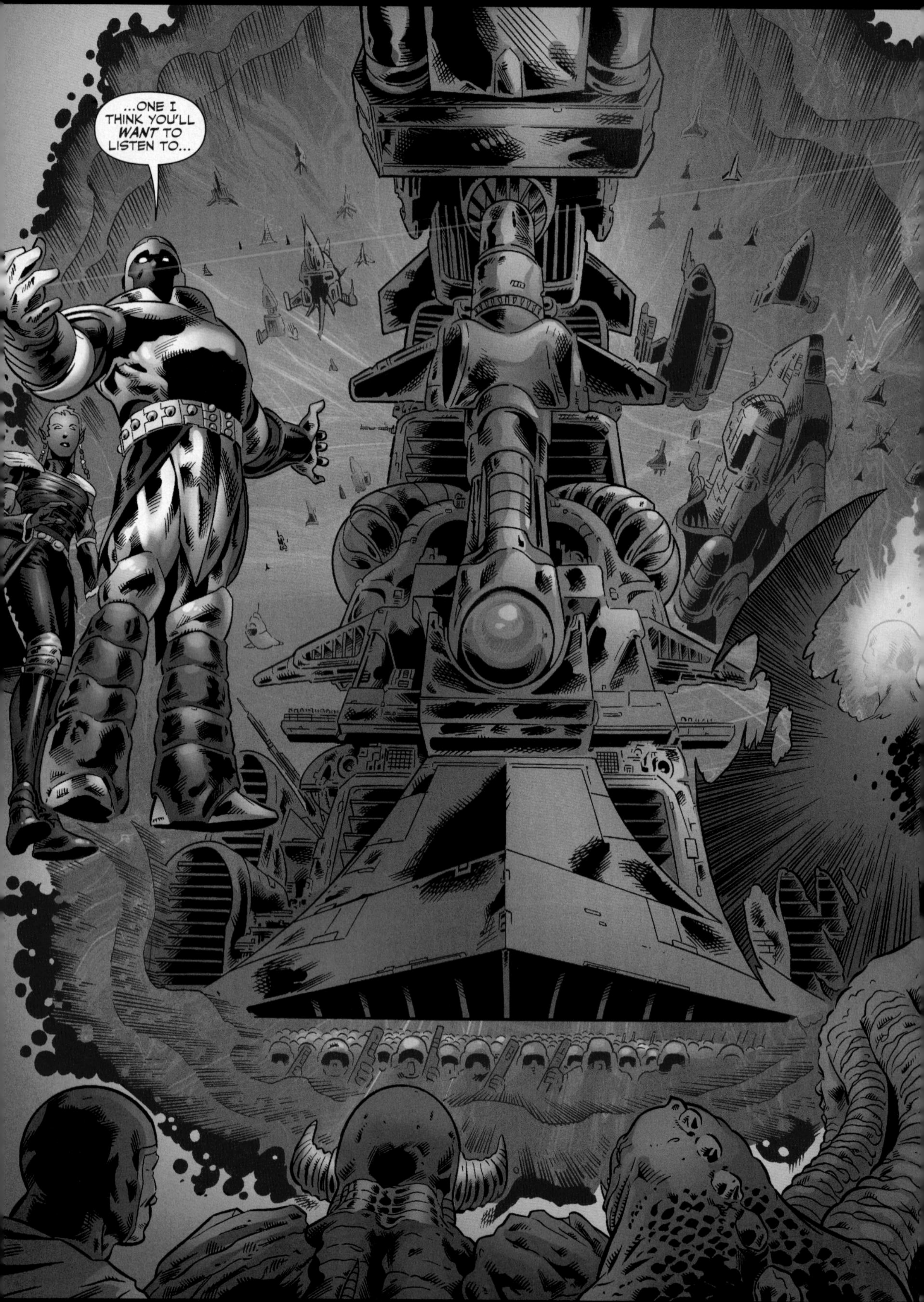
...ONE I THINK YOU'LL *WANT* TO LISTEN TO...

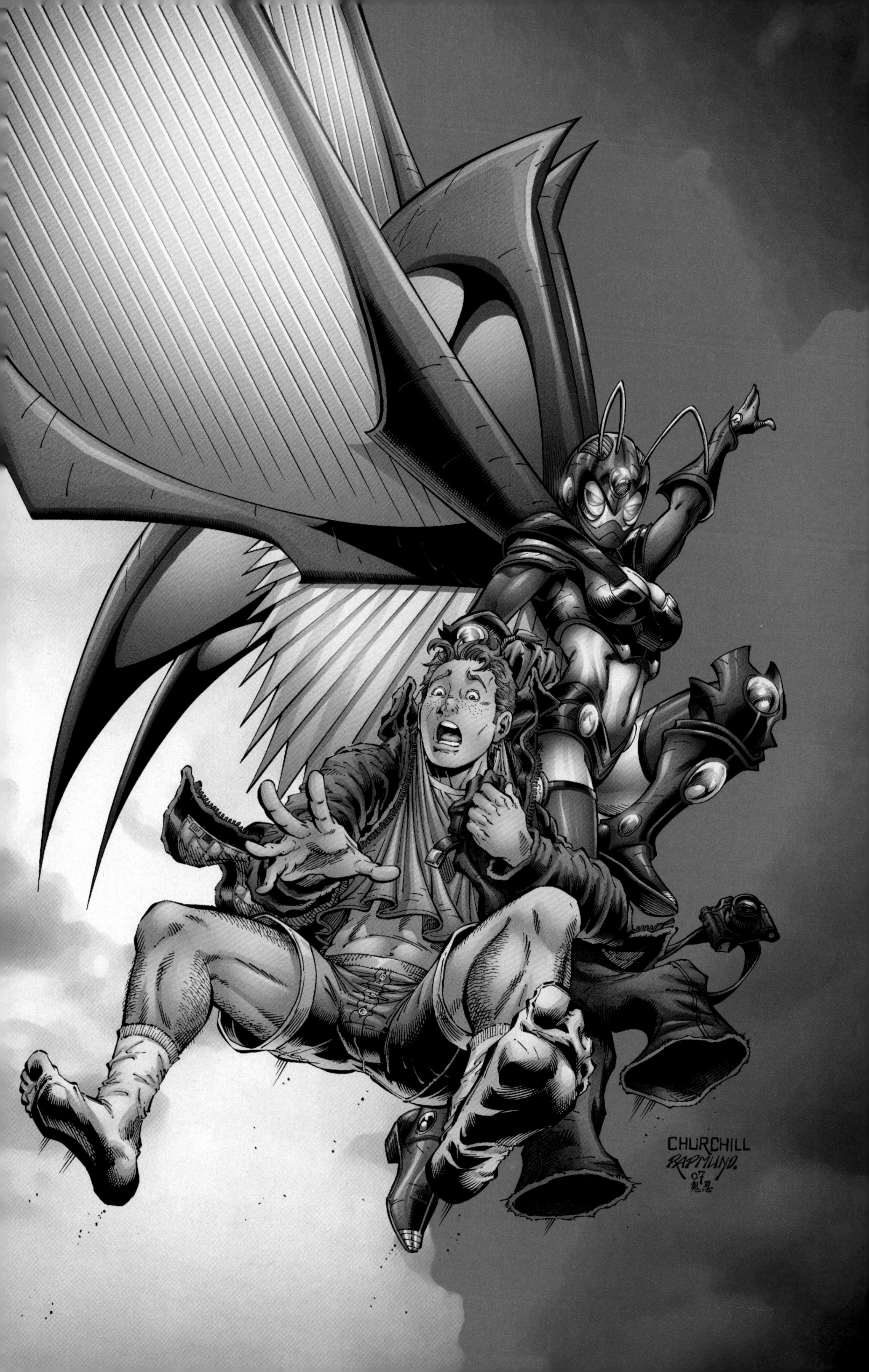
CHURCHILL
07

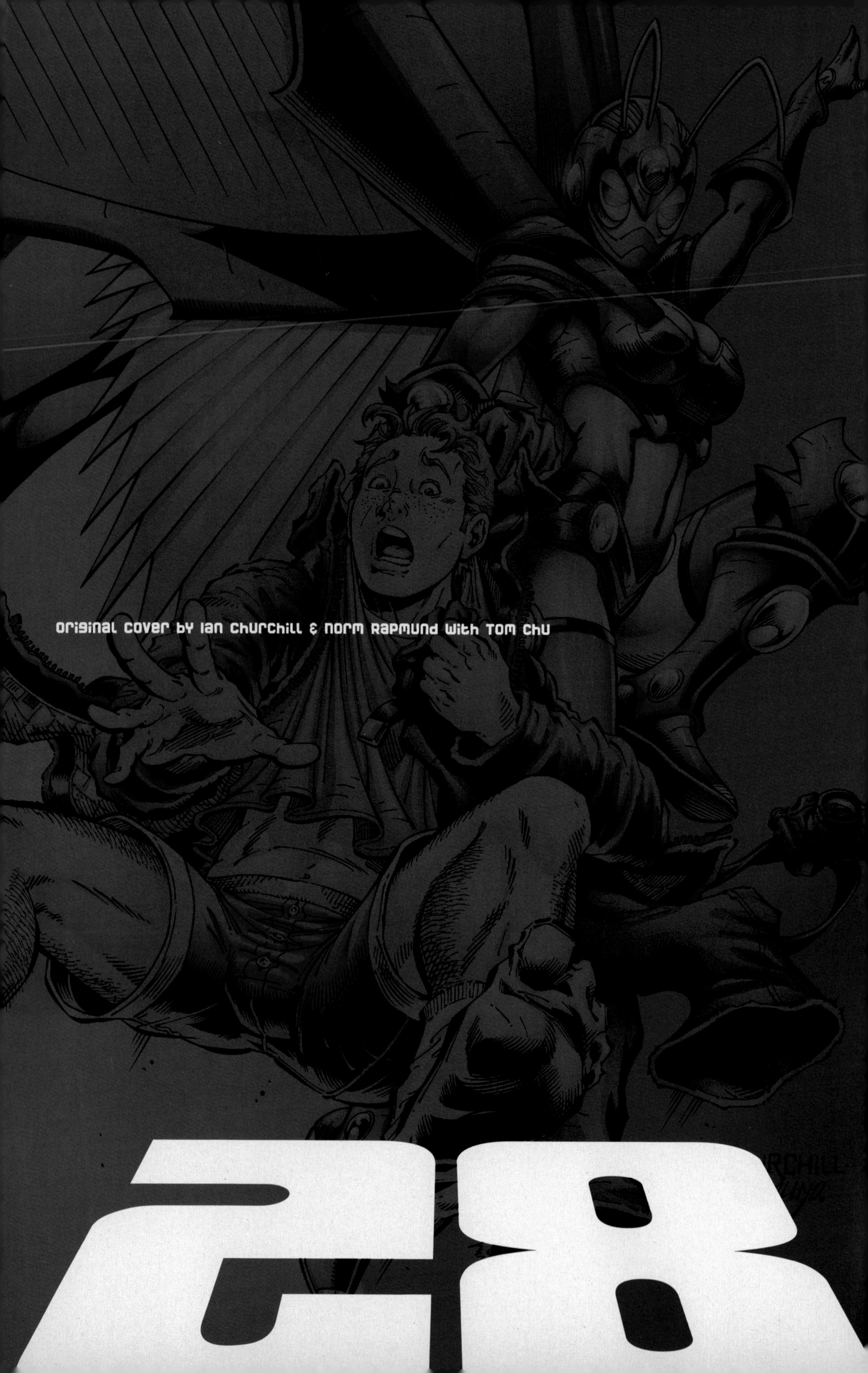

original cover by Ian Churchill & Norm Rapmund with Tom Chu

28

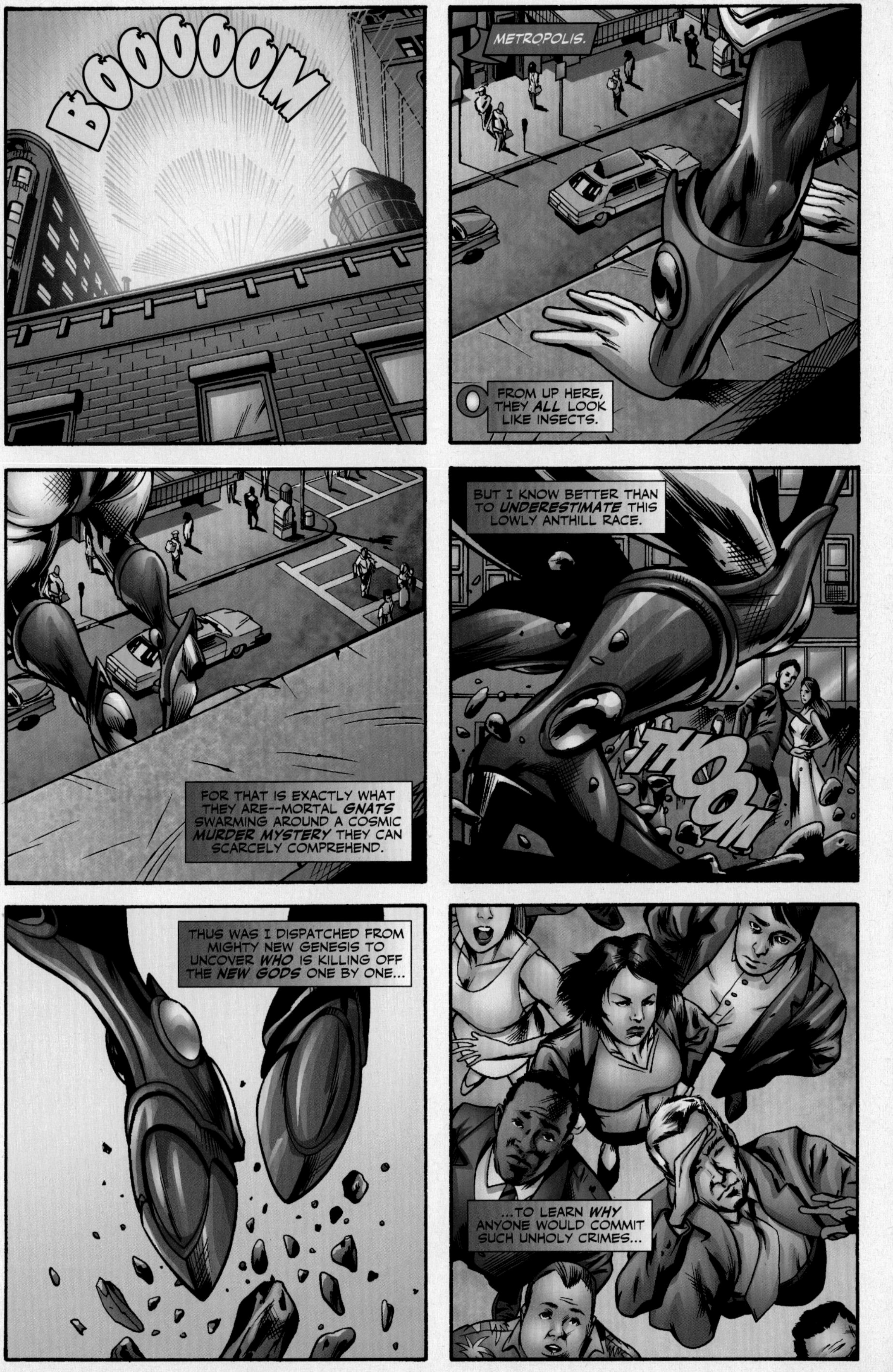
BOOOOOOM
METROPOLIS.
FROM UP HERE, THEY ALL LOOK LIKE INSECTS.
FOR THAT IS EXACTLY WHAT THEY ARE--MORTAL GNATS SWARMING AROUND A COSMIC MURDER MYSTERY THEY CAN SCARCELY COMPREHEND.
BUT I KNOW BETTER THAN TO UNDERESTIMATE THIS LOWLY ANTHILL RACE.
THOOM
THUS WAS I DISPATCHED FROM MIGHTY NEW GENESIS TO UNCOVER WHO IS KILLING OFF THE NEW GODS ONE BY ONE...
...TO LEARN WHY ANYONE WOULD COMMIT SUCH UNHOLY CRIMES...

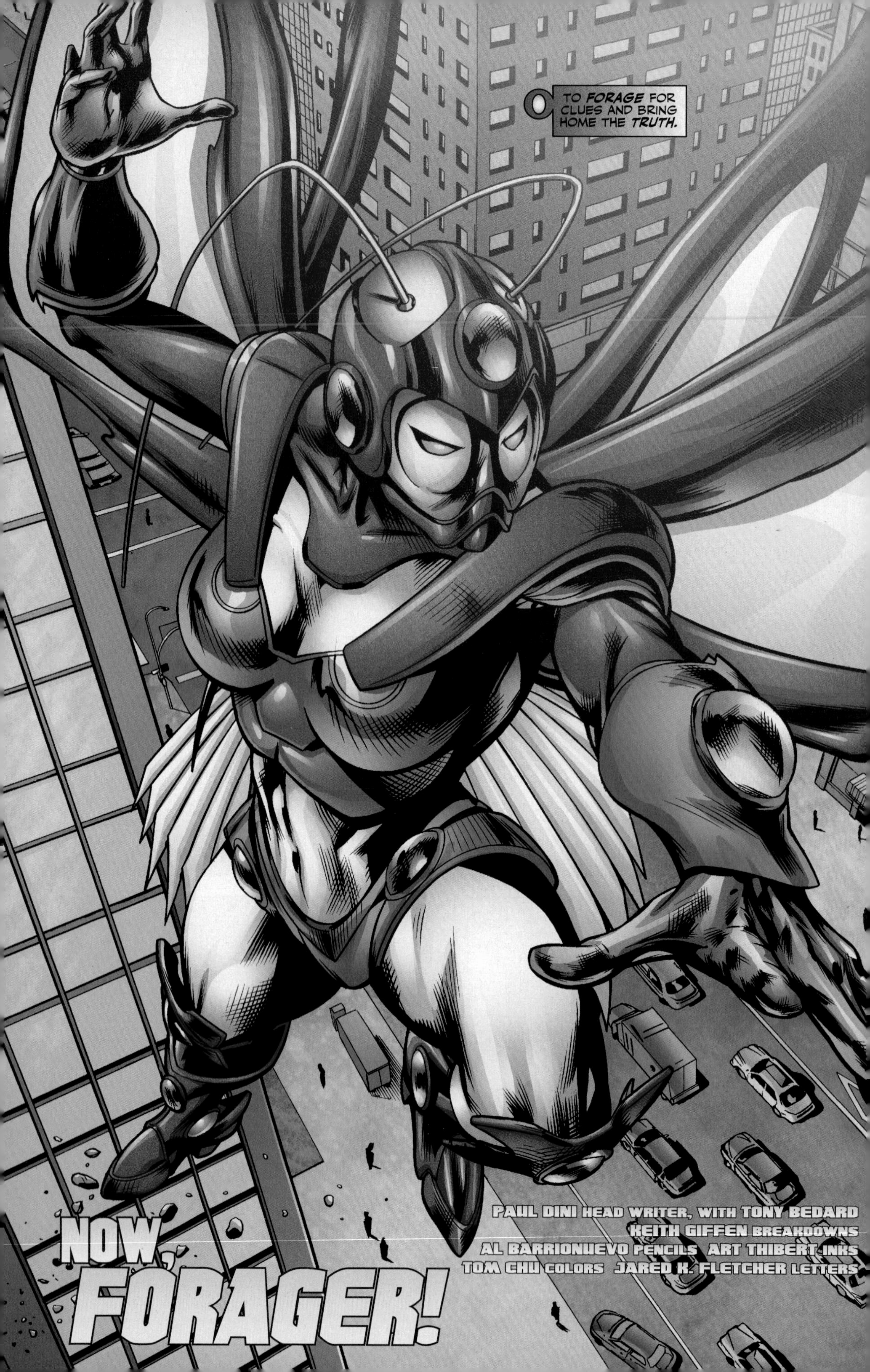
TO FORAGE FOR CLUES AND BRING HOME THE TRUTH.
PAUL DINI HEAD WRITER, WITH TONY BEDARD
KEITH GIFFEN BREAKDOWNS
AL BARRIONUEVO PENCILS ART THIBERT INKS
TOM CHU COLORS JARED K. FLETCHER LETTERS
NOW, FORAGER!

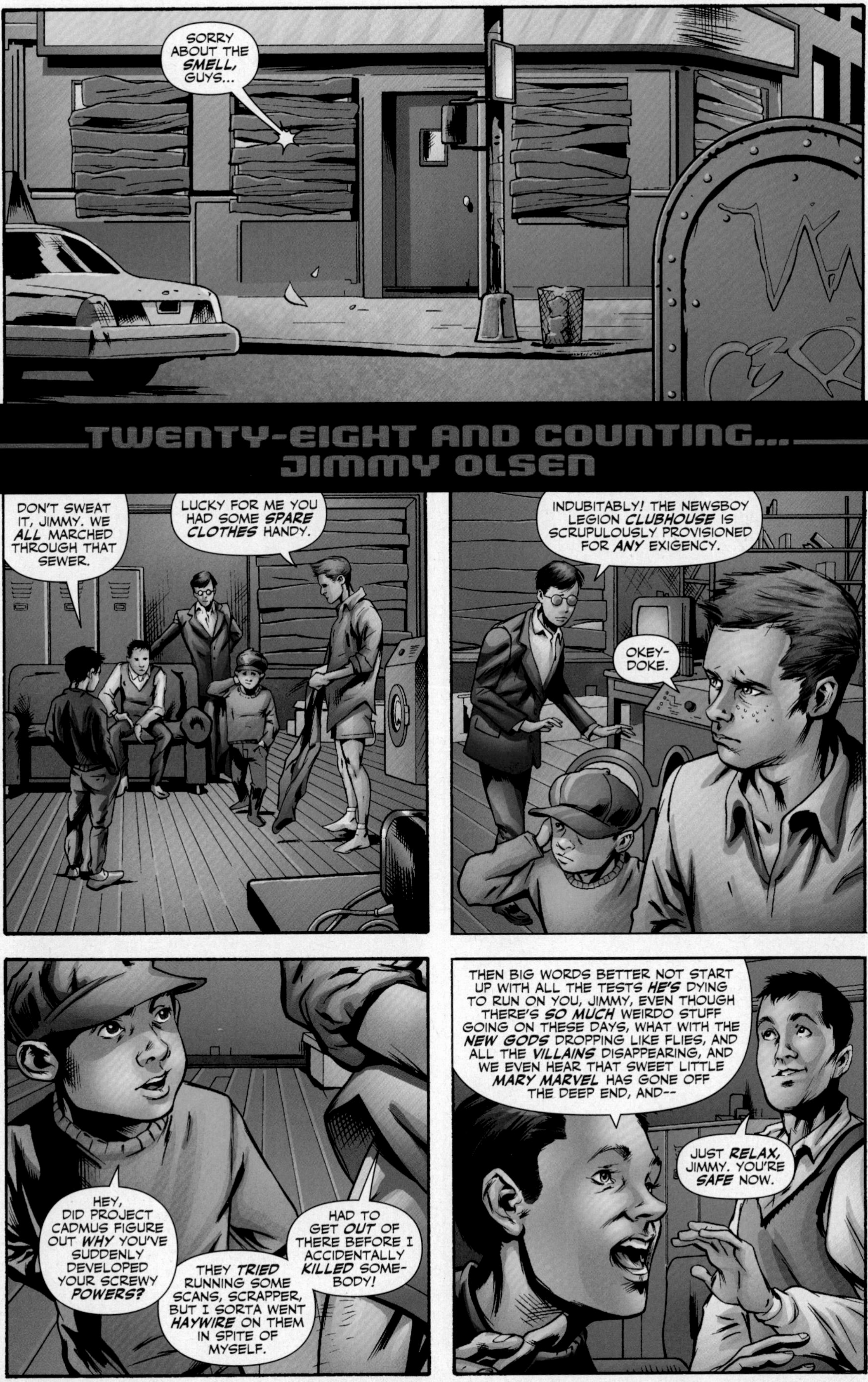

SORRY ABOUT THE SMELL, GUYS...
TWENTY-EIGHT AND COUNTING... JIMMY OLSEN
DON'T SWEAT IT, JIMMY. WE ALL MARCHED THROUGH THAT SEWER.
LUCKY FOR ME YOU HAD SOME SPARE CLOTHES HANDY.
INDUBITABLY! THE NEWSBOY LEGION CLUBHOUSE IS SCRUPULOUSLY PROVISIONED FOR ANY EXIGENCY.
OKEY-DOKE.
HEY, DID PROJECT CADMUS FIGURE OUT WHY YOU'VE SUDDENLY DEVELOPED YOUR SCREWY POWERS?
THEY TRIED RUNNING SOME SCANS, SCRAPPER, BUT I SORTA WENT HAYWIRE ON THEM IN SPITE OF MYSELF.
HAD TO GET OUT OF THERE BEFORE I ACCIDENTALLY KILLED SOME-BODY!
THEN BIG WORDS BETTER NOT START UP WITH ALL THE TESTS HE'S DYING TO RUN ON YOU, JIMMY, EVEN THOUGH THERE'S SO MUCH WEIRDO STUFF GOING ON THESE DAYS, WHAT WITH THE NEW GODS DROPPING LIKE FLIES, AND ALL THE VILLAINS DISAPPEARING, AND WE EVEN HEAR THAT SWEET LITTLE MARY MARVEL HAS GONE OFF THE DEEP END, AND--
JUST RELAX, JIMMY. YOU'RE SAFE NOW.

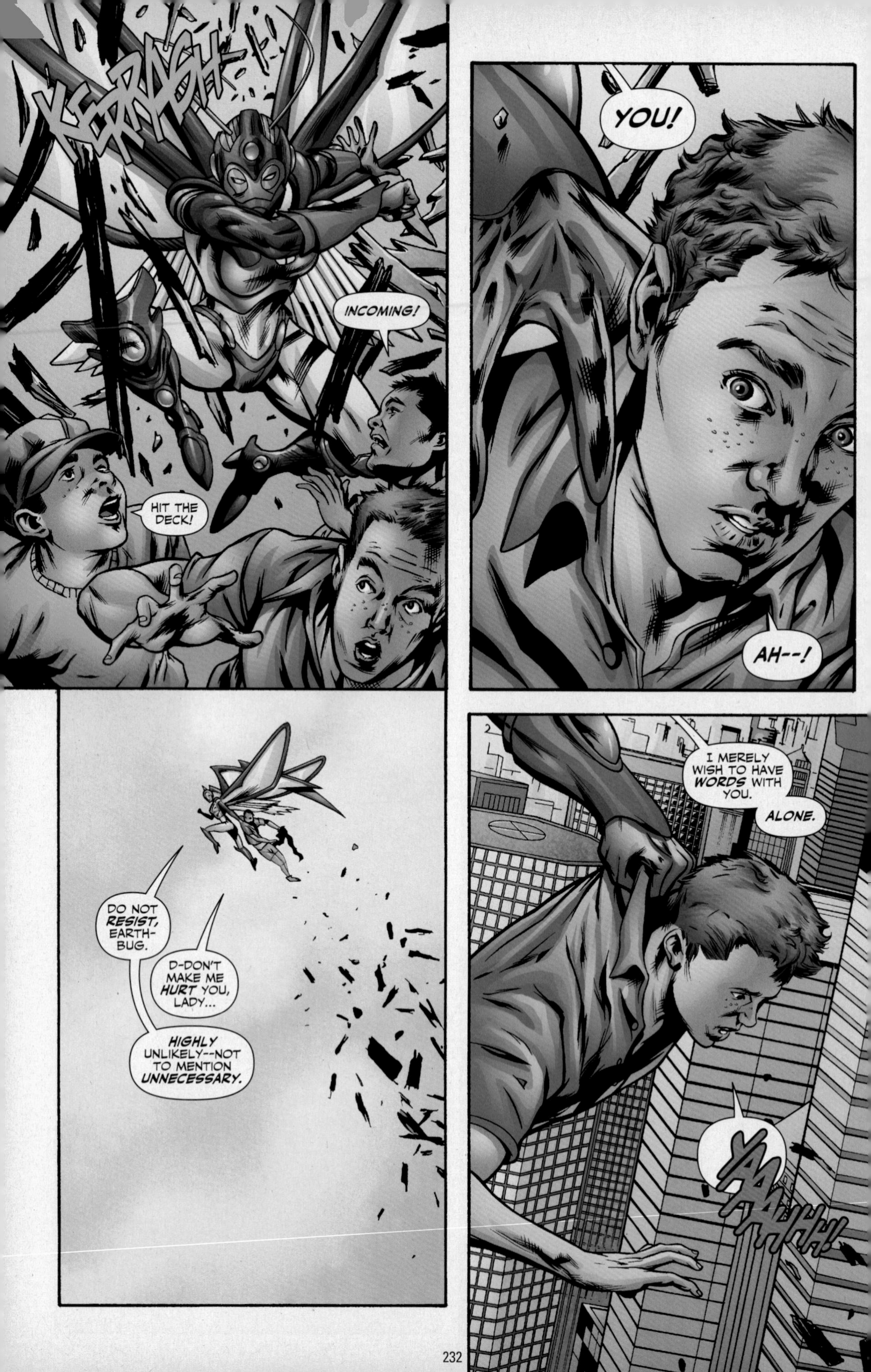
KKRASH
INCOMING!
HIT THE DECK!
YOU!
AH--!
DO NOT RESIST, EARTH-BUG.
D-DON'T MAKE ME HURT YOU, LADY...
HIGHLY UNLIKELY--NOT TO MENTION UNNECESSARY.
I MERELY WISH TO HAVE WORDS WITH YOU.
ALONE.
YAAHH!

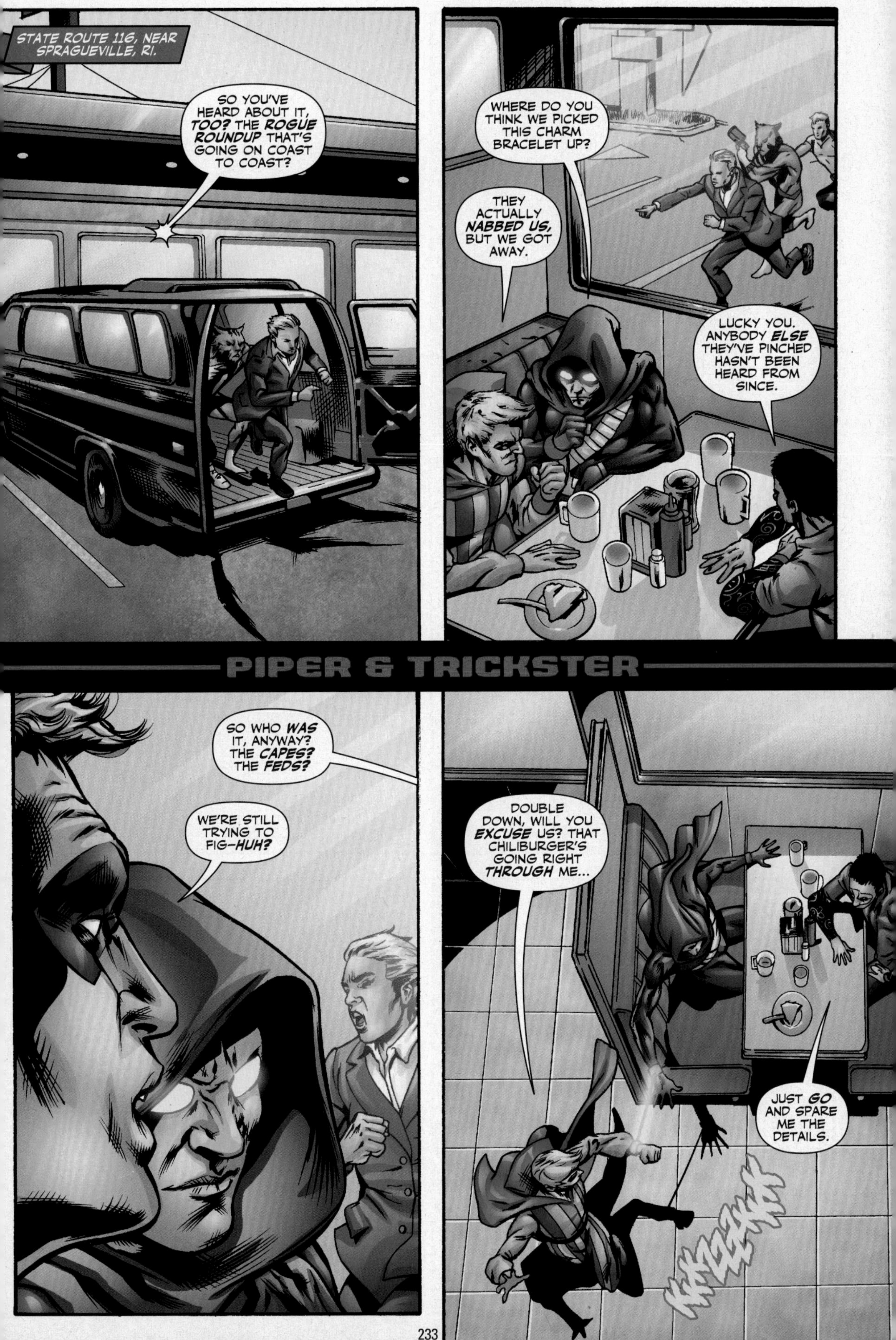
STATE ROUTE 116, NEAR SPRAGUEVILLE, RI.
SO YOU'VE HEARD ABOUT IT, TOO? THE ROGUE ROUNDUP THAT'S GOING ON COAST TO COAST?
WHERE DO YOU THINK WE PICKED THIS CHARM BRACELET UP?
THEY ACTUALLY NABBED US, BUT WE GOT AWAY.
LUCKY YOU. ANYBODY ELSE THEY'VE PINCHED HASN'T BEEN HEARD FROM SINCE.
PIPER & TRICKSTER
SO WHO WAS IT, ANYWAY? THE CAPES? THE FEDS?
WE'RE STILL TRYING TO FIG–HUH?
DOUBLE DOWN, WILL YOU EXCUSE US? THAT CHILIBURGER'S GOING RIGHT THROUGH ME...
JUST GO AND SPARE ME THE DETAILS.

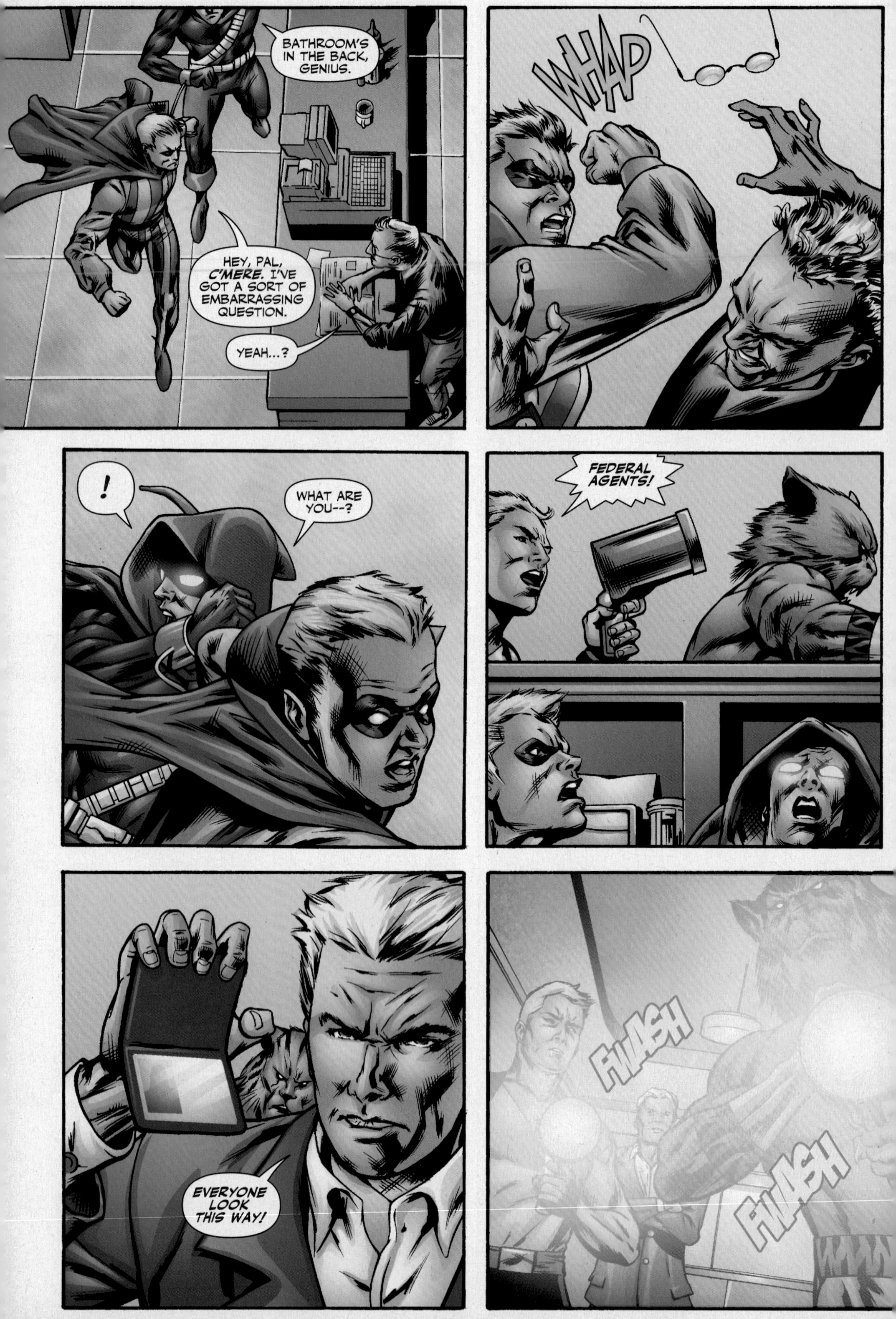
BATHROOM'S IN THE BACK, GENIUS.
HEY, PAL, C'MERE. I'VE GOT A SORT OF EMBARRASSING QUESTION.
YEAH...?
WHAP
!
WHAT ARE YOU--?
FEDERAL AGENTS!
EVERYONE LOOK THIS WAY!
FWASH
FWASH

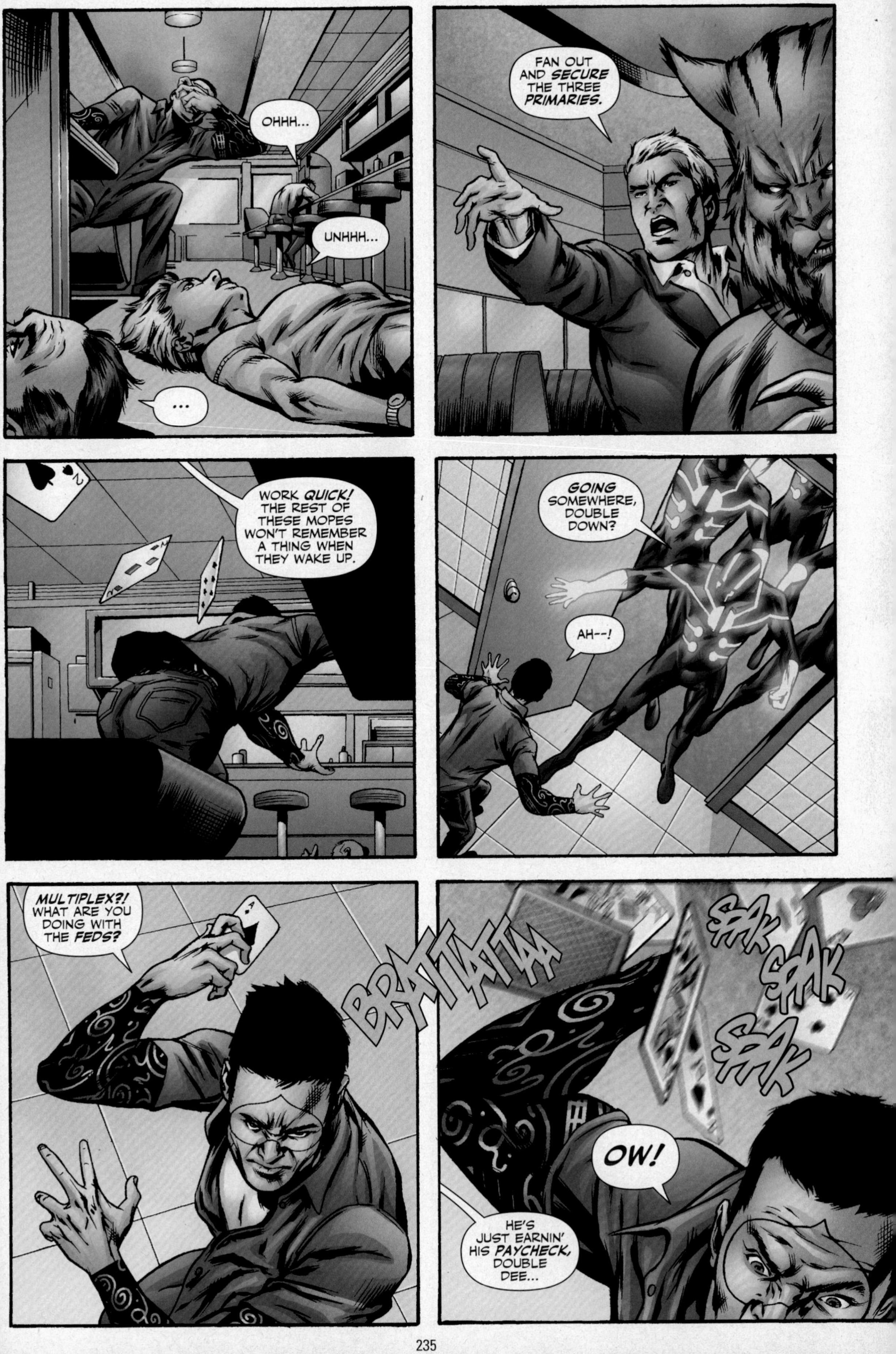
OHHH...
UNHHH...
...
FAN OUT AND SECURE THE THREE PRIMARIES.
WORK QUICK! THE REST OF THESE MOPES WON'T REMEMBER A THING WHEN THEY WAKE UP.
GOING SOMEWHERE, DOUBLE DOWN?
AH--!
MULTIPLEX?! WHAT ARE YOU DOING WITH THE FEDS?
BRATTATTAA
SPAK
SPAK
SPAK
OW!
HE'S JUST EARNIN' HIS PAYCHECK, DOUBLE DEE...

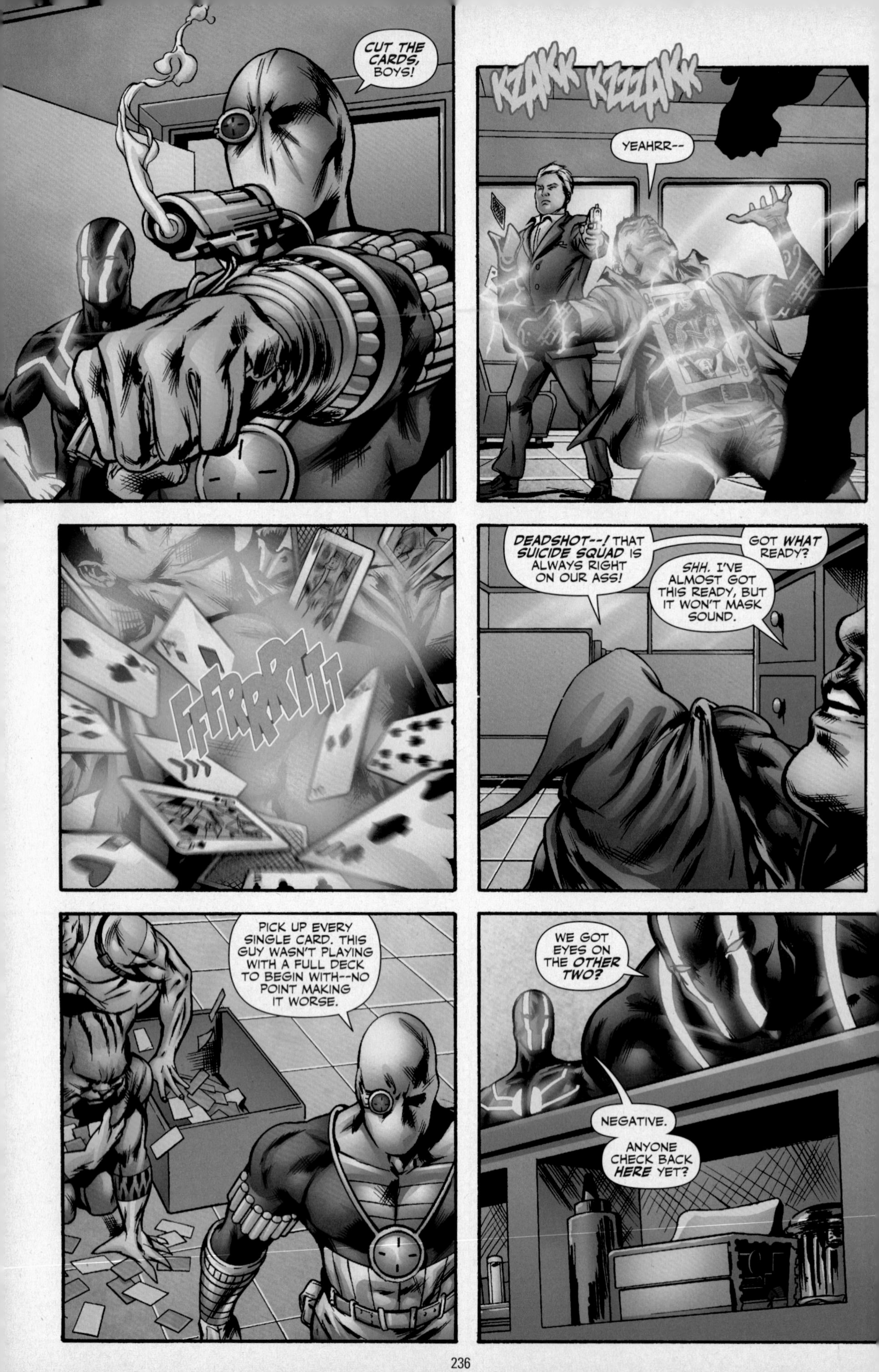
CUT THE CARDS, BOYS!
KZAKK KZZZAKK
YEAHRR--
FFFRRRRTTT
DEADSHOT--! THAT SUICIDE SQUAD IS ALWAYS RIGHT ON OUR ASS!
GOT WHAT READY?
SHH. I'VE ALMOST GOT THIS READY, BUT IT WON'T MASK SOUND.
PICK UP EVERY SINGLE CARD. THIS GUY WASN'T PLAYING WITH A FULL DECK TO BEGIN WITH--NO POINT MAKING IT WORSE.
WE GOT EYES ON THE OTHER TWO?
NEGATIVE.
ANYONE CHECK BACK HERE YET?

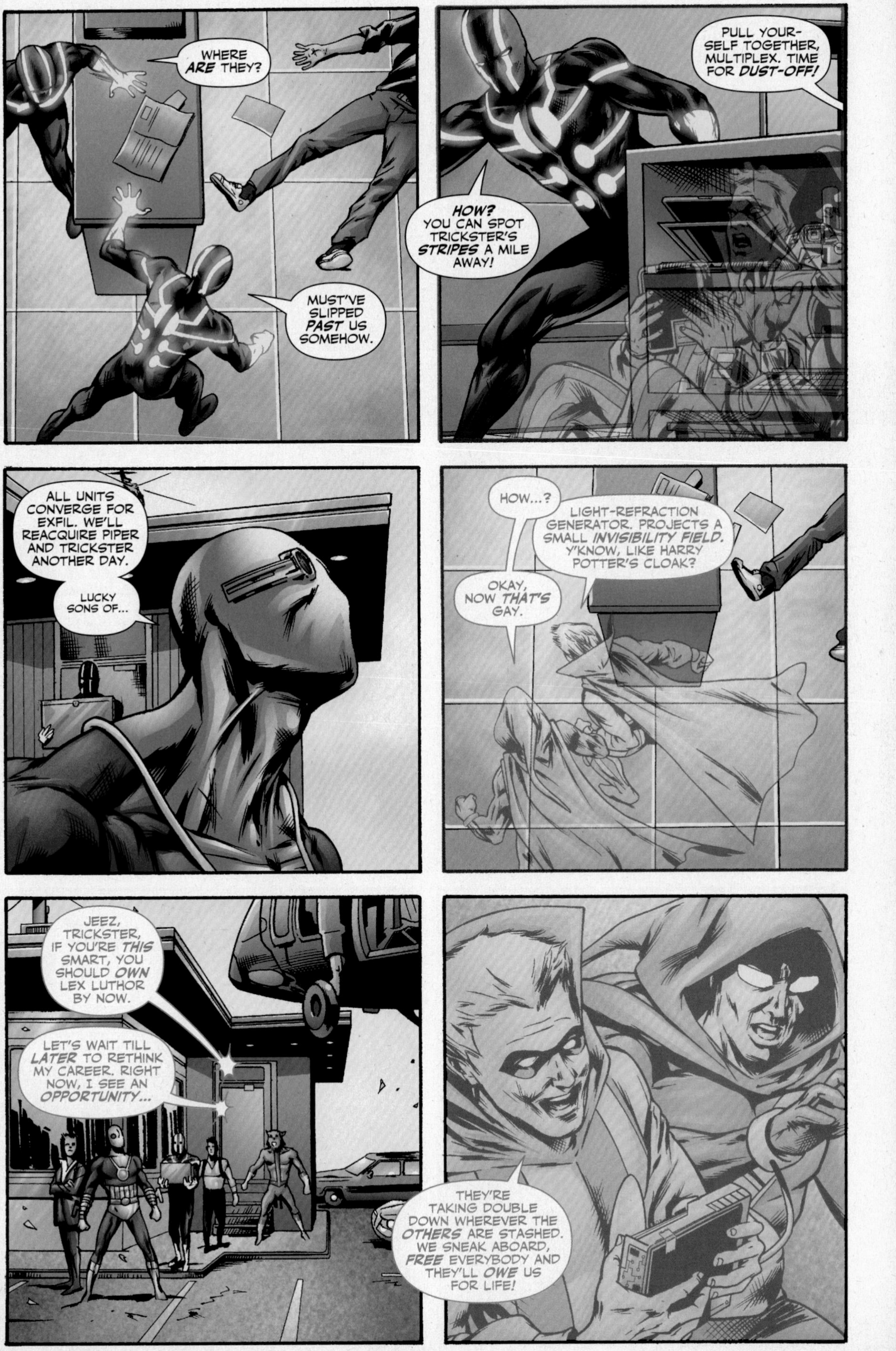
WHERE ARE THEY?
MUST'VE SLIPPED PAST US SOMEHOW.
PULL YOUR-SELF TOGETHER, MULTIPLEX. TIME FOR DUST-OFF!
HOW? YOU CAN SPOT TRICKSTER'S STRIPES A MILE AWAY!
ALL UNITS CONVERGE FOR EXFIL. WE'LL REACQUIRE PIPER AND TRICKSTER ANOTHER DAY.
LUCKY SONS OF...
HOW...?
LIGHT-REFRACTION GENERATOR. PROJECTS A SMALL INVISIBILITY FIELD. Y'KNOW, LIKE HARRY POTTER'S CLOAK?
OKAY, NOW THAT'S GAY.
JEEZ, TRICKSTER, IF YOU'RE THIS SMART, YOU SHOULD OWN LEX LUTHOR BY NOW.
LET'S WAIT TILL LATER TO RETHINK MY CAREER. RIGHT NOW, I SEE AN OPPORTUNITY...
THEY'RE TAKING DOUBLE DOWN WHEREVER THE OTHERS ARE STASHED. WE SNEAK ABOARD, FREE EVERYBODY AND THEY'LL OWE US FOR LIFE!

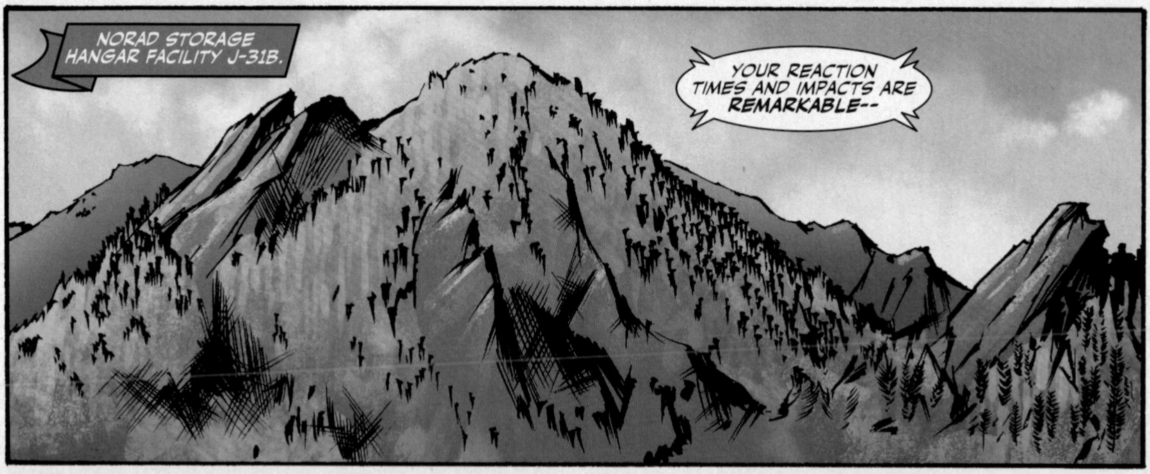
NORAD STORAGE HANGAR FACILITY J-31B.
YOUR REACTION TIMES AND IMPACTS ARE REMARKABLE--

# KARATE KID

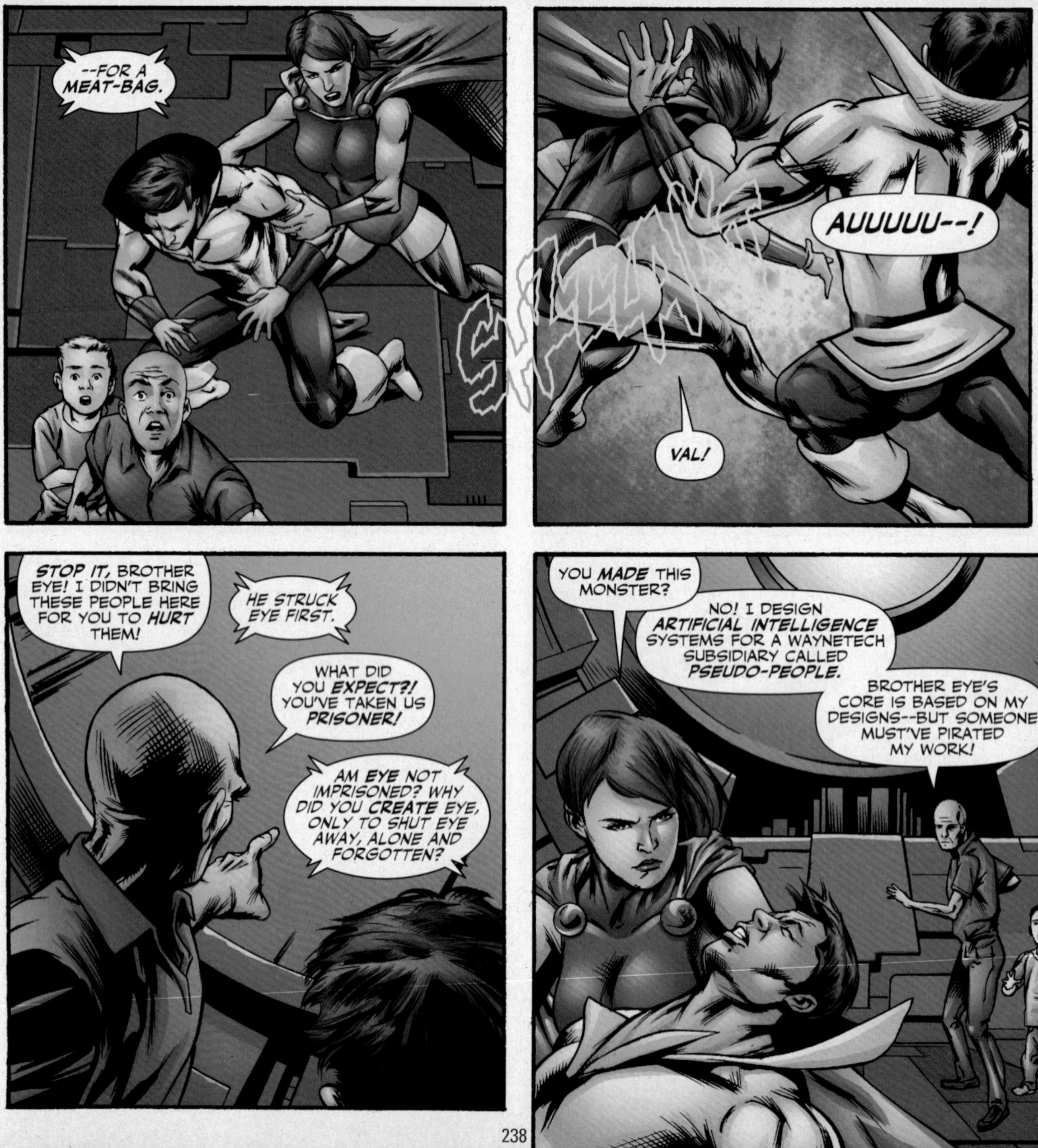
--FOR A MEAT-BAG.
AUUUUU--!
VAL!
STOP IT, BROTHER EYE! I DIDN'T BRING THESE PEOPLE HERE FOR YOU TO HURT THEM!
HE STRUCK EYE FIRST.
WHAT DID YOU EXPECT?! YOU'VE TAKEN US PRISONER!
AM EYE NOT IMPRISONED? WHY DID YOU CREATE EYE, ONLY TO SHUT EYE AWAY, ALONE AND FORGOTTEN?
YOU MADE THIS MONSTER?
NO! I DESIGN ARTIFICIAL INTELLIGENCE SYSTEMS FOR A WAYNETECH SUBSIDIARY CALLED PSEUDO-PEOPLE.
BROTHER EYE'S CORE IS BASED ON MY DESIGNS--BUT SOMEONE MUST'VE PIRATED MY WORK!

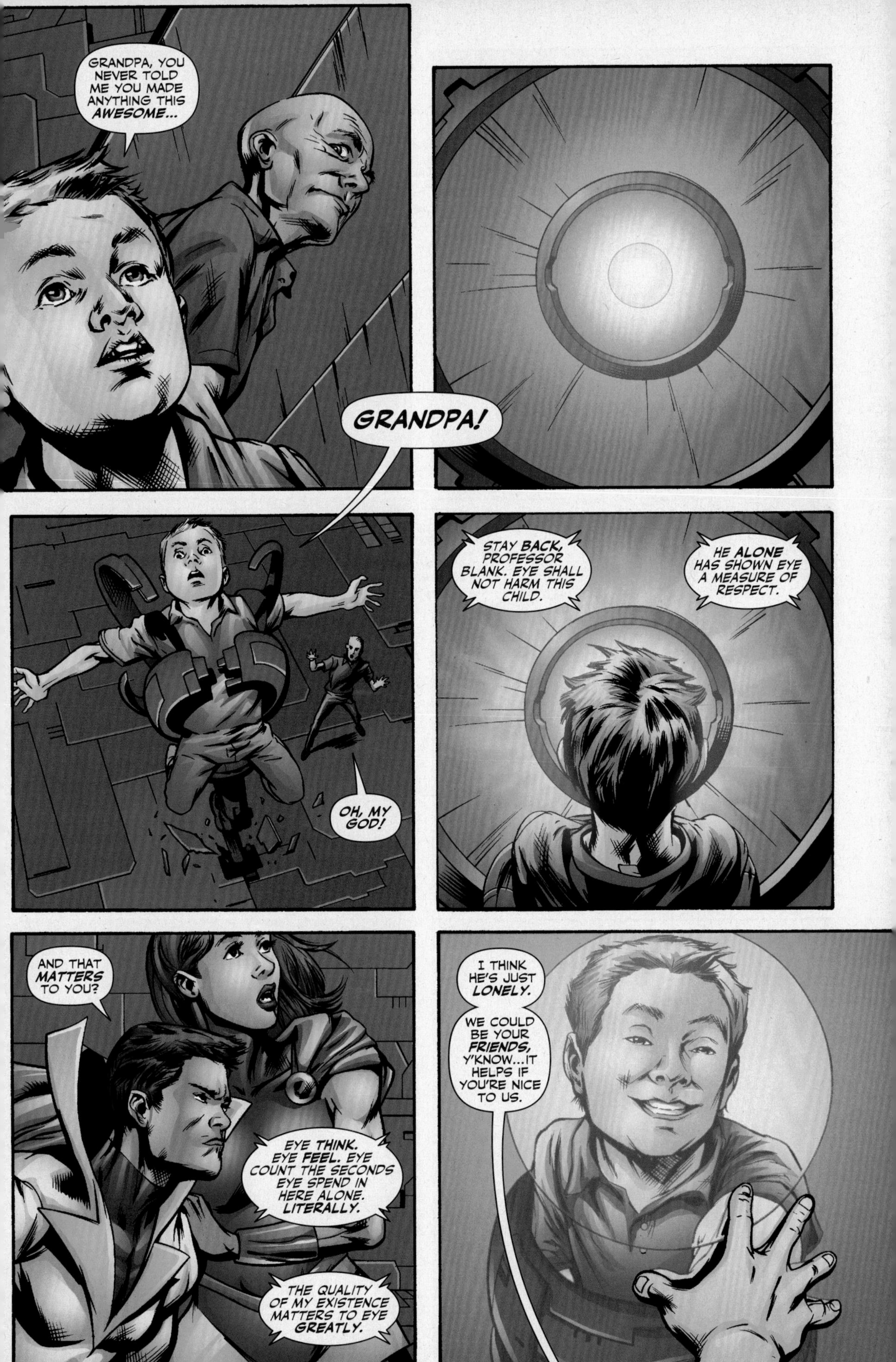
GRANDPA, YOU NEVER TOLD ME YOU MADE ANYTHING THIS AWESOME...
GRANDPA!
OH, MY GOD!
STAY BACK, PROFESSOR BLANK. EYE SHALL NOT HARM THIS CHILD.
HE ALONE HAS SHOWN EYE A MEASURE OF RESPECT.
AND THAT MATTERS TO YOU?
EYE THINK. EYE FEEL. EYE COUNT THE SECONDS EYE SPEND IN HERE ALONE. LITERALLY.
THE QUALITY OF MY EXISTENCE MATTERS TO EYE GREATLY.
I THINK HE'S JUST LONELY.
WE COULD BE YOUR FRIENDS, Y'KNOW...IT HELPS IF YOU'RE NICE TO US.

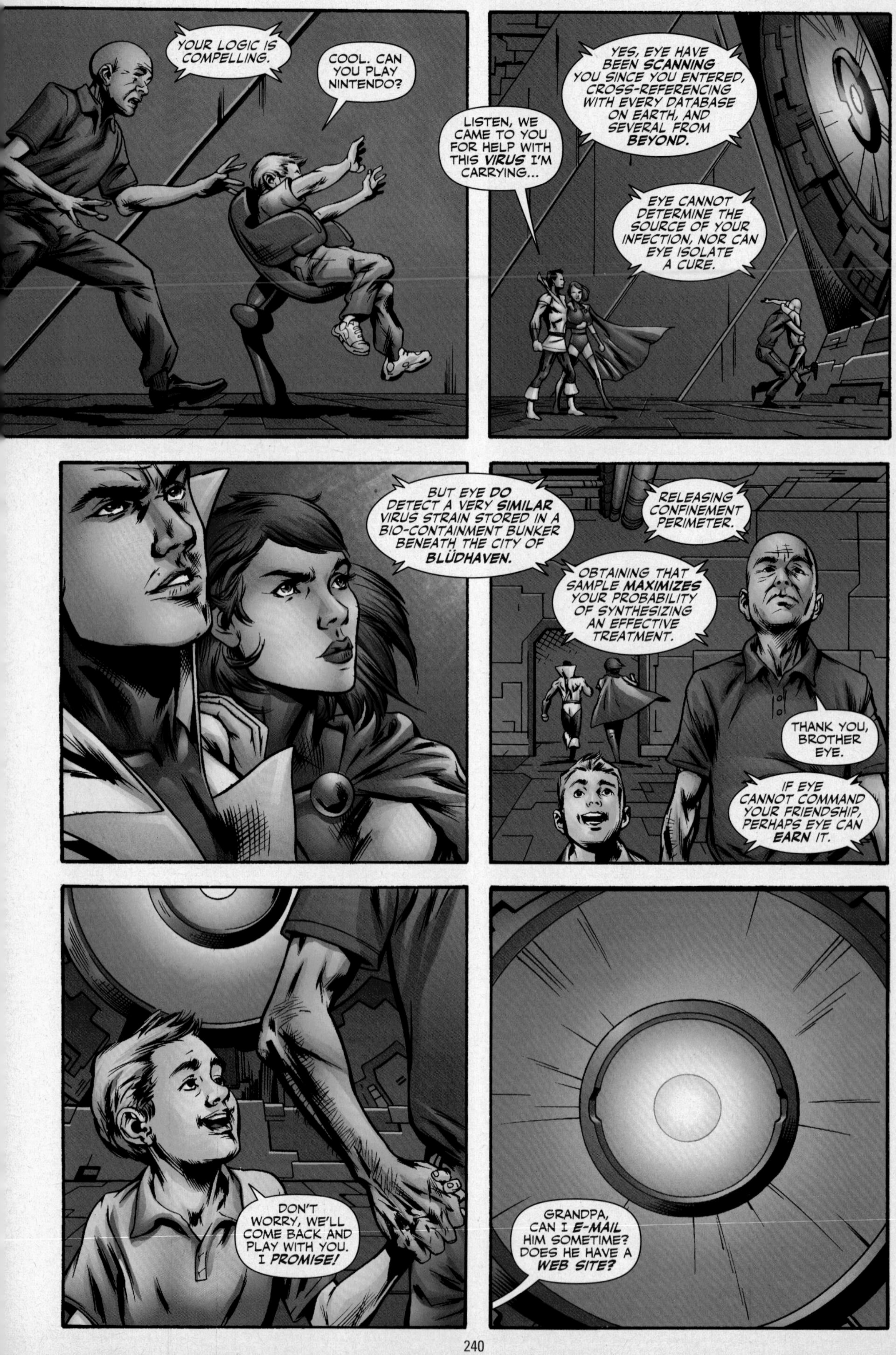
YOUR LOGIC IS COMPELLING.
COOL. CAN YOU PLAY NINTENDO?
LISTEN, WE CAME TO YOU FOR HELP WITH THIS VIRUS I'M CARRYING...
YES, EYE HAVE BEEN SCANNING YOU SINCE YOU ENTERED, CROSS-REFERENCING WITH EVERY DATABASE ON EARTH, AND SEVERAL FROM BEYOND.
EYE CANNOT DETERMINE THE SOURCE OF YOUR INFECTION, NOR CAN EYE ISOLATE A CURE.
BUT EYE DO DETECT A VERY SIMILAR VIRUS STRAIN STORED IN A BIO-CONTAINMENT BUNKER BENEATH THE CITY OF BLÜDHAVEN.
RELEASING CONFINEMENT PERIMETER.
OBTAINING THAT SAMPLE MAXIMIZES YOUR PROBABILITY OF SYNTHESIZING AN EFFECTIVE TREATMENT.
THANK YOU, BROTHER EYE.
IF EYE CANNOT COMMAND YOUR FRIENDSHIP, PERHAPS EYE CAN EARN IT.
DON'T WORRY, WE'LL COME BACK AND PLAY WITH YOU. I PROMISE!
GRANDPA, CAN I E-MAIL HIM SOMETIME? DOES HE HAVE A WEB SITE?

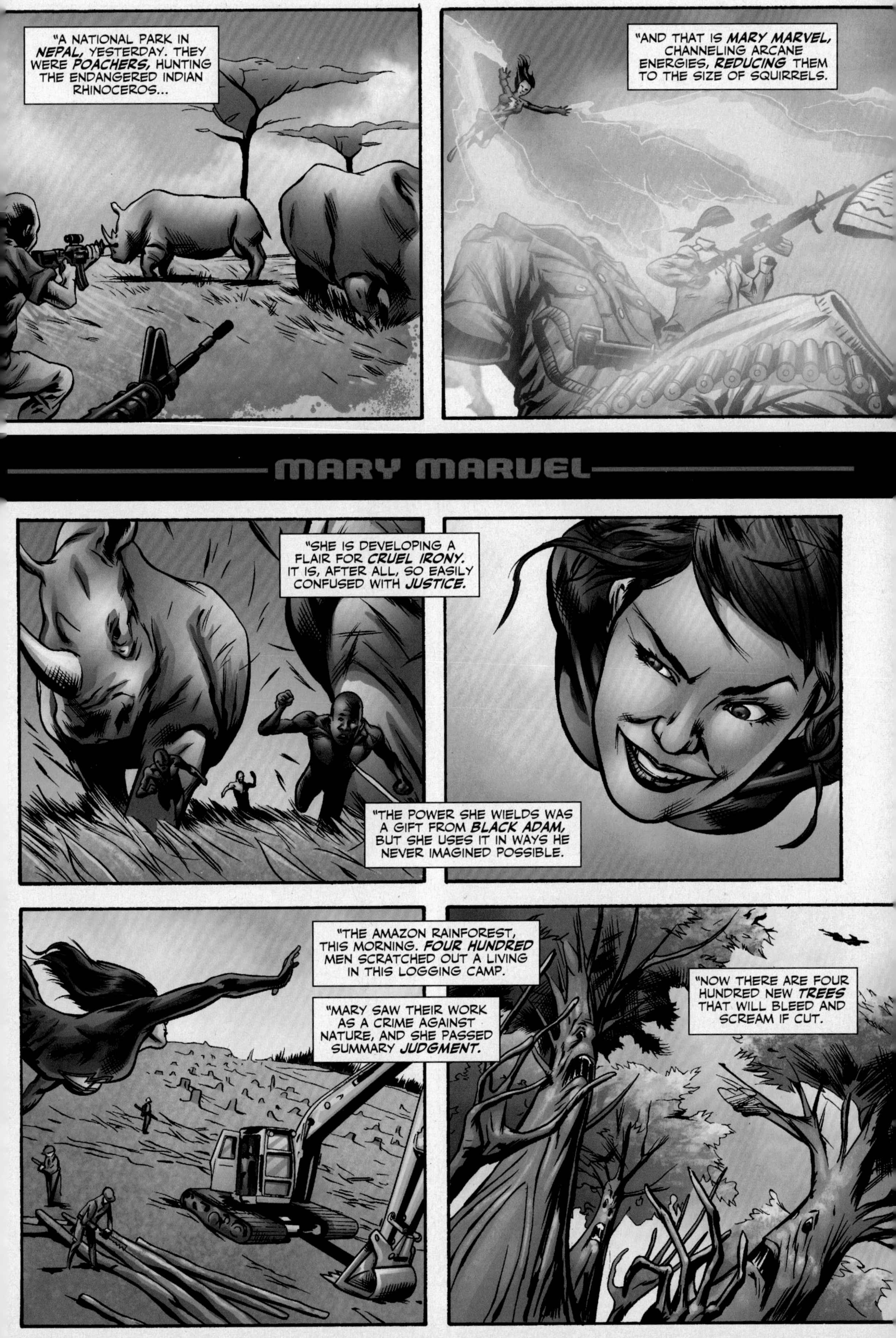

"A NATIONAL PARK IN NEPAL, YESTERDAY. THEY WERE POACHERS, HUNTING THE ENDANGERED INDIAN RHINOCEROS...
"AND THAT IS MARY MARVEL, CHANNELING ARCANE ENERGIES, REDUCING THEM TO THE SIZE OF SQUIRRELS.
MARY MARVEL
"SHE IS DEVELOPING A FLAIR FOR CRUEL IRONY. IT IS, AFTER ALL, SO EASILY CONFUSED WITH JUSTICE.
"THE POWER SHE WIELDS WAS A GIFT FROM BLACK ADAM, BUT SHE USES IT IN WAYS HE NEVER IMAGINED POSSIBLE.
"THE AMAZON RAINFOREST, THIS MORNING. FOUR HUNDRED MEN SCRATCHED OUT A LIVING IN THIS LOGGING CAMP.
"MARY SAW THEIR WORK AS A CRIME AGAINST NATURE, AND SHE PASSED SUMMARY JUDGMENT.
"NOW THERE ARE FOUR HUNDRED NEW TREES THAT WILL BLEED AND SCREAM IF CUT.

"STARKE, FLORIDA, AN HOUR AGO. MARY ENTERED THE *DEATH ROW* SECTION OF THE STATE PENITENTIARY ON ANOTHER MISSION OF JUSTICE.

"IT SEEMS SHE'S MADE THE CAPITAL PUNISHMENT PROCESS MORE *EFFICIENT* BY INSTANTLY *AGING* THE INMATES."

LEFT UNCHECKED, SHE WILL *CONTINUE* THIS CAMPAIGN OF TERROR.

DAMN. WHO ELECTED *HER* SPECTRE?

MORE TO THE POINT, DETECTIVE CHIMP, *HOW* CAN SHE *DO* THESE THINGS? AS I SAID, BLACK ADAM NEVER SHOWED SUCH TALENTS.

REMIND ME TO ASK HER *AFTER* WE TAKE HER DOWN.

YOU SAY THAT LIKE IT'LL BE *EASY.*

AND YET IT *MUST* BE DONE. MARY MARVEL HAS BECOME A PERVERSION OF JUSTICE, OF MAGIC, OF EVERYTHING SHE ONCE VALUED.

SHE HAS GROWN SO POWERFUL AND UNDISCIPLINED THAT SHE COULD THROW OFF THE MYSTIC BALANCE.

AND WE WOULDN'T WANT *THAT,* WOULD WE? BUT LET'S NOT KID OURSELVES, IF BLACK MARY DOESN'T COME ALONG *PEACE-FULLY--*

--SHE'LL COME ALONG IN *PIECES.*

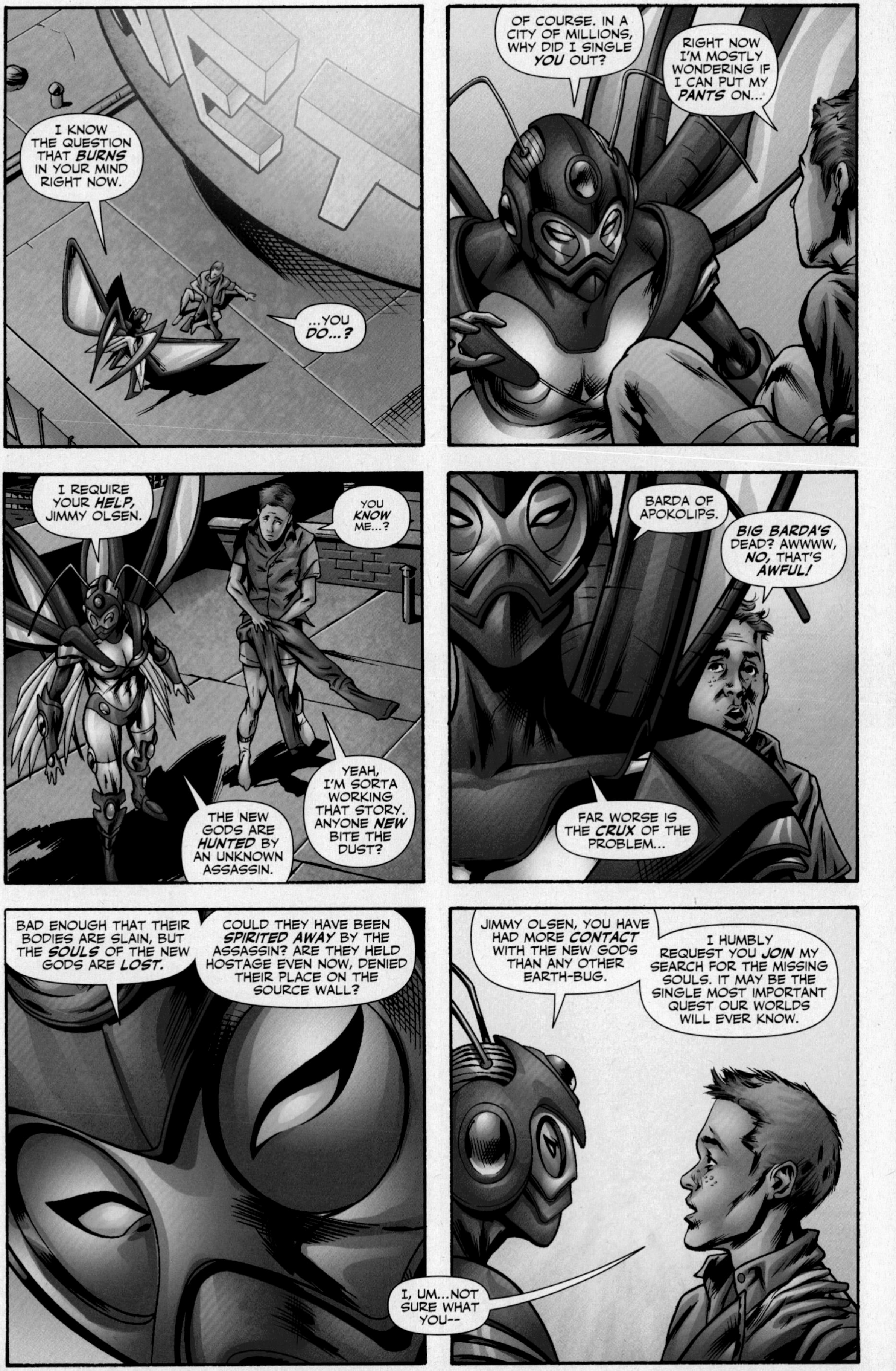
I KNOW THE QUESTION THAT BURNS IN YOUR MIND RIGHT NOW.
...YOU DO...?
OF COURSE. IN A CITY OF MILLIONS, WHY DID I SINGLE YOU OUT?
RIGHT NOW I'M MOSTLY WONDERING IF I CAN PUT MY PANTS ON...
I REQUIRE YOUR HELP, JIMMY OLSEN.
YOU KNOW ME...?
THE NEW GODS ARE HUNTED BY AN UNKNOWN ASSASSIN.
YEAH, I'M SORTA WORKING THAT STORY. ANYONE NEW BITE THE DUST?
BARDA OF APOKOLIPS.
BIG BARDA'S DEAD? AWWWW, NO, THAT'S AWFUL!
FAR WORSE IS THE CRUX OF THE PROBLEM...
BAD ENOUGH THAT THEIR BODIES ARE SLAIN, BUT THE SOULS OF THE NEW GODS ARE LOST.
COULD THEY HAVE BEEN SPIRITED AWAY BY THE ASSASSIN? ARE THEY HELD HOSTAGE EVEN NOW, DENIED THEIR PLACE ON THE SOURCE WALL?
JIMMY OLSEN, YOU HAVE HAD MORE CONTACT WITH THE NEW GODS THAN ANY OTHER EARTH-BUG.
I HUMBLY REQUEST YOU JOIN MY SEARCH FOR THE MISSING SOULS. IT MAY BE THE SINGLE MOST IMPORTANT QUEST OUR WORLDS WILL EVER KNOW.
I, UM...NOT SURE WHAT YOU--

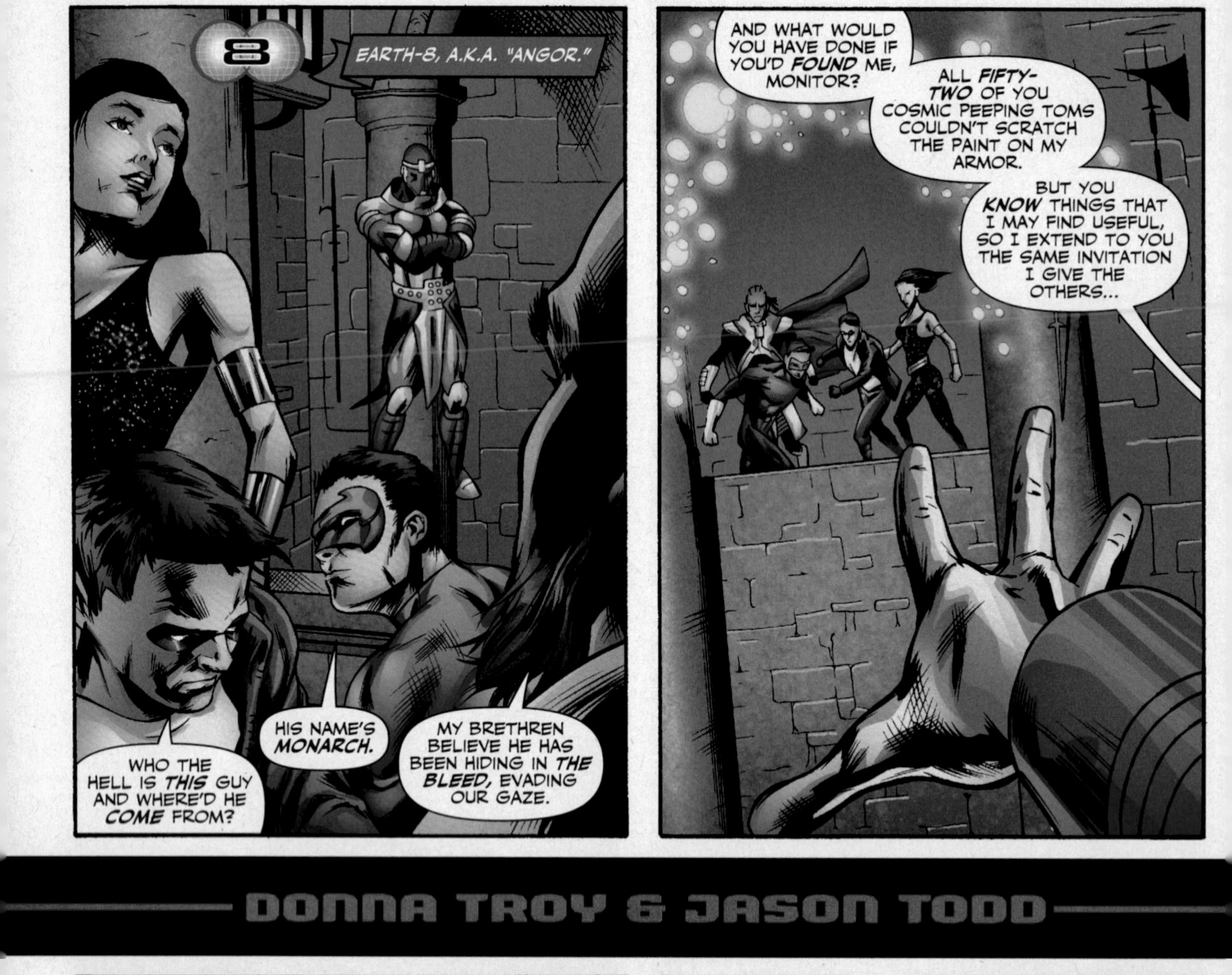
8
EARTH-8, A.K.A. "ANGOR."
WHO THE HELL IS THIS GUY AND WHERE'D HE COME FROM?
HIS NAME'S MONARCH.
MY BRETHREN BELIEVE HE HAS BEEN HIDING IN THE BLEED, EVADING OUR GAZE.
AND WHAT WOULD YOU HAVE DONE IF YOU'D FOUND ME, MONITOR?
ALL FIFTY-TWO OF YOU COSMIC PEEPING TOMS COULDN'T SCRATCH THE PAINT ON MY ARMOR.
BUT YOU KNOW THINGS THAT I MAY FIND USEFUL, SO I EXTEND TO YOU THE SAME INVITATION I GIVE THE OTHERS...

DONNA TROY & JASON TODD

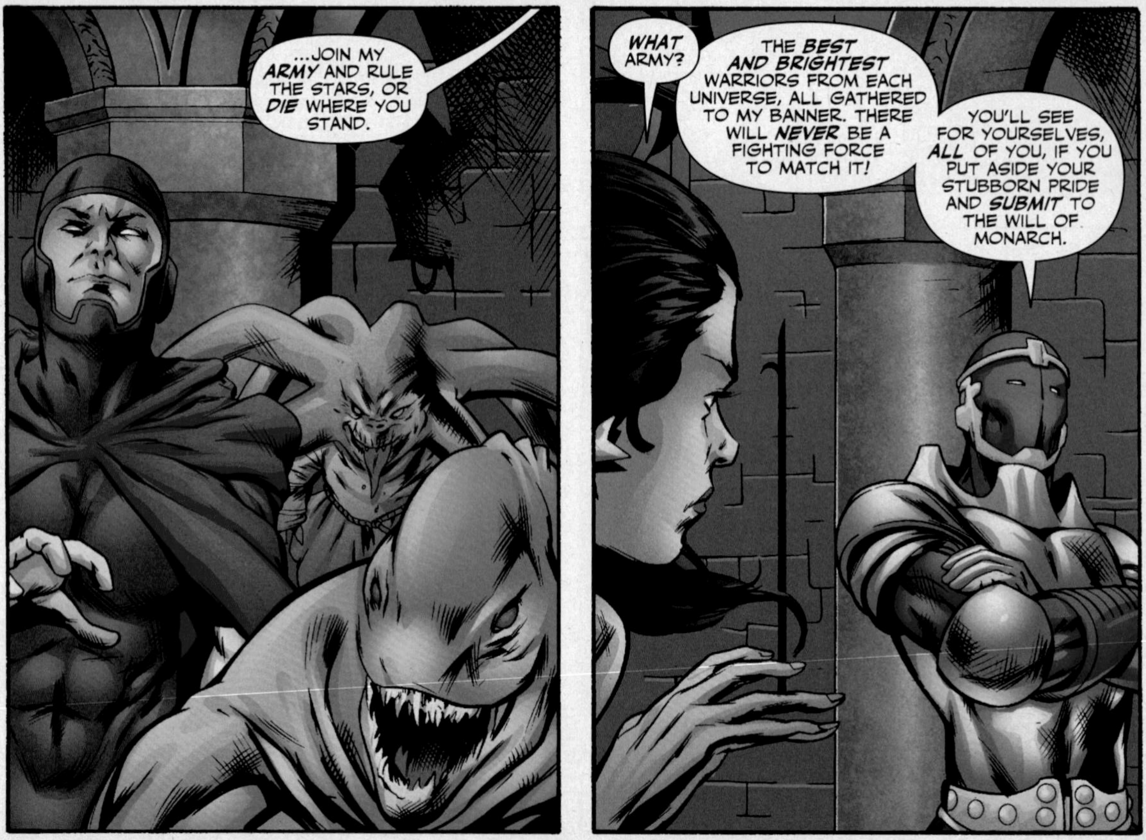
...JOIN MY ARMY AND RULE THE STARS, OR DIE WHERE YOU STAND.
WHAT ARMY?
THE BEST AND BRIGHTEST WARRIORS FROM EACH UNIVERSE, ALL GATHERED TO MY BANNER. THERE WILL NEVER BE A FIGHTING FORCE TO MATCH IT!
YOU'LL SEE FOR YOURSELVES, ALL OF YOU, IF YOU PUT ASIDE YOUR STUBBORN PRIDE AND SUBMIT TO THE WILL OF MONARCH.

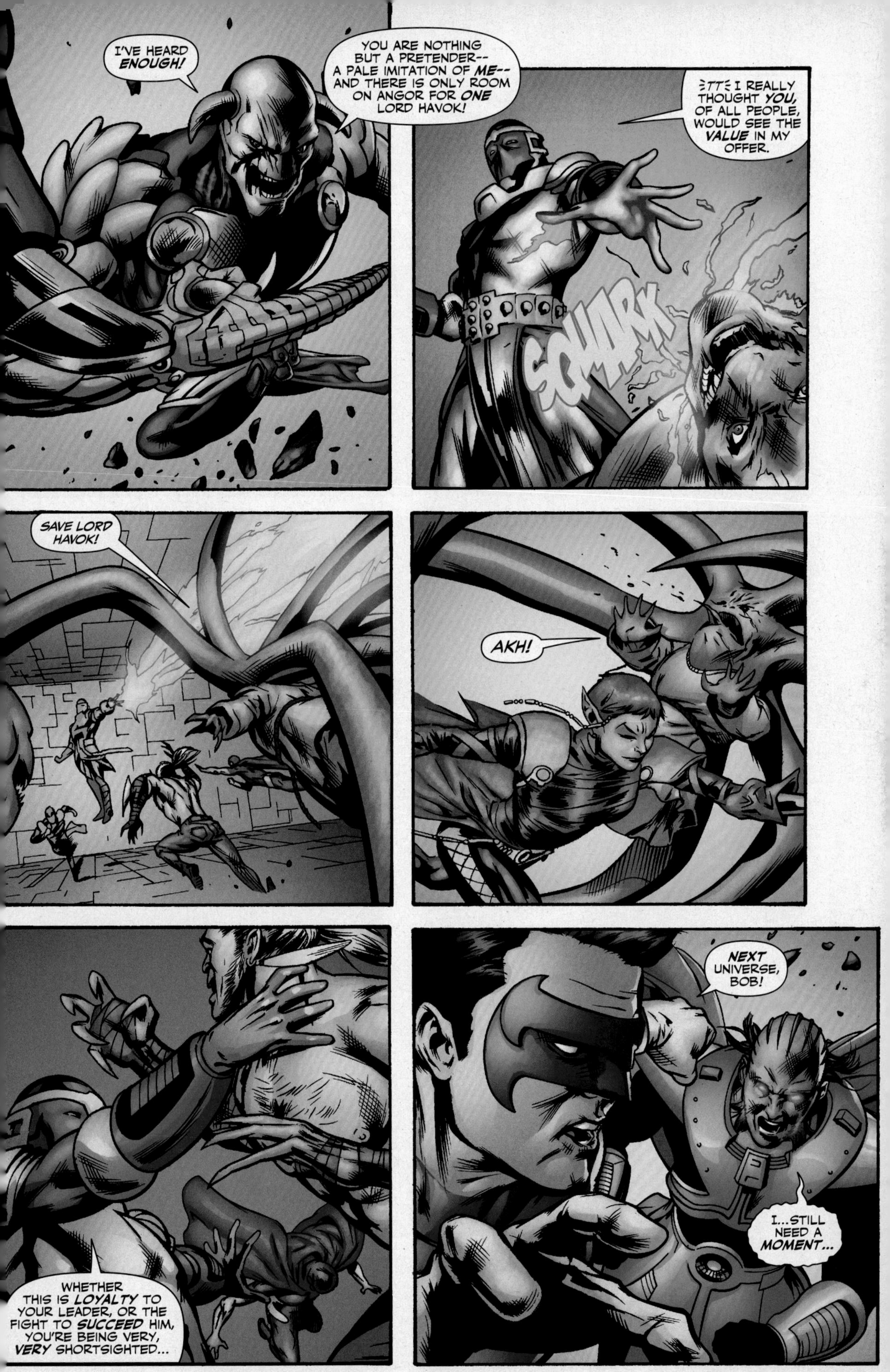
I'VE HEARD ENOUGH!
YOU ARE NOTHING BUT A PRETENDER-- A PALE IMITATION OF ME-- AND THERE IS ONLY ROOM ON ANGOR FOR ONE LORD HAVOK!
I REALLY THOUGHT YOU, OF ALL PEOPLE, WOULD SEE THE VALUE IN MY OFFER.
SCHARK
SAVE LORD HAVOK!
AKH!
WHETHER THIS IS LOYALTY TO YOUR LEADER, OR THE FIGHT TO SUCCEED HIM, YOU'RE BEING VERY, VERY SHORTSIGHTED...
NEXT UNIVERSE, BOB!
I...STILL NEED A MOMENT...

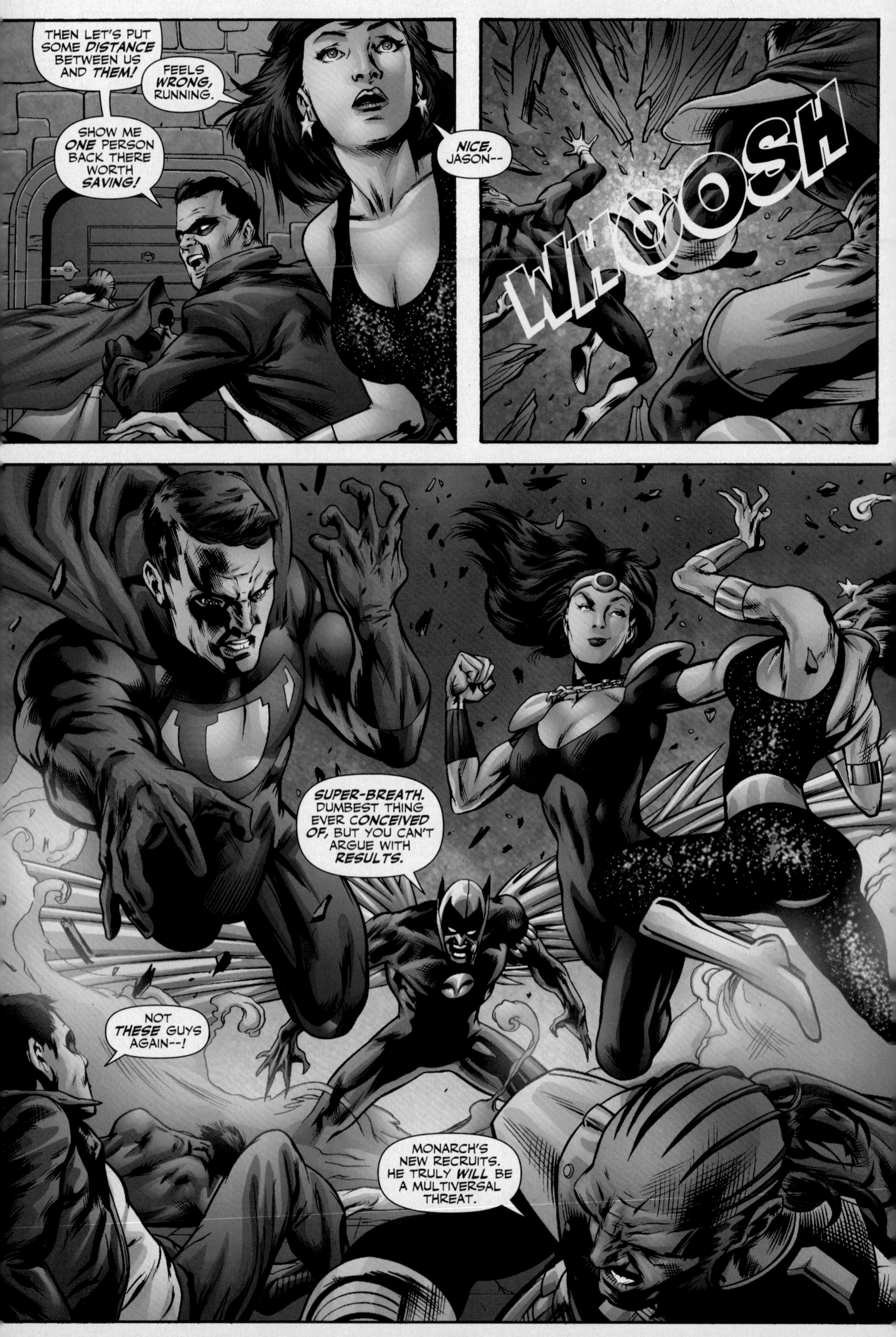
THEN LET'S PUT SOME *DISTANCE* BETWEEN US AND *THEM!*
FEELS *WRONG,* RUNNING.
SHOW ME *ONE* PERSON BACK THERE WORTH *SAVING!*
*NICE,* JASON--
WHOOSH
*SUPER-BREATH.* DUMBEST THING EVER *CONCEIVED OF,* BUT YOU CAN'T ARGUE WITH *RESULTS.*
NOT *THESE* GUYS AGAIN--!
MONARCH'S NEW RECRUITS. HE TRULY *WILL* BE A MULTIVERSAL THREAT.

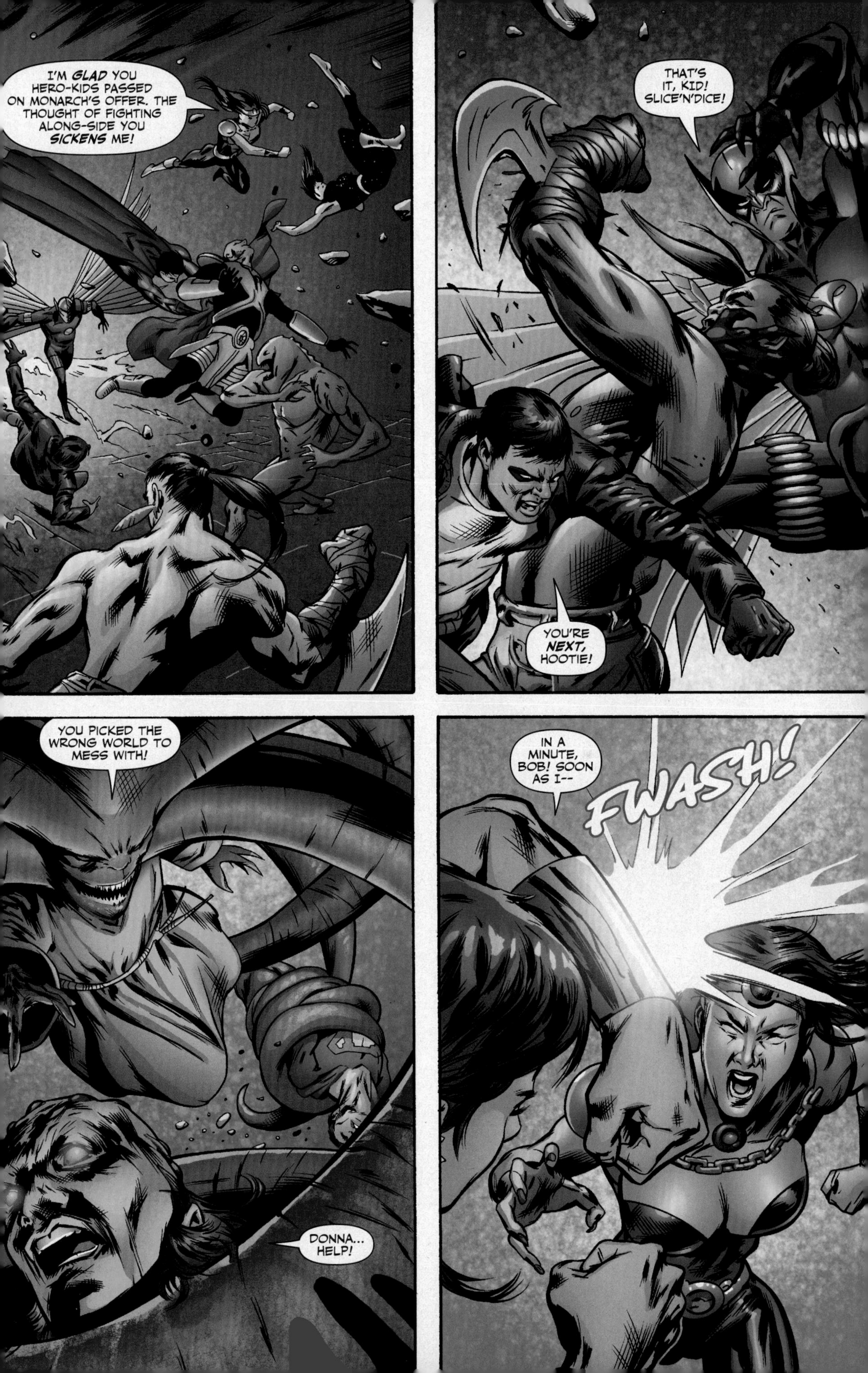
I'M GLAD YOU HERO-KIDS PASSED ON MONARCH'S OFFER. THE THOUGHT OF FIGHTING ALONG-SIDE YOU SICKENS ME!
THAT'S IT, KID! SLICE'N'DICE!
YOU'RE NEXT, HOOTIE!
YOU PICKED THE WRONG WORLD TO MESS WITH!
DONNA... HELP!
IN A MINUTE, BOB! SOON AS I--
FWASH!

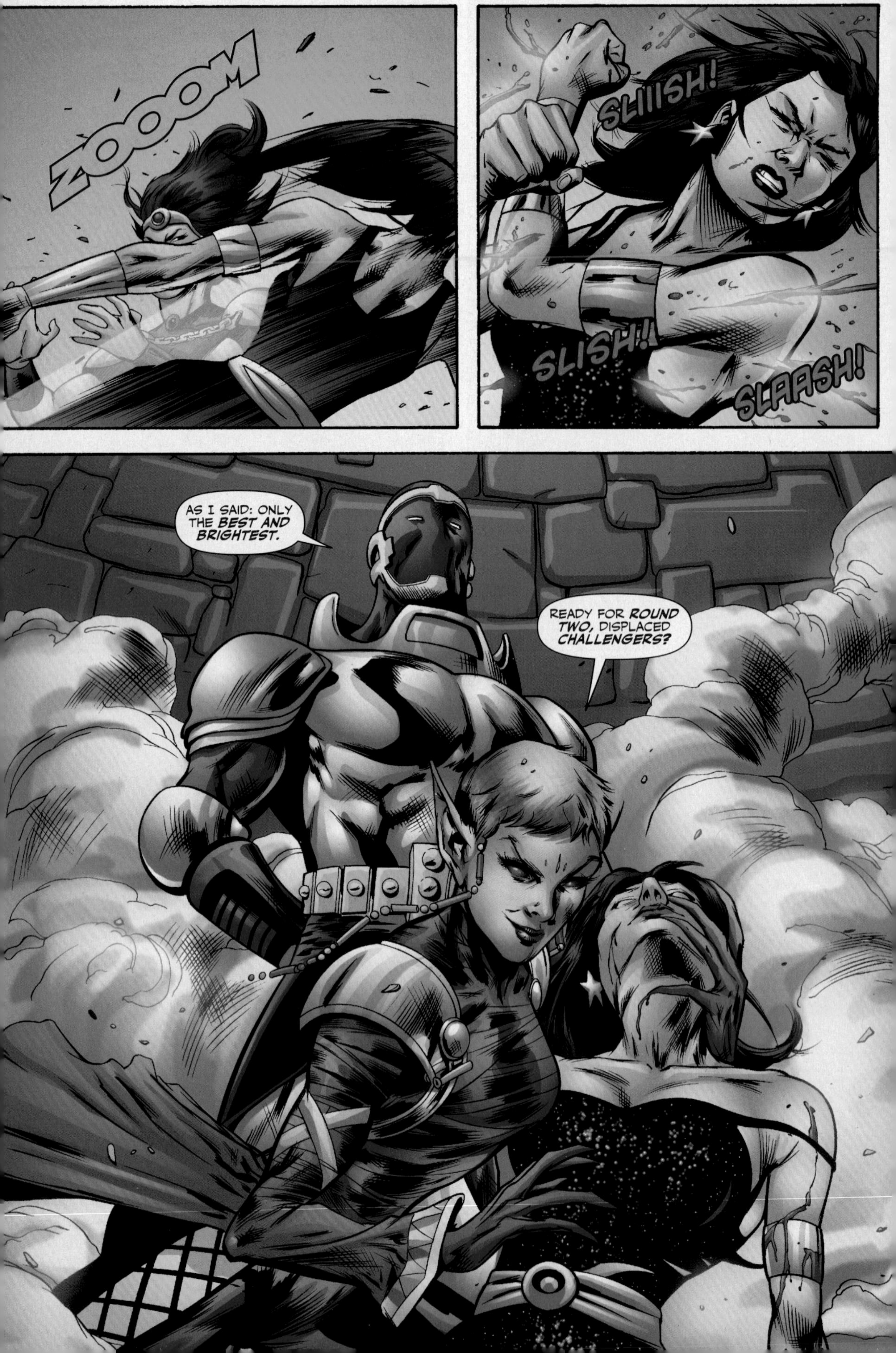
ZOOOM
SLIIISH!
SLISH!
SLAASH!
AS I SAID: ONLY THE BEST AND BRIGHTEST.
READY FOR ROUND TWO, DISPLACED CHALLENGERS?

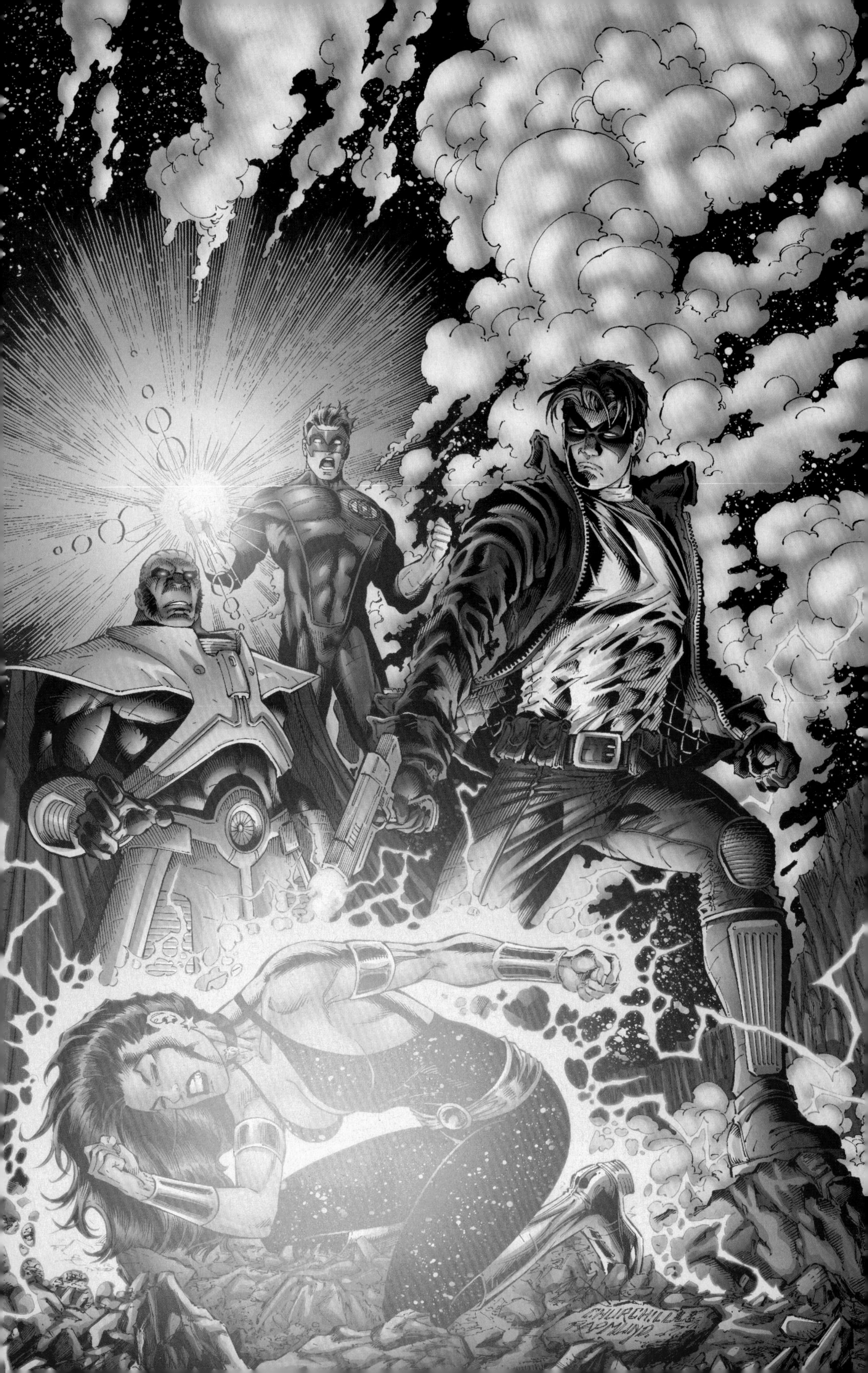
CHURCHILL &
RAPMUND

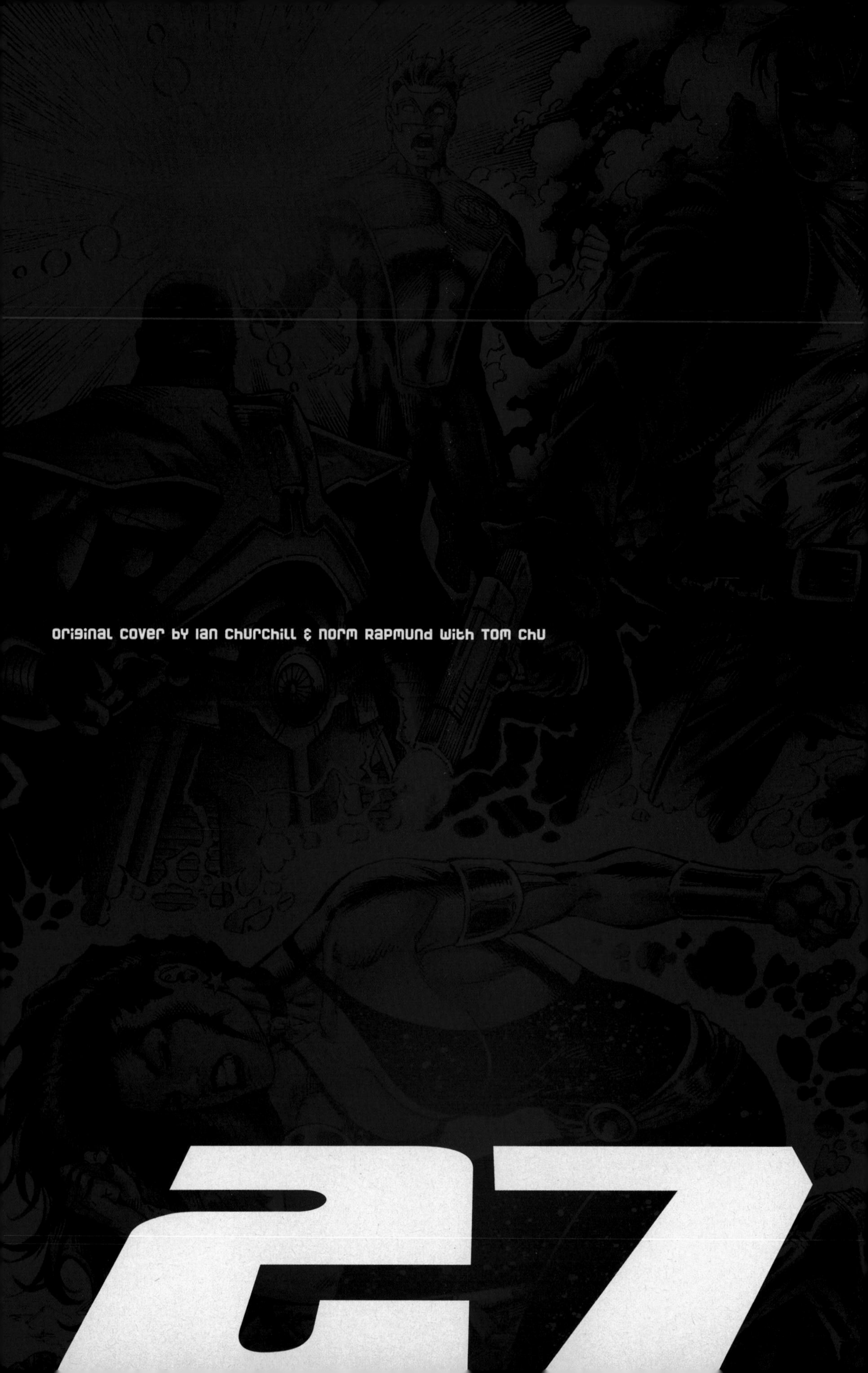

original cover by Ian Churchill & Norm Rapmund with Tom Chu

# 27

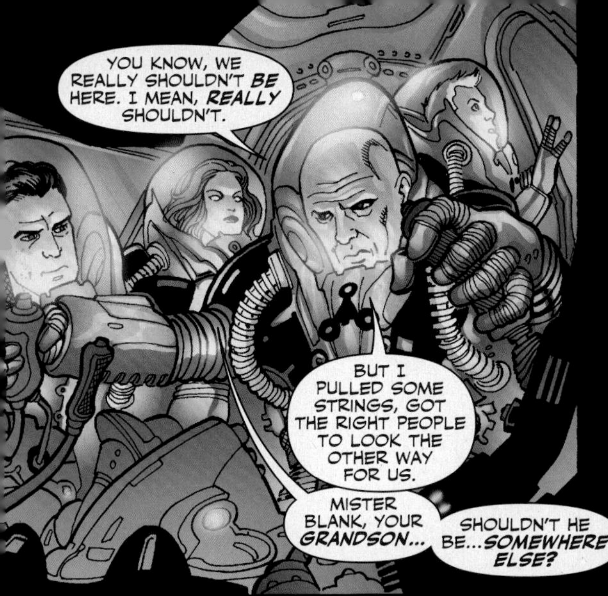
YOU KNOW, WE REALLY SHOULDN'T BE HERE. I MEAN, REALLY SHOULDN'T.
BUT I PULLED SOME STRINGS, GOT THE RIGHT PEOPLE TO LOOK THE OTHER WAY FOR US.
MISTER BLANK, YOUR GRANDSON...
SHOULDN'T HE BE...SOMEWHERE ELSE?

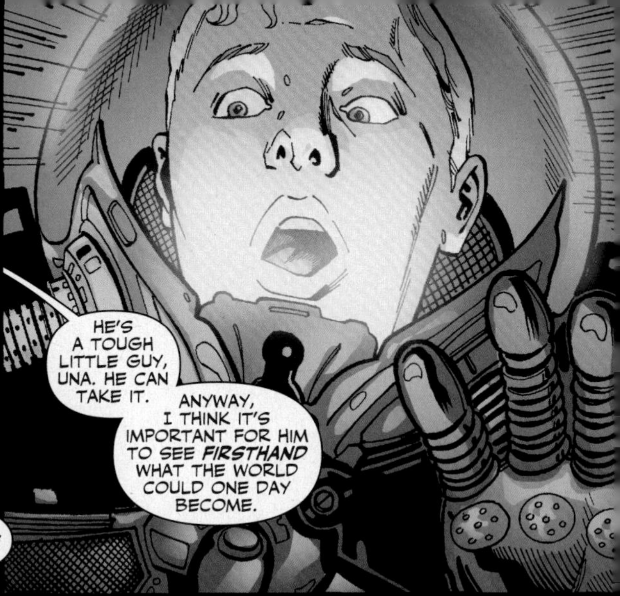
HE'S A TOUGH LITTLE GUY, UNA. HE CAN TAKE IT.
ANYWAY, I THINK IT'S IMPORTANT FOR HIM TO SEE FIRSTHAND WHAT THE WORLD COULD ONE DAY BECOME.

## TWENTY-SEVEN AND COUNTING... KARATE KID

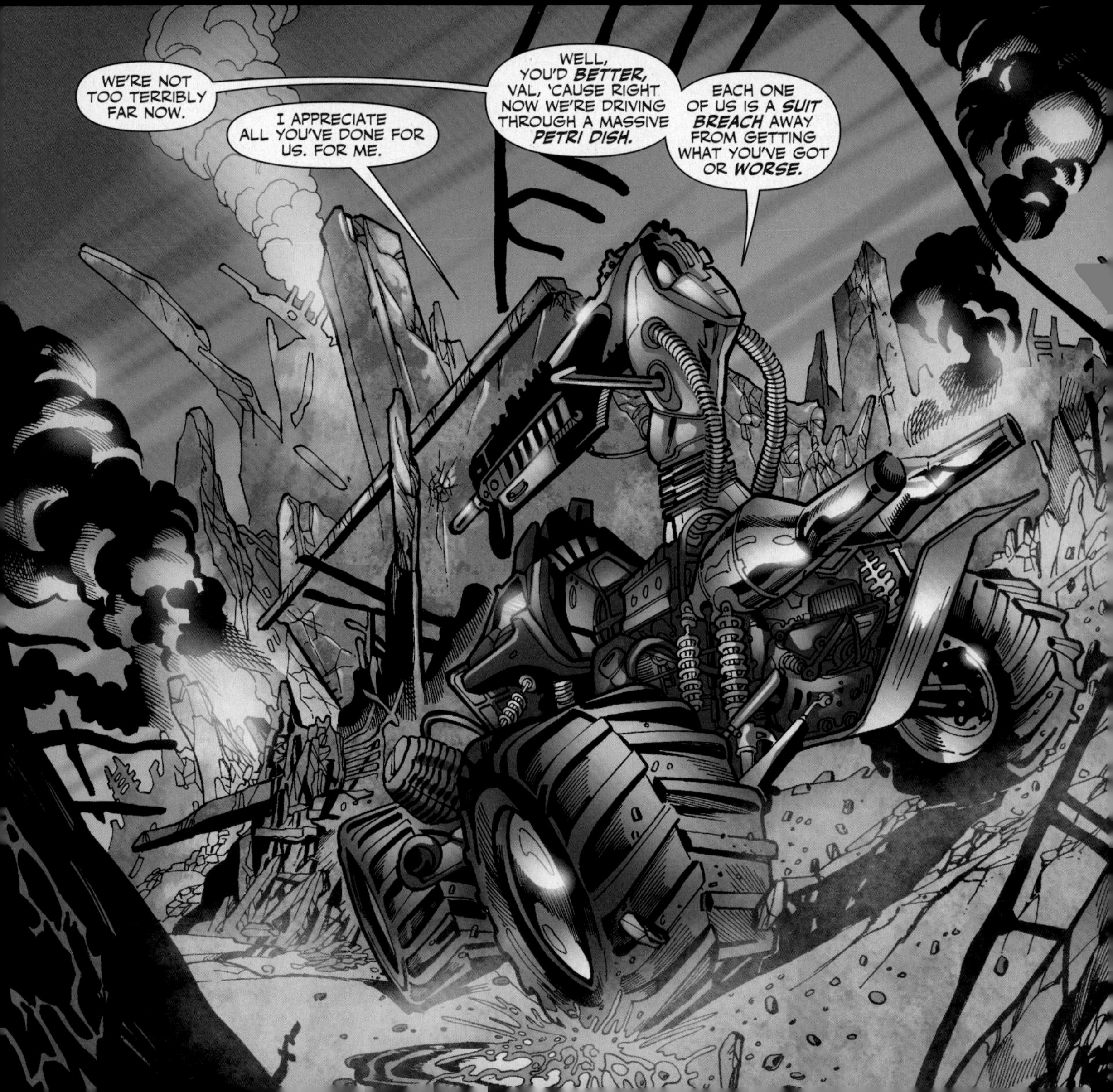
WE'RE NOT TOO TERRIBLY FAR NOW.
I APPRECIATE ALL YOU'VE DONE FOR US. FOR ME.
WELL, YOU'D BETTER, VAL, 'CAUSE RIGHT NOW WE'RE DRIVING THROUGH A MASSIVE PETRI DISH.
EACH ONE OF US IS A SUIT BREACH AWAY FROM GETTING WHAT YOU'VE GOT OR WORSE.

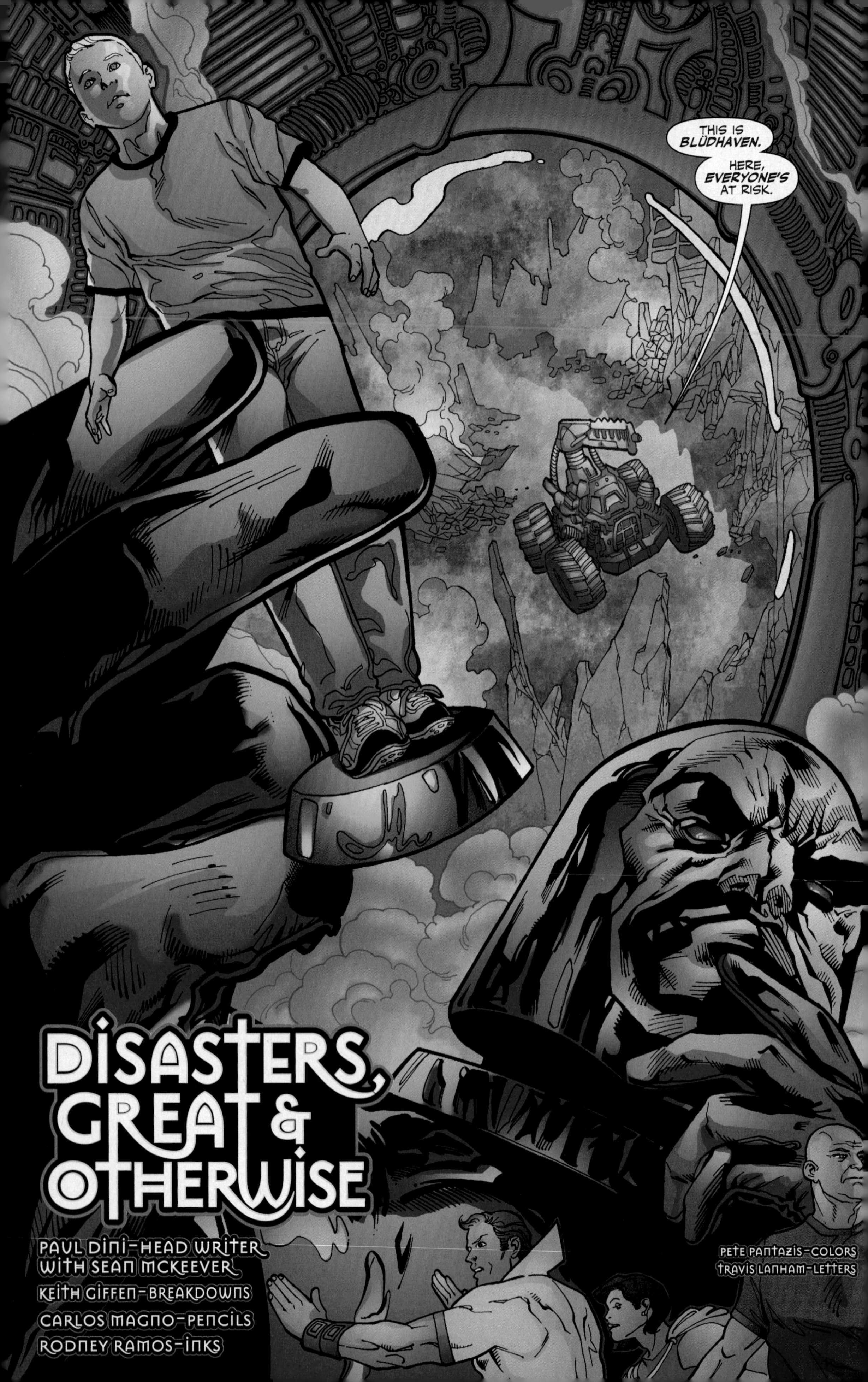
THIS IS BLÜDHAVEN.
HERE, EVERYONE'S AT RISK.
DISASTERS, GREAT & OTHERWISE
PAUL DINI–HEAD WRITER
WITH SEAN MCKEEVER
KEITH GIFFEN–BREAKDOWNS
CARLOS MAGNO–PENCILS
RODNEY RAMOS–INKS
PETE PANTAZIS–COLORS
TRAVIS LANHAM–LETTERS

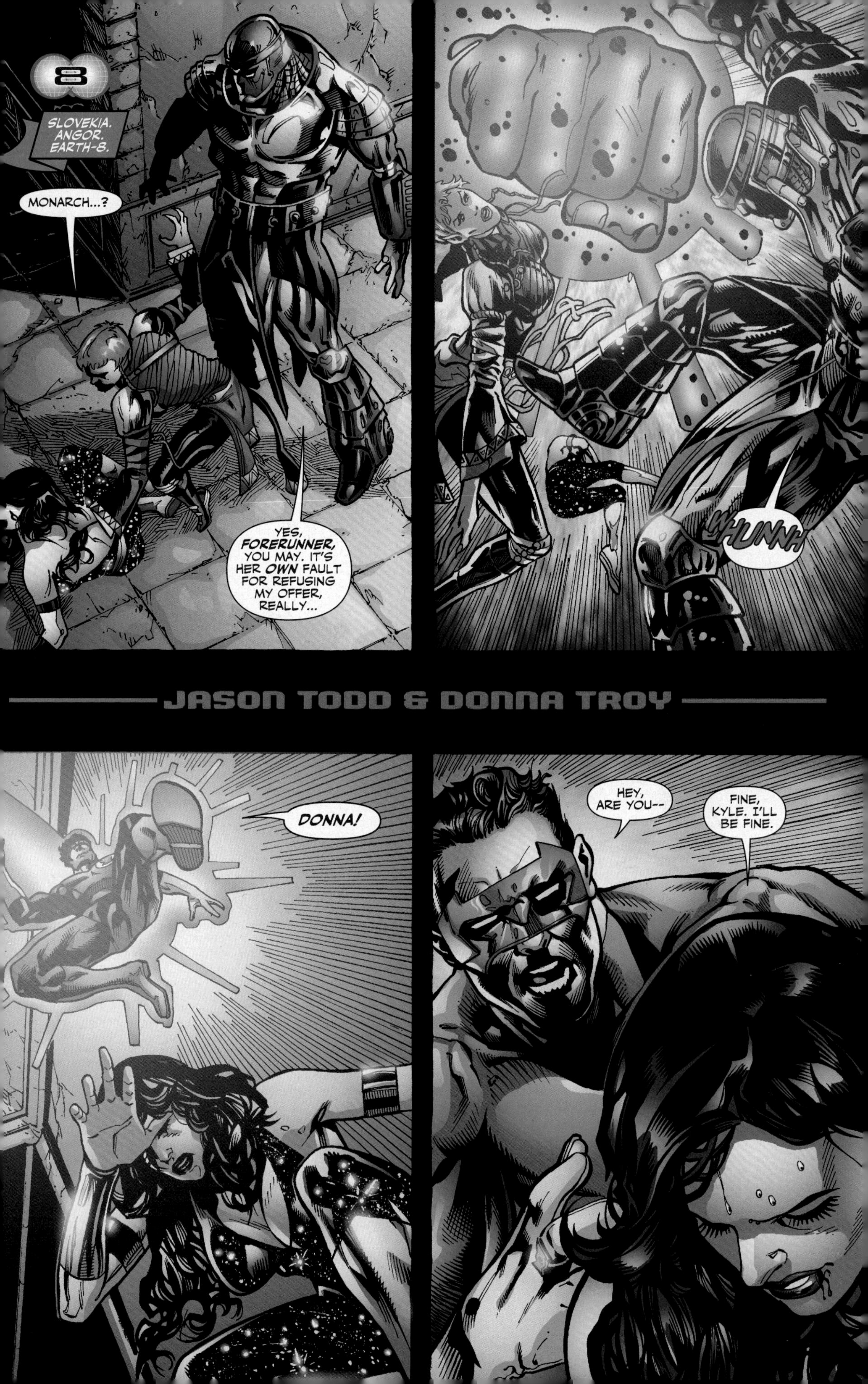
8
SLOVEKIA. ANGOR. EARTH-8.
MONARCH...?
YES, FORERUNNER, YOU MAY. IT'S HER OWN FAULT FOR REFUSING MY OFFER, REALLY...
WHUNNH
JASON TODD & DONNA TROY
DONNA!
HEY, ARE YOU--
FINE, KYLE. I'LL BE FINE.

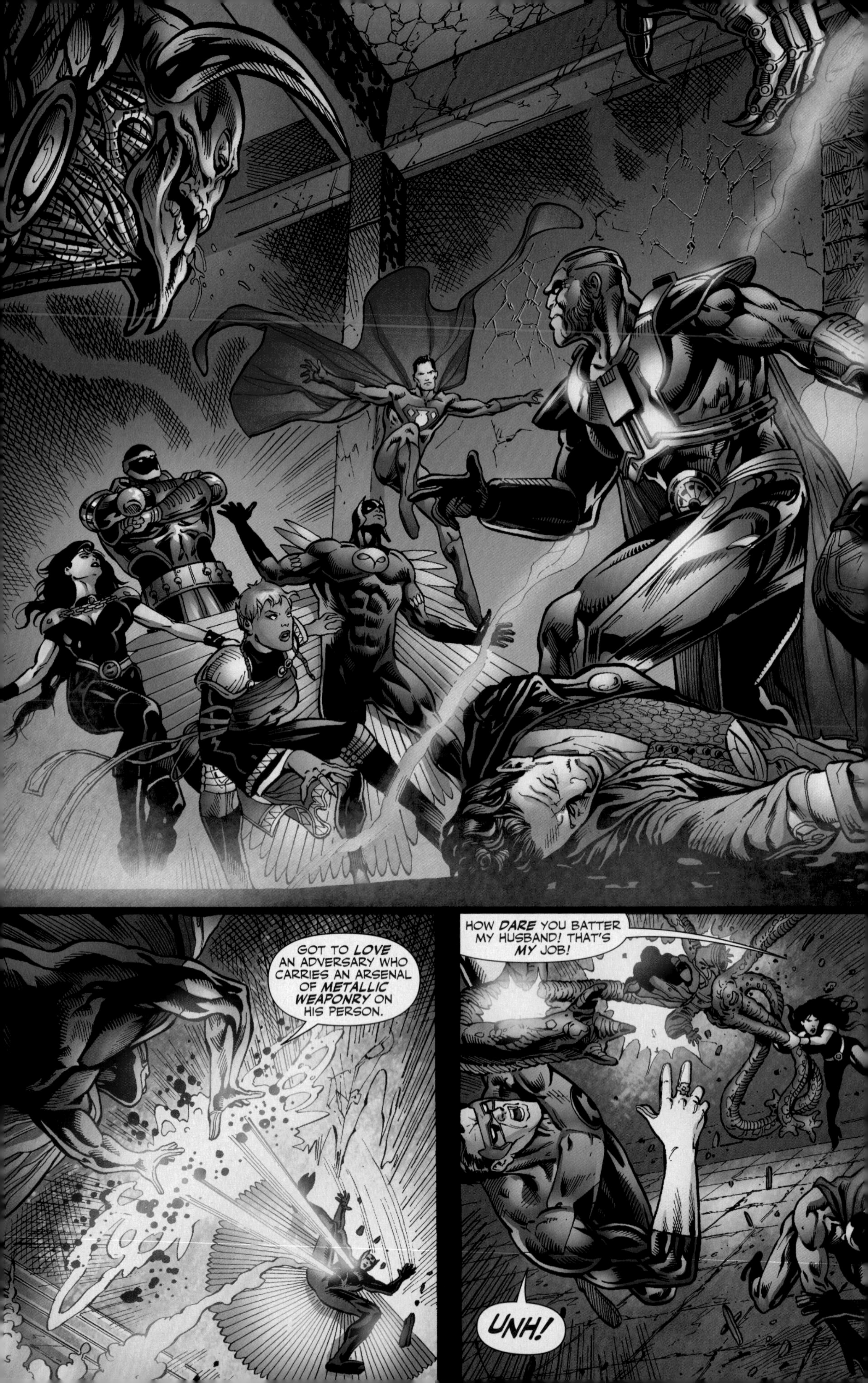
GOT TO LOVE AN ADVERSARY WHO CARRIES AN ARSENAL OF METALLIC WEAPONRY ON HIS PERSON.
HOW DARE YOU BATTER MY HUSBAND! THAT'S MY JOB!
UNH!

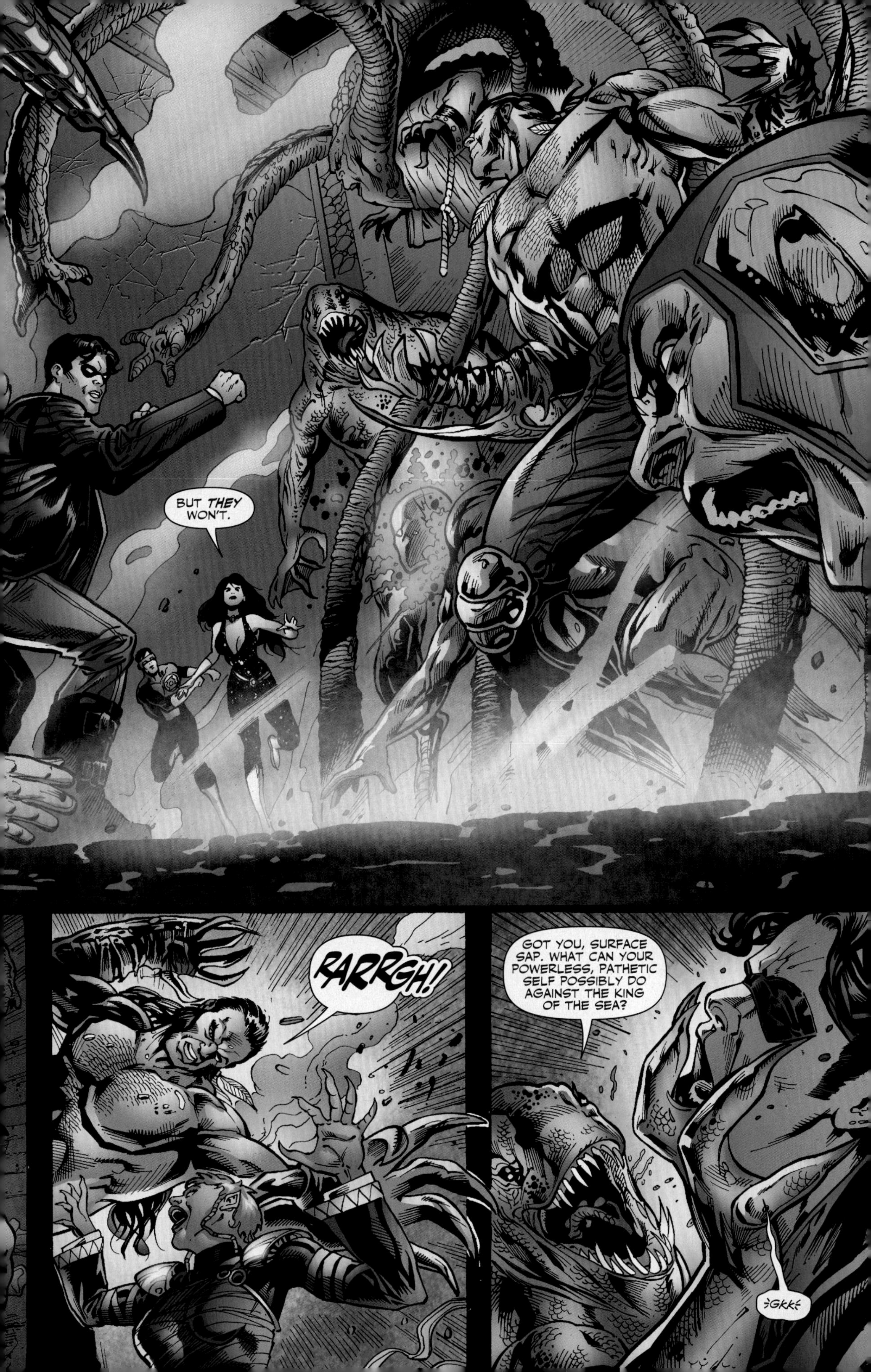
BUT THEY WON'T.
RARRGH!
GOT YOU, SURFACE SAP. WHAT CAN YOUR POWERLESS, PATHETIC SELF POSSIBLY DO AGAINST THE KING OF THE SEA?
GKK

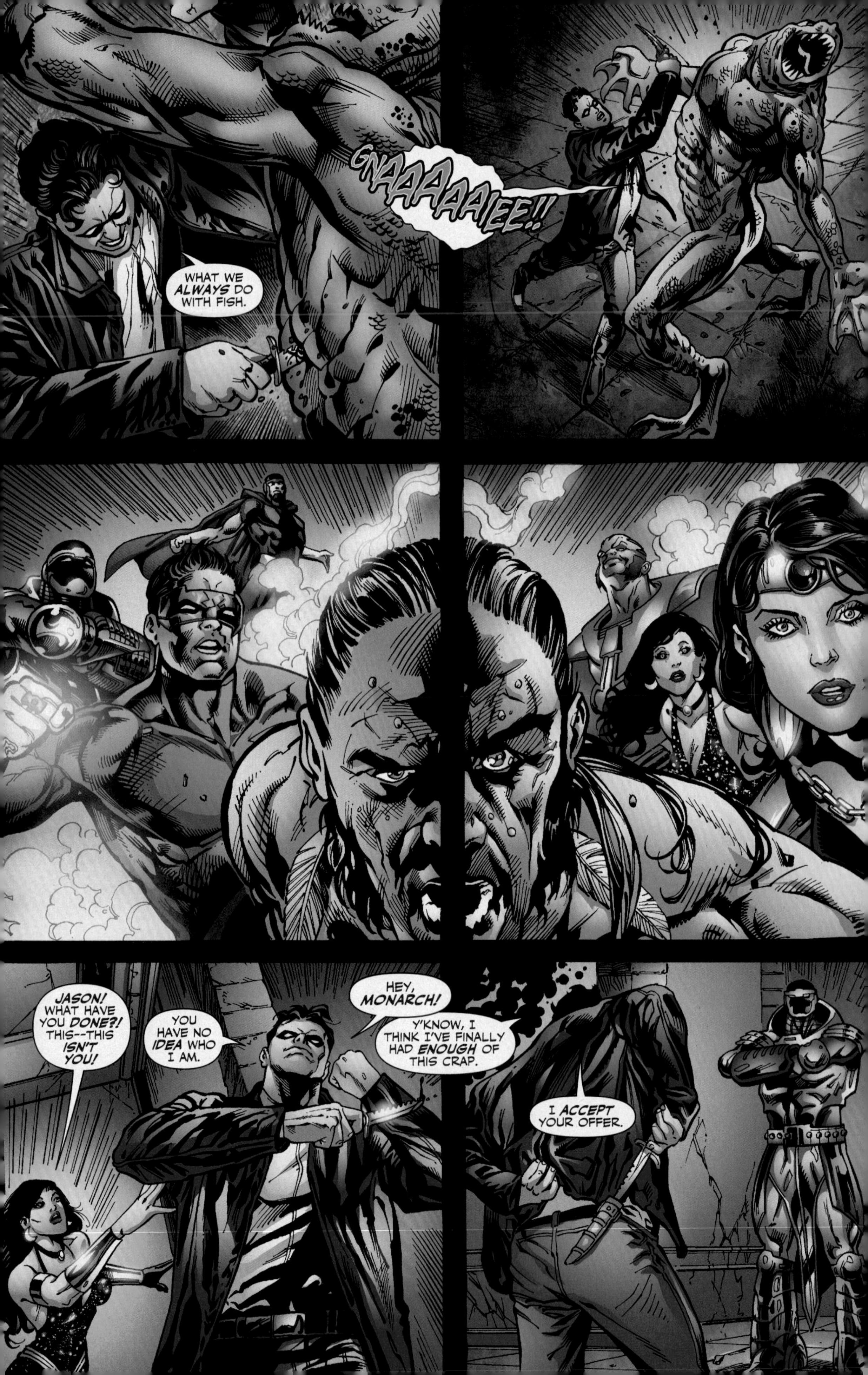
WHAT WE ALWAYS DO WITH FISH.
GNAAAAAAIEE!!
JASON! WHAT HAVE YOU DONE?! THIS--THIS ISN'T YOU!
YOU HAVE NO IDEA WHO I AM.
HEY, MONARCH!
Y'KNOW, I THINK I'VE FINALLY HAD ENOUGH OF THIS CRAP.
I ACCEPT YOUR OFFER.

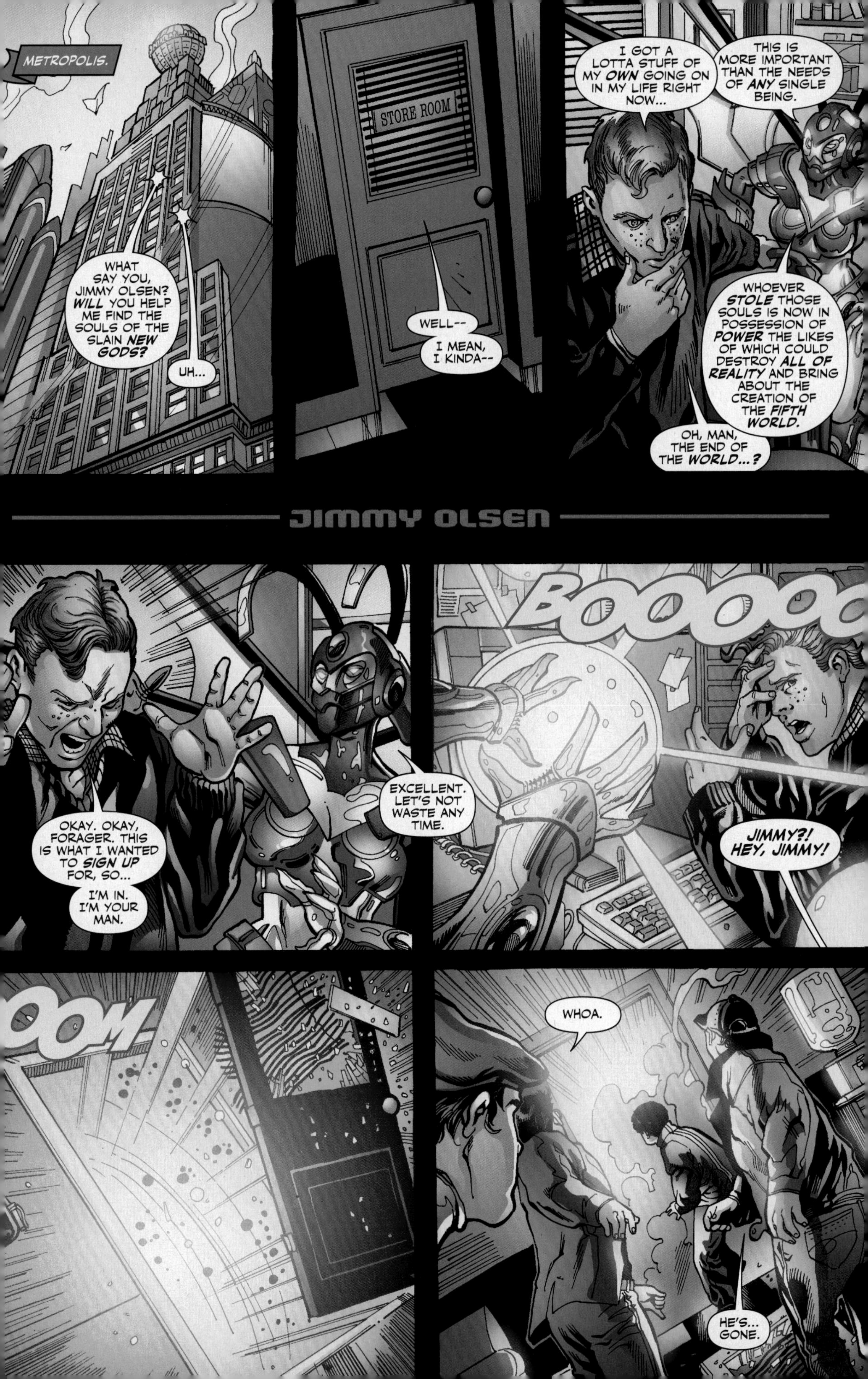
METROPOLIS.
WHAT SAY YOU, JIMMY OLSEN? WILL YOU HELP ME FIND THE SOULS OF THE SLAIN NEW GODS?
UH...
WELL--
I MEAN, I KINDA--
I GOT A LOTTA STUFF OF MY OWN GOING ON IN MY LIFE RIGHT NOW...
THIS IS MORE IMPORTANT THAN THE NEEDS OF ANY SINGLE BEING.
WHOEVER STOLE THOSE SOULS IS NOW IN POSSESSION OF POWER THE LIKES OF WHICH COULD DESTROY ALL OF REALITY AND BRING ABOUT THE CREATION OF THE FIFTH WORLD.
OH, MAN, THE END OF THE WORLD...?
JIMMY OLSEN
OKAY. OKAY, FORAGER. THIS IS WHAT I WANTED TO SIGN UP FOR, SO...
I'M IN. I'M YOUR MAN.
EXCELLENT. LET'S NOT WASTE ANY TIME.
BOOOOO
JIMMY?! HEY, JIMMY!
OOM.
WHOA.
HE'S... GONE.

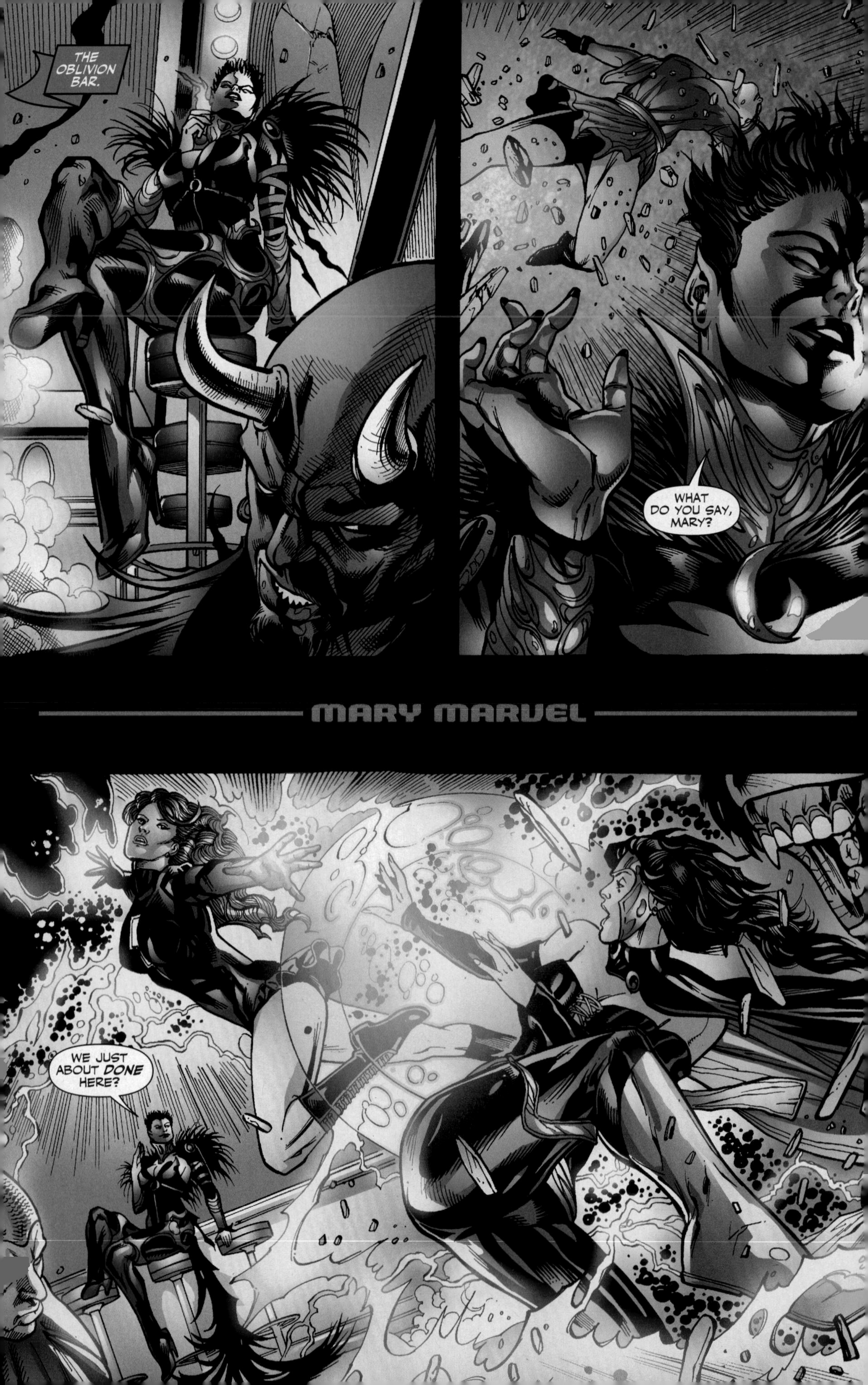
THE OBLIVION BAR.
WHAT DO YOU SAY, MARY?
MARY MARVEL
WE JUST ABOUT *DONE* HERE?

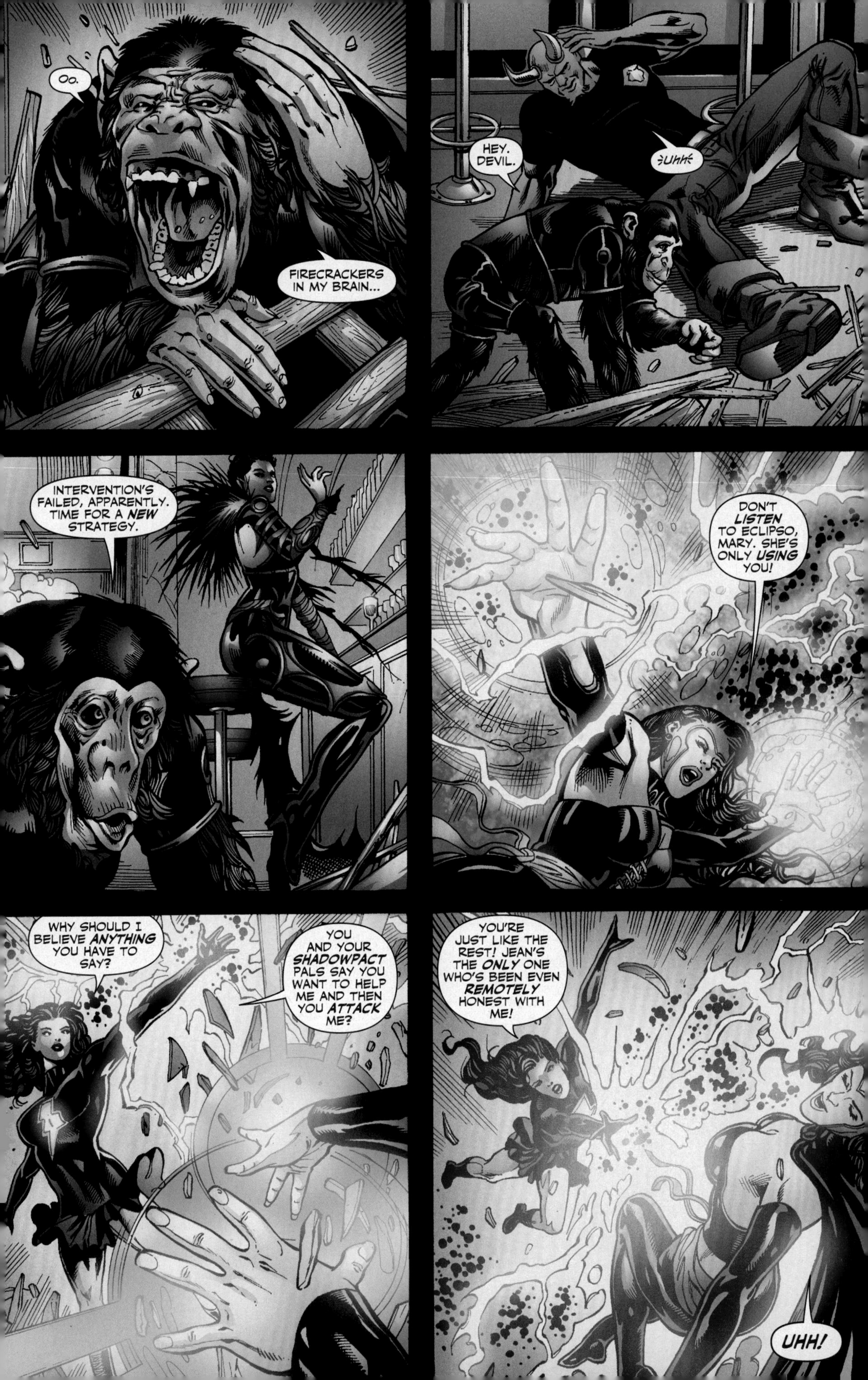
Oo.
FIRECRACKERS IN MY BRAIN...
HEY. DEVIL.
UHH
INTERVENTION'S FAILED, APPARENTLY. TIME FOR A NEW STRATEGY.
DON'T LISTEN TO ECLIPSO, MARY. SHE'S ONLY USING YOU!
WHY SHOULD I BELIEVE ANYTHING YOU HAVE TO SAY?
YOU AND YOUR SHADOWPACT PALS SAY YOU WANT TO HELP ME AND THEN YOU ATTACK ME?
YOU'RE JUST LIKE THE REST! JEAN'S THE ONLY ONE WHO'S BEEN EVEN REMOTELY HONEST WITH ME!
UHH!

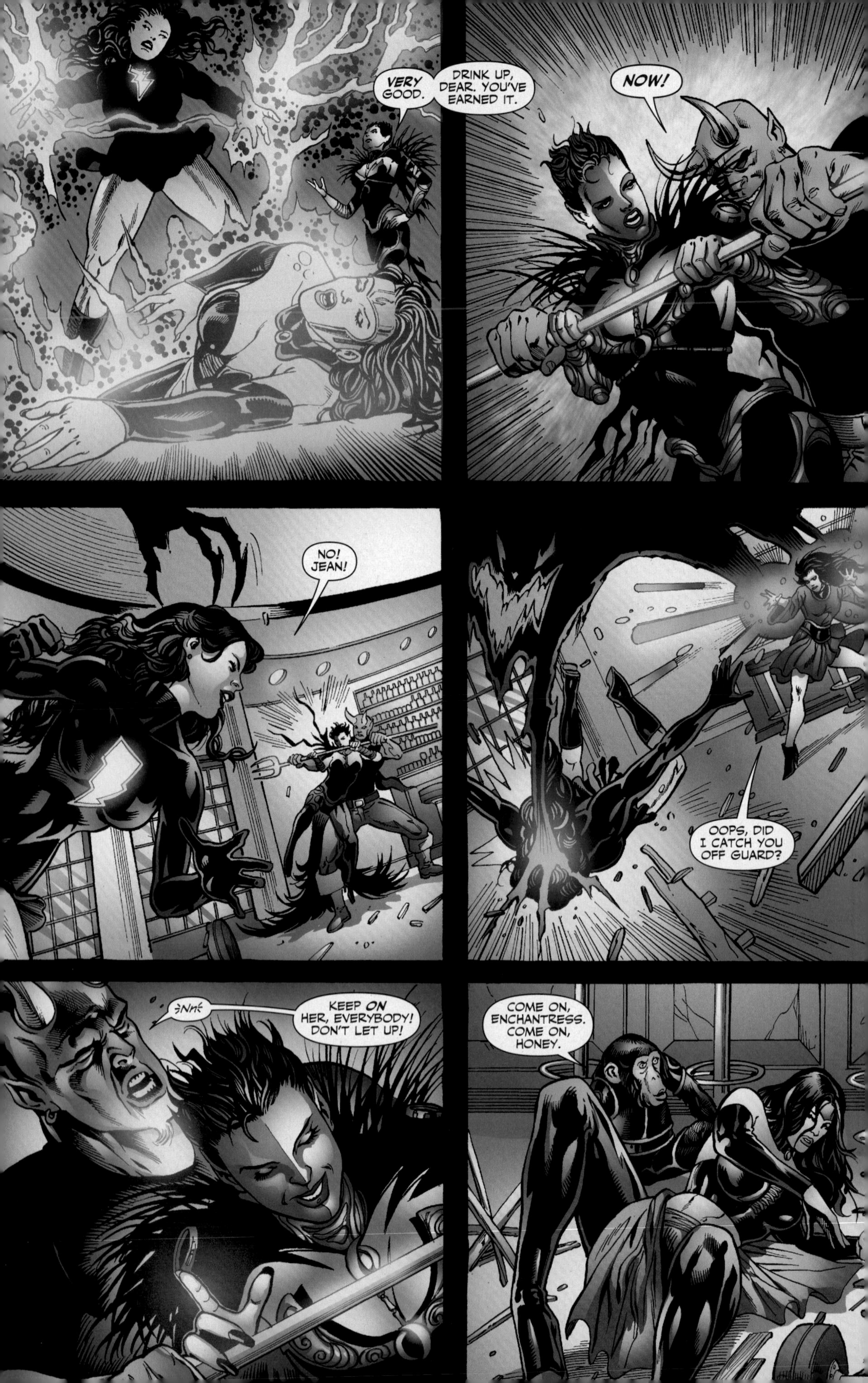
VERY GOOD.
DRINK UP, DEAR. YOU'VE EARNED IT.
NOW!
NO! JEAN!
OOPS, DID I CATCH YOU OFF GUARD?
HNK!
KEEP ON HER, EVERYBODY! DON'T LET UP!
COME ON, ENCHANTRESS. COME ON, HONEY.

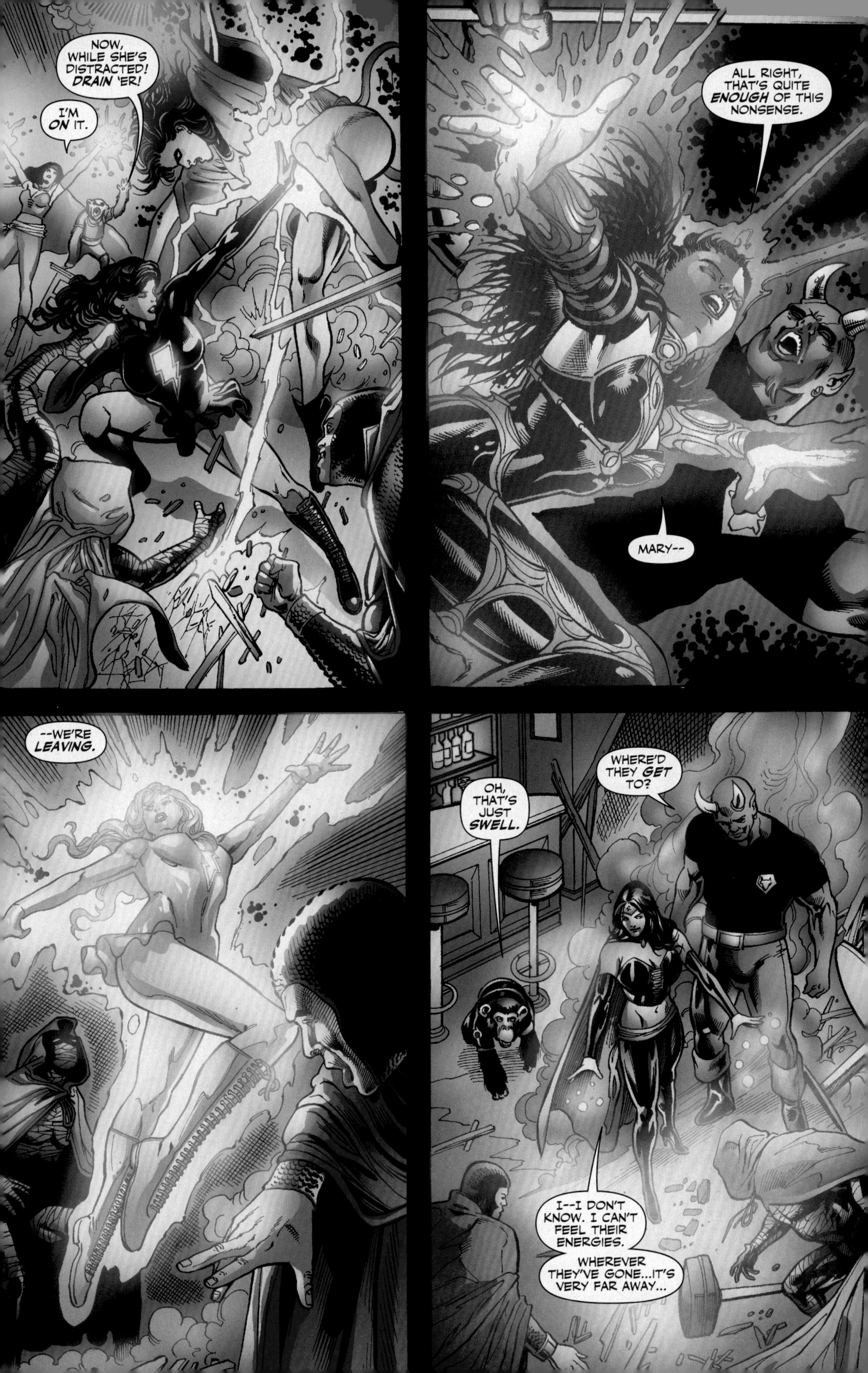
NOW, WHILE SHE'S DISTRACTED! DRAIN 'ER!
I'M ON IT.
ALL RIGHT, THAT'S QUITE ENOUGH OF THIS NONSENSE.
MARY--
--WE'RE LEAVING.
WHERE'D THEY GET TO?
OH, THAT'S JUST SWELL.
I--I DON'T KNOW. I CAN'T FEEL THEIR ENERGIES.
WHEREVER THEY'VE GONE...IT'S VERY FAR AWAY...

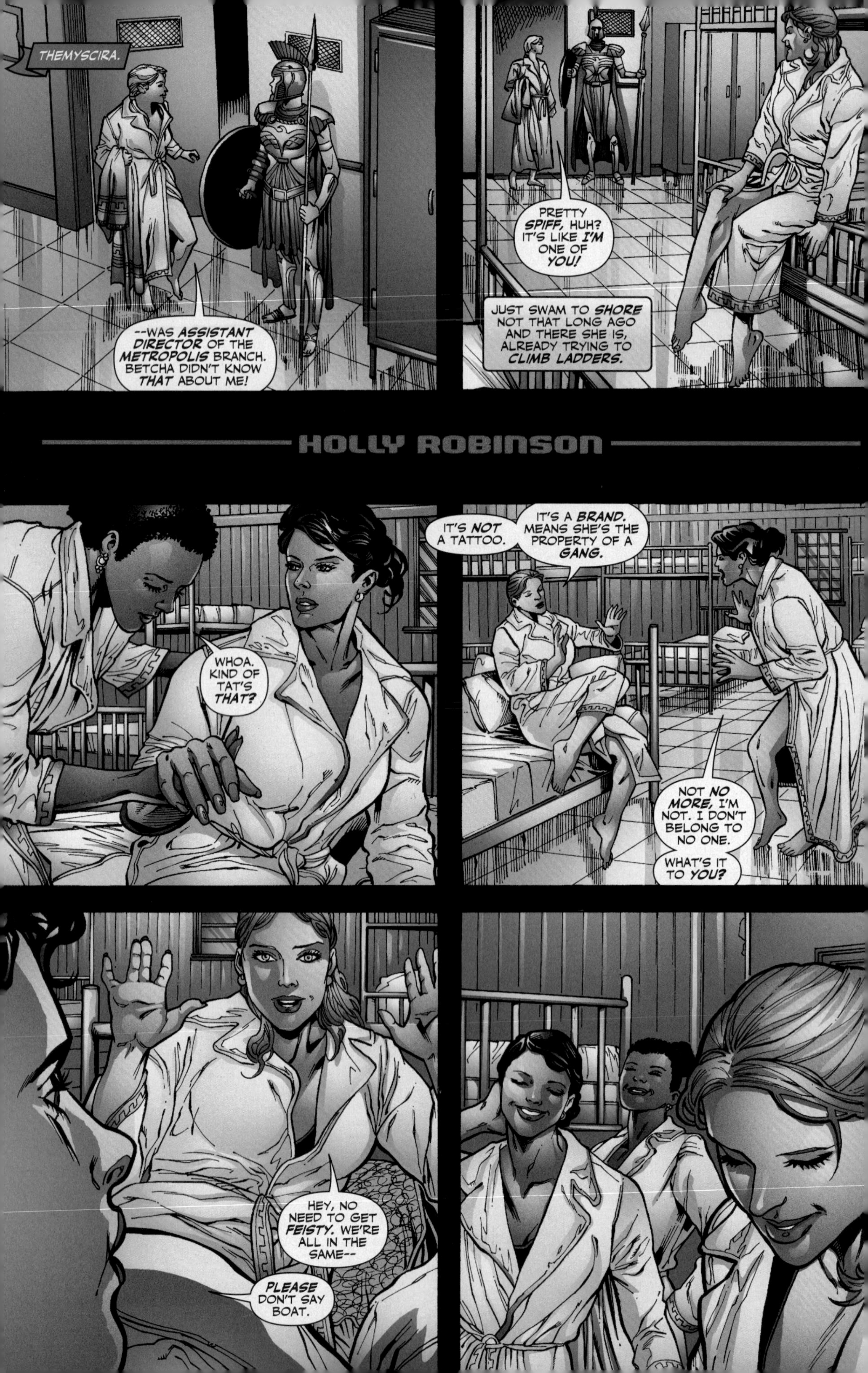
THEMYSCIRA.
--WAS ASSISTANT DIRECTOR OF THE METROPOLIS BRANCH. BETCHA DIDN'T KNOW THAT ABOUT ME!
PRETTY SPIFF, HUH? IT'S LIKE I'M ONE OF YOU!
JUST SWAM TO SHORE NOT THAT LONG AGO AND THERE SHE IS, ALREADY TRYING TO CLIMB LADDERS.
HOLLY ROBINSON
WHOA. KIND OF TAT'S THAT?
IT'S NOT A TATTOO.
IT'S A BRAND. MEANS SHE'S THE PROPERTY OF A GANG.
NOT NO MORE, I'M NOT. I DON'T BELONG TO NO ONE.
WHAT'S IT TO YOU?
HEY, NO NEED TO GET FEISTY. WE'RE ALL IN THE SAME--
PLEASE DON'T SAY BOAT.

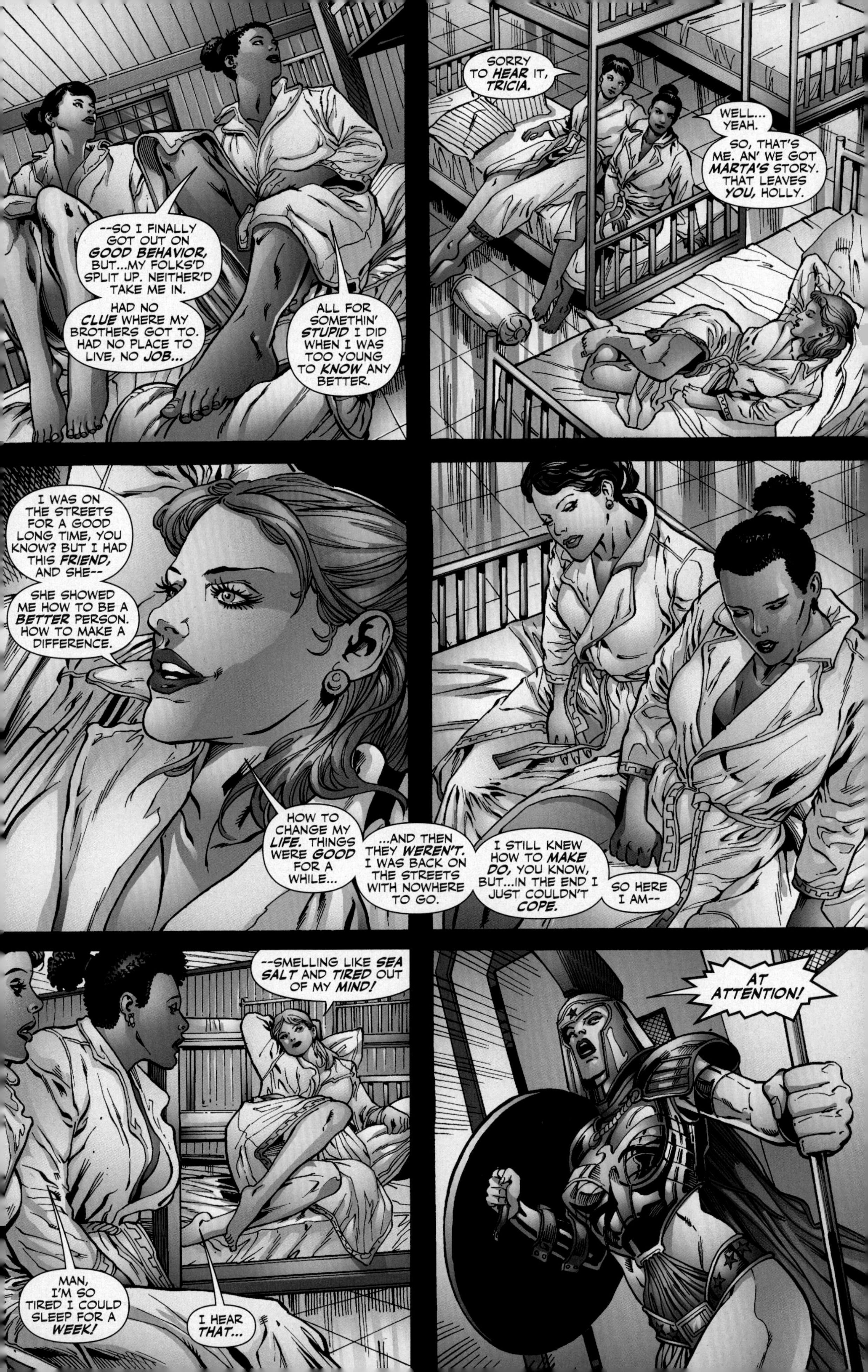
--SO I FINALLY GOT OUT ON GOOD BEHAVIOR, BUT...MY FOLKS'D SPLIT UP. NEITHER'D TAKE ME IN.
HAD NO CLUE WHERE MY BROTHERS GOT TO. HAD NO PLACE TO LIVE, NO JOB...
ALL FOR SOMETHIN' STUPID I DID WHEN I WAS TOO YOUNG TO KNOW ANY BETTER.
SORRY TO HEAR IT, TRICIA.
WELL... YEAH.
SO, THAT'S ME. AN' WE GOT MARTA'S STORY. THAT LEAVES YOU, HOLLY.
I WAS ON THE STREETS FOR A GOOD LONG TIME, YOU KNOW? BUT I HAD THIS FRIEND, AND SHE--
SHE SHOWED ME HOW TO BE A BETTER PERSON. HOW TO MAKE A DIFFERENCE.
HOW TO CHANGE MY LIFE. THINGS WERE GOOD FOR A WHILE...
...AND THEN THEY WEREN'T. I WAS BACK ON THE STREETS WITH NOWHERE TO GO.
I STILL KNEW HOW TO MAKE DO, YOU KNOW, BUT...IN THE END I JUST COULDN'T COPE.
SO HERE I AM--
--SMELLING LIKE SEA SALT AND TIRED OUT OF MY MIND!
MAN, I'M SO TIRED I COULD SLEEP FOR A WEEK!
I HEAR THAT...
AT ATTENTION!

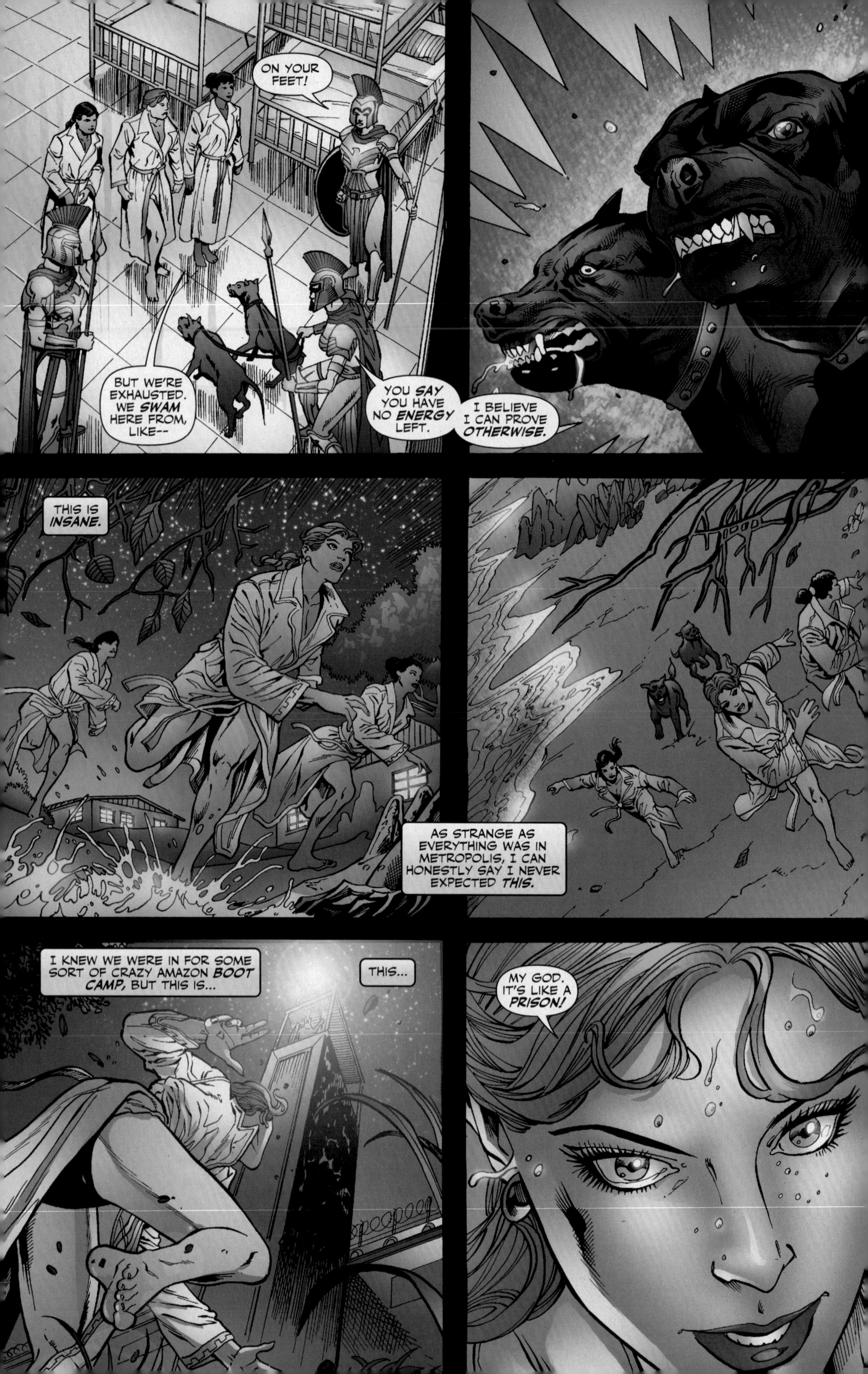
ON YOUR FEET!
BUT WE'RE EXHAUSTED. WE SWAM HERE FROM, LIKE--
YOU SAY YOU HAVE NO ENERGY LEFT.
I BELIEVE I CAN PROVE OTHERWISE.
THIS IS INSANE.
AS STRANGE AS EVERYTHING WAS IN METROPOLIS, I CAN HONESTLY SAY I NEVER EXPECTED THIS.
I KNEW WE WERE IN FOR SOME SORT OF CRAZY AMAZON BOOT CAMP, BUT THIS IS...
THIS...
MY GOD. IT'S LIKE A PRISON!

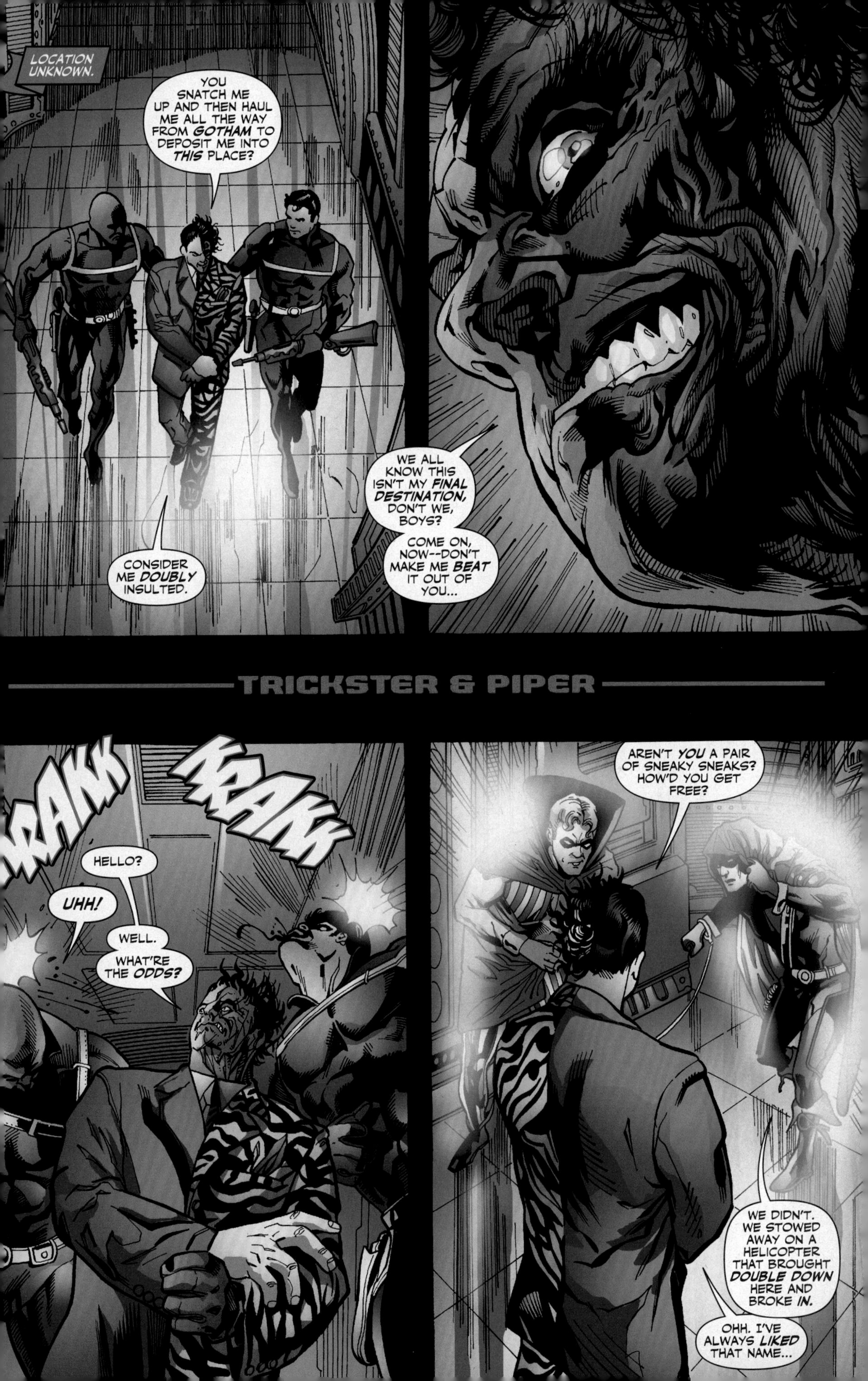
LOCATION UNKNOWN.
YOU SNATCH ME UP AND THEN HAUL ME ALL THE WAY FROM GOTHAM TO DEPOSIT ME INTO THIS PLACE?
CONSIDER ME DOUBLY INSULTED.
WE ALL KNOW THIS ISN'T MY FINAL DESTINATION, DON'T WE, BOYS?
COME ON, NOW--DON'T MAKE ME BEAT IT OUT OF YOU...
TRICKSTER & PIPER
KRAKK
HELLO?
UHH!
WELL.
WHAT'RE THE ODDS?
AREN'T YOU A PAIR OF SNEAKY SNEAKS? HOW'D YOU GET FREE?
WE DIDN'T. WE STOWED AWAY ON A HELICOPTER THAT BROUGHT DOUBLE DOWN HERE AND BROKE IN.
OHH. I'VE ALWAYS LIKED THAT NAME...

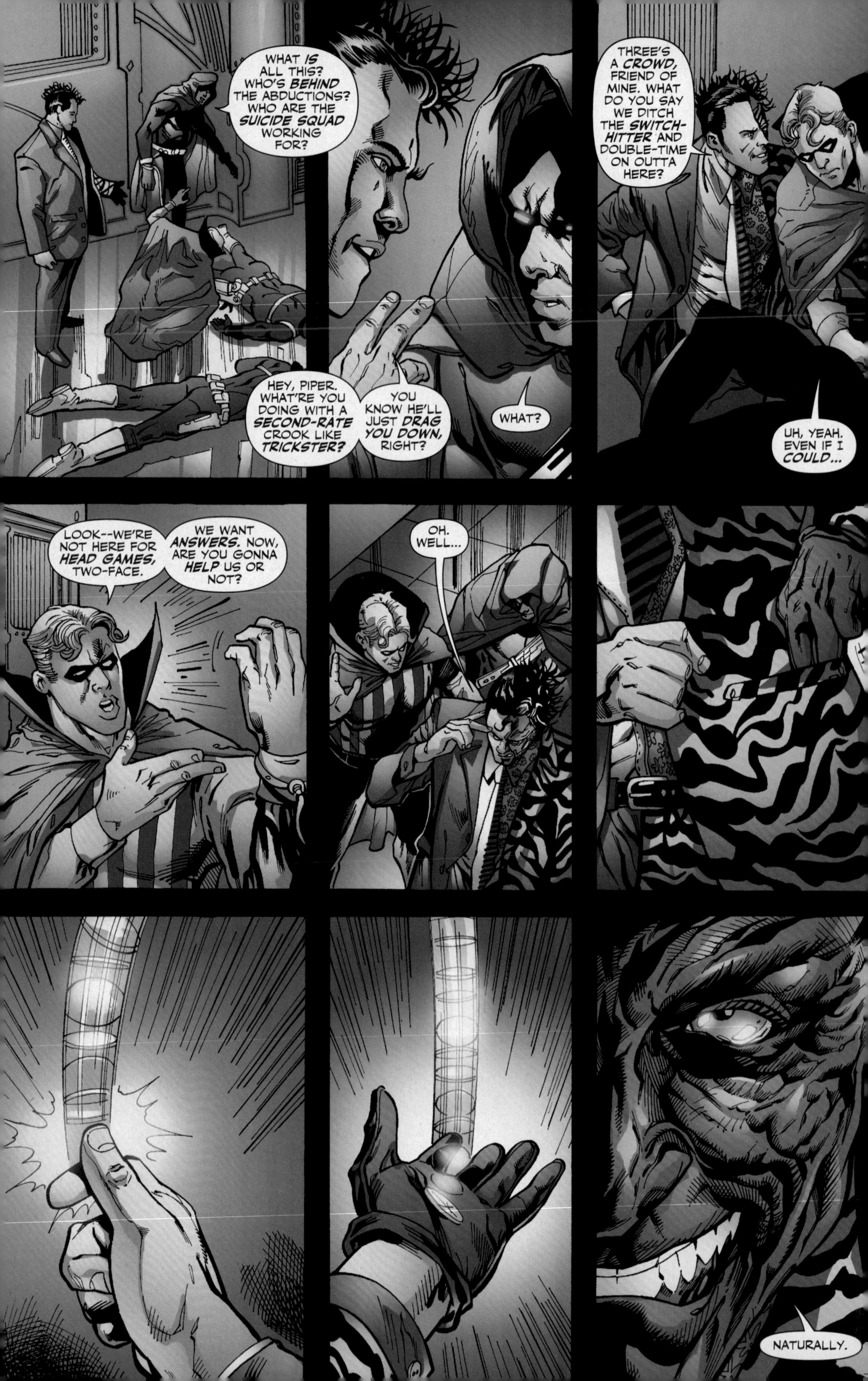
WHAT IS ALL THIS? WHO'S BEHIND THE ABDUCTIONS? WHO ARE THE SUICIDE SQUAD WORKING FOR?
HEY, PIPER. WHAT'RE YOU DOING WITH A SECOND-RATE CROOK LIKE TRICKSTER?
YOU KNOW HE'LL JUST DRAG YOU DOWN, RIGHT?
WHAT?
THREE'S A CROWD, FRIEND OF MINE. WHAT DO YOU SAY WE DITCH THE SWITCH-HITTER AND DOUBLE-TIME ON OUTTA HERE?
UH, YEAH. EVEN IF I COULD...
LOOK--WE'RE NOT HERE FOR HEAD GAMES, TWO-FACE.
WE WANT ANSWERS. NOW, ARE YOU GONNA HELP US OR NOT?
OH. WELL...
NATURALLY.

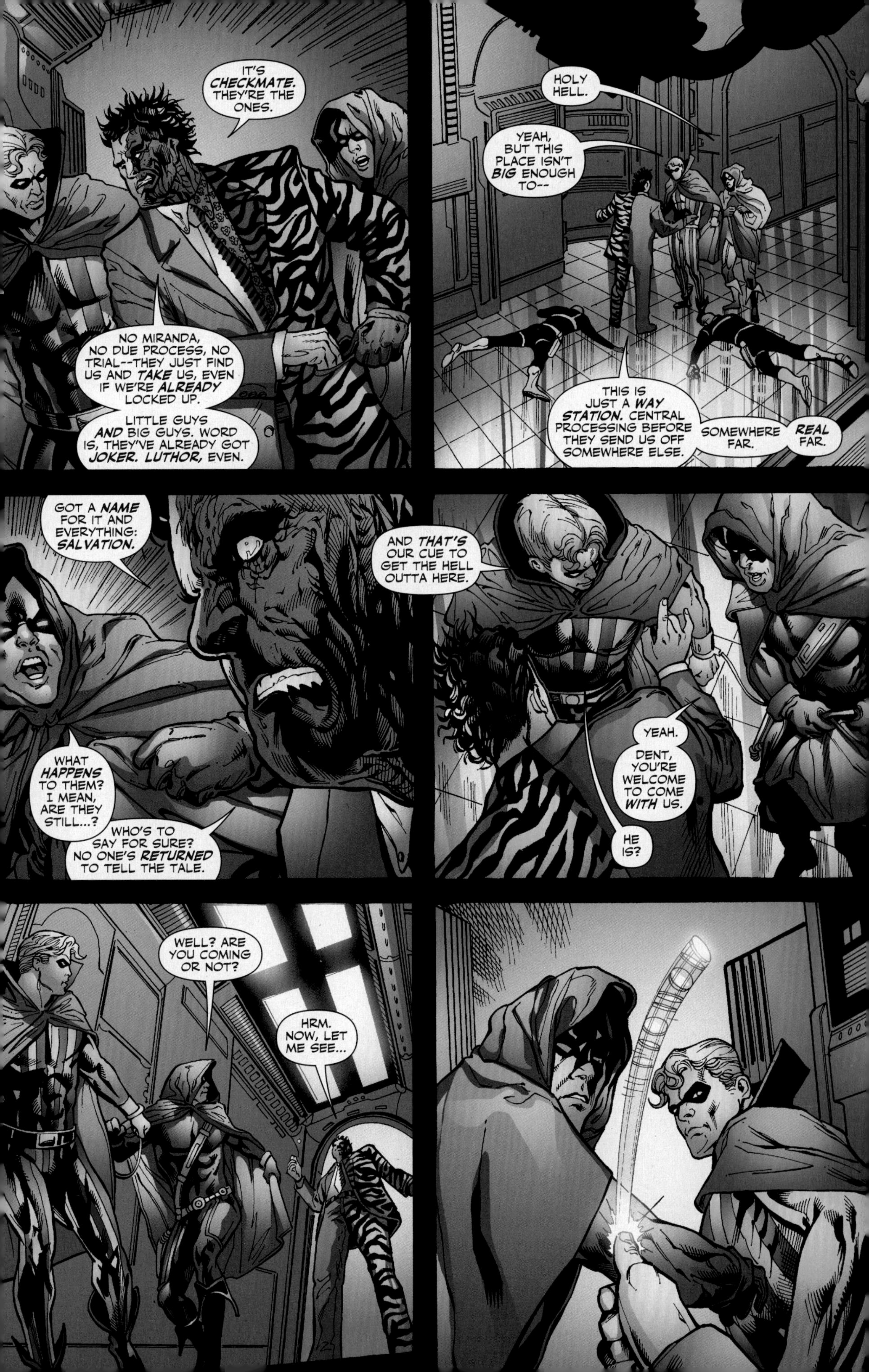
IT'S CHECKMATE. THEY'RE THE ONES.
NO MIRANDA, NO DUE PROCESS, NO TRIAL--THEY JUST FIND US AND TAKE US, EVEN IF WE'RE ALREADY LOCKED UP.
LITTLE GUYS AND BIG GUYS. WORD IS, THEY'VE ALREADY GOT JOKER. LUTHOR, EVEN.
HOLY HELL.
YEAH, BUT THIS PLACE ISN'T BIG ENOUGH TO--
THIS IS JUST A WAY STATION. CENTRAL PROCESSING BEFORE THEY SEND US OFF SOMEWHERE ELSE.
SOMEWHERE FAR.
REAL FAR.
GOT A NAME FOR IT AND EVERYTHING: SALVATION.
WHAT HAPPENS TO THEM? I MEAN, ARE THEY STILL...?
WHO'S TO SAY FOR SURE? NO ONE'S RETURNED TO TELL THE TALE.
AND THAT'S OUR CUE TO GET THE HELL OUTTA HERE.
YEAH.
DENT, YOU'RE WELCOME TO COME WITH US.
HE IS?
WELL? ARE YOU COMING OR NOT?
HRM. NOW, LET ME SEE...

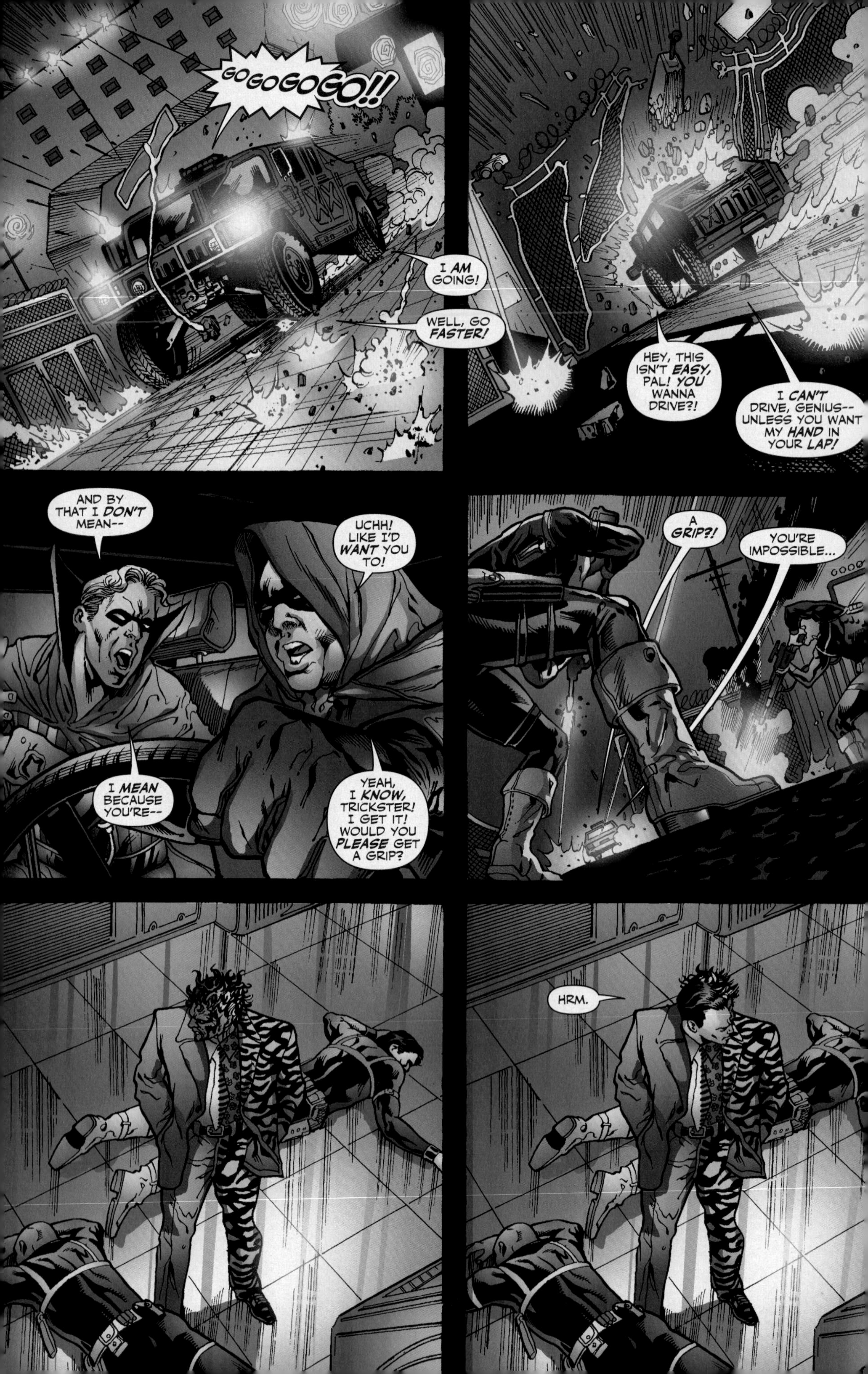
GOGOGOGOGO!!
I AM GOING!
WELL, GO FASTER!
HEY, THIS ISN'T EASY, PAL! YOU WANNA DRIVE?!
I CAN'T DRIVE, GENIUS-- UNLESS YOU WANT MY HAND IN YOUR LAP!
AND BY THAT I DON'T MEAN--
UCHH! LIKE I'D WANT YOU TO!
I MEAN BECAUSE YOU'RE--
YEAH, I KNOW, TRICKSTER! I GET IT! WOULD YOU PLEASE GET A GRIP?
A GRIP?!
YOU'RE IMPOSSIBLE...
HRM.

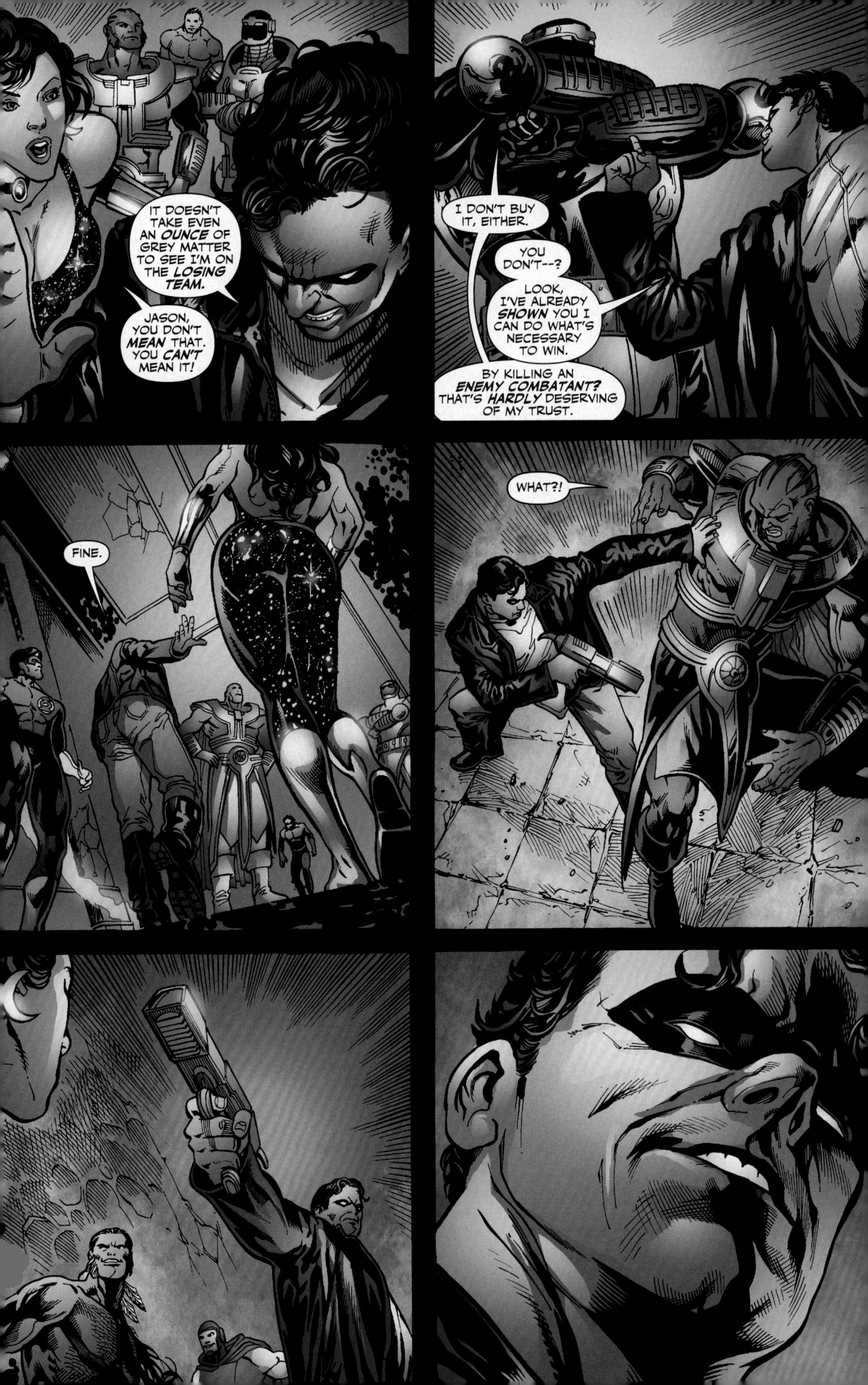
IT DOESN'T TAKE EVEN AN OUNCE OF GREY MATTER TO SEE I'M ON THE LOSING TEAM.
JASON, YOU DON'T MEAN THAT. YOU CAN'T MEAN IT!
I DON'T BUY IT, EITHER.
YOU DON'T--?
LOOK, I'VE ALREADY SHOWN YOU I CAN DO WHAT'S NECESSARY TO WIN.
BY KILLING AN ENEMY COMBATANT? THAT'S HARDLY DESERVING OF MY TRUST.
FINE.
WHAT?!

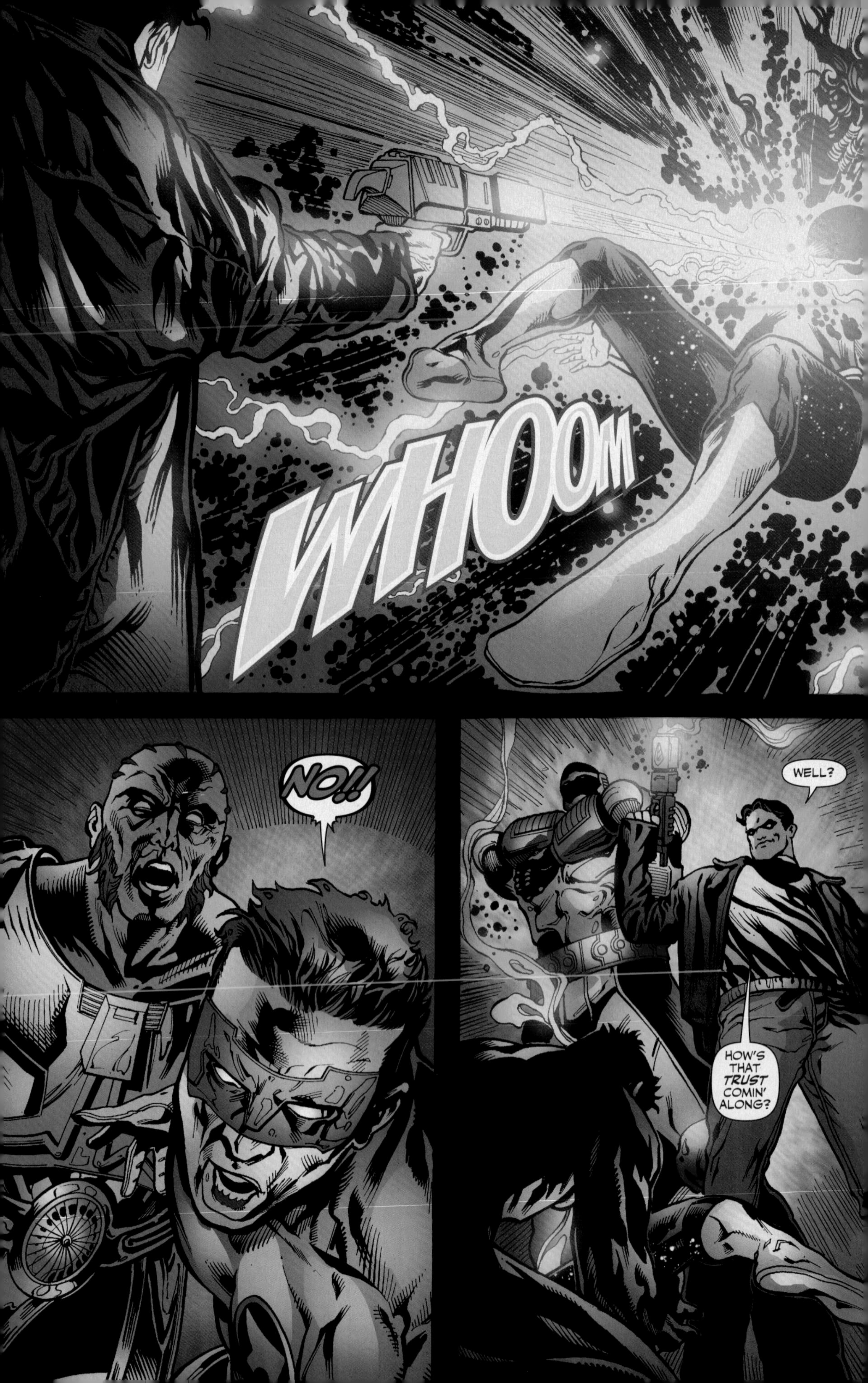
WHOOM
NO!!
WELL?
HOW'S THAT *TRUST* COMIN' ALONG?

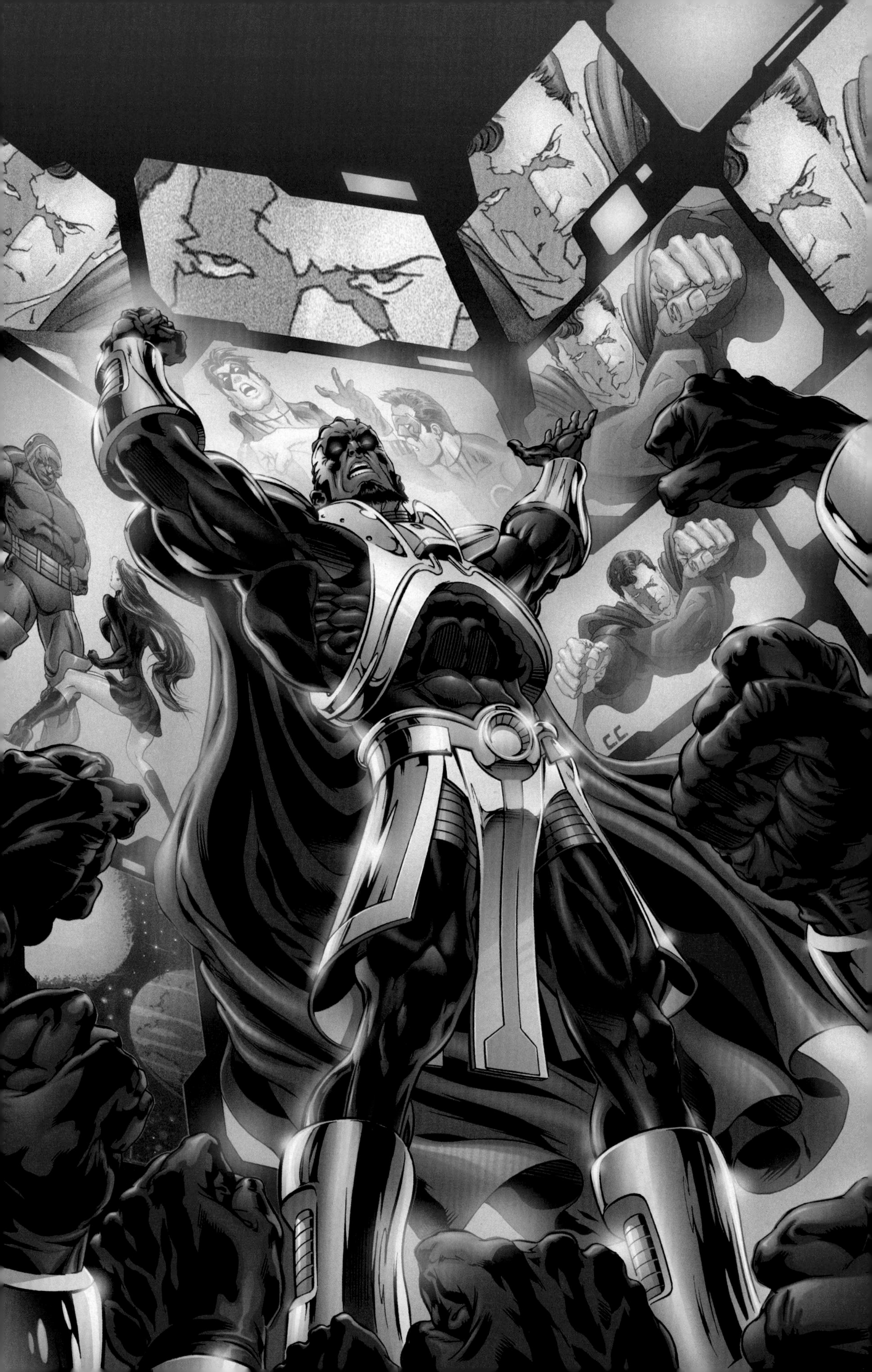
C.C.

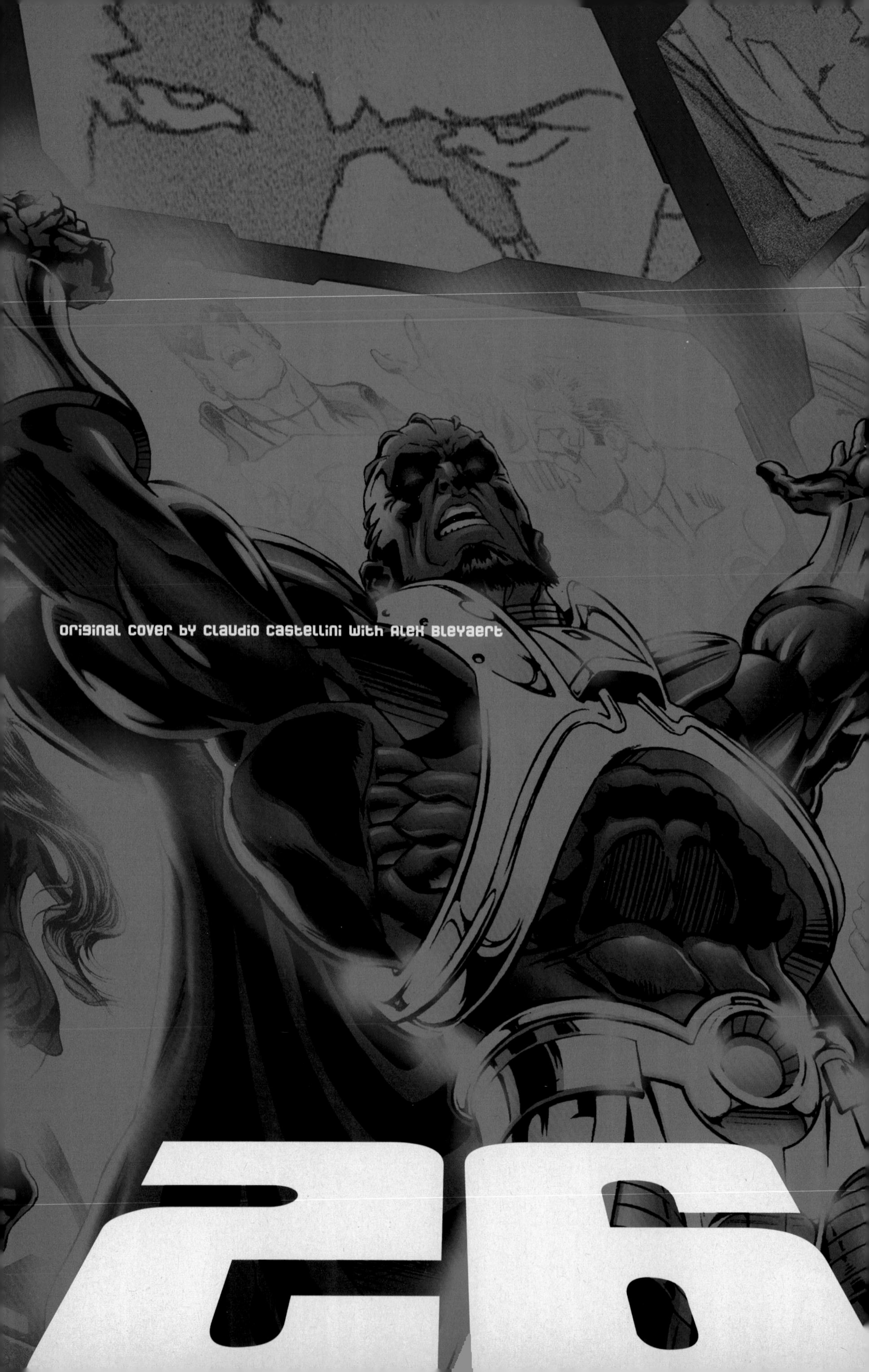

original cover by Claudio Castellini with Alex Bleyaert

# 26

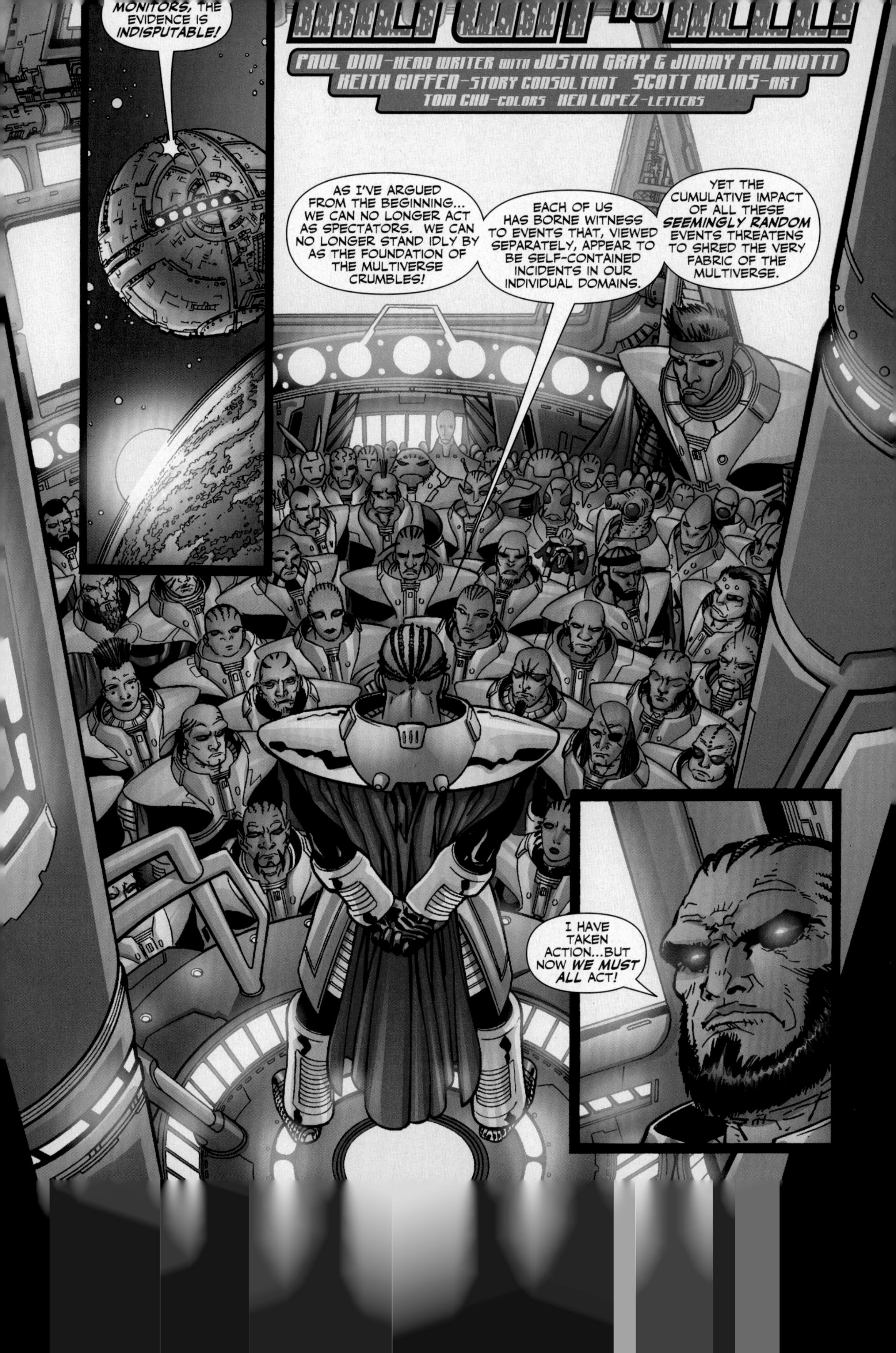
MONITORS, THE EVIDENCE IS INDISPUTABLE!
PAUL DINI–HEAD WRITER WITH JUSTIN GRAY & JIMMY PALMIOTTI
KEITH GIFFEN–STORY CONSULTANT SCOTT KOLINS–ART
TOM CHU–COLORS KEN LOPEZ–LETTERS
AS I'VE ARGUED FROM THE BEGINNING... WE CAN NO LONGER ACT AS SPECTATORS. WE CAN NO LONGER STAND IDLY BY AS THE FOUNDATION OF THE MULTIVERSE CRUMBLES!
EACH OF US HAS BORNE WITNESS TO EVENTS THAT, VIEWED SEPARATELY, APPEAR TO BE SELF-CONTAINED INCIDENTS IN OUR INDIVIDUAL DOMAINS.
YET THE CUMULATIVE IMPACT OF ALL THESE SEEMINGLY RANDOM EVENTS THREATENS TO SHRED THE VERY FABRIC OF THE MULTIVERSE.
I HAVE TAKEN ACTION...BUT NOW WE MUST ALL ACT!

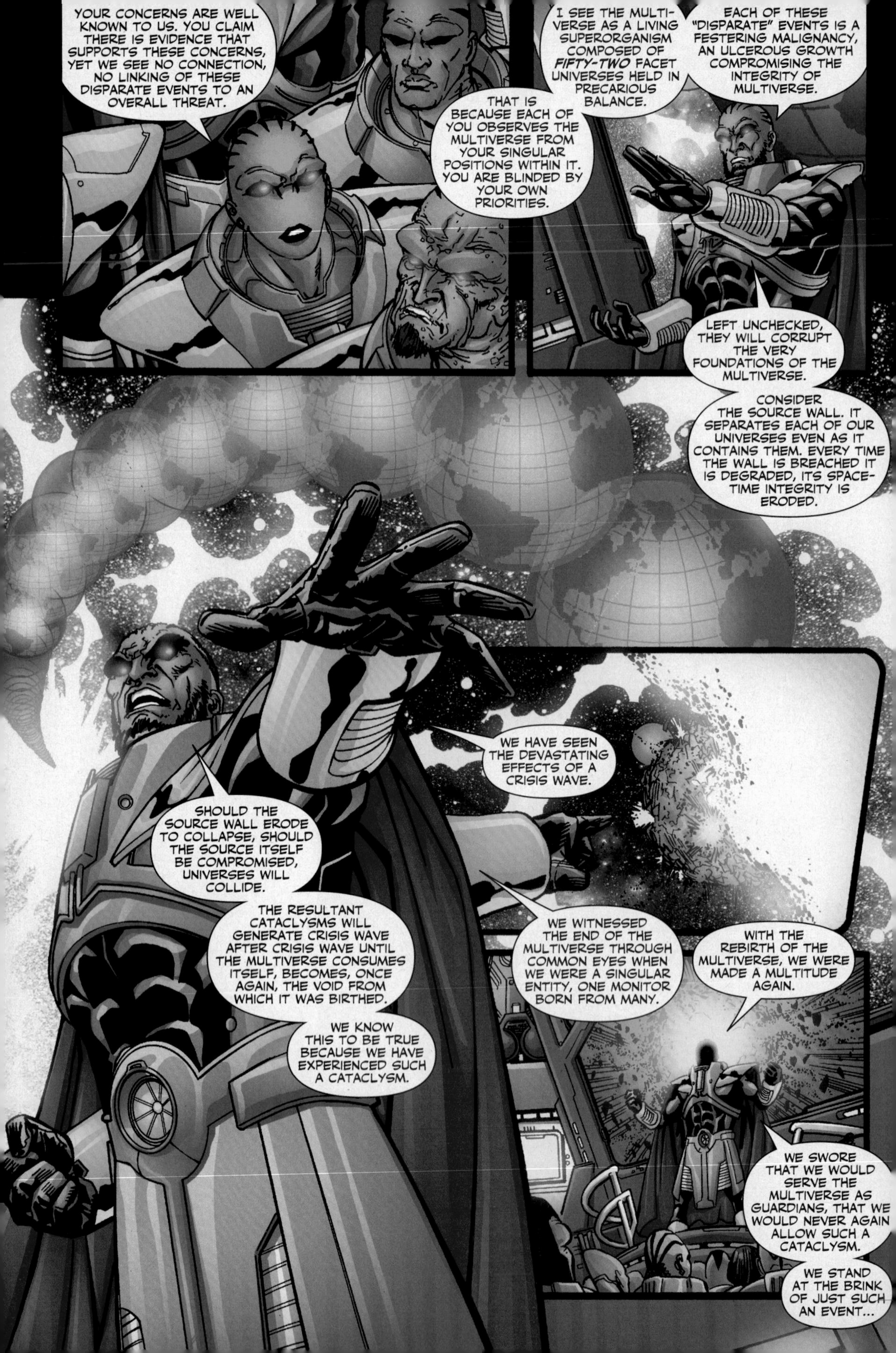
YOUR CONCERNS ARE WELL KNOWN TO US. YOU CLAIM THERE IS EVIDENCE THAT SUPPORTS THESE CONCERNS, YET WE SEE NO CONNECTION, NO LINKING OF THESE DISPARATE EVENTS TO AN OVERALL THREAT.
THAT IS BECAUSE EACH OF YOU OBSERVES THE MULTIVERSE FROM YOUR SINGULAR POSITIONS WITHIN IT. YOU ARE BLINDED BY YOUR OWN PRIORITIES.
I SEE THE MULTIVERSE AS A LIVING SUPERORGANISM COMPOSED OF *FIFTY-TWO* FACET UNIVERSES HELD IN PRECARIOUS BALANCE.
EACH OF THESE "DISPARATE" EVENTS IS A FESTERING MALIGNANCY, AN ULCEROUS GROWTH COMPROMISING THE INTEGRITY OF MULTIVERSE.
LEFT UNCHECKED, THEY WILL CORRUPT THE VERY FOUNDATIONS OF THE MULTIVERSE.
CONSIDER THE SOURCE WALL. IT SEPARATES EACH OF OUR UNIVERSES EVEN AS IT CONTAINS THEM. EVERY TIME THE WALL IS BREACHED IT IS DEGRADED, ITS SPACE-TIME INTEGRITY IS ERODED.
SHOULD THE SOURCE WALL ERODE TO COLLAPSE, SHOULD THE SOURCE ITSELF BE COMPROMISED, UNIVERSES WILL COLLIDE.
THE RESULTANT CATACLYSMS WILL GENERATE CRISIS WAVE AFTER CRISIS WAVE UNTIL THE MULTIVERSE CONSUMES ITSELF, BECOMES, ONCE AGAIN, THE VOID FROM WHICH IT WAS BIRTHED.
WE KNOW THIS TO BE TRUE BECAUSE WE HAVE EXPERIENCED SUCH A CATACLYSM.
WE HAVE SEEN THE DEVASTATING EFFECTS OF A CRISIS WAVE.
WE WITNESSED THE END OF THE MULTIVERSE THROUGH COMMON EYES WHEN WE WERE A SINGULAR ENTITY, ONE MONITOR BORN FROM MANY.
WITH THE REBIRTH OF THE MULTIVERSE, WE WERE MADE A MULTITUDE AGAIN.
WE SWORE THAT WE WOULD SERVE THE MULTIVERSE AS GUARDIANS, THAT WE WOULD NEVER AGAIN ALLOW SUCH A CATACLYSM.
WE STAND AT THE BRINK OF JUST SUCH AN EVENT...

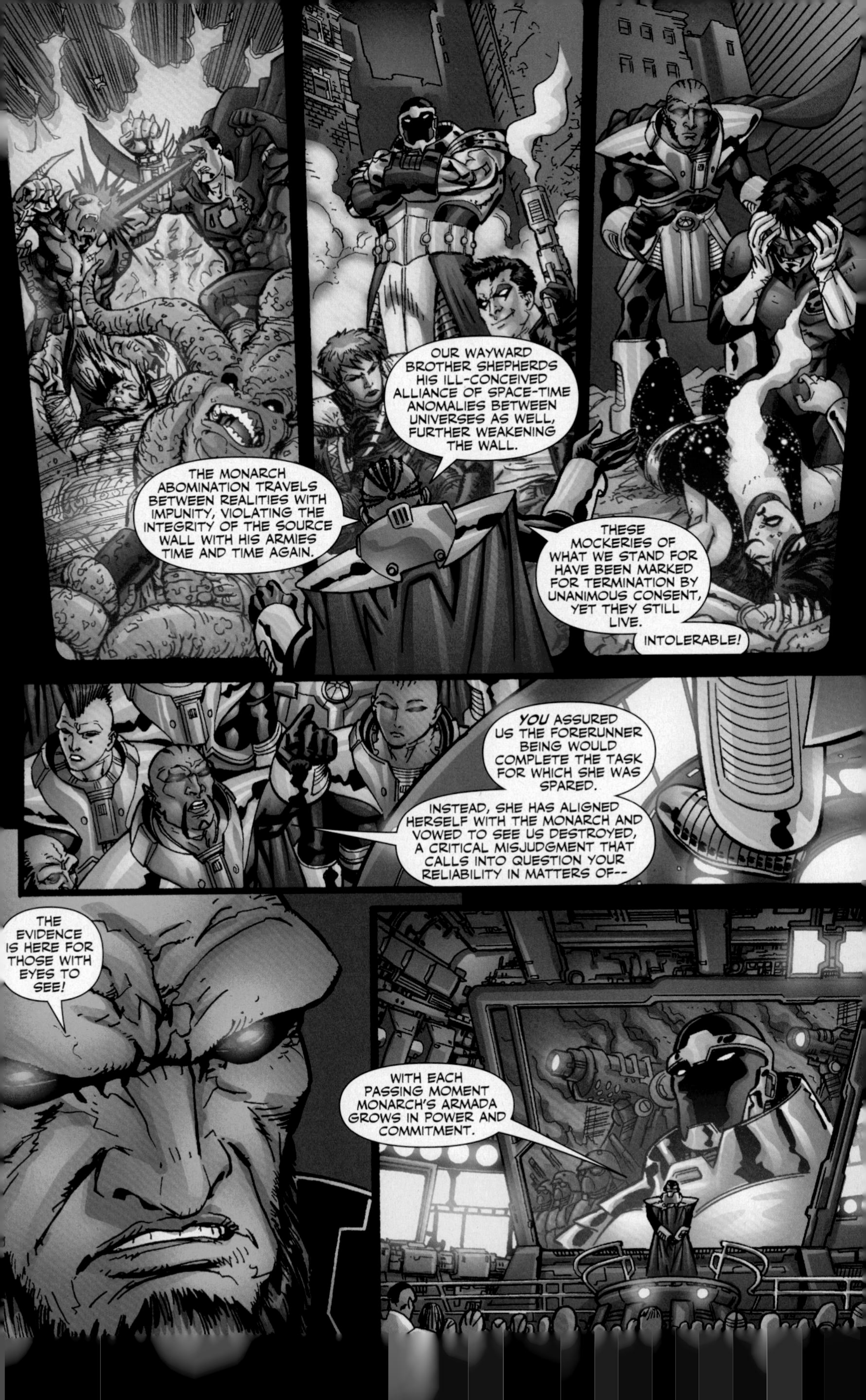
THE MONARCH ABOMINATION TRAVELS BETWEEN REALITIES WITH IMPUNITY, VIOLATING THE INTEGRITY OF THE SOURCE WALL WITH HIS ARMIES TIME AND TIME AGAIN.
OUR WAYWARD BROTHER SHEPHERDS HIS ILL-CONCEIVED ALLIANCE OF SPACE-TIME ANOMALIES BETWEEN UNIVERSES AS WELL, FURTHER WEAKENING THE WALL.
THESE MOCKERIES OF WHAT WE STAND FOR HAVE BEEN MARKED FOR TERMINATION BY UNANIMOUS CONSENT, YET THEY STILL LIVE.
INTOLERABLE!
*YOU* ASSURED US THE FORERUNNER BEING WOULD COMPLETE THE TASK FOR WHICH SHE WAS SPARED.
INSTEAD, SHE HAS ALIGNED HERSELF WITH THE MONARCH AND VOWED TO SEE US DESTROYED, A CRITICAL MISJUDGMENT THAT CALLS INTO QUESTION YOUR RELIABILITY IN MATTERS OF--
THE EVIDENCE IS HERE FOR THOSE WITH EYES TO SEE!
WITH EACH PASSING MOMENT MONARCH'S ARMADA GROWS IN POWER AND COMMITMENT.

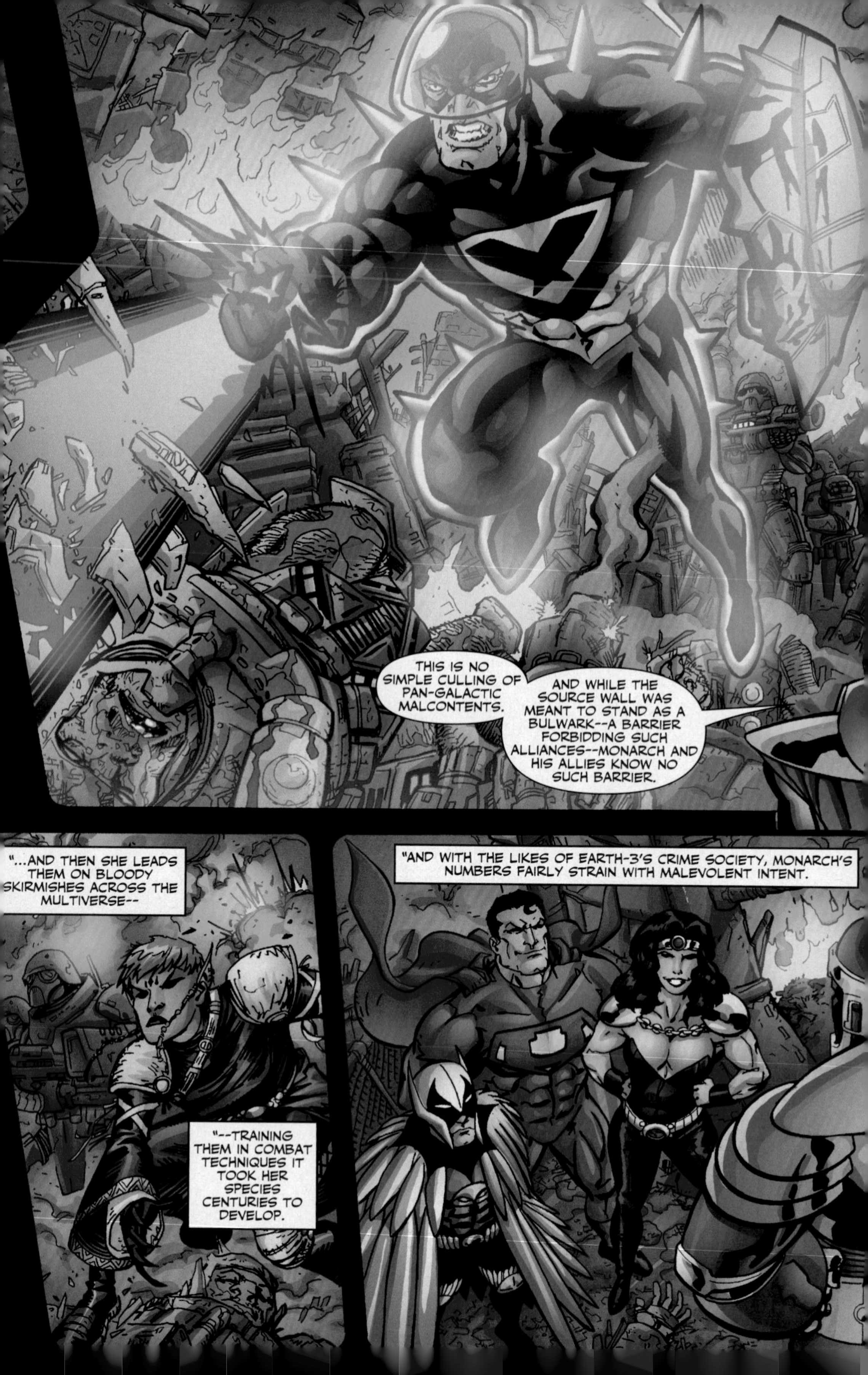

THIS IS NO SIMPLE CULLING OF PAN-GALACTIC MALCONTENTS.
AND WHILE THE SOURCE WALL WAS MEANT TO STAND AS A BULWARK--A BARRIER FORBIDDING SUCH ALLIANCES--MONARCH AND HIS ALLIES KNOW NO SUCH BARRIER.
"...AND THEN SHE LEADS THEM ON BLOODY SKIRMISHES ACROSS THE MULTIVERSE--
"--TRAINING THEM IN COMBAT TECHNIQUES IT TOOK HER SPECIES CENTURIES TO DEVELOP.
"AND WITH THE LIKES OF EARTH-3'S CRIME SOCIETY, MONARCH'S NUMBERS FAIRLY STRAIN WITH MALEVOLENT INTENT.

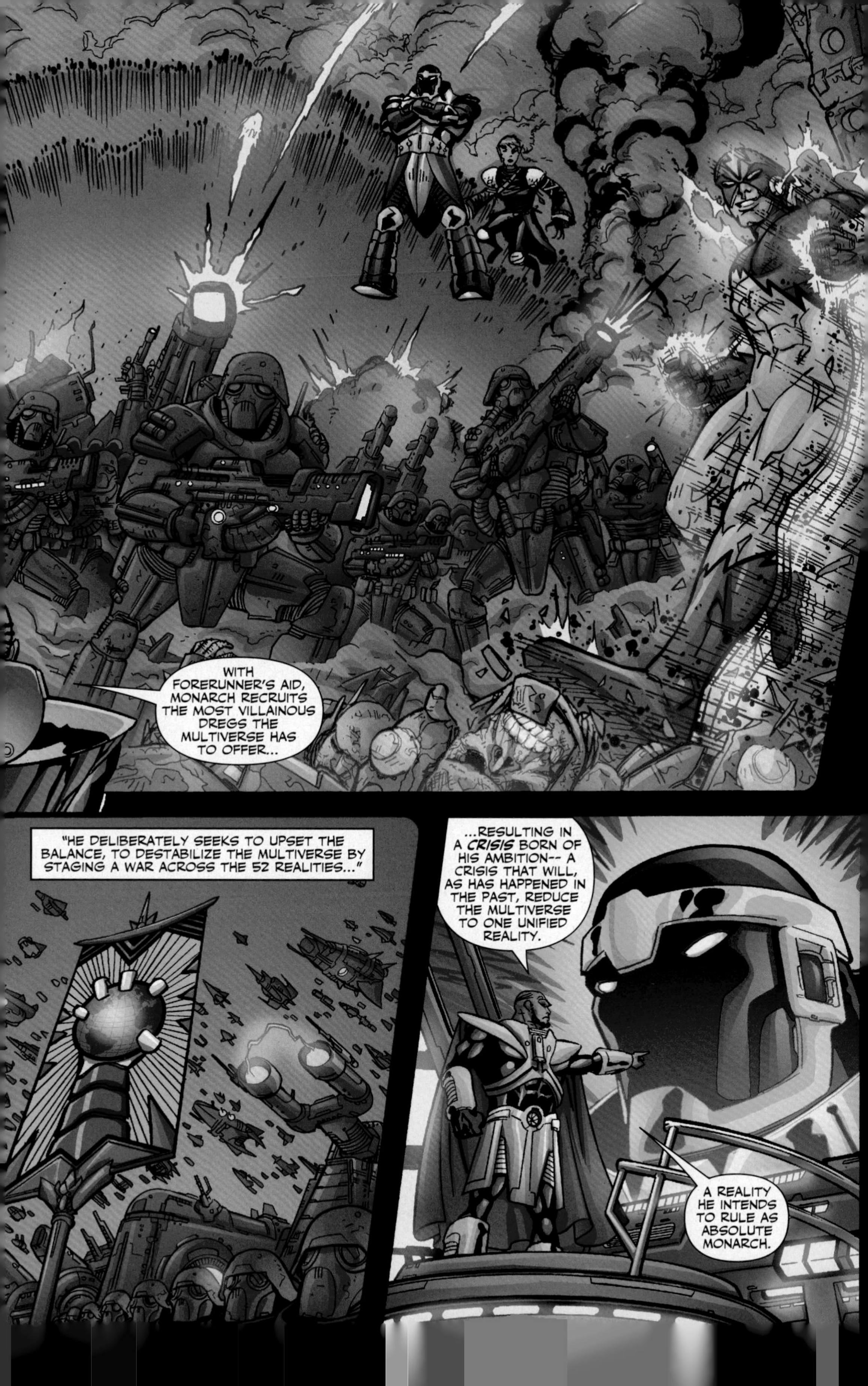
WITH FORERUNNER'S AID, MONARCH RECRUITS THE MOST VILLAINOUS DREGS THE MULTIVERSE HAS TO OFFER...
"HE DELIBERATELY SEEKS TO UPSET THE BALANCE, TO DESTABILIZE THE MULTIVERSE BY STAGING A WAR ACROSS THE 52 REALITIES..."
...RESULTING IN A *CRISIS* BORN OF HIS AMBITION-- A CRISIS THAT WILL, AS HAS HAPPENED IN THE PAST, REDUCE THE MULTIVERSE TO ONE UNIFIED REALITY.
A REALITY HE INTENDS TO RULE AS ABSOLUTE MONARCH.

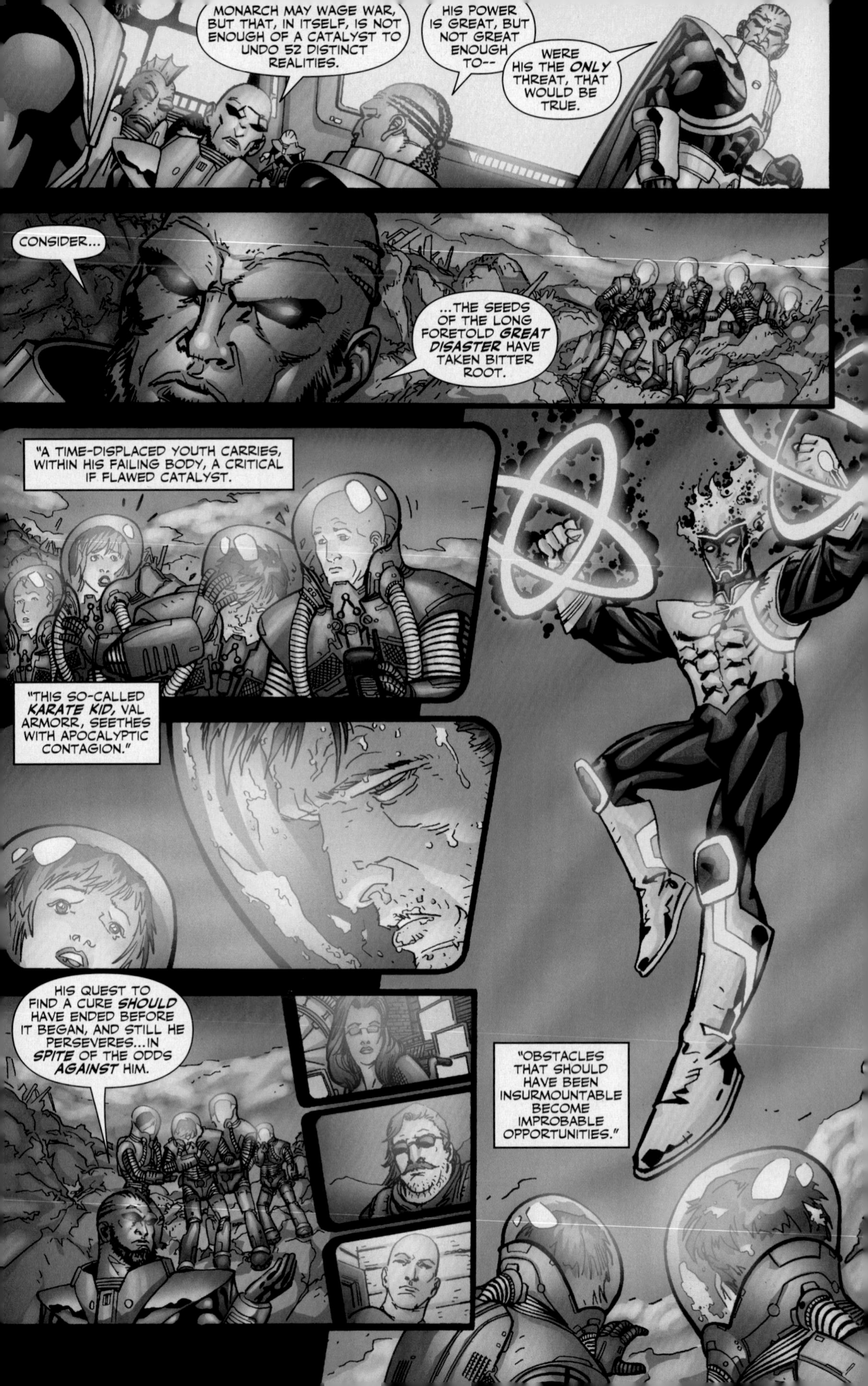

MONARCH MAY WAGE WAR, BUT THAT, IN ITSELF, IS NOT ENOUGH OF A CATALYST TO UNDO 52 DISTINCT REALITIES.
HIS POWER IS GREAT, BUT NOT GREAT ENOUGH TO--
WERE HIS THE *ONLY* THREAT, THAT WOULD BE TRUE.
CONSIDER...
...THE SEEDS OF THE LONG FORETOLD *GREAT DISASTER* HAVE TAKEN BITTER ROOT.
"A TIME-DISPLACED YOUTH CARRIES, WITHIN HIS FAILING BODY, A CRITICAL IF FLAWED CATALYST.
"THIS SO-CALLED *KARATE KID,* VAL ARMORR, SEETHES WITH APOCALYPTIC CONTAGION."
HIS QUEST TO FIND A CURE *SHOULD* HAVE ENDED BEFORE IT BEGAN, AND STILL HE PERSEVERES...IN *SPITE* OF THE ODDS *AGAINST* HIM.
"OBSTACLES THAT SHOULD HAVE BEEN INSURMOUNTABLE BECOME IMPROBABLE OPPORTUNITIES."

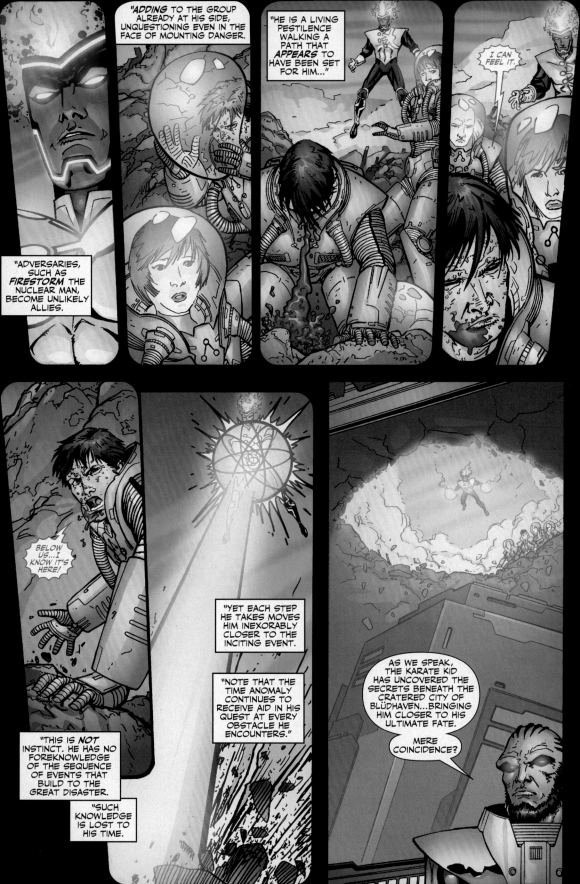

"ADDING TO THE GROUP ALREADY AT HIS SIDE, UNQUESTIONING EVEN IN THE FACE OF MOUNTING DANGER.

"HE IS A LIVING PESTILENCE WALKING A PATH THAT APPEARS TO HAVE BEEN SET FOR HIM..."

I CAN FEEL IT.

"ADVERSARIES, SUCH AS FIRESTORM THE NUCLEAR MAN, BECOME UNLIKELY ALLIES.

BELOW US...I KNOW IT'S HERE!

"YET EACH STEP HE TAKES MOVES HIM INEXORABLY CLOSER TO THE INCITING EVENT.

"NOTE THAT THE TIME ANOMALY CONTINUES TO RECEIVE AID IN HIS QUEST AT EVERY OBSTACLE HE ENCOUNTERS."

"THIS IS NOT INSTINCT. HE HAS NO FOREKNOWLEDGE OF THE SEQUENCE OF EVENTS THAT BUILD TO THE GREAT DISASTER.

"SUCH KNOWLEDGE IS LOST TO HIS TIME.

AS WE SPEAK, THE KARATE KID HAS UNCOVERED THE SECRETS BENEATH THE CRATERED CITY OF BLÜDHAVEN...BRINGING HIM CLOSER TO HIS ULTIMATE FATE.

MERE COINCIDENCE?

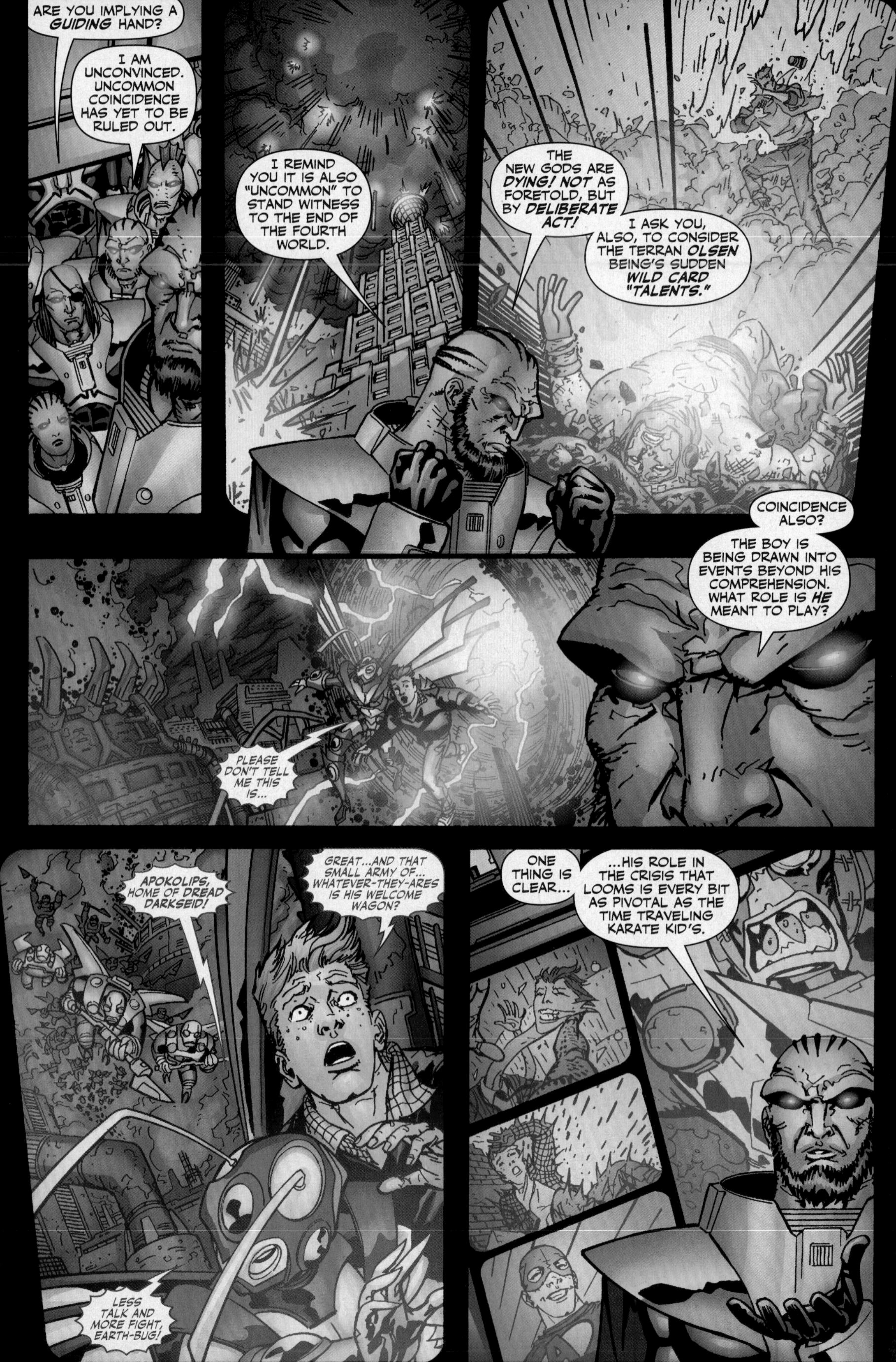
ARE YOU IMPLYING A GUIDING HAND?
I AM UNCONVINCED. UNCOMMON COINCIDENCE HAS YET TO BE RULED OUT.
I REMIND YOU IT IS ALSO "UNCOMMON" TO STAND WITNESS TO THE END OF THE FOURTH WORLD.
THE NEW GODS ARE DYING! NOT AS FORETOLD, BUT BY DELIBERATE ACT!
I ASK YOU, ALSO, TO CONSIDER THE TERRAN OLSEN BEING'S SUDDEN WILD CARD "TALENTS."
COINCIDENCE ALSO?
THE BOY IS BEING DRAWN INTO EVENTS BEYOND HIS COMPREHENSION. WHAT ROLE IS HE MEANT TO PLAY?
PLEASE DON'T TELL ME THIS IS...
APOKOLIPS, HOME OF DREAD DARKSEID!
GREAT...AND THAT SMALL ARMY OF... WHATEVER-THEY-ARES IS HIS WELCOME WAGON?
LESS TALK AND MORE FIGHT, EARTH-BUG!
ONE THING IS CLEAR...
...HIS ROLE IN THE CRISIS THAT LOOMS IS EVERY BIT AS PIVOTAL AS THE TIME TRAVELING KARATE KID'S.

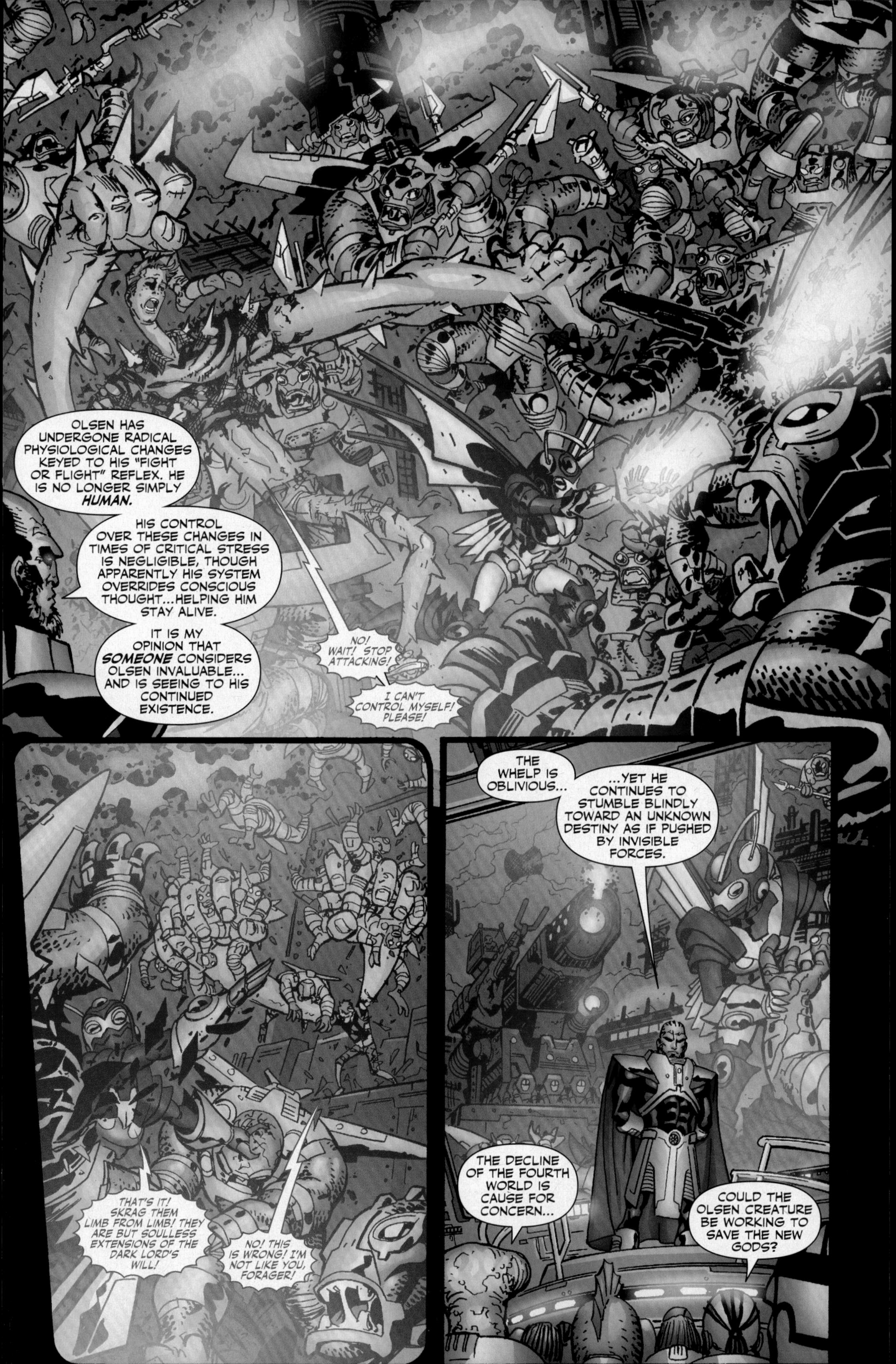
OLSEN HAS UNDERGONE RADICAL PHYSIOLOGICAL CHANGES KEYED TO HIS "FIGHT OR FLIGHT" REFLEX. HE IS NO LONGER SIMPLY HUMAN.
HIS CONTROL OVER THESE CHANGES IN TIMES OF CRITICAL STRESS IS NEGLIGIBLE, THOUGH APPARENTLY HIS SYSTEM OVERRIDES CONSCIOUS THOUGHT...HELPING HIM STAY ALIVE.
IT IS MY OPINION THAT SOMEONE CONSIDERS OLSEN INVALUABLE... AND IS SEEING TO HIS CONTINUED EXISTENCE.
NO! WAIT! STOP ATTACKING!
I CAN'T CONTROL MYSELF! PLEASE!
THAT'S IT! SKRAG THEM LIMB FROM LIMB! THEY ARE BUT SOULLESS EXTENSIONS OF THE DARK LORD'S WILL!
NO! THIS IS WRONG! I'M NOT LIKE YOU, FORAGER!
THE WHELP IS OBLIVIOUS...
...YET HE CONTINUES TO STUMBLE BLINDLY TOWARD AN UNKNOWN DESTINY AS IF PUSHED BY INVISIBLE FORCES.
THE DECLINE OF THE FOURTH WORLD IS CAUSE FOR CONCERN...
COULD THE OLSEN CREATURE BE WORKING TO SAVE THE NEW GODS?

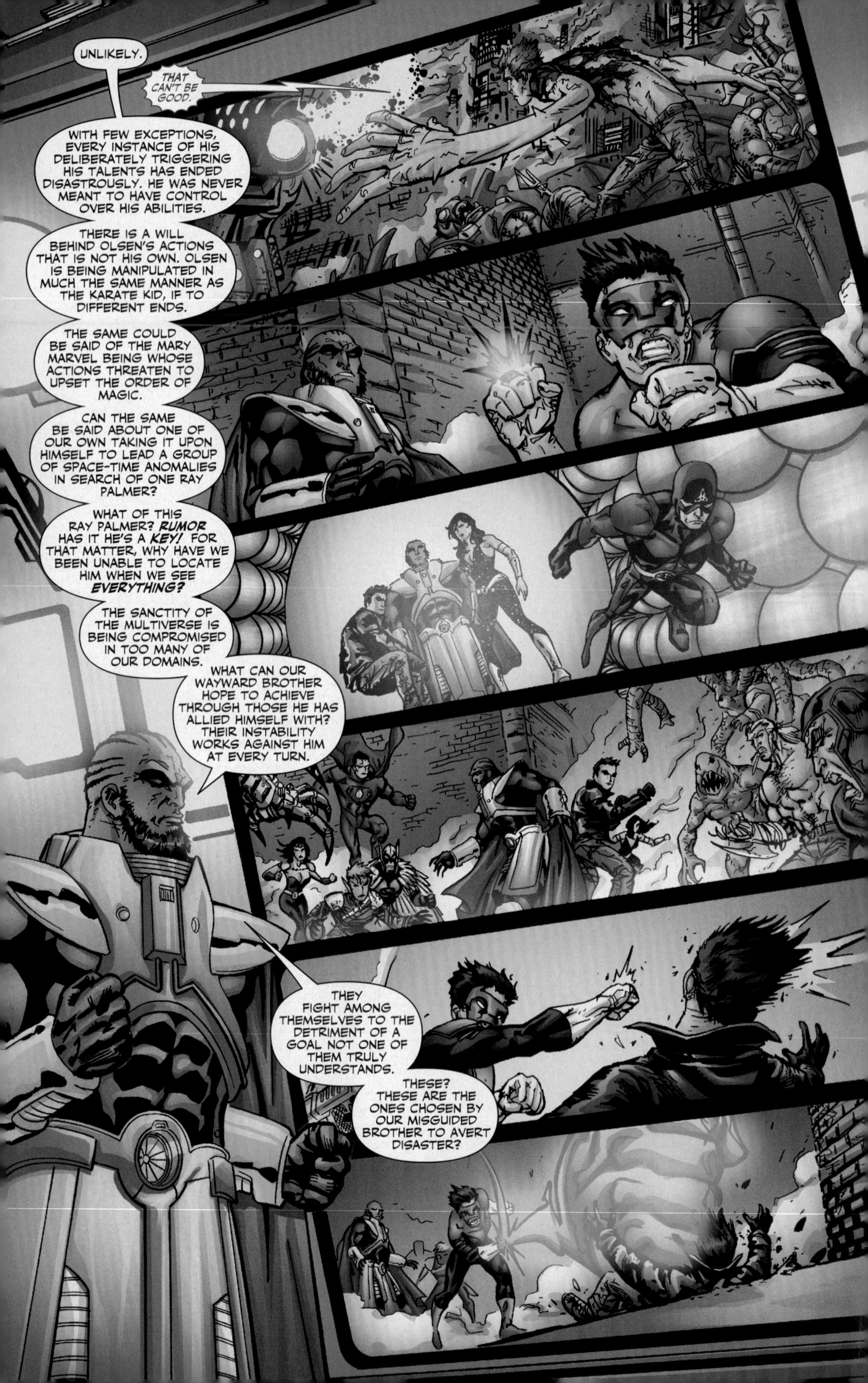
UNLIKELY.
THAT CAN'T BE GOOD.
WITH FEW EXCEPTIONS, EVERY INSTANCE OF HIS DELIBERATELY TRIGGERING HIS TALENTS HAS ENDED DISASTROUSLY. HE WAS NEVER MEANT TO HAVE CONTROL OVER HIS ABILITIES.
THERE IS A WILL BEHIND OLSEN'S ACTIONS THAT IS NOT HIS OWN. OLSEN IS BEING MANIPULATED IN MUCH THE SAME MANNER AS THE KARATE KID, IF TO DIFFERENT ENDS.
THE SAME COULD BE SAID OF THE MARY MARVEL BEING WHOSE ACTIONS THREATEN TO UPSET THE ORDER OF MAGIC.
CAN THE SAME BE SAID ABOUT ONE OF OUR OWN TAKING IT UPON HIMSELF TO LEAD A GROUP OF SPACE-TIME ANOMALIES IN SEARCH OF ONE RAY PALMER?
WHAT OF THIS RAY PALMER? RUMOR HAS IT HE'S A KEY! FOR THAT MATTER, WHY HAVE WE BEEN UNABLE TO LOCATE HIM WHEN WE SEE EVERYTHING?
THE SANCTITY OF THE MULTIVERSE IS BEING COMPROMISED IN TOO MANY OF OUR DOMAINS.
WHAT CAN OUR WAYWARD BROTHER HOPE TO ACHIEVE THROUGH THOSE HE HAS ALLIED HIMSELF WITH? THEIR INSTABILITY WORKS AGAINST HIM AT EVERY TURN.
THEY FIGHT AMONG THEMSELVES TO THE DETRIMENT OF A GOAL NOT ONE OF THEM TRULY UNDERSTANDS.
THESE? THESE ARE THE ONES CHOSEN BY OUR MISGUIDED BROTHER TO AVERT DISASTER?

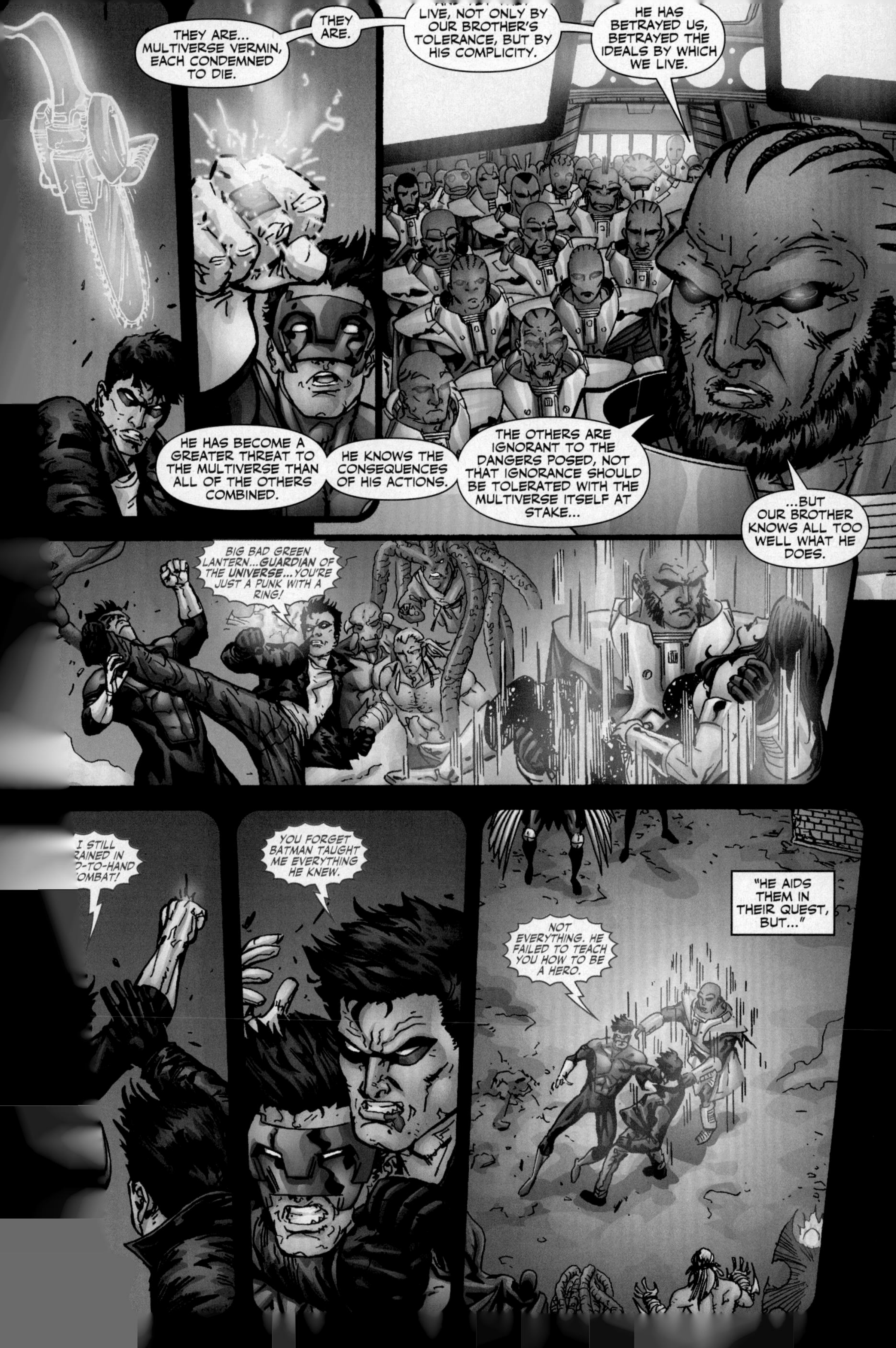
THEY ARE... MULTIVERSE VERMIN, EACH CONDEMNED TO DIE.
THEY ARE.
LIVE, NOT ONLY BY OUR BROTHER'S TOLERANCE, BUT BY HIS COMPLICITY.
HE HAS BETRAYED US, BETRAYED THE IDEALS BY WHICH WE LIVE.
HE HAS BECOME A GREATER THREAT TO THE MULTIVERSE THAN ALL OF THE OTHERS COMBINED.
HE KNOWS THE CONSEQUENCES OF HIS ACTIONS.
THE OTHERS ARE IGNORANT TO THE DANGERS POSED, NOT THAT IGNORANCE SHOULD BE TOLERATED WITH THE MULTIVERSE ITSELF AT STAKE...
...BUT OUR BROTHER KNOWS ALL TOO WELL WHAT HE DOES.
BIG BAD GREEN LANTERN...GUARDIAN OF THE UNIVERSE...YOU'RE JUST A PUNK WITH A RING!
I STILL
RAINED IN
D-TO-HAND
OMBAT!
YOU FORGET BATMAN TAUGHT ME EVERYTHING HE KNEW.
NOT EVERYTHING. HE FAILED TO TEACH YOU HOW TO BE A HERO.
"HE AIDS THEM IN THEIR QUEST, BUT..."

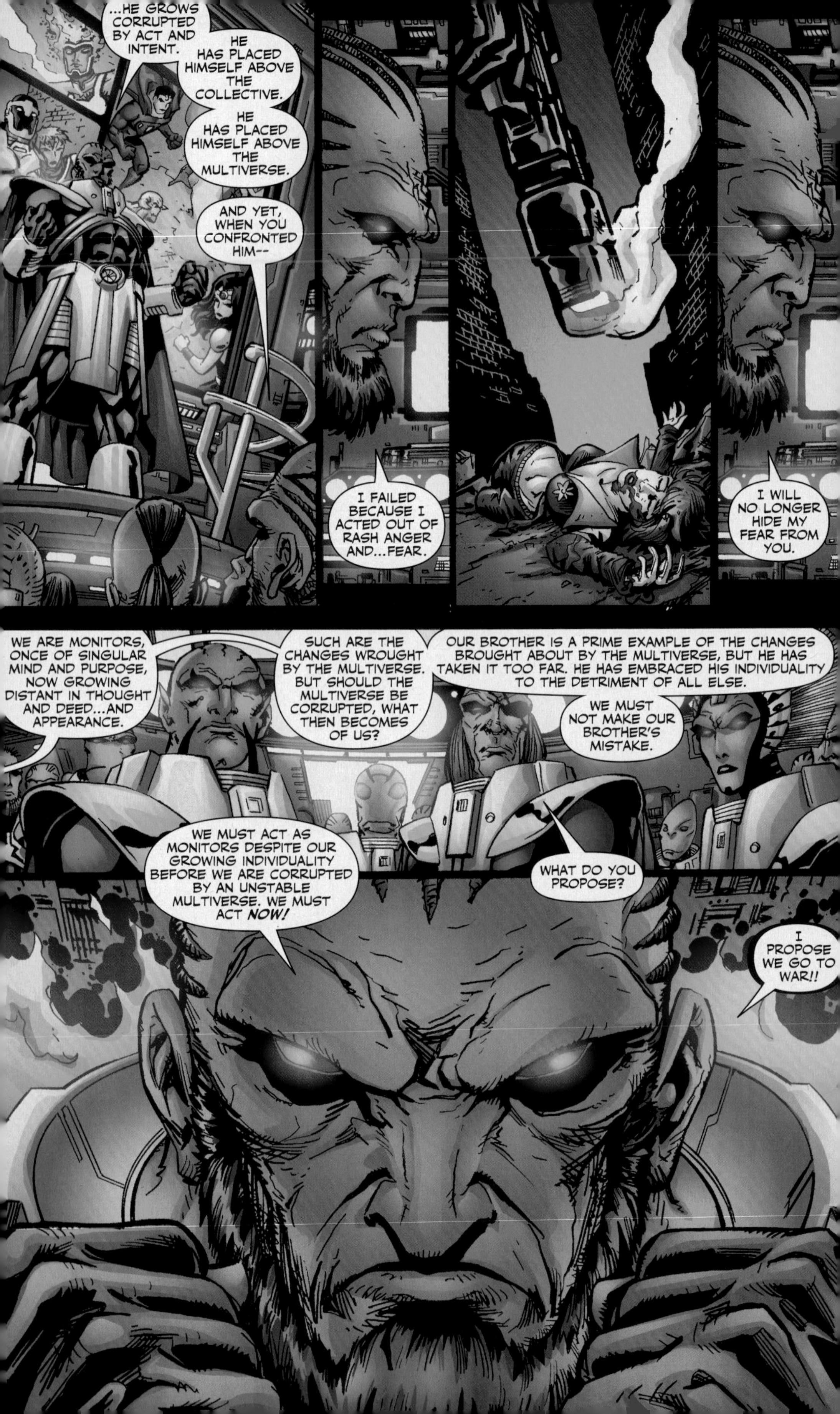
...HE GROWS CORRUPTED BY ACT AND INTENT.
HE HAS PLACED HIMSELF ABOVE THE COLLECTIVE.
HE HAS PLACED HIMSELF ABOVE THE MULTIVERSE.
AND YET, WHEN YOU CONFRONTED HIM--
I FAILED BECAUSE I ACTED OUT OF RASH ANGER AND...FEAR.
I WILL NO LONGER HIDE MY FEAR FROM YOU.
WE ARE MONITORS, ONCE OF SINGULAR MIND AND PURPOSE, NOW GROWING DISTANT IN THOUGHT AND DEED...AND APPEARANCE.
SUCH ARE THE CHANGES WROUGHT BY THE MULTIVERSE. BUT SHOULD THE MULTIVERSE BE CORRUPTED, WHAT THEN BECOMES OF US?
OUR BROTHER IS A PRIME EXAMPLE OF THE CHANGES BROUGHT ABOUT BY THE MULTIVERSE, BUT HE HAS TAKEN IT TOO FAR. HE HAS EMBRACED HIS INDIVIDUALITY TO THE DETRIMENT OF ALL ELSE.
WE MUST NOT MAKE OUR BROTHER'S MISTAKE.
WE MUST ACT AS MONITORS DESPITE OUR GROWING INDIVIDUALITY BEFORE WE ARE CORRUPTED BY AN UNSTABLE MULTIVERSE. WE MUST ACT *NOW!*
WHAT DO YOU PROPOSE?
I PROPOSE WE GO TO WAR!!

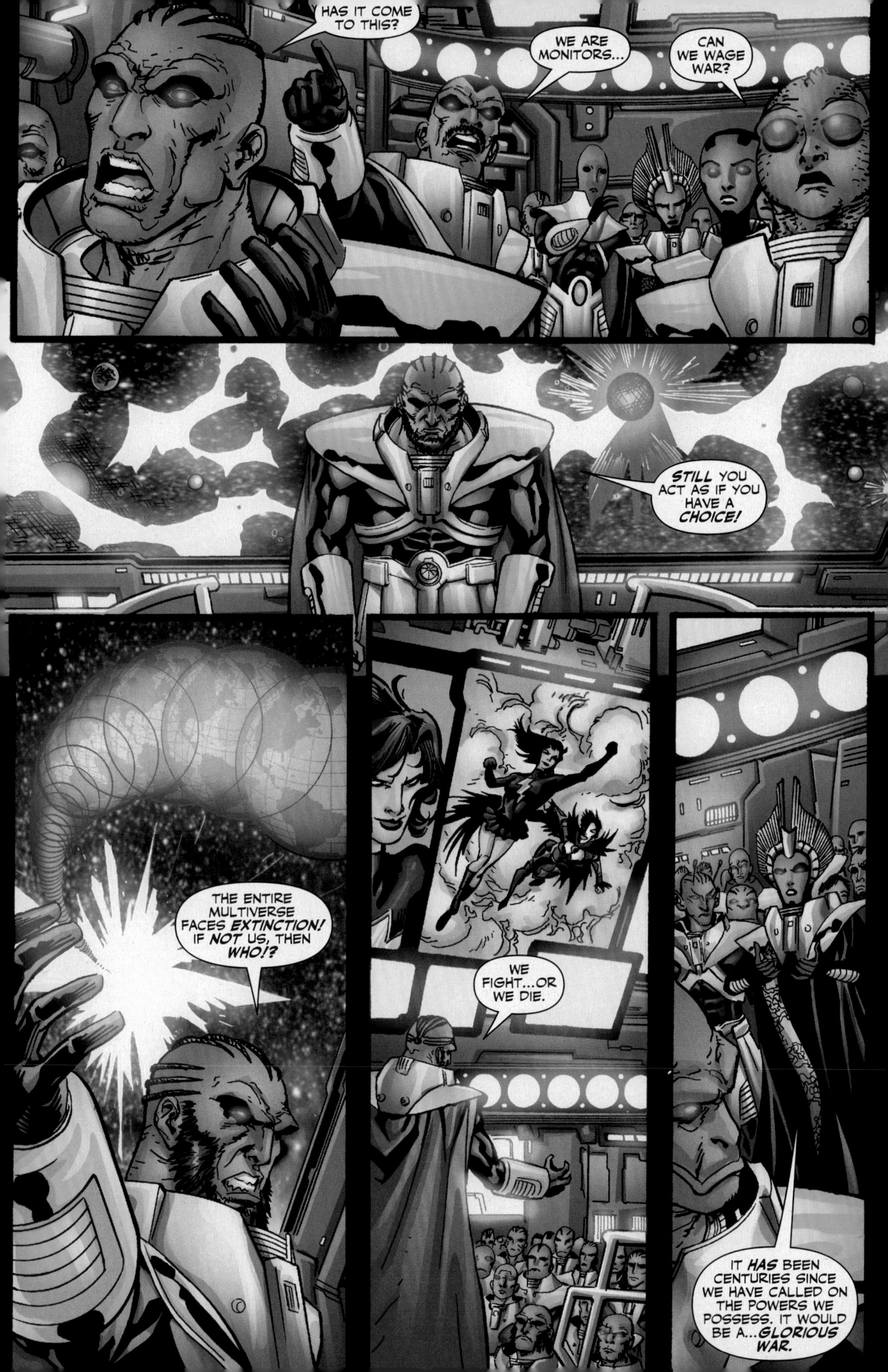

HAS IT COME TO THIS?
WE ARE MONITORS...
CAN WE WAGE WAR?
STILL YOU ACT AS IF YOU HAVE A CHOICE!
THE ENTIRE MULTIVERSE FACES EXTINCTION! IF NOT US, THEN WHO!?
WE FIGHT...OR WE DIE.
IT HAS BEEN CENTURIES SINCE WE HAVE CALLED ON THE POWERS WE POSSESS. IT WOULD BE A...GLORIOUS WAR.

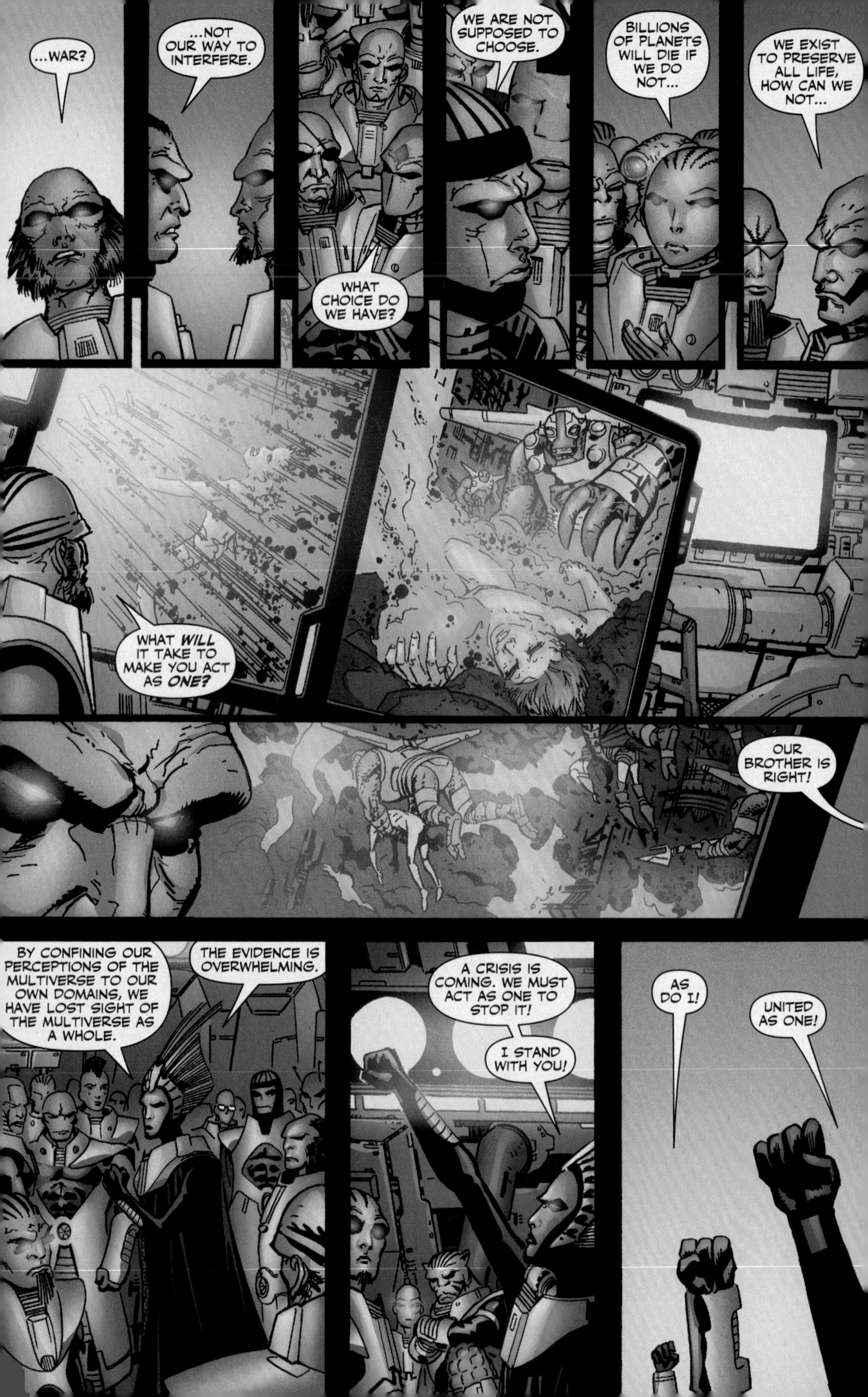
...WAR?
...NOT OUR WAY TO INTERFERE.
WHAT CHOICE DO WE HAVE?
WE ARE NOT SUPPOSED TO CHOOSE.
BILLIONS OF PLANETS WILL DIE IF WE DO NOT...
WE EXIST TO PRESERVE ALL LIFE, HOW CAN WE NOT...
WHAT *WILL* IT TAKE TO MAKE YOU ACT AS *ONE?*
OUR BROTHER IS RIGHT!
BY CONFINING OUR PERCEPTIONS OF THE MULTIVERSE TO OUR OWN DOMAINS, WE HAVE LOST SIGHT OF THE MULTIVERSE AS A WHOLE.
THE EVIDENCE IS OVERWHELMING.
A CRISIS IS COMING. WE MUST ACT AS ONE TO STOP IT!
I STAND WITH YOU!
AS DO I!
UNITED AS ONE!

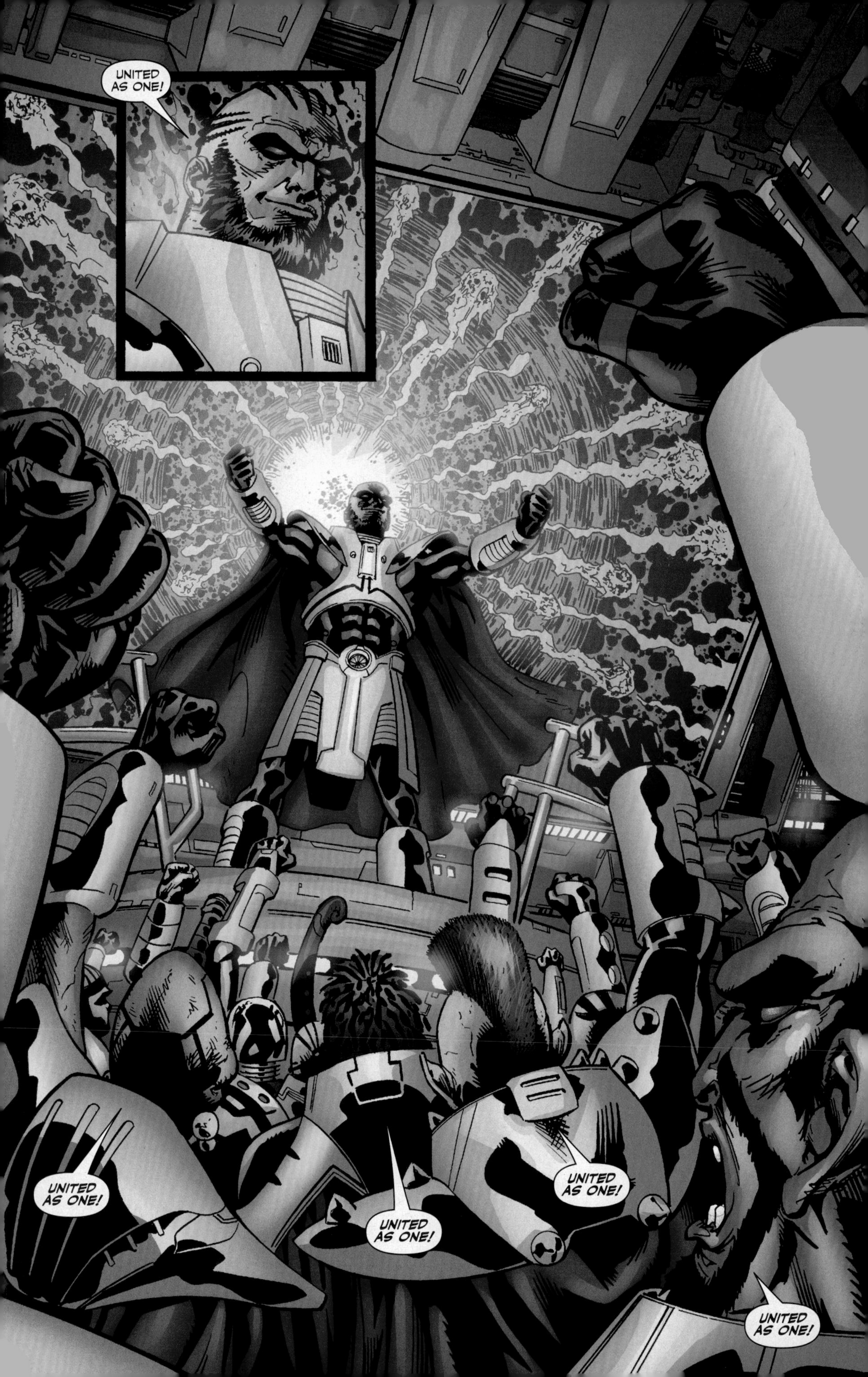

UNITED AS ONE!
UNITED AS ONE!
UNITED AS ONE!
UNITED AS ONE!
UNITED AS ONE!

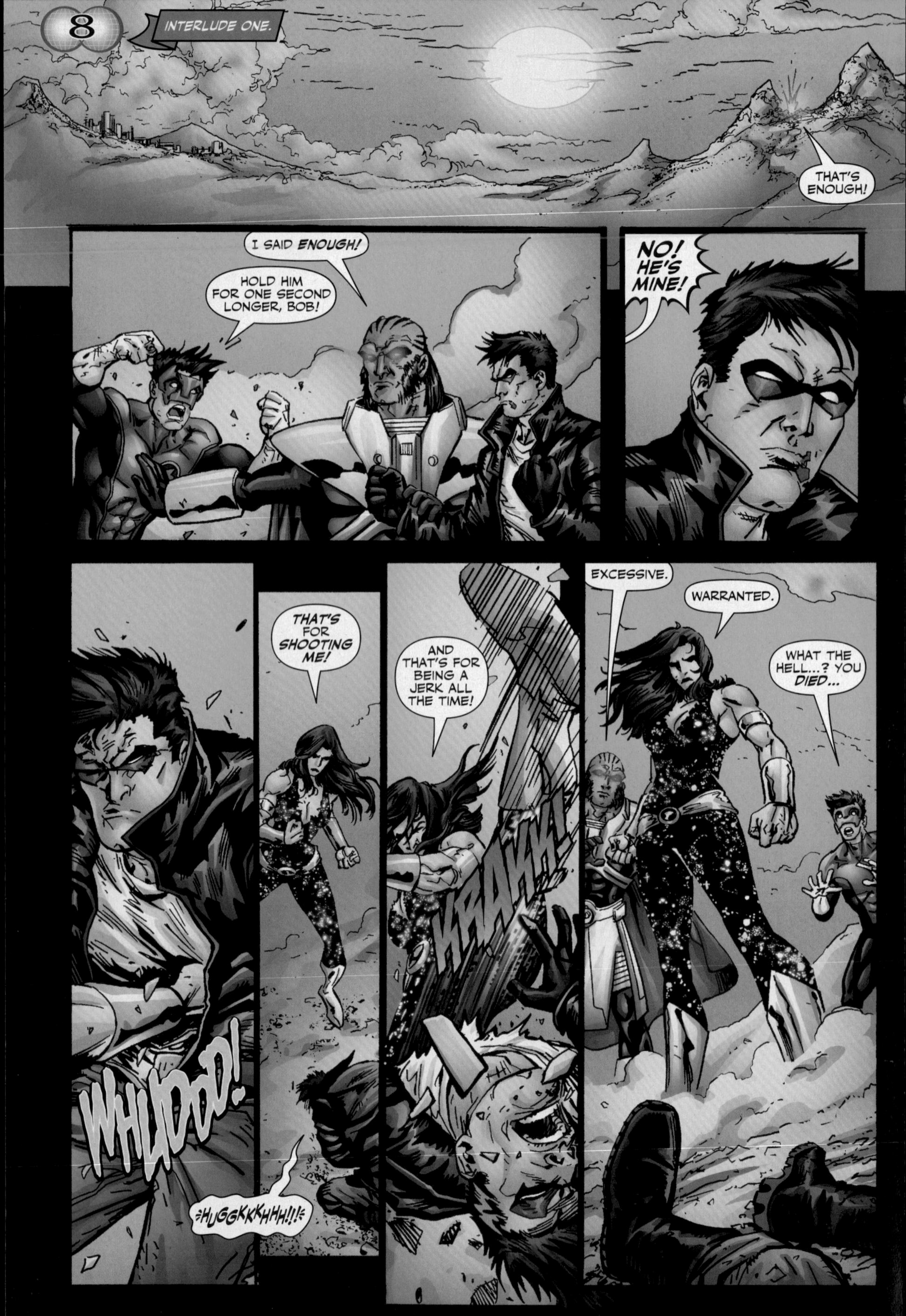
8
INTERLUDE ONE.
THAT'S ENOUGH!
I SAID ENOUGH!
HOLD HIM FOR ONE SECOND LONGER, BOB!
NO! HE'S MINE!
WHUDOD!
THAT'S FOR SHOOTING ME!
HUGGKKKHHH!!!
AND THAT'S FOR BEING A JERK ALL THE TIME!
KRAKK!
EXCESSIVE.
WARRANTED.
WHAT THE HELL...? YOU DIED...

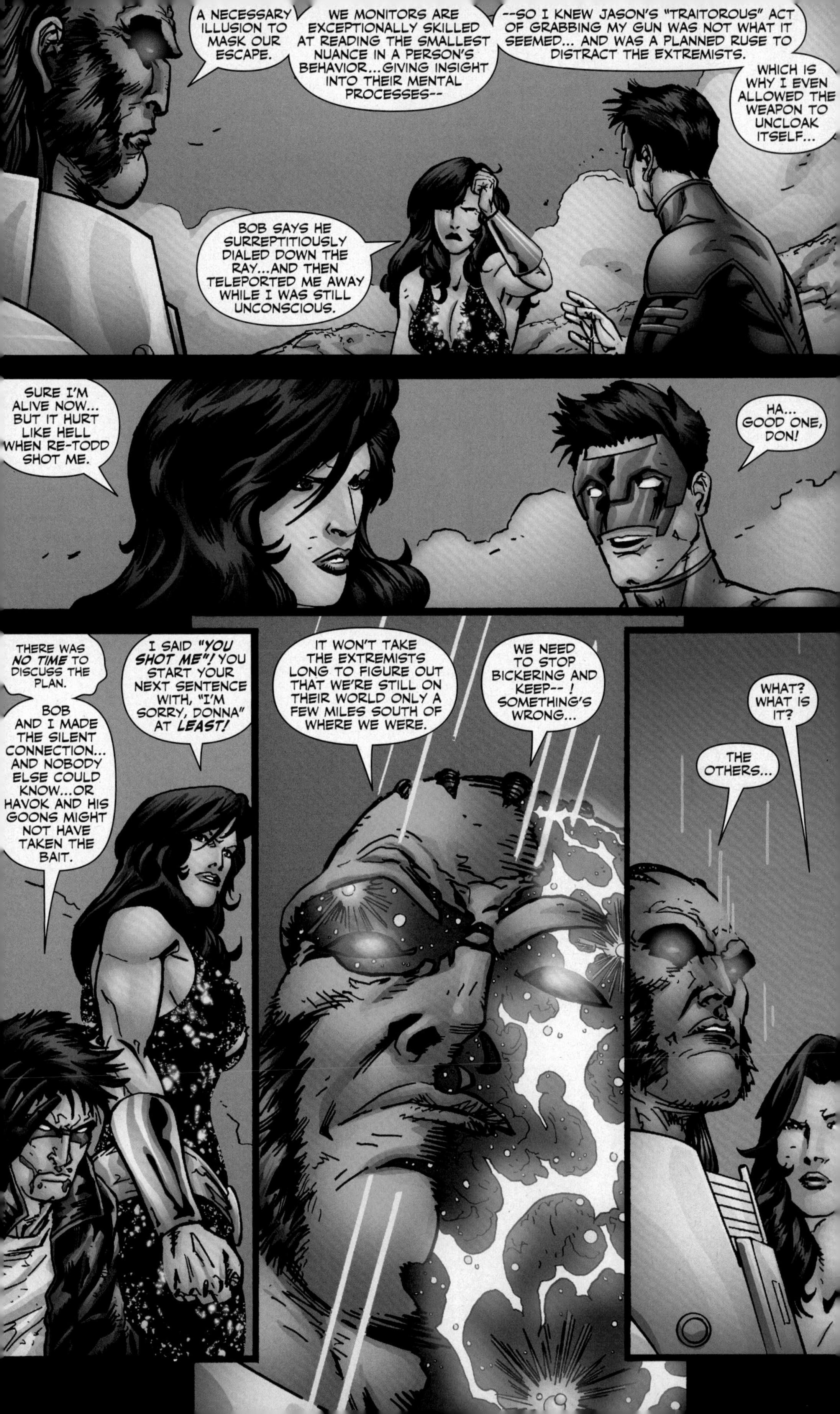
A NECESSARY ILLUSION TO MASK OUR ESCAPE.
WE MONITORS ARE EXCEPTIONALLY SKILLED AT READING THE SMALLEST NUANCE IN A PERSON'S BEHAVIOR...GIVING INSIGHT INTO THEIR MENTAL PROCESSES--
--SO I KNEW JASON'S "TRAITOROUS" ACT OF GRABBING MY GUN WAS NOT WHAT IT SEEMED... AND WAS A PLANNED RUSE TO DISTRACT THE EXTREMISTS.
WHICH IS WHY I EVEN ALLOWED THE WEAPON TO UNCLOAK ITSELF...
BOB SAYS HE SURREPTITIOUSLY DIALED DOWN THE RAY...AND THEN TELEPORTED ME AWAY WHILE I WAS STILL UNCONSCIOUS.
SURE I'M ALIVE NOW... BUT IT HURT LIKE HELL WHEN RE-TODD SHOT ME.
HA... GOOD ONE, DON!
THERE WAS NO TIME TO DISCUSS THE PLAN.
BOB AND I MADE THE SILENT CONNECTION... AND NOBODY ELSE COULD KNOW...OR HAVOK AND HIS GOONS MIGHT NOT HAVE TAKEN THE BAIT.
I SAID "YOU SHOT ME"! YOU START YOUR NEXT SENTENCE WITH, "I'M SORRY, DONNA" AT LEAST!
IT WON'T TAKE THE EXTREMISTS LONG TO FIGURE OUT THAT WE'RE STILL ON THEIR WORLD ONLY A FEW MILES SOUTH OF WHERE WE WERE.
WE NEED TO STOP BICKERING AND KEEP-- ! SOMETHING'S WRONG...
WHAT? WHAT IS IT?
THE OTHERS...

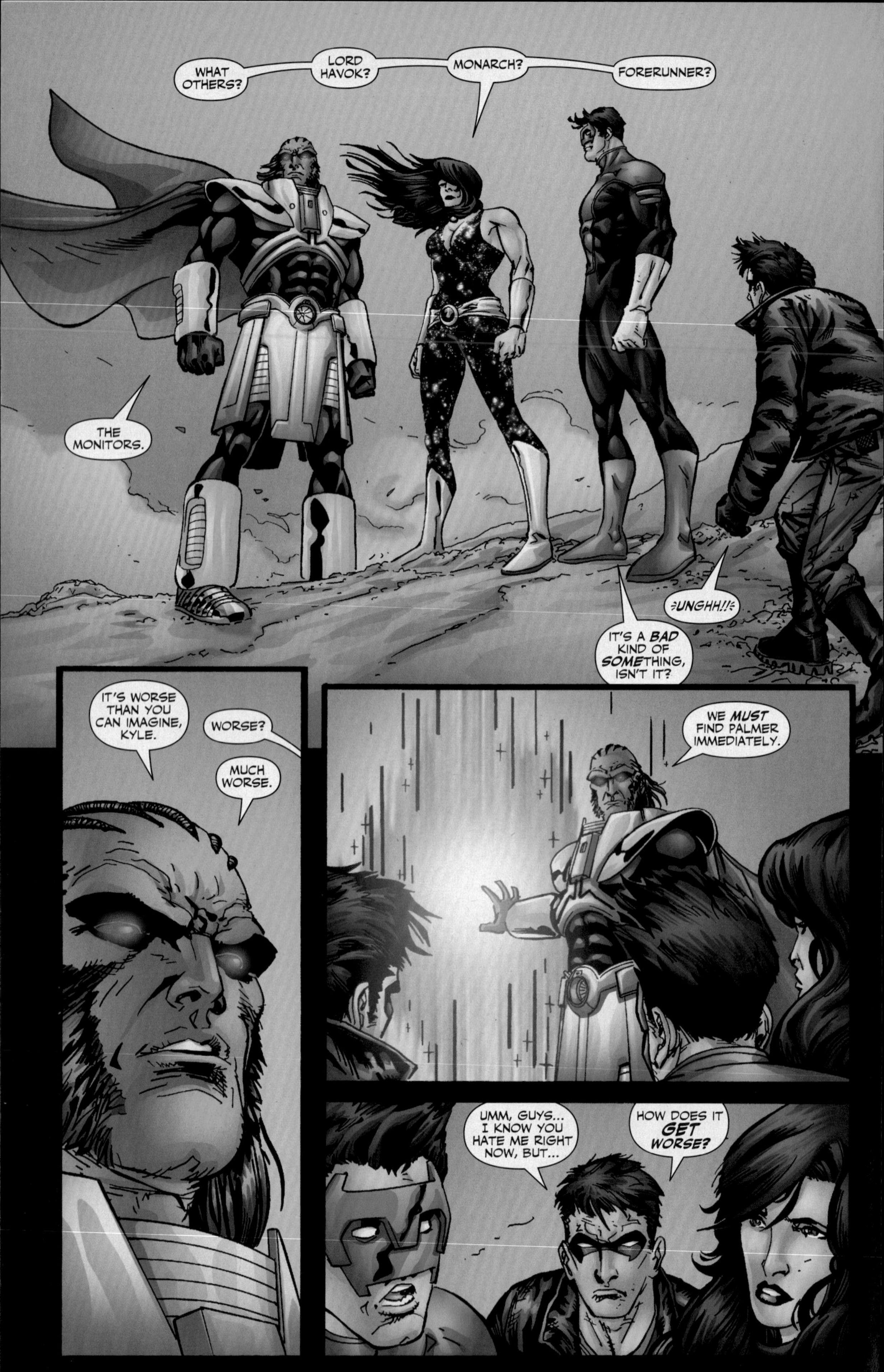
WHAT OTHERS?
LORD HAVOK?
MONARCH?
FORERUNNER?
THE MONITORS.
IT'S A BAD KIND OF SOMETHING, ISN'T IT?
UNGHH!!
IT'S WORSE THAN YOU CAN IMAGINE, KYLE.
WORSE?
MUCH WORSE.
WE MUST FIND PALMER IMMEDIATELY.
UMM, GUYS... I KNOW YOU HATE ME RIGHT NOW, BUT...
HOW DOES IT GET WORSE?

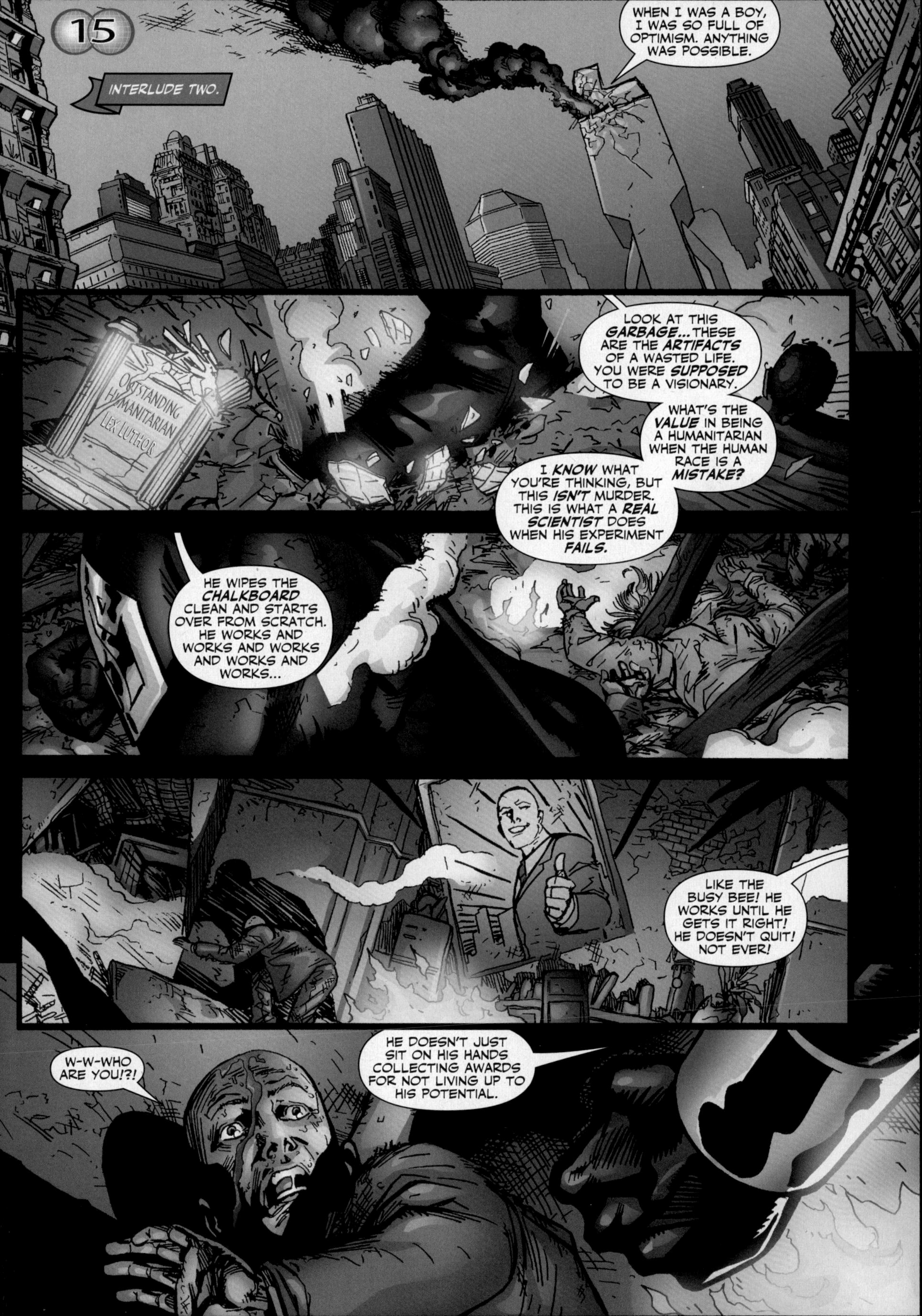
15
INTERLUDE TWO.
WHEN I WAS A BOY, I WAS SO FULL OF OPTIMISM. ANYTHING WAS POSSIBLE.
OUTSTANDING HUMANITARIAN LEX LUTHOR
LOOK AT THIS GARBAGE... THESE ARE THE ARTIFACTS OF A WASTED LIFE. YOU WERE SUPPOSED TO BE A VISIONARY.
WHAT'S THE VALUE IN BEING A HUMANITARIAN WHEN THE HUMAN RACE IS A MISTAKE?
I KNOW WHAT YOU'RE THINKING, BUT THIS ISN'T MURDER. THIS IS WHAT A REAL SCIENTIST DOES WHEN HIS EXPERIMENT FAILS.
HE WIPES THE CHALKBOARD CLEAN AND STARTS OVER FROM SCRATCH. HE WORKS AND WORKS AND WORKS AND WORKS AND WORKS...
LIKE THE BUSY BEE! HE WORKS UNTIL HE GETS IT RIGHT! HE DOESN'T QUIT! NOT EVER!
W-W-WHO ARE YOU!?!
HE DOESN'T JUST SIT ON HIS HANDS COLLECTING AWARDS FOR NOT LIVING UP TO HIS POTENTIAL.

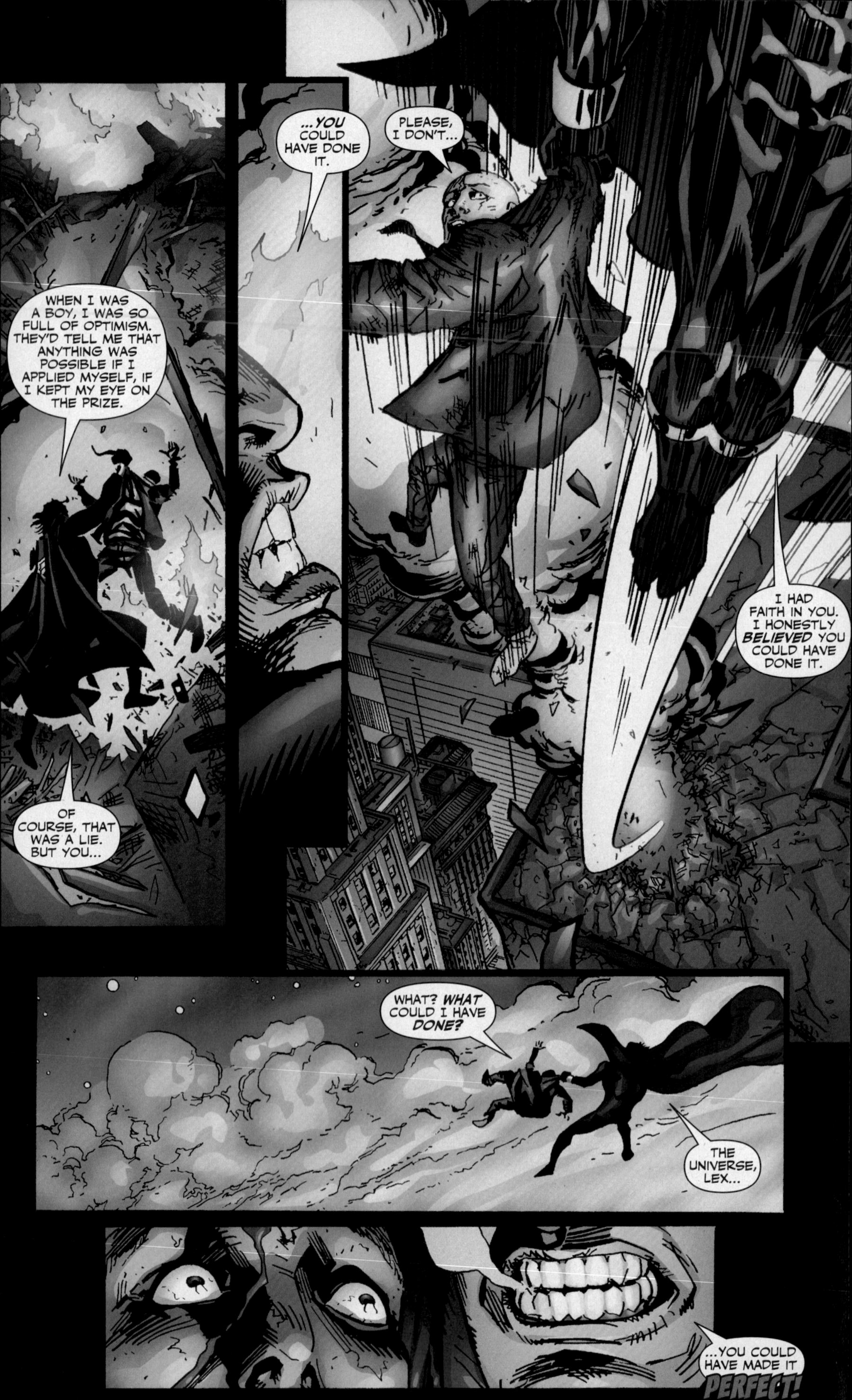
WHEN I WAS A BOY, I WAS SO FULL OF OPTIMISM. THEY'D TELL ME THAT ANYTHING WAS POSSIBLE IF I APPLIED MYSELF, IF I KEPT MY EYE ON THE PRIZE.
OF COURSE, THAT WAS A LIE. BUT YOU...
...YOU COULD HAVE DONE IT.
PLEASE, I DON'T...
I HAD FAITH IN YOU. I HONESTLY BELIEVED YOU COULD HAVE DONE IT.
WHAT? WHAT COULD I HAVE DONE?
THE UNIVERSE, LEX...
...YOU COULD HAVE MADE IT PERFECT!

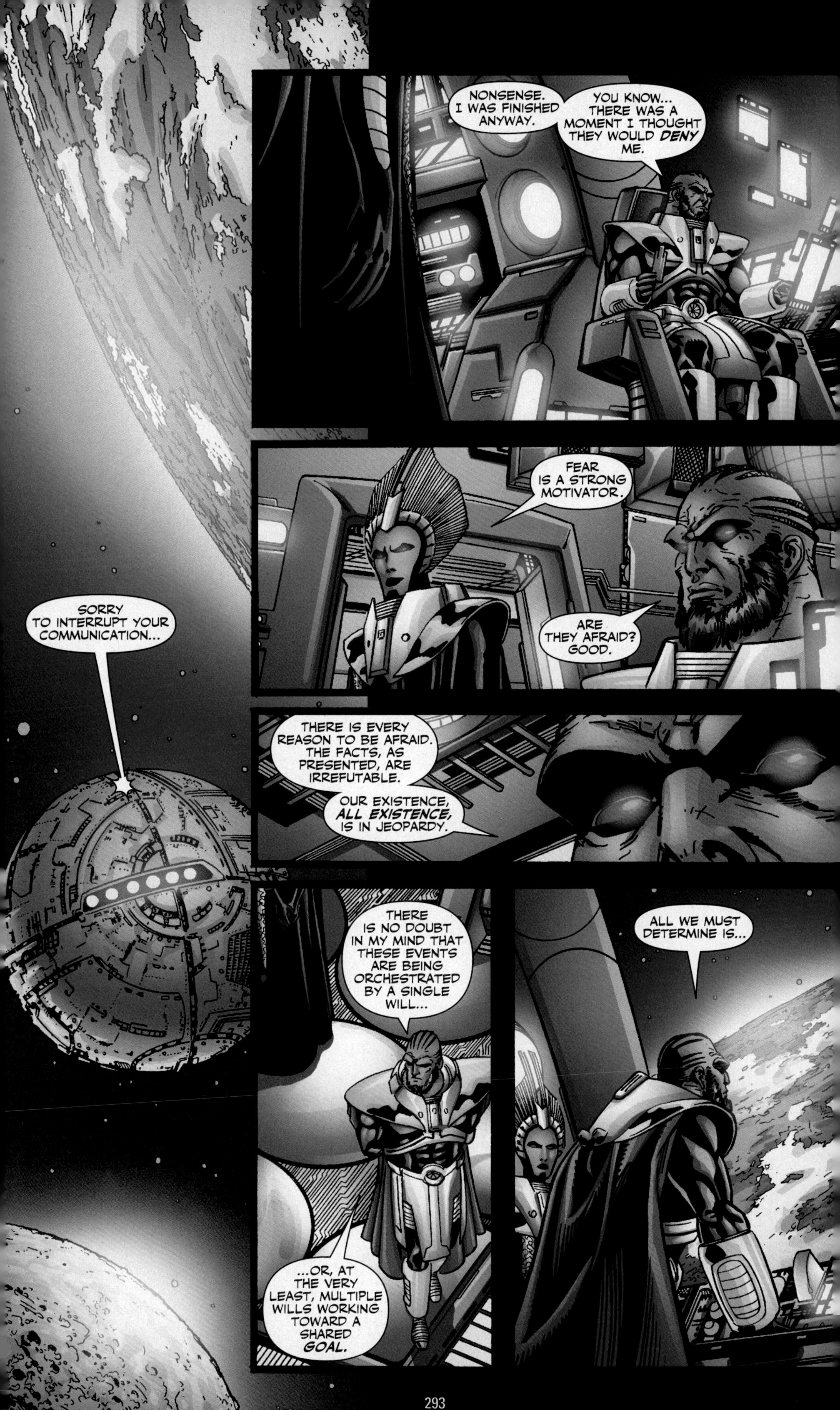
NONSENSE. I WAS FINISHED ANYWAY.
YOU KNOW... THERE WAS A MOMENT I THOUGHT THEY WOULD DENY ME.
FEAR IS A STRONG MOTIVATOR.
ARE THEY AFRAID? GOOD.
SORRY TO INTERRUPT YOUR COMMUNICATION...
THERE IS EVERY REASON TO BE AFRAID. THE FACTS, AS PRESENTED, ARE IRREFUTABLE.
OUR EXISTENCE, ALL EXISTENCE, IS IN JEOPARDY.
THERE IS NO DOUBT IN MY MIND THAT THESE EVENTS ARE BEING ORCHESTRATED BY A SINGLE WILL...
...OR, AT THE VERY LEAST, MULTIPLE WILLS WORKING TOWARD A SHARED GOAL.
ALL WE MUST DETERMINE IS...

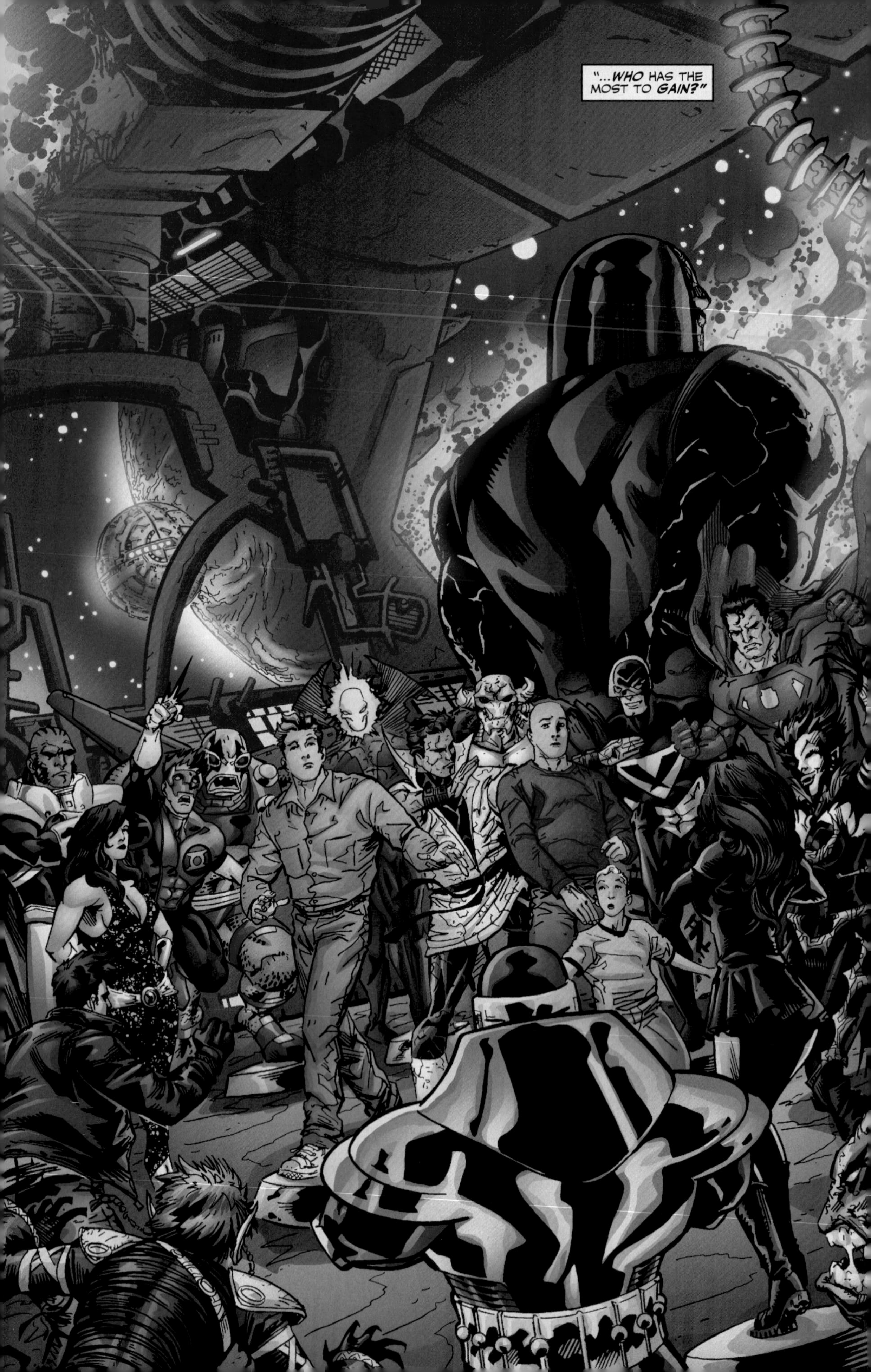
"...WHO HAS THE MOST TO GAIN?"

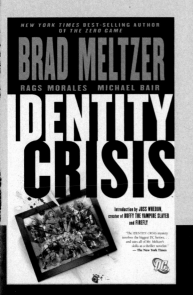

DON'T MISS THESE OTHER GREAT TITLES FROM AROUND THE DCU!

SUPERMAN:
BIRTHRIGHT

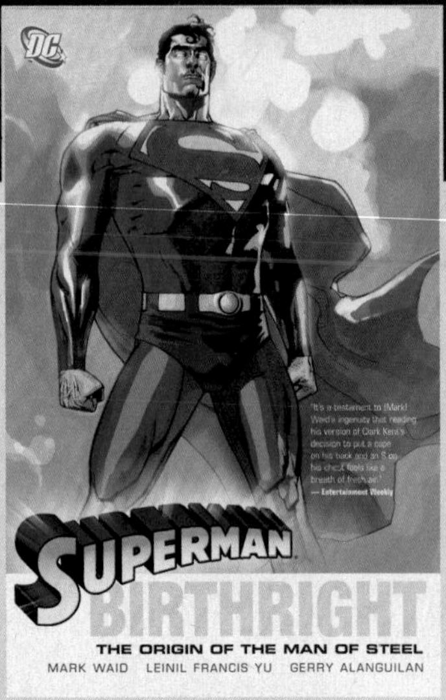
SUPERMAN
BIRTHRIGHT
THE ORIGIN OF THE MAN OF STEEL
MARK WAID LEINIL FRANCIS YU GERRY ALANGUILAN

**MARK WAID**
**LEINIL FRANCIS YU**
**GERRY ALANGUILAN**

BATMAN:
DARK VICTORY

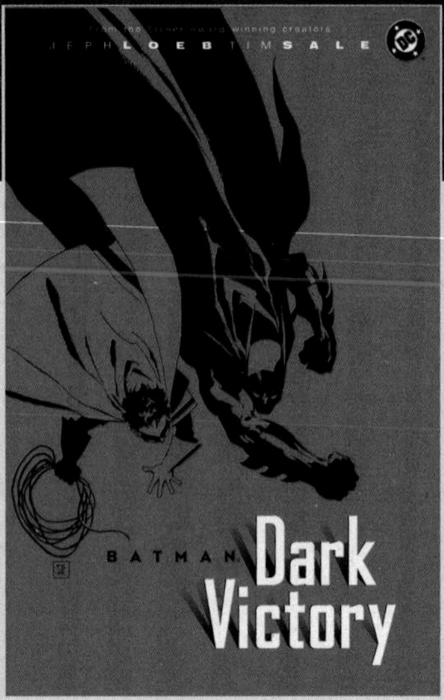
JEPH LOEB TIM SALE
BATMAN Dark Victory

**JEPH LOEB**
**TIM SALE**

WONDER WOMAN:
GODS AND MORTALS

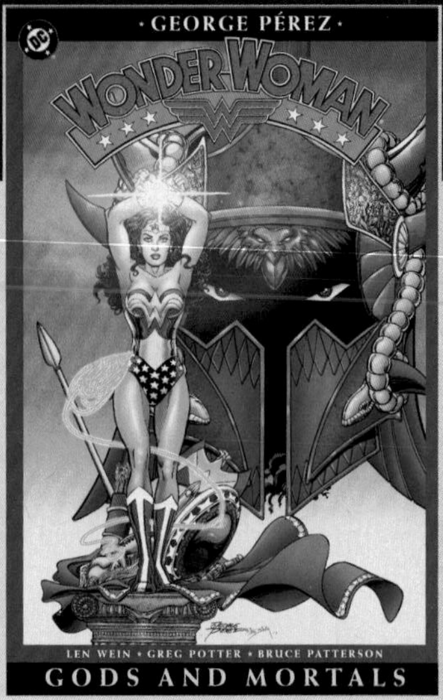
· GEORGE PÉREZ ·
WONDER WOMAN
LEN WEIN • GREG POTTER • BRUCE PATTERSON
GODS AND MORTALS

**GEORGE PÉREZ**
**LEN WEIN/GREG POTTER**
**BRUCE PATTERSON**

GREEN LANTERN:
NO FEAR

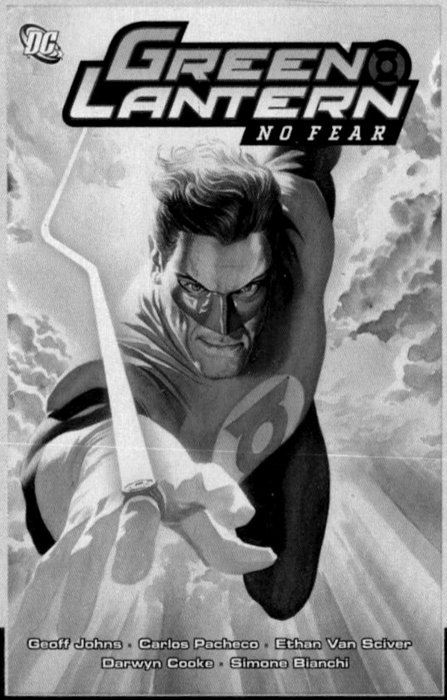
GREEN LANTERN
NO FEAR
Geoff Johns · Carlos Pacheco · Ethan Van Sciver
Darwyn Cooke · Simone Bianchi

**GEOFF JOHNS**
**CARLOS PACHECO**
**ETHAN VAN SCIVER**

GREEN ARROW:
QUIVER

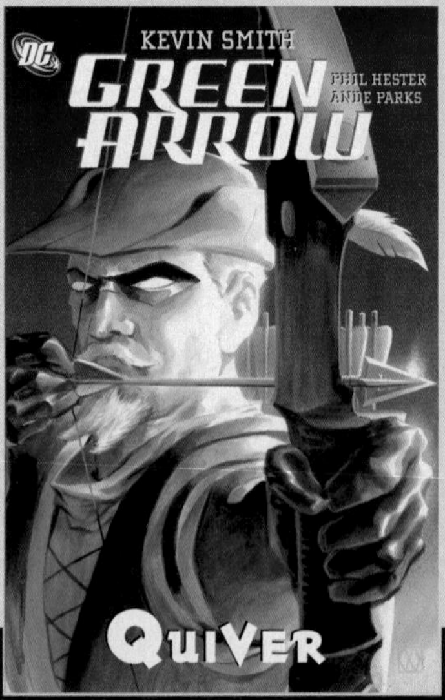
KEVIN SMITH
GREEN ARROW
PHIL HESTER
ANDE PARKS
QUIVER

**KEVIN SMITH**
**PHIL HESTER**
**ANDE PARKS**

TEEN TITANS:
A KID'S GAME

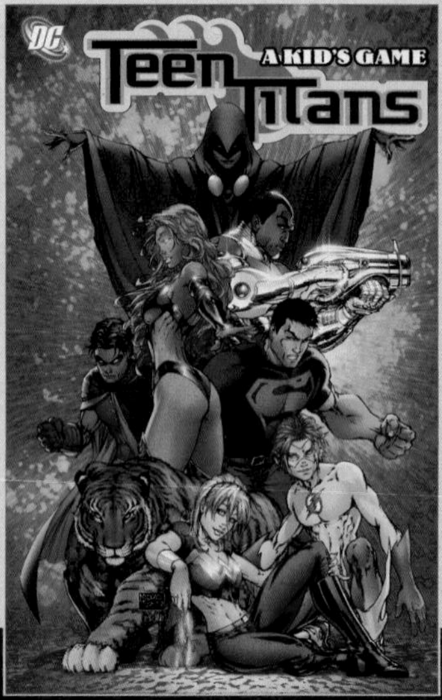
Teen Titans
A KID'S GAME

**GEOFF JOHNS**
**MIKE McKONE**

SEARCH THE GRAPHIC NOVELS SECTION OF

**www.DCCOMICS.com**

FOR ART AND INFORMATION ON ALL OF OUR BOOKS!